26.10

MIRRORS

An Introduction to Literature

MIRRORS
An Introduction to Literature

SECOND EDITION

EDITED BY

John R. Knott, Jr.
University of Michigan

Christopher R. Reaske
Junior College of Albany

HARPER & ROW, PUBLISHERS
New York Hagerstown Philadelphia San Francisco London

Library of Congress Cataloging in Publication Data

Knott, John Ray, 1937-   comp.
    Mirrors.

    Includes index.
    1. Literature—Collections. I. Reaske, Christopher
Russell, joint comp. II. Title.
PN6014.K63   1975   808.8   75-15586
ISBN 0-06-384701-9

Cover and interior art by Heather Kortebein

Credits

ANONYMOUS, "Into my head rose," from *Selected Translations* by W. S. Merwin. Copyright © 1967 by W. S. Merwin. Reprinted by permission of Atheneum Publishers.

W. H. AUDEN, "In Memory of W. B. Yeats," "Musee des Beaux Arts," "The Unknown Citizen," from *Collected Shorter Poems 1927–1957* by W. H. Auden. Copyright 1940 and renewed 1968 by W. H. Auden. Reprinted by permission of Random House, Inc. Canadian rights by Faber and Faber Ltd.

TONI CADE BAMBARA, "The Lesson." From *Gorilla, My Love,* by Toni Cade Bambara. Copyright © 1972 by Toni Cade Bambara. Reprinted by permission of Random House, Inc.

DONALD BARTHELME, "The School." Reprinted by permission of International Famous Agency and Donald Barthelme. Copyright © 1974 by The New Yorker Magazine, Inc.

BASHO, "The Sea Darkening," by Basho from *Japanese Haiku*. Translated by Peter Beilenson. © Peter Pauper Press. Reprinted by permission of Peter Pauper Press.

(credits continued on page 532)

PREFACE

For the second edition of *Mirrors* we have continued our practice of including an unusually large number of selections from contemporary literature. We have not ignored the classics. Shakespeare is now represented in the Drama section by *King Lear,* and we have added stories by Chekhov, Kafka, Faulkner, and Hemingway. But we have made a particular effort to add representative works by younger writers like Toni Cade Bambara, Erica Jong, Nikki Giovanni, Al Young, and others likely to engage student interest (Kurt Vonnegut, Robert Bly).

As before, we have gone outside the Anglo-American literary tradition in order to expose students to unfamiliar cultures and sensibilities. Thus the Poetry section includes leading Latin American and Eastern European poets and anonymous Eskimo and American Indian poets as well as more predictable figures. Also, we have tried to stretch the student's sense of the possibilities of literature. Under the heading of "Love" we have gathered poems as diverse as the "Song of Solomon," translations from Petrarch, verse by the Mexican poet Octavio Paz, and Gregory Corso's "Marriage."

Both the Poetry and Fiction sections open with works chosen for their immediacy and then proceed to selections and commentary intended to introduce students to useful critical terminology. In general, the movement is from simple to complex. We offer thematic groupings of poems as well as sections designed to illustrate the way poems work, because we feel that both kinds of organization serve important purposes.

Each section includes commentary by an author on his or her work. Joyce Carol Oates describes how she writes and comments on her story, "Where Are You Going, Where Have You Been?" Robert Hayden discusses the process of writing poetry and explains the origins of a particular poem. Ibsen's notes for *Hedda Gabler* offer revealing glimpses of his views of the characters and their dramatic situation.

We believe that this is a lively book and one that reflects the needs and interests of students as well as our own sense of what literature is worth studying.

JOHN R. KNOTT, JR.
CHRISTOPHER R. REASKE
Ann Arbor, Michigan
Albany, New York

Acknowledgments

The second edition of this book, like the first, profited greatly from the criticisms and suggestions of Myrna Harrison of Contra Costa College, who served as advisory editor. We would also like to thank Audrey Roth of Miami Dade Community College for her contributions to the "Writing about Literature" section that appears for the first time in this edition. Joyce Carol Oates kindly permitted us to reprint our interview with her from the first edition of the book, and Robert Hayden showed his customary generosity in allowing us to reprint excerpts from a previously published interview. We are grateful to the editorial and production staff of Canfield Press for their patience and continuing support: Ann Ludwig, Linda Mandeville, and Janet Wondra in particular. Finally, we want to thank our wives, Anne and Mary K., for their forbearance, and especially Mary K., who contributed editorial services far beyond the call of wifely duty.

CONTENTS

POETRY

DRAMA

At times in the afternoons a face
Looks at us from the depths of a mirror;
Art must be like that mirror
That reveals to us this face of ours.

JORGE LUIS BORGES

FICTION

We have Art that we may not perish from Truth.

FRIEDRICH NIETZSCHE

The story . . . should magnetize the imagination and give pleasure—of however disturbing, complex, or painful a kind.

ELIZABETH BOWEN

There is no prejudice that the work of art does not finally overcome.

ANDRÉ GIDE

[The artist] speaks to our capacity for delight and wonder, to the sense of mystery surrounding our lives . . . to the latent feeling of fellowship with all creation.

JOSEPH CONRAD

Introductory

Because it is so easy to get caught up in the imaginary life of fiction, we sometimes forget that the writer carefully chose every detail that contributes to the nature of that fictional life. What we may experience as a representation of everyday life is actually a highly selective vision in which we see as much, or as little, as the writer allows us to see. The novelist E. M. Forster has this to say about the fictional character:

> He is generally born off [stage], he is capable of dying on, he wants little food or sleep, he is tirelessly occupied with human relationships. And—most important—we can know more about him than we can about any of our fellow creatures, because his creator and narrator are one.

Eudora Welty puts it this way:

> It [is] the business of writing, and the responsibility of the writer, to disentangle the significant —in character, incident, setting, mood, everything—from the random and meaningless and irrelevant that in real life surround and beset it.

Why should a writer show a character eating? Only if his eating contributes something to our knowledge of the character or to the action in which he figures. Writers of short stories, particularly, have so little space that they can afford to show the reader only what is significant about a character, screening out details that are irrelevant to the meaning of the story. We generally know such characters better than we know our friends. What they say and do reveals them, and the writer lets us into their consciousness.

The fictional character is preoccupied with human relationships, as Forster says, because they give a story direction and point. The writer frequently puts these relationships under pressure in order to give a story its significance: he may force a crisis, or a character's recognition of some truth about himself or his experience. Some writers are less preoccupied with illuminating human relationships than others. For example, a detective story may simply march a set of stereotyped characters through a complicated series of adventures, entertaining the reader by keeping him in doubt about the outcome without offering him any insights into the characters. But the best fiction demands an alert

3

reader who will ask himself how everything in the story contributes to its meaning. Why does the story begin the way it does? Why does the author give a character a particular gesture? Why does he describe the furniture of the room, or the rain outside?

In the following pages we introduce some of the terms often used to describe how fiction works: suspense, point of view, irony, and symbolism. Although we associate each of these terms with a particular group of stories, all of them may be applied to any given story. They are simply ways of talking about or naming various aspects of a story, ways of breaking down a complex whole into parts.

By seeing how a story is put together, you can develop a better sense of its meaning. This meaning is not something that can be extracted and set down in a sentence, however. Attempts to state the "theme" of a story only distort it, as Flannery O'Connor recognized:

> *People talk about the theme of a story as if the theme were like the string that a sack of chicken feed is tied with. They think that if you can pick out the theme, the way you pick the right thread in the chicken-feed sack, you can rip the story open and feed the chickens. But this is not the way meaning works in fiction. . . . The meaning of a story has to be embodied in it, has to be made concrete in it. A story is a way to say something that can't be said in any other way, and it takes every word in the story to say what the meaning is.*

If we followed O'Connor's advice strictly, we would not talk about stories at all, we would only reread them. But one of the best ways of learning to read good stories with the close attention they deserve is to talk about them—remembering that the writer chose the exact words he used, all of them, for a reason.

4

Suspense

The oldest requirement of a story is that it hold the attention of its audience, and the surest way for the storyteller to command this attention is through the use of suspense. If we want to know what happens next, we will keep reading. The three stories that follow all rely heavily upon suspense. In each case the plot—the sequence of events by which the story develops—keeps the reader guessing about what will happen up to the end, or even beyond. The stories build in tension, and they shock or surprise us by their conclusions.

Joyce Carol Oates uses the suspense created by the sudden appearance of an ominous visitor in a teenage girl's driveway to hold her story together, but the underlying concern of "Where Are You Going, Where Have You Been?" is with the disturbing potential of the life Connie hides from her parents. Arnold Friend acts as a mirror in which Connie's values and wants are distorted, and his threatening presence forces the reader to ask how well Connie understands herself and the sexuality with which she has been toying.

Eudora Welty's "A Piece of News" suggests that a story need not be built around a shocking event in order to create suspense. What fails to happen in the relationship between Ruby and her husband Clyde is more important than the shooting Ruby reads about in a newspaper. Miss Welty has said that "plots are what we see with. What's seen is what we're interested in." What's "seen" in this case, by the aid of a plot so slight that it could be summarized in a sentence or two, is the way in which a man and a woman are confronted by the possibility of rediscovering their love.

William Faulkner's "A Rose for Emily" works by slowly arousing the reader's curiosity about Miss Emily's peculiar habits and then suddenly opening a door that gives an indecently revealing view of her private self. In this story suspense is generated by tension between the conventional expectations of the community, with which the reader is led to identifiy, and Miss Emily's determined independence. Faulkner's way of telling Miss Emily's story makes it clear that if we are to understand her bizarre fate we must understand the town, and the family, into which she was born.

5

The first two stories raise questions about the relationship of fiction to fact. Joyce Carol Oates, commenting on her story, in an interview that appears after her story, mentions having been influenced by a magazine account of "a killer in some southwestern state." A brief excerpt from the *Life* magazine article about this person, who provided a model for Arnold Friend, follows the story. It gives an indication of the way Miss Oates was able to create a story and a memorable character out of actual events, transforming fact into something that is perhaps more interesting and revealing.

Eudora Welty's use of a newspaper item in "A Piece of News" invites speculation about the kind of truth that fiction offers us. The newspaper story presents facts without explanations. We know that a woman named Ruby Fisher was shot in the leg by her husband. But what were the circumstances? Did the gun go off when he was loading it? Did he catch her in bed with another man? And what do we know about this "Ruby Fisher" and her husband anyway? Obviously the "truth" of such a news story is severely limited. Miss Welty's story embodies a larger truth—a truth about human nature and the possibilities for loneliness and love—because she provides a *context*. It is in terms of this context that Ruby Fisher's identification with the woman in the newspaper story becomes meaningful.

WHERE ARE YOU GOING,
WHERE HAVE YOU BEEN?*

for Bob Dylan

Her name was Connie. She was fifteen and she had a quick nervous giggling habit of craning her neck to glance into mirrors, or checking other people's faces to make sure her own was all right. Her mother, who noticed everything and knew everything and who hadn't much reason any longer to look at her own face, always scolded Connie about it. "Stop gawking at yourself, who are you? You think you're so pretty?" she would say. Connie would raise her eyebrows at these familiar complaints and look right through her mother, into a shadowy vision of herself as she was right at that moment: she knew she was pretty and that was everything. Her mother had been pretty once too, if you could believe those old snapshots in the album, but now her looks were gone and that was why she was always after Connie.

"Why don't you keep your room clean like your sister? How've you got your hair fixed —what the hell stinks? Hair spray? You don't see your sister using that junk."

Her sister June was twenty-four and still lived at home. She was a secretary in the high school Connie attended, and if that wasn't bad enough—with her in the same building— she was so plain and chunky and steady that Connie had to hear her praised all the time by her mother and her mother's sisters. June did this, June did that, she saved money and helped clean the house and cooked and Connie couldn't do a thing, her mind was all

filled with trashy daydreams. Their father was away at work most of the time and when he came home he wanted supper and he read the newspaper at supper and after supper he went to bed. He didn't bother talking much to them, but around his bent head Connie's mother kept picking at her until Connie wished her mother was dead and she herself was dead and it was all over. "She makes me want to throw up sometimes," she complained to her friends. She had a high, breathless, amused voice which made everything she said sound a little forced, whether it was sincere or not.

There was one good thing: June went places with girl friends of hers, girls who were just as plain and steady as she, and so when Connie wanted to do that her mother had no objections. The father of Connie's best girl friend drove the girls the three miles to town and left them off at a shopping plaza, so that they could walk through the stores or go to a movie, and when he came to pick them up again at eleven he never bothered to ask what they had done.

They must have been familiar sights, walking around that shopping plaza in their shorts and flat ballerina slippers that always scuffed the sidewalk, with charm bracelets jingling on their thin wrists; they would lean together to whisper and laugh secretly if someone passed by who amused or interested them. Connie had long dark blond hair that drew anyone's eye to it, and she wore part of it pulled up on her head and puffed out and the rest of it she let fall down her back. She wore

*An interview with Miss Oates appears at the end of this story.

a pull-over jersey blouse that looked one way when she was at home and another way when she was away from home. Everything about her had two sides to it, one for home and one for anywhere that was not home: her walk that could be childlike and bobbing, or languid enough to make anyone think she was hearing music in her head, her mouth which was pale and smirking most of the time, but bright and pink on these evenings out, her laugh which was cynical and drawling at home—"Ha, ha, very funny"—but high-pitched and nervous anywhere else, like the jingling of the charms on her bracelet.

Sometimes they did go shopping or to a movie, but sometimes they went across the highway, ducking fast across the busy road, to a drive-in restaurant where older kids hung out. The restaurant was shaped like a big bottle, though squatter than a real bottle, and on its cap was a revolving figure of a grinning boy who held a hamburger aloft. One night in mid-summer they ran across, breathless with daring, and right away someone leaned out a car window and invited them over, but it was just a boy from high school they didn't like. It made them feel good to be able to ignore him. They went up through the maze of parked and cruising cars to the bright-lit, fly-infested restaurant, their faces pleased and expectant as if they were entering a sacred building that loomed out of the night to give them what haven and what blessing they yearned for. They sat at the counter and crossed their legs at the ankles, their thin shoulders rigid with excitement, and listened to the music that made everything so good: the music was always in the background like music at a church service, it was something to depend on.

A boy named Eddie came in to talk with them. He sat backwards on his stool, turning himself jerkily around in semi-circles and then stopping and turning again, and after a while he asked Connie if she would like something to eat. She said she did and so she tapped her friend's arm on her way out—her friend pulled her face up into a brave droll look—

and Connie said she would meet her at eleven, across the way. "I just hate to leave her like that," Connie said earnestly, but the boy said that she wouldn't be alone for long. So they went out to his car and on the way Connie couldn't help but let her eyes wander over the windshields and faces all around her, her face gleaming with a joy that had nothing to do with Eddie or even this place; it might have been the music. She drew her shoulders up and sucked in her breath with the pure pleasure of being alive, and just at that moment she happened to glance at a face just a few feet from hers. It was a boy with shaggy black hair, in a convertible jalopy painted gold. He stared at her and then his lips widened into a grin. Connie slit her eyes at him and turned away, but she couldn't help glancing back and there he was still watching her. He wagged a finger and laughed and said, "Gonna get you, baby," and Connie turned away again without Eddie noticing anything.

She spent three hours with him, at the restaurant where they ate hamburgers and drank Cokes in wax cups that were always sweating, and then down an alley a mile or so away, and when he left her off at five to eleven only the movie house was still open at the plaza. Her girl friend was there, talking with a boy. When Connie came up the two girls smiled at each other and Connie said, "How was the movie?" and the girl said, "*You* should know." They rode off with the girl's father, sleepy and pleased, and Connie couldn't help but look at the darkened shopping plaza with its big empty parking lot and its signs that were faded and ghostly now, and over at the drive-in restaurant where cars were still circling tirelessly. She couldn't hear the music at this distance.

Next morning June asked her how the movie was and Connie said, "So-so."

She and that girl and occasionally another girl went out several times a week that way, and the rest of the time Connie spent around the house—it was summer vacation—getting in her mother's way and thinking, dreaming, about the boys she met. But all the boys fell back and dissolved into a single face that was not even a face, but an idea, a feeling, mixed up with the urgent insistent pounding of the music and the humid night air of July. Connie's mother kept dragging her back to the daylight by finding things for her to do or saying, suddenly, "What's this about the Pettinger girl?"

And Connie would say nervously, "Oh, her. That dope." She always drew thick clear lines between herself and such girls, and her mother was simple and kindly enough to believe her. Her mother was so simple, Connie thought, that it was maybe cruel to fool her so much. Her mother went scuffling around the house in old bedroom slippers and complained over the telephone to one sister about the other, then the other called up and the two of them complained about the third one. If June's name was mentioned her mother's tone was approving, and if Connie's name was mentioned it was disapproving. This did not really mean she disliked Connie and actually Connie thought that her mother preferred her to June because she was prettier, but the two of them kept up a pretense of exasperation, a sense that they were tugging and struggling over something of little value to either of them. Sometimes, over coffee, they were almost friends, but something would come up—some vexation that was like a fly buzzing suddenly around their heads— and their faces went hard with contempt.

One Sunday Connie got up at eleven— none of them bothered with church—and washed her hair so that it could dry all day long, in the sun. Her parents and sisters were going to a barbecue at an aunt's house and Connie said no, she wasn't interested, rolling her eyes to let mother know just what she thought of it. "Stay home alone then," her mother said sharply. Connie sat out back in a lawn chair and watched them drive away, her father quiet and bald, hunched around so that he could back the car out, her mother with a look that was still angry and not at all softened through the windshield, and in the

back seat poor old June all dressed up as if she didn't know what a barbecue was, with all the running yelling kids and the flies. Connie sat with her eyes closed in the sun, dreaming and dazed with the warmth about her as if this were a kind of love, the caresses of love, and her mind slipped over onto thoughts of the boy she had been with the night before and how nice he had been, how sweet it always was, not the way someone like June would suppose but sweet, gentle, the way it was in movies and promised in songs; and when she opened her eyes she hardly knew where she was, the back yard ran off into weeds and a fence-line of trees and behind it the sky was perfectly blue and still. The asbestos "ranch house" that was now three years old startled her—it looked small. She shook her head as if to get awake.

It was too hot. She went inside the house and turned on the radio to drown out the quiet. She sat on the edge of her bed, barefoot, and listened for an hour and a half to a program called XYZ Sunday Jamboree, record after record of hard, fast, shrieking songs she sang along with, interspersed by exclamations from "Bobby King": "An' look here you girls at Napoleon's—Son and Charley want you to pay real close attention to this song coming up!"

And Connie paid close attention herself, bathed in a glow of slow-pulsed joy that seemed to rise mysteriously out of the music itself and lay languidly about the airless little room, breathed in and breathed out with each gentle rise and fall of her chest.

After a while she heard a car coming up the drive. She sat up at once, startled, because it couldn't be her father so soon. The gravel kept crunching all the way in from the road —the driveway was long—and Connie ran to the window. It was a car she didn't know. It was an open jalopy, painted a bright gold that caught the sunlight opaquely. Her heart began to pound and her fingers snatched at her hair, checking it, and she whispered "Christ. Christ," wondering how bad she looked. The car came to a stop at the side door and the horn sounded four short taps as if this were a signal Connie knew.

She went into the kitchen and approached the door slowly, then hung out the screen door, her bare toes curling down off the step. There were two boys in the car and now she recognized the driver: he had shaggy, shabby black hair that looked crazy as a wig and he was grinning at her.

"I ain't late, am I?" he said.

"Who the hell do you think you are?" Connie said.

"Toldja I'd be out, didn't I?"

"I don't even know who you are."

She spoke sullenly, careful to show no interest or pleasure, and he spoke in a fast bright monotone. Connie looked past him to the other boy, taking her time. He had fair brown hair, with a lock that fell onto his forehead. His sideburns gave him a fierce, embarrassed look, but so far he hadn't even bothered to glance at her. Both boys wore sunglasses. The driver's glasses were metallic and mirrored everything in miniature.

"You wanta come for a ride?" he said.

Connie smirked and let her hair fall loose over one shoulder.

"Don'tcha like my car? New paint job," he said. "Hey."

"What?"

"You're cute."

She pretended to fidget, chasing flies away from the door.

"Don'tcha believe me, or what?" he said.

"Look, I don't even know who you are," Connie said in disgust.

"Hey, Ellie's got a radio, see. Mine's broke down." He lifted his friend's arm and showed her the little transistor the boy was holding, and now Connie began to hear the music. It was the same program that was playing inside the house.

"Bobby King?" she said.

"I listen to him all the time. I think he's great."

"He's kind of great," Connie said reluctantly.

"Listen, that guy's *great*. He knows where the action is."

Connie blushed a little, because the glasses made it impossible for her to see just what this boy was looking at. She couldn't decide if she liked him or if he was just a jerk, and so she dawdled in the doorway and wouldn't come down or go back inside. She said, "What's all that stuff painted on your car?"

"Can'tcha read it?" He opened the door very carefully, as if he was afraid it might fall off. He slid out just as carefully, planting his feet firmly on the ground, the tiny metallic world in his glasses slowing down like gelatine hardening and in the midst of it Connie's bright green blouse. "This here is my name, to begin with," he said. ARNOLD FRIEND was written in tar-like black letters on the side, with a drawing of a round grinning face that reminded Connie of a pumpkin, except it wore sunglasses. "I wanta introduce myself, I'm Arnold Friend and that's my real name and I'm gonna be your friend, honey, and inside the car's Ellie Oscar, he's kinda shy." Ellie brought his transistor radio up to his shoulder and balanced it there. "Now these numbers are a secret code, honey," Arnold Friend explained. He read off the numbers 33, 19, 17 and raised his eyebrows at her to see what she thought of that, but she didn't think much of it. The left rear fender had been smashed and around it was written, on the gleaming gold background: DONE BY CRAZY WOMAN DRIVER. Connie had to laugh at that. Arnold Friend was pleased at her laughter and looked up at her. "Around the other side's a lot more—you wanta come and see them?"

"No."

"Why not?"

"Why should I?"

"Don'tcha wanta see what's on the car? Don'tcha wanta go for a ride?"

"I don't know."

"Why not?"

"I got things to do."

"Like what?"

Since we are introduced to him earlier, we want to know how he knows what he does about her.

"Things."

He laughed as if she had said something funny. He slapped his thighs. He was standing in a strange way, leaning back against the car as if he were balancing himself. He wasn't tall, only an inch or so taller than she would be if she came down to him. Connie liked the way he was dressed, which was the way all of them dressed: tight faded jeans stuffed into black, scuffed boots, a belt that pulled his waist in and showed how lean he was, and a white pull-over shirt that was a little soiled and showed the hard small muscles of his arms and shoulders. He looked as if he probably did hard work, lifting and carrying things. Even his neck looked muscular. And his face was a familiar face, somehow: the jaw and chin and cheeks slightly darkened, because he hadn't shaved for a day or two, and the nose long and hawk-like, sniffing as if she were a treat he was going to gobble up and it was all a joke.

"Connie, you ain't telling the truth. This is your day set aside for a ride with me and you know it," he said, still laughing. The way he straightened and recovered from his fit of laughing showed that it had been all fake.

"How do you know what my name is?" she said suspiciously.

"It's Connie."

"Maybe and maybe not."

"I know my Connie," he said, wagging his finger. Now she remembered him even better, back at the restaurant, and her cheeks warmed at the thought of how she sucked in her breath just at the moment she passed him —how she must have looked to him. And he had remembered her. "Ellie and I come out here especially for you," he said. "Ellie can sit in back. How about it?"

"Where?"

"Where what?"

"Where're we going?"

He looked at her. He took off the sunglasses and she saw how pale the skin around his eyes was, like holes that were not in shadow but instead in light. His eyes were like chips of broken glass that catch the light in an amiable way. He smiled. It was as if the idea of going for a ride somewhere, to some place, was a new idea to him.

"Just for a ride, Connie sweetheart."

"I never said my name was Connie," she said.

"But I know what it is. I know your name and all about you, lots of things," Arnold Friend said. He had not moved yet but stood still leaning back against the side of his jalopy. "I took a special interest in you, such a pretty girl, and found out all about you like I know your parents and sister are gone somewheres and I know where and how long they're going to be gone, and I know who you were with last night, and your best girl friend's name is Betty. Right?"

He spoke in a simple lilting voice, exactly as if he were reciting the words to a song. His smile assured her that everything was fine. In the car Ellie turned up the volume on his radio and did not bother to look around at them.

"Ellie can sit in the back seat," Arnold Friend said. He indicated his friend with a casual jerk of his chin, as if Ellie did not count and she should not bother with him.

"How'd you find out all that stuff?" Connie said.

"Listen: Betty Schultz and Tony Fitch and Jimmy Pettinger and Nancy Pettinger," he said, in a chant. "Raymond Stanley and Bob Hutter—"

"Do you know all those kids?"

"I know everybody."

"Look, you're kidding. You're not from around here."

"Sure."

"But—how come we never saw you before?"

"Sure you saw me before," he said. He looked down at his boots, as if he were a little offended. "You just don't remember."

"I guess I'd remember you," Connie said.

"Yeah?" He looked up at this, beaming. He was pleased. He began to mark time with the music from Ellie's radio, tapping his fists lightly together. Connie looked away from his smile to the car, which was painted so bright it almost hurt her eyes to look at it. She looked at that name, ARNOLD FRIEND. And up at the front fender was an expression that was familiar—MAN THE FLYING SAUCERS. It was an expression kids had used the year before, but didn't use this year. She looked at it for a while as if the words meant something to her that she did not yet know.

"What're you thinking about? Huh?" Arnold Friend demanded. "Not worried about your hair blowing around in the car, are you?"

"No."

"Think I maybe can't drive good?"

"How do I know?"

"You're a hard girl to handle. How come?" he said. "Don't you know I'm your friend? Didn't you see me put my sign in the air when you walked by?"

"What sign?"

"My sign." And he drew an X in the air, leaning out toward her. They were maybe ten feet apart. After his hand fell back to his side the X was still in the air, almost visible. Connie let the screen door close and stood perfectly still inside it, listening to the music from her radio and the boy's blend together. She stared at Arnold Friend. He stood there so stiffly relaxed, pretending to be relaxed, with one hand idly on the door handle as if he were keeping himself up that way and had no intention of ever moving again. She recognized most things about him, the tight jeans that showed his thighs and buttocks and the greasy leather boots and the tight shirt, and even that slippery friendly smile of his, that sleepy dreamy smile that all the boys used to get across ideas they didn't want to put into words. She recognized all this and also the singsong way he talked, slightly mocking, kidding, but serious and a little melancholy, and she recognized the way he tapped one fist against the other in homage to the per-petual music behind him. But all these things did not come together.

She said suddenly, "Hey, how old are you?"

His smile faded. She could see then that he wasn't a kid, he was much older—thirty, maybe more. At this knowledge her heart began to pound faster.

"That's a crazy thing to ask. Can'tcha see I'm your own age?"

"Like hell you are."

"Or maybe a coupla years older, I'm eighteen."

"Eighteen?" she said doubtfully.

He grinned to reassure her and lines appeared at the corners of his mouth. His teeth were big and white. He grinned so broadly his eyes became slits and she saw how thick the lashes were, thick and black as if painted with a black tar-like material. Then he seemed to become embarrassed, abruptly, and looked over his shoulder at Ellie. "*Him*, he's crazy," he said. "Ain't he a riot, he's a nut, a real character." Ellie was still listening to the music. His sunglasses told nothing about what he was thinking. He wore a bright orange shirt unbuttoned halfway to show his chest, which was a pale, bluish chest and not muscular like Arnold Friend's. His shirt collar was turned up all around and the very tips of the collar pointed out past his chin as if they were protecting him. He was pressing the transistor radio up against his ear and sat there in a kind of daze, right in the sun.

"He's kinda strange," Connie said.

"Hey, she says you're kinda strange! Kinda strange!" Arnold Friend cried. He pounded on the car to get Ellie's attention. Ellie turned for the first time and Connie saw with shock that he wasn't a kid either—he had a fair, hairless face, cheeks reddened slightly as if the veins grew too close to the surface of his skin, the face of a forty-year-old baby. Connie felt a wave of dizziness rise in her at this sight and she stared at him as if waiting for something to change the shock of the moment, make it all right again. Ellie's lips kept shaping words, mumbling along with the words blasting in his ear.

"Maybe you two better go away," Connie said faintly.

"What? How come?" Arnold Friend cried. "We come out here to take you for a ride. It's Sunday." He had the voice of the man on the radio now. It was the same voice, Connie thought. "Don'tcha know it's Sunday all day and honey, no matter who you were with last night today you're with Arnold Friend and don't you forget it!—Maybe you better step out here," he said, and this last was in a different voice. It was a little flatter, as if the heat was finally getting to him.

"No. I got things to do."

"Hey."

"You two better leave."

"We ain't leaving until you come with us."

"Like hell I am—"

"Connie, don't fool around with me. I mean, don't fool *around*," he said, shaking his head. He laughed incredulously. He placed his sunglasses on top of his head, carefully, as if he were indeed wearing a wig, and brought the stems down behind his ears. Connie stared at him, another wave of dizziness and fear rising in her so that for a moment he wasn't even in focus but was just a blur, standing there against his gold car, and she had the idea that he had driven up the driveway all right but had come from nowhere before that and belonged nowhere and that everything about him and even about the music that was so familiar to her was only half real.

"If my father comes and sees you—"

"He ain't coming. He's at a barbecue."

"How do you know that?"

"Aunt Tillie's. Right now they're—uh—they're drinking. Sitting around," he said vaguely, squinting as if he were staring all the way to town and over to Aunt Tillie's back yard. Then the vision seemed to get clear and he nodded energetically. "Yeah. Sitting around. There's your sister in a blue dress, huh? And high heels, the poor sad bitch—nothing like you, sweetheart! And your mother's helping some fat woman with the corn, they're cleaning the corn—husking the corn—"

"What fat woman?" Connie cried.

"How do I know what fat woman, I don't know every goddam fat woman in the world!" Arnold Friend laughed.

"Oh, that's Mrs. Hornby. . . . Who invited her?" Connie said. She felt a little light-headed. Her breath was coming quickly.

"She's too fat. I don't like them fat. I like them the way you are, honey," he said smiling sleepily at her. They stared at each other for a while, through the screen door. He said softly, "Now what you're going to do is this: you're going to come out that door. You're going to sit up front with me and Ellie's going to sit in the back, the hell with Ellie, right? This isn't Ellie's date. You're my date. I'm your lover, honey."

"What? You're crazy—"

"Yes, I'm your lover. You don't know what that is but you will," he said. "I know that too. I know all about you. But look: it's real nice and you couldn't ask for nobody better than me, or more polite. I always keep my word. I'll tell you how it is, I'm always nice at first, the first time. I'll hold you so tight you won't think you have to try to get away or pretend anything because you'll know you can't. And I'll come inside you where it's all secret and you'll give in to me and you'll love me—"

"Shut up! You're crazy!" Connie said. She backed away from the door. She put her hands against her ears as if she'd heard something terrible, something not meant for her. "People don't talk like that, you're crazy," she muttered. Her heart was almost too big now for her chest and its pumping made sweat break out all over her. She looked out to see Arnold Friend pause and then take a step toward the porch lurching. He almost fell. But, like a clever drunken man, he managed to catch his balance. He wobbled in his high boots and grabbed hold of one of the porch posts.

"Honey?" he said. "You still listening?"

"Get the hell out of here!"

"Be nice, honey. Listen."

"I'm going to call the police—"

He wobbled again and out of the side of his mouth came a fast spat curse, an aside not meant for her to hear. But even this "Christ!" sounded forced. Then he began to smile again. She watched this smile come, awkward as if he were smiling from inside a mask. His whole face was a mask, she thought wildly, tanned down onto his throat but then running out as if he had plastered make-up on his face but had forgotten about his throat.

"Honey—? Listen, here's how it is. I always tell the truth and I promise you this: I ain't coming in that house after you."

"You better not! I'm going to call the police if you—if you don't—"

"Honey," he said, talking right through her voice, "honey, I'm not coming in there but you are coming out here. You know why?"

She was panting. The kitchen looked like a place she had never seen before, some room she had run inside but which wasn't good enough, wasn't going to help her. The kitchen window had never had a curtain, after three years, and there were dishes in the sink for her to do—probably—and if you ran your hand across the table you'd probably feel something sticky there.

"You listening, honey? Hey?"

"—going to call the police—"

"Soon as you touch the phone I don't need to keep my promise and can come inside. You won't want that."

She rushed forward and tried to lock the door. Her fingers were shaking. "But why lock it," Arnold Friend said gently, talking right into her face. "It's just a screen door. It's just nothing." One of his boots was at a strange angle, as if his foot wasn't in it. It pointed out to the left, bent at the ankle. "I mean, anybody can break through a screen door and glass and wood and iron or any-

thing else if he needs to, anybody at all and specially Arnold Friend. If the place got lit up with a fire honey you'd come running out into my arms, right into my arms and safe at home—like you knew I was your lover and'd stopped fooling around. I don't mind a nice shy girl but I don't like no fooling around." Part of those words were spoken with a slight rhythmic lilt, and Connie somehow recognized them—the echo of a song from last year, about a girl rushing into her boy friend's arms and coming home again—

Connie stood barefoot on the linoleum floor, staring at him. "What do you want?" she whispered.

"I want you," he said.

"What?"

"Seen you that night and thought, that's the one, yes sir. I never needed to look any more."

"But my father's coming back. He's coming to get me. I had to wash my hair first—" She spoke in a dry, rapid voice, hardly raising it for him to hear.

"No, your daddy is not coming and yes, you had to wash your hair and you washed it for me. It's nice and shining and all for me, I thank you, sweetheart," he said, with a mock bow, but again he almost lost his balance. He had to bend and adjust his boots. Evidently his feet did not go all the way down; the boots must have been stuffed with something so that he would seem taller. Connie stared out at him and behind him Ellie in the car, who seemed to be looking off toward Connie's right, into nothing. This Ellie said, pulling the words out of the air one after another as if he were just discovering them, "You want me to pull out the phone?"

"Shut your mouth and keep it shut," Arnold Friend said, his face red from bending over or maybe from embarrassment because Connie had seen his boots. "This ain't none of your business."

"What—what are you doing? What do you want?" Connie said. "If I call the police they'll get you, they'll arrest you—"

"Promise was not to come in unless you

touch that phone, and I'll keep that promise," he said. He resumed his erect position and tried to force his shoulders back. He sounded like a hero in a movie, declaring something important. He spoke too loudly and it was as if he were speaking to someone behind Connie. "I ain't made plans for coming in that house where I don't belong but just for you to come out to me, the way you should. Don't you know who I am?"

"You're crazy," she whispered. She backed away from the door but did not want to go into another part of the house, as if this would give him permission to come through the door. "What do you. . . . You're crazy, you . . ."

"Huh? What're you saying, honey?"

Her eyes darted everywhere in the kitchen. She could not remember what it was, this room.

"This is how it is, honey: you come out and we'll drive away, have a nice ride. But if you don't come out we're gonna wait till your people come home and then they're all going to get it."

"You want that telephone pulled out?" Ellie said. He held the radio away from his ear and grimaced, as if without the radio the air was too much for him.

"I toldja shut up, Ellie," Arnold Friend said, "you're deaf, get a hearing aid, right? Fix yourself up. This little girl's no trouble and's gonna be nice to me, so Ellie keep to yourself, this ain't your date—right? Don't hem in on me. Don't hog. Don't crush. Don't bird dog. Don't trail me," he said in a rapid meaningless voice, as if he were running through all the expressions he'd learned but was no longer sure which one of them was in style, then rushing on to new ones, making them up with his eyes closed, "Don't crawl under my fence, don't squeeze in my chipmunk hole, don't sniff my glue, suck my popsicle, keep your own greasy fingers on yourself!" He shaded his eyes and peered in at Connie, who was backed against the kitchen table. "Don't mind him honey he's just a creep. He's a dope. Right? I'm the boy for you and like I said you come out here nice like a lady and give me your hand, and nobody else gets hurt, I mean, your nice old bald-headed daddy and your mummy and your sister in her high heels. Because listen: why bring them in this?"

"Leave me alone," Connie whispered.

"Hey, you know that old woman down the road, the one with the chickens and stuff—you know her?"

"She's dead!"

"Dead? What? You know her?" Arnold Friend said.

"She's dead—"

"Don't you like her?"

"She's dead—she's—she isn't here any more—"

"But don't you like her, I mean, you got something against her? Some grudge or something?" Then his voice dipped as if he were conscious of a rudeness. He touched the sunglasses perched on top of his head as if to make sure they were still there. "Now you be a good girl."

"What are you going to do?"

"Just two things, or maybe three," Arnold Friend said. "But I promise it won't last long and you'll like me that way you get to like people you're close to. You will. It's all over for you here, so come on out. You don't want your people in any trouble, do you?"

She turned and bumped against a chair or something, hurting her leg, but she ran into the back room and picked up the telephone. Something roared in her ear, a tiny roaring and she was so sick with fear that she could do nothing but listen to it—the telephone was clammy and very heavy and her fingers groped down to the dial but were too weak to touch it. She began to scream into the phone, into the roaring. She cried out, she cried for her mother, she felt her breath start jerking back and forth in her lungs as if it were something Arnold Friend were stabbing her with again and again with no tenderness. A noisy sorrowful wailing rose all about her and she was locked inside it the way she was locked inside this house.

After a while she could hear again. She was sitting on the floor with her wet back against the wall.

Arnold Friend was saying from the door, "That's a good girl. Put the phone back."

She kicked the phone away from her.

"No, honey. Pick it up. Put it back right."

She picked it up and put it back. The dial tone stopped.

"That's a good girl. Now you come outside."

She was hollow with what had been fear, but what was now just an emptiness. All that screaming had blasted it out of her. She sat, one leg cramped under her, and deep inside her brain was something like a pinpoint of light that kept going and would not let her relax. She thought, I'm not going to see my mother again. She thought, I'm not going to sleep in my bed again. Her bright green blouse was all wet.

Arnold Friend said, in a gentle-loud voice that was like a stage voice, "The place where you came from ain't there any more, and where you had in mind to go is cancelled out. This place you are now—inside your daddy's house—is nothing but a cardboard box I can knock down any time. You know that and always did know it. You hear me?"

She thought, I have got to think. I have to know what to do.

"We'll go out to a nice field, out in the country here where it smells so nice and it's sunny," Arnold Friend said. "I'll have my arms tight around you so you won't need to try to get away and I'll show you what love is like, what it does. The hell with this house! It looks solid all right," he said. He ran a fingernail down the screen and the noise did not make Connie shiver, as it would have the day before. "Now put your hand on your heart, honey. Feel that? That feels solid too but we know better, be nice to me, be sweet like you can because what else is there for a girl like you but to be sweet and pretty and give in?—and get away before her people come back?"

She felt her pounding heart. Her hand seemed to enclose it. She thought for the first time in her life that it was nothing that was hers, that belonged to her, but just a pounding, living thing inside this body that wasn't really hers either.

"You don't want them to get hurt," Arnold Friend went on. "Now get up, honey. Get up all by yourself."

She stood.

"Now turn this way. That's right. Come over here to me—Ellie, put that away, didn't I tell you? You dope. You miserable creepy dope," Arnold Friend said. His words were not angry but only part of an incantation. The incantation was kindly. "Now come out through the kitchen to me honey and let's see a smile, try it, you're a brave sweet little girl and now they're eating corn and hotdogs cooked to bursting over an outdoor fire, and they don't know one thing about you and never did and honey you're better than them because not a one of them would have done this for you."

Connie felt the linoleum under her feet; it was cool. She brushed her hair back out of her eyes. Arnold Friend let go of the post tentatively and opened his arms for her, his elbows pointing in toward each other and his wrists limp, to show that this was an embarrassed embrace and a little mocking, he didn't want to make her self-conscious.

She put out her hand against the screen. She watched herself push the door slowly open as if she were safe back somewhere in the other doorway, watching this body and this head of long hair moving out into the sunlight where Arnold Friend waited.

"My sweet little blue-eyed girl," he said, in a half-sung sigh that had nothing to do with her brown eyes but was taken up just the same by the vast sunlit reaches of the land behind him and on all sides of him, so much land that Connie had never seen before and did not recognize except to know that she was going to it.

The March 4, 1966, issue of *Life* magazine tells the story of Charles Schmid, who talked tough and disguised his height (five feet, three inches) by stuffing old rags and tin cans in the bottoms of his boots. Schmid was eventually convicted of murder. The *Life* article begins this way:

The Pied Piper of Tucson

Sullen and unshaved, 23 years old and arrested for murder, Charles Schmid did not now look like a hero. But to many of the teen-agers in Tucson, Arizona, he had been someone to admire and emulate. He was different. He was Smitty, with mean, "beautiful" eyes and an interesting way of talking, and if he sometimes did weird things, at least he wasn't dull. He had his own house where he threw good parties, he wore crazy make-up, he was known at all the joints up and down Tucson's Speedway, and girls dyed their hair blond for him. Three of the girls who knew him wound up dead in the desert outside of town.

1. How is Arnold Friend like Charles Schmid? How is he different? How does the effect of the story differ from that of the magazine article (insofar as you can judge from the excerpt above)?

2. Why does Connie listen to Arnold Friend at all? At one point she recognizes that he has all the right clothes, gestures, and words, "But all these things did not come together." What is wrong with the way he looks and acts? Why does Arnold Friend seem dangerous?

3. What does Connie's failure to resist reveal about her social education? ("What else is there for a girl like you but to be sweet and pretty and give in?")

INTERVIEW WITH JOYCE CAROL OATES

I

EDITORS: Could you give us some idea of the way you work—how you get ideas for stories and how the stories develop?

MISS OATES: The "ideas" seem to come out of nowhere, perhaps originally as dreams, or day-dreams. There is sometimes a crowd of people, or of images, or sounds—difficult to explain—and, in me, a sense of restlessness and disorder, which must be made sensible, coherent, in some way explicable. When the sensations become "ideas" they have already been distorted to some extent, and when they become formal works of art they are further distorted.

EDITORS: What kinds of conditions do you need to write?

MISS OATES: Relative privacy and quiet, I suppose. I can write when I am feeling upset, though; good health is evidently not that important.

EDITORS: Maureen, in your novel *Them*, is excited by reading novels, perceiving their worlds as more real than hers, the characters' suffering greater than her own. What is *your* feeling about the characters you create versus real people?

MISS OATES: A question I find difficult to answer: the people are "real" to me as many people I know are not real, and they are more "interesting" because less predictable.

So many of my characters are actually based upon real people . . . just as most of the plots are "real" plots, taken over from life and fixed up slightly. . . .

EDITORS: Willa Cather once wrote: "there are only two or three human stories, and they go on repeating themselves as if they had never happened before." As you write more and more, do you find yourself returning to the same themes?

MISS OATES: Not consciously, but I suppose I am under an enchantment to repeat certain patterns until I am free of them. Once I finish a story or a novel I feel rather melancholy because I will never write about those people again, but at the same time I am impatient to get on with the next work, because I always feel rather crowded and harassed with things that I should be working on. This sensation of "crowding" might have some psychological (psychopathological?) explanation.

EDITORS: In 1961, the year before his own novel *Letting Go* was published, Philip Roth wrote an article in which he argued that current fiction was failing to deal with the very real horrors of American society. Do you think, a decade later, that some of those horrors are being met more completely?

MISS OATES: As I recall the article, Roth said that reality had outstripped fiction because it was more horrible. . . . But reality has always been horrible, and fiction has always been able to deal with it.

EDITORS: Do your characters generally turn out the way you expect them to? How clear an idea of Arnold Friend did you have, for example, before you wrote the story?

MISS OATES: My characters and the way they "turn out" are inseparable. They *are* their destinies, their plots. "Arnold Friend" is what he is because he does what he does; every word of his, every aspect of his physical being, is imagined with his actions in mind.

EDITORS: Lillian Hellman said, in a *Paris Review* interview, "I don't really know much about the process of creation and I don't like talking about it." Do you feel the same way, or would you like to comment on the creative process?

MISS OATES: Unlike Miss Hellman, I am fascinated with the "creative process" though, like her, I don't know much about it. It is a mystery. Analyzed, argued over, categorized, still it remains a mystery, like our dreams—in which we are all artists.

WHERE ARE YOU GOING, WHERE HAVE YOU BEEN?

II

EDITORS: How did you get the idea for the story?

MISS OATES: The story as it was originally published in *Epoch* was not dedicated to anyone, but after that I dedicated it "to Bob Dylan." I will explain this: after hearing for some weeks Dylan's song "It's All Over Now, Baby Blue," and after having read about a killer in some Southwestern state, and after having thought about

18

the old legends and folk songs of Death and the Maiden, the story came to me more or less in a piece. Dylan's song is very beautiful, very disturbing.

EDITORS: How does Arnold Friend know so much about what Connie's parents are doing? About the woman down the street?

MISS OATES: Arnold Friend is a fantastic figure: he is Death, he is the "elf-Knight" of the ballads, he is the Imagination, he is a Dream, he is a Lover, a Demon, *and all that*. The story was originally called "Death and the Maiden," but I thought the title too pompous, too literary.

It is always frustrating to attempt to explain these things . . . the mind goes dead, the voice keeps on supplying words, familiar terms, a system of explanations. But the explanations are false, or inadequate. What is so terrifying about the world of dreams is its indeterminate quality; raised to a verbal level (what is verbalized is less of a threat. . . ?) so much is lost, at least to the rational mind. Still, it will not do to suggest that one writes in a trance, the way Jackson Pollock evidently did some of his violent paintings, because writing and painting (his kind of painting) are two quite different things. But the "writing" I do is a kind of reporting, a recalling, an approximation of things that have already happened. I never write until these things have already happened, and then I try to do justice to them.

A PIECE OF NEWS

She had been out in the rain. She stood in
front of the cabin fireplace, her legs wide
apart, bending over, shaking her wet yellow
head crossly, like a cat reproaching itself for
not knowing better. She was talking to herself—only a small fluttering sound, hard to
lay hold of in the sparsity of the room.

"The pouring-down rain, the pouring-
down rain"—was that what she was saying
over and over, like a song? She stood turning
in little quarter turns to dry herself, her head
bent forward and the yellow hair hanging out
streaming and tangled. She was holding her
skirt primly out to draw the warmth in.

Then, quite rosy, she walked over to the
table and picked up a little bundle. It was a
sack of coffee, marked "Sample" in red letters, which she unwrapped from a wet newspaper. But she handled it tenderly.

"Why, how come he wrapped it in a newspaper!" she said, catching her breath, looking
from one hand to the other. She must have
been lonesome and slow all her life, the way
things would take her by surprise.

She set the coffee on the table, just in the
center. Then she dragged the newspaper by
one corner in a dreamy walk across the floor,
spread it all out, and lay down full length on
top of it in front of the fire. Her little song
about the rain, her cries of surprise, had been
only a preliminary, only playful pouting with
which she amused herself when she was alone.
She was pleased with herself now. As she
sprawled close to the fire, her hair began to
slide out of its damp tangles and hung all dis-
played down her back like a piece of bargain
silk. She closed her eyes. Her mouth fell into
a deepness, into a look of unconscious cunning. Yet in her very stillness and pleasure she

seemed to be hiding there, all alone. And at
moments when the fire stirred and tumbled
in the grate, she would tremble, and her hand
would start out as if in impatience or despair.

Presently she stirred and reached under her
back for the newspaper. Then she squatted
there, touching the printed page as if it were
fragile. She did not merely look at it—she
watched it, as if it were unpredictable, like a
young girl watching a baby. The paper was
still wet in places where her body had lain.
Crouching tensely and patting the creases
away with small cracked red fingers, she
frowned now and then at the blotched drawing of something and big letters that spelled
a word underneath. Her lips trembled, as if
looking and spelling so slowly had stirred her
heart.

All at once she laughed.

She looked up.

"Ruby Fisher!" she whispered.

An expression of utter timidity came over
her flat blue eyes and her soft mouth. Then a
look of fright. She stared about. . . . What eye
in the world did she feel looking in on her?
She pulled her dress down tightly and began
to spell through a dozen words in the newspaper.

The little item said:

"Mrs. Ruby Fisher had the misfortune to
be shot in the leg by her husband this week."

As she passed from one word to the next she
only whispered; she left the long word, "misfortune," until the last, and came back to it,
then she said it all over out loud, like conversation.

"That's me," she said softly, with defer-
ence, very formally.

The fire slipped and suddenly roared in the

house already deafening with the rain which beat upon the roof and hung full of lightning and thunder outside.

"You Clyde!" screamed Ruby Fisher at last, jumping to her feet. "Where are you, Clyde Fisher?"

She ran straight to the door and pulled it open. A shudder of cold brushed over her in the heat, and she seemed striped with anger and bewilderment. There was a flash of lightning, and she stood waiting, as if she half thought that would bring him in, a gun leveled in his hand.

She said nothing more and, backing against the door, pushed it closed with her hip. Her anger passed like a remote flare of elation. Neatly avoiding the table where the bag of coffee stood, she began to walk nervously about the room, as if a teasing indecision, an untouched mystery, led her by the hand. There was one window, and she paused now and then, waiting, looking out at the rain. When she was still, there was a passivity about her, or a deception of passivity, that was not really passive at all. There was something in her that never stopped.

At last she flung herself onto the floor, back across the newspaper, and looked at length into the fire. It might have been a mirror in the cabin, into which she could look deeper and deeper as she pulled her fingers through her hair, trying to see herself and Clyde coming up behind her.

"Clyde?"

But of course her husband, Clyde, was still in the woods. He kept a thick brushwood roof over his whisky still, and he was mortally afraid of lightning like this, and would never go out in it for anything.

And then, almost in amazement, she began to comprehend her predicament: it was unlike Clyde to take up a gun and shoot her.

She bowed her head toward the heat, onto her rosy arms, and began to talk and talk to herself. She grew voluble. Even if he heard about the coffee man, with a Pontiac car, she did not think he would shoot her. When Clyde would make her blue, she would go out onto the road, some car would slow down, and if it had a Tennessee license, the lucky kind, the chances were that she would spend the afternoon in the shed of the empty gin. (Here she rolled her head about on her arms and stretched her legs tiredly behind her, like a cat.) And if Clyde got word, he would slap her. But the account in the paper was wrong. Clyde had never shot her, even once. There had been a mistake made.

A spark flew out and nearly caught the paper on fire. Almost in fright she beat it out with her fingers. Then she murmured and lay back more firmly upon the pages.

There she stretched, growing warmer and warmer, sleepier and sleepier. She began to wonder out loud how it would be if Clyde shot her in the leg. . . . If he were truly angry, might he shoot her through the heart?

At once she was imagining herself dying. She would have a nightgown to lie in, and a bullet in her heart. Anyone could tell, to see her lying there with that deep expression about her mouth, how strange and terrible that would be. Underneath a brand-new nightgown her heart would be hurting with every beat, many times more than her toughened skin when Clyde slapped at her. Ruby began to cry softly, the way she would be crying from the extremity of pain; tears would run down in a little stream over the quilt. Clyde would be standing there above her, as he once looked, with his wild black hair hanging to his shoulders. He used to be very handsome and strong!

He would say, "Ruby, I done this to you."

She would say—only a whisper—"That is the truth, Clyde—you done this to me."

Then she would die; her life would stop right there.

She lay silently for a moment, composing her face into a look which would be beautiful, desirable, and dead.

Clyde would have to buy her a dress to bury her in. He would have to dig a deep hole behind the house, under the cedar, a grave. He would have to nail her up a pine coffin and lay her inside. Then he would have to carry her to the grave, lay her down and cover her up. All the time he would be wild, shouting, and all distracted, to think he could never touch her one more time.

She moved slightly, and her eyes turned toward the window. The white rain splashed down. She could hardly breathe, for thinking that this was the way it was to fall on her grave, where Clyde would come and stand, looking down in the tears of some repentance.

A whole tree of lightning stood in the sky. She kept looking out the window, suffused with the warmth from the fire and with the pity and beauty and power of her death. The thunder rolled.

Then Clyde was standing there, with dark streams flowing over the floor where he had walked. He poked at Ruby with the butt of his gun, as if she were asleep.

"What's keepin' supper?" he growled.

She jumped up and darted away from him. Then, quicker than lightning, she put away the paper. The room was dark, except for the firelight. From the long shadow of his steamy presence she spoke to him glibly and lighted the lamp.

He stood there with a stunned, yet rather good-humored look of delay and patience in his face, and kept on standing there. He stamped his mud-red boots, and his enormous hands seemed weighted with the rain that fell from him and dripped down the barrel of the gun. Presently he sat down with dignity in the chair at the table, making a little tumult of his rightful wetness and hunger. Small streams began to flow from him everywhere.

Ruby was going through the preparations for the meal gently. She stood almost on tiptoe in her bare, warm feet. Once as she knelt at the safe, getting out the biscuits, she saw Clyde looking at her and she smiled and bent her head tenderly. There was some way she began to move her arms that was mysteriously sweet and yet abrupt and tentative, a delicate and vulnerable manner, as though her breasts gave her pain. She made many unnecessary trips back and forth across the floor, circling Clyde where he sat in his steamy silence, a knife and fork in his fists.

"Well, where you been, anyway?" he grumbled at last, as she set the first dish on the table.

"Nowheres special."

"Don't you talk back to me. You been hitchhikin' again, ain't you?" He almost chuckled.

She gave him a quick look straight into his eyes. She had not even heard him. She was filled with happiness. Her hand trembled when she poured the coffee. Some of it splashed on his wrist.

At that he let his hand drop heavily down upon the table and made the plates jump.

"Some day I'm goin to smack the livin' devil outa you," he said.

Ruby dodged mechanically. She let him eat. Then, when he had crossed his knife and fork over his plate, she brought him the newspaper. Again she looked at him in delight. It excited her even to touch the paper with her hand, to hear its quiet secret noise when she carried it, the rustle of surprise.

"A newspaper!" Clyde snatched it roughly and with a grabbing disparagement. "Where'd you git that? Hussy."

"Look at this-here," said Ruby in her small sing-song voice. She opened the paper while he held it and pointed gravely to the paragraph.

Reluctantly, Clyde began to read it. She watched his damp bald head slowly bend and turn.

Then he made a sound in his throat and said, "It's a lie."

"That's what's in the newspaper about me," said Ruby, standing up straight. She took up his plate and gave him that look of joy.

He put his big crooked finger on the paragraph and poked at it.

"Well, I'd just like to see the place I shot you!" he cried explosively. He looked up, his face blank and bold.

But she drew herself in, still holding the

empty plate, faced him straightened and hard, and they looked at each other. The moment filled full with their helplessness. Slowly they both flushed, as though with a double shame and a double pleasure. It was as though Clyde might really have killed Ruby, and as though Ruby might really have been dead at his hand. Rare and wavering, some possibility stood timidly like a stranger between them and made them hang their heads.

Then Clyde walked over in his water-soaked boots and laid the paper on the dying fire. It floated there a moment and then burst into flame. They stood still and watched it burn. The whole room was bright.

"Look," said Clyde suddenly. "It's a Tennessee paper. See 'Tennessee'? That wasn't none of you it wrote about." He laughed, to show that he had been right all the time.

"It was Ruby Fisher!" cried Ruby. "My name is Ruby Fisher!" she declared passionately to Clyde.

"Oho, it was another Ruby Fisher—in Tennessee," cried her husband. "Fool me, huh? Where'd you get that paper?" He spanked her good-humoredly across her backside.

Ruby folded her still trembling hands into her skirt. She stood stooping by the window until everything, outside and in, was quieted before she went to her supper.

It was dark and vague outside. The storm had rolled away to faintness like a wagon crossing a bridge.

1. The setting of a story—the background against which the action takes place—helps define the characters and the action in which they are involved by locating them in a limited world. Eudora Welty locates the events of "A Piece of News" in the rural South but reveals very little of Ruby Fisher's world: the cabin in which she lives, the highway where she hitchhikes, Clyde's still in the woods. How does what you see of the cabin and its simple furnishings affect your view of Ruby's life? The storm outside is part of the background of the action. What does it contribute to the mood of the story?

2. Do you get to know Ruby better through her gestures or through the statements that Miss Welty makes about her?

3. The action of a good story grows naturally out of the relationships of the characters—usually out of a tension, or conflict, between them. This action typically moves toward a moment at which the central character or characters make some kind of discovery. The turning point of "A Piece of News" comes when Ruby and Clyde flush "as though with a double shame and double pleasure." What is the "possibility" that stands between them? Is it realized or not?

A ROSE FOR EMILY

I

When Miss Emily Grierson died, our whole town went to her funeral: the men through a sort of respectful affection for a fallen monument, the women mostly out of curiosity to see the inside of her house, which no one save an old manservant—a combined gardener and cook—had seen in at least ten years.

It was a big, squarish frame house that had once been white, decorated with cupolas and spires and scrolled balconies in the heavily lightsome style of the seventies, set on what had once been our most select street. But garages and cotton gins had encroached and obliterated even the august names of that neighborhood; only Miss Emily's house was left, lifting its stubborn and coquettish decay above the cotton wagons and the gasoline pumps—an eyesore among eyesores. And now Miss Emily had gone to join the representatives of those august names where they lay in the cedar-bemused cemetery among the ranked and anonymous graves of Union and Confederate soldiers who fell at the battle of Jefferson.

Alive, Miss Emily had been a tradition, a duty, and a care; a sort of hereditary obligation upon the town, dating from that day in 1894 when Colonel Sartoris, the mayor—he who fathered the edict that no Negro woman should appear on the streets without an apron —remitted her taxes, the dispensation dating from the death of her father on into perpetuity. Not that Miss Emily would have accepted charity. Colonel Sartoris invented an involved tale to the effect that Miss Emily's father had loaned money to the town, which the town, as a matter of business, preferred this way of repaying. Only a man of Colonel Sartoris' generation and thought could have

invented it, and only a woman could have believed it.

When the next generation, with its more modern ideas, became mayors and aldermen, this arrangement created some little dissatisfaction. On the first of the year they mailed her a tax notice. February came, and there was no reply. They wrote her a formal letter, asking her to call at the sheriff's office at her convenience. A week later the mayor wrote her himself, offering to call or to send his car for her, and received in reply a note on paper of an archaic shape, in a thin, flowing calligraphy in faded ink, to the effect that she no longer went out at all. The tax notice was also enclosed, without comment.

They called a special meeting of the Board of Aldermen. A deputation waited upon her, knocked at the door through which no visitor had passed since she ceased giving china-painting lessons eight or ten years earlier. They were admitted by the old Negro into a dim hall from which a stairway mounted into still more shadow. It smelled of dust and disuse—a close, dank smell. The Negro led them into the parlor. It was furnished in heavy, leather-covered furniture. When the Negro opened the blinds of one window, they could see that the leather was cracked; and when they sat down, a faint dust rose sluggishly about their thighs, spinning with slow motes in the single sunray. On a tarnished gilt easel before the fireplace stood a crayon portrait of Miss Emily's father.

They rose when she entered—a small, fat woman in black, with a thin gold chain descending to her waist and vanishing into her belt, leaning on an ebony cane with a tarnished gold head. Her skeleton was small and spare; perhaps that was why what would have been merely plumpness in another was obesity in her. She looked bloated, like a body long submerged in motionless water, and of that pallid hue. Her eyes, lost in the fatty ridges of her face, looked like two small pieces of coal pressed into a lump of dough as they moved from one face to another while the visitors stated their errand.

She did not ask them to sit. She just stood in the door and listened quietly until the spokesman came to a stumbling halt. Then they could hear the invisible watch ticking at the end of the gold chain.

Her voice was dry and cold. "I have no taxes in Jefferson. Colonel Sartoris explained it to me. Perhaps one of you can gain access to the city records and satisfy yourselves."

"But we have. We are the city authorities, Miss Emily. Didn't you get a notice from the sheriff, signed by him?"

"I received a paper, yes," Miss Emily said. "Perhaps he considers himself the sheriff. . . I have no taxes in Jefferson."

"But there is nothing on the books to show that, you see. We must go by the—"

"See Colonel Sartoris. I have no taxes in Jefferson."

"But, Miss Emily—"

"See Colonel Sartoris." (Colonel Sartoris had been dead almost ten years.) "I have no taxes in Jefferson. Tobe!" The Negro appeared. "Show these gentlemen out."

II

So she vanquished them, horse and foot, just as she had vanquished their fathers thirty years before about the smell. That was two years after her father's death and a short time after her sweetheart—the one we believed would marry her—had deserted her. After her father's death she went out very little; after her sweetheart went away, people hardly saw her at all. A few of the ladies had the temerity to call, but were not received, and the only sign of life about the place was the Negro man—a young man then—going in and out with a market basket.

"Just as if a man—any man—could keep a kitchen properly," the ladies said; so they were not surprised when the smell developed. It was another link between the gross, teeming world and the high and mighty Griersons.

A neighbor, a woman, complained to the mayor, Judge Stevens, eighty years old.

"But what will you have me do about it, madam?" he said.

"Why, send her word to stop it," the woman said. "Isn't there a law?"

"I'm sure that won't be necessary," Judge Stevens said. "It's probably just a snake or a rat that nigger of hers killed in the yard. I'll speak to him about it."

The next day he received two more complaints, one from a man who came in diffident deprecation. "We really must do something about it, Judge. I'd be the last one in the world to bother Miss Emily, but we've got to do something." That night the Board of Aldermen met—three graybeards and one younger man, a member of the rising generation.

"It's simple enough, " he said. "Send her word to have her place cleaned up. Give her a certain time to do it in, and if she don't . . . ."

"Dammit, sir," Judge Stevens said, "will you accuse a lady to her face of smelling bad?"

So the next night, after midnight, four men crossed Miss Emily's lawn and slunk about the house like burglars, sniffing along the base of the brickwork and at the cellar openings while one of them performed a regular sowing motion with his hand out of a sack slung from his shoulder. They broke open the cellar door and sprinkled lime there, and in all the outbuildings. As they recrossed the lawn, a window that had been dark was lighted and Miss Emily sat in it, the light behind her, and her upright torso motionless as that of an idol. They crept quietly across the lawn and into the shadow of the locusts that lined the street. After a week or two the smell went away.

That was when people had begun to feel really sorry for her. People in our town, remembering how old lady Wyatt, her great-aunt, had gone completely crazy at last, believed that the Griersons held themselves a little too high for what they really were. None of the young men were quite good enough to Miss Emily and such. We had long thought of them as a tableau; Miss Emily a slender figure in white in the background, her father a spraddled silhouette in the foreground, his back to her and clutching a horsewhip, the two of them framed by the back-flung front door. So when she got to be thirty and was single, we were not pleased exactly, but vindicated; even with insanity in the family she wouldn't have turned down all of her chances if they had really materialized.

When her father died, it got about that the house was all that was left to her; and in a way, people were glad. At last they could pity Miss Emily. Being left alone, and a pauper, she had become humanized. Now she too would know the old thrill and the old despair of a penny more or less.

The day after his death all the ladies prepared to call at the house and offer condolence and aid, as is our custom. Miss Emily met them at the door, dressed as usual and with no trace of grief on her face. She told them that her father was not dead. She did that for three days, with the ministers calling on her, and the doctors, trying to persuade her to let them dispose of the body. Just as they were about to resort to law and force, she broke down, and they buried her father quickly.

We did not say she was crazy then. We believed she had to do that. We remembered all the young men her father had driven away, and we knew that with nothing left, she would have to cling to that which had robbed her, as people will.

III

She was sick for a long time. When we saw her again, her hair was cut short, making her look like a girl, with a vague resemblance to those angels in colored church windows—sort of tragic and serene.

The town had just let the contracts for paving the sidewalks, and in the summer after her father's death they began the work.

The construction company came with niggers and mules and machinery, and a foreman named Homer Barron, a Yankee—a big, dark, ready man, with a big voice and eyes lighter than his face. The little boys would follow in groups to hear him cuss the niggers, and the niggers singing in time to the rise and fall of picks. Pretty soon he knew everybody in town. Whenever you heard a lot of laughing anywhere about the square, Homer Barron would be in the center of the group. Presently we began to see him and Miss Emily on Sunday afternoons driving in the yellow-wheeled buggy and the matched team of bays from the livery stable.

At first we were glad that Miss Emily would have an interest, because the ladies all said, "Of course a Grierson would not think seriously of a Northerner, a day laborer." But there were still others, older people, who said that even grief could not cause a real lady to forget *noblesse oblige*—without calling it *noblesse oblige*. They just said, "Poor Emily. Her kinsfolk should come to her." She had some kin in Alabama; but years ago her father had fallen out with them over the estate of old lady Wyatt, the crazy woman, and there was no communication between the two families. They had not even been represented at the funeral.

And as soon as the old people said, "Poor Emily," the whispering began. "Do you suppose it's really so?" they said to one another. "Of course it is. What else could . . ." This behind their hands; rustling of craned silk and satin behind jalousies closed upon the sun of Sunday afternoon as the thin, swift clop-clop-clop of the matched team passed: "Poor Emily."

She carried her head high enough—even when we believed that she was fallen. It was as if she demanded more than ever the recognition of her dignity as the last Grierson; as if it had wanted that touch of earthiness to reaffirm her imperviousness. Like when she bought the rat poison, the arsenic. That was over a year after they had begun to say "Poor Emily," and while the two female cousins were visiting her.

"I want some poison," she said to the druggist. She was over thirty then, still a slight woman, though thinner than usual, with cold, haughty black eyes in a face the flesh of which was strained across the temples and about the eye-sockets as you imagine a lighthouse-keeper's face ought to look. "I want some poison," she said.

"Yes, Miss Emily. What kind? For rats and such? I'd recom—"

"I want the best you have. I don't care what kind."

The druggist named several. "They'll kill anything up to an elephant. But what you want is—"

"Arsenic," Miss Emily said. "Is that a a good one?"

"Is . . . arsenic? Yes, ma'am. But what you want—"

"I want arsenic."

The druggist looked down at her. She looked back at him, erect, her face like a strained flag. "Why, of course," the druggist said. "If that's what you want. But the law requires you to tell what you are going to use it for."

Miss Emily just stared at him, her head tilted back in order to look him eye for eye, until he looked away and went and got the arsenic and wrapped it up. The Negro delivery boy brought her the package; the druggist didn't come back. When she opened the package at home there was written on the box, under the skull and bones: "For rats."

IV

So the next day we all said, "She will kill herself"; and we said it would be the best thing. When she had first begun to be seen with Homer Barron, we had said, "She will marry him." Then we said, "She will persuade him yet," because Homer himself had remarked—he liked men, and it was known that he drank with the younger men in the Elks' Club—that he was not a marrying man. Later we said, "Poor Emily" behind the jalousies as they passed on Sunday afternoon in the glittering buggy, Miss Emily with her head high and Homer Barron with his hat cocked and a cigar in his teeth, reins and whip in a yellow glove.

Then some of the ladies began to say that it was a disgrace to the town and a bad example to the young people. The men did not want to interfere, but at last the ladies forced the Baptist minister—Miss Emily's people were Episcopal—to call upon her. He would never divulge what happened during that interview, but he refused to go back again. The next Sunday they again drove about the streets, and the following day the minister's wife wrote to Miss Emily's relations in Alabama.

So she had blood-kin under her roof again and we sat back to watch developments. At first nothing happened. Then we were sure that they were to be married. We learned that Miss Emily had been to the jeweler's and ordered a man's toilet set in silver, with the letters H. B. on each piece. Two days later we learned that she had bought a complete outfit of men's clothing, including a nightshirt, and we said, "They are married." We were really glad. We were glad because the two female cousins were even more Grierson than Miss Emily had ever been.

So we were not surprised when Homer Barron—the streets had been finished some time since—was gone. We were a little disappointed that there was not a public blowing-off, but we believed that he had gone on to prepare for Miss Emily's coming, or to give her a chance to get rid of the cousins. (By that time it was a cabal, and we were all Miss Emily's allies to help circumvent the cousins.) Sure enough, after another week they departed. And, as we had expected all along, within three days Homer Barron was back in town. A neighbor saw the Negro man admit him at the kitchen door at dusk one evening.

And that was the last we saw of Homer Barron. And of Miss Emily for some time. The Negro man went in and out with the market basket, but the front door remained closed. Now and then we would see her at a window for a moment, as the men did that night when they sprinkled the lime, but for almost six months she did not appear on the streets. Then we knew that this was to be expected too; as if that quality of her father which had thwarted her woman's life so many times had been too virulent and too furious to die.

When we next saw Miss Emily, she had grown fat and her hair was turning gray. During the next few years it grew grayer and grayer until it attained an even pepper-and-salt iron-gray, when it ceased turning. Up to the day of her death at seventy-four it was still that vigorous iron-gray, like the hair of an active man.

From that time on her front door remained closed, save for a period of six or seven years, when she was about forty, during which she gave lessons in china-painting. She fitted up a studio in one of the downstairs rooms, where the daughters and granddaughters of Colonel Sartoris' contemporaries were sent to her with the same regularity and in the same spirit that they were sent to church on Sundays with a twenty-five cent piece for the collection plate. Meanwhile her taxes had been remitted.

Then the newer generation became the backbone and the spirit of the town, and the painting pupils grew up and fell away and did not send their children to her with boxes of color and tedious brushes and pictures cut from the ladies' magazines. The front door closed upon the last one and remained closed for good. When the town got free postal delivery, Miss Emily alone refused to let them fasten the metal numbers above her door and attach a mailbox to it. She would not listen to them.

Daily, monthly, yearly we watched the Negro grow grayer and more stooped, going in and out with the market basket. Each December we sent her a tax notice, which would be returned by the post office a week later, unclaimed. Now and then we would see her in one of the downstairs windows— she had evidently shut up the top floor of the house— like the carven torso of an idol in a niche, looking or not looking at us, we could never tell which. Thus she passed from generation to generation—dear, inescapable, impervious, tranquil, and perverse.

And so she died. Fell·ill in the house filled with dust and shadows, with only a doddering Negro man to wait on her. We did not even know she was sick; we had long since given up trying to get any information from the Negro. He talked to no one, probably not even to her, for his voice had grown harsh and rusty, as if from disuse.

She died in one of the downstairs rooms, in a heavy walnut bed with a curtain, her gray head propped on a pillow yellow and moldy with age and lack of sunlight.

V

The Negro met the first of the ladies at the front door and let them in, with their hushed, sibilant voices and their quick, curious glances, and then he disappeared. He walked right through the house and out the back and was not seen again.

The two female cousins came at once. They held the funeral on the second day, with the town coming to look at Miss Emily beneath a mass of bought flowers, with the crayon face of her father musing profoundly above the bier and the ladies sibilant and macabre; and the very old men—some in their brushed Confederate uniforms—on the porch and the lawn, talking of Miss Emily as if she had been a contemporary of theirs, believing that they had danced with her and courted her perhaps, confusing time with its mathematical progression, as the old do, to whom all the past is not a diminishing road but, instead, a huge meadow which no winter ever quite touches, divided from them now by the narrow bottle-neck of the most recent decade of years.

Already we knew that there was one room in that region above stairs which no one had seen in forty years, and which would have to be forced. They waited until Miss Emily was decently in the ground before they opened it.

The violence of breaking down the door seemed to fill this room with pervading dust. A thin, acrid pall as of the tomb seemed to lie everywhere upon this room decked and furnished as for a bridal: upon the valence curtains of faded rose color, upon the rose-shaded lights, upon the dressing table, upon the delicate array of crystal and the man's toilet things backed with tarnished silver, silver so tarnished that the monogram was obscured. Among them lay a collar and tie, as if they had just been removed, which, lifted, left upon the surface a pale crescent in the dust. Upon a chair hung the suit, carefully folded; beneath it the two mute shoes and the discarded socks.

The man himself lay in the bed.

For a long while we just stood there, looking down at the profound and fleshless grin. The body had apparently once lain in the attitude of an embrace, but now the long sleep that outlasts love, that conquers even the grimace of love, had cuckolded him. What was left of him, rotted beneath what was left of the nightshirt, had become inextricable from the bed in which he lay; and upon him and upon the pillow beside him lay that even coating of the patient and biding dust.

Then we noticed that in the second pillow was the indentation of a head. One of us lifted something from it, and leaning forward, that faint and invisible dust dry and acrid in the nostrils, we saw a long strand of iron-gray hair.

1. What part does the setting, a small, close-knit Southern town, play in Faulkner's story? Why can't the aldermen make Miss Emily pay her taxes? How would you describe the attitude of the ladies of the town toward her?

2. How does Faulkner define Miss Emily's character? What are we meant to think of her in the end? Of the ladies?

Point of View

Every story has a narrator, who presents the action from a particular, identifiable point of view. The narrator may be a character in the story who speaks in the first person. More often, the narrator views the action from a vantage point outside the story, speaking in the third person. When such a narrator appears to know everything about all the characters, he may be called omniscient. Sometimes a narrator will seem to know everything about only one character, offering a kind of selective omniscience. We see the action primarily as it affects the consciousness of this character.

Leonard Michaels's story, "The Deal," is told by an omniscient narrator who occasionally interprets (as in suggesting that the boys have "a common corruption in their bones") but who, for the most part, avoids commenting on the action. The reader is allowed to judge the characters for himself. Like a skillful director guiding a cameraman, the narrator zeroes in on details that fix the scene: the way Miss Carlyle carries her purse, the pattern of tar and cobblestones, a pock-marked face. He says enough to capture the precise sensations of the characters—for example, Miss Carlyle's reaction as she sees bright teeth, eyes, and fingers coming toward her.

In "Lucy Grange" Doris Lessing uses selective omniscience to let the reader into the mind of the title character and at the same time to evaluate her responses. We learn how Lucy orders her life, how she reacts to her visitor, even what she says to herself when she looks in the mirror. We see the travelling insurance salesman solely as he appears to her:

> She looked down at the greasy dark head, the red folded neck, and stood rigid, thinking of the raw, creased neck of vultures.

Because we understand Lucy's feelings so well, we are prepared to accept her recognition of the kind of future which will result from having yielded to him.

The point of view in Yuli Daniel's "Hands" is that of the central character, who tells his own story to his friend Sergey. With no "outside" narrator to comment on the characters or reveal their thoughts, the reader must rely entirely on the narrator's words. First-person narration can be extremely revealing, especially when the narrator is insensitive to the implications of his experience. What the narrator says—in this case about the way he carried out his duties as a member of a firing squad—may be less important than what he fails to say. The reader is free to draw his own conclusions about why the narrator's experience with the priest he is unable to kill is so terrible, and about why his hands shake uncontrollably.

THE DEAL

Tense story drama well-handled

Twenty were jammed together on the stoop; tiers of heads made one central head, and the wings rested along the banisters: a raggedy monster of boys studying her approach. Her white face and legs. She passed without looking, poked her sunglasses against the bridge of her nose and tucked her bag between her arm and ribs. She carried it at her hip like a rifle stock. On her spine forty eyes hung like poison berries. Bone dissolved beneath her lank beige silk, and the damp circle of her belt cut her in half. Independent legs struck toward the points of her shoes. Her breasts lifted and rode the air like porpoises. She would cross to the grocery as usual, buy cigarettes, then cross back despite their eyes. As if the neighborhood hadn't changed one bit. She slipped the bag forward to crack it against her belly and pluck out keys and change. In the gesture she was home from work. Her keys jangled in the sun as if they opened everything and the air received her. The monster, watching, saw the glove fall away.

Pigeons looped down to whirl between buildings, and a ten-wheel truck came slowly up the street. As it passed she emerged from the grocery, then stood at the curb opposite the faces. She glanced along the street where she had crossed it. No glove. Tar reticulated between the cobbles. A braid of murky water ran against the curb, twisting bits of flotsam toward the drain. She took off her sunglasses, dropped them with her keys into the bag, then stepped off the curb toward the faces. Addressing them with a high, friendly voice, she said: "Did you guys see a glove? I dropped it a moment ago."

The small ones squinted up at her from the bottom step. On the middle steps sat boys fourteen or fifteen years old. The oldest ones made the wings. Dandies and introverts, they sprawled, as if with a common corruption in their bones. In the center, his eyes level with hers, a boy waited for her attention in the matter of gloves. To his right sat a very thin boy with a pocked face. A narrow-brimmed hat tipped toward his nose and shaded the continuous activity of his eyes. She spoke to the green eyes of the boy in the center and held up the glove she had: "Like this."

Teeth appeared below the hat, then everywhere as the boys laughed. Did she hold up a fish? Green eyes said: "Hello, Miss Calile."

She looked around at the faces, then laughed with them at her surprise. "You know my name?"

"I see it on the mailbox," said the hat. "He can't read. I see it."

"My name is Duke Francisco." said the illiterate.

"My name is Abbe Carlyle," she said to him.

The hat smirked. "His name Francisco Lopez."

Green eyes turned to the hat. "Shut you mouth, baby. I tell her my name, not you."

"His name Francisco Lopez," the hat repeated.

She saw pocks and teeth, the thin oily face and the hat, as he spoke again, nicely to her: "My name Francisco Pacheco, the Prince. I seen your name on the mailbox."

"Did either of you . . ."

"You name is shit," said green eyes to the hat.

"My name is Tito." A small one on the bottom step looked up for the effect of his name. She looked down at him. "I am Tito," he said.

"Did you see my glove, Tito?"

"This is Tomato," he answered, unable to bear her attention. He nudged the boy to his left. Tomato nudged back, stared at the ground.

"I am happy to know you, Tito," she said, "and you, Tomato. Both of you." She looked back up to green eyes and the hat. The hat acknowledged her courtesy. He tilted back to show her his eyes, narrow and black except for bits of white reflected in the corners. His face was thin, high-boned and fragile. She pitied the riddled skin.

"This guy," he said, pointing his thumb to the right, "is Monkey," and then to the left beyond green eyes, "and this guy is Beans." She nodded to the hat, then Monkey, then Beans, measuring the respect she offered, doling it out in split seconds. Only one of them had the glove.

"Well, did any of you guys see my glove?"

Every tier grew still, like birds in a tree waiting for a sign that would move them all at once.

Tito's small dark head snapped forward. She heard the slap an instant late. The body lurched after the head and pitched off the stoop at her feet. She saw green eyes sitting back slowly. Tito gaped up at her from the concrete. A sacrifice to the lady. She stepped back as if rejecting it and frowned at green eyes. He gazed indifferently at Tito, who was up, facing him with coffee-bean fists. Tito screamed, "I tell her you got it, dick-head."

The green eyes swelled in themselves like a light blooming in the ocean. Tito's fists opened, he turned, folded quickly and sat back into the mass. He began to rub his knees.

"May I have my glove, Francisco?" Her voice was still pleasant and high. She now held her purse in the crook of her arm and pressed it against her side.

Some fop had a thought and giggled in the wings. She glanced up at him immediately. He produced a toothpick. With great delicacy he stuck it into his ear. She looked away. Green eyes again waited for her. A cup of

darkness formed in the hollow that crowned his chestbone. His soiled gray polo shirt hooked below it. "You think I have you glove?" She didn't answer. He stared between his knees, between heads and shoulders to the top of Tito's head. "Hey, Tito, you tell her I got the glove?"

"I didn't tell nothing," muttered Tito rubbing his knees harder as if they were still bitter from his fall.

"He's full of shit, Miss Calile. I break his head later. What kind of glove you want?"

"This kind," she said wearily, "a white glove like this."

"Too hot." he grinned.

"Yes, too hot, but I need it."

"What for? Too hot." He gave her full green concern.

"It's much too hot, but the glove is mine, mister."

She rested her weight on one leg and wiped her brow with the glove she had. They watched her do it, the smallest of them watched her, and she moved the glove slowly to her brow again and drew it down her cheek and neck. She could think of nothing to say, nothing to do without expressing impatience. Green eyes changed the subject. "You live there." He pointed toward her building.

"That's right."

A wooden front door with a window in it showed part of the shadowy lobby, mailboxes, and a second door. Beyond her building and down the next street were warehouses. Beyond them, the river. A meat truck started toward them from a packing house near the river. It came slowly, bug-eyed with power. The driver saw the lady standing in front of the boys. He yelled as the truck went past. Gears yowled, twisting the sound of his voice. She let her strength out abruptly: "Give me the glove, Francisco."

The boy shook his head at the truck, at her lack of civilization. "What you give me?"

That tickled the hat. "*Vaya*, baby. What she give you, eh?" He spoke fast, his tone decorous and filthy.

"All right, baby," she said fast as the hat,

33

"what do you want?" The question had New York and much man in it. The hat swiveled to the new sound. A man of honor, let him understand the terms. He squinted at her beneath the hat brim.

"Come on, Francisco, make your deal." She presented brave, beautiful teeth, smiling hard as a skull.

"Tell her, Duke. Make the deal." The hat lingered on "deal," grateful to the lady for this word.

The sun shone in his face and the acknowledged duke sat dull, green eyes blank with possibilities. Her question, not "deal," held him. It had come too hard, too fast. He laughed in contempt of something and glanced around at the wings. They offered nothing. "I want a dollar," he said.

That seemed obvious to the hat: he sneered, "He wants a dollar." She had to be stupid not to see it.

"No deal. Twenty-five cents." Her gloves were worth twenty dollars. She had paid ten for them at a sale. At the moment they were worth green eyes' life.

"I want ten dollars," said green eyes flashing the words like extravagant meaningless things; gloves of his own. He lifted his arms, clasped his hands behind his head and leaned against the knees behind him. His belly filled with air, the polo shirt rolled out on its curve. He made a fat man doing business. "Ten dollars." Ten fingers popped up behind his head like grimy spikes. Keeper of the glove, cocky duke of the stoop. The number made him happy: it bothered her. He drummed the spikes against his head: "I wan' you ten dol-lar." Beans caught the beat in his hips and rocked it on the stoop.

"Francisco," she said, hesitated, then said, "dig me, please. You will get twenty-five cents. Now let's have the glove." Her bag snapped open, her fingers hooked, stiffened on the clasp. Monkey leered at her and bongoed his knees with fists. "The number is ten dol-lar." She waited, said nothing. The spikes continued drumming, Monkey rocked his hips. Beans pummeled his knees. The hat

sang sadly: "Twany fyiv not d'nummer, not d'nummer, not d'nummer." He made claves of his fingers and palms, tocked, clicked his tongue against the beat. "Twan-ny fyiv—na t'nomma." She watched green eyes. He was quiet now in the center of the stoop, sitting motionless, waiting, as though seconds back in time his mind still touched the question: what did he want? He seemed to wonder, now that he had the formula, what *did* he want? The faces around him, dopey in the music, wondered nothing, grinned at her, nodded, clicked, whined the chorus: "Twany fyiv not t'nomma, twany fyiv not t'nomma."

Her silk blouse stained and stuck flat at her breasts and shoulders. Water chilled her sides.

"Ten dol-lar iss t'nomma."

She spread her feet slightly, taking better possession of the sidewalk and resting on them evenly, the bag held open for green eyes. She could see he didn't want that, but she insisted in her silence he did. Tito spread his little feet and lined the points of his shoes against hers. Tomato noticed the imitation and cackled at the concrete. The music went on, the beat feeding on itself, pulverizing words, smearing them into liquid submission: "Iss t'nomma twany fyiv? Dat iss not t'nomma."

"Twenty-five cents," she said again.

Tito whined, "Gimme twenty-five cents."

"Shut your mouth," said the hat, and turned a grim face to his friend. In the darkness of his eyes there were deals. The music ceased. "Hey, baby, you got no manners? Tell what you want." He spoke in a dreamy voice, as if to a girl.

"I want a kiss," said green eyes.

She glanced down with this at Tito and studied the small shining head. "Tell him to give me my glove, Tito," she said cutely, nervously. The wings shuffled and looked down bored. Nothing was happening. Twisting backwards Tito shouted up to green eyes, "Give her the glove." He twisted front again and crouched over his knees. He shoved Tomato for approval and smiled. Tomato

34

shoved him back, snarled at the concrete and spit between his feet at a face which had taken shape in the grains.

"I want a kiss," said the boy again.

She sighed, giving another second to helplessness. The sun was low above the river and the street three quarters steeped in shade. Sunlight cut across the building tops where pigeons swept by loosely and fluttered in to pack the stone foliage of the eaves. Her bag snapped shut. Her voice was business: "Come on, Francisco. I'll give you the kiss."

He looked shot among the faces.

"Come on," she said, "it's a deal."

The hat laughed out loud with childish insanity. The others shrieked and jiggled, except for the wings. But they ceased to sprawl, and seemed to be getting bigger, to fill with imminent motion. "Gimme a kiss, gimme a kiss," said the little ones on the lowest step. Green eyes sat with a quiet, open mouth.

"Let's go," she said. "I haven't all day."

"Where I go?"

"That doorway." she pointed to her building and took a step toward it. "You know where I live, don't you?"

"I don't want no kiss."

"What's the matter now?"

"You scared?" asked the hat. "Hey, Duke, you scared?"

The wings leaned toward the center, where green eyes hugged himself and made a face.

"Look, Mr. Francisco, you made a deal."

"Yeah," said the wings.

"Now come along."

I'm not scared," he shouted and stood up among them. He sat down. "I don't want no kiss."

"You're scared?" she said.

"You scared chicken," said the hat.

"Yeah," said the wings. "Hey, punk. Fairy. Hey, Duke Chicken."

"Duke scared," mumbled Tito. Green eyes stood up again. The shoulders below him separated. Tito leaped clear of the stoop and trotted into the street. Green eyes passed through the place he had vacated and stood

at her side, his head not so high as her shoulder. She nodded at him, tucked her bag up and began walking toward her building. A few others stood up on the stoop and the hat started down. She turned. "Just him." Green eyes shuffled after her. The hat stopped on the sidewalk. Someone pushed him forward. He resisted, but called after them, "He's my cousin." She walked on, the boy came slowly after her. They were yelling from the stoop, the hat yelling his special point, "He's my brother." He stepped after them and the others swarmed behind him down the stoop and onto the sidewalk. Tito jumped out of the street and ran alongside the hat. He yelled, "He's got the glove." They all moved down the block, the wings trailing sluggishly, the young ones jostling, punching each other, laughing, shrieking things in Spanish after green eyes and the lady. She heard him, a step behind her. "I give you the glove and take off."

She put her hand out to the side a little. The smaller hand touched hers and took it. "You made a deal."

She tugged him through the doorway into the tight, square lobby. The hand snapped free and he swung by, twisting to face her as if to meet a blow. He put his back against the second door, crouched a little. His hands pressed the sides of his legs. The front door shut slowly and the shadows deepened in the lobby. He crouched lower, his eyes level with her breasts, as she took a step toward him. The hat appeared, a black rock in the door window. Green eyes saw it, straightened up, one hand moving quickly toward his pants pocket. The second and third head, thick dark bulbs, lifted beside the hat in the window. Bodies piled against the door behind her. Green eyes held up the glove. "Here, you lousy glove."

She smiled and put out her hand. The hat screamed, "Hey, you made a deal, baby. Hey, you got no manners."

"Don't be scared," she whispered, stepping closer.

The glove lifted toward her and hung in

the air between them, gray, languid as smoke. She took it and bent toward his face. "I won't kiss you. Run." The window went black behind her, the lobby solid in darkness, silent but for his breathing, <u>the door breathing against the pressure of the bodies</u>, and the scraping of fingers spread about them like rats in the walls. She felt his shoulder, touched the side of his neck, bent the last inch and kissed him. White light cut the walls. They tumbled behind it, screams and bright teeth. Spinning to face them she was struck, pitched against green eyes and the second door. He twisted hard, shoved away from her as the faces piled forward popping eyes and lights, their fingers accumulating in the air, coming at her. She raised the bag, brought it down swishing into the faces, and wrenched and twisted to get free of the fingers, screaming against their shrieks, "Stop it, stop it, stop it." The bag sprayed papers and coins, and the sunglasses flew over their heads and cracked against the brass mailboxes. She dropped amid shrieks, "Gimme a kiss, gimme a kiss," squirming down the door onto her knees to get fingers out from under her and she thrust up with the bag into bellies and thighs until a fist banged her mouth. She cursed, flailed at nothing.

There was light in the lobby and leather scraping on concrete as they crashed out the door into the street. She shut her eyes instantly as the fist came again, big as her face. Then she heard running in the street. The lobby was silent. The door shut slowly, the shadows deepened. She could feel the darkness getting thicker. She opened her eyes. Standing in front of her was the hat.

He bowed slightly. "I get those guys for you. They got no manners." The hat shook amid the shadows, slowly, sadly.

She pressed the smooth leather of her bag against her cheek where the mouths had kissed it. Then she tested the clasp, snapping it open and shut. The hat shifted his posture and waited. <u>"You hit me," she whispered and did not look up at him.</u> The hat bent and picked up her keys and the papers. He handed the keys to her, then the papers, and bent again for the coins. She dropped the papers into her bag and stuffed them together in the bottom. "Help me up!" She took his hands and got to her feet without looking at him. As she put the key against the lock of the second door she began to shiver. The key rattled against the slot. "Help me!" The hat leaned over the lock, his long thin fingers squeezing the key. It caught, angled with a click. She pushed him aside. "You give me something? Hey, you give me something?" The door shut on his voice.

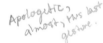

Apologetic, almost, this last gesture.

1. Point out phrases and sentences that indicate that "The Deal" is told by an omniscient narrator. How would the story change if it were told by Abbe Carlyle?

2. Why does Miss Carlyle say "Give me the glove, Francisco" after the driver of the meat truck yells at her? What do you think of the way she handles the boys? Why do they attack her?

3. Why does "the hat" stay after the others have run away? What does he want? Why does Miss Carlyle shut the door on him?

Vascillates between strength and helplessness.

LUCY GRANGE

The farm was fifty miles from the nearest town, in a maize-growing district. The mealie lands[1] began at a stone's throw from the front door of the farmhouse. At the back were several acres of energetic and colourful domestic growth: chicken runs, vegetables, pumpkins. Even on the verandah there were sacks of grain and bundles of hoes. The life of the farm, her husband's life, washed around the house, leaving old scraps of iron on the front step where the children played wagon-and-driver, or a bottle of medicine for a sick animal on her dressing-table among the bottles of Elizabeth Arden.

One walked straight from the verandah of this gaunt, iron-roofed, brick barracks of a house into a wide drawing-room that was shaded in green and orange Liberty linens.

"Stylish?" said the farmers' wives when they came on formal calls, asking the question of themselves while they discussed with Lucy Grange the price of butter and servants' aprons and their husbands discussed the farm with George Grange. They never "dropped over" to see Lucy Grange; they never rang her up with invitations to "spend the day." They would finger the books on child psychology, politics, art; gaze guiltily at the pictures on her walls, which they felt they ought to be able to recognise; and say: "I can see you are a great reader, Mrs. Grange."

There were years of discussing her among themselves before their voices held the good-natured amusement of acceptance: "I found Lucy in the vegetable patch wearing gloves full of cold cream." "Lucy has ordered another dress pattern from town." And later

still, with self-consciously straightened shoulders, eyes directly primly before them, discreet non-committal voices: "Lucy is very attractive to men."

One can imagine her, when they left at the end of those mercifully short visits, standing on the verandah and smiling bitterly after the satisfactory solid women with their straight tailored dresses, made by the Dutch-woman at the store at seven-and-six a time, buttoned loosely across their well-used breasts; with their untidy hair permanent-waved every six months in town; with their feminity which was asserted once and for all by a clumsy scrawl of red across the mouth. One can imagine her clenching her fists and saying fiercely to the mealie fields that rippled greenly all around her, cream-topped like the sea: "I won't. I simply won't. He needn't imagine that I will!"

"Do you like my new dress, George?"

"You're the best-looking woman in the district, Lucy." So it seemed, on the face of it, that he didn't expect, or even want, that she should. . . .

Meanwhile she continued to order cook-books from town, to make new recipes of pumpkin and green mealies and chicken, to put skin food on her face at night; she constructed attractive nursery furniture out of packing-cases enameled white—the farm wasn't doing too well; and discussed with George how little Betty's cough was probably psychological.

"I'm sure you're right, my dear."

Then the rich, over-controlled voice: "Yes darling. No, my sweetheart. Yes, of course, I'll play bricks with you, but you must have your lunch first." Then it broke, hard and

[1] Maize (corn) fields.

37

shrill: "*Don't* make all that noise, darling. I can't stand it. Go on, go and play in the garden and leave me in peace."

Sometimes, storms of tears. Afterwards: "Really, George, didn't your mother ever tell you that all women cry sometimes? It's as good as a tonic. Or a holiday." And a lot of high laughter and gay explanations at which George hastened to guffaw. He liked her gay. She usually was. For instance, she was a good mimic. She would "take off," deliberately trying to relieve his mind of farm worries, the visiting policemen, who toured the district once a month to see if the natives were behaving themselves, or the Government agricultural officials.

"Do you want to see my husband?"

That was what they had come for, but they seldom pressed the point. They sat far longer than they had intended, drinking tea, talking about themselves. They would go away and say at the bar in the village: "Mrs. Grange is a smart woman, isn't she?"

And Lucy would be acting, for George's benefit, how a khaki-clad, sun-raw youth had bent into her room, looking around him with comical surprise; had taken a cup of tea, thanking her three times; had knocked over an ashtray, stayed for lunch and afternoon tea, and left saying with awkward gallantry: "It's a real treat to meet a lady like you who is interested in things."

"You shouldn't be so hard on us poor Colonials, Lucy."

Finally one can imagine how one day, when the houseboy came to her in the chicken runs to say that there was a baas[2] waiting to see her at the house, it was no sweating policeman, thirsty after fifteen dusty miles on a motorcycle, to whom she must be gracious.

He was a city man, of perhaps forty or forty-five, dressed in city clothes. At first glance she felt a shudder of repulsion. It was a coarse face, and sensual; and he looked like a patient vulture as the keen, heavy-lidded eyes travelled up and down her body.

[2]White man.

"Are you looking for my husband, perhaps? He's in the cowsheds this morning."

"No, I don't think I am. I was."

She laughed. It was as if he had started playing a record she had not heard for a long time, and which started her feet tapping. It was years since she had played this game. "I'll get you some tea," she said hurriedly and left him in her pretty drawing-room.

Collecting the cups, her hands were clumsy. Why, Lucy! she said to herself, archly. She came back, very serious and responsible, to find him standing in front of the picture that filled half the wall at one end of the room. "I should have thought you had sunflowers enough here," he said, in his heavy, over-emphasised voice, which made her listen for meanings behind his words. And when he turned away from the wall and came to sit down, leaning forward, examining her, she suppressed an impulse to apologise for the picture: Van Gogh is obvious, but he's rather effective, she might have said; and she felt that the whole room was that: effective but obvious. But she was pleasantly conscious of how she looked: graceful and cool in her green linen dress, with her corn-coloured hair knotted demurely on her neck. She lifted wide, serious eyes to his face and asked, "Milk? Sugar?" and knew that the corners of her mouth were tight with self-consciousness.

When he left, three hours later, he turned her hand over and lightly kissed the palm. She looked down at the greasy dark head, the red folded neck, and stood rigid, thinking of the raw, creased necks of vultures.

Then he straightened up and said with simple kindliness, "You must be lonely here, my dear"; and she was astounded to find her eyes full of tears.

"One does what one can to make a show of it." She kept her lids lowered and her voice light. Inside she was weeping with gratitude. Embarrassed, she said quickly, "You know, you haven't yet said what you came for."

"I sell insurance. And besides, I've heard people talk of you."

She imagined the talk and smiled stiffly. "You don't seem to take your work very seriously.

"If I may, I'll come back another time and try again?"

She did not reply. He said, "My dear, I'll tell you a secret: one of the reasons I chose this district was because of you. Surely there aren't so many people in this country one can really talk to that we can afford not to take each other seriously?"

He touched her cheek with his hand, smiled, and went.

She heard the last thing he had said like a parody of the things she often said and felt a violent revulsion. *Self-consciousness*

She went to her bedroom, where she found herself in front of the mirror. Her hands went to her cheeks and she drew in her breath with the shock. "Why, Lucy, whatever is the matter with you?" Her eyes were dancing, her mouth smiled irresistibly. Yet she heard the archness of her "Why, Lucy," and thought: I'm going to pieces. I must have gone to pieces without knowing it.

Later she found herself singing in the pantry as she made a cake, stopped herself; made herself look at the insurance salesman's face against her closed eyelids; and instinctively wiped the palms of her hands against her skirt.

He came three days later. Again, in the first shock of seeing him stand at the door, smiling familiarly, she thought, It's the face of an old animal. He probably chose this kind of work because of the opportunities it gives him.

He talked of London, where he had lately been on leave; about the art galleries and the theatres.

She could not help warming, because of her hunger for this kind of talk. She could not help an apologetic note in her voice, because she knew that after so many years in this exile she must seem provincial. She liked him

because he associated himself with her abdication from her standards by saying: "Yes, yes, my dear, in a country like this we all learn to accept the second-rate." *Convinces her that it is second-rate, even if she doesn't really believe it.*

While he talked his eyes were roving. He was listening. Outside the window the turkeys were scraping in the dust and gobbling. In the next room the houseboy was moving; then there was silence because he had gone to get his midday meal. The children had had their lunch and gone off to the garden with the nurse.

No, she said to herself. No, no, no.

"Does your husband come back for lunch?"

"He takes it on the lands at this time of the year, he's so busy."

He came over and sat beside her. "Well, shall we console each other?" She was crying in his arms. She could feel their impatient and irritable tightening.

In the bedroom she kept her eyes shut. His hand travelled up and down her back. "What's the matter, little one? What's the matter?"

His voice was a sedative. She could have fallen asleep and lain there for a week inside the anonymous, comforting arms. But he was looking at his watch over her shoulder. "We'd better get dressed, hadn't we?"

"Of course."

She sat naked on the bed, covering herself with her arms, looking at his white hairy body in loathing, and then at the creased red neck. She became extremely gay; and in the living-room they sat side by side on the big sofa, being ironical. Then he put his arm around her, and she curled up inside it and cried again. She clung to him and felt him going away from her; and in a few minutes he stood up, saying, "Wouldn't do for your old man to come in and find us like this, would it?" Even while she was hating him for the "old man," she put her arms around him and said, "You'll come back soon."

"I couldn't keep away." The voice purred caressingly over her head, and she said: "You know, I'm very lonely." *The whole problem*

"Darling, I'll come as soon as I can. I've a living to make, you know."

She let her arms drop, and smiled, and watched him drive away down the rutted red-rust farm road, between the rippling sea-coloured mealies.

She knew he would come again, and next time she would not cry; she would stand again like this, watching him go, hating him, thinking of how he had said: In this country we learn to accept the second-rate. And he would come again and again and again; and she would stand here, watching him go and hating him.

1. What sentences or phrases show that the story is told from Lucy Grange's point of view? Are we told anything from the salesman's point of view?

2. Why does Lucy resist becoming like the other farm wives? Should she try to be different? What do you think of her stylishness?

3. Why does Lucy respond to the salesman and begin to play his "game" of flirtation?

4. At one point Lucy sees the salesman's civilized talk as a parody of things she has said. In what sense do his attitudes call into question her own? Why does she allow him to seduce her and to keep coming back? Whose fault is it that the relationship gets started? Why does she hate him?

3rd person limited omniscience.

HANDS

You're an educated man, Sergey, you've got manners. So you don't ask questions, you keep quiet, not like our chaps at the factory —they ask me straight out: 'Is it drink that's given you the shakes?' My hands, they mean. Think I didn't notice how you looked at them and turned away? And now, too, you keep trying to look past them. I realise it's because you're tactful, you don't want to embarrass me. But I don't mind, you can look as much as you like. It's not every day you see such a thing. And it's not drink, let me tell you. Actually, I don't drink much—when I do, it's more for company, or to mark an occasion like now with you. We couldn't meet again after all this time and not have a drink. I remember all about those days. How we went on recce,[1] and how you talked French to that White Guard, and how we captured Yaroslavl . . . Remember that meeting you addressed? You took me by the hand—I happened to be next to you—and you said: 'With these very hands' . . . Come on, Sergey, pour us a drink or I might go to pieces. I've forgotten what they call these shakes, there's a medical word for it. But I've got it written down, I'll show you afterwards . . . Anyway, I'll tell you how it happened. It was all because of an incident. But to take things in their right order: as soon as we were demobbed after the Civil War, in that victorious year 1921, I went back to my old factory. I got a grand welcome—you know how it was—a revolutionary hero . . . And then I was a Party member, a politically conscious worker as they say. I used to straighten people out. There was a lot of talk in those days: 'What have we been fighting for? Can't we manage better than

this? No bread, nothing . . .' I'd always cut them short. I was always firm. I never fell for that kind of Menshevik muck. Go on, pour yourself a drink, don't wait for me. But hardly had I worked for a year when— bang—they summoned me to the Regional Committee. 'Here you are, Malinin, here's your travel permit,' they said. 'The Party is mobilising you, Vasily Malinin, into the ranks of the glorious Cheka, to fight against Counter-Revolution. We wish you success,' they said, 'in the struggle with the world bourgeoisie, and if you meet Comrade Dzerzhinsky, give him our greetings.' 'Well, I'm a Party man. I'm at the Party's orders,' I said. I took the travel permit, dropped in at the factory to say goodbye to the chaps, and went off. As I went, I kept thinking of how I would mercilessly hunt down those counter-revolutionaries, so they shouldn't make a mess of our young Soviet regime. Well, I arrived, and I did see Felix Edmundovich Dzerzhinsky,[2] and gave him the message from the Regional Committee. He shook me by the hand and thanked me. Then he drew us all up in a row—about thirty of us Party members who had been mobilised— and he told us: 'You can't build a house on a swamp. First you have to dry the swamp, and while you're doing that, you've got to destroy the vermin that's there. That's an iron necessity,' he said. 'And each of you must put his hand to it . . .' He told it like a story or a fable but it was all quite clear. He looked very stern while he was saying it,

[2] Dzerzhinsky, first head of the Cheka (Extraordinary Commission), set up in 1917 to combat counter-revolution. This body has often changed its name: 1922, G.P.U. (State Political Administration); 1924–34, O.G.P.U. (Unified G.P.U.). Today, its powers reduced since Stalin's death, it is called the K.G.B. (Committee of State Security).

[1] Reconnaisance.

he never smiled once. After that, they sorted us out, to know who was to go where. 'How much schooling have you had?' they asked me. Well, you know how it was—my schooling was the German War, the Civil War, the factory—all I'd done before that was two years at the parish school . . . So they assigned me to a Special Duties Section—or to put it plainly, the firing squad, the one that carries out executions. You wouldn't say it was a difficult job exactly, but it wasn't easy either. It affects your heart. It's one thing at the front, you understand: there it's either him or you. But here . . . still, you get used to it of course. You follow your man across the yard and you say to yourself: 'You've got to do it, Vasily, you've *got* to. If you don't finish him off now, the rat will do in our whole Soviet Republic.' I got used to it. I drank a bit of course. They issued us with alcohol. All these stories about special rations—rolls and chocolate for the Cheka— they were nothing but bourgeois lies. Our rations were the ordinary soldier's rations— bread and gruel and salted fish. But they did issue us with alcohol. You couldn't do without it, you understand. Well anyway, that was how I worked for seven months, and then there was this incident. We were ordered to liquidate a group of priests. For counter-revolutionary propaganda. With intent. They'd been subverting their parishioners. On account of Tikhon,[3] I suppose. Or perhaps they were just against socialism—I don't know. Anyway, they were enemies. There were twelve of them. Our commander gave us the orders: 'You, Malinin, take three,' he said, 'and you, Vlasenko, the next three, and you, Golovchiner, the next, and you . . .' I can't remember what the fourth was called. He was a Lett, he had a strange name, not like one of ours. He and Golovchiner went first. The arrangements were like this: the guardroom was in the middle: on one side of it was the room where the condemned were kept, and on the other was the yard. We took them one by one. When you finished with one in the yard, you

and the chaps dragged him out of the way and you returned for the next. They had to be dragged out of the way because otherwise when you led the next one out and he saw the corpse he might struggle and try to break free, and give you no end of trouble—as was only natural of course. It's better when they keep quiet. Well, that day, Golovchiner and the Lett finished with theirs, and it came to my turn. I'd already had a drink by then. Not that I was afraid, or religious or anything like that. I'm a Party man, I'm hard, I don't believe in any of those gods or angels or archangels—but all the same I somehow didn't feel myself. It was easier for Golovchiner, he's a Jew, people say they don't have ikons, I don't know if that's true— but I sat and drank, and all sorts of foolishness kept passing through my head: how my mother, when she was alive, used to take me to the village church, and how I'd kiss the hand of our parish priest, Father Vasily— he was an old man and he always used to joke with me and call me his namesake . . . Well anyway, I went to fetch the first one and took him out and finished him off. Then I came back and had a smoke, and did the second one. I came back and had a drink and I didn't feel too well, so I said to the chaps: 'Wait a minute, I'll be back.' I put the Mauser on the table, and went out. I

[3]Patriarch Tikhon, 1863–1925. In 1921, when the country was suffering from famine, Tikhon instructed the Parish Councils to surrender all articles of value in the Churches for the benefit of the starving, with the exception of objects used for the sacraments, the surrender of which he forbade. When the seizures began there were many brawls which resulted in a number of arrests and executions. He himself was placed under house arrest and forbidden to carry out his duties. In the circumstances, he agreed to hand over his authority temporarily to a group of secular priests. These abolished the Patriarchate, reduced Tikhon to the status of a lay-man and founded the so-called Living Church, which cooperated closely with the State authorities. In 1923 Tikhon drew up a statement deploring his offences against the regime and was released. Many parishes returned to the obedience of the Patriarchate. Tikhon died on 7th April 1925; three hundred thousand people attended his funeral.

must have had too much to drink, I thought. I'll stick my fingers in my throat and make myself sick, and have a wash, and I'll be all right. I did all that, but I still didn't feel better. All right, I said to myself, to hell with it, I'll finish the job and I'll go and have a sleep. I picked up the Mauser and went for the third one. The third one was young— a big, hefty, good-looking young priest. I led him along the corridor, and I noticed how he lifted the hem of his cassock—it was down to his heels—as he crossed the threshold, and somehow I felt sick, I couldn't understand what was happening to me. We came out into the yard. He stuck his beard in the air and looked at the sky. 'Walk on, Father,' I said, 'don't look back. You prayed for heaven and you'll soon be there.' I was just joking to keep my spirits up, why I don't know. It had never happened to me in my life before to talk to the condemned. Well, I let him walk three paces ahead, as we always did, and put the barrel of my gun between his shoulder blades and fired. You know what a Mauser shot is like—a crash like a cannon, and it kicks so that it nearly dislocates your arm. But when I looked there was my shot priest turning round and walking back at me. It's true of course that every case is different: some people fall flat, others spin round, and a few start pacing, reeling like drunks. But this one was walking towards me with short steps, as though floating in his cassock, just as though I hadn't shot him. 'Stop it, Father' I said, 'Halt!' and I shot him again—this time in the chest. But he tore his cassock open over his chest— he had a hairy, ugly chest—and walked straight on, shouting at the top of his voice: 'Shoot at me! Antichrist! Kill me, your Christ!' I lost my head, I fired again and again. But he kept coming on! No wound, no blood, he was walking along and praying aloud: 'Lord, you have stopped a bullet armed by evil hands. I accept to die for Your sake! ... No one can murder a living soul!' and something else of that sort ... I don't remember how many times I fired;

all I know is I couldn't have missed, I was firing at point blank. There he stood before me, his eyes burning like a wolf's, his chest bare, and a kind of halo round his head— it occurred to me afterwards that he was standing against the sun and the sun was setting. 'Your hands,' he shouted, 'your hands covered with blood! Look at your hands!' I threw the Mauser down and ran into the guard room, knocked someone over in the doorway and ran inside—the chaps were all looking at me as if I were mad, and laughing, I grabbed a rifle from the stack and yelled: 'take me this minute to Dzerzhinsky or I'll bayonet the lot of you!' Well, they took the rifle away from me and they led me off quick march. I walked into his study and broke free from the chaps and I said to him, trembling all over and stuttering: 'Shoot me, Felix Edmundovich,' I said, 'I can't kill a priest!' That's what I said, and fell down, and that's all I can remember. I came to myself in hospital. The doctors said: 'nervous shock'. They looked after me well, I must say. I got treatment, and the place was clean, and the food was good considering the times. They cured me—all but my hands, you see how they won't keep still. I suppose that nervous shock went to my hands. I was sacked from the Cheka of course—those sort of hands are no use to them. Nor of course could I go back to minding a machine. So they made me factory storekeeper. Well, it's a useful job. I can't do any paper work, of course—can't fill any forms, because of my hands. They gave me an assistant for that, a good sensible girl. That's how it is with me now. As for the priest, I discovered afterwards. There wasn't anything divine about it. It was just that, when I went to the washroom, the chaps took the bullets out of the cartridge clip and filled it with blanks. Just for a joke. Oh well, I'm not angry with them—they were young, and it wasn't pleasant for them either, so they thought this up. No, I'm not cross with them. It's just that my hands ... they're no good for any work.

1. The point of view in the story is that of the first-person (I) narrator. Point out places in the story where the reader understands things the narrator doesn't.

2. How does Daniel keep the reader aware of the narrator's hands?

3. Does the narrator question Dzerzhinsky's explanation of why people must be shot (when you dry a swamp, you have to destroy the vermin that are there)? How would you argue with this kind of explanation?

4. Why does the narrator regard the priests as "enemies"? How do you think he feels about shooting people?

5. Why is the narrator uneasy about shooting the last priest? What effect do you think the priest's accusations have on him?

6. Why is the narrator willing to forgive the people who played the joke on him and accept his disability?

Irony

In conversation a person's attitude toward what he is talking about is partly revealed through his tone of voice. The most ordinary expression ("Really!") can be used to communicate anything from wonder to sarcasm. A writer, unable to rely on inflection, must find verbal means of establishing a tone that will convey his attitude toward his subject. This tone lets the reader know how he is meant to regard a particular character. By the way she describes Connie's self-conscious walk and her "nervous giggling habit of craning her neck to glance into mirrors" Joyce Carol Oates suggests how young Connie really is. Doris Lessing hints that we are to question Lucy Grange's values and feelings by saying that she speaks to her child in a "rich, over-controlled voice."

An ironic tone depends upon a contrast between what the writer's words seem to say and what they really mean. To grasp the true meaning we must read between the lines. Verbal irony can take various forms, some easier to detect than others. In "The Princess and the Tin Box" James Thurber mocks the stock devices of fairy tales by exaggerating them to the point of absurdity. His heroine is the "prettiest princess in the world," with a throat that makes "the swan look dusty"; her toys are "all made of gold or platinum or diamonds or emeralds"; only the nightingale is allowed to sing for her.

In "The Balek Scales" Heinrich Böll uses a more subtle kind or irony, which depends upon understatement. He talks about the happiness of the peasants in a manner that seems to be approving yet is, in fact, a severe indictment of the economic and social system perpetuated by the local aristocracy. By his irony Böll turns what appears to be a simple folktale into a commentary on the injustices suffered by the poor of the world.

> *For five generations they had been breathing in the dust which arose from the crushed flax stalks, letting themselves be killed off by slow degrees, a race of long-suffering, cheerful people who ate goat cheese, potatoes, and now and then a rabbit.*

His narrative calls into question all the paternalistic customs by which the Baleks keep the workers in their place.

45

The irony that Flannery O'Connor employs in "Everything That Rises Must Converge" is both sharper and more complex than that of Böll or Thurber. Miss O'Connor has Julian's mother say things that reveal perfectly her genteel, old-South complacency about social inferiors and black people:

"Of course," she said, "if you know who you are, you can go anywhere." She said this every time he took her to the reducing class. "Most of them in it are not our kind of people," she said, "but I can be gracious to anybody. I know who I am."

But she reserves her most cutting irony for Julian, who continually reminds himself of his moral superiority to his mother and fails to see her as a human being in need of love until it is too late. In this story multiple ironies bring out the human complexity of the relationship between Julian and his mother, revealing the blind spots of each.

Not all irony is verbal. Miss O'Connor uses an irony of situation in having a black woman get on the bus wearing a hat identical to Julian's mother's. Böll also creates an ironic situation by having the Baleks walk into church unaware that the peasants have discovered their justice to be false. And Thurber's mock fairy tale depends upon the ironic fact that the princess chooses the most expensive present after all.

JAMES THURBER (1894–1961)

THE PRINCESS AND THE TIN BOX

Once upon a time, in a far country, there lived a king whose daughter was the prettiest princess in the world. Her eyes were like the cornflower, her hair was sweeter than the hyacinth, and her throat made the swan look dusty.

From the time she was a year old, the princess had been showered with presents. Her nursery looked like Cartier's window. Her toys were all made of gold or platinum or diamonds or emeralds. She was not permitted to have wooden blocks or china dolls or rubber dogs or linen books, because such materials were considered cheap for the daughter of a king.

When she was seven, she was allowed to attend the wedding of her brother and throw real pearls at the bride instead of rice. Only the nightingale, with his lyre of gold, was permitted to sing for the princess. The common blackbird, with his boxwood flute, was kept out of the palace grounds. She walked in silver-and-samite slippers to a sapphire-and-topaz bathroom and slept in an ivory bed inlaid with rubies.

On the day the princess was eighteen, the king sent a royal ambassador to the courts of five neighboring kingdoms to announce that he would give his daughter's hand in marriage to the prince who brought her the gift she liked the most.

The first prince to arrive at the palace rode a swift white stallion and laid at the feet of the princess an enormous apple made of solid gold which he had taken from a dragon who had guarded it for a thousand years. It was placed on a long ebony table set up to hold the gifts of the princess's suitors. The second prince, who came on a gray charger, brought her a nightingale made of a thousand diamonds, and it was placed beside the golden apple. The third prince, riding on a black horse, carried a great jewel box made of platinum and sapphires, and it was placed next to the diamond nightingale. The fourth prince, astride a fiery yellow horse, gave the princess a gigantic heart made of rubies and pierced by an emerald arrow. It was placed next to the platinum-and-sapphire jewel box.

Now the fifth prince was the strongest and handsomest of all the five suitors, but he was the son of a poor king whose realm had been overrun by mice and locusts and wizards and mining engineers so that there was nothing much of value left in it. He came plodding up to the palace of the princess on a plow horse and he brought her a small tin box filled with mica and feldspar and hornblende which he had picked up on the way.

The other princes roared with disdainful laughter when they saw the tawdry gift the fifth prince had brought to the princess. But she examined it with great interest and squealed with delight, for all her life she had been glutted with precious stones and priceless metals, but she had never seen tin before or mica or feldspar or hornblende. The tin box was placed next to the ruby heart pierced with an emerald arrow.

"Now," the king said to his daughter, "you must select the gift you like best and marry the prince that brought it."

The princess smiled and walked up to the table and picked up the present she liked the most. It was the platinum-and-sapphire jewel box, the gift of the third prince.

"The way I figure it," she said, "is this. It is a very large and expensive box, and when I am married, I will meet many admirers who will give me precious gems with which to fill it to the top. Therefore, it is the most valuable of all the gifts my suitors have brought me and I like it the best."

The princess married the third prince that very day in the midst of great merriment and high revelry. More than a hundred thousand pearls were thrown at her and she loved it.

Moral: All those who thought the princess was going to select the tin box filled with worthless stones instead of one of the other gifts will kindly stay after class and write one hundred times on the blackboard "I would rather have a hunk of aluminum silicate than a diamond necklace."

THE BALEK SCALES

Translated by Leila Vennewitz

Where my grandfather came from, most of the people lived by working in the flax sheds. For five generations they had been breathing in the dust which rose from the crushed flax stalks, letting themselves be killed off by slow degrees, a race of long-suffering, cheerful people who ate goat cheese, potatoes, and now and then a rabbit; in the evening they would sit at home spinning and knitting; they sang, drank mint tea and were happy. During the day they would carry the flax stalks to the antiquated machines, with no protection from the dust and at the mercy of the heat which came pouring out of the drying kilns. Each cottage contained only one bed, standing against the wall like a closet and reserved for the parents, while the children slept all round the room on benches. In the morning the room would be filled with the odor of thin soup; on Sundays there was stew, and on feast days the children's faces would light up with pleasure as they watched the black acorn coffee turning paler and paler from the milk their smiling mother poured into their coffee mugs.

The parents went off early to the flax sheds, the housework was left to the children: they would sweep the room, tidy up, wash the dishes and peel the potatoes, precious pale-yellow fruit whose thin peel had to be produced afterwards to dispel any suspicion of extravagance or carelessness.

As soon as the children were out of school they had to go off into the woods and, depending on the season, gather mushrooms and herbs: woodruff and thyme, caraway, mint and foxglove, and in summer, when they had brought in the hay from their meager fields, they gathered hayflowers. A kilo of hayflowers was worth one pfennig, and they were sold by the apothecaries in town for twenty pfennigs a kilo to highly strung ladies. The mushrooms were highly prized: they fetched twenty pfennigs a kilo and were sold in the shops in town for one mark twenty. The children would crawl deep into the green darkness of the forest during the autumn when dampness drove the mushrooms out of the soil, and almost every family had its own places where it gathered mushrooms, places which were handed down in whispers from generation to generation.

The woods belonged to the Baleks, as well as the flax sheds, and in my grandfather's village the Baleks had a chateau, and the wife of the head of the family had a little room next to the dairy where mushrooms, herbs and hayflowers were weighed and paid for. There on the table stood the great Balek scales, an old-fashioned, ornate bronze-gilt contraption, which my grandfather's grandparents had already faced when they were children, their grubby hands holding their little baskets of mushrooms, their paper bags of hayflowers, breathlessly watching the number of weights Frau Balek had to throw on the scale before the swinging pointer came to rest exactly over the black line, that thin line of justice which had to be redrawn every year. Then Frau Balek would take the big book covered in brown leather, write down the weight, and pay out the money, pfennigs or ten-pfennig pieces and very, very occasionally, a mark. And when my grandfather was a child there was a big glass jar

49

of lemon drops standing there, the kind that cost one mark a kilo, and when Frau Balek—whichever one happened to be presiding over the little room—was in a good mood, she would put her hand into this jar and give each child a lemon drop, and the children's faces would light up with pleasure, the way they used to when on feast days their mother poured milk into their coffee mugs, milk that made the coffee turn paler and paler until it was as pale as the flaxen pigtails of the little girls.

One of the laws imposed by the Baleks on the village was: no one was permitted to have any scales in the house. The law was so ancient that nobody gave a thought as to when and how it had arisen, and it had to be obeyed, for anyone who broke it was dismissed from the flax sheds, he could not sell his mushrooms or his thyme or his hay-flowers, and the power of the Baleks was so far-reaching that no one in the neighboring villages would give him work either, or buy his forest herbs. But since the days when my grandfather's parents had gone out as small children to gather mushrooms and sell them in order that they might season the meat of the rich people of Prague or be baked into game pies, it had never occurred to anyone to break this law: flour could be measured in cups, eggs could be counted, what they had spun could be measured by the yard, and besides, the old-fashioned bronze-gilt, ornate Balek scales did not look as if there was anything wrong with them, and five generations had entrusted the swinging black pointer with what they had gone out as eager children to gather from the woods.

True, there were some among these quiet people who flouted the law, poachers bent on making more money in one night than they could earn in a whole month in the flax sheds, but even these people apparently never thought of buying scales or making their own. My grandfather was the first person bold enough to test the justice of the Baleks, the family who lived in the chateau and drove two carriages, who always main-tained one boy from the village while he studied theology at the seminary in Prague, the family with whom the priest played taroc every Wednesday, on whom the local reeve, in his carriage emblazoned with the Imperial coat-of-arms, made an annual New Year's Day call and on whom the Emperor conferred a title on the first day of the year 1900.

My grandfather was hard-working and smart: he crawled further into the woods than the children of his clan had crawled before him, he penetrated as far as the thicket where, according to legend, Bilgan the Giant was supposed to dwell, guarding a treasure. But my grandfather was not afraid of Bilgan: he worked his way deep into the thicket, even when he was quite little, and brought out great quantities of mushrooms; he even found truffles, for which Frau Balek paid thirty pfennigs a pound. Everything my grandfather took to the Baleks he entered on the back of a torn-off calendar page: every pound of mushrooms, every gram of thyme, and on the right-hand side, in his childish handwriting, he entered the amount he received for each item; he scrawled in every pfennig, from the age of seven to the age of twelve, and by the time he was twelve the year 1900 had arrived, and because the Baleks had been raised to the aristocracy by the Emperor, they gave every family in the village a quarter of a pound of real coffee, the Brazilian kind; there was also free beer and tobacco for the men, and at the chateau there was a great banquet; many carriages stood in the avenue of poplars leading from the entrance gates to the chateau.

But the day before the banquet the coffee was distributed in the little room which had housed the Balek scales for almost a hundred years, and the Balek family was now called Balek von Bilgan because, according to legend, Bilgan the Giant used to have a great castle on the site of the present Balek estate.

My grandfather often used to tell me how he went there after school to fetch the coffee for four families: the Cechs, the Weidlers, the Vohlas and his own, the Brüchers. It was the afternoon of New Year's Eve: there were the front rooms to be decorated, the baking to be done, and the families did not want to spare four boys and have each of them go all the way to the chateau to bring back a quarter of a pound of coffee.

And so my grandfather sat on the narrow wooden bench in the little room while Gertrud the maid counted out the wrapped four-ounce packages of coffee, four of them, and he looked at the scales and saw that the pound weight was still lying on the left-hand scale; Frau Balek von Bilgan was busy with preparations for the banquet. And when Gertrud was about to put her hand into the jar with the lemon drops to give my grandfather one, she discovered it was empty: it was refilled once a year, and held one kilo of the kind that cost a mark.

Gertrud laughed and said: "Wait here while I get the new lot," and my grandfather waited with the four four-ounce packages which had been wrapped and sealed in the factory, facing the scales on which someone had left the pound weight, and my grandfather took the four packages of coffee, put them on the empty scale, and his heart thudded as he watched the black finger of justice come to rest on the left of the black line: the scale with the pound weight stayed down, and the pound of coffee remained up in the air; his heart thudded more than if he had been lying behind a bush in the forest waiting for Bilgan the Giant, and he felt in his pocket for the pebbles he always carried with him so he could use his catapult to shoot the sparrows which pecked away at his mother's cabbage plants—he had to put three, four, five pebbles beside the packages of coffee before the scale with the pound weight rose and the pointer at last came to rest over the black line. My grandfather took the coffee from the scale, wrapped the five pebbles in his kerchief, and when Gertrud came back with the big kilo bag of lemon drops which had to last for another whole year in order to make the children's faces light up with pleasure, when

Gertrud let the lemon drops rattle into the glass jar, the pale little fellow was still standing there, and nothing seemed to have changed. My grandfather only took three of the packages, then Gertrud looked in startled surprise at the white-faced child who threw the lemon drop onto the floor, ground it under his heel, and said: "I want to see Frau Balek."

"Balek von Bilgan, if you please," said Gertrud.

"All right, Frau Balek von Bilgan," but Gertrud only laughed at him, and he walked back to the village in the dark, took the Cechs, the Weidlers and the Vohlas their coffee, and said he had to go and see the priest.

Instead he went out into the dark night with his five pebbles in his kerchief. He had to walk a long way before he found someone who had scales, who was permitted to have them; no one in the villages of Blaugau and Bernau had any, he knew that, and he went straight through them till, after two hours' walking, he reached the little town of Dielheim where Honig the apothecary lived. From Honig's house came the smell of fresh pancakes, and Honig's breath, when he opened the door to the half-frozen boy, already smelled of punch, there was a moist cigar between his narrow lips, and he clasped the boy's cold hands firmly for a moment, saying: "What's the matter, has your father's lung got worse?"

"No, I haven't come for medicine, I wanted . . ." My grandfather undid his kerchief, took out the five pebbles, held them out to Honig and said: "I wanted to have these weighed." He glanced anxiously into Honig's face, but when Honig said nothing and did not get angry, or even ask him anything, my grandfather said: "It is the amount that is short of justice," and now, as he went into the warm room, my grandfather realized how wet his feet were. The snow had soaked through his cheap shoes, and in the forest the branches had showered him with snow which was now melting, and he was tired and hungry and suddenly began to cry because he thought of the quantities of mushrooms, the herbs, the flowers, which had been weighed on the scales which were short five pebbles' worth of justice. And when Honig, shaking his head and holding the five pebbles, called his wife, my grandfather thought of the generations of his parents, his grandparents, who had all had to have their mushrooms, their flowers, weighed on the scales, and he was overwhelmed by a great wave of injustice, and began to sob louder than ever, and, without waiting to be asked, he sat down on a chair, ignoring the pancakes, the cup of hot coffee which nice plump Frau Honig put in front of him, and did not stop crying till Honig himself came out from the shop at the back and, rattling the pebbles in his hand, said in a low voice to his wife: "Fifty-five grams, exactly."

My grandfather walked the two hours home through the forest, got a beating at home, said nothing, not a single word, when he was asked about the coffee, spent the whole evening doing sums on the piece of paper on which he had written down everything he had sold to Frau Balek, and when midnight struck, and the cannon could be heard from the chateau, and the whole village rang with shouting and laughter and the noise of rattles, when the family kissed and embraced all round, he said into the New Year silence: "The Baleks owe me eighteen marks and thirty-two pfennigs." And again he thought of all the children there were in the village, of his brother Fritz who had gathered so many mushrooms, of his sister Ludmilla; he thought of the many hundreds of children who had all gathered mushrooms for the Baleks, and herbs and flowers, and this time he did not cry but told his parents and brothers and sisters of his discovery.

When the Baleks von Bilgan went to High Mass on New Year's Day, their new coat-of-arms—a giant crouching under a fir tree—already emblazoned in blue and gold on their carriage, they saw the hard, pale faces of the people all staring at them. They had expected garlands in the village, a song in their honor, cheers and hurrahs, but the village was completely deserted as they drove through it, and in church the pale faces of the people were turned toward them, mute and hostile, and when the priest mounted the pulpit to deliver his New Year's sermon he sensed the chill in those otherwise quiet and peaceful faces, and he stumbled painfully through his sermon and went back to the altar drenched in sweat. And as the Baleks von Bilgan left the church after Mass, they walked through a lane of mute, pale faces. But young Frau Balek von Bilgan stopped in front of the children's pews, sought out my grandfather's face, pale little Franz Brücher, and asked him, right there in the church: "Why didn't you take the coffee for your mother?" And my grandfather stood up and said: "Because you owe me as much money as five kilos of coffee would cost." And he pulled the five pebbles from his pocket, held them out to the young woman and said: "This much, fifty-five grams, is short in every pound of your justice"; and before the woman could say anything the men and women in the church lifted up their voices and sang: "The justice of this earth, O Lord, hath put Thee to death. . . ."

While the Baleks were at church, Wilhelm Vohla, the poacher, had broken into the little room, stolen the scales and the big fat leather-bound book in which had been entered every kilo of mushrooms, every kilo of hayflowers, everything bought by the Baleks in the village, and all afternoon of that New Year's Day the men of the village sat in my great-grandparents' front room and calculated, calculated one tenth of everything that had been bought —but when they had calculated many thousands of talers and had still not come to an end, the reeve's gendarmes arrived, made their way into my great-grandfather's front room, shooting and stabbing as they came, and removed the scales and the book by force. My grandfather's little sister Ludmilla lost her life, a few men were wounded, and one of the gendarmes was stabbed to death by Wilhelm Vohla the poacher.

Our village was not the only one to rebel: Blaugau and Bernau did too, and for almost a week no work was done in the flax sheds. But a great many gendarmes appeared, and the men and women were threatened with prison, and the Baleks forced the priest to display the scales publicly in the school and demonstrate that the finger of justice swung to and fro accurately. And the men and women went back to the flax sheds—but no one went to the school to watch the priest: he stood there all alone, helpless and forlorn with his weights, scales, and packages of coffee.

And the children went back to gathering mushrooms, to gathering thyme, flowers and foxglove, but every Sunday, as soon as the Baleks entered the church, the hymn was struck up: "The justice of this earth, O Lord, hath put Thee to death," until the reeve ordered it proclaimed in every village that the singing of this hymn was forbidden.

My grandfather's parents had to leave the village, and the new grave of their little daughter; they became basket weavers, but did not stay long anywhere because it pained them to see how everywhere the finger of justice swung falsely. They walked along behind their cart, which crept slowly over the country roads, taking their thin goat with them, and passers-by could sometimes hear a voice from the cart singing: "The justice of this earth, O Lord, hath put Thee to death." And those who wanted to listen could hear the tale of the Baleks von Bilgan, whose justice lacked a tenth part. But there were few who listened.

1. What details suggest that we are meant to read the description of "happy village life" ironically?

2. Why does Böll so carefully establish the "ancient" nature of the scales? How does this affect your response to the discovery that the Baleks had been cheating?

3. What significance does the hymn have? What do the last two lines imply about people's reactions to injustice?

EVERYTHING THAT RISES
MUST CONVERGE

Her doctor had told Julian's mother that she must lose twenty pounds on account of her blood pressure, so on Wednesday nights Julian had to take her downtown on the bus for a reducing class at the Y. The reducing class was designed for working girls over fifty, who weighed from 165 to 200 pounds. His mother was one of the slimmer ones, but she said ladies did not tell their age or weight. She would not ride the buses by herself at night since they had been integrated, and because the reducing class was one of her few pleasures, necessary for her health, and *free*, she said Julian could at least put himself out to take her, considering all she did for him. Julian did not like to consider all she did for him, but every Wednesday night he braced himself and took her.

She was almost ready to go, standing before the hall mirror, putting on her hat, while he, his hands behind him, appeared pinned to the door frame, waiting like Saint Sebastian for the arrows to begin piercing him. The hat was new and had cost her seven dollars and a half. She kept saying, "Maybe I shouldn't have paid that for it. No, I shouldn't have. I'll take it off and return it tomorrow. I shouldn't have bought it."

Julian raised his eyes to heaven. "Yes, you should have bought it," he said. "Put it on and let's go." It was a hideous hat. A purple velvet flap came down on one side of it and stood up on the other; the rest of it was green and looked like a cushion with the stuffing out. He decided it was less comical than jaunty and pathetic. Everything that gave her pleasure was small and depressed him.

She lifted the hat one more time and set it down slowly on top of her head. Two wings of gray hair protruded on either side of her florid face, but her eyes, sky-blue, were as innocent and untouched by experience as they must have been when she was ten. Were it not that she was a widow who had struggled fiercely to feed and clothe and put him through school and who was supporting him still, "until he got on his feet," she might have been a little girl that he had to take to town.

"It's all right, it's all right," he said. "Let's go." He opened the door himself and started down the walk to get her going. The sky was a dying violet and the houses stood out darkly against it, bulbous liver-colored monstrosities of a uniform ugliness though no two were alike. Since this had been a fashionable neighborhood forty years ago, his mother persisted in thinking they did well to have an apartment in it. Each house had a narrow collar of dirt around it in which sat, usually, a grubby child. Julian walked with his hands in his pockets, his head down and thrust forward and his eyes glazed with the determination to make himself completely numb during the time he would be sacrificed to her pleasure.

The door closed and he turned to find the dumpy figure, surmounted by the atrocious hat, coming toward him. "Well," she said, "you only live once and paying a little more for it, I at least won't meet myself coming and going."

"Some day I'll start making money," Julian said gloomily—he knew he never would—"and you can have one of those jokes whenever you take the fit." But first they would move. He visualized a place where the nearest neighbors would be three miles away on either side.

"I think you're doing fine," she said, drawing on her gloves. "You've only been out of school a year. Rome wasn't built in a day."

She was one of the few members of the Y reducing class who arrived in hat and gloves and who had a son who had been to college. "It takes time," she said, "and the world is in such a mess. This hat looked better on me than any of the others, though when she brought it out I said, 'Take that thing back. I wouldn't have it on my head,' and she said, 'Now wait till you see it on,' and when she put it on me, I said, 'We-ull,' and she said, 'If you ask me, that hat does something for you and you do something for the hat, and besides,' she said, 'with that hat, you won't meet yourself coming and going.' "

Julian thought he could have stood his lot better if she had been selfish, if she had been an old hag who drank and screamed at him. He walked along, saturated in depression, as if in the midst of his martyrdom he had lost his faith. Catching sight of his long, hopeless, irritated face, she stopped suddenly with a grief-stricken look, and pulled back on his arm. "Wait on me," she said. "I'm going back to the house and take this thing off and tomorrow I'm going to return it. I was out of my head. I can pay the gas bill with that seven-fifty."

He caught her arm in a vicious grip. "You are not going to take it back," he said. "I like it."

"Well," she said, "I don't think I ought . . ."

"Shut up and enjoy it," he muttered, more depressed than ever.

"With the world in the mess it's in," she said, "it's a wonder we can enjoy anything. I tell you, the bottom rail is on the top."

Julian sighed.

"Of course," she said, "if you know who you are, you can go anywhere." She said this every time he took her to the reducing class. "Most of them in it are not our kind of people," she said, "but I can be gracious to anybody. I know who I am."

"They don't give a damn for your graciousness," Julian said savagely. "Knowing who you are is good for one generation only. You haven't the foggiest idea where you stand now or who you are."

She stopped and allowed her eyes to flash at him. "I most certainly do know who I am," she said, "and if you don't know who you are, I'm ashamed of you."

"Oh hell," Julian said.

"Your great-grandfather was a former governor of this state," she said. "Your grandfather was a prosperous landowner. Your grandmother was a Godhigh."

"Will you look around you," he said tensely, "and see where you are now?" and he swept his arm jerkily out to indicate the neighborhood, which the growing darkness at least made less dingy.

"You remain what you are," she said. "Your great-grandfather had a plantation and two hundred slaves."

"There are no more slaves," he said irritably.

"They were better off when they were," she said. He groaned to see that she was off on that topic. She rolled onto it every few days like a train on an open track. He knew every stop, every junction, every swamp along the way, and knew the exact point at which her conclusion would roll majestically into the station: "It's ridiculous. It's simply not realistic. They should rise, yes, but on their own side of the fence."

"Let's skip it," Julian said.

"The ones I feel sorry for," she said, "are the ones that are half white. They're tragic."

"Will you skip it?"

"Suppose we were half white. We would certainly have mixed feelings.

"I have mixed feelings now," he groaned.

"Well let's talk about something pleasant," she said. "I remember going to Grandpa's when I was a little girl. Then the house had double stairways that went up to what was really the second floor—all the cooking was done on the first. I used to like to stay down in the kitchen on account of the way the walls smelled. I would sit with my nose pressed against the plaster and take deep breaths. Actually the place belonged to the Godhighs but your grandfather Chestny paid the mortgage and saved it for them. They were in reduced circumstances," she said, "but reduced or not, they never forgot who they were."

"Doubtless that decayed mansion reminded them," Julian muttered. He never spoke of it without contempt or thought of it without longing. He had seen it once when he was a child before it had been sold. The double stairways had rotted and been torn down. Negroes were living in it. But it remained in his mind as his mother had known it. It appeared in his dreams regularly. He would stand on the wide porch, listening to the rustle of oak leaves, then wander through the high-ceilinged hall into the parlor that opened onto it and gaze at the worn rugs and faded draperies. It occurred to him that it was he, not she, who could have appreciated it. He preferred its threadbare elegance to anything he could name and it was because of it that all the neighborhoods they had lived in had been a torment to him—whereas she had hardly known the difference. She called her insensitivity "being adjustable."

"And I remember the old darky who was my nurse, Caroline. There was no better person in the world. I've always had a great respect for my colored friends," she said. "I'd do anything in the world for them and they'd . . ."

"Will you for God's sake get off that subject?" Julian said. When he got on a bus by himself, he made it a point to sit down beside a Negro, in reparation as it were for his mother's sins.

"You're mighty touchy tonight," she said. "Do you feel all right?"

"Yes I feel all right," he said. "Now lay off."

She pursed her lips. "Well, you certainly are in a vile humor," she observed. "I just won't speak to you at all."

They had reached the bus stop. There was no bus in sight and Julian, his hands still jammed in his pockets and his head thrust forward, scowled down the empty street. The frustration of having to wait on the bus as well as ride on it began to creep up his neck like a hot hand. The presence of his mother was borne in upon him as she gave a pained sigh. He looked at her bleakly. She was holding herself very erect under the preposterous hat, wearing it like a banner of her imaginary dignity. There was in him an evil urge to break her spirit. He suddenly unloosened his tie and pulled it off and put it in his pocket.

She stiffened. "Why must you look like *that* when you take me to town?" she said. "Why must you deliberately embarrass me?"

"If you'll never learn where you are," he said, "you can at least learn where I am."

"You look like a—thug," she said.

"Then I must be one," he murmured.

"I'll just go home," she said. "I will not bother you. If you can't do a little thing like that for me . . ."

Rolling his eyes upward, he put his tie back on. "Restored to my class," he muttered. He thrust his face toward her and hissed, "True culture is in the mind, the *mind*," he said, and tapped his head, "the mind."

"It's in the heart," she said, "and in how you do things and how you do things is because of who you *are*."

"Nobody in the damn bus cares who you are."

"I care who I am," she said icily.

The lighted bus appeared on top of the next hill and as it approached, they moved out into the street to meet it. He put his hand under her elbow and hoisted her up on the creaking step. She entered with a little smile, as if she were going into a drawing room where everyone had been waiting for her. While he put in the tokens, she sat down on one of the broad front seats for three which faced the aisle. A thin woman with protruding teeth and long yellow hair was sitting on the end of it. His mother moved up beside her and left room for Julian beside herself. He sat down and looked at the floor across the aisle where a pair of thin feet in red and white canvas sandals were planted.

His mother immediately began a general conversation meant to attract anyone who felt like talking. "Can it get any hotter?" she said and removed from her purse a folding fan, black with a Japanese scene on it, which she began to flutter before her.

"I reckon it might could," the woman with the protruding teeth said, "but I know for a fact my apartment couldn't get no hotter."

"It must get the afternoon sun," his mother said. She sat forward and looked up and down the bus. It was half filled. Everybody was white. "I see we have the bus to ourselves," she said. Julian cringed.

"For a change," said the woman across the aisle, the owner of the red and white canvas sandals. "I come on one the other day and they were thick as fleas—up front and all through."

"The world is in a mess everywhere," his mother said. "I don't know how we've let it get in this fix."

"What gets my goat is all those boys from good families stealing automobile tires," the woman with the protruding teeth said. "I told my boy, I said you may not be rich but you been raised right and if I ever catch you in any such mess, they can send you on to the reformatory. Be exactly where you belong."

"Training tells," his mother said. "Is your boy in high school?"

"Ninth grade," the woman said.

"My son just finished college last year. He wants to write but he's selling typewriters until he gets started," his mother said.

The woman leaned forward and peered at Julian. He threw her such a malevolent look that she subsided against the seat. On the floor across the aisle there was an abandoned newspaper. He got up and got it and opened it out in front of him. His mother discreetly continued the conversation in a lower tone but the woman across the aisle said in a loud voice, "Well that's nice. Selling typewriters is close to writing. He can go right from one to the other."

"I tell him," his mother said, "that Rome wasn't built in a day."

Behind the newspaper Julian was withdrawing into the inner compartment of his mind where he spent most of his time. This was a kind of mental bubble in which he established himself when he could not bear to be a part of what was going on around him. From it he could see out and judge but in it he was safe from any kind of penetration from without. It was the only place where he felt free of the general idiocy of his fellows. His mother had never entered it but from it he could see her with absolute clarity.

The old lady was clever enough and he thought that if she had started from any of the right premises, more might have been expected of her. She lived according to the laws of her fantasy world, outside of which he had never seen her set foot. The law of it was to sacrifice herself for him after she had first created the necessity to do so by making a mess of things. If he had permitted her sacrifices, it was only because her lack of foresight had made them necessary. All of her life had been a struggle to act like a Chestny without the Chestny goods, and to give him everything she thought a Chestny ought to have; but since, said she, it was fun to struggle, why complain? And when you had won, as she had won, what fun to look back on the hard times! He could not forgive her that she had enjoyed the struggle and that she thought *she* had won.

What she meant when she said she had won was that she had brought him up successfully and had sent him to college and that he had turned out so well—good looking (her teeth had gone unfilled so that his could be straightened), intelligent (he realized he was too intelligent to be a success), and with a future ahead of him (there was of course no future ahead of him). She excused his gloominess on the grounds that he was still growing up and his radical ideas on his lack of practical experience. She said he didn't yet know a thing about "life," that he hadn't even entered the real world—when already he was as disenchanted with it as a man of fifty.

The further irony of all this was that in spite of her, he had turned out so well. In spite of going to only a third-rate college, he had, on his own initiative, come out with a first-rate education; in spite of growing up dominated by a small mind, he had ended up with a large one; in spite of all her foolish views, he was free of prejudice and unafraid to face facts. Most miraculous of all, instead of being blinded by love for her as she was for him, he had cut himself emotionally free of her and could see her with complete objectivity. He was not dominated by his mother.

The bus stopped with a sudden jerk and shook him from his meditation. A woman from the back lurched forward with little steps and barely escaped falling in his newspaper as she righted herself. She got off and a large Negro got on. Julian kept his paper lowered to watch. It gave him a certain satisfaction to see injustice in daily operation. It confirmed his view that with a few exceptions there was no one worth knowing within a radius of three hundred miles. The Negro was well dressed and carried a briefcase. He looked around and then sat down on the other end of the seat where the woman with the red and white canvas sandals was sitting. He immediately unfolded a newspaper and obscured himself behind it. Julian's mother's elbow at once prodded insistently into his ribs. "Now you see why I won't ride on these buses by myself," she whispered.

The woman with the red and white canvas sandals had risen at the same time the Negro sat down and had gone further back in the bus and taken the seat of the woman who had got off. His mother leaned forward and cast her an approving look.

Julian rose, crossed the aisle, and sat down in the place of the woman with the canvas sandals. From this position, he looked serenely across at his mother. Her face had turned an angry red. He stared at her, making his eyes the eyes of a stranger. He felt his tension suddenly lift as if he had openly declared war on her.

He would have liked to get in conversation with the Negro and to talk with him about art or politics or any subject that would be above the comprehension of those around them, but the man remained entrenched behind his paper. He was either ignoring the change of seating or had never noticed it. There was no way for Julian to convey his sympathy.

His mother kept her eyes fixed reproachfully on his face. The woman with the protruding teeth was looking at him avidly as if he was a type of monster new to her.

"Do you have a light?" he asked the Negro.

Without looking away from his paper, the man reached in his pocket and handed him a packet of matches.

"Thanks," Julian said. For a moment he held the matches foolishly. A NO SMOKING sign looked down upon him from over the door. This alone would not have deterred him; he had no cigarettes. He had quit smoking some months before because he could not afford it. "Sorry," he muttered and handed back the matches. The Negro lowered the paper and gave him an annoyed look. He took the matches and raised the paper again.

His mother continued to gaze at him but she did not take advantage of his momentary discomfort. Her eyes retained their battered look. Her face seemed to be unnaturally red, as if her blood pressure had risen. Julian allowed no glimmer of sympathy to show on his face. Having got the advantage, he wanted desperately to keep it and carry it through.

He would have liked to teach her a lesson that would last her a while, but there seemed no way to continue the point. The Negro refused to come out from behind his paper.

Julian folded his arms and looked stolidly before him, facing her but as if he did not see her, as if he had ceased to recognize her existence. He visualized a scene in which, the bus having reached their stop, he would remain in his seat and when she said, "Aren't you going to get off?" he would look at her as at a stranger who had rashly addressed him. The corner they got off on was usually deserted, but it was well lighted and it would not hurt her to walk by herself the four blocks to the Y. He decided to wait until the time came and then decide whether or not he would let her get off by herself. He would have to be at the Y at ten to bring her back, but he could leave her wondering if he was going to show up. There was no reason for her to think she could always depend on him.

He retired again into the high-ceilinged room sparsely settled with large pieces of antique furniture. His soul expanded momentarily but then he became aware of his mother across from him and the vision shriveled. He studied her coldly. Her feet in little pumps dangled like a child's and did not quite reach the floor. She was training on him an exaggerated look of reproach. He felt completely detached from her. At that moment he could with pleasure have slapped her as he would have slapped a particularly obnoxious child in his charge.

He began to imagine various unlikely ways by which he could teach her a lesson. He might make friends with some distinguished Negro professor or lawyer and bring him home to spend the evening. He would be entirely justified but her blood pressure would rise to 300. He could not push her to the extent of making her have a stroke, and moreover, he had never been successful at making any Negro friends. He had tried to strike up an acquaintance on the bus with some of the better types, with ones that looked like pro-

fessors or ministers or lawyers. One morning he had sat down next to a distinguished-looking dark brown man who had answered his questions with a sonorous solemnity but who had turned out to be an undertaker. Another day he had sat down beside a cigar-smoking Negro with a diamond ring on his finger, but after a few stilted pleasantries, the Negro had rung the buzzer and risen, slipping two lottery tickets into Julian's hand as he climbed over him to leave.

He imagined his mother lying desperately ill and his being able to secure only a Negro doctor for her. He toyed with that idea for a few minutes and then dropped it for a momentary vision of himself participating as a sympathizer in a sit-in demonstration. This was possible but he did not linger with it. Instead, he approached the ultimate horror. He brought home a beautiful suspiciously Negroid woman. Prepare yourself, he said. There is nothing you can do about it. This is the woman I've chosen. She's intelligent, dignified, even good, and she's suffered and she hasn't thought it *fun*. Now persecute us, go ahead and persecute us. Drive her out of here, but remember, you're driving me too. His eyes were narrowed and through the indignation he had generated, he saw his mother across the aisle, purple-faced, shrunken to the dwarf-like proportions of her moral nature, sitting like a mummy beneath the ridiculous banner of her hat.

He was tilted out of his fantasy again as the bus stopped. The door opened with a sucking hiss and out of the dark a large, gaily dressed, sullen-looking colored woman got on with a little boy. The child, who might have been four, had on a short plaid suit and a Tyrolean hat with a blue feather in it. Julian hoped that he would sit down beside him and that the woman would push in beside his mother. He could think of no better arrangement.

As she waited for her tokens, the woman was surveying the seating possibilities—he hoped with the idea of sitting where she was least wanted. There was something familiar-looking about her but Julian could not place what it was. She was a giant of a woman. Her face was set not only to meet opposition but to seek it out. The downward tilt of her large lower lip was like a warning sign: DON'T TAMPER WITH ME. Her bulging figure was encased in a green crepe dress and her feet overflowed in red shoes. She had on a hideous hat. A purple velvet flap came down on one side of it and stood up on the other; the rest of it was green and looked like a cushion with the stuffing out. She carried a mammoth red pocketbook that bulged throughout as if it were stuffed with rocks.

To Julian's disappointment, the little boy climbed up on the empty seat beside his mother. His mother lumped all children, black or white, into the common category, "cute," and she thought little Negroes were on the whole cuter than little white children. She smiled at the little boy as he climbed on the seat.

Meanwhile the woman was bearing down upon the empty seat beside Julian. To his annoyance, she squeezed herself into it. He saw his mother's face change as the woman settled herself next to him and he realized with satisfaction that this was more objectionable to her than it was to him. Her face seemed almost gray and there was a look of dull recognition in her eyes, as if suddenly she had sickened at some awful confrontation. Julian saw that it was because she and the woman had, in a sense, swapped sons. Though his mother would not realize the symbolic significance of this, she would feel it. His amusement showed plainly on his face.

The woman next to him muttered something unintelligible to herself. He was conscious of a kind of bristling next to him, a muted growling like that of an angry cat. He could not see anything but the red pocketbook upright on the bulging green thighs. He visualized the woman as she had stood waiting for her tokens—the ponderous figure, rising from the red shoes upward over the solid hips, the mammoth bosom, the haughty face, to the green and purple hat.

His eyes widened.

The vision of the two hats, identical, broke upon him with the radiance of a brilliant sunrise. His face was suddenly lit with joy. He could not believe that Fate had thrust upon his mother such a lesson. He gave a loud chuckle so that she would look at him and see that he saw. She turned her eyes on him slowly. The blue in them seemed to have turned a bruised purple. For a moment he had an uncomfortable sense of her innocence, but it lasted only a second before principle rescued him. Justice entitled him to laugh. His grin hardened until it said to her as plainly as if he were saying aloud: Your punishment exactly fits your pettiness. This should teach you a permanent lesson.

Her eyes shifted to the woman. She seemed unable to bear looking at him and to find the woman preferable. He became conscious again of the bristling presence at his side. The woman was rumbling like a volcano about to become active. His mother's mouth began to twitch slightly at one corner. With a sinking heart, he saw incipient signs of recovery on her face and realized that this was going to strike her suddenly as funny and was going to be no lesson at all. She kept her eyes on the woman and an amused smile came over her face as if the woman were a monkey that had stolen her hat. The little Negro was looking up at her with large fascinated eyes. He had been trying to attract her attention for some time.

"Carver!" the woman said suddenly. "Come heah!"

When he saw that the spotlight was on him at last, Carver drew his feet up and turned himself toward Julian's mother and giggled.

"Carver!" the woman said. "You heah me? Come heah!"

Carver slid down from the seat but remained squatting with his back against the base of it, his head turned slyly around toward Julian's mother, who was smiling at him. The woman reached a hand across the aisle and snatched him to her. He righted himself and hung backwards on her knees, grinning at Julian's mother. "Isn't he cute?" Julian's mother said to the woman with the protruding teeth.

"I reckon he is," the woman said without conviction.

The Negress yanked him upright but he eased out of her grip and shot across the aisle and scrambled, giggling wildly, onto the seat beside his love.

"I think he likes me," Julian's mother said, and smiled at the woman. It was the smile she used when she was being particularly gracious to an inferior. Julian saw everything lost. The lesson had rolled off her like rain on a roof.

The woman stood up and yanked the little boy off the seat as if she were snatching him from contagion. Julian could feel the rage in her at having no weapon like his mother's smile. She gave the child a sharp slap across his leg. He howled once and then thrust his head into her stomach and kicked his feet against her shins. "Be-have," she said vehemently.

The bus stopped and the Negro who had been reading the newspaper got off. The woman moved over and set the little boy down with a thump between herself and Julian. She held him firmly by the knee. In a moment he put his hands in front of his face and peeped at Julian's mother through his fingers.

"I see yooooooo!" she said and put her hand in front of her face and peeped at him.

The woman slapped his hand down. "Quit yo' foolishness," she said, "before I knock the living Jesus out of you!"

Julian was thankful that the next stop was theirs. He reached up and pulled the cord. The woman reached up and pulled it at the same time. Oh my God, he thought. He had the terrible intuition that when they got off the bus together, his mother would open her purse and give the little boy a nickel. The gesture would be as natural to her as breathing. The bus stopped and the woman got up and lunged to the front, dragging the child, who wished to stay on, after her. Julian and

his mother got up and followed. As they neared the door, Julian tried to relieve her of her pocketbook.

"No," she murmured, "I want to give the little boy a nickel."

"No!" Julian hissed. "No!"

She smiled down at the child and opened her bag. The bus door opened and the woman picked him up by the arm and descended with him, hanging at her hip. Once in the street she set him down and shook him.

Julian's mother had to close her purse while she got down the bus step but as soon as her feet were on the ground, she opened it again and began to rummage inside. "I can't find but a penny," she whispered, "but it looks like a new one."

"Don't do it!" Julian said fiercely between his teeth. There was a streetlight on the corner and she hurried to get under it so that she could better see into her pocketbook. The woman was heading off rapidly down the street with the child still hanging backward on her hand.

"Oh little boy!" Julian's mother called and took a few quick steps and caught up with him just beyond the lamp post. "Here's a bright new penny for you," and she held out the coin, which shone bronze in the dim light.

The huge woman turned and for a moment stood, her shoulders lifted and her face frozen with frustrated rage, and stared at Julian's mother. Then all at once she seemed to explode like a piece of machinery that had been given one ounce of pressure too much. Julian saw the black fist swing out with the red pocketbook. He shut his eyes and cringed as he heard the woman shout, "He don't take nobody's pennies!" When he opened his eyes, the woman was disappearing down the street with the little boy staring wide-eyed over her shoulder. Julian's mother was sitting on the sidewalk.

"I told you not to do that," Julian said angrily. "I told you not to do that!"

He stood over her for a minute, gritting his teeth. Her legs were stretched out in front of her and her hat was on her lap. He squatted down and looked her in the face. It was totally expressionless. "You got exactly what you deserved," he said. "Now get up."

He picked up her pocketbook and put what had fallen out back in it. He picked the hat up off her lap. The penny caught his eye on the sidewalk and he picked that up and let it drop before her eyes into the purse. Then he stood up and leaned over and held his hands out to pull her up. She remained immobile. He sighed. Rising above them on either side were black apartment buildings, marked with irregular rectangles of light. At the end of the block a man came out of a door and walked off in the opposite direction. "All right," he said, "suppose somebody happens by and wants to know why you're sitting on the sidewalk?"

She took the hand and, breathing hard, pulled heavily up on it and then stood for a moment, swaying slightly as if the spots of light in the darkness were circling around her. Her eyes, shadowed and confused, finally settled on his face. He did not try to conceal his irritation. "I hope this teaches you a lesson," he said. She leaned forward and her eyes raked his face. She seemed trying to determine his identity. Then, as if she found nothing familiar about him, she started off with a headlong movement in the wrong direction.

"Aren't you going to the Y?" he asked.

"Home," she muttered.

"Well, are we walking?"

For answer she kept going. Julian followed along, his hands behind him. He saw no reason to let the lesson she had had go without backing it up with an explanation of its meaning. She might as well be made to understand what had happened to her. "Don't think that was just an uppity Negro woman," he said. "That was the whole colored race which will no longer take your condescending pennies. That was your black double. She can wear the same hat as you, and to be sure," he added gratuitously (because he thought it was funny), "it looked

better on her than it did on you. What all this means," he said, "is that the old world is gone. The old manners are obsolete and your graciousness is not worth a damn." He thought bitterly of the house that had been lost for him. "You aren't who you think you are," he said.

She continued to plow ahead, paying no attention to him. Her hair had come undone on one side. She dropped her pocketbook and took no notice. He stooped and picked it up and handed it to her but she did not take it.

"You needn't act as if the world had come to an end," he said, "because it hasn't. From now on you've got to live in a new world and face a few realities for a change. Buck up," he said, "it won't kill you."

She was breathing fast.

"Let's wait on the bus," he said.

"Home," she said thickly.

"I hate to see you behave like this," he said. "Just like a child. I should be able to expect more of you." He decided to stop where he was and make her stop and wait for a bus. "I'm not going any farther," he said, stopping. "We're going on the bus."

She continued to go on as if she had not heard him. He took a few steps and caught her arm and stopped her. He looked into her face and caught his breath. He was looking into a face he had never seen before. "Tell Grandpa to come get me," she said.

He stared, stricken.

"Tell Caroline to come get me," she said.

Stunned, he let her go and she lurched forward again, walking as if one leg were shorter than the other. A tide of darkness seemed to be sweeping her from him. "Mother!" he cried. "Darling, sweetheart, wait!" Crumpling, she fell to the pavement. He dashed forward and fell at her side, crying, "Mamma, Mamma!" He turned her over. Her face was fiercely distorted. One eye, large and staring, moved slightly to the left as if it had become unmoored. The other remained fixed on him, raked his face again, found nothing and closed.

"Wait here, wait here!" he cried and jumped up and began to run for help toward a cluster of lights he saw in the distance ahead of him. "Help, help!" he shouted, but his voice was thin, scarcely a thread of sound. The lights drifted farther away the faster he ran and his feet moved numbly as if they carried him nowhere. The tide of darkness seemed to sweep him back to her, postponing from moment to moment his entry into the world of guilt and sorrow.

1. How does Miss O'Connor's irony work in a passage such as the following?

   In spite of growing up dominated by a small mind, he had ended up with a large one; in spite of all her foolish views, he was free of prejudice and unafraid to face facts. Most miraculous of all, instead of being blinded by love for her as she was for him, he had cut himself emotionally free of her with complete objectivity. He was not dominated by his mother.

   Does Julian need his mother? Why does he live at home?

2. Julian's mother defines her identity in terms of her ancestors and the code of gentility that she was brought up to believe in. How does Julian define his identity? Why does he spend most of his time in "the inner compartment of his mind"?

3. What does the hat mean to Julian's mother? Why does Julian detest it? What is the significance of the fact that the black woman is wearing the same hat?

4. Could Julian have done anything to prevent his mother's death? What do you think the last sentence of the story means?

Symbolism

A symbol stands for something: a dove for peace, a cross for Christianity, a policeman's badge for his legal authority. Such symbols have a basic meaning that we take for granted, though occasionally people invest an old symbol, such as the American flag, with new meaning. Literary symbols have no fixed meaning independent of the work in which they appear. The context that the writer establishes determines their significance. Scales are an ancient symbol of justice; but in Heinrich Böll's story the "old-fashioned, ornate, bronze-gilt" scales symbolize the hypocrisy of the Balek family and the false standard of justice by which this family has exploited several generations of village children.

All stories—except those that present the plainest, most factual kind of narrative—are symbolic to some degree. A particular object or action may embody an intensified kind of meaning that the writer cannot convey in other ways. In "Where Are You Going, Where Have You Been?" Arnold Friend's gold-painted jalopy, with all its decorations, suggests the grotesque way he apes teenage styles. In "Everything That Rises Must Converge," the angry gesture of the black woman who knocks Julian's mother down with her purse effectively demonstrates her pride.

D. H. Lawrence's stories often seem to be more concerned with the emotional forces involved in human relationships than with his characters themselves. At the beginning of "The Horse Dealer's Daughter," it seems impossible for Mabel to escape the bleak conditions of her life—symbolized in part by the desolate house, the "winter-dark fields," the town "clustered like smouldering ash"—yet she is mysteriously transfigured by the experience of being rescued by Dr. Fergusson. After attempting to drown herself in the "dead, cold pond"

64

with its bottom of rotten clay, Mabel awakens to a new emotional life. Lawrence presents her immersion in the cold waters, and that of Dr. Fergusson, in such a way as to suggest that both experience a symbolic death and rebirth. He is talking about a death of the self that must precede the birth of love in two individuals unused to giving themselves in an intimate human relationship.

The short story form has been used by some writers as a vehicle for concerns that have little to do with problems of character and human interaction. Hawthorne's story, "Young Goodman Brown," is only superficially concerned with the relationship of the central character and his young wife. Its real subject is the difficulty of holding onto faith when confronted by the prospect that "Evil is the nature of mankind." Goodman Brown can be regarded as everyman, his wife as an allegorical representation of the ideal of faith. By questioning whether Goodman Brown may have dreamed his experience in the forest, Hawthorne suggests that we need not regard the action of the story as literally true; what matters is that we consider the validity of his vision of evil.

In his story, "The South," Jorge Luis Borges raises questions about the way we perceive and understand the apparent destiny of an individual. Juan Dahlmann, like Goodman Brown, makes a symbolic journey, not into a forest where moral values are confused but into the Argentine pampas of his ancestors. His train ride becomes a journey into the past and into a different mode of life. It may not even be a literal journey at all, but a sick man's dream of the heroic way in which he would prefer to die. Borges presents the action in such a way as to leave the reader wondering about his conceptions of time and causality. His story shares with Hawthorne's a profound ambiguity that points finally to the mysteriousness of human life.

THE HORSE DEALER'S DAUGHTER

"Well, Mabel, and what are you going to do with yourself?" asked Joe, with foolish flippancy. He felt quite safe himself. Without listening for an answer, he turned aside, worked a grain of tobacco to the tip of his tongue, and spat it out. He did not care about anything, since he felt safe himself.

The three brothers and the sister sat round the desolate breakfast table, attempting some sort of desultory consultation. The morning's post had given the final tap to the family fortunes, and all was over. The dreary dining-room itself, with its heavy mahogany furniture, looked as if it were waiting to be done away with.

But the consultation amounted to nothing. There was a strange air of ineffectuality about the three men, as they sprawled at table, smoking and reflecting vaguely on their own condition. The girl was alone, a rather short, sullen-looking young woman of twenty-seven. She did not share the same life as her brothers. She would have been good-looking, save for the impassive fixity of her face, "bull-dog," as her brothers called it.

There was a confused tramping of horses' feet outside. The three men all sprawled round in their chairs to watch. Beyond the dark holly-bushes that separated the strip of lawn from the highroad, they could see a cavalcade of shire horses swinging out of their own yard, being taken for exercise. This was the last time. These were the last horses that would go through their hands. The young men watched with critical, callous look. They were all frightened at the collapse of their lives, and the sense of disaster in which they were involved left them no inner freedom.

Yet they were three fine, well-set fellows enough. Joe, the eldest, was a man of thirty-three, broad and handsome in a hot, flushed way. His face was red, he twisted his black moustache over a thick finger, his eyes were shallow and restless. He had a sensual way of uncovering his teeth when he laughed, and his bearing was stupid. Now he watched the horses with a glazed look of helplessness in his eyes, a certain stupor of downfall.

The great draught-horses swung past. They were tied head to tail, four of them, and they heaved along to where a lane branched off from the highroad, planting their great hoofs floutingly in the fine black mud, swinging their great rounded haunches sumptuously, and trotting a few sudden steps as they were led into the lane, round the corner. Every movement showed a massive, slumbrous strength, and a stupidity which held them in subjection. The groom at the head looked back, jerking the leading rope. And the cavalcade moved out of sight up the lane, the tail of the last horse, bobbed up tight and stiff, held out taut from the swinging great haunches as they rocked behind the hedges in a motionlike sleep.

Joe watched with glazed hopeless eyes. The horses were almost like his own body to him. He felt he was done for now. Luckily he was engaged to a woman as old as himself, and therefore her father, who was steward of a neighboring estate, would provide him with a job. He would marry and go into harness. His life was over, he would be a subject animal now.

He turned uneasily aside, the retreating steps of the horses echoing in his ears. Then, with foolish restlessness, he reached for the scraps of bacon-rind from the plates, and making a faint whistling sound, flung them to the terrier that lay against the fender. He watched the dog swallow them, and waited till the creature looked into his eyes. Then a faint grin came on his face, and in a high, foolish voice he said:

"You won't get much more bacon, shall you, you little b———?"

The dog faintly and dismally wagged its tail, then lowered its haunches, circled round, and lay down again.

There was another helpless silence at the table. Joe sprawled uneasily in his seat, not willing to go till the family conclave was dissolved. Fred Henry, the second brother, was erect, clean-limbed, alert. He had watched the passing of the horses with more *sangfroid*. If he was an animal, like Joe, he was an animal which controls, not one which is controlled. He was master of any horse, and he carried himself with a well-tempered air of mastery. But he was not master of the situations of life. He pushed his coarse brown moustache upwards, off his lip, and glanced irritably at his sister, who sat impassive and inscrutable.

You'll go and stop with Lucy for a bit, shan't you?" he asked. The girl did not answer.

"I don't see what else you can do," persisted Fred Henry.

"Go as a skivvy," Joe interpolated laconically.

The girl did not move a muscle.

"If I was her, I should go in for training for a nurse," said Malcolm, the youngest of them all. He was the baby of the family, a young man of twenty-two, with a fresh, jaunty *museau*.

But Mabel did not take any notice of him. They had talked at her and round her for so many years, that she hardly heard them at all.

The marble clock on the mantel-piece softly chimed the half-hour, the dog rose uneasily from the hearthrug and looked at the party at the breakfast table. But still they sat on in ineffectual conclave.

"Oh, all right," said Joe suddenly, *à propos* of nothing. "I'll get a move on."

He pushed back his chair, straddled his knees with a downward jerk, to get them free, in horsey fashion, and went to the fire. Still he did not go out of the room; he was curious to know what the others would do or say. He began to charge his pipe, looking down at the dog and saying, in a high, affected voice:

"Going wi' me? Going wi' me are ter? Tha'rt goin' further than tha counts on just now, dost hear?"

The dog faintly wagged its tail, the man stuck out his jaw and covered his pipe with his hands, and puffed intently, losing himself in the tobacco, looking down all the while at the dog, with an absent brown eye. The dog looked up at him in mournful distrust. Joe stood with his knees stuck out, in real horsey fashion.

"Have you had a letter from Lucy?" Fred Henry asked of his sister.

"Last week," came the neutral reply.

"And what does she say?"

There was no answer.

"Does she *ask* you to go and stop there?" persisted Fred Henry.

"She says I can if I like."

"Well, then, you'd better. Tell her you'll come on Monday."

This was received in silence.

"That's what you'll do then, is it?" said Fred Henry, in some exasperation.

But she made no answer. There was a silence of futility and irritation in the room. Malcolm grinned fatuously.

"You'll have to make up your mind between now and next Wednesday," said Joe loudly, "or else find yourself lodgings on the kerbstone."

The face of the young woman darkened, but she sat on immutable.

"Here's Jack Fergusson!" exclaimed Malcolm, who was looking aimlessly out of the window.

"Where?" exclaimed Joe, loudly.

"Just gone past."

"Coming in?"

Malcolm craned his neck to see the gate.

"Yes," he said.

There was silence. Mabel sat on like one condemned, at the head of the table. Then a whistle was heard from the kitchen. The dog got up and barked sharply. Joe opened the door and shouted:

"Come on."

After a moment, a young man entered. He was muffled up in overcoat and a purple woollen scarf, and his tweed cap, which he did not remove, was pulled down on his head. He was of medium height, his face was rather long and pale, his eyes looked tired.

"Hello Jack! Well Jack!" exclaimed Malcolm and Joe. Fred Henry merely said "Jack!"

"What's doing?" asked the newcomer, evidently addressing Fred Henry.

"Same. We've got to be out by Wednesday. —Got a cold?"

"I have—got it bad, too."

"Why don't you stop in?"

"*Me* stop in? When I can't stand on my legs, perhaps I shall have a chance." The young man spoke huskily. He had a slight Scotch accent.

"It's a knock-out, isn't it," said Joe boisterously, "if a doctor goes round croaking with a cold. Looks bad for the patients, doesn't it?"

The young doctor looked at him slowly.

"Anything the matter with *you* then?" he asked, sarcastically.

"Not as I know of. Damn your eyes, I hope not. Why?"

"I thought you were very concerned about the patients, wondered if you might be one yourself."

"Damn it, no, I've never been patient to no flaming doctor, and hope I never shall be," returned Joe.

At this point Mabel rose from the table, and they all seemed to become aware of her existence. She began putting the dishes together. The young doctor looked at her, but

did not address her. He had not greeted her. She went out of the room with the tray, her face impassive and unchanged.

"When are you off then, all of you?" asked the doctor.

"I'm catching the eleven-forty," replied Malcolm. "Are you goin' down wi' th' trap, Joe?"

"Yes, I've told you I'm going down wi' th' trap, haven't I?"

"We'd better be getting her in then.—So long, Jack, if I don't see you before I go," said Malcolm, shaking hands.

He went out, followed by Joe, who seemed to have his tail between his legs.

"Well, this is the devil's own," exclaimed the doctor, when he was left alone with Fred Henry. "Going before Wednesday, are you?"

"That's the orders," replied the other.

"Where, to Northampton?"

"That's it."

"The devil!" exclaimed Fergusson, with quiet chagrin.

And there was silence between the two.

"All settled up, are you?" asked Fergusson.

"About."

There was another pause.

"Well, I shall miss yer, Freddy boy," said the young doctor.

"And I shall miss thee, Jack," returned the other.

"Miss you like hell," mused the doctor.

Fred Henry turned aside. There was nothing to say. Mabel came in again, to finish clearing the table.

"What are *you* going to do then, Miss Pervin?" asked Fergusson. "Going to your sister's are you?"

Mabel looked at him with her steady, dangerous eyes, that always made him uncomfortable, unsettling his superficial ease.

"No," she said.

"Well, what in the name of fortune *are* you going to do? Say what you *mean* to do," cried Fred Henry, with futile intensity.

But she only averted her head, and continued her work. She folded the white tablecloth, and put on the chenille cloth.

68

"The sulkiest bitch that ever trod!" muttered her brother.

But she finished her task with perfectly impassive face, the young doctor watching her interestedly all the while. Then she went out.

Fred Henry stared after her, clenching his lips, his blue eyes fixing in sharp antagonism, as he made a grimace of sour exasperation.

"You could bray her into bits, and that's all you'd get out of her," he said, in a small, narrowed tone.

The doctor smiled faintly.

"What's she *going* to do then?" he asked.

"Strike me if *I* know!" returned the other.

There was a pause. Then the doctor stirred.

"I'll be seeing you to-night, shall I?" he said to his friend.

"Ay—where's it to be? Are we going over to Jessdale?"

"I don't know. I've got such a cold on me. I'll come round to the Moon and Stars, anyway."

"Let Lizzie and May miss their night for once, eh?"

"That's it—if I feel as I do now."

"All's one———"

The two young men went through the passage and down to the back door together. The house was large, but it was servantless now, and desolate. At the back was a small bricked house-yard, and beyond that a big square, gravelled fine and red, and having stables on two sides. Sloping, dank, winter-dark fields stretched away on the open sides.

But the stables were empty. Joseph Pervin, the father of the family, had been a man of no education, who had become a fairly large horse dealer. The stables had been full of horses, there was a great turmoil and come-and-go of horses and of dealers and grooms. Then the kitchen was full of servants. But of late things had declined. The old man had married a second time, to retrieve his fortunes. Now he was dead and everything was gone to the dogs, there was nothing but debt and threatening.

For months, Mabel had been servantless in the big house, keeping the home together in penury for her ineffectual brothers. She had kept house for ten years. But previously, it was with unstinted means. Then, however brutal and coarse everything was, the sense of money had kept her proud, confident. The men might be foulmouthed, the women in the kitchen might have bad reputations, her brothers might have illegitimate children. But so long as there was money, the girl felt herself established, and brutally proud, reserved.

No company came to the house, save dealers and coarse men. Mabel had no associates of her own sex, after her sister went away. But she did not mind. She went regularly to church, she attended to her father. And she lived in the memory of her mother, who had died when she was fourteen, and whom she had loved. She had loved her father, too, in a different way, depending upon him, and feeling secure in him, until at the age of fifty-four he married again. And then she had set hard against him. Now he had died and left them all hopelessly in debt.

She had suffered badly during the period of poverty. Nothing, however, could shake the curious sullen, animal pride that dominated each member of the family. Now, for Mabel, the end had come. Still she would not cast about her. She would follow her own way just the same. She would always hold the keys of her own situation. Mindless and persistent, she endured from day to day. Why should she think? Why should she answer anybody? It was enough that this was the end, and there was no way out. She need not pass any more darkly along the main street of the small town, avoiding every eye. She need not demean herself any more, going into the shops and buying the cheapest food. This was at an end. She thought of nobody, not even of herself. Mindless and persistent, she seemed in a sort of ecstasy to be coming nearer to her fulfilment, her own glorification, approaching her dead mother, who was glorified.

In the afternoon she took a little bag, with shears and sponge and a small scrubbing brush, and went out. It was a grey, wintry day, with saddened, dark-green fields and an atmosphere blackened by the smoke of foundries not far off. She went quickly, darkly along the causeway, heeding nobody, through the town to the churchyard.

There she always felt secure, as if no one could see her, although as a matter of fact she was exposed to the stare of everyone who passed along under the churchyard wall. Nevertheless, once under the shadow of the great looming church, among the graves, she felt immune from the world, reserved within the thick churchyard wall as in another country.

Carefully she clipped the grass from the grave, and arranged the pinky-white, small chrysanthemums in the tin cross. When this was done, she took an empty jar from a neighbouring grave, brought water, and carefully, most scrupulously sponged the marble headstone and the coping-stone.

It gave her sincere satisfaction to do this. She felt in immediate contact with the world of her mother. She took minute pains, went through the park in a state bordering on pure happiness, as if in performing this task she came into a subtle, intimate connection with her mother. For the life she followed here in the world was far less real than the world of death she inherited from her mother.

The doctor's house was just by the church. Fergusson, being a mere hired assistant, was slave to the countryside. As he hurried now to attend to the outpatients in the surgery, glancing across the graveyard with his quick eye, he saw the girl at her task at the grave. She seemed so intent and remote, it was like looking into another world. Some mystical element was touched in him. He slowed down as he walked, watching her as if spell-bound.

She lifted her eyes, feeling him looking. Their eyes met. And each looked again at once, each feeling, in some way, found out by the other. He lifted his cap and passed on down the road. There remained distinct in his consciousness, like a vision, the memory of her face, lifted from the tombstone in the churchyard, and looking at him with slow, large, portentous eyes. It *was* portentous, her face. It seemed to mesmerise him. There was a heavy power in her eyes which laid hold of his whole being, as if he had drunk some powerful drug. He had been feeling weak and done before. Now the life came back into him, he felt delivered from his own fretted, daily self.

He finished his duties at the surgery as quickly as might be, hastily filling up the bottles of the waiting people with cheap drugs. Then, in perpetual haste, he set off again to visit several cases in another part of his round, before teatime. At all times he preferred to walk, if he could, but particularly when he was not well. He fancied the motion restored him.

The afternoon was falling. It was grey, deadened, and wintry, with a slow, moist, heavy coldness sinking in and deadening all the faculties. But why should he think or notice? He hastily climbed the hill and turned across the dark-green fields, following the black cinder-track. In the distance, across a shallow dip in the country, the small town was clustered like smouldering ash, a tower, a spire, a heap of low, raw, extinct houses. And on the nearest fringe of the town, sloping into the dip, was Oldmeadow, the Pervins' house. He could see the stables and the outbuildings distinctly, as they lay towards him on the slope. Well, he would not go there many more times! Another resource would be lost to him, another place gone: the only company he cared for in the alien, ugly little town he was losing. Nothing but work, drudgery, constant hastening from dwelling to dwelling among the colliers and the iron-workers. It wore him out, but at the same time he had a craving for it. It was a stimulant to him to be in the homes of the working people, moving as it were through the innermost body of their life. His nerves were excited and gratified. He could come so near, into the very lives of the rough, inarticulate, powerfully emotional men and women. He grumbled, he said he hated the hellish hole.

But as a matter of fact it excited him, the contact with the rough, strongly-feeling people was a stimulant applied direct to his nerves.

Below Oldmeadow, in the green, shallow, soddened hollow of fields, lay a square, deep pond. Roving across the landscape, the doctor's quick eye detected a figure in black passing through the gate of the field, down towards the pond. He looked again. It would be Mabel Pervin. His mind suddenly became alive and attentive.

Why was she going down there? He pulled up on the path on the slope above, and stood staring. He could just make sure of the small black figure moving in the hollow of the failing day. He seemed to see her in the midst of such obscurity, that he was like a clairvoyant, seeing rather with the mind's eye than with ordinary sight. Yet he could see her positively enough, whilst he kept his eye attentive. He felt, if he looked away from her, in the thick, ugly falling dusk, he would lose her altogether.

He followed her minutely as she moved, direct and intent, like something transmitted rather than stirring in voluntary activity, straight down the field towards the pond. There she stood on the bank for a moment. She never raised her head. Then she waded slowly into the water.

He stood motionless as the small black figure walked slowly and deliberately towards the centre of the pond, very slowly, gradually moving deeper into the motionless water, and still moving forward as the water got up to her breast. Then he could see her no more in the dusk of the dead afternoon.

"There!" he exclaimed. "Would you believe it?"

And he hastened straight down, running over the wet, soddened fields, pushing through the hedges, down into the depression of callous wintry obscurity. It took him several minutes to come to the pond. He stood on the bank, breathing heavily. He could see nothing. His eyes seemed to penetrate the dead water. Yes, perhaps that was the dark shadow of her black clothing beneath the surface of the water.

He slowly ventured into the pond. The bottom was deep, soft clay, he sank in, and the water clasped dead cold round his legs. As he stirred he could smell the cold, rotten clay that fouled up into the water. It was objectionable in his lungs. Still, repelled and yet not heeding, he moved deeper into the pond. The cold water rose over his thighs, over his loins, upon his abdomen. The lower part of his body was all sunk in the hideous cold element. And the bottom was so deeply soft and uncertain, he was afraid of pitching with his mouth underneath. He could not swim, and was afraid.

He crouched a little, spreading his hands under the water and moving them round, trying to feel for her. The dead cold pond swayed upon his chest. He moved again, a little deeper, and again, with his hands underneath, he felt all around under the water. And he touched her clothing. But it evaded his fingers. He made a desperate effort to grasp it.

And so doing he lost his balance, and went under, horribly, suffocating in the foul earthy water, struggling madly for a few moments. At last, after what seemed an eternity, he got his footing, rose again into the air and looked around. He gasped, and knew he was in the world. Then he looked at the water. She had risen near him. He grasped her clothing, and drawing her nearer, turned to take his way to land again.

He went very slowly, carefully, absorbed in the slow progress. He rose higher, climbing out of the pond. The water was now only about his legs; he was thankful, full of relief to be out of the clutches of the pond. He lifted her and staggered on to the bank, out of the horror of wet, grey clay.

He laid her down on the bank. She was quite unconscious and running with water. He made the water come from her mouth, he worked to restore her. He did not have to work very long before he could feel the breathing begin again in her; she was breathing naturally. He worked a little longer. He could feel her live beneath his hands; she was coming back. He wiped her face, wrapped her in his overcoat, looked round into the dim, dark-grey world, then lifted her and staggered down the bank and across the fields.

It seemed an unthinkably long way, and his burden so heavy he felt he would never get to the house. But at last he was in the stable-yard, and then in the house-yard. He opened the door and went into the house. In the kitchen he laid her down on the hearth-rug, and called. The house was empty. But the fire was burning in the grate.

Then again he kneeled to attend to her. She was breathing regularly, her eyes were wide open and as if conscious, but there seemed something missing in her look. She was conscious in herself, but unconscious of her surroundings.

He ran upstairs, took blankets from a bed, and put them before the fire to warm. Then he removed her saturated, earthy-smelling clothing, rubbed her dry with a towel, and wrapped her naked in the blankets. Then he went into the dining-room, to look for spirits. There was a little whiskey. He drank a gulp himself, and put some into her mouth.

The effect was instantaneous. She looked full into his face, as if she had been seeing him for some time, and yet had only just become conscious of him.

"Dr. Fergusson?" she said.

"What?" he answered.

He was divesting himself of his coat, intending to find some dry clothing upstairs. He could not bear the smell of the dead, clayey water, and he was mortally afraid for his own health.

"What did I do?" she asked.

"Walked into the pond," he replied. He had begun to shudder like one sick, and could hardly attend to her. Her eyes remained full on him, he seemed to be going dark in his mind, looking back at her helplessly. The shuddering became quieter in him, his life came back to him, dark and unknowing, but strong again.

"Was I out of my mind?" she asked, while her eyes were fixed on him all the time.

"Maybe, for the moment," he replied. He felt quiet, because his strength had come back. The strange fretful strain had left him.

"Am I out of my mind now?" she asked.

"Are you?" he reflected a moment. "No," he answered truthfully, "I don't see that you are." He turned his face aside. He was afraid, now, because he felt dazed, and felt dimly that her power was stronger than his, in this issue. And she continued to look at him fixedly all the time. "Can you tell me where I shall find some dry things to put on?" he asked.

"Did you dive into the pond for me?" she asked.

"No," he answered. "I walked in. But I went in overhead as well."

There was silence for a moment. He hesitated. He very much wanted to go upstairs to get into dry clothing. But there was another desire in him. And she seemed to hold him. His will seemed to have gone to sleep, and left him, standing there slack before her. But he felt warm inside himself. He did not shudder at all, though his clothes were sodden on him.

"Why did you?" she asked.

"Because I didn't want you to do such a foolish thing," he said.

"It wasn't foolish," she said, still gazing at him as she lay on the floor, with a sofa cushion under her head. "It was the right thing to do. *I* knew best, then."

"I'll go and shift these wet things," he said. But still he had not the power to move out of her presence, until she sent him. It was as if she had the life of his body in her hands, and he could not extricate himself. Or perhaps he did not want to.

Suddenly she sat up. Then she became aware of her own immediate condition. She felt the blankets about her, she knew her own limbs. For a moment it seemed as if her reason were going. She looked round, with wild eye, as if seeking something. He stood still with fear. She saw her clothing lying scattered.

"Who undressed me?" she asked, her eyes resting full and inevitable on his face.

"I did," he replied, "to bring you round."

For some moments she sat and gazed at him awfully, her lips parted.

"Do you love me then?" she asked.

He only stood and stared at her, fascinated. His soul seemed to melt.

She shuffled forward on her knees, and put her arms round him, round his legs, as he stood there, pressing her breasts against his knees and thighs, clutching him with strange, convulsive certainty, pressing his thighs against her, drawing him to her face, her throat, as she looked up at him with flaring, humble eyes of transfiguration, triumphant in first possession.

"You love me," she murmured, in strange transport, yearning and triumphant and confident. "You love me. I know you love me, I know."

And she was passionately kissing his knees, through the wet clothing, passionately and indiscriminately kissing his knees, his legs, as if unaware of everything.

He looked down at the tangled wet hair, the wild, bare, animal shoulders. He was amazed, bewildered, and afraid. He had never thought of loving her. He had never wanted to love her. When he rescued her and restored her, he was a doctor, and she was a patient. He had had no single personal thought of her. Nay, this introduction of the personal element was very distasteful to him, a violation of his professional honour. It was horrible to have her there embracing his knees. It was horrible. He revolted from it, violently. And yet—and yet—he had not the power to break away.

She looked at him again, with the same supplication of powerful love, and that same transcendent, frightening light of triumph. In view of the delicate flame which seemed to come from her face like a light, he was powerless. And yet he had never intended to love her. He had never intended. And something stubborn in him could not give way.

"You love me," she repeated, in a murmur of deep, rhapsodic assurance. "You love me."

Her hands were drawing him, drawing him down to her. He was afraid, even a little horrified. For he had, really, no intention of loving her. Yet her hands were drawing him towards her. He put out his hand quickly to steady himself, and grasped her bare shoulder. A flame seemed to burn the hand that grasped her soft shoulder. He had no intention of loving her: his whole will was against his yielding. It was horrible—And yet wonderful was the touch of her shoulder, beautiful the shining of her face. Was she perhaps mad? He had a horror of yielding to her. Yet something in him ached also.

He had been staring away at the door, away from her. But his hand remained on her shoulder. She had gone suddenly very still. He looked down at her. Her eyes were now wide with fear, with doubt, the light was dying from her face, a shadow of terrible greyness was returning. He could not bear the touch of her eyes' question upon him, and the look of death behind the question.

With an inward groan he gave way, and let his heart yield towards her. A sudden gentle smile came on his face. And her eyes, which never left his face, slowly, slowly filled with tears. He watched the strange water rise in her eyes, like some slow fountain coming up. And his heart seemed to burn and melt away in his breast.

He could not bear to look at her any more. He dropped on his knees and caught her head with his arms and pressed her face against his throat. She was very still. His heart, which seemed to have broken, was burning with a kind of agony in his breast. And he felt her slow, hot tears wetting his throat. But he could not move.

He felt the hot tears wet his neck and the hollows of his neck, and he remained motionless, suspended through one of man's eternities. Only now it had become indispensable to him to have her face pressed close to him; he could never let her go again. He could never let her head go away from the close clutch of his arm. He wanted to remain like that for ever, with his heart hurting him in a pain that was also life to him. Without knowing, he was looking down on her damp, soft brown hair.

Then, as it were suddenly, he smelt the horrid stagnant smell of that water. And at the same moment she drew away from him and looked at him. Her eyes were wistful and unfathomable. He was afraid of them, and he fell to kissing her, not knowing what he was doing. He wanted her eyes not to have that terrible, wistful, unfathomable look.

When she turned her face to him again, a faint delicate flush was glowing, and there was again dawning that terrible shining of joy in her eyes, which really terrified him, and yet which he now wanted to see, because he feared the look of doubt still more.

"You love me?" she said, rather faltering.

"Yes." The word cost him a painful effort. Not because it wasn't true. But because it was too newly true, the *saying* seemed to tear open again his newly-torn heart. And he hardly wanted it to be true, even now.

She lifted her face to him, and he bent forward and kissed her on the mouth, gently, with the one kiss that is an eternal pledge. And as he kissed her his heart strained again in his breast. He never intended to love her. But now it was over. He had crossed over the gulf to her, and all that he had left behind had shrivelled and become void.

After the kiss, her eyes again slowly filled with tears. She sat still, away from him, with her face drooped aside, and her hands folded in her lap. The tears fell very slowly. There was complete silence. He too sat there motionless and silent on the hearthrug. The strange pain of his heart that was broken seemed to consume him. That he should love her? That this was love! That he should be ripped open in this way!—Him, a doctor!—How they would all jeer if they knew!—It was agony to him to think they might know.

In the curious naked pain of the thought he looked again to her. She was sitting there drooped into a muse. He saw a tear fall, and his heart flared hot. He saw for the first time

that one of her shoulders was quite uncovered, one arm bare, he could see one of her small breasts; dimly, because it had become almost dark in the room.

"Why are you crying?" he asked, in an altered voice.

She looked up at him, and behind her tears the consciousness of her situation for the first time brought a dark look of shame to her eyes.

"I'm not crying, really," she said, watching him half frightened.

He reached his hand, and softly closed it on her bare arm.

"I love you! I love you!" he said in a soft, low, vibrating voice, unlike himself.

She shrank, and dropped her head. The soft, penetrating grip of his hand on her arm distressed her. She looked up at him.

"I want to go," she said. "I want to go and get you some dry things."

"Why?" he said. "I'm all right."

"But I want to go," she said. "And I want you to change your things."

He released her arm, and she wrapped herself in the blanket, looking at him rather frightened. And still she did not rise.

"Kiss me," she said wistfully.

He kissed her, but briefly, half in anger.

Then, after a second, she rose nervously, all mixed up in the blanket. He watched her in her confusion, as she tried to extricate herself and wrap herself up so that she could walk. He watched her relentlessly, as she knew. And as she went, the blanket trailing, and as he saw a glimpse of her feet and her white leg, he tried to remember her as she was when he had wrapped her in the blanket. But then he didn't want to remember, because she had been nothing to him then, and his nature revolted from remembering her as she was when she was nothing to him.

A tumbling muffled noise from within the dark house startled him. Then he heard her voice:—"There are clothes." He rose and went to the foot of the stairs, and gathered up the garments she had thrown down. Then he came back to the fire, to rub himself down and dress. He grinned at his own appearance, when he had finished.

The fire was sinking, so he put on coal. The house was now quite dark, save for the light of a street-lamp that shone in faintly from beyond the holly trees. He lit the gas with matches he found on the mantel-piece. Then he emptied the pockets of his own clothes, and threw all his wet things in a heap into the scullery. After which he gathered up her sodden clothes, gently, and put them in a separate heap on the copper-top in the scullery.

It was six o'clock on the clock. His own watch had stopped. He ought to go back to the surgery. He waited, and still she did not come down. So he went to the foot of the stairs and called:

"I shall have to go."

Almost immediately he heard her coming down. She had on her best dress of black voile, and her hair was tidy, but still damp. She looked at him—and in spite of herself, smiled.

"I don't like you in those clothes," she said.

"Do I look a sight?" he answered.

They were shy of one another.

"I'll make you some tea," she said.

"No, I must go."

"Must you?" And she looked at him again with the wide, strained, doubtful eyes. And again, from the pain of his breast, he knew how he loved her. He went and bent to kiss her, gently, passionately, with his heart's painful kiss.

"And my hair smells so horrible," she murmured in distraction. "And I'm so awful, I'm so awful! Oh, no, I'm too awful." And she broke into bitter, heartbroken sobbing. "You can't want to love me, I'm horrible."

"Don't be silly, don't be silly," he said, trying to comfort her, kissing her, holding her in his arms. "I want you, I want to marry you, we're going to be married, quickly, quickly—to-morrow if I can."

But she only sobbed terribly, and cried:

"I feel awful. I feel awful. I feel I'm horrible to you."

"No, I want you, I want you," was all he answered, blindly, with that terrible intonation which frightened her almost more than her horror lest he should *not* want her.

---

1. In what ways do the horses resemble the members of the family?

2. How does going into the pond to rescue Mabel affect Dr. Fergusson? Why does he continue to think of himself as a doctor (in reviving her and wrapping her in a blanket)?

3. Why is it difficult for Dr. Fergusson to yield to Mabel's influence after he has rescued her? How would you describe her love and its effect on him? Why is she frightened by the prospect of having his love (when he says "I want you, I want you" at the end of the story)?

4. What is Lawrence saying about the nature of love?

YOUNG GOODMAN BROWN

Young Goodman Brown came forth at sunset into the street at Salem village; but put his head back, after crossing the threshold, to exchange a parting kiss with his young wife. And Faith, as the wife was aptly named, thrust her own pretty head into the street, letting the wind play with the pink ribbons of her cap while she called to Goodman Brown.

"Dearest heart," whispered she, softly and rather sadly, when her lips were close to' his ear, "prithee put off your journey until sunrise and sleep in your own bed to-night. A lone woman is troubled with such dreams and such thoughts that she's afeard of herself sometimes. Pray tarry with me this night, dear husband, of all nights in the year."

"My love and my Faith," replied young Goodman Brown, "of all nights in the year, this one night must I tarry away from thee. My journey, as thou callest it, forth and back again, must needs be done 'twixt now and sunrise. What, my sweet, pretty wife, dost thou doubt me already, and we but three months married?"

"Then God bless you!" said Faith, with the pink ribbons; "and may you find all well when you come back."

"Amen!" cried Goodman Brown. "Say thy prayers, dear Faith, and go to bed at dusk, and no harm will come to thee."

So they parted; and the young man pursued his way until, being about to turn the corner by the meeting-house, he looked back and saw the head of Faith still peeping after him with a melancholy air, in spite of her pink ribbons.

"Poor little Faith!" thought he, for his heart smote him. "What a wretch am I to leave her on such an errand! She talks of dreams, too. Methought as she spoke there was trouble in her face, as if a dream had warned her what work is to be done to-night. But no, no; 't would kill her to think it. Well, she's a blessed angel on earth; and after this one night I'll cling to her skirts and follow her to heaven."

With this excellent resolve for the future, Goodman Brown felt himself justified in making more haste on his present evil purpose. He had taken a dreary road, darkened by all the gloomiest trees of the forest, which barely stood aside to let the narrow path creep through, and closed immediately behind. It was all as lonely as could be; and there is this peculiarity in such a solitude, that the traveller knows not who may be concealed by the innumerable trunks and the thick boughs overhead; so that with lonely footsteps he may yet be passing through an unseen multitude.

"There may be a devilish Indian behind every tree," said Goodman Brown to himself; and he glanced fearfully behind him as he added, "What if the devil himself should be at my very elbow!"

His head being turned back, he passed a crook of the road, and, looking forward again, beheld the figure of a man, in grave and decent attire, seated at the foot of an old tree. He arose at Goodman Brown's approach and walked onward side by side with him.

"You are late, Goodman Brown," said he. "The clock of the Old South was striking as I came through Boston, and that is full fifteen minutes agone."

"Faith kept me back a while," replied the young man, with a tremor in his voice, caused by the sudden appearance of his companion, though not wholly unexpected.

It was now deep dusk in the forest, and deepest in that part of it where these two were journeying. As nearly as could be discerned, the second traveller was about fifty years old, apparently in the same rank of life as Goodman Brown, and bearing a considerable resemblance to him, though perhaps more in expression than features. Still they might have been taken for father and son. And yet, though the elder person was as simply clad as the younger, and as simple in manner too, he had an indescribable air of one who knew the world, and who would not have felt abashed at the governor's dinner table or in King William's court, were it possible that his affairs should call him thither. But the only thing about him that could be fixed upon as remarkable was his staff, which bore the likeness of a great black snake, so curiously wrought that it might almost be seen to twist and wriggle itself like a living serpent. This, of course, must have been an ocular deception, assisted by the uncertain light.

"Come, Goodman Brown," cried his fellow-traveller, "this is a dull pace for the beginning of a journey. Take my staff, if you are so soon weary."

"Friend," said the other, exchanging his slow pace for a full stop, "having kept covenant by meeting thee here, it is my purpose now to return whence I came. I have scruples touching the matter thou wot'st of."

"Sayest thou so?" replied he of the serpent, smiling apart. "Let us walk on, nevertheless, reasoning as we go; and if I convince thee not thou shalt turn back. We are but a little way in the forest yet."

"Too far! too far!" exclaimed the goodman, unconsciously resuming his walk. "My father never went into the woods on such an errand, nor his father before him. We have been a race of honest men and good Christians since the days of the martyrs; and shall I be the first of the name of Brown that ever took this path and kept"—

"Such company, thou wouldst say," observed the elder person, interpreting his pause. "Well said, Goodman Brown! I have been as well acquainted with your family as with ever a one among the Puritans; and that's no trifle to say. I helped your grandfather, the constable, when he lashed the Quaker woman so smartly through the streets of Salem; and it was I that brought your father a pitch-pine knot, kindled at my own hearth, to set fire to an Indian village, in King Philip's war. They were my good friends, both; and many a pleasant walk have we had along this path, and returned merrily after midnight. I would fain be friends with you for their sake."

"If it be as thou sayest," replied Goodman Brown, "I marvel they never spoke of these matters; or, verily, I marvel not, seeing that the least rumor of the sort would have driven them from New England. We are a people of prayer, and good works to boot, and abide no such wickedness."

"Wickedness or not," said the traveller with the twisted staff, "I have a very general acquaintance here in New England. The deacons of many a church have drunk the communion wine with me; the selectmen of divers towns make me their chairman; and a majority of the Great and General Court are firm supporters of my interest. The governor and I, too—But these are state secrets."

"Can this be so?" cried Goodman Brown, with a stare of amazement at his undisturbed companion. "Howbeit, I have nothing to do with the governor and council; they have their own ways, and are no rule for a simple husbandman like me. But, were I to go on with thee, how should I meet the eye of that good old man, our minister, at Salem village? Oh, his voice would make me tremble both Sabbath day and lecture day."

Thus far the elder traveller had listened with due gravity; but now burst into a fit of irrepressible mirth, shaking himself so violently that his snake-like staff actually seemed to wriggle in sympathy.

"Ha! ha! ha!" shouted he again and again; then composing himself, "Well, go on, Goodman Brown, go on; but, prithee, don't kill me with laughing."

"Well, then, to end the matter at once," said Goodman Brown, considerably nettled, "there is my wife, Faith. It would break her dear little heart; and I'd rather break my own."

"Nay, if that be the case," answered the other, "e'en go thy ways, Goodman Brown. I would not for twenty old women like the one hobbling before us that Faith should come to any harm."

As he spoke he pointed his staff at a female figure on the path, in whom Goodman Brown recognized a very pious and exemplary dame, who had taught him his catechism in youth, and was still his moral and spiritual adviser, jointly with the minister and Deacon Gookin.

"A marvel, truly, that Goody Cloyse should be so far in the wilderness at night-fall," said he. "But with your leave, friend, I shall take a cut through the woods until we have left this Christian woman behind. Being a stranger to you, she might ask whom I was consorting with and whither I was going."

"Be it so," said his fellow-traveller. "Betake you to the woods, and let me keep the path."

Accordingly the young man turned aside, but took care to watch his companion, who advanced softly along the road until he had come within a staff's length of the old dame. She, meanwhile, was making the best of her way, with singular speed for so aged a woman, and mumbling some indistinct words—a prayer, doubtless—as she went. The traveller put forth his staff and touched her withered neck with what seemed the serpent's tail.

"The devil!" screamed the pious old lady.

"Then Goody Cloyse knows her old friend?" observed the traveller, confronting her and leaning on his writhing stick.

"Ah, forsooth, and is it your worship indeed?" cried the good dame. "Yea, truly is it, and in the very image of my old gossip, Goodman Brown, the grandfather of the silly fellow that now is. But—would your worship believe it?—my broomstick hath strangely disappeared, stolen, as I suspect, by that unhanged witch, Goody Cory, and that, too, when I was all anointed with the juice of smallage, and cinquefoil, and wolf's bane"—

"Mingled with fine wheat and the fat of a new-born babe," said the shape of old Goodman Brown.

"Ah, your worship knows the recipe," cried the old lady, cackling aloud. "So, as I was saying, being all ready for the meeting, and no horse to ride on, I made up my mind to foot it; for they tell me there is a nice young man to be taken into communion to-night. But now your good worship will lend me your arm, and we shall be there in a twinkling."

"That can hardly be," answered her friend. "I may not spare you my arm, Goody Cloyse; but here is my staff, if you will."

So saying, he threw it down at her feet, where, perhaps, it assumed life, being one of the rods which its owner had formerly lent to the Egyptian magi. Of this fact, however, Goodman Brown could not take cognizance. He had cast up his eyes in astonishment, and, looking down again, beheld neither Goody Cloyse nor the serpentine staff, but his fellow-traveller alone, who waited for him as calmly as if nothing had happened.

"That old woman taught me my catechism," said the young man; and there was a world of meaning in this simple comment.

They continued to walk onward, while the elder traveller exhorted his companion to make good speed and persevere in the path, discoursing so aptly that his arguments seemed rather to spring up in the bosom of his auditor than to be suggested by himself. As they went, he plucked a branch of maple to serve for a walking stick, and began to strip it of the twigs and little boughs, which were wet with evening dew. The moment his fingers touched them they became strangely withered and dried up as with a week's sunshine. Thus the pair proceeded, at a good free pace, until suddenly, in a gloomy hollow of the road, Goodman Brown sat himself down on the stump of a tree and refused to go any farther.

"Friend," said he, stubbornly, "my mind is made up. Not another step will I budge on this errand. What if a wretched old woman do choose to go to the devil when I thought she was going to heaven; is that any reason why I should quit my dear Faith and go after her?"

"You will think better of this by and by," said his acquaintance, composedly. "Sit here and rest yourself a while; and when you feel like moving again, there is my staff to help you along."

Without more words, he threw his companion the maple stick, and was as speedily out of sight as if he had vanished into the deepening gloom. The young man sat a few moments by the roadside, applauding himself greatly, and thinking with how clear a conscience he should meet the minister in his morning walk, nor shrink from the eye of good old Deacon Gookin. And what calm sleep would be his that very night, which was to have been spent so wickedly, but so purely and sweetly now, in the arms of Faith! Amidst these pleasant and praiseworthy meditations, Goodman Brown heard the tramp of horses along the road, and deemed it advisable to conceal himself within the verge of the forest, conscious of the guilty purpose that had brought him thither, though now so happily turned from it.

On came the hoof tramps and the voices of the riders, two grave old voices, conversing soberly as they drew near. These mingled sounds appeared to pass along the road, within a few yards of the young man's hiding-place; but, owing doubtless to the depth of the gloom at that particular spot, neither the travellers nor their steeds were visible. Though their figures brushed the small boughs by the wayside, it could not be seen that they intercepted, even for a moment, the faint gleam from the strip of bright sky athwart which they must have passed. Goodman Brown alternately crouched and stood on tiptoe, pulling aside the branches and thrusting forth his head as far as he durst without discerning so much as a shadow. It vexed him the more, because he could have sworn, were such a thing possible, that he recognized the voices of the minister and Deacon Gookin, jogging along quietly, as they were wont to do, when bound to some ordination or ecclesiastical council. While yet within hearing, one of the riders stopped to pluck a switch.

"Of the two, reverend sir," said the voice like the deacon's, "I had rather miss an ordination dinner than to-night's meeting. They tell me that some of our community are to be here from Falmouth and beyond, and others from Connecticut and Rhode Island, besides several of the Indian pow-wows, who, after their fashion, know almost as much deviltry as the best of us. Moreover, there is a goodly young woman to be taken into communion."

"Mighty well, Deacon Gookin!" replied the solemn old tones of the minister. "Spur up, or we shall be late. Nothing can be done, you know, until I get on the ground."

The hoofs clattered again; and the voices, talking so strangely in the empty air, passed on through the forest, where no church had ever been gathered or solitary Christian prayed. Whither, then, could these holy men be journeying so deep into the heathen wilderness? Young Goodman Brown caught hold of a tree for support, being ready to sink down on the ground, faint and overburdened with the heavy sickness of his heart. He looked up to the sky, doubting whether there really was a heaven above him. Yet there was the blue arch, and the stars brightening in it.

"With heaven above and Faith below, I will yet stand firm against the devil!" cried Goodman Brown.

While he still gazed upward into the deep arch of the firmament and had lifted his hands to pray, a cloud, though no wind was stirring, hurried across the zenith and hid the brightening stars. The blue sky was still visible, except directly overhead, where this black mass of cloud was sweeping swiftly northward. Aloft in the air, as if from the depths of the cloud, came a confused and doubtful sound of voices. Once the listener fancied that he could distinguish the accents of towns-people of his own, men and women, both pious and ungodly, many of whom he had met at the communion table, and had seen others rioting at the tavern. The next moment, so indistinct were the sounds, he doubted whether he had heard aught but the murmur of the old forest, whispering without a wind. Then came a stronger swell of those familiar tones, heard daily in the sunshine of Salem village, but never until now from a cloud of night. There was one voice, of a young woman, uttering lamentations, yet with an uncertain sorrow, and entreating for some favor, which, perhaps, it would grieve her to obtain; and all the unseen multitude, both saints and sinners, seemed to encourage her onward.

"Faith!" shouted Goodman Brown, in a voice of agony and desperation; and the echoes of the forest mocked him, crying, "Faith! Faith!" as if bewildered wretches were seeking her all through the wilderness.

The cry of grief, rage, and terror was yet piercing the night, when the unhappy husband held his breath for a response. There was a scream, drowned immediately in a louder murmur of voices, fading into far off laughter, as the dark cloud swept away, leaving the clear and silent sky above Goodman Brown. But something fluttered lightly down through the air and caught on the branch of a tree. The young man seized it, and beheld a pink ribbon.

"My Faith is gone!" cried he, after one stupefied moment. "There is no good on earth; and sin is but a name. Come, devil; for to thee is this world given."

And, maddened with despair, so that he laughed loud and long, did Goodman Brown grasp his staff and set forth again, at such a rate that he seemed to fly along the forest path rather than to walk or run. The road grew wilder and drearier and more faintly traced, and vanished at length, leaving him in the heart of the dark wilderness, still rushing onward with the instinct that guides mortal man to evil. The whole forest was peopled with frightful sounds—the creaking of the trees, the howling of wild beasts, and

the yell of Indians; while sometimes the wind tolled like a distant church bell, and sometimes gave a broad roar around the traveller, as if all Nature were laughing him to scorn. But he was himself the chief horror of the scene, and shrank not from its other horrors.

"Ha! ha! ha!" roared Goodman Brown when the wind laughed at him. "Let us hear which will laugh loudest. Think not to frighten me with your deviltry. Come, witch, come wizard, come Indian powwow, come devil himself, and here comes Goodman Brown. You may as well fear him as he fear you."

In truth, all through the haunted forest there could be nothing more frightful than the figure of Goodman Brown. On he flew among the black pines, brandishing his staff with frenzied gestures, now giving vent to an inspiration of horrid blasphemy, and now shouting forth such laughter as set all the echoes of the forest laughing like demons around him. The fiend in his own shape is less hideous than when he rages in the breast of man. Thus sped the demoniac on his course, until, quivering among the trees, he saw a red light before him, as when the felled trunks and branches of a clearing have been set on fire, and throw up their lurid blaze against the sky, at the hour of midnight. He paused, in a lull of the tempest that had driven him onward, and heard the swell of what seemed a hymn, rolling solemnly from a distance with the weight of many voices. He knew the tune; it was a familiar one in the choir of the village meeting-house. The verse died heavily away, and was lengthened by a chorus, not of human voices, but of all the sounds of the benighted wilderness pealing in awful harmony together. Goodman Brown cried out, and his cry was lost to his own ear by its unison with the cry of the desert.

In the interval of silence he stole forward until the light glared full upon his eyes. At one extremity of an open space, hemmed in by the dark wall of the forest, arose a rock, bearing some rude, natural resemblance either to an altar or a pulpit, and surrounded by four blazing pines, their tops aflame, their stems untouched, like candles at an evening meeting. The mass of foliage that had overgrown the summit of the rock was all on fire, blazing high into the night and fitfully illuminating the whole field. Each pendent twig and leafy festoon was in a blaze. As the red light arose and fell, a numerous congregation alternately shone forth, then disappeared in shadow, and again grew, as it were, out of the darkness, peopling the heart of the solitary woods at once.

"A grave and dark-clad company," quoth Goodman Brown.

In truth they were such. Among them, quivering to and fro between gloom and splendor, appeared faces that would be seen next day at the council board of the province, and others which, Sabbath after Sabbath, looked devoutly heavenward, and benignantly over the crowded pews, from the holiest pulpits in the land. Some affirm that the lady of the governor was there. At least there were high dames well known to her, and wives of honored husbands, and widows, a great multitude, and ancient maidens, all of excellent repute, and fair young girls, who trembled lest their mothers should espy them. Either the sudden gleams of light flashing over the obscure field bedazzled Goodman Brown, or he recognized a score of the church members of Salem village famous for their especial sanctity. Good old Deacon Gookin had arrived, and waited at the skirts of that venerable saint, his revered pastor. But, irreverently consorting with these grave, reputable, and pious people, these elders of the church, these chaste dames and dewy virgins, there were men of dissolute lives and women of spotted fame, wretches given over to all mean and filthy vice, and suspected even of horrid crimes. It was strange to see that the good shrank not from the wicked, nor were the sinners abashed by the saints. Scattered also among their pale-faced enemies were the Indian priests, or powwows, who had often scared their native forest with more hideous incantations than any known to English witchcraft.

"But where is Faith?" thought Goodman Brown; and, as hope came into his heart, he trembled.

Another verse of the hymn arose, a slow and mournful strain, such as the pious love, but joined to words which expressed all that our nature can conceive of sin, and darkly hinted at far more. Unfathomable to mere mortals is the lore of fiends. Verse after verse was sung; and still the chorus of the desert swelled between like the deepest tone of a mighty organ; and with the final peal of that dreadful anthem there came a sound, as if the roaring wind, the rushing streams, the howling beasts, and every other voice of the unconcerted wilderness were mingling and according with the voice of guilty man in homage to the prince of all. The four blazing pines threw up a loftier flame, and obscurely discovered shapes and visages of horror on the smoke wreaths above the impious assembly. At the same moment the fire on the rock shot redly forth and formed a glowing arch above its base, where now appeared a figure. With reverence be it spoken, the figure bore no slight similitude, both in garb and manner, to some grave divine of the New England churches.

"Bring forth the converts!" cried a voice that echoed through the field and rolled into the forest.

At the word, Goodman Brown stepped forth from the shadow of the trees and approached the congregation, with whom he felt a loathful brotherhood by the sympathy of all that was wicked in his heart. He could have well-nigh sworn that the shape of his own dead father beckoned him to advance, looking downward from a smoke wreath, while a woman, with dim features of despair, threw out her hand to warn him back. Was it his mother? But he had no power to retreat one step, nor to resist, even in thought, when the minister and good old Deacon Gookin seized his arms and led him to the blazing rock. Thither came also the slender form of a veiled female, led between Goody Cloyse, that pious teacher of the catechism, and

Martha Carrier, who had received the devil's promise to be queen of hell. A rampant hag was she. And there stood the proselytes beneath the canopy of fire.

"Welcome, my children," said the dark figure, "to the communion of your race. Ye have found thus young your nature and your destiny. My children, look behind you!"

They turned; and flashing forth, as it were, in a sheet of flame, the fiend worshippers were seen; the smile of welcome gleamed darkly on every visage.

"There," resumed the sable form, "are all whom ye have reverenced from youth. Ye deemed them holier than yourselves, and shrank from your own sin, contrasting it with their lives of righteousness and prayerful aspirations heavenward. Yet here are they all in my worshipping assembly. This night it shall be granted you to know their secret deeds: how hoarybearded elders of the church have whispered wanton words to the young maids of their households; how many a woman, eager for widows' weeds, has given her husband a drink at bedtime and let him sleep his last sleep in her bosom; how beardless youths have made haste to inherit their fathers' wealth; and how fair damsels—blush not, sweet ones—have dug little graves in the garden, and bidden me, the sole guest, to an infant's funeral. By the sympathy of your human hearts for sin ye shall scent out all the places—whether in church, bed-chamber, street, field, or forest—where crime has been committed, and shall exult to behold the whole earth one stain of guilt, one mighty blood spot. Far more than this. It shall be yours to penetrate, in every bosom, the deep mystery of sin, the fountain of all wicked arts, and which inexhaustibly supplies more evil impulses than human power—than my power at its utmost—can make manifest in deeds. And now, my children, look upon each other."

They did so; and, by the blaze of the hell-kindled torches, the wretched man beheld his Faith, and the wife her husband, trembling before that unhallowed altar.

"Lo, there ye stand, my children," said the figure, in a deep and solemn tone, almost sad with its despairing awfulness, as if his once angelic nature could yet mourn for our miserable race. "Depending upon one another's hearts, ye had still hoped that virtue were not all a dream. Now are ye undeceived. Evil is the nature of mankind. Evil must be your only happiness. Welcome again, my children, to the communion of your race."

"Welcome," repeated the fiend worshippers, in one cry of despair and triumph.

And there they stood, the only pair, as it seemed, who were yet hesitating on the verge of wickedness in this dark world. A basin was hollowed, naturally, in the rock. Did it contain water, reddened by the lurid light? or was it blood? or, perchance, a liquid flame? Herein did the shape of evil dip his hand and prepare to lay the mark of baptism upon their foreheads, that they might be partakers of the mystery of sin, more conscious of the secret guilt of others, both in deed and thought, than they could now be of their own. The husband cast one look at his pale wife, and Faith at him. What polluted wretches would the next glance show them to each other, shuddering alike at what they disclosed and what they saw!

"Faith! Faith!" cried the husband, "look up to heaven, and resist the wicked one."

Whether Faith obeyed he knew not. Hardly had he spoken when he found himself amid calm night and solitude, listening to a roar of the wind which died heavily away through the forest. He staggered against the rock, and felt it chill and damp; while a hanging twig, that had been all on fire, besprinkled his cheek with the coldest dew.

The next morning young Goodman Brown came slowly into the street of Salem village, staring around him like a bewildered man. The good old minister was taking a walk along the graveyard to get an appetite for breakfast and meditate his sermon, and bestowed a blessing, as he passed, on Goodman Brown. He shrank from the venerable saint as if to avoid an anathema. Old Deacon

Gookin was at domestic worship, and the holy words of his prayer were heard through the open window: "What God doth the wizard pray to?" quoth Goodman Brown. Goody Cloyse, that excellent old Christian, stood in the early sunshine at her own lattice, catechizing a little girl who had brought her a pint of morning's milk. Goodman Brown snatched away the child as from the grasp of the fiend himself. Turning the corner by the meeting house, he spied the head of Faith, with the pink ribbons, gazing anxiously forth, and bursting into such joy at sight of him that she skipped along the street and almost kissed her husband before the whole village. But Goodman Brown looked sternly and sadly into her face, and passed on without a greeting.

Had Goodman Brown fallen asleep in the forest and only dreamed a wild dream of a witch-meeting?

Be it so if you will; but, alas! it was a dream of evil omen for young Goodman Brown. A stern, a sad, a darkly meditative, a distrustful, if not a desperate man did he become from the night of that fearful dream. On the Sabbath day, when the congregation were singing a holy psalm, he could not listen because an anthem of sin rushed loudly upon his ear and drowned all the blessed strain. When the minister spoke from the pulpit with power and fervid eloquence, and, with his hand on the open Bible, of the sacred truths of our religion, and of saint-like lives and triumphant deaths, and of future bliss or misery unutterable, then did Goodman Brown turn pale, dreading lest the roof should thunder down upon the gray blasphemer and his hearers. Often, awaking suddenly at midnight, he shrank from the bosom of Faith; and at morning or eventide, when the family knelt down at prayer, he scowled and muttered to himself, and gazed sternly at his wife, and turned away. And when he had lived long, and was borne to his grave a hoary corpse, followed by Faith, an aged woman, and children and grandchildren, a goodly procession, besides neighbors not a few, they carved no hopeful verse upon his tombstone, for his dying hour was gloom.

1. What symbolic use is made throughout the story of the name Faith? How do the clothing, gestures, and actions of Goodman Brown's wife, Faith, symbolize characteristics of religious faith?

2. How does Hawthorne establish the forest as a place of evil? How does he contrast night and day in the story?

3. Why does Goodman Brown go into the forest? To what extent is he responsible for his initiation into the "mystery of sin"?

4. Does the last paragraph of the story imply that Goodman Brown's distrust is unfounded? Does it suggest that he would be better off without his doubts, even if they are justified?

THE SOUTH

Translated by Anthony Kerrigan

The man who landed in Buenos Aires in 1871 bore the name of Johannes Dahlmann and he was a minister in the Evangelical Church. In 1939, one of his grandchildren, Juan Dahlmann, was secretary of a municipal library on Calle Córdoba, and he considered himself profoundly Argentinian. His maternal grandfather had been that Francisco Flores, of the Second Line-Infantry Division, who had died on the frontier of Buenos Aires, run through with a lance by Indians from Catriel; in the discord inherent between his two lines of descent, Juan Dahlmann (perhaps driven to it by his Germanic blood) chose the line represented by his romantic ancestor, his ancestor of the romantic death. An old sword, a leather frame containing the daguerreotype of a blank-faced man with a beard, the dash and grace of certain music, the familiar strophes of *Martín Fierro*, the passing years, boredom and solitude, all went to foster this voluntary, but never ostentatious nationalism. At the cost of numerous small privations, Dahlmann had managed to save the empty shell of a ranch in the South which had belonged to the Flores family; he continually recalled the image of the balsamic eucalyptus trees and the great rose-colored house which had once been crimson. His duties, perhaps even indolence, kept him in the city. Summer after summer he contented himself with the abstract idea of possession and with the certitude that his ranch was waiting for him on a precise site in the middle of the plain. Late in February, 1939, something happened to him.

Blind to all fault, destiny can be ruthless at one's slightest distraction. Dahlmann had succeeded in acquiring, on that very afternoon, an imperfect copy of Weil's edition of *The Thousand and One Nights*. Avid to examine this find, he did not wait for the elevator but hurried up the stairs. In the obscurity, something brushed by his forehead: a bat, a bird? On the face of the woman who opened the door to him he saw horror engraved, and the hand he wiped across his face came away red with blood. The edge of a recently painted door which someone had forgotten to close had caused this wound. Dahlmann was able to fall asleep, but from the moment he awoke at dawn the savor of all things was atrociously poignant. Fever wasted him and the pictures in *The Thousand and One Nights* served to illustrate nightmares. Friends and relatives paid him visits and, with exaggerated smiles, assured him that they thought he looked fine. Dahlmann listened to them with a kind of feeble stupor and he marveled at their not knowing that he was in hell. A week, eight days passed, and they were like eight centuries. One afternoon, the usual doctor appeared, accompanied by a new doctor, and they carried him off to a sanitarium on the Calle Ecuador, for it was necessary to X-ray him. Dahlmann, in the hackney coach which bore them away, thought that he would, at last, be able to sleep in a room different from his own. He felt happy and communicative. When he arrived at his destination, they undressed him, shaved his head, bound him with metal fastenings to a stretcher; they shone bright lights on him until he was blind and dizzy, auscultated him, and a masked man stuck a needle into his arm. He awoke with a feeling of nausea, covered with a bandage, in a cell with something of a well about it; in the days and nights which followed the operation he came to realize that he had merely been, up until then, in a suburb of hell. Ice in his mouth did not leave the least trace of freshness. During these days Dahlmann hated himself in minute detail: he hated his identity, his bodily necessities, his humiliation, the beard which bristled upon his face. He stoically endured the curative measures, which were painful, but when the surgeon told him he had been on the point of death from septicemia, Dahlmann dissolved in tears of self-pity for his fate. Physical wretchedness and the incessant anticipation of horrible nights had not allowed him time to think of anything so abstract as death. On another day, the surgeon told him he was healing and that, very soon, he would be able to go to his ranch for convalescence. Incredibly enough, the promised day arrived.

Reality favors symmetries and slight anachronisms: Dahlmann had arrived at the sanitarium in a hackney coach and now a hackney coach was to take him to the Constitución station. The first fresh tang of autumn, after the summer's oppressiveness, seemed like a symbol in nature of his rescue and release from fever and death. The city, at seven in the morning, had not lost that air of an old house lent it by the night; the streets seemed like long vestibules, the plazas were like patios. Dahlmann recognized the city with joy on the edge of vertigo: a second before his eyes registered the phenomena themselves, he recalled the corners, the billboards, the modest variety of Buenos Aires. In the yellow light of the new day, all things returned to him.

Every Argentine knows that the South begins at the other side of Rivadavia. Dahlmann was in the habit of saying that this was no mere convention, that whoever crosses this street enters a more ancient and sterner world. From inside the carriage he sought out, among the new buildings, the iron grill window, the brass knocker, the arched door, the entrance way, the intimate patio.

At the railroad station he noted that he still had thirty minutes. He quickly recalled that in a café on the Calle Brazil (a few dozen feet from Yrigoyen's house) there was an enormous cat which allowed itself to be caressed as if it were a disdainful divinity. He entered the café. There was the cat, asleep. He ordered a cup of coffee, slowly stirred the sugar, sipped it (this pleasure had been denied him in the clinic), and thought, as he smoothed the cat's black coat, that this contact was an illusion and that the two beings, man and cat, were as good as separated by a glass, for man lives in time, in succession, while the magical animal lives in the present, in the eternity of the instant.

Along the next to the last platform the train lay waiting. Dahlmann walked through the coaches until he found one almost empty. He arranged his baggage in the network rack. When the train started off, he took down his valise and extracted, after some hesitation, the first volume of *The Thousand and One Nights*. To travel with this book, which was so much a part of the history of his ill-fortune, was a kind of affirmation that his ill-fortune had been annulled; it was a joyous and secret defiance of the frustrated forces of evil.

Along both sides of the train the city dissipated into suburbs; this sight, and then a view of the gardens and villas, delayed the beginning of his reading. The truth was that Dahlmann read very little. The magnetized mountain and the genie who swore to kill his benefactor are—who would deny it?—marvelous, but not so much more than the morning itself and the mere fact of being. The joy of life distracted him from paying attention to Scheherezade and her superfluous miracles. Dahlmann closed his book and allowed himself to live.

Lunch—the bouillon served in shining metal bowls, as in the remote summers of childhood—was one more peaceful and rewarding delight.

Tomorrow I'll wake up at the ranch, he thought, and it was as if he was two men at a time: the man who traveled through the autumn day and across the geography of the

85

fatherland, and the other one, locked up in a sanitarium and subject to methodical servitude. He saw unplastered brick houses, long and angled, timelessly watching the trains go by; he saw horsemen along the dirt roads; he saw gullies and lagoons and ranches; he saw great luminous clouds that resembled marble; and all these things were accidental, casual, like dreams of the plain. He also thought he recognized trees and crop fields; but he would not have been able to name them, for his actual knowledge of the countryside was quite inferior to his nostalgic and literary knowledge.

From time to time he slept, and his dreams were animated by the impetus of the train. The intolerable white sun of high noon had already become the yellow sun which precedes nightfall, and it would not be long before it would turn red. The railroad car was now also different; it was not the same as the one which had quit the station siding at Constitución; the plain and the hours had transfigured it. Outside, the moving shadow of the railroad car stretched toward the horizon. The elemental earth was not perturbed either by settlements or other signs of humanity. The country was vast but at the same time intimate and, in some measure, secret. The limitless country sometimes contained only a solitary bull. The solitude was perfect, perhaps hostile, and it might have occurred to Dahlmann that he was traveling into the past and not merely south. He was distracted from these considerations by the railroad inspector who, on reading his ticket, advised him that the train would not let him off at the regular station but at another: an earlier stop, one scarcely known to Dahlmann. (The man added an explanation which Dahlmann did not attempt to understand, and which he hardly heard, for the mechanism of events did not concern him.)

The train laboriously ground to a halt, practically in the middle of the plain. The station lay on the other side of the tracks; it was not much more than a siding and a shed. There was no means of conveyance to be seen, but the station chief supposed that the traveler might secure a vehicle from a general store and inn to be found some ten or twelve blocks away.

Dahlmann accepted the walk as a small adventure. The sun had already disappeared from view, but a final splendor exalted the vivid and silent plain, before the night erased its color. Less to avoid fatigue than to draw out his enjoyment of these sights, Dahlmann walked slowly, breathing in the odor of clover with sumptuous joy.

The general store at one time had been painted a deep scarlet, but the years had tempered this violent color for its own good. Something in its poor architecture recalled a steel engraving, perhaps one from an old edition of *Paul et Virginie*. A number of horses were hitched up to the paling. Once inside, Dahlmann thought he recognized the shopkeeper. Then he realized that he had been deceived by the man's resemblance to one of the male nurses in the sanitarium. When the shopkeeper heard Dahlmann's request, he said he would have the shay made up. In order to add one more event to that day and to kill time, Dahlmann decided to eat at the general store.

Some country louts, to whom Dahlmann did not at first pay any attention, were eating and drinking at one of the tables. On the floor, and hanging on to the bar, squatted an old man, immobile as an object. His years had reduced and polished him as water does a stone or the generations of men do a sentence. He was dark, dried up, diminutive, and seemed outside time, situated in eternity. Dahlmann noted with satisfaction the kerchief, the thick poncho, the long *chiripá*, and the colt boots, and told himself, as he recalled futile discussions with people from the Northern counties or from the province of Entre Rios, that gauchos like this no longer existed outside the South.

Dahlmann sat down next to the window. The darkness began overcoming the plain, but the odor and sound of the earth penetrated the iron bars of the window. The shop owner brought him sardines, followed by some roast meat. Dahlmann washed the meal down with several glasses of red wine. Idling, he relished the tart savor of the wine, and let his gaze, now grown somewhat drowsy, wander over the shop. A kerosene lamp hung from a beam. There were three customers at the other table: two of them appeared to be farm workers; the third man, whose features hinted at Chinese blood, was drinking with his hat on. Of a sudden, Dahlmann felt something brush lightly against his face. Next to the heavy glass of turbid wine, upon one of the stripes in the table cloth, lay a spit ball of breadcrumb. That was all: but someone had thrown it there.

The men at the other table seemed totally cut off from him. Perplexed, Dahlmann decided that nothing had happened, and he opened the volume of *The Thousand and One Nights*, by way of suppressing reality. After a few moments another little ball landed on his table, and now the *peones* laughed outright. Dahlmann said to himself that he was not frightened, but he reasoned that it would be a major blunder if he, a convalescent, were to allow himself to be dragged by strangers into some chaotic quarrel. He determined to leave, and had already gotten to his feet when the owner came up and exhorted him in an alarmed voice:

"*Señor* Dahlmann, don't pay any attention to those lads; they're half high."

Dahlmann was not surprised to learn that the other man, now, knew his name. But he felt that these conciliatory words served only to aggravate the situation. Previous to this moment, the *peones*' provocation was directed against an unknown face, against no one in particular, almost against no one at all. Now it was an attack against him, against his name, and his neighbors knew it. Dahlmann pushed the owner aside, confronted the *peones*, and demanded to know what they wanted of him.

The tough with a Chinese look staggered heavily to his feet. Almost in Juan Dahlmann's face he shouted insults, as if he had been a long way off. His game was to exaggerate his drunkness, and this extravagance constituted a ferocious mockery. Between curses and obscenities, he threw a long knife into the air, followed it with his eyes, caught and juggled it, and challenged Dahlmann to a knife fight. The owner objected in a tremulous voice, pointing out that Dahlmann was unarmed. At this point, something unforeseeable occurred.

From a corner of the room, the old ecstatic gaucho—in whom Dahlmann saw a summary and cipher of the South (his South)—threw him a naked dagger, which landed at his feet. It was as if the South had resolved that Dahlmann should accept the duel. Dahlmann bent over to pick up the dagger, and felt two things. The first, that this almost instinctive act bound him to fight. The second, that the weapon, in his torpid hand, was no defense at all, but would merely serve to justify his murder. He had once played with a poniard, like all men, but his idea of fencing and knifeplay did not go further than the notion that all strokes should be directed upwards, with the cutting edge held inwards. *They would not have allowed such things to happen to me in the sanitarium*, he thought.

"Let's get on our way," said the other man.

They went out and if Dahlmann was without hope, he was also without fear. As he crossed the threshold, he felt that to die in a knife fight, under the open sky, and going forward to the attack, would have been a liberation, a joy, and a festive occasion, on the first night in the sanitarium, when they stuck him with the needle. He felt that if he had been able to choose, then, or to dream his death, this would have been the death he would have chosen or dreamt.

Firmly clutching his knife, which he perhaps would not know how to wield, Dahlmann went out into the plain.

1. Juan Dahlmann has two lines of ancestry, one Argentinean (Juan), and one German (Dahlmann). How does the symbolism of these two lines work itself out in the story? How does his reading of *The Thousand and One Nights* fit into this symbolic pattern?

2. In this story Borges offers a number of generalizations:

   Blind to all fault, destiny can be ruthless at one's slightest distraction.

   Reality favors symmetries and slight anachronisms.

   . . . man lives in time, in succession, while the magical animal lives in the instant, in the eternity of the instant.

   How do such generalizations affect the way you view the events of the story?

3. Borges writes that "it might have occurred to Dahlmann that he was traveling into the past and not merely South." How does this tentative association of the South and the past connect with the old gaucho who is "dark, dried up, diminutive . . . outside time, situated in eternity"? Why does Dahlmann accept the knife the gaucho throws him? What does Dahlmann experience in the South that he does not in Buenos Aires?

4. In conversation Borges once made the following remark:

   Coincidences are given to us so that we may feel there is a pattern—that there is a pattern in life, that things mean something. Of course, there is a pattern in the sense that we have night and day, the four seasons, being born, living and dying, the stars and so on, but there may be a more subtle kind of pattern, no?

   How many coincidences can you find in the story? What kind of pattern does Dahlmann's life have? Can we understand it?

Further Stories

HEARTACHE

Translated by Robert Payne

To whom shall I tell my sorrow?

Evening Twilight. Thick flakes of wet snow were circling lazily round the newly lighted street lamps, settling in thin soft layers on rooftops, on the horses' backs, and on people's shoulders and caps. The cabdriver Iona Potapov was white as a ghost, and bent double as much as any human body can be bent double, sitting very still on his box. Even if a whole snowdrift had fallen on him, he would have found no need to shake it off. The little mare, too, was white, and quite motionless. Her immobility, and the fact that she was all sharp angles and sticklike legs, gave her a resemblance to one of those gingerbread horses which can be bought for a kopeck. No doubt the mare was plunged in deep thought. So would you be if you were torn from the plow, snatched away from familiar, gray surroundings, and thrown into a whirlpool of monstrous illuminations, ceaseless uproar, and people scrambling hither and thither.

For a long while neither Iona nor the little mare had made the slightest motion. They had driven out of the stableyard before dinner, and so far not a single fare had come to them. The evening mist fell over the city. The pale glow of the street lamps grew brighter, more intense, as the street noises grew louder.

Iona heard some one saying "Driver—you, there!—take me to Vyborg District!"

Iona started, and through his sown-laden eyelashes he made out an officer wearing a military overcoat with a hood.

"Vyborg!" the officer repeated. "Are you asleep, eh? Get on with it—Vyborg!"

To show he had heard, Iona pulled at the reins, sending whole layers of snow flying from the horse's back and from his own shoulders. The officer sat down in the sleigh. The driver clucked with his tongue, stretched out his neck like a swan, rose in his seat, and more from habit than necessity, he flourished his whip. The little horse also stretched her neck, crooked her sticklike legs, and started off irresolutely. . . .

"Where are you going, you fool!" Iona was being assailed with shouts from some massive, dark object wavering to and fro in front of him. "Where the devil are you going? Stay on the right side of the road!"

"You don't know how to drive! Stay on the right side!" the officer shouted angrily.

A coachman driving a private carriage was swearing at him, and a pedestrian, running across the road and brushing his shoulder against the mare's nose, glanced up at him and shook the snow from his sleeve. Iona shifted about on the box, as though sitting on needles, thrust out his elbows, rolled his eyes like a madman, as though he did not understand where he was or what he was doing there.

"They're all scoundrels," the officer laughed. "All trying to shove into you, or fall under your horse. Quite a conspiracy!"

The driver turned towards the officer, his lips moving. He appeared about to say something, but the only sound coming from him was a hoarse wheezing cough.

"What is it?" the officer asked.

Iona's lips twitched into a smile, and he

strained his throat and croaked: "My son, sir. He died this week."

"Hm, what did he die of?"

Iona turned his whole body round to face his fare.

"Who knows? They say it was fever. . . . . He was in the hospital only three days, and then he died. It was God's will!"

"Get over, damn you!" came a sudden shout out of the darkness. "Have you gone blind, you old idiot? Keep your eyes skinned!"

"Keep going," the officer said. "This way we won't get there till tomorrow morning. Put the whip to her!"

Once more the driver stretched his neck, rose in his seat, and with heavy grace flourished the whip. Several times he turned to watch his fare, but the officer's eyes were closed and apparently he was in no mood to listen. And then, letting off the passenger in the Vyborg District, the driver stopped by a tavern, and again he remained motionless, doubled up on his box. And again the wet snow splashed him and his mare with its white paint. An hour passed, and then another.

Then three young men came loudly pounding the sidewalk in galoshes, quarreling furiously among themselves. Two were tall and slender, the third was a small hunchback.

"Driver, to the Police Bridge!" the hunchback shouted in a cracked voice. "The three of us for twenty kopecks!"

Iona tugged at the reins and smacked his lips. Twenty kopecks was not a fair price, but he did not care any more. Whether it was a ruble or five kopecks no longer mattered, so long as he had a fare. The young men, jostling and cursing one another, came up to the sleigh, and all three of them tried to jump onto the seat, and then they began to argue about which two should sit down, and who should be the one to stand up. After a long, fantastic, and ill-natured argument they decided that the hunchback would have to stand, because he was the shortest.

"Let's go!" cried the hunchback in his cracked voice, taking his place and breathing down Iona's neck. "Get going! Eh, brother, what a funny cap you're wearing. You won't find a worse one anywhere in St. Petersburg!"

"Hee-hee-hee," Iona giggled. "Yes, it's a funny cap."

"Then get a move on! Are you going to crawl along all this time at the same pace? Do you want to get it in the neck?"

"My head's splitting!" said one of the tall ones. "Yesterday at the Dukmassovs', I drank all of four bottles of cognac with Vaska."

"I don't know why you have to tell lies," the other tall one said angrily. "You lie like a swine!"

"May God strike me dead if I am not telling the truth!"

"A flea coughs the truth, too."

"Hee-hee-hee," Iona giggled. "What a lot of merry gentlemen. . . ."

"Pfui!" the hunchback exclaimed indignantly. "Damn you for an old idiot! Will you get a move on, or won't you? Is that how to drive? Use the whip, dammit! Go on, you old devil, give it to her!"

Iona could feel at his back the hunchback's wriggling body, and the tremble in the voice. He heard the insults which were being hurled at him, he saw the people in the street, and little by little the feeling of loneliness was lifted from his heart. The hunchback went on swearing until he choked on an elaborate six-story-high oath, and then was overcome with a fit of coughing. The tall ones began to talk about a certain Nadezhda Petrovna. Iona looked round at them. He waited until there was a short pause in the conversation, and then he turned again and murmured: "My son died—he died this week. . . ."

"We all die," sighed the hunchback, wiping his lips after his fit of coughing. "Keep going, eh? Gentlemen, we simply can't go any further like this. We'll never get there!"

"Give him a bit of encouragement. Hit him in the neck!"

"Did you hear that, old pest? You'll get it in the neck all right. One shouldn't stand on ceremony with people like you—one might just as well walk. Do you hear me, you old snake? I don't suppose you care a tinker's damn about what we are saying."

Then Iona heard rather than felt a thud on the nape of his neck.

"Hee-hee-hee," he laughed. "Such merry gentlemen! God bless them!"

"Driver, are you married?" one of the tall men asked.

"Me, am I married? Hee-hee-hee. You're all such merry gentlemen. There's only one wife left to me now—the damp earth. Hee-ho-ho. The grave, that's what's left for me. My son is dead, and I'm alive. Strange how death comes by the wrong door. It didn't come for me, it came for my son. . . ."

Iona turned round to tell them how his son died, but at that moment the hunchback gave a little sigh of relief and announced that, thank God, they had come to the end of the journey. Having received his twenty kopecks, Iona gazed after the revelers for a long time, even after they had vanished through a dark gateway. Once more he was alone, once more silence fell on him. The grief he had kept at bay for a brief while now returned to wrench his heart with still greater force. With an expression of anxiety and torment, he gazed at the crowds hurrying along both sides of the street, wondering whether there was anyone among those thousands of people who would listen to him. But the crowds hurried past, paying no attention to him or to his grief. His grief was vast, boundless. If his heart could break, and the grief could pour out of it, it would flow over the whole world; but no one would see it. It had found a hiding place invisible to all: even in broad daylight, even if you held a candle to it, you wouldn't see it.

There was a doorman carrying some kind of sack, and Iona decided to talk to him.

"What time is it, my dear fellow?" he asked.

"Ten o'clock. What the devil are you standing there for? Get a move on!"

Iona drove along the street a bit. His body was bent, and he was surrendering to his grief. He felt it was useless to turn to people for help, but in less than five minutes he had straightened himself up, shaking his head as though he felt a sharp pang of pain, and then he pulled at the reins. He could bear it no longer.

"Back to the stables," he thought. "Back to the stables."

The little mare, as though she read his thoughts, started off at a trot.

An hour and a half later Iona was sitting by a large dirty stove. On the stove, on the floor, on benches, men were snoring. The air was noisome, suffocating. Iona found himself gazing at the sleeping people. He scratched himself, and he was sorry he had come back so early.

"I haven't earned enough even for the hay," he thought. "There's grief for you. But a man who knows his work, and has a full belly, and a well-fed horse besides, he's at peace with the world all his days."

From one of the corners a young driver rose, grunting sleepily as he reached for the water bucket.

"You thirsty?" Iona asked him.

"Reckon so."

"Well, it's a good thing to be thirsty, but as for me, brother, my son is dead. Did you hear me? This week, at the hospital. . . . Such a lot of trouble!"

Iona looked to see whether the words were producing any effect, but saw none—the young man had covered up his face and was a-sleep again. The old man sighed and scratched himself. Just as the young man wanted to drink, so he wanted to talk. Soon it would be a week since his son died, and still no one had let him talk about it properly. He would have to tell it slowly, very carefully. He would tell them how his son fell ill, how he suffered, what he said before he died, how he died. He would have to describe the funeral, and how he went to the hospital to collect his son's clothes. His daughter Anissya was still in the country. He wanted to talk about her, too. Yes, there was so much to talk about. And the listener would have to gasp and sigh and bewail the fate of the dead man. And maybe it would be better to talk about it to women. Even though women are so foolish, you can bring the tears to their eyes with a few words.

"Now I'll go and look at my horse," Iona thought to himself. "There's always time for sleep—nothing there to be afraid of."

He threw on his coat and went down to the stable to look after her, thinking about such things as hay, oats, and the weather. Alone, he dared not let his mind dwell on his son. He could talk about him to anyone, but alone, thinking about him, conjuring up his living presence, no—no, that was too painful for words.

"Filling your belly, eh?" he said, seeing the mare's shining eyes. "Well, eat up! We haven't earned enough for oats, but we can eat hay. Oh, I'm too old to be driving. My son should be driving, not me. He was a real cabdriver, and he should be alive now. . . ."

Iona was silent for a moment, and then he went on: "That's how it is, old girl. My son, Kuzma Ionich, is no more. He died on us. Now let's say you had a foal, and you were the foal's mother, and suddenly, let's say, the same little foal departed this life. You'd be sorry, eh?"

The little mare munched and listened and breathed on his hands.

Surrendering to his grief, Iona told her the whole story.

A HUNGER ARTIST

During these last decades the interest in professional fasting has markedly diminished. It used to pay very well to stage such great performances under one's own management, but today that is quite impossible. We live in a different world now. At one time the whole town took a lively interest in the hunger artist; from day to day of his fast the excitement mounted; everybody wanted to see him at least once a day; there were people who bought season tickets for the last few days and sat from morning till night in front of his small barred cage; even in the nighttime there were visiting hours, when the whole effect was heightened by torch flares; on fine days the cage was set out in the open air, and then it was the children's special treat to see the hunger artist; for their elders he was often just a joke that happened to be in fashion, but the children stood open-mouthed, holding each other's hands for greater security, marveling at him as he sat there pallid in black tights, with his ribs sticking out so prominently, not even on a seat but down among straw on the ground, sometimes giving a courteous nod, answering questions with a constrained smile, or perhaps stretching an arm through the bars so that one might feel how thin it was, and then again withdrawing deep into himself, paying no attention to anyone or anything, not even to the all-important striking of the clock that was the only piece of furniture in his cage, but merely staring into vacancy with half-shut eyes, now and then taking a sip from a tiny glass of water to moisten his lips.

Besides casual onlookers there were also relays of permanent watchers selected by the public, usually butchers, strangely enough, and it was their task to watch the hunger artist day and night, three of them at a time, in case he should have some secret recourse to nourishment. This was nothing but a formality, instituted to reassure the masses, for the initiates knew well enough that during his fast the artist would never in any circumstances, not even under forcible compulsion, swallow the smallest morsel of food; the honor of his profession forbade it. Not every watcher, of course, was capable of understanding this, there were often groups of night watchers who were very lax in carrying out their duties and deliberately huddled together in a retired corner to play cards with great absorption, obviously intending to give the hunger artist the chance of a little refreshment, which they supposed he could draw from some private hoard. Nothing annoyed the artist more than such watchers; they made him miserable; they made his fast seem unendurable; sometimes he mastered his feebleness sufficiently to sing during their watch for as long as he could keep going, to show them how unjust their suspicions were. But that was of little use; they only wondered at his cleverness in being able to fill his mouth even while singing. Much more to his taste were the watchers who sat close up to the bars, who were not content with the dim night lighting of the hall but focused him in the full glare of the electric pocket torch given them by the impresario. The harsh light did not trouble him at all. In any case he could never sleep properly, and he could always drowse a little, whatever the light, at any hour, even when the hall was thronged with noisy onlookers. He was quite happy at the prospect of spending a sleepless night

94

with such watchers; he was ready to exchange jokes with them, to tell them stories out of his nomadic life, anything at all to keep them awake and demonstrate to them again that he had no eatables in his cage and that he was fasting as not one of them could fast. But his happiest moment was when the morning came and an enormous breakfast was brought them, at his expense, on which they flung themselves with the keen appetite of healthy men after a weary night of wakefulness. Of course there were people who argued that this breakfast was an unfair attempt to bribe the watchers, but that was going rather too far, and when they were invited to take on a night's vigil without a breakfast, merely for the sake of the cause, they made themselves scarce, although they stuck stubbornly to their suspicions.

Such suspicions, anyhow, were a necessary accompaniment to the profession of fasting. No one could possibly watch the hunger artist continuously, day and night, and so no one could produce first-hand evidence that the fast had really been rigorous and continuous; only the artist himself could know that; he was therefore bound to be the sole completely satisfied spectator of his own fast. Yet for other reasons he was never satisfied; it was not perhaps mere fasting that had brought him to such skeleton thinness that many people had regretfully to keep away from his exhibitions, because the sight of him was too much for them, perhaps it was dissatisfaction with himself that had worn him down. For he alone knew, what no other initiate knew, how easy it was to fast. It was the easiest thing in the world. He made no secret of this, yet people did not believe him; at the best they set him down as modest. Most of them, however, thought he was out for publicity or else was some kind of cheat who found it easy to fast because he had discovered a way of making it easy, and then had the impudence to admit the fact, more or less. He had to put up with all that, and in the course of time had got used to it, but his inner dissatisfaction always rankled, and never yet, after

any term of fasting—this must be granted to his credit—had he left the cage of his own free will. The longest period of fasting was fixed by his impresario at forty days, beyond that term he was not allowed to go, not even in great cities, and there was good reason for it, too. Experience had proved that for about forty days the interest of the public could be stimulated by a steadily increasing pressure of advertisement, but after that the town began to lose interest, sympathetic support began notably to fall off; there were of course local variations as between one town and another or one country and another, but as a general rule forty days marked the limit. So on the fortieth day the flower-bedecked cage was opened, enthusiastic spectators filled the hall, a military band played, two doctors entered the cage to measure the results of the fast, which were announced through a megaphone, and finally two young ladies appeared, blissful at having been selected for the honor, to help the hunger artist down the few steps leading to a small table on which was spread a carefully chosen invalid repast. And at this very moment the artist always turned stubborn. True, he would entrust his bony arms to the outstretched helping hands of the ladies bending over him, but stand up he would not. Why stop fasting at this particular moment, after forty days of it? He had held out for a long time, an illimitably long time; why stop now, when he was in his best fasting form, or rather, not yet quite in his best fasting form? Why should he be cheated of the fame he would get for fasting longer, for being not only the record hunger artist of all time, which presumably he was already, but for beating his own record by a performance beyond human imagination, since he felt that there were no limits to his capacity for fasting? His public pretended to admire him so much, why should it have so little patience with him; if he could endure fasting longer, why shouldn't the public endure it? Besides, he was tired, he was comfortable sitting in the straw, and now he was supposed to lift himself to his full height and go down to a meal the very thought of which gave him a nausea that only the presence of the ladies kept him from betraying, and even that with an effort. And he looked up into the eyes of the ladies who were apparently so friendly and in reality so cruel, and shook his head, which felt too heavy on its strengthless neck. But then there happened yet again what always happened. The impresario came forward, without a word—for the band made speech impossible—lifted his arms in the air above the artist, as if inviting Heaven to look down upon its creature here in the straw, this suffering martyr, which indeed he was, although in quite another sense; grasped him round the emaciated waist, with exaggerated caution, so that the frail condition he was in might be appreciated; and committed him to the care of the blenching ladies, not without secretly giving him a shaking so that his legs and body tottered and swayed. The artist now submitted completely; his head lolled on his breast as if it had landed there by chance; his body was hollowed out; his legs in a spasm of self-preservation clung close to each other at the knees, yet scraped on the ground as if it were not really solid ground, as if they were only trying to find solid ground; and the whole weight of his body, a featherweight after all, relapsed onto one of the ladies, who, looking round for help and panting a little—this post of honor was not at all what she had expected it to be—first stretched her neck as far as she could to keep her face at least free from contact with the artist, then finding this impossible, and her more fortunate companion not coming to her aid but merely holding extended on her own trembling hand the little bunch of knucklebones that was the artist's, to the great delight of the spectators burst into tears and had to be replaced by an attendant who had long been stationed in readiness. Then came the food, a little of which the impresario managed to get between the artist's lips, while he sat in a kind of half-fainting trance, to the accompaniment of cheerful patter designed to distract the public's attention from the artist's condition; after that, a toast was drunk to the public, supposedly prompted by a whisper from the artist in the impresario's ear; the band confirmed it with a mighty flourish, the spectators melted away, and no one had any cause to be dissatisfied with the proceedings, no one except the hunger artist himself, he only, as always.

So he lived for many years, with small regular intervals of recuperation, in visible glory, honored by the world, yet in spite of that troubled in spirit, and all the more troubled because no one would take his trouble seriously. What comfort could he possibly need? What more could he possibly wish for? And if some good-natured person, feeling sorry for him, tried to console him by pointing out that his melancholy was probably caused by fasting, it could happen, especially when he had been fasting for some time, that he reacted with an outburst of fury and to the general alarm began to shake the bars of his cage like a wild animal. Yet the impresario had a way of punishing these outbreaks which he rather enjoyed putting into operation. He would apologize publicly for the artist's behavior, which was only to be excused, he admitted, because of the irritability caused by fasting; a condition hardly to be understood by well-fed people; then by natural transition he went on to mention the artist's equally incomprehensible boast that he could fast for much longer than he was doing; he praised the high ambition, the good will, the great self-denial undoubtedly implicit in such a statement; and then quite simply countered it by bringing out photographs, which were also on sale to the public, showing the artist on the fortieth day of a fast lying in bed almost dead from exhaustion. This perversion of the truth, familiar to the artist though it was, always unnerved him afresh and proved too much for him. What was a consequence of the premature ending of his fast was here presented as the cause of it! To fight against this lack of understanding, against a whole world of non-understanding, was impossible. Time and again in good faith he stood by the bars listening to the impresario, but as soon as the photographs appeared he always let go and sank with a groan back on to his straw, and the reassured public could once more come close and gaze at him.

A few years later when the witnesses of such scenes called them to mind, they often failed to understand themselves at all. For meanwhile the aforementioned change in public interest had set in; it seemed to happen almost overnight; there may have been profound causes for it, but who was going to bother about that; at any rate the pampered hunger artist suddenly found himself deserted one fine day by the amusement seekers, who went streaming past him to other more favored attractions. For the last time the impresario hurried him over half Europe to discover whether the old interest might still survive here and there; all in vain; everywhere, as if by secret agreement, a positive revulsion from professional fasting was in evidence. Of course it could not really have sprung up so suddenly as all that, and many premonitory symptoms which had not been sufficiently remarked or suppressed during the rush and glitter of success now came retrospectively to mind, but it was now too late to take any countermeasures. Fasting would surely come into fashion again at some future date, yet that was no comfort for those living in the present. What, then, was the hunger artist to do? He had been applauded by thousands in his time and could hardly come down to showing himself in a street booth at village fairs, and as for adopting another profession, he was not only too old for that but too fanatically devoted to fasting. So he took leave of the impresario, his partner in an unparalleled career, and hired himself to a large circus; in order to spare his own feelings he avoided reading the conditions of his contract.

A large circus with its enormous traffic in replacing and recruiting men, animals and apparatus can always find a use for people at any time, even for a hunger artist, provided of course that he does not ask too much, and in this particular case anyhow it was not only the artist who was taken on but his famous and long-known name as well; indeed considering the peculiar nature of his performance, which was not impaired by advancing age, it could not be objected that here was an artist past his prime, no longer at the height of his professional skill, seeking a refuge in some quiet corner of a circus; on the contrary, the hunger artist averred that he could fast as well as ever, which was entirely credible; he even alleged that if he were allowed to fast as he liked, and this was at once promised him without more ado, he could astound the world by establishing a record never yet achieved, a statement which certainly provoked a smile among the other professionals, since it left out of account the change in public opinion, which the hunger artist in his zeal conveniently forgot.

He had not, however, actually lost his sense of the real situation and took it as a matter of course that he and his cage should be stationed, not in the middle of the ring as a main attraction, but outside, near the animal cages, on a site that was after all easily accessible. Large and gaily painted placards made a frame for the cage and announced what was to be seen inside it. When the public came thronging out in the intervals to see the animals, they could hardly avoid passing the hunger artist's cage and stopping there for a moment, perhaps they might even have stayed longer had not those pressing behind them in the narrow gangway, who did not understand why they should be held up on their way towards the excitements of the menagerie, made it impossible for anyone to stand gazing quietly for any length of time. And that was the reason why the hunger artist, who had of course been looking forward to these visiting hours as the main achievement of his life, began instead to shrink from them. At first he could hardly wait for the intervals; it was exhilarating to watch the crowds come streaming his way, until only too soon—not even the most obstinate self-deception, clung to almost consciously, could hold out against the fact—the conviction was borne in upon him that these people, most of them, to judge from their actions, again and again, without exception, were all on their way to the menagerie. And the first sight of them from the distance remained the best. For when they reached his cage he was at once deafened by the storm of shouting and abuse that arose from the two contending factions, which renewed themselves continuously, of those who wanted to stop and stare at him—he soon began to dislike them more than the others—not out of real interest but only out of obstinate self-assertiveness, and those who wanted to go straight on to the animals. When the first great rush was past, the stragglers came along, and these, whom nothing could have prevented from stopping to look at him as long as they had breath, raced past with long strides, hardly even glancing at him, in their haste to get to the menagerie in time. And all too rarely did it happen that he had a stroke of luck, when some father of a family fetched up before him with his children, pointed a finger at the hunger artist and explained at length what the phenomenon meant, telling stories of earlier years when he himself had watched similar but much more thrilling performances, and the children, still rather uncomprehending, since neither inside nor outside school had they been sufficiently prepared for this lesson—what did they care about fasting?—yet showed by the brightness of their intent eyes that new and better times might be coming. Perhaps, said the hunger artist to himself many a time, things would be a little better if his cage were set not quite so near the menagerie. That made it too easy for people to make their choice, to say nothing of what he suffered from the stench of the menagerie, the animals' restlessness by night, the carrying past of raw lumps of flesh for the beasts of prey, the roaring at feeding times, which depressed him continually. But he did not dare to lodge a complaint with the management; after all, he had the animals to thank for the troops of people who passed his cage, among whom there might always be one here and there to take an interest in him, and who could tell where they might seclude him if he called attention to his existence and thereby to the fact that, strictly speaking, he was only an impediment on the way to the menagerie.

A small impediment, to be sure, one that grew steadily less. People grew familiar with the strange idea that they could be expected, in times like these, to take an interest in a hunger artist, and with this familiarity the verdict went out against him. He might fast as much as he could, and he did so; but nothing could save him now, people passed him by. Just try to explain to anyone the art of fasting! Anyone who has no feeling for it cannot be made to understand it. The fine placards grew dirty and illegible, they were torn down; the little notice board telling the number of fast days achieved, which at first was changed carefully every day, had long stayed at the same figure, for after the first few weeks even this small task seemed pointless to the staff; and so the artist simply fasted on and on, as he had once dreamed of doing, and it was no trouble to him, just as he had always foretold, but no one counted the days, no one, not even the artist himself, knew what records he was already breaking, and his heart grew heavy. And when once in a time some leisurely passer-by stopped, made merry over the old figure on the board and spoke of swindling, that was in its way the stupidest lie ever invented by indifference and inborn malice, since it was not the hunger artist who was cheating; he was working honestly, but the world was cheating him of his reward.

Many more days went by, however, and that too came to an end. An overseer's eye fell on the cage one day and he asked the attendants why this perfectly good cage should be left standing there unused with dirty straw inside it; nobody knew, until one man, helped out by the notice board, remembered about the hunger artist. They poked into the straw with sticks and found him in it. "Are you still fasting?" asked the overseer. "When on earth do you mean to stop?" "Forgive me, everybody," whispered the hunger artist; only the overseer, who had his ear to the bars, understood him. "Of course," said the overseer, and tapped his forehead with a finger to let the attendants know what state the man was in, "we forgive you." "I always wanted you to admire my fasting," said the hunger artist. "We do admire it," said the overseer, affably. "But you shouldn't admire it," said the hunger artist. "Well, then we don't admire it," said the overseer, "but why shouldn't we admire it?" "Because I have to fast, I can't help it," said the hunger artist. "What a fellow you are," said the overseer, "and why can't you help it?" "Because," said the hunger artist, lifting his head a little and speaking, with his lips pursed, as if for a kiss, into the overseer's ear, so that no syllable might be lost, "because I couldn't find the food I liked. If I had found it, believe me, I should have made no fuss and stuffed myself like you or anyone else." These were his last words, but in his dimming eyes remained the firm though no longer proud persuasion that he was still continuing to fast.

"Well, clear this out now!" said the overseer, and they buried the hunger artist, straw and all. Into the cage they put a young panther. Even the most insensitive felt it refreshing to see this wild creature leaping around the cage that had so long been dreary. The panther was all right. The food he liked was brought him without hesitation by the attendants; he seemed not even to miss his freedom; his noble body, furnished almost to the bursting point with all that it needed, seemed to carry freedom around with it too; somewhere in his jaws it seemed to lurk; and the joy of life streamed with such ardent passion from his throat that for the onlookers it was not easy to stand the shock of it. But they braced themselves, crowded round the cage, and did not want ever to move away.

Just like they had once crowded around his cage.

THE JILTING OF GRANNY WEATHERALL

She flicked her wrist neatly out of Doctor Harry's pudgy careful fingers and pulled the sheet up to her chin. The brat ought to be in knee breeches. Doctoring around the country with spectacles on his nose! "Get along now, take your schoolbooks and go. There's nothing wrong with me."

Doctor Harry spread a warm paw like a cushion on her forehead where the forked green vein danced and made her eyelids twitch. "Now, now, be a good girl, and we'll have you up in no time."

"That's no way to speak to a woman nearly eighty years old just because she's down. I'd have you respect your elders, young man."

"Well, Missy, excuse me." Doctor Harry patted her cheek. "But I've got to warn you, haven't I? You're a marvel, but you must be careful or you're going to be good and sorry."

"Don't tell me what I'm going to be. I'm on my feet now, morally speaking. It's Cornelia. I had to go to bed to get rid of her."

Her bones felt loose, and floated around in her skin, and Doctor Harry floated like a balloon around the foot of the bed. He floated and pulled down his waistcoat and swung his glasses on a cord. "Well, stay where you are, it certainly can't hurt you."

"Get along and doctor your sick," said Granny Weatherall. "Leave a well woman alone. I'll call for you when I want you. . . Where were you forty years ago when I pulled through milk-leg and double pneumonia? You weren't even born. Don't let Cornelia lead you on," she shouted, because Doctor Harry appeared to float up to the ceiling and out. "I pay my own bills, and I don't throw my money away on nonsense!"

She meant to wave good-by, but it was too much trouble. Her eyes closed of themselves, it was like a dark curtain drawn around the bed. The pillow rose and floated under her, pleasant as a hammock in a light wind. She listened to the leaves rustling outside the window. No, somebody was swishing newspapers: no, Cornelia and Doctor Harry were whispering together. She leaped broad awake, thinking they whispered in her ear.

"She was never like this, *never* like this!" "Well, what can we expect?" "Yes, eighty years old. . ."

Well, and what if she was? She still had ears. It was like Cornelia to whisper around doors. She always kept things secret in such a public way. She was always being tactful and kind. Cornelia was dutiful; that was the trouble with her. Dutiful and good: "So good and dutiful," said Granny, "that I'd like to spank her." She saw herself spanking Cornelia and making a fine job of it.

"What'd you say, Mother?"

Granny felt her face tying up in hard knots.

"Can't a body think, I'd like to know?"

"I thought you might want something."

"I do. I want a lot of things. First off, go away and don't whisper."

She lay and drowsed, hoping in her sleep that the children would keep out and let her rest a minute. It had been a long day. Not that she was tired. It was always pleasant to snatch a minute now and then. There was always so much to be done, let me see: tomorrow.

Tomorrow was far away and there was nothing to trouble about. Things were finished somehow when the time came; thank God there was always a little margin over for peace: then a person could spread out the plan of life and tuck in the edges orderly. It was good to have everything clean and folded away, with the hair brushes and tonic bottles sitting straight on the white embroidered linen: the day started without fuss and the pantry shelves laid out with rows of jelly glasses and brown jugs and white stone-china jars with blue whirligigs and words painted on them: coffee, tea, sugar, ginger, cinnamon, allspice: and the bronze clock with the lion on top nicely dusted off. The dust that lion could collect in twenty-four hours! The box in the attic with all those letters tied up, well, she'd have to go through that tomorrow. All those letters—George's letters and John's letters and her letters to them both—lying around for the children to find afterwards made her uneasy. Yes, that would be tomorrow's business. No use to let them know how silly she had been once.

While she was rummaging around she found death in her mind and it felt clammy and unfamiliar. She had spent so much time preparing for death there was no need for bringing it up again. Let it take care of itself now. When she was sixty she had felt very old, finished, and went around making farewell trips to see her children and grandchildren, with a secret in her mind: This is the very last of your mother, children! Then she made her will and came down with a long fever. That was all just a notion like a lot of other things, but it was lucky too, for she had once for all got over the idea of dying for a long time. Now she couldn't be worried. She hoped she had better sense now. Her father had lived to be one hundred and two years old and had drunk a noggin of strong hot toddy on his last birthday. He told the reporters it was his daily habit, and he owed his long life to that. He had made quite a scandal and was very pleased about it. She believed she'd just plague Cornelia a little.

"Cornelia! Cornelia!" No footsteps, but a sudden hand on her cheek. "Bless you, where have you been?"

"Here, Mother."

"Well, Cornelia, I want a noggin of hot toddy."

"Are you cold, darling?"

"I'm chilly, Cornelia. Lying in bed stops the circulation. I must have told you that a thousand times."

Well, she could just hear Cornelia telling her husband that Mother was getting a little childish and they'd have to humor her. The thing that most annoyed her was that Cornelia thought she was deaf, dumb, and blind. Little hasty glances and tiny gestures tossed around her and over her head saying, "Don't cross her, let her have her way, she's eighty years old," and she sitting there as if she lived in a thin glass cage. Sometimes Granny almost made up her mind to pack up and move back to her own house where nobody could remind her every minute that she was old. Wait, wait, Cornelia, till your own children whisper behind your back!

In her day she had kept a better house and had got more work done. She wasn't too old yet for Lydia to be driving eighty miles for advice when one of the children jumped the track, and Jimmy still dropped in and talked things over: "Now, Mammy, you've a good business head, I want to know what you think of this? . . ." Old. Cornelia couldn't change the furniture around without asking. Little things, little things! They had been so sweet when they were little. Granny wished the old days were back again with the children young and everything to be done over. It had been a hard pull, but not too much for her. When she thought of all the food she had cooked, and all the clothes she had cut and sewed, and all the gardens she had made—well, the children showed it. There they were, made out of her, and they couldn't get away from that. Sometimes she wanted to see John again and point to them and say, Well, I didn't do so badly, did I? But that would have to wait. That was for tomorrow. She used to think of him as a man, but now all the children were older than their father, and he would be a child beside her if she saw him now. It seemed strange and there was something wrong in the idea. Why, he couldn't possibly recognize her. She had fenced in a hundred acres once, digging the post holes herself and clamping the wires with just a Negro boy to help. That changed a woman. John would be looking for a young woman with the peaked Spanish comb in her hair and the painted fan. Digging post holes changed a woman. Riding country roads in the winter when women had their babies was another thing: sitting up nights with sick horses and sick Negroes and sick children and hardly ever losing one. John, I hardly ever lost one of them! John would see that in a minute, that would be something he could understand, she wouldn't have to explain anything!

It made her feel like rolling up her sleeves and putting the whole place to rights again. No matter if Cornelia was determined to be everywhere at once, there were a great many things left undone on this place. She would start tomorrow and do them. It was good to be strong enough for everything, even if all you made melted and changed and slipped under your hands, so that by the time you finished you almost forgot what you were working for. What was it I set out to do? she asked herself intently, but she could not remember. A fog rose over the valley, she saw it marching across the creek swallowing the trees and moving up the hill like an army of ghosts. Soon it would be at the near edge of the orchard, and then it was time to go in and light the lamps. Come in, children, don't stay out in the night air.

Lighting the lamps had been beautiful. The children huddled up to her and breathed like little calves waiting at the bars in the twilight. Their eyes followed the match and watched the flame rise and settle in a blue curve, then they moved away from her. The lamp, was lit, they didn't have to be scared and hang on to mother any more. Never, never, never more. God, for all my life I thank Thee. Without Thee, my God, I could never have done it. Hail, Mary, full of grace.

I want you to pick all the fruit this year

and see that nothing is wasted. There's always someone who can use it. Don't let good things rot for want of using. You waste life when you waste good food. Don't let things get lost. It's bitter to lose things. Now, don't let me get to thinking, not when I am tired and taking a little nap before supper. . . .

The pillow rose about her shoulders and pressed against her heart and the memory was being squeezed out of it: oh, push down the pillow, somebody: it would smother her if she tried to hold it. Such a fresh breeze blowing and such a green day with no threats in it. But he had not come, just the same. What does a woman do when she has put on the white veil and set out the white cake for a man and he doesn't come? She tried to remember. No, I swear he never harmed me but in that. He never harmed me but in that . . . and what if he did? There was the day, the day, but a whirl of dark smoke rose and covered it, crept up and over into the bright field where everything was planted so carefully in orderly rows. That was hell, she knew hell when she saw it. For sixty years she had prayed against remembering him and against losing her soul in the deep pit of hell, and now the two things were mingled in one and the thought of him was a smoky cloud from hell that moved and crept in her head when she had just got rid of Doctor Harry and was trying to rest a minute. Wounded vanity, Ellen, said a sharp voice in the top of her mind. Don't let your wounded vanity get the upper hand of you. Plenty of girls get jilted. You were jilted, weren't you? Then stand up to it. Her eyelids wavered and let in streamers of blue-gray light like tissue paper over her eyes. She must get up and pull the shades down or she'd never sleep. She was in bed again and the shades were not down. How could that happen? Better turn over, hide from the light, sleeping in the light gave you nightmares. "Mother, how do you feel now?" And a stinging wetness on her forehead. But I don't like having my face washed in cold water!

Hapsy? George? Lydia? Jimmy? No, Cornelia, and her features were swollen and full of little puddles. "They're coming, darling, they'll all be here soon." Go wash your face, child, you look funny.

Instead of obeying, Cornelia knelt down and put her head on the pillow. She seemed to be talking but there was no sound. "Well, are you tongue-tied? Whose birthday is it? Are you going to give a party?"

Cornelia's mouth moved urgently in strange shapes. "Don't do that, you bother me, daughter."

"Oh, no, Mother. Oh, no . . ."

Nonsense. It was strange about children. They disputed your every word. "No what, Cornelia?"

"Here's Doctor Harry."

"I won't see that boy again. He just left five minutes ago."

"That was this morning, Mother. It's night now. Here's the nurse."

"This is Doctor Harry, Mrs. Weatherall. I never saw you look so young and happy!"

"Ah, I'll never be young again— but I'd be happy if they'd let me lie in peace and get rested."

She thought she spoke up loudly, but no one answered. A warm weight on her forehead, a warm bracelet on her wrist, and a breeze went on whispering, trying to tell her something. A shuffle of leaves in the everlasting hand of God, He blew on them and they danced and rattled. "Mother, don't mind, we're going to give you a little hypodermic." "Look here, daughter, how do ants get in this bed? I saw sugar ants yesterday." Did you send for Hapsy too?

It was Hapsy she really wanted. She had to go a long way back through a great many rooms to find Hapsy standing with a baby on her arm. She seemed to herself to be Hapsy also, and the baby on Hapsy's arm was Hapsy and himself and herself, all at once, and there was no surprise in the meeting. Then Hapsy melted from within and turned flimsy as gray gauze and the baby was a gauzy shadow, and Hapsy came up close and said, "I thought you'd never come," and

looked at her very searchingly and said, "You haven't changed a bit!" They leaned forward to kiss, when Cornelia began whispering from a long way off, "Oh, is there anything you want to tell me? Is there anything I can do for you?"

Yes, she had changed her mind after sixty years and she would like to see George. I want you to find George. Find him and be sure to tell him I forgot him. I want him to know I had my husband just the same and my children and my house like any other woman. A good house too and a good husband that I loved and fine children out of him. Better than I hoped for even. Tell him I was given back everything he took away and more. Oh, no, oh, God, no, there was something else besides the house and the man and the children. Oh, surely they were not all? What was it? Something not given back. . . . Her breath crowded down under her ribs and grew into a monstrous frightening shape with cutting edges; it bored up into her head, and the agony was unbelievable: Yes, John, get the doctor now, no more talk, my time has come.

When this one was born it should be the last. The last. It should have been born first, for it was the one she had truly wanted. Everything came in good time. Nothing left out, left over. She was strong, in three days she would be as well as ever. Better. A woman needed milk in her to have her full health.

"Mother, do you hear me?"

"I've been telling you—"

"Mother, Father Connolly's here."

"I went to Holy Communion only last week. Tell him I'm not so sinful as all that."

"Father just wants to speak to you."

He could speak as much as he pleased. It was like him to drop in and inquire about her soul as if it were a teething baby, and then stay on for a cup of tea and a round of cards and gossip. He always had a funny story of some sort, usually about an Irishman who made his little mistakes and confessed them, and the point lay in some absurd thing he would blurt out in the confessional showing his struggles between native piety and original sin. Granny felt easy about her soul. Cornelia, where are your manners? Give Father Connolly a chair. She had her secret comfortable understanding with a few favorite saints who cleared a straight road to God for her. All as surely signed and sealed as the papers for the new Forty Acres. Forever . . . heirs and assigns forever. Since the day the wedding cake was not cut, but thrown out and wasted. The whole bottom dropped out of the world, and there she was blind and sweating with nothing under her feet and the walls falling away. His hand had caught her under the breast, she had not fallen, there was the freshly polished floor with the green rug on it, just as before. He had cursed like a sailor's parrot and said, "I'll kill him for you." Don't lay a hand on him, for my sake leave something to God. "Now, Ellen, you must believe what I tell you. . . ."

So there was nothing, nothing to worry about any more, except sometimes in the night one of the children screamed in a nightmare, and they both hustled out shaking and hunting for the matches and calling, "There, wait a minute, here we are!" John, get the doctor now, Hapsy's time has come. But there was Hapsy standing by the bed in a white cap. "Cornelia, tell Hapsy to take off her cap. I can't see her plain."

Her eyes opened very wide and the room stood out like a picture she had seen somewhere. Dark colors with the shadows rising toward the ceiling in long angles. The tall black dresser gleamed with nothing on it but John's picture, enlarged from a little one, with John's eyes very black when they should have been blue. You never saw him, so how do you know how he looked? But the man insisted the copy was perfect, it was very rich and handsome. For a picture, yes, but it's not my husband. The table by the bed had a linen cover and a candle and a crucifix. The light was blue from Cornelia's silk lampshades. No sort of light at all, just frippery. You had to live forty years with kerosene lamps to appreciate honest electricity. She

felt very strong and she saw Doctor Harry with a rosy nimbus around him.

"You look like a saint, Doctor Harry, and I vow that's as near as you'll ever come to it."

"She's saying something."

"I heard you, Cornelia. What's all this carrying-on?"

"Father Connolly's saying—"

Cornelia's voice staggered and bumped like a cart in a bad road. It rounded corners and turned back again and arrived nowhere. Granny stepped up in the cart very lightly and reached for the reins, but a man sat beside her and she knew him by his hands, driving the cart. She did not look in his face, for she knew without seeing, but looked instead down the road where the trees leaned over and bowed to each other and a thousand birds were singing a Mass. She felt like singing too, but she put her hand in the bosom of her dress and pulled out a rosary, and Father Connolly murmured Latin in a very solemn voice and tickled her feet. My God, will you stop that nonsense? I'm a married woman. What if he did run away and leave me to face the priest by myself? I found another a whole world better. I wouldn't have exchanged my husband for anybody except Saint Michael himself, and you may tell him that for me with a thank you in the bargain.

Light flashed on her closed eyelids, and a deep roaring shook her. Cornelia, is that lightning? I hear thunder. There's going to be a storm. Close all the windows. Call the children in. . . . "Mother, here we are, all of us." "Is that you, Hapsy?" "Oh, no, I'm Lydia. We drove as fast as we could." Their faces drifted above her, drifted away. The rosary fell out of her hands and Lydia put it back. Jimmy tried to help, their hands fumbled together, and Granny closed two fingers around Jimmy's thumb. Beads wouldn't do, it must be something alive. She was so amazed her thoughts ran round and round. So, my dear Lord, this is my death and I wasn't even thinking about it. My children have come to see me die. But I can't, it's not time. Oh, I always hated surprises. I wanted to give Cornelia the amethyst set—Cornelia, you're to have the amethyst set, but Hapsy's to wear it when she wants, and, Doctor Harry, do shut up. Nobody sent for you. Oh, my dear Lord, do wait a minute. I meant to do something about the Forty Acres, Jimmy doesn't need it and Lydia will later on, with that worthless husband of hers. I meant to finish the altar cloth and send six bottles of wine to Sister Borgia for her dyspepsia. I want to send six bottles of wine to Sister Borgia, Father Connolly, now don't let me forget.

Cornelia's voice made short turns and tilted over and crashed. "Oh, Mother, oh, Mother, oh, Mother . . ."

"I'm not going, Cornelia. I'm taken by surprise. I can't go."

You'll see Hapsy again. What about her? "I thought you'd never come." Granny made a long journey outward, looking for Hapsy. What if I don't find her? What then? Her heart sank down and down, there was no bottom to death, she couldn't come to the end of it. The blue light from Cornelia's lampshade drew into a tiny point in the center of her brain, it flickered and winked like an eye, quietly it fluttered and dwindled. Granny lay curled down within herself, amazed and watchful, staring at the point of light that was herself; her body now only a deeper mass of shadow in an endless darkness and this darkness would curl around the light and swallow it up. God, give a sign!

For the second time there was no sign. Again no bridegroom and the priest in the house. She could not remember any other sorrow because this grief wiped them all away. Oh, no, there's nothing more cruel than this—I'll never forgive it. She stretched herself with a deep breath and blew out the light.

INDIAN CAMP

At the lake shore there was another rowboat drawn up. The two Indians stood waiting.

Nick and his father got in the stern of the boat and the Indians shoved it off and one of them got in to row. Uncle George sat in the stern of the camp rowboat. The young Indian shoved the camp boat off and got in to row Uncle George.

The two boats started off in the dark. Nick heard the oarlocks of the other boat quite a way ahead of them in the mist. The Indians rowed with quick choppy strokes. Nick lay back with his father's arm around him. It was cold on the water. The Indian who was rowing them was working very hard, but the other boat moved further ahead in the mist all the time.

"Where are we going, Dad?" Nick asked.

"Over to the Indian camp. There is an Indian lady very sick."

"Oh," said Nick.

Across the bay they found the other boat beached. Uncle George was smoking a cigar in the dark. The young Indian pulled the boat way up on the beach. Uncle George gave both the Indians cigars.

They walked up from the beach through a meadow that was soaking wet with dew, following the young Indian who carried a lantern. Then they went into the woods and followed a trail that led to the logging road that ran back into the hills. It was much lighter on the logging road as the timber was cut away on both sides. The young Indian stopped and blew out his lantern and they all walked on along the road.

They came around a bend and a dog came out barking. Ahead were the lights of the shanties where the Indian bark-peelers lived. More dogs rushed out at them. The two Indians sent them back to the shanties. In the shanty nearest the road there was a light in the window. An old woman stood in the doorway holding a lamp.

Inside on a wooden bunk lay a young Indian woman. She had been trying to have her baby for two days. All the old women in the camp had been helping her. The men had moved off up the road to sit in the dark and smoke out of range of the noise she made. She screamed just as Nick and the two Indians followed his father and Uncle George into the shanty. She lay in the lower bunk, very big under a quilt. Her head was turned to one side. In the upper bunk was her husband. He had cut his foot very badly with an ax three days before. He was smoking a pipe. The room smelled very bad.

Nick's father ordered some water to be put on the stove, and while it was heating he spoke to Nick.

"This lady is going to have a baby, Nick," he said.

"I know," said Nick.

"You don't know," said his father. "Listen to me. What she is going through is called being in labor. The baby wants to be born and she wants it to be born. All her muscles are trying to get the baby born. That is what is happening when she screams."

"I see," Nick said.

Just then the woman cried out.

"Oh, Daddy, can't you give her something to make her stop screaming?" asked Nick.

"No. I haven't any anaesthetic," his father said. "But her screams are not important. I don't hear them because they are not important."

The husband in the upper bunk rolled over against the wall.

The woman in the kitchen motioned to the

106

↳A doctor can't concentrate on the pain.

doctor that the water was hot. Nick's father went into the kitchen and poured about half of the water out of the big kettle into a basin. Into the water left in the kettle he put several things he unwrapped from a handkerchief.

"Those must boil," he said, and began to scrub his hands in the basin of hot water with a cake of soap he had brought from the camp. Nick watched his father's hands scrubbing each other with the soap. While his father washed his hands very carefully and thoroughly, he talked.

"You see, Nick, babies are supposed to be born head first but sometimes they're not. When they're not they make a lot of trouble for everybody. Maybe I'll have to operate on this lady. We'll know in a little while."

When he was satisfied with his hands he went in and went to work.

"Pull back that quilt, will you, George?" he said. "I'd rather not touch it."

Later when he started to operate Uncle George and three Indian men held the woman still. She bit Uncle George on the arm and Uncle George said, "Damn squaw bitch!" and the young Indian who had rowed Uncle George over laughed at him. Nick held the basin for his father. It all took a long time.

His father picked the baby up and slapped it to make it breathe and handed it to the old woman.

"See, it's a boy, Nick," he said. "How do you like being an interne?"

Nick said, "All right." He was looking away so as not to see what his father was doing.

"There. That gets it," said his father and put something into the basin.

Nick didn't look at it.

"Now," his father said, "there's some stitches to put in. You can watch this or not, Nick, just as you like. I'm going to sew up the incision I made."

Nick did not watch. His curiosity had been gone for a long time. *Understatement. Overwhelmed.*

His father finished and stood up. Uncle George and the three Indian men stood up. Nick put the basin out in the kitchen.

Uncle George looked at his arm. The young Indian smiled reminiscently.

"I'll put some peroxide on that, George," the doctor said.

He bent over the Indian woman. She was quiet now and her eyes were closed. She looked very pale. She did not know what had become of the baby or anything.

"I'll be back in the morning," the doctor said, standing up. "The nurse should be here from St. Ignace by noon and she'll bring everything we need."

He was feeling exalted and talkative as football players are in the dressing room after a game.

"That's one for the medical journal, George," he said. "Doing a Caesarian with a jack-knife and sewing it up with nine-foot, tapered gut leaders."

Uncle George was standing against the wall, looking at his arm.

"Oh, you're a great man, all right," he said.

"Ought to have a look at the proud father. They're usually the worst sufferers in these little affairs," the doctor said. "I must say he took it all pretty quietly."

He pulled back the blanket from the Indian's head. His hand came away wet. He mounted on the edge of the lower bunk with the lamp in one hand and looked in. The Indian lay with his face toward the wall. His throat had been cut from ear to ear. The blood had flowed down into a pool where his body sagged the bunk. His head rested on his left arm. The open razor lay, edge up, in the blankets.

"Take Nick out of the shanty, George," the doctor said.

There was no need of that. Nick, standing in the door of the kitchen, had a good view of the upper bunk when his father, the lamp in one hand, tipped the Indian's head back.

It was just beginning to be daylight when they walked along the logging road back toward the lake.

"I'm terribly sorry I brought you along, Nickie," said his father, all his post-operative exhilaration gone. "It was an awful mess to put you through."

107

"Do ladies always have such a hard time having babies?" Nick asked.

"No, that was very, very exceptional."

"Why did he kill himself, Daddy?"

"I don't know, Nick. He couldn't stand things, I guess."

"Do many men kill themselves, Daddy?"

"Not very many, Nick."

"Do many women?"

"Hardly ever."

"Don't they ever?"

"Oh, yes. They do sometimes."

"Daddy?"

"Yes."

"Where did Uncle George go?"

"He'll turn up all right."

"Is dying hard, Daddy?"

"No, I think it's pretty easy, Nick. It all depends."

They were seated in the boat, Nick in the stern, his father rowing. The sun was coming up over the hills. A bass jumped, making a circle in the water. Nick trailed his hand in the water. It felt warm in the sharp chill of the morning.

In the early morning on the lake sitting in the stern of the boat with his father rowing, he felt quite sure that he would never die.

Birth & Death
Pain in both cuts

↑↓

Depression of the Indian Camp?

A child learns of life & death

Kuvad- father's sympathetic labor pains

Nick- between 8 and 12

Nice relationship between father and son.

Understatement

BRIGHT AND MORNING STAR

South in the late 20's or 30's during the Depression. Communism had a great appeal then; seemed to get at the root of economic problems.

I *Reva comes History of faith*

She stood with her black face some six inches from the moist windowpane and wondered when on earth would it ever stop raining. It might keep up like this all week, she thought. She heard rain droning upon the roof and high up in the wet sky her eyes followed the silent rush of a bright shaft of yellow that swung from the airplane beacon in far off Memphis. Momently she could see it cutting through the rainy dark; it would hover a second like a gleaming sword above her head, then vanish. She sighed, troubling, Johnny-Boys been tramp'n in this slop all day wid no decent shoes on his feet. . . . Through the window she could see the rich black earth sprawling outside in the night. There was more rain than the clay could soak up; pools stood everywhere. She yawned and mumbled: "Rains good n bad. It kin make seeds bus up thu the groun, er it kin bog things down lika watah-soaked coffin." Her hands were folded loosely over her stomach and the hot air of the kitchen traced a filmy veil of sweat on her forehead. From the cook stove came the soft singing of burning wood and now and then a throaty bubble rose from a pot of simmering greens.

"Shucks, Johnny-Boy coulda let somebody else do all tha runnin in the rain. Theres others bettah fixed fer it than he is. But, naw! Johnny-Boy ain the one t trust nobody t do nothin. Hes gotta do it *all* hissef. . . ."

She glanced at a pile of damp clothes in a zinc tub. Waal, Ah bettah git t work. She turned, lifted a smoothing iron with a thick pad of cloth, touched a spit-wet finger to it with a quick, jerking motion: *smiiitz!* Yeah;

its hot! Stooping, she took a blue workshirt from the tub and shook it out. With a deft twist of her shoulder she caught the iron in her right hand; the fingers of her left hand took a piece of wax from a tin box and a frying sizzle came as she smeared the bottom. She was thinking of nothing now; her hands followed a life-long ritual of toil. Spreading a sleeve, she ran the hot iron to and fro until the wet cloth became stiff. She was deep in the midst of her work when a song rose up out of the far off days of her childhood and broke through half-parted lips:

Hes the Lily of the Valley, the Bright n Mawnin Star
Hes the Fairest of Ten Thousan t mah soul . . .

A symbol striven toward

A gust of wind dashed rain against the window. Johnny-Boy oughta c mon home n eat his suppah. Aw, Lawd! Itd be fine ef Sug could eat wid us tonight! Itd be like ol times! Mabbe aftah all it wont be long fo he comes back. Tha lettah Ah got from im las week said *Don give up hope.* . . . Yeah; we gotta live in hope. Then both of her sons, Sug and Johnny-Boy, would be back with her.

With an involuntary nervous gesture, she stopped and stood still, listening. But the only sound was the lulling fall of rain. Shucks, ain no usa me ackin this way, she thought. Ever time they gits ready to hol them meetings Ah gits jumpity. Ah been a lil scared ever since Sug went t jail. She heard the clock ticking and looked. Johnny-Boys a *hour* late! He sho mus be havin a time doin all tha trampin, trampin thu the mud. . . . But her fear was a quiet one; it was more like an intense brooding than a fear; it was a sort of hugging of hated facts so closely that

109

she could feel their grain, like letting cold water run over her hand from a faucet on a winter morning.

She ironed again, faster now, as if she felt the more she engaged her body in work the less she would think. But how could she forget Johnny-Boy out there on those wet fields rounding up white and black Communists for a meeting tomorrow? And that was just what Sug had been doing when the sheriff had caught him, beat him, and tried to make him tell who and where his comrades were. Po Sug! They sho musta beat the boy somethin awful! But, thank Gawd, he didnt talk! He ain no weaklin, Sug ain! Hes been lion-hearted all his life long.

That had happened a year ago. And now each time those meetings came around the old terror surged back. While shoving the iron a cluster of toiling days returned; days of washing and ironing to feed Johnny-Boy and Sug so they could do party work; days of carrying a hundred pounds of white folks' clothes upon her head across fields sometimes wet and sometimes dry. But in those days a hundred pounds was nothing to carry carefully balanced upon her head while stepping by instinct over the corn and cotton rows. The only time it had seemed heavy was when she had heard of Sug's arrest. She had been coming home one morning with a bundle upon her head, her hands swinging idly by her sides, walking slowly with her eyes in front of her, when Bob, Johnny-Boy's pal, had called from across the fields and had come and told her that the sheriff had got Sug. That morning the bundle had become heavier than she could ever remember.

And with each passing week now, though she spoke of it to no one, things were becoming heavier. The tubs of water and the smoothing iron and the bundle of clothes were becoming harder to lift, with her back aching so; and her work was taking longer, all because Sug was gone and she didn't know just when Johnny-Boy would be taken too. To ease the ache of anxiety that was swelling her heart, she hummed, then sang softly:

> *He walks wid me, He talks wid me*
> *He tells me Ahm His own. . . .*

Guiltily, she stopped and smiled. Looks like Ah jus cant seem t fergit them ol songs, no mattah how hard Ah tries. . . . She had learned them when she was a little girl living and working on a farm. Every Monday morning from the corn and cotton fields the slow strains had floated from her mother's lips, lonely and haunting; and later, as the years had filled with gall, she had learned their deep meaning. Long hours of scrubbing floors for a few cents a day had taught her who Jesus was, what a great boon it was to cling to Him, to be like Him and suffer without a mumbling word. She had poured the yearning of her life into the songs, feeling buoyed with a faith beyond this world. The figure of the Man nailed in agony to the Cross, His burial in a cold grave, His transfigured Resurrection, His being breath and clay, God and Man—all had focused her feelings upon an imagery which had swept her life into a wondrous vision.

But as she had grown older, a cold white mountain, the white folks and their laws, had swum into her vision and shattered her songs and their spell of peace. To her that white mountain was temptation, something to lure her from her Lord, a part of the world God had made in order that she might endure it and come through all the stronger, just as Christ had risen with greater glory from the tomb. The days crowded with trouble had enhanced her faith and she had grown to love hardship with a bitter pride; she had obeyed the laws of the white folks with a soft smile of secret knowing.

After her mother had been snatched up to heaven in a chariot of fire, the years had brought her a rough workingman and two black babies, Sug and Johnny-Boy, all three of whom she had wrapped in the charm and

she has the flaw of hubris

magic of her vision. Then she was tested by no less than God; her man died, a trial which she bore with the strength shed by the grace of her vision; finally even the memory of her man faded into the vision itself, leaving her with two black boys growing tall, slowly into manhood.

Then one day grief had come to her heart when Johnny-Boy and Sug had walked forth demanding their lives. She had sought to fill their eyes with her vision, but they would have none of it. And she had wept when they began to boast of the strength shed by a new and terrible vision.

But she had loved them, even as she loved them now; bleeding, her heart had followed them. She could have done no less, being an old woman in a strange world. And day by day her sons had ripped from her startled eyes her old vision, and image by image had given her a new one, different, but great and strong enough to fling her into the light of another grace. The wrongs and sufferings of black men had taken the place of Him nailed to the Cross; the meager beginnings of the party had become another Resurrection; and the hate of those who would destroy her new faith had quickened in her a hunger to feel how deeply her new strength went. *Her emotional senses are still in the old. She overacts to show she believes in the new order.*

"Lawd, Johnny-Boy," she would sometimes say, "Ah just wan them white folks t try t make me tell *who* is *in* the party n who *ain*! Ah just wan em t try, n Ahll show em somethin they never thought a black woman could have!"

But sometimes like tonight, while lost in the forgetfulness of work, her past and the present would become mixed in her; while toiling under a strange star for a new freedom the old songs would slip from her lips with their beguiling sweetness.

The iron was getting cold. She put more wood into the fire, stood again at the window and watched the yellow blade of light cut through the wet darkness. Johnny-Boy ain here yit. . . . Then, before she was aware of it, she was still, listening for sounds. Under the drone of rain she heard the slosh of feet in mud. Tha ain Johnny-Boy. She knew his long, heavy footsteps in a million. She heard feet come on the porch. Some woman. . . . She heard bare knuckles knock three times, then once. Thas some of them comrades! She unbarred the door, cracked it a few inches, and flinched from the cold rush of damp wind.

"Whos tha?"

"Its me!"

"Who?"

"Me, Reva!"

She flung the door open.

"Lawd, chile c mon in!"

She stepped to one side and a thin, blond-haired white girl ran through the door; as she slid the bolt she heard the girl gasping and shaking her wet clothes. Somethings wrong! Reva wouldna walked a mile t mah house in all this slop fer nothin! Tha gals stuck onto Johnny-Boy. Ah wondah ef anything happened t im?

"Git on inter the kitchen, Reva, where its warm."

"Lawd, Ah sho is wet!"

"How yuh reckon yuhd be, in all tha rain?"

"Johnny-Boy ain here *yit*?" asked Reva.

"Naw! N ain no usa yuh worryin bout im. Jus yuh git them shoes off! Yuh wanna ketch yo deatha col?" She stood looking absently. Yeah; its somethin about the party er Johnny-Boy thas gone wrong. Lawd, Ah wondah ef her pa knows how she feels bout Johnny-Boy? "Honey, yuh hadnt oughta come out in sloppy weather like this."

"Ah had t come, An Sue."

She led Reva to the kitchen.

"Git them shoes off n git close t the stove so yuhll git dry!"

"An Sue, Ah got somethin t tell yuh . . ."

The words made her hold her breath. Ah bet its somethin bout Johnny-Boy!

"Whut, honey?"

Star — Flag, Freedom

111

"The sheriff wuz by our house tonight. He come t see pa."

"Yeah?"

"He done got word from somewheres bout tha meetin tomorrow."

"Is it Johnny-Boy, Reva?"

"Aw, naw, An Sue! Ah ain hearda word bout im. Ain yuh seen im tonight?"

"He ain come home t eat yit."

"Where kin he be?"

"Lawd knows, chile."

"Somebodys gotta tell them comrades tha meetings off," said Reva. "The sheriffs got men watchin our house. Ah had t slip out t git here widout em followin me."

"Reva?"

"Hunh?"

"Ahma ol woman n Ah wans yuh t tell me the truth."

"Whut, An Sue?"

"Yuh ain tryin t fool me, is yuh?"

"*Fool* yuh?"

"Bout Johnny-Boy?"

"Lawd, naw, An Sue!"

"Ef theres anythin wrong jus tell me, chile. Ah kin stan it."

She stood by the ironing board, her hands as usual folded loosely over her stomach, watching Reva pull off her water-clogged shoes. She was feeling that Johnny-Boy was already lost to her; she was feeling the pain that would come when she knew it for certain; and she was feeling that she would have to be brave and bear it. She was like a person caught in a swift current of water and knew where the water was sweeping her and did not want to go on but had to go on to the end.

"It ain nothin bout Johnny-Boy, An Sue," said Reva. "But we gotta do somethin er we'll all git inter trouble."

"How the sheriff know about tha meetin?"

"Thas whut pa wans t know."

"Somebody done turned Judas."

"Sho looks like it."

"Ah bet it wuz some of them new ones," she said.

"Its hard t tell," said Reva.

"Lissen, Reva, yuh oughta stay here n git dry, but yuh bettah get back n tell yo pa Johnny-Boy ain here n Ah don know when hes gonna show up. *Some*bodys gotta tell them comrades t stay erway from yo pas house."

She stood with her back to the window, looking at Reva's wide, blue eyes. Po critter! Gotta go back thu all tha slop! Though she felt sorry for Reva, not once did she think that it would not have to be done. Being a woman, Reva was not suspect; she would *have* to go. It was just as natural for Reva to go back through the cold rain as it was for her to iron night and day, or for Sug to be in jail. Right now, Johnny-Boy was out there on those dark fields trying to get home. Lawd, don let em git im tonight! In spite of herself her feelings became torn. She loved her son and, loving him, she loved what he was trying to do. Johnny-Boy was happiest when he was working for the party, and her love for him was for his happiness. She frowned, trying hard to fit something together in her feelings: for her to try to stop Johnny-Boy was to admit that all the toil of years meant nothing; and to let him go meant that sometime or other he would be caught, like Sug. In facing it this way she felt a little stunned, as though she had come suddenly upon a blank wall in the dark. But outside in the rain were people, white and black, whom she had known all her life. Those people depended upon Johnny-Boy, loved him and looked to him as a man and leader. Yeah; hes gotta keep on; he cant stop now. . . . She looked at Reva; she was crying and pulling her shoes back on with reluctant fingers.

"Whut yuh carryin on tha way fer, chile?"

"Yuh done los Sug, now yuh sendin Johnny-Boy . . ."

"Ah got t, honey."

She was glad she could say that. Reva believed in black folks and not for anything in the world would she falter before her. In Reva's trust and acceptance of her she had found her first feelings of humanity; Reva's love was her refuge from shame and degradation. If in the early days of her life the white mountain had driven her back from the earth, then in her last days Reva's love was drawing her toward it, like the beacon that swung through the night outside. She heard Reva sobbing.

"Hush, honey!"

"Mah brothers in jail too! Ma cries ever day . . ."

"Ah know, honey."

She helped Reva with her coat; her fingers felt the scant flesh of the girl's shoulders. She don git ernuff t eat, she thought. She slipped her arms around Reva's waist and held her close for a moment.

"Now, yuh stop that cryin."

"A-a-ah c-c-cant hep it. . . ."

"Everythingll be awright; Johnny-Boyll be back."

"Yuh think so?"

"Sho, chile. Cos he will."

Neither of them spoke again until they stood in the doorway. Outside they could hear water washing through the ruts of the street.

"Be sho n send Johnny-Boy t tell the folks t stay erway from pas house," said Reva.

"Ahll tell im. Don yuh worry."

"Good-bye!"

"Good-bye!"

Leaning against the door jamb, she shook her head slowly and watched Reva vanish through the falling rain.

II Johnny-Boy comes

She was back at her board, ironing, when she heard feet sucking in the mud of the back yard; feet she knew from long years of listening were Johnny-Boy's. But tonight, with all the rain and fear, his coming was like a leaving, was almost more than she could bear. Tears welled to her eyes and she blinked them away. She felt that he was coming so that she could give him up; to see him now was to say good-bye. But it was a good-bye she knew she could never say; they were not that way toward each other. All day long

they could sit in the same room and not speak; she was his mother and he was her son. Most of the time a nod or a grunt would carry all the meaning that she wanted to convey to him, or he to her. She did not even turn her head when she heard him come stomping into the kitchen. She heard him pull up a chair, sit, sigh, and draw off his muddy shoes; they fell to the floor with heavy thuds. Soon the kitchen was full of the scent of his drying socks and his burning pipe. Tha boys hongry! She paused and looked at him over her shoulder; he was puffing at his pipe with his head tilted back and his feet propped up on the edge of the stove; his eyelids drooped and his wet clothes steamed from the heat of the fire. Lawd, tha boy gits mo like his pa ever day he lives, she mused, her lips breaking in a slow faint smile. Hols tha pipe in his mouth just like his pa usta hol his. Wondah how they woulda got erlong ef his pa hada lived? They oughta liked each other, they so mucha like. She wished there could have been other children besides Sug, so Johnny-Boy would not have to be so much alone. A man needs a woman by his side. . . . She thought of Reva; she liked Reva; the brightest glow her heart had ever known was when she had learned that Reva loved Johnny-Boy. But beyond Reva were cold white faces. Ef theys caught it means *death*. . . . She jerked around when she heard Johnny-Boy's pipe clatter to the floor. She saw him pick it up, smile sheepishly at her, and wag his head.

"Gawd, Ahm sleepy," he mumbled.

She got a pillow from her room and gave it to him.

"Here," she said.

"Hunh," he said, putting the pillow between his head and the back of the chair.

They were silent again. Yes, she would have to tell him to go back out into the cold rain and slop; maybe to get caught; maybe for the last time; she didn't know. But she would let him eat and get dry before telling him that the sheriff knew of the meeting to be held at Lem's tomorrow. And she would make him take a big dose of soda before he went out; soda always helped to stave off a cold. She looked at the clock. It was eleven. Theres time yit. Spreading a newspaper on the apron of the stove, she placed a heaping plate of greens upon it, a knife, a fork, a cup of coffee, a slab of cornbread, and a dish of peach cobbler.

"Yo suppahs ready," she said.

"Yeah," he said.

He did not move. She ironed again. Presently, she heard him eating. When she could no longer hear his knife tinkling against the edge of the plate, she knew he was through. It was almost twelve now. She would let him rest a little while longer before she told him. Till one er'clock, mabbe. Hes so tired. . . . She finished her ironing, put away the board, and stacked the clothes in her dresser drawer. She poured herself a cup of black coffee, drew up a chair, sat down and drank.

"Yuh almos dry," she said, not looking around.

"Yeah," he said, turning sharply to her.

The tone of voice in which she had spoken had let him know that more was coming. She drained her cup and waited a moment longer.

"Reva wuz here."

"Yeah?"

"She lef bout a hour ergo."

"Whut she say?"

"She said ol man Lem hada visit from the sheriff today."

"Bout the meetin?"

"Yeah."

She saw him stare at the coals glowing red through the crevices of the stove and run his fingers nervously through his hair. She knew he was wondering how the sheriff had found out. In the silence he would ask a wordless question and in the silence she would answer wordlessly. Johnny-Boys too trustin, she thought. Hes trying t make the party big n hes takin in folks fastern he kin get t know em. You cant trust ever white man yuh meet. . . .

"Yuh know, Johnny-Boy, yuh been takin in a lotta them white folks lately . . ."

"Aw, ma!"

"But, Johnny-Boy . . ."

"Please, don talk t me bout tha now, ma."

"Yuh ain t ol t lissen n learn, son," she said.

"Ah know whut yuh gonna say, ma. N yuh wrong. Yuh cant judge folks jus by how yuh feel bout em n by how long yuh done knowed em. Ef we start tha we wouldnt have *no*body in the party. When folks pledge they word t be with us, then we gotta take em in. Wes too weak t be choosy."

He rose abruptly, rammed his hands into his pockets, and stood facing the window; she looked at his back in a long silence. She knew his faith; it was deep. He had always said that black men could not fight the rich bosses alone; a man could not fight with every hand against him. But he believes so hard hes blind, she thought. At odd times they had had these arguments before; always she would be pitting her feelings against the hard necessity of his thinking, and always she would lose. She shook her head. Po Johnny-Boy; he dont know . . .

"But ain nona our folks tol, Johnny-Boy," she said.

"How yuh know?" he asked. His voice came low and with a tinge of anger. He still faced the window and now and then the yellow blade of light flicked across the sharp outline of his black face.

"Cause Ah know em," she said.

"*Any*body mighta tol," he said.

"It wuznt nona *our* folks," she said again.

She saw his hand sweep in a swift arc of disgust.

"*Our* folks! Ma, who in Gawds name is *our* folks?"

"The folks we wuz born n raised wid, son. The folks we *know*!"

"We cant make the party grow tha way, ma."

"It mighta been Booker," she said.

"Yuh don know."

". . . er Blattberg . . ."

"Fer Chrissakes!"

". . . er any of the fo-five others whut joined las week."

"Ma, yuh jus don wan me t go out tonight," he said.

"Yo ol ma wans yuh t be careful, son."

"Ma, when yuh start doubtin folks in the party, then there ain no end."

"Son, Ah knows ever black man n woman in this parta the country," she said, standing too. "Ah watched em grow up; Ah even heped birth n nurse some of em; Ah knows em *all* from way back. There ain none of em that *coulda* tol! The folks Ah know jus don open they dos n ast death t walk in! Son, it wuz some of them *white* folks! Yuh jus mark mah word n wait n see!"

"Why is it gotta be *white* folks?" he asked. "Ef they tol, then theys jus Judases, thas all."

"Son, look at whuts befo yuh."

He shook his head and sighed.

"Ma, Ah done tol yuh a hundred times. Ah cant see white n Ah cant see black," he said. "Ah sees rich men n Ah sees po men."

She picked up his dirty dishes and piled them in a pan. Out of the corners of her eyes she saw him sit and pull on his wet shoes. Hes goin! When she put the last dish away he was standing fully dressed, warming his hands over the stove. Jus a few mo minutes now n he'll be gone, like Sug, mabbe. Her throat tightened. This black mans fight takes *everthin*! Looks like Gawd put us in this worl jus t beat us down!

"Keep this, ma," he said.

She saw a crumpled wad of money in his outstretched fingers.

"Naw; yuh keep it. Yuh might need it."

"It ain mine, ma. It berlongs t the party."

"But, Johnny-Boy, yuh might hafta go erway!"

"Ah kin make out."

"Don fergit yosef too much, son."

"Ef Ah don come back theyll need it."

He was looking at her face and she was looking at the money.

"Yuh keep tha," she said slowly. "Ahll give em the money."

"From where?"

"Ah got some."

"Where yuh git it from?"

She sighed.

"Ah been savin a dollah a week for Sug ever since hes been in jail."

"Lawd, ma!"

She saw the look of puzzled love and wonder in his eyes. Clumsily, he put the money back into his pocket.

"Ahm gone," he said.

"Here; drink this glass of soda watah."

She watched him drink, then put the glass away.

"Waal," he said.

"Take the stuff outta yo pockets!"

She lifted the lid of the stove and he dumped all the papers from his pocket into the fire. She followed him to the door and made him turn round.

"Lawd, yuh tryin to maka revolution n yuh cant even keep yo coat buttoned." Her nimble fingers fastened his collar high around his throat. "There!"

He pulled the brim of his hat low over his eyes. She opened the door and with the suddenness of the cold gust of wind that struck her face, he was gone. She watched the black fields and the rain take him, her eyes burning. When the last faint footstep could no longer be heard, she closed the door, went to her bed, lay down, and pulled the cover over her while fully dressed. Her feelings coursed with the rhythm of the rain: Hes gone! Lawd, Ah *know* hes gone! Her blood felt cold.

III

She was floating in a grey void somewhere between sleeping and dreaming and then suddenly she was wide awake, hearing and feeling in the same instant the thunder of the door crashing in and a cold wind filling the room. It was pitch black and she stared, resting her elbows, her mouth open, not breathing, her ears full of the sound of tramping

115

feet and booming voices. She knew at once: They lookin fer im! Then, filled with her will, she was on her feet, rigid, waiting, listening.

"The lamps burnin!"

"Yuh see her?"

"Naw!"

"Look in the kitchen!"

"Gee, this place smells like niggers!"

"Say, somebodys here er been here!"

"Yeah; theres fire in the stove!"

"Mabbe hes been here n gone?"

"Boy, look at these jars of jam!"

"Niggers make good jam!"

"Git some bread!"

"Heres some cornbread!"

"Say, lemme git some!"

"Take it easy! Theres plenty here!"

"Ahma take some of this stuff home!"

"Look, heres a pota greens!"

"N some hot cawffee!"

"Say, yuh guys! Cmon! Cut it out! We didnt come here fer a feas!"

She walked slowly down the hall. They lookin fer im, but they ain got im yit! She stopped in the doorway, her gnarled, black hands as always folded over her stomach, but tight now, so tightly the veins bulged. The kitchen was crowded with white men in glistening raincoats. Though the lamp burned, their flashlights still glowed in red fists. Across her floor she saw the muddy tracks of their boots.

"Yuh white folks git outta mah house!"

There was quick silence; every face turned toward her. She saw a sudden movement, but did not know what it meant until something hot and wet slammed her squarely in the face. She gasped, but did not move. Calmly, she wiped the warm, greasy liquor of greens from her eyes with her left hand. One of the white men had thrown a handful of greens out of the pot at her.

"How they taste, ol bitch?"

"Ah ast yuh t git outta mah house!"

She saw the sheriff detach himself from the crowd and walk toward her.

"Now, Anty . . ."

"White man, don yuh *Anty* me!"

"Yuh ain got the right sperit!"

"Sperit hell! Yuh git these men outta mah house!"

"Yuh ack like yuh don like it!"

"Naw, Ah don like it, n yuh knows dam waal Ah don!"

"Whut yuh gonna do bout it?"

"Ahm tellin yuh git outta mah house!"

"Gittin sassy?"

"Ef telling yuh t git outta mah house is sass, then Ahm sassy!"

Her words came in a tense whisper, but beyond, back of them, she was watching, thinking, judging the men.

"Listen, Anty," the sheriff's voice came soft and low. "Ahm here t hep yuh. How come yuh wanna ack this way?"

"Yuh ain never heped yo *own* sef since yuh been born," she flared. "How kin the likes of yuh hep me?"

One of the white men came forward and stood directly in front of her.

"Lissen, nigger woman, yuh talkin t *white* men!"

"Ah don care who Ahm talkin t!"

"Yuhll wish some day yuh did!"

"Not t the likes of yuh!"

"Yuh need somebody t teach yuh how t be a good nigger!"

"*Yuh* cant teach it t me!"

"Yuh gonna change yo tune."

"Not longs mah bloods warm!"

"Don git smart now!"

"Yuh git outta mah house!"

"Spose we don go?" the sheriff asked.

They were crowded around her. She had not moved since she had taken her place in the doorway. She was thinking only of Johnny-Boy as she stood there giving and taking words; and she knew that they, too, were thinking of Johnny-Boy. She knew they wanted him, and her heart was daring them to take him from her.

"Spose we don go?" the sheriff asked again.

"Twenty of yuh runnin over one ol woman! Now, ain yuh white men glad yuh so brave?"

The sheriff grabbed her arm.

"C mon, now! Yuh done did ernuff sass fer one night. Wheres tha nigger son of yos?"

"Don yuh wished yuh knowed?"

"Yuh wanna git slapped?"

"Ah ain never seen one of yo kind tha wuznt too low fer . . ."

The sheriff slapped her straight across her face with his open palm. She fell back against a wall and sank to her knees.

"Is tha whut white men do t nigger women?"

She rose slowly and stood again, not even touching the place that ached from his blow, her hands folded over her stomach.

"Ah ain never seen one of yo kind tha wuznt too low fer . . ."

He slapped her again; she reeled backward several feet and fell on her side.

"Is tha whut we too low t do?"

She stood before him again, dry-eyed, as though she had not been struck. Her lips were numb and her chin was wet with blood.

"Aw, let her go! Its the nigger we wan!" said one.

"Wheres that nigger son of yos?" the sheriff asked.

"Find im," she said.

"By Gawd, ef we hafta find im we'll kill im!"

"He wont be the only nigger yuh ever killed," she said.

She was consumed with a bitter pride. There was nothing on this earth, she felt then, that they could not do to her but that she could take. She stood on a narrow plot of ground from which she would die before she was pushed. And then it was, while standing there feeling warm blood seeping down her throat, that she gave up Johnny-Boy, gave him up to the white folks. She gave him up because they had come tramping into her heart demanding him, thinking they could get him by beating her, thinking they could scare her into making her tell where he was. She gave him up because she wanted them to know that they could not get what they wanted by bluffing and killing.

"Wheres this meetin gonna be?" the sheriff asked.

"Don yuh wish yuh knowed?"

"Ain there gonna be a meetin?"

"How come yuh astin me?"

"There *is* gonna be a meetin," said the sheriff.

"Is it?"

"Ah gotta great mind t choke it outta yuh!"

"Yuh so smart," she said.

"We ain playin wid yuh!"

"Did Ah say yuh wuz?"

"Tha nigger son of yos is erroun here somewheres n we aim t find im," said the sheriff. "Ef yuh tell us where he is n ef he talks, mabbe he'll git off easy. But ef we hafta find im, we'll kill im! Ef we hafta find im, then yuh git a sheet t put over im in the mawnin, see? Gut yuh a sheet, cause hes gonna be dead!"

"He wont be the only nigger yuh ever killed," she said again.

The sheriff walked past her. The others followed. Yuh didn't git whut yuh wanted! she thought exultingly. N yuh ain gonna *never* git it! Hotly, something ached in her to make them feel the intensity of her pride and freedom; her heart groped to turn the bitter hours of her life into words of a kind that would make them feel that she had taken all they had done to her in her stride and could still take more. Her faith surged so strongly in her she was all but blinded. She walked behind them to the door, knotting and twisting her fingers. She saw them step to the muddy ground. Each whirl of the yellow beacon revealed glimpses of slanting rain. Her lips moved, then she shouted:

"Yuh didnt git whut yuh wanted! N yuh ain gonna nevah git it!"

The sheriff stopped and turned; his voice came low and hard.

"Now, by Gawd, thas ernuff outta yuh!"

"Ah know when Ah done said ernuff!"

"Aw, naw, yuh don!" he said. "Yuh don know when yuh done said ernuff, but Ahma teach yuh ternight!"

He was up the steps and across the porch with one bound. She backed into the hall, her eyes full on his face.

"Tell me when yuh gonna stop talkin!" he said, swinging his fist.

The blow caught her high on the cheek; her eyes went blank; she fell flat on her face. She felt the hard heel of his wet shoes coming into her temple and stomach.

"Lemme hear yuh talk some mo!"

She wanted to, but could not; pain numbed and choked her. She lay still and somewhere out of the grey void of unconsciousness she heard someone say: *aw fer chrissakes leave her erlone its the nigger we wan....*

IV Tells Booker

She never knew how long she had lain huddled in the dark hallway. Her first returning feeling was of a nameless fear crowding the inside of her, then a deep pain spreading from her temple downward over her body. Her ears were filled with the drone of rain and she shuddered from the cold wind blowing through the door. She opened her eyes and at first saw nothing. As if she were imagining it, she knew she was half-lying and half-sitting in a corner against a wall. With difficulty she twisted her neck and what she saw made her hold her breath—a vast white blur was suspended directly above her. For a moment she could not tell if her fear was from the blur or if the blur was from her fear. Gradually the blur resolved itself into a huge white face that slowly filled her vision. She was stone still, conscious really of the effort to breathe, feeling somehow that she existed only by the mercy of that white face. She had seen it before; its fear had gripped her many times; it had for her the fear of all the white faces she had ever seen in her life. *Sue* . . . As from a great distance, she heard her name being called. She was regaining consciousness now, but the fear was coming with her. She looked into the face of a white man, wanting to scream out for him to go; yet accepting his presence because she felt she had to. Though

some remote part of her mind was active, her limbs were powerless. It was as if an invisible knife had split her in two, leaving one half of her lying there helpless, while the other half shrank in dread from a forgotten but familiar enemy. *Sue its me Sue its me* . . . Then all at once the voice came clearly.

"Sue, its me! Its Booker!"

And she heard an answering voice speaking inside of her, Yeah, its Booker . . . The one whut jus joined . . . She roused herself, struggling for full consciousness; and as she did so she transferred to the person of Booker the nameless fear she felt. It seemed that Booker towered above her as a challenge to her right to exist upon the earth.

"Yuh awright?"

She did not answer; she started violently to her feet and fell.

"Sue, yuh hurt!"

"Yeah," she breathed.

"Where they hit yuh?"

"Its mah head," she whispered.

She was speaking even though she did not want to; the fear that had hold of her compelled her.

"They beat yuh?"

"Yeah."

"Them bastards! Them Gawddam bastards!"

She heard him saying it over and over; then she felt herself being lifted.

"Naw!" she gasped.

"Ahma take yuh t the kitchen!"

"Put me down!"

"But yuh cant stay here like this!"

She shrank in his arms and pushed her hands against his body; when she was in the kitchen she freed herself, sank into a chair, and held tightly to its back. She looked wonderingly at Booker. There was nothing about him that should frighten her so, but even that did not ease her tension. She saw him go to the water bucket, wet his handkerchief, wring it, and offer it to her. Distrustfully, she stared at the damp cloth.

"Here; put this on yo fohead . . ."

"Naw!"

"C mon; itll make yuh feel bettah!"

She hesitated in confusion. What right had she to be afraid when someone was acting as kindly as this toward her? Reluctantly, she leaned forward and pressed the damp cloth to her head. It helped. With each passing minute she was catching hold of herself, yet wondering why she felt as she did.

"Whut happened?"

"Ah don know."

"Yuh feel bettah?"

"Yeah."

"Who all wuz here?"

"Ah don know," she said again.

"Yo head still hurt?"

"Yeah."

"Gee, Ahm sorry."

"Ahm awright," she sighed and buried her face in her hands.

She felt him touch her shoulder.

"Sue, Ah got some bad news fer yuh . . ."

She knew; she stiffened and grew cold. It had happened; she stared dry-eyed, with compressed lips.

"Its mah Johnny-Boy," she said.

"Yeah; Ahm awful sorry t hafta tell yuh this way. But Ah thought yuh oughta know . . ."

Her tension eased and a vacant place opened up inside of her. A voice whispered, Jesus, hep me!

"W-w-where is he?"

"They got im out t Foleys Woods tryin t make im tell who the others is."

"He ain gonna tell," she said. "They just as waal kill im, cause he ain gonna nevah tell."

"Ah hope he don," said Booker. "But he didnt hava chance t tell the others. They grabbed im jus as he got t the woods."

Then all the horror of it flashed upon her; she saw flung out over the rainy countryside an array of shacks where white and black comrades were sleeping; in the morning they would be rising and going to Lem's; then they would be caught. And that meant terror, prison, and death. The comrades would have to be told; she would have to tell them; she could not entrust Johnny-Boy's work to another, and especially not to Booker as long

as she felt toward him as she did. Gripping the bottom of the chair with both hands, she tried to rise; the room blurred and she swayed. She found herself resting in Booker's arms.

"Lemme go!"

"Sue, yuh too weak t walk!"

"Ah gotta tell em!" she said.

"Set down, Sue! Yuh hurt! Yuh sick!"

When seated, she looked at him helplessly.

"Sue, lissen! Johnny-Boys caught. Ahm here. Yuh tell me who they is n Ahll tell em."

She stared at the floor and did not answer. Yes; she was too weak to go. There was no way for her to tramp all those miles through the rain tonight. But should she tell Booker? If only she had somebody like Reva to talk to! She did not want to decide alone; she must make no mistake about this. She felt Booker's fingers pressing on her arm and it was as though the white mountain was pushing her to the edge of a sheer height; she again exclaimed inwardly, Jesus, hep me! Booker's white face was at her side, waiting. Would she be doing right to tell him? Suppose she did not tell and then the comrades were caught? She could not ever forgive herself for doing a thing like that. But maybe she was wrong; maybe her fear was what Johnny-Boy had always called "jus foolishness." She remembered his saying, Ma we cant make the party grow ef we start doubtin everbody. . . .

"Tell me who they is, Sue, n Ahll tell em. Ah jus joined n Ah don know who they is."

"Ah don know who they is," she said.

"Yuh *gotta* tell me who they is, Sue!"

"Ah tol yuh Ah don know!"

"Yuh *do* know! C mon! Set up n talk!"

"Naw!"

"Yuh wan em all t git *killed?*"

She shook her head and swallowed. Lawd, Ah don blieve in this man!

"Lissen, Ahll call the names n yuh tell me which ones is in the party n which ones ain, see?"

"Naw!"

"Please, Sue!"

"Ah don know," she said.

"Sue, yuh ain doin right by em. Johnny-Boy wouldnt wan yuh t be this way. Hes out there holdin up his end. Les hol up ours . . ."

"Lawd, Ah don know . . ."

"Is yuh scareda me cause Ahm *white*? Johnny-Boy ain like tha. Don let all the work we done go fer nothin."

She gave up and bowed her head in her hands.

"It it Johnson? Tell me, Sue?"

"Yeah," she whispered in horror; a mounting horror of feeling herself being undone.

"Is it Green?"

"Yeah."

"Murphy?"

"Lawd, Ah don know!"

"Yuh gotta tell me, Sue!"

"Mistah Booker, please leave me er-lone . . ."

"Is it Murphy?"

She answered yes to the names of Johnny-Boy's comrades; she answered until he asked her no more. Then she thought, How he know the sheriffs men is watchin Lems house? She stood up and held onto her chair, feeling something sure and firm within her.

"How yuh know bout Lem?"

"Why . . . How Ah know?"

"Whut yuh doin here this tima night? How yuh know the sheriffs got Johnny-Boy?"

"Sue, don yuh blieve in me?"

She did not, but she could not answer. She stared at him until her lips hung open; she was searching deep within herself for certainty.

"You meet Reva?" she asked.

"Reva?"

"Yeah; Lems gal?"

"Oh, yeah. Sho, Ah met Reva."

"She tell yuh?"

She asked the question more of herself than of him; she longed to believe.

"Yeah," he said softly. "Ah reckon Ah oughta be goin t tell em now."

"Who?" she asked. "Tell *who*?"

The muscles of her body were stiff as she waited for his answer; she felt as thought life depended upon it.

"The comrades," he said.

"Yeah," she sighed.

She did not know when he left; she was not looking or listening. She just suddenly saw the room empty and from her the thing that had made her fearful was gone.

V

For a space of time that seemed to her as long as she had been upon the earth, she sat huddled over the cold stove. One minute she would say to herself, They both gone now; Johnny-Boy n Sug . . . Mabbe Ahll never see em ergin. Then a surge of guilt would blot out her longing. "Lawd, Ah shouldna tol!" she mumbled. "But no man kin be so low-down as to do a thing like that . . ." Several times she had an impulse to try to tell the comrades herself; she was feeling a little better now. But what good would that do? She had told Booker the names. He jus couldn't be a Judas to po folks like us . . . He *couldnt!*

"An Sue!"

Thas Reva! Her heart leaped with an anxious gladness. She rose without answering and limped down the dark hallway. Through the open door, against the background of rain, she saw Reva's face lit now and then to whiteness by the whirling beams of the beacon. She was about to call, but a thought checked her. Jesus, hep me! Ah gotta tell her bout Johnny-Boy . . . Lawd, Ah cant!

"An Sue, yuh there?"

"C mon in, chile!"

She caught Reva and held her close for a moment without speaking.

"Lawd, Ahm sho glad yuh here," she said at last.

"Ah thought somethin had happened t yuh," said Reva, pulling away. "Ah saw the do open . . . Pa tol me to come back n stay wid yuh tonight . . .'" Reva paused and started. "W-w-whuts the mattah?"

120

She was so full of having Reva with her that she did not understand what the question meant.

"Hunh?"

"Yo neck . . ."

"Aw, it ain nothin, chile. C mon in the kitchen."

"But theres blood on yo neck!"

"The sheriff wuz here . . ."

"Them fools! Whut they wanna bother yuh fer? Ah could kill em! So help me Gawd, Ah could!"

"It ain nothin," she said.

She was wondering how to tell Reva about Johnny-Boy and Booker. Ahll wait a lil while longer, she thought. Now that Reva was here, her fear did not seem as awful as before.

"C mon, lemme fix yo head, An Sue. Yuh hurt."

They went to the kitchen. She sat silent while Reva dressed her scalp. She was feeling better now; in just a little while she would tell Reva. She felt the girl's finger pressing gently upon her head.

"Tha hurt?"

"A lil, chile."

"Yuh po thing."

"It ain nothin."

"Did Johnny-Boy come?"

She hesitated.

"Yeah."

"He done gone t tell the others?"

Reva's voice sounded so clear and confident that it mocked her. Lawd, Ah cant tell this chile . . .

"Yuh tol im, didnt yuh, An Sue?"

"Y-y-yeah . . ."

"Gee! Thas good! Ah tol pa he didnt hafta worry ef Johnny-Boy got the news. Mabbe thingsll come out awright."

"Ah hope . . ."

She could not go on; she had gone as far as she could. For the first time that night she began to cry.

"Hush, An Sue! Yuh awways been brave. Itll be awright!"

"Ain nothin awright, chile. The worls jus too much fer us, Ah reckon."

"Ef yuh cry that way itll make me cry."

She forced herself to stop. Naw; Ah cant carry on this way in fronta Reva . . . Right now she had a deep need for Reva to believe in her. She watched the girl get pine-knots from behind the stove, rekindle the fire, and put on the coffee pot.

"Yuh wan some cawffee?" Reva asked.

"Naw, honey."

"Aw, c mon, An Sue."

"Jusa lil, honey."

"Thas the way to be. Oh, say, Ah fergot," said Reva, measuring out spoonsful of coffee. "Pa tol me t tell yuh t watch out fer tha Booker man. Hes a stool."

She showed not one sign of outward movement or expression, but as the words fell from Reva's lips she went limp inside.

"Pa tol me soon as Ah got back home. He got word from town . . ."

She stopped listening. She felt as though she had been slapped to the extreme outer edge of life, into a cold darkness. She knew now what she had felt when she had looked up out of her fog of pain and had seen Booker. It was the image of all the white folks, and the fear that went with them, that she had seen and felt during her lifetime. And again, for the second time that night, something she had felt had come true. All she could say to herself was, Ah didnt like im! Gawd knows, Ah didn't! Ah tol Johnny-Boy it wuz some of them white folks . . .

"Here; drink yo cawffee . . ."

She took the cup; her fingers trembled, and the steaming liquid spilt onto her dress and leg.

"Ahm sorry, An Sue!"

Her leg was scalded, but the pain did not bother her.

"Its awright," she said.

"Wait; lemme put some lard on tha burn!"

"It don hurt."

"Yuh worried bout somethin."

"Naw, honey."

"Lemme fix yuh so mo cawffee."

"Ah don wan nothin now, Reva."

"Waal, buck up. Don be tha way . . ."

They were silent. She heard Reva drinking. No; she would not tell Reva; Reva was all she had left. But she had to do something, some way, somehow. She was undone too much as it was; and to tell Reva about Booker or Johnny-Boy was more than she was equal to; it would be too coldly shameful. She wanted to be alone and fight this thing out with herself.

"Go t bed, honey. Yuh tired."

"Naw; Ahm awright, An Sue."

She heard the bottom of Reva's empty cup clank against the top of the stove. Ah *got* t make her go t bed! Yes; Booker would tell the names of the comrades to the sheriff. If she could only stop him some way! That was the answer, the point, the star that grew bright in the morning of new hope. Soon, maybe half an hour from now, Booker would reach Foley's Woods. Hes boun t go the long way, cause he don know no short cut, she thought. Ah could wade the creek n beat im there . . . But what would she do after that?

"Reva, honey, go t bed. Ahm awright. Yuh need res."

"Ah ain sleepy, An Sue."

"Ah knows whuts bes fer yuh, chile. Yuh tired n wet."

"Ah wanna stay up wid yuh."

She forced a smile and said:

"Ah don think they gonna hurt Johnny-Boy . . ."

"Fer *real*, An Sue?"

"Sho, honey."

"But Ah wanna wait up wid yuh."

"Thas mah job, honey. Thas whut a mas fer, t wait up fer her chullun."

"Good night, An Sue."

"Good night, honey."

She watched Reva pull up and leave the kitchen; presently she heard the shucks in the mattress whispering, and she knew that Reva had gone to bed. She was alone. Through the cracks of the stove she saw the fire dying to grey ashes; the room was growing cold again. The yellow beacon continued to flit past the window and the rain still drummed. Yes; she was alone; she had done this awful thing alone; she must find some way out, alone. Like touching a festering sore, she put her finger upon that moment when she had shouted her defiance to the sheriff, when she had shouted to feel her strength. She had lost Sug to save others; she had let Johnny-Boy go to save others; and then in a moment of weakness that came from too much strength she had lost all. If she had not shouted to the sheriff, she would have been strong enough to have resisted Booker; she would have been able to tell the comrades herself. Something tightened in her as she remembered and understood the fit of fear she had felt on coming to herself in the dark hallway. A part of her life she thought she had done away with forever had had hold of her then. She had thought the soft, warm past was over; she had thought that it did not mean much when now she sang: "*Hes the Lily of the Valley, the Bright n Mawnin Star*" . . . The days when she had sung that song were the days when she had not hoped for anything on this earth, the days when the cold mountain had driven her into the arms of Jesus. She had thought that Sug and Johnny-Boy had taught her to forget Him, to fix her hope upon the fight of black men for freedom. Through the gradual years she had believed and worked with them, had felt strength shed from the grace of their terrible vision. That grace had been upon her when she had let the sheriff slap her down; it had been upon her when she had risen time and again from the floor and faced him. But she had trapped herself with her own hunger; to water the long dry thirst of her faith her pride had made a bargain which her flesh could not keep. Her having told the names of Johnny-Boy's comrades was but an incident in a deeper horror. She stood up and looked at the floor while call and counter-call, loyalty and counter-loyalty struggled in her soul. Mired she was between two abandoned worlds, living, but dying without the strength of the grace that either gave. The clearer she felt it the fuller did something well up from the depths of her for release; the more urgent did she feel the need to fling into her black sky another star, another hope, one more terrible vision to give her the strength to live and act. Softly and restlessly she walked about the kitchen, feeling herself naked against the night, the rain, the world; and shamed whenever the thought of Reva's love crossed her mind. She lifted her empty hands and looked at her writhing fingers. Lawd, whut kin Ah do now? She could still wade the creek and get to Foley's Woods before Booker. And then what? How could she manage to see Johnny-Boy or Booker? Again she heard the sheriff's threatening voice: Git yuh a sheet, cause hes gonna be dead! The sheet! Thas it, the *sheet*! Her whole being leaped with will; the long years of her life bent toward a moment of focus, a point. Ah kin go wid mah sheet! Ahll be doin whut he said! Lawd Gawd in Heaven, Ahma go lika nigger woman wid mah windin sheet t git mah dead son! But then what? She stood straight and smiled grimly; she had in her heart the whole meaning of her life; her entire personality was poised on the brink of a total act. Ah know! Ah *know*! She thought of Johnny-Boy's gun in the dresser drawer. Ahll hide the gun in the sheet n go aftah Johnny-Boys body. . . . She tiptoed to her room, eased out the dresser drawer, and got a sheet. Reva was sleeping; the darkness was filled with her quiet breathing. She groped in the drawer and found the gun. She wound the gun in the sheet and held them both under her apron. Then she stole to the bedside and watched Reva. Lawd, hep her! But mabbe shes bettah off. This had t happen sometimes . . . She n Johnny-Boy couldna been together in this here South . . . N Ah couldnt tell her bout Booker. Itll come out awright n she wont nevah know. Reva's trust would never be shaken. She caught her breath as the shucks in the mattress rustled dryly; then all was quiet and she breathed easily again. She tiptoed to the door, down the hall, and stood on the porch. Above her the yellow beacon whirled through the rain. She went over muddy ground, mounted a slope, stopped and looked back at her house. The lamp glowed in her window, and the yellow beacon that swung every few seconds seemed to feed it with light. She turned and started across the fields, holding the gun and sheet tightly, thinking, Po Reva . . . Po critter . . . Shes fas ersleep . . .

VI   Climax

For the most part she walked with her eyes half shut, her lips tightly compressed, leaning her body against the wind and the driving rain, feeling the pistol in the sheet sagging cold and heavy in her fingers. Already she was getting wet; it seemed that her feet found every puddle of water that stood between the corn rows.

She came to the edge of the creek and paused, wondering at what point was it low. Taking the sheet from under her apron, she wrapped the gun in it so that her finger could be upon the trigger. Ahll cross here, she thought. At first she did not feel the water; her feet were already wet. But the water grew cold as it came up to her knees; she gasped when it reached her waist. Lawd, this creeks high! When she had passed the middle, she knew that she was out of danger. She came out of the water, climbed a grassy hill, walked on, turned a bend and saw the lights of autos gleaming ahead. Yeah; theys still there! She hurried with her head down. Wondah did Ah beat im here? Lawd, Ah *hope* so! A vivid image of Booker's white face hovered a moment before her eyes and a surging will rose up in her so hard and strong that it vanished. She was among the autos now. From nearby came the hoarse voices of the men.

"Hey, yuh!"

She stopped, nervously clutching the sheet.

123

Two white men with shotguns came toward her.

"Whut in hell yuh doin out here?"

She did not answer.

"Didnt yuh hear somebody speak t yuh?"

"Ahm comin aftah mah son," she said humbly.

"Yo *son?*"

"Yessuh."

"Whut yo son doin out here?"

"The sheriffs got im."

"Holy Scott! Jim, its the niggers ma!"

"Whut yuh got there?" asked one.

"A sheet."

"A *sheet?*"

"Yessuh."

"Fer whut?"

"The sheriff tol me t bring a sheet t git his body."

"Waal, waal . . ."

"Now, ain tha somethin?"

The white men looked at each other.

"These niggers sho love one ernother," said one.

"N tha ain no lie," said the other.

"Take me t the sheriff," she begged.

"Yuh ain givin us *orders*, is yuh?"

"Nawsuh."

"We'll take yuh when wes good n ready."

"Yessuh."

"So yuh wan his body?"

"Yessuh."

"Waal, he ain dead yit."

"They gonna kill im," she said.

"Ef he talks they wont."

"He ain gonna talk," she said.

"How yuh know?"

"Cause he ain."

"We got ways of makin niggers talk."

"Yuh ain got no way fer im."

"Yuh thinka a lot of that black Red, don yuh?"

"Hes mah son."

"Why don yuh teach im some sense?"

"Hes mah son," she said again.

"Lissen, ol nigger woman, yuh stand there wid yo hair white. Yuh got bettah sense than t believe tha niggers kin make a revolution . . ."

"A black republic," said the other one, laughing.

"Take me t the sheriff," she begged.

"Yuh his ma," said one. "Yuh kin make im talk n tell whos in this thing wid im."

"He ain gonna talk," she said.

"Don yuh wan im t live?"

She did not answer.

"Cmon, les take her t Bradley."

They grabbed her arms and she clutched hard at the sheet and gun; they led her toward the crowd in the woods. Her feelings were simple; Booker would not tell; she was there with the gun to see to that. The louder became the voices of the men the deeper became her feeling of wanting to right the mistake she had made; of wanting to fight her way back to solid ground. She would stall for time until Booker showed up. Oh, ef theyll only lemme git close t Johnny-Boy! As they led her near the crowd she saw white faces turning and looking at her and heard a rising clamor of voices.

"Whos tha?"

"A nigger woman!"

"Whut she doin out here?"

"This is his ma!" called one of the men.

"Whut she wans?"

"She brought a sheet t cover his body!"

"He ain dead yit!"

"They tryin t make im talk!"

"But he will be dead soon ef he don open up!"

"Say, look! The niggers ma brought a sheet t cover up his body!"

"Now, ain that sweet?"

"Mabbe she wans t hol a prayer meetin!"

"Did she git a preacher?"

"Say, go git Bradley!"

"O.K.!"

The crowd grew quiet. They looked at her curiously; she felt their cold eyes trying to detect some weakness in her. Humbly, she stood with the sheet covering the gun. She had already accepted all that they could do to her.

The sheriff came.

"So yuh brought yo sheet, hunh?"

"Yessuh," she whispered.

"Looks like them slaps we gave yuh learned yuh some sense, didnt they?"

She did not answer.

"Yuh don need tha sheet. Yo son ain dead yit," he said, reaching toward her.

She backed away, her eyes wide.

"Naw!"

"Now, lissen, Anty!" he said. "There ain no use in yuh ackin a fool! Go in there n tell tha nigger son of yos t tell us whos in this wid im, see? Ah promise we wont kill im ef he talks. We'll let im git outta town."

"There ain nothin Ah kin tell im," she said.

"Yuh wan us t kill im?"

She did not answer. She saw someone lean toward the sheriff and whisper.

"Bring her erlong," the sheriff said.

They led her to a muddy clearing. The rain streamed down through the ghostly glare of the flashlights. As the men formed a semi-circle she saw Johnny-Boy lying in a trough of mud. He was tied with rope; he lay hunched and one side of his face rested in a pool of black water. His eyes were staring questioningly at her.

"Speak t im," said the sheriff.

If she could only tell him why she was here! But that was impossible; she was close to what she wanted and she stared straight before her with compressed lips.

"Say, nigger!" called the sheriff, kicking Johnny-Boy. "Heres yo ma!"

Johnny-Boy did not move or speak. The sheriff faced her again.

"Lissen, Anty," he said. "Yuh got mo say wid im than anybody. Tell im t talk n hava chance. Whut he wanna pertect the other niggers n white folks fer?"

She slid her finger about the trigger of the gun and looked stonily at the mud.

"Go t him," said the sheriff.

She did not move. Her heart was crying out to answer the amazed question in Johnny-Boy's eyes. But there was no way now.

"Waal, yuhre astin fer it. By Gawd, we gotta way to *make* yuh talk t im," he said, turning away. "Say, Tim, git one of them logs n turn that nigger upside-down n put his legs on it!"

A murmur of assent ran through the crowd. She bit her lips; she knew what that meant.

"Yuh wan yo nigger son crippled?" she heard the sheriff ask.

She did not answer. She saw them roll the log up; they lifted Johnny-Boy and laid him on his face and stomach, then they pulled his legs over the log. His knee-caps rested on the sheer top of the log's back and the toes of his shoes pointed groundward. So absorbed was she in watching that she felt that it was she who was being lifted and made ready for torture.

"Git a crowbar!" said the sheriff.

A tall, lank man got a crowbar from a nearby auto and stood over the log. His jaws worked slowly on a wad of tobacco.

"Now, its up t yuh, Anty," the sheriff said. "Tell the man whut t do!"

She looked into the rain. The sheriff turned.

"Mabbe she think wes playin. Ef she don say nothin, then break em at the knee-caps!"

"O.K., Sheriff!"

She stood waiting for Booker. Her legs felt weak; she wondered if she would be able to wait much longer. Over and over she said to herself, Ef he came now Ahd kill em both!

"She ain sayin nothin, Sheriff!"

"Waal, Gawddammit, let im have it!"

The crowbar came down and Johnny-Boy's body lunged in the mud and water. There was a scream. She swayed, holding tight to the gun and sheet.

"Hol im! Git the other leg!"

The crowbar fell again. There was another scream.

"Yuh break em?" asked the sheriff.

The tall man lifted Johnny-Boy's legs and let them drop limply again, dropping rearward from the kneecaps. Johnny-Boy's body lay still. His head had rolled to one side and she could not see his face.

"Jus lika broke sparrow wing," said the man, laughing softly.

Then Johnny-Boy's face turned to her; he

screamed.

"Go way, ma! Go way!"

It was the first time she had heard his voice since she had come out to the woods; she all but lost control of herself. She started violently forward, but the sheriff's arm checked her.

"Aw, naw! Yuh had yo chance!" He turned to Johnny-Boy. "She kin go ef yuh talk."

"Mistah, he ain gonna talk," she said.

"Go way, ma!" said Johnny-Boy.

"Shoot im! Don make im suffah so," she begged.

"He'll either talk or he'll never hear yuh ergin," the sheriff said. "Theres other things we kin do t im."

She said nothing.

"What yuh come here fer, ma?" Johnny-Boy sobbed.

"Ahm gonna split his eardrums," the sheriff said. "Ef yuh got anythin t say t im yuh bettah say it *now*!"

She closed her eyes. She heard the sheriff's feet sucking in mud. Ah could save im! She opened her eyes; there were shouts of eagerness from the crowd as it pushed in closer.

"Bus em, Sheriff!"

"Fix im so he cant hear!"

"He knows how t do it, too!"

"He busted a Jew boy tha way once!"

She saw the sheriff stoop over Johnny-Boy, place his flat palm over one ear and strike his fist against it with all his might. He placed his palm over the other ear and struck again. Johnny-Boy moaned, his head rolling from side to side, his eyes showing white amazement in a world without sound.

"Yuh wouldnt talk t im when yuh had the chance," said the sheriff. "Try n talk now."

She felt warm tears on her cheeks. She longed to shoot Johnny-Boy and let him go. But if she did that they would take the gun from her, and Booker would tell who the others were. Lawd, hep me! The men were talking loudly now, as though the main business was over. It seemed ages that she stood there watching Johnny-Boy roll and whimper in his world of silence.

"Say, Sheriff, heres somebody lookin fer yuh!"

"Who is it?"

"Ah don know!"

"Bring em in!"

She stiffened and looked around wildly, holding the gun tight. Is tha Booker? Then she held still, feeling that her excitement might betray her. Mabbe Ah kin shoot em both! Mabbe Ah kin shoot *twice*! The sheriff stood in front of her, waiting. The crowd parted and she saw Booker hurrying forward.

"Ah know em all, Sheriff!" he called.

He came full into the muddy clearing where Johnny-Boy lay.

"Yuh mean yuh got the names?"

"Sho! The ol nigger . . ."

She saw his lips hang open and silent when he saw her. She stepped forward and raised the sheet.

"Whut . . ."

She fired, once; then, without pausing, she turned, hearing them yell. She aimed at Johnny-Boy, but they had their arms around her, bearing her to the ground, clawing at the sheet in her hand. She glimpsed Booker lying sprawled in the mud, on his face, his hands stretched out before him; then a cluster of yelling men blotted him out. She lay without struggling, looking upward through the rain at the white faces above her. And she was suddenly at peace; they were not a white mountain now; they were not pushing her any longer to the edge of life. Its awright . . .

"She shot Booker!"

"She hada gun in the sheet!"

"She shot im right thu the head!"

"Whut she shoot im fer?"

"Kill the bitch!"

"Ah *thought* somethin wuz wrong bout her!"

"Ah wuz fer givin it t her from the firs!"

"Thas whut yuh git fer treatin a nigger nice!"

"Say, Bookers dead!"

She stopped looking into the white faces, stopped listening. She waited, giving up her life before they took it from her; she had done what she wanted. Ef only Johnny-Boy . . . She looked at him; he lay looking at her with tired eyes. Ef she could only tell im! But he lay already buried in a grave of silence.

"Whut yuh kill im fer, hunh?"

It was the sheriff's voice; she did not answer.

"Mabbe she wuz shootin at yuh, Sheriff?"

"Whut yuh kill im fer?"

She felt the sheriff's foot come into her side; she closed her eyes.

"Yuh black bitch!"

"Let her have it!"

"Yuh reckon she foun out bout Booker?"

"She mighta."

"Jesus Chris, whut yuh dummies *waitin* on!"

"Yeah; kill her!"

"Kill em *both*!"

"Let her know her nigger sons dead firs!"

She turned her head toward Johnny-Boy; he lay looking puzzled in a world beyond the reach of voices. At leas he cant hear, she thought.

"C mon, let im have it!"

She listened to hear what Johnny-Boy could not. They came, two of them, one right behind the other; so close together that they sounded like one shot. She did not look at Johnny-Boy now; she looked at the white faces of the men, hard and wet in the glare of the flashlights.

"Yuh hear tha, nigger woman?"

"Did tha surprise im? Hes in hell now wonderin whut hit im!"

"C mon! Give it t her, Sheriff!"

"Lemme shoot her, Sheriff! It wuz mah pal she shot!"

"Awright, Pete! Thas fair ernuff!"

She gave up as much of her life as she could before they took it from her. But the sound of the shot and the streak of fire that tore its way through her chest forced her to live again, intensely. She had not moved, save for the slight jarring impact of the bullet. She felt the heat of her own blood warming her cold, wet back. She yearned suddenly to talk. "Yuh didnt git whut yuh wanted! N yuh ain gonna nevah git it! Yuh didnt kill me; Ah come here by mahsef . . ." She felt rain falling into her wide-open, dimming eyes and heard faint voices. Her lips moved soundlessly. *Yuh didnt git yuh didnt yuh didnt* . . . Focused and pointed she was, buried in the depths of her star, swallowed in its peace and strength; and not feeling her flesh growing cold, cold as the rain that fell from the invisible sky upon the doomed living and the dead that never dies.

[handwritten marginal notes:]
Rain: mourning

Revolution never wins, never dies

Better to have the old faith she believed in
Bright & morning star

The strength of her personal faith, but also the tragedy of it.

KING OF THE BINGO GAME

The woman in front of him was eating roasted peanuts that smelled so good that he could barely contain his hunger. He could not even sleep and wished they'd hurry and begin the bingo game. There, on his right, two fellows were drinking wine out of a bottle wrapped in a paper bag, and he could hear soft gurgling in the dark. His stomach gave a low, gnawing growl. "If this was down South," he thought, "all I'd have to do is lean over, and say, 'Lady, gimme a few of those peanuts, please ma'am,' and she'd pass me the bag and never think nothing of it." Or he could ask the fellows for a drink in the same way. Folks down South stuck together that way; they didn't even have to know you. But up here it was different. Ask somebody for something, and they'd think you were crazy. Well, I ain't crazy. I'm just broke, 'cause I got no birth certificate to get a job, and Laura 'bout to die 'cause we got no money for a doctor. But I ain't crazy. And yet a pinpoint of doubt was focused in his mind as he glanced toward the screen and saw the hero stealthily entering a dark room and sending the beam of a flashlight along a wall of bookcases. This is where he finds the trapdoor, he remembered. The man would pass abruptly through the wall and find the girl tied to a bed, her legs and arms spread wide, and her clothing torn to rags. He laughed softly to himself. He had seen the picture three times, and this was one of the best scenes.

On his right the fellow whispered wide-eyed to his companion, "Man, look a-yonder!"

"Damn!"

"Wouldn't I like to have her tied up like that . . ."

"Hey! That fool's letting her loose!"

"Aw, man, he loves her."

"Love or no love!"

The man moved impatiently beside him, and he tried to involve himself in the scene. But Laura was on his mind. Tiring quickly of watching the picture he looked back to where the white beam filtered from the projection room above the balcony. It started small and grew large, specks of dust dancing in its whiteness as it reached the screen. It was strange how the beam always landed right on the screen and didn't mess up and fall somewhere else. But they had it all fixed. Everything was fixed. Now suppose when they showed that girl with her dress torn the girl started taking off the rest of her clothes, and when the guy came in he didn't untie her but kept her there and went to taking off his own clothes? *That* would be something to see. If a picture got out of hand like that those guys up there would go nuts. Yeah, and there'd be so many folks in here you couldn't find a seat for nine months! A strange sensation played over his skin. He shuddered. Yesterday he'd seen a bedbug on a woman's neck as they walked out into the bright street. But exploring his thigh through a hole in his pocket he found only goose pimples and old scars.

The bottle gurgled again. He closed his eyes. Now a dreamy music was accompanying the film and train whistles were sounding in the distance, and he was a boy again walking along a railroad trestle down South, and seeing the train coming, and running back as fast as he could go, and hearing the whistle blowing, and getting off the trestle to solid ground just in time, with the earth trembling beneath his feet, and feeling relieved as he ran down the cinder-strewn embankment onto the highway, and looking back and seeing with terror that the train had left the track and was following him right down the middle of the street, and all the white people laughing as he ran screaming . . .

"Wake up there, buddy! What the hell do you mean hollering like that? Can't you see we trying to enjoy this here picture?"

He stared at the man with gratitude.

"I'm sorry, old man," he said. "I musta been dreaming."

"Well, here, have a drink. And don't be making no noise like that, damn!"

His hands trembled as he tilted his head. It was not wine, but whiskey. Cold rye whiskey. He took a deep swoller, decided it was better not to take another, and handed the bottle back to its owner.

"Thanks, old man," he said.

Now he felt the cold whiskey breaking a warm path straight through the middle of him, growing hotter and sharper as it moved. He had not eaten all day, and it made him light-headed. The smell of the peanuts stabbed him like a knife, and he got up and found a seat in the middle aisle. But no sooner did he sit than he saw a row of intense-faced young girls, and got up again, thinking, "You chicks musta been Lindy-hopping somewhere." He found a seat several rows ahead as the lights came on, and he saw the screen disappear behind a heavy red and gold curtain; then the curtain rising, and the man with the microphone and a uniformed attendant coming on the stage.

He felt for his bingo cards, smiling. The guy at the door wouldn't like it if he knew about his having *five* cards. Well, not everyone played the bingo game; and even with five cards he didn't have much of a chance. For Laura, though, he had to have faith. He studied the cards, each with its different numerals, punching the free center hole in each and spreading them neatly across his lap; and when the lights faded he sat slouched in his seat so that he could look from his cards to the bingo wheel with but a quick shifting of his eyes.

Ahead, at the end of the darkness, the man with the microphone was pressing a button attached to a long cord and spinning the bingo wheel and calling out the number each time the wheel came to rest. And each time the voice rang out his finger raced over the cards for the number. With five cards he had to move fast. He became nervous; there were too many cards, and the man went too fast with his grating voice. Perhaps he should just select one and throw the others away. But he was afraid. He became warm. Wonder how much Laura's doctor would cost? Damn that, watch the cards! And with despair he heard the man call three in a row which he missed on all five cards. This way he'd never win . . .

When he saw the row of holes punched across the third card, he sat paralyzed and heard the man call three more numbers before he stumbled forward, screaming,

"Bingo! Bingo!"

"Let that fool up there," someone called.

"Get up there, man!"

He stumbled down the aisle and up the steps to the stage into a light so sharp and bright that for a moment it blinded him, and he felt that he had moved into the spell of some strange, mysterious power. Yet it was as familar as the sun, and he knew it was the perfectly familiar bingo.

The man with the microphone was saying something to the audience as he held out his card. A cold light flashed from the man's finger as the card left his hand. His knees trembled. The man stepped closer, checking the card against the numbers chalked on the board. Suppose he had made a mistake? The pomade on the man's hair made him feel faint, and he backed away. But the man was checking the card over the microphone now, and he had to stay. He stood tense, listening.

"Under the O, forty-four," the man chanted. "Under the I, seven. Under the G, three. Under the B, ninety-six. Under the N, thirteen!"

His breath came easier as the man smiled at the audience.

"Yessir, ladies and gentlemen, he's one of the chosen people!"

The audience rippled with laughter and applause.

"Step right up to the front of the stage."

He moved slowly forward, wishing that the light was not so bright.

"To win tonight's jackpot of $36.90 the wheel must stop between the double zero, understand?"

He nodded, knowing the ritual from the many days and nights he had watched the winners march across the stage to press the button that controlled the spinning wheel and receive the prizes. And now he followed the instructions as though he'd crossed the slippery stage a million prize-winning times.

The man was making some kind of a joke, and he nodded vacantly. So tense had he become that he felt a sudden desire to cry and shook it away. He felt vaguely that his whole life was determined by the bingo wheel; not only that which would happen now that he was at last before it, but all that had gone before, since his birth, and his mother's birth and the birth of his father. It had always been there, even though he had not been aware of it, handing out the unlucky cards and numbers of his days. The feeling persisted, and he started quickly away. I better get down from here before I make a fool of myself, he thought.

"Here, boy," the man called. "You haven't started yet."

Someone laughed as he went hesitantly back.

"Are you all reet?"

He grinned at the man's jive talk, but no words would come, and he knew it was not a convincing grin. For suddenly he knew that he stood on the slippery brink of some terrible embarrassment.

"Where are you from, boy?" the man asked.

"Down South."

"He's from down South, ladies and gentlemen," the man said. "Where from? Speak right into the mike."

"Rocky Mont," he said. "Rock' Mont, North Car'lina."

"So you decided to come down off that mountain to the U.S.," the man laughed. He felt that the man was making a fool of him, but then something cold was placed in his hand, and the lights were no longer behind him.

Standing before the wheel he felt alone, but that was somehow right, and he remembered his plan. He would give the wheel a short quick twirl. Just a touch of the button. He had watched it many times, and always it came close to double zero when it was short and quick. He steeled himself; the fear had left, and he felt a profound sense of promise, as though he were about to be repaid for all the things he'd suffered all his life. Trembling, he pressed the button. There was a whirl of lights, and in a second he realized with finality that though he wanted to, he could not stop. It was as though he held a high-powered line in his naked hand. His nerves tightened. As the wheel increased its speed it seemed to draw him more and more into his power, as though it held his fate; and with it came a deep need to submit, to whirl, to lose himself in its swirl of color. He could not stop it now, he knew. So let it be.

The button rested snugly in his palm where the man had placed it. And now he became aware of the man beside him, advising him through the microphone, while behind the shadowy audience hummed with noisy voices. He shifted his feet. There was still that feeling of helplessness within him, making part of him desire to turn back, even now that the jackpot was right in his hand. He squeezed the button until his fist ached. Then, like the sudden shriek of a subway whistle, a doubt tore through his head. Suppose he did not spin the wheel long enough? What could he do, and how could he tell? And then he knew, even as he wondered, that as long as he pressed the button, he could control the jackpot. He and only he could determine whether or not it was to be his. Not even the man with the microphone could do anything about it now. He felt drunk. Then, as though he had come down from a high hill into a valley of people, he heard the audience yelling.

"Come down from there, you jerk!"

"Let somebody else have a chance . . ."

"Ole Jack thinks he done found the end of the rainbow . . ."

The last voice was not unfriendly, and he turned and smiled dreamily into the yelling mouths. Then he turned his back squarely on them.

"Don't take too long, boy," a voice said.

He nodded. They were yelling behind him. Those folks did not understand what had happened to him. They had been playing the bingo game day in and night out for years, trying to win rent money or hamburger change. But not one of those wise guys had discovered this wonderful thing. He watched the wheel whirling past the numbers and experienced a burst of exaltation: This is God! This is the really truly God! He said it aloud, "This is God!"

He said it with such absolute conviction that he feared he would fall fainting into the footlights. But the crowd yelled so loud that they could not hear. Those fools, he thought. I'm here trying to tell them the most wonderful secret in the world, and they're yelling like they gone crazy. A hand fell upon his shoulder.

"You'll have to make a choice now, boy. "You've taken too long."

He brushed the hand violently away.

"Leave me alone, man. I know what I'm doing!"

The man looked surprised and held on to the microphone for support. And because he did not wish to hurt the man's feelings he smiled, realizing with a sudden pang that there was no way of explaining to the man just why he had to stand there pressing the button forever.

"Come here," he called tiredly.

The man approached, rolling the heavy microphone across the stage.

"Anybody can play this bingo game, right?" he said.

"Sure, but . . ."

He smiled, feeling inclined to be patient with this slick looking white man with his blue sport shirt and his sharp gabardine suit.

"That's what I thought," he said. "Anybody can win the jackpot as long as they get the lucky number, right?"

"That's the rule, but after all . . ."

"That's what I thought," he said. "And the big prize goes to the man who knows how to win it?"

The man nodded speechlessly.

"Well then, go on over there and watch me win like I want to. I ain't going to hurt nobody," he said, "and I'll show you how to win. I mean to show the whole world how it's got to be done."

And because he understood, he smiled again to let the man know that he held nothing against him for being white and impatient. Then he refused to see the man any longer and stood pressing the button, the voices of the crowd reaching him like sounds in distant streets. Let them yell. All the Negroes down there were just ashamed because he was black like them. He smiled inwardly, knowing how it was. Most of the time he was ashamed of what Negroes did himself. Well, let them be ashamed for something this time. Like him. He was like a long thin black wire that was being stretched and wound upon the bingo wheel; wound until he wanted to scream; wound, but this time himself controlling the winding and the sadness and the shame, and because he did, Laura would be all right. Suddenly the lights flickered. He staggered backwards. Had something gone wrong? All this noise. Didn't they know that although he controlled the wheel, it also controlled him, and unless he pressed the button forever and forever and ever it would stop, leaving him high and dry, dry and high on this hard high slippery hill and Laura dead? There was only one chance; he had to do whatever the wheel demanded. And gripping the button in despair, he discovered with surprise that it imparted a nervous energy. His spine tingled. He felt a certain power.

Now he faced the raging crowd with defiance, its screams penetrating his eardrums like trumpets shrieking from a juke-box. The vague faces glowing in the bingo lights gave him a sense of himself that he had never known before. He was running the show, by God! They had to react to him, for he was their luck. This is *me*, he thought. Let the bastards yell. Then someone was laughing inside him, and he realized that somehow he had forgotten his own name. It was a sad, lost feeling to lose your name, and a crazy thing to do. That name had been given him by the white man who had owned his grandfather a long lost time ago down South. But maybe those wise guys knew his name.

"Who am I?" he screamed.

"Hurry up and bingo, you jerk!"

They didn't know either, he thought sadly. They didn't even know their own names, they were all poor nameless bastards. Well, he didn't need that old name; he was reborn. For as long as he pressed the button he was The-man-who-pressed-the-button-who-held-the-prize-who-was-the-King-of-Bingo. That was the way it was, and he'd have to press the button even if nobody understood, even though Laura did not understand.

"Live!" he shouted.

The audience quieted like the dying of a huge fan.

"Live, Laura, baby. I got holt of it now, sugar. Live!"

He screamed it, tears streaming down his face. "I got nobody but YOU!"

The screams tore from his very guts. He felt as though the rush of blood to his head would burst out in baseball seams of small red droplets, like a head beaten by police clubs.

Bending over he saw a trickle of blood splashing the toe of his shoe. With his free hand he searched his head. It was his nose. God, suppose something has gone wrong? He felt that the whole audience had somehow entered him and was stamping its feet in his stomach and he was unable to throw them out. They wanted the prize, that was it. They wanted the secret for themselves. But they'd never get it; he would keep the bingo wheel whirling forever, and Laura would be safe in the wheel. But would she? It had to be, because if she were not safe the wheel would cease to turn; it could not go on. He had to get away, *vomit* all, and his mind formed an image of himself running with Laura in his arms down the tracks of the subway just ahead of an A train, running desperately *vomit* with people screaming for him to come out but knowing no way of leaving the tracks because to stop would bring the train crushing down upon him and to attempt to leave across the other tracks would mean to run into a hot third rail as high as his waist which threw blue sparks that blinded his eyes until he could hardly see.

He heard singing and the audience was clapping its hands.

> *Shoot the liquor to him, Jim, boy!*
> *Clap-clap-clap*
> *Well a-calla the cop*
> *He's blowing his top!*
> *Shoot the liquor to him, Jim, boy!*

Bitter anger grew within him at the singing. They think I'm crazy. Well let 'em laugh. I'll do what I got to do.

He was standing in an attitude of intense listening when he saw that they were watching something on the stage behind him. He felt weak. But when he turned he saw no one. If only his thumb did not ache so. Now they were applauding. And for a moment he thought that the wheel had stopped. But that was impossible, his thumb still pressed the button. Then he saw them. Two men in uniform beckoned from the end of the stage. They were coming toward him, walking in step, slowly, like a tap-dance team returning for a third encore. But their shoulders shot forward, and he backed away, looking wildly about. There was nothing to fight them with. He had only the long black cord which led to a plug somewhere back stage, and he couldn't use that because it operated the bingo wheel. He backed slowly, fixing the men with his eyes as his lips stretched over his teeth in a tight, fixed grin; moved toward the end of the stage and realizing that he couldn't go much further, for suddenly the cord became taut and he couldn't afford to break the cord. But he had to do something. The audience was howling. Suddenly he stopped dead, seeing the men halt, their legs lifted as in an interrupted step of a slow-motion dance. There was nothing to do but run in the other direction and he dashed forward, slipping and sliding. The men fell back, surprised. He struck out violently going past.

"Grab him!"

He ran, but all too quickly the cord tightened, resistingly, and he turned and ran back again. This time he slipped them, and discovered by running in a circle before the wheel he could keep the cord from tightening. But this way he had to flail his arms to keep the men away. Why couldn't they leave a man alone? He ran, circling.

"Ring down the curtain," someone yelled. But they couldn't do that. If they did the wheel flashing from the projection room would be cut off. But they had him before he could tell them so, trying to pry open his fist, and he was wrestling and trying to bring his knees into the fight and holding on to the button, for it was his life. And now he was down, seeing a foot coming down, crushing his wrist cruelly, down, as he saw the wheel whirling serenely above.

"I can't give it up," he screamed. Then quietly, in a confidential tone, "Boys, I really can't give it up."

It landed hard against his head. And in the blank moment they had it away from him, completely now. He fought them trying to pull him up from the stage as he watched the wheel spin slowly to a stop. Without sur-prise he saw it rest at double-zero.

"You see," he pointed bitterly.

"Sure, boy, sure, it's O.K.," one of the men said smiling.

And seeing the man bow his head to someone he could not see, he felt very, very happy; he would receive what all the winners received.

But as he warmed in the justice of the man's tight smile he did not see the man's slow wink, nor see the bow-legged man behind him step clear of the swiftly descending curtain and set himself for a blow. He only felt the dull pain exploding in his skull, and he knew even as it slipped out of him that his luck had run out on the stage.

God: luck
Wheel of fate and fortune
Power over it

133

HARRISON BERGERON

The year was 2081, and everybody was finally equal. They weren't only equal before God and the law. They were equal every which way. Nobody was smarter than anybody else. Nobody was better looking than anybody else. Nobody was stronger or quicker than anybody else. All this equality was due to the 211th, 212th, and 213th Amendments to the Constitution, and to the unceasing vigilance of agents of the United States Handicapper General.

Some things about living still weren't quite right, though. April, for instance, still drove people crazy by not being springtime. And it was in that clammy month that the H-G men took George and Hazel Bergeron's fourteen-year-old son, Harrison, away.

It was tragic, all right, but George and Hazel couldn't think about it very hard. Hazel had a perfectly average intelligence, which meant she couldn't think about anything except in short bursts. And George, while his intelligence was way above normal, had a little mental handicap radio in his ear. He was required by law to wear it at all times. It was tuned to a government transmitter. Every twenty seconds or so, the transmitter would send out some sharp noise to keep people like George from taking unfair advantage of their brains.

George and Hazel were watching television. There were tears on Hazel's cheeks, but she'd forgotten for the moment what they were about.

On the television screen were ballerinas.

A buzzer sounded in George's head. His thoughts fled in panic, like bandits from a burglar alarm.

"That was a real pretty dance, that dance they just did," said Hazel.

"Huh?" said George.

"That dance—it was nice," said Hazel.

"Yup," said George. He tried to think a little about the ballerinas. They weren't really very good—no better than anybody else would have been, anyway. They were burdened with sashweights and bags of birdshot, and their faces were masked, so that no one, seeing a free and graceful gesture or a pretty face, would feel like something the cat drug in. George was toying with the vague notion that maybe dancers shouldn't be handicapped. But he didn't get very far with it before another noise in his ear radio scattered his thoughts.

George winced. So did two out of the eight ballerinas.

Hazel saw him wince. Having no mental handicap herself, she had to ask George what the latest sound had been.

"Sounded like somebody hitting a milk bottle with a ball peen hammer," said George.

"I'd think it would be real interesting, hearing all the different sounds," said Hazel, a little envious. "All the things they think up."

"Um," said George.

"Only, if I was Handicapper General, you know what I would do?" said Hazel. Hazel, as a matter of fact, bore a strong resemblance to the Handicapper General, a woman named Diana Moon Glampers. "If I was Diana Moon Glampers," said Hazel, "I'd have chimes on Sunday—just chimes. Kind of in honor of religion."

"I could think, if it was just chimes," said George.

"Well—maybe make 'em real loud," said Hazel. "I think I'd make a good Handicapper General."

"Good as anybody else," said George.

"Who knows better'n I do what normal is?" said Hazel.

"Right," said George. He began to think glimmeringly about his abnormal son who was now in jail, about Harrison, but a twenty-one-gun salute in his head stopped that.

"Boy!" said Hazel, "that was a doozy, wasn't it?"

It was such a doozy that George was white and trembling, and tears stood on the rims of his red eyes. Two of the eight ballerinas had collapsed to the studio floor, were holding their temples.

"All of a sudden you look so tired," said Hazel. "Why don't you stretch out on the sofa, so's you can rest your handicap bag on the pillows, honeybunch." She was referring to the forty-seven pounds of birdshot in a canvas bag, which was padlocked around George's neck. "Go on and rest the bag for a little while," she said. "I don't care if you're not equal to me for a while."

George weighed the bag with his hands. "I don't mind it, " he said. "I don't notice it any more. It's just a part of me."

"You been so tired lately—kind of wore out," said Hazel. "If there was just some way we could make a little hole in the bottom of the bag, and just take out a few of them lead balls. Just a few."

"Two years in prison and two thousand dollars fine for every ball I took out," said George. "I don't call that a bargain."

"If you could just take a few out when you came home from work," said Hazel. "I mean —you don't compete with anybody around here. You just set around."

"If I tried to get away with it," said George, "then other people'd get away with it—and pretty soon we'd be right back to the dark ages again, with everybody competing against everybody else. You wouldn't like that, would you?"

"I'd hate it," said Hazel.

"There you are," said George. "The minute people start cheating on laws, what do you think happens to society?"

If Hazel hadn't been able to come up with an answer to this question, George couldn't have supplied one. A siren was going off in his head.

"Reckon it'd fall all apart," said Hazel.

"What would?" said George blankly.

"Society," said Hazel uncertainly. "Wasn't that what you just said?"

"Who knows?" said George.

The television program was suddenly interrupted for a news bulletin. It wasn't clear at first as to what the bulletin was about, since the announcer, like all announcers, had a serious speech impediment. For about half a minute, and in a state of high excitement, the announcer tried to say, "Ladies and gentlemen—"

He finally gave up, handed the bulletin to a ballerina to read.

"That's all right—" Hazel said of the announcer, "he tried. That's the big thing. He tried to do the best he could with what God gave him. He should get a nice raise for trying so hard."

"Ladies and gentlemen—" said the ballerina, reading the bulletin. She must have been extraordinarily beautiful, because the mask she wore was hideous. And it was easy to see that she was the strongest and most graceful of all the dancers, for her handicap bags were as big as those worn by two-hundred-pound men.

And she had to apologize at once for her voice, which was a very unfair voice for a woman to use. Her voice was a warm, luminous, timeless melody. "Excuse me—" she said, and she began again, making her voice absolutely uncompetitive.

"Harrison Bergeron, age fourteen," she said in a grackle squawk, "has just escaped from jail, where he was held on suspicion of plotting to overthrow the government. He is a genius and an athlete, is under-handicapped, and should be regarded as extremely dangerous."

A police photograph of Harrison Bergeron was flashed on the screen upside down, then sideways, upside down again, then right side up. The picture showed the full length of Harrison against a background calibrated in feet and inches. He was exactly seven feet tall.

The rest of Harrison's appearance was Halloween and hardware. Nobody had ever born heavier handicaps. He had outgrown hindrances faster than the H-G men could think them up. Instead of a little ear radio for a mental handicap, he wore a tremendous pair of earphones, and spectacles with thick wavy lenses. The spectacles were intended to make him not only half blind, but to give him whanging headaches besides.

Scrap metal was hung all over him. Ordinarily, there was a certain symmetry, a military neatness to the handicaps issued to strong people, but Harrison looked like a walking junkyard. In the race of life, Harrison carried three hundred pounds.

And to offset his good looks, the H-G men required that he wear at all times a red rubber ball for a nose, keep his eyebrows shaved off, and cover his even white teeth with black caps at snaggle-tooth random.

"If you see this boy," said the ballerina, "do not—I repeat, do not—try to reason with him."

There was the shriek of a door being torn from its hinges.

Screams and barking cries of consternation came from the television set. The photograph of Harrison Bergeron on the screen jumped again and again, as though dancing to the tune of an earthquake.

George Bergeron correctly identified the earthquake, and well he might have—for many was the time his own home had danced to the same crashing tune. "My God—" said George, "that must be Harrison!"

The realization was blasted from his mind instantly by the sound of an automobile collision in his head.

When George could open his eyes again, the photograph of Harrison was gone. A living, breathing Harrison filled the screen.

Clanking, clownish, and huge, Harrison stood in the center of the studio. The knob of the uprooted studio door was still in his hand. Ballerinas, technicians, musicians, and announcers cowered on their knees before him, expecting to die.

"I am the Emperor!" cried Harrison. "Do you hear? I am the Emperor! Everybody must do what I say at once!" He stamped his foot and the studio shook.

"Even as I stand here—" he bellowed, "crippled, hobbled, sickened—I am a greater ruler than any man who ever lived! Now watch me become what I *can* become!"

Harrison tore the straps of his handicap harness like wet tissue paper, tore straps guaranteed to support five thousand pounds.

Harrison's scrap-iron handicaps crashed to the floor.

Harrison thrust his thumbs under the bar of the padlock that secured his head harness. The bar snapped like celery. Harrison smashed his headphones and spectacles against the wall.

He flung away his rubber-ball nose, revealed a man that would have awed Thor, the god of thunder.

"I shall now select my Empress!" he said, looking down on the cowering people. "Let the first woman who dares rise to her feet claim her mate and her throne!"

A moment passed, and then a ballerina arose, swaying like a willow.

Harrison plucked the mental handicap from her ear, snapped off her physical handicaps with marvelous delicacy. Last of all, he removed her mask.

She was blindingly beautiful.

"Now—" said Harrison, taking her hand, "shall we show the people the meaning of the word dance? Music!" he commanded.

The musicians scrambled back into their chairs, and Harrison stripped them of their handicaps, too. "Play your best," he told them, "and I'll make you barons and dukes and earls."

The music began. It was normal at first—cheap, silly, false. But Harrison snatched two musicians from their chairs, waved them like batons as he sang the music as he wanted it played. He slammed them back into their chairs.

The music began again and was much improved.

Harrison and his Empress merely listened to the music for a while—listened gravely, as though synchronizing their heartbeats with it.

They shifted their weights to their toes.

Harrison placed his big hands on the girl's tiny waist, letting her sense the weightlessness that would soon be hers.

And then in an explosion of joy and grace, into the air they sprang!

Not only were the laws of the land abandoned, but the law of gravity and the laws of motion as well.

They reeled, whirled, swiveled, flounced, capered, gamboled, and spun.

They leaped like deer on the moon.

The studio ceiling was thirty feet high, but each leap brought the dancers nearer to it.

It became their obvious intention to kiss the ceiling.

They kissed it.

And then, neutralizing gravity with love and pure will, they remained suspended in air inches below the ceiling, and they kissed each other for a long, long time.

It was then that Diana Moon Glampers, the Handicapper General, came into the studio with a double-barreled ten-gauge shotgun. She fired twice, and the Emperor and the Empress were dead before they hit the floor.

Diana Moon Glampers loaded the gun again. She aimed it at the musicians and told them they had ten seconds to get their handicaps back on.

It was then that the Bergerons' television tube burned out.

Hazel turned to comment about the blackout to George. But George had gone out into the kitchen for a can of beer.

George came back in with the beer, paused while a handicap signal shook him up. And then he sat down again.

"You been crying?" he said to Hazel.

"Yup," she said.

"What about?" he said.

"I forget," she said. "Something real sad on television."

"What was it?" he said.

"It's all kind of mixed up in my mind," said Hazel.

"Forget sad things," said George.

"I always do," said Hazel.

"That's my girl," said George. He winced. There was the sound of a rivetting gun in his head.

"Gee—I could tell that one was a doozy," said Hazel.

"You can say that again," said George.

"Gee—" said Hazel, "I could tell that one was a doozy."

THE SCHOOL

Well, we had all these children out planting trees, see, because we figured that . . . that was part of their education, to see how, you know, the root systems . . . and also the sense of responsibility, taking care of things, being individually responsible. You know what I mean. And the trees all died. They were orange trees. I don't know why they died, they just died. Something wrong with the soil possibly or maybe the stuff we got from the nursery . . . wasn't the best. We complained about it. So we've got thirty kids there, each kid had his or her own little tree to plant, and we've got these thirty trees. All these kids looking at these little brown sticks, it was depressing.

It wouldn't have been so bad except that . . . Before that, just a couple of weeks before the thing with the trees, the snakes all died. But I think that the snakes—well, the reason that the snakes kicked off was that . . . you remember, the boiler was shut off for four days because of the strike, and that was explicable. It was something you could explain to the kids because of the strike. I mean, none of their parents would let them cross the picket line and they knew there was a strike going on and what it meant. So when things got started up again and we found the snakes they weren't too disturbed.

With the herb gardens it was probably a case of overwatering, and at least now they know not to overwater. The children were very conscientious with the herb gardens and some of them probably . . . you know, slipped them a little extra water when we weren't looking. Or maybe . . . well, I don't like to think about sabotage, although it did occur to us. I mean, it was something that crossed our minds. We were thinking that way probably because before that the gerbils had died, and the white mice had died, and the salamander . . . well, now they know not to carry them around in plastic bags.

Of course we *expected* the tropical fish to die, that was no surprise. Those numbers, you look at them crooked and they're belly-up on the surface. But the lesson plan called for a tropical-fish input at that point, there was nothing we could do, it happens every year, you just have to hurry past it.

We weren't even supposed to have a puppy.

We weren't even supposed to have one, it was just a puppy the Murdoch girl found under a Gristede's truck one day and she was afraid the truck would run over it when the driver had finished making his delivery, so she stuck it in her knapsack and brought it to school with her. So we had this puppy. As soon as I saw the puppy I thought, Oh Christ, I bet it will live for about two weeks and then . . . And that's what it did. It wasn't supposed to be in the classroom at all, there's some kind of regulation about it, but you can't tell them they can't have a puppy when the puppy is already there, right in front of them, running around on the floor and yap yap yapping. They named it Edgar—that is, they named it after me. They had a lot of fun running after it and yelling, "Here, Edgar! Nice Edgar!" Then they'd laugh like hell. They enjoyed the ambiguity. I enjoyed it myself. I don't mind being kidded. They made a little house for it in the supply closet and all that. I don't know what it died of. Distemper, I guess. It probably hadn't had any shots. I got it out of there before the kids got to school. I checked the supply closet each morning, routinely, because I knew what was going to happen. I gave it to the custodian.

And then there was this Korean orphan that the class adopted through the Help the Children program, all the kids brought in a quarter a month, that was the idea. It was an unfortunate thing, the kid's name was Kim and maybe we adopted him too late or something. The cause of death was not stated in the letter we got, they suggested we adopt another child instead and sent us some interesting case histories, but we didn't have the heart. The class took it pretty hard, they began (I think; nobody ever said anything to me directly) to feel that maybe there was something wrong with the school. But I don't think there's anything wrong with the school, particularly, I've seen better and I've seen worse. It was just a run of bad luck. We had an extraordinary number of parents passing away, for instance. There were I think two heart attacks and two suicides, one drowning, and four killed together in a car accident. One stroke, and we had the usual heavy mortality rate among the grandparents, or maybe it was heavier this year, it seemed so. And finally the tragedy.

The tragedy occurred when Matthew Wein and Tony Mavrogordo were playing over where they're excavating for the new federal office building. There were all these big wooden beams stacked, you know, at the edge of the excavation. There's a court case coming out of that, the parents are claiming that the beams were poorly stacked. I don't know what's true and what's not. It's been a strange year.

I forgot to mention Billy Brandt's father, who was knifed fatally when he grappled with a masked intruder in his home.

One day, we had a discussion in class. They asked me, where did they go? The trees, the salamander, the tropical fish, Edgar, the poppas and mommas, Matthew and Tony, where did they go? And I said, I don't know, I don't know. And they said, who knows? and I said, nobody knows. And they said, is death that which gives meaning to life? and I said, no, life is that which gives meaning to life. Then they said, but isn't death, considered as a fundamental datum, the means by which the taken-for-granted mundanity of the everyday may be transcended in the direction of—

I said, yes, maybe.

They said, we don't like it.

I said, that's sound.

They said, it's a bloody shame!

I said, it is.

They said, will you make love now with Helen (our teaching assistant) so that we can see how it is done? We know you like Helen.

I do like Helen but I said that I would not.

We've heard so much about it, they said, but we've never seen it.

I said I would be fired and that it was never, or almost never, done as a demonstration. Helen looked out of the window.

They said, please, please make love with Helen, we require an assertion of value, we are frightened.

I said that they shouldn't be frightened (although I am often frightened) and that there was value everywhere. Helen came and embraced me. I kissed her a few times on the brow. We held each other. The children were excited. Then there was a knock on the door, I opened the door, and the new gerbil walked in. The children cheered wildly.

OF CABBAGES AND KINGS

Claude Sheats had been in the Brotherhood all his life, and then he had tried to get out. Some of his people and most of his friends were still in the Brotherhood and were still very good members, but Claude was no longer a good member because he had tried to get out after over twenty years. To get away from the Brotherhood and all his friends who were still active in it, he moved to Washington Square and took to reading about being militant. But, living there, he developed a craving for whiteness the way a nicely broke-in virgin craves sex. In spite of this, he maintained a steady black girl, whom he saw at least twice a month to keep up appearances, and once he took both of us with him when he visited his uncle in Harlem who was still in the Brotherhood.

"She's a nice girl, Claude," his uncle's wife had told him that night, because the girl, besides being attractive, had some very positive ideas about the Brotherhood. Her name was Marie, she worked as a secretary in my office, and it was on her suggestion that I moved in with Claude Sheats.

"I'm glad to see you don't waste your time on hippies," the uncle had said. "All our young men are selling out these days."

The uncle was the kind of fellow who had played his cards right. He was much older than his wife, and I had the impression that night that he must have given her time to experience enough and to become bored enough before he overwhelmed her with his success. He wore glasses and combed his hair back and had that oily composure that made me think of a waiter waiting to be tipped. He was very proud of his English, I observed, and how he always ended his words with just

the right sound. He must have felt superior to people who didn't. He must have felt superior to Claude because he was still with the Brotherhood and Claude had tried to get out.

Claude did not like him and always seemed to feel guilty whenever we visited his uncle's house. "Don't mention any of my girls to him," he told me after our first visit.

"Why would I do that?" I said.

"He'll try to psych you into telling him."

"Why should he suspect you? He never comes over to the apartment."

"He just likes to know what I'm doing. I don't want him to know about my girls."

"I won't say anything," I promised.

He was almost twenty-three and had no steady girls except Marie. He was well built so that he had no trouble in the Village area. It was like going to the market for him. During my first days in the apartment the process had seemed like a game. And once, when he was going out, I said: "Bring back two."

Half an hour later he came back with two girls. He got their drinks, and then he called me into his room to meet them.

"This is Doris," he said, pointing to the smaller one, "and I forgot your name," he said to the big blonde.

"Jane," she said.

"This is Howard," he told her.

"Hi," I said. Neither one of them smiled. The big blonde in white pants sat on the big bed, and the little one sat on a chair near the window. He had given them his worst bourbon.

"Excuse me a minute," Claude said to the girls. "I want to talk to Howard for a minute." He put on a record before we went outside into the hall between our rooms. He was always extremely polite and gentle, and he was very soft-spoken in spite of his size.

"Listen," he said to me outside, "you can have the blonde."

"What can I do with that amazon?"

"I don't care. Just get her out of the room."

"She's dirty," I said.

"So you can give her a bath."

"It wouldn't help much."

"Well, just take her out and talk to her," he told me. "Remember, you asked for her."

We went back in. "Where you from?" I said to the amazon.

"Brighton."

"What school?"

"No. I just got here."

"From where?"

"*Brighton!*"

"Where's that?" I said.

"*England*," she said. Claude Sheats looked at me.

"How did you find Washington Square so fast?"

"I got friends."

She was very superior about it all and showed the same slight irritation of a professional theater critic waiting for a late performance to begin. The little one sat on the chair, her legs crossed, staring at the ceiling. Her white pants were dirty too. Both girls looked as though they would have been relieved if we had taken off our clothes and danced for them around the room and across the bed, and made hungry sounds in our throats with our mouths slightly opened.

I said that I had to go out to the drugstore and would be back very soon; but once outside, I walked a whole hour in one direction, and then I walked back. I passed them a block away from our apartment. They were walking fast and did not slow down or speak when I passed them.

Claude Sheats was drinking heavily when I came into the apartment.

"What the hell are you trying to pull?" he said.

"I couldn't find a drugstore open."

He got up from the living room table and walked toward me. "You should have asked me," he said. "I got more than enough."

"I wanted some mouthwash too," I said.

He fumed a while longer, and then told me how I had ruined his evening because the amazon would not leave the room to wait for me and the little one would not do anything with the amazon around. He suddenly thought of going down and bringing them back, and he went out for a while. But he came back without them, saying that they had been picked up again.

"When a man looks out for you, you got to look out for him," he warned me.

"I'm sorry."

"A hell of a lot of good *that* does. And that's the last time I look out for *you*, baby," he said. "From now on it's *me* all the way."

"Thanks," I said.

"If she was too much for you I could of taken the amazon."

"It didn't matter that much," I said.

"You could of had Doris if you couldn't handle the amazon."

"They were both too much," I told him.

But Claude Sheats did not answer. He just looked at me.

After two months of living with him I concluded that Claude hated whites as much as he loved them. And he hated himself with the very same passion. He hated the country and his place in it, and he loved the country and his place in it. He loved the Brotherhood and all that being in it had taught him, and he still believed in what he had been taught, even after he had left it and did not have to believe in anything.

"This Man is going *down*, Howard," he would announce with conviction.

"Why?" I would ask.

"Because it's the Black Man's time to rule again. They had five thousand years, now we get five thousand years."

"What if I don't *want* to rule?" I asked. "What happens if I don't want to take over?"

He looked at me with pity in his face. "You go down with the rest of the country."

"I guess I wouldn't mind much anyway," I said. "It would be a hell of a place with nobody to hate."

But I could never get him to smile about it the way I tried to smile about it. He was always serious. And once, when I questioned the mysticism in the teachings of the Brotherhood, Claude almost attacked me. "Another man might kill you for saying that," he had said. "Another man might not let you get away with saying something like that." He was quite deadly, and he stood over me with an air of patient superiority. And because he he could afford to be generous and forgiving, being one of the saved, he sat down at the table with me under the single light bulb and began to teach me. He told me the stories about how it was in the beginning before the whites took over, and about all the little secret significances of black, and about the subtle infiltration of white superiority into everyday objects.

"You've never seen me eat white bread or white sugar, have you?"

"No," I said. He used brown bread and brown sugar.

"Or use bleached flour or white rice?"

"No."

"You know why, don't you?" he waited expectantly.

"No," I finally said. "I don't know why."

He was visibly shocked, so much so that he dropped that line of instruction and began to draw on a pad before him on the living room table. He moved his big shoulders over the yellow pad to conceal his drawings and looked across the table at me. "Now I'm going to tell you something that white men have paid thousands of dollars to learn," he said. "Men have been killed for telling this, but I'm telling you for nothing. I'm warning you not to repeat it because if the whites find out, you know, you could be killed too."

"You know me," I said. "I wouldn't repeat any secrets."

He gave me a long, thoughtful look.

I gave him back a long, eager, honest look. Then he leaned across the table, and whispered: "Kennedy isn't buried in this country. He was the only President who never had his coffin opened during the funeral. The body was in state all that time, and they never opened the coffin once. You know why?"

"No."

"Because he's not *in it!* They buried an empty coffin. Kennedy was a Thirty-third Degree Mason. His body is in Jerusalem right now."

"How do you know?" I asked.

"If I told you, it would put your life in danger."

"Did his family know about it?"

"No. His lodge kept it secret."

"No one knew?"

"I'm telling you, *no!*"

"Then how did you find out?"

He sighed, more from tolerance than from boredom with my inability to comprehend the mysticism of pure reality in its most unadulterated form. Of course I could not believe him, and we argued about it, back and forth; but to cap all my uncertainties he drew the thirty-three-degree circle, showed me the secret signs that men had died to learn, and spoke about the time when our black ancestors chased an evil genius out of their kingdom and across a desert and onto an island somewhere in the sea; from which, hundreds of years later, this same evil genius sent forth a perfected breed of white-skinned and evil creatures who, through trickery, managed to enslave for five thousand years the onetime Black Masters of the world. He further explained the significance of the East and why all the saved must go there once during their lifetime, and possibly be buried there, as Kennedy had been.

It was dark and late at night, and the glaring bulb cast his great shadow into the corners so that there was the sense of some outraged spirit, fuming in the halls and dark places of our closets, waiting to extract some terrible and justifiable revenge from him for disclosing to me, an unbeliever, the closest-kept of secrets. But I was aware of them only for an instant, and then I did not believe him again.

The most convincing thing about it all was that he was very intelligent and had an orderly, well-regimented life-style, and yet *he* had no trouble with believing. He believed in the certainty of statistical surveys, which was his work; the nutritional value of wheat germ sprinkled on eggs; the sensuality of gin; and the dangers inherent in smoking. He was stylish in that he did not believe in God, but he was extremely moral and warm and kind; and I wanted sometimes to embrace him for his kindness and bigness and gentle manners. He lived his life so carefully that no matter what he said, I could not help believing him sometimes. But I did not want to, because I knew that once I started I could not stop; and then there would be no purpose to my own beliefs and no real conviction or direction in my own efforts to achieve when always, in the back of my regular thoughts, there would be a sense of futility and a fear of the unknown all about me. So, for the sake of necessity, I chose not to believe him.

He felt that the country was doomed and that the safe thing to do was to make enough money as soon as possible and escape to the Far East. He forecast summer riots in certain Northern cities and warned me, religiously, to avoid all implicating ties with whites so that I might have a chance to be saved when that time came. And I asked him about *his* ties, and the girls, and how it was never a movie date with coffee afterwards but always his room and the cover-all blanket of Motown sounds late into the night.

"A man has different reasons for doing certain things," he had said.

He never seemed to be comfortable with any of the girls. He never seemed to be in control. And after my third month in the apartment I had concluded that he used his virility as a tool and forged, for however long it lasted, a little area of superiority which could never, it seemed, extend itself beyond the certain confines of his room, no matter

how late into the night the records played. I could see him fighting to extend the area, as if an increase in the number of girls he saw could compensate for what he had lost in duration. He saw many girls: curious students, unexpected bus-stop pickups and assorted other one-nighters. And his rationalizations allowed him to believe that each one was an actual conquest, a physical affirmation of a psychological victory over all he hated and loved and hated in the little world of his room.

But then he seemed to have no happiness, even in this. Even here I sensed some intimations of defeat. After each girl, Claude would almost immediately come out of his room, as if there were no need for aftertalk; as if, after it was over, he felt a brooding, silent emptiness that quickly intensified into nervousness and instantaneous shyness and embarrassment, so that the cold which sets in after that kind of emotional drain came in very sharp against his skin, and he could not bear to have her there any longer. And when the girl had gone, he would come into my room to talk. These were the times when he was most like a little boy; and these were the times when he really began to trust me.

"That bitch called me everything but the son of God," he would chuckle. And I would put aside my papers brought home from the office, smile at him, and listen.

He would always eat or drink afterward, and in those early days I was glad for his companionship and the return of his trust, and sometimes we drank and talked until dawn. During these times he would tell me more subtleties about the Man and would repredict the fall of the country. Once he warned me, in a fatherly way, about reading life from books before experiencing it; and another night he advised me on how to schedule girls so that one could run them without being run in return. These were usually good times of good-natured arguments and predictions; but as we drank more often he tended to grow excited and quick-tempered, especially after he had just entertained. Sometimes he would seethe with hate, and every drink he took gave life to increasingly bitter condemnations of the present system and our place in it. There were actually flying saucers, he told me once, piloted by things from other places in the universe, which would eventually destroy the country for what it had done to the black man. He had run into his room on that occasion, and had brought out a book by a man who maintained that the government was deliberately withholding from the public overwhelming evidence of flying saucers and strange creatures from other galaxies that walked among us every day. Claude emphasized the fact that the writer was a Ph.D. who must know what he was talking about, and insisted that the politicians withheld the information because they knew that their time was almost up and if they made it public, the black man would know that he had outside friends who would help him take over the world again. Nothing I said could make him reconsider the slightest bit of his information.

"What are we going to use for weapons when we take over?" I asked him once.

"We've got atomic bombs stockpiled and waiting for the day."

"How can you believe that crap?"

He did not answer, but said instead: "You are the living example of what the Man has done to my people."

"I just try to think things out for myself," I said.

"You can't think. The handkerchief over your head is too big."

I smiled.

"I know," he continued. "I know all there is to know about whites because I've been studying them all my life."

I smiled some more.

"I ought to know," he said slowly. "I have supernatural powers."

"I'm tired," I told him. "I want to go to sleep now."

Claude started to leave the room, then he turned. "Listen," he said at the door. He pointed his finger at me to emphasize the gravity of his pronouncement. "I predict that within the next week something is going to happen to this country that will hurt it even more than Kennedy's assassination."

"Good-night," I said as he closed the door.

He opened it again. "Remember that I predicted it when it happens," he said. For the first time I noticed that he had been deadly serious all along.

Two days later several astronauts burned to death in Florida. He raced into my room hot with the news.

"Do you believe in me *now?*" he said. "Just two days and look what happened."

I tried to explain, as much to myself as to him, that in any week of the year something unfortunate was bound to occur. But he insisted that this was only part of a divine plan to bring the country to its knees. He said that he intended to send a letter off right away to Jeane Dixon in D.C. to let her know that she was not alone because he also had the same power. Then he thought that he had better not because the FBI knew that he had been active in the Brotherhood before he got out.

At first it was good fun believing that someone important cared enough to watch us. And sometimes when the telephone was dead a long time before the dial tone sounded, I would knock on his door and together we would run through our telephone conversations for that day to see if either of us had said anything implicating or suspect, just in case they were listening. This feeling of persecution brought us closer together, and soon the instruction sessions began to go on almost every night. At this point I could not help believing him a little. And he began to trust me again, like a tolerable little brother, and even confided that the summer riots would break out simultaneously in Harlem and Watts during the second week in August. For some reason, something very difficult to put into words, I spent three hot August nights on the streets of Harlem, waiting for the riot to start.

144

In the seventh month of our living together, he began to introduce me to his girls again when they came in. Most of them came only once, but all of them received the same mechanical treatment. He discriminated only with liquor, the quality of which improved with the attractiveness or reluctance of the girl: gin for slow starters, bourbon for momentary strangers, and the scotch he reserved for those he hoped would come again. There was first the trek into his room, his own trip out for the ice and glasses while classical music was played within; then after a while the classical piece would be replaced by several Motowns. Finally, there was her trip to the bathroom, his calling a cab in the hall, and the sound of both their feet on the stairs as he walked her down to the cab. Then he would come to my room in his red bathrobe, glass in hand, for the aftertalk.

Then in the ninth month the trouble started. It would be very easy to pick out one incident, one day, one area of misunderstanding in that month and say: "That was where it began." It would be easy, but not accurate. It might have been one instance or a combination of many. It might have been the girl who came into the living room when I was going over the proposed blueprints for a new settlement house, and who lingered too long outside his room in conversation because her father was a builder somewhere. Or it might have been nothing at all. But after that time he warned me about being too friendly with his company.

Another night, when I was leaving the bathroom in my shorts, he came out of his room with a girl who smiled. "Hi," she said to me.

I nodded hello as I ducked back into the bathroom.

When he had walked her down to the door he came to my room and knocked. He did not have a drink. "Why didn't you speak to my company?" he demanded.

"I was in my shorts."

"She felt bad about it. She asked what the hell was wrong with you. What could I tell her—'He got problems'?"

"I'm sorry," I said. "But I didn't want to stop in my shorts."

"I see through you, Howard," he said. "You're just jealous of me and try to insult my girls to get to me."

"Why should I be jealous of you?"

"Because I'm a man and you're not."

"What makes a man anyway?" I said. "Your fried eggs and wheat germ? Why should I be jealous of you *or* what you bring in?"

"Some people don't need a reason. You're a black devil and you'll get yours. I predict that you'll get yours."

"Look," I told him, "I'm sorry about the girl. Tell her I'm sorry when you see her again."

"You treated her so bad she probably won't come back."

I said nothing more, and he stood there silently for a long time before he turned to leave the room. But at the door he turned again and said: "I see through you, Howard. You're a black devil."

It should have ended there, and it might have with anyone else. I took great pains to speak to his girls after that, even though he tried to get them into the room as quickly as possible. But a week later he accused me of walking about in his room after he had gone out some two weeks before.

"I swear I wasn't in your room," I protested.

"I saw your shadow on the blinds from across the street at the bus stop," he insisted.

"I've *never* been in your room when you weren't there," I told him.

"I *saw* you!"

We went into his room, and I tried to explain how, even if he could see the window from the bus stop, the big lamp next to the window prevented any shadow from being cast on the blinds. But he was convinced in his mind that at every opportunity I plundered his closets and drawers. He had no respect for simple logic in these matters, no sense of the absurdity of his accusations, and the affair finally ended with my confessing that I might have done it without actually knowing, and if I had, I would not do it again.

But what had been a gesture for peace on my part became a vindication for him, proof that I *was* a black devil, capable of lying and lying until he confronted me with the inescapable truth of the situation. And so he persisted in creating situations from which, if he insisted on a point long enough and with enough self-righteousness, he could draw my inevitable confession.

And I confessed eagerly, goaded on by the necessity of maintaining peace. I confessed to mixing white sugar crystals in with his own brown crystals so that he could use it and violate the teachings of the Brotherhood; I confessed to cleaning the bathroom all the time merely because I wanted to make him feel guilty for not having ever cleaned it. I confessed to telling the faithful Marie, who brought a surprise dinner over for him, that he was working late at his office in order to implicate him with the girls who worked there. I confessed to leaving my papers about the house so that his company could ask about them and develop an interest in me. And I pleaded guilty to a record of other little infamies, which multiplied into countless others, and again subdivided into hundreds of little subtleties until my every movement was a threat to him. If I had a girlfriend to dinner, we should eat in my room instead of at the table because he had to use the bathroom a lot, and he was embarrassed to be seen going to the bathroom.

If I protested, he would fly into a tantrum and shake his big finger at me vigorously. And so I retreated, step by step, into my room, from which I emerged only to go to the bathroom or kitchen or out of the house. I tried to stay out on nights when he had company. But he had company so often that I could not always help being in my room after he had walked her to the door. Then he would knock on my door for his talk. He might offer me a drink, and if I refused, he would go to his room for a while and then come back. He would pace about for a while, like a big little boy who wants to ask for money over his allowance. At these times my mind would move feverishly over all our contacts for as far back as I could make it reach, searching and attempting to pull out that one incident which would surely be the point of his attack. But it was never any use.

"Howard, I got something on my chest, and I might as well get it off."

"What is it?" I asked from my bed.

"You been acting strange lately. Haven't been talking to me. If you got something on your chest, get it off now."

"I have nothing on my chest," I said.

"Then why don't you talk?"

I did not answer.

"You hardly speak to me in the kitchen. If you have something against me, tell me now."

"I have nothing against you."

"Why don't you talk, then?" He looked directly at me. "If a man doesn't talk, you think *something's* wrong!"

"I've been nervous lately, that's all. I got problems, and I don't want to talk."

"Everybody's got problems. That's no reason for going around making a man feel guilty."

"For God's sake, I don't want to talk."

"I know what's wrong with you. Your conscience is bothering you. You're so evil that your conscience is giving you trouble. You got everybody fooled but *me*. I know you're a black devil."

"I'm a black devil," I said. "Now will you let me sleep?"

He went to the door. "You dish it out, but you can't take it," he said. "That's *your* trouble."

"I'm a black devil," I said.

I lay there, after he left, hating myself but thankful that he hadn't called me into his room for the fatherly talk as he had done another time. That was the worst. He had come to the door and said: "Come out of there, I want to talk to you." He had walked ahead of me into his room and had sat down in his big leather chair next to the lamp with his legs spread wide and his big hands in his lap. He had said: "Don't be afraid. I'm not going to hurt you. Sit down. I'm not going to argue. What are you so nervous about? Have a drink," in his kindest, most fatherly way, and that had been the worst of all. That was the time he had told me to eat in my room. Now I could hear him pacing about in the hall, and I knew that it was not over for the night. I began to pray that I could sleep before he came. I did not care what he did as long as I did not have to face him. I resolved to confess to anything he accused me of if it would make him leave sooner. I was about to go out into the hall for my confession when the door was kicked open and he charged into the room.

"You black son of a bitch!" he said. "I ought to *kill* you." He stood over the bed in the dark room and shook his big fist over me. And I lay there hating the overpowering cowardice in me, which kept my body still and my eyes closed, and hoping that he would kill all of it when his heavy fist landed.

"First you insult a man's company, then you ignore him. I been *good* to you. I let you live here, I let you eat my uncle's food, and I taught you things. But you're a ungrateful m-f. I ought to *kill* you right now!"

And I still lay there, as he went on, not hearing him, with nothing in me but a loud throbbing which pulsed through the length of my body and made the sheets move with its pounding. I lay there secure and safe in cowardice for as long as I looked up at him with my eyes and my body twitching and my mind screaming out to him that it was all right, and I thanked him, because now I truly believed in the new five thousand years of Black Rule.

It is night again. I am in bed again, and I can hear the new blond girl closing the bathroom door. I know that in a minute he will come out in his red robe and call a cab. His muffled voice through my closed door will

seem very tired, but just as kind and patient to the dispatcher as it is to everyone, and as it was to me in those old times. I am afraid, because when they came up the stairs earlier they caught me working at the living room table with my back to them. I had not expected him back so soon; but then I should have known that he would not go out. I had turned around in the chair, and she smiled and said hello, and I said "Hi" before he hurried her into the room. I *did* speak, and I know that she heard. But I also know that I must have done something wrong; if not to her, then to him earlier today or yesterday or last week, because he glared at me before following her into the room, and he almost paused to say something when he came out to get the glasses and ice. I wish that I could remember just what it was. But it does not matter. I *am* guilty, and he knows it.

Now that he knows about me I am afraid. I could move away from the apartment and hide my guilt from him, but I know that he would find me. The brainwashed part of my mind tells me to call the police while he is still busy with her, but what could I charge him with when I know that he is only trying to help me? I could move the big ragged yellow chair in front of the door, but that would not stop him, and it might make him impatient with me. Even if I pretended to be asleep and ignored him, it would not help when he comes. He has not bothered to knock for weeks.

In the black shadows over my bed and in the corners I can sense the outraged spirits who help him when they hover about his arms as he gestures, with his lessons, above my bed. I am determined now to lie here and take it. It is the price I must pay for all the black secrets I have learned, and all the evil I have learned about myself. I *am* jealous of him, of his learning, of his girls. I am not the same handkerchief-head I was nine months ago. I have Marie to thank for that, and Claude, and the spirits. They know about me, and perhaps it is they who make him do it and he cannot help himself. I believe in the

147

spirits now, just as I believe most of the time that I am a black devil.

They are going down to the cab now.

I will not ever blame him for it. He is helping me. But I blame the girls. I blame them for not staying on afterward, and for letting all the good nice happy love talk cut off automatically after it is over. *I* need to have them there, after it is over. And he needs it; he needs it much more and much longer than they could ever need what he does for them. He should be able to teach them, as he has taught me. And he should have their appreciation, as he has mine. I blame them. I blame them for letting him try and try and never get just a little of the love there is left in the world.

I can hear him coming back from the cab.

THE LESSON Diction

Back in the days when everyone was old and stupid or young and foolish and me and Sugar were the only ones just right, this lady moved on our block with nappy hair and proper speech and no makeup. And quite naturally we laughed at her, laughed the way we did at the junk man who went about his business like he was some big-time president and his sorry-ass horse his secretary. And we kinda hated her too, hated the way we did the winos who cluttered up our parks and pissed on our handball walls and stank up our hallways and stairs so you couldn't halfway play hide-and-seek without a goddamn gas mask. Miss Moore was her name. The only woman on the block with no first name. And she was black as hell, cept for her feet, which were fish-white and spooky. And she was always planning these boring-ass things for us to do, us being my cousin, mostly, who lived on the block cause we all moved North the same time and to the same apartment then spread out gradual to breathe. And our parents would yank our heads into some kinda shape and crisp up our clothes so we'd be presentable for travel with Miss Moore, who always looked like she was going to church, though she never did. Which is just one of things the grownups talked about when they talked behind her back like a dog. But when she came calling with some sachet she'd sewed up or some gingerbread she'd made or some book, why then they'd all be too embarrassed to turn her down and we'd get handed over all spruced up. She'd been to college and said it was only right that she should take responsibility for the young ones' education, and she not even related by marriage or blood. So they'd go for it. Specially Aunt Gretchen. She was the main gofer in the family. You got some ole dumb shit foolishness you want somebody to go for, you send for Aunt Gretchen. She been screwed into the go-along for so long, it's a blood-deep natural thing with her. Which is how she got saddled with me and Sugar and Junior in the first place while our mothers were in a la-de-da apartment up the block having a good ole time.

So this one day Miss Moore rounds us all up at the mailbox and it's puredee hot and she's knockin herself out about arithmetic. And school suppose to let up in summer I heard, but she don't never let up. And the starch in my pinafore scratching the shit outta me and I'm really hating this nappy-head bitch and her goddamn college degree. I'd much rather go to the pool or to the show where it's cool. So me and Sugar leaning on the mailbox being surly, which is a Miss Moore word. And Flyboy checking out what everybody brought for lunch. And Fat Butt already wasting his peanut-butter-and-jelly sandwich like the pig he is. And Junebug punchin on Q.T.'s arm for potato chips. And Rosie Giraffe shifting from one hip to the other waiting for somebody to step on her foot or ask her if she from Georgia so she can kick ass, preferably Mercedes'. And Miss Moore asking us do we know what money is, like we a bunch of retards. I mean real money, she say, like it's only poker chips or monopoly papers we lay on the grocer. So right away I'm tired of this and say so. And would much rather snatch Sugar and go to the Sunset and terrorize the West Indian kids and take their hair ribbons and their money too. And Miss Moore files that remark away for next week's lesson on brotherhood, I can tell. And finally I say we oughta get to the subway cause it's cooler and besides we might meet some cute boys. Sugar done swiped her mama's lipstick, so we ready.

So we heading down the street and she's boring us silly about what things cost and what our parents make and how much goes for rent and how money ain't divided up right in this country. And then she gets to the part about we all poor and live in the slums, which I don't feature. And I'm ready to speak on that, but she steps out in the street and hails two cabs just like that. Then she hustles half the crew in with her and hands me a five-dollar bill and tells me to calculate 10 percent tip for the driver. And we're off. Me and Sugar and Junebug and Flyboy hangin out the window and hollering to everybody, putting lipstick on each other cause Flyboy a faggot anyway, and making farts with our sweaty armpits. But I'm mostly trying to figure how to spend this money. But they all fascinated with the meter ticking and Junebug starts laying bets as to how much it'll read when Flyboy can't hold his breath no more. Then Sugar lays bets as to how much it'll be when we get there. So I'm stuck. Don't nobody want to go for my plan, which is to jump out at the next light and run off to the first bar-b-que we can find. Then the driver tells us to get the hell out cause we there already. And the meter reads eighty-five cents. And I'm stalling to figure out the tip and Sugar say give him a dime. And I decide he don't need it bad as I do, so later for him. But then he tries to take off with Junebug foot still in the door so we talk about his mama something ferocious. Then we check out that we on Fifth Avenue and everybody dressed up in stockings. One lady in a fur coat, hot as it is. White folks crazy.

"This is the place," Miss Moore say, presenting it to us in the voice she uses at the museum. "Let's look in the windows before we go in."

"Can we steal?" Sugar asks very serious like she's getting the ground rules squared away before she plays. "I beg your pardon," say Miss Moore, and we fall out. So she leads us around the windows of the toy store and me and Sugar screamin, "This is mine, that's mine, I gotta have that, that was made for me, I was born for that," till Big Butt drowns us out.

"Hey, I'm goin to buy that there."

"That there? You don't even know what it is, stupid."

"I do so," he say punchin on Rosie Giraffe. "It's a microscope."

"Whatcha gonna do with a microscope, fool?"

"Look at things."

"Like what, Ronald?" ask Miss Moore. And Big Butt ain't got the first notion. So here go Miss Moore gabbing about the thousands of bacteria in a drop of water and the somethinorother in a speck of blood and the million and one living things in the air around us is invisible to the naked eye. And what she say that for? Junebug go to town on that "naked" and we rolling. Then Miss Moore ask what it cost. So we all jam into the window smudgin it up and the price tag say $300. So then she ask how long'd take for Big Butt and Junebug to save up their allowances. "Too long," I say. "Yeh," adds Sugar, "outgrown it by that time." And Miss Moore say no, you never outgrow learning instruments. "Why, even medical students and interns and, " blah, blah, blah. And we ready to choke Big Butt for bringing it up in the first damn place.

"This here costs four hundred eighty dollars," say Rosie Giraffe. So we pile up all over her to see what she pointin out. My eyes tell me it's a chunk of glass cracked with something heavy, and different-color inks dripped into the splits, then the whole thing put into a oven or something. But for $480 it don't make sense.

"That's a paperweight made of semi-precious stones fused together under tremendous pressure," she explains slowly, with her hands doing the mining and all the factory work.

"So what's a paperweight?" asks Rosie Giraffe.

"To weigh paper with, dumbbell," say Flyboy, the wise man from the East.

"Not exactly," say Miss Moore, which is what she say when you warm or way off too. "It's to weigh paper down so it won't scatter and make your desk untidy." So right away me and Sugar curtsy to each other and then to Mercedes who is more the tidy type.

"We don't keep paper on top of the desk in my class," say Junebug, figuring Miss Moore crazy or lyin one.

"At home, then," she say. "Don't you have a calendar and a pencil case and a blotter and a letter-opener on your desk at home where you do your homework?" And she know damn well what our homes look like cause she nosys around in them every chance she gets.

"I don't even have a desk," say Junebug. "Do we?"

"No. And I don't get no homework neither," say Big Butt.

"And I don't even have a home," say Flyboy like he do at school to keep the white folks off his back and sorry for him. Send this poor kid to camp posters, is his specialty.

"I do," says Mercedes. "I have a box of stationery on my desk and a picture of my cat. My godmother bought the stationery and the desk. There's a big rose on each sheet and the envelopes smell like roses."

"Who wants to know about your smelly-ass stationery," say Rosie Giraffe fore I can get my two cents in.

"It's important to have a work area all your own so that . . ."

"Will you look at this sailboat, please," say Flyboy, cuttin her off and pointin to the thing like it was his. So once again we tumble all over each other to gaze at this magnificent thing in the toy store which is just big enough to maybe sail two kittens across the pond if you strap them to the posts tight. We all start reciting the price tag like we in assembly. "Handcrafted sailboat of fiberglass at one thousand one hundred ninety-five dollars."

"Unbelievable," I hear myself say and am really stunned. I read it again for myself just in case the group recitation put me in a trance. Same thing. For some reason this pisses me off. We look at Miss Moore and she lookin at us, waiting for I dunno what.

Who'd pay all that when you can buy a sailboat set for a quarter at Pop's, a tube of glue for a dime, and a ball of string for eight cents? "It must have a motor and a whole lot else besides," I say. "My sailboat cost me *calculates* about fifty cents."

"But will it take water?" say Mercedes with her smart ass.

"Took mine to Alley Pond Park once," say Flyboy. "String broke, lost it. Pity."

"Sailed mine in Central Park and it keeled over and sank. Had to ask my father for another dollar."

"And you got the strap," laugh Big Butt. "The jerk didn't even have a string on it. My old man wailed on his behind."

Little Q.T. was staring hard at the sailboat and you could see he wanted it bad. But he too little and somebody'd just take it from him. So what the hell. "This boat for kids, Miss Moore?"

"Parents silly to buy something like that just to get all broke up," say Rosie Giraffe.

"That much money it should last forever," I figure.

"My father'd buy it for me if I wanted it."

"Your father, my ass," say Rosie Giraffe getting a chance to finally push Mercedes.

"Must be rich people shop here," say Q.T.

"You are a very bright boy," say Flyboy. "What was your first clue?" And he rap him on the head with the back of his knuckles, since Q.T. the only one he could get away with. Though Q.T. liable to come up behind you years later and get his licks in when you half expect it.

"What I want to know is, " I says to Miss Moore though I never talk to her, I wouldn't give the bitch that satisfaction, "is how much a real boat costs? I figure a thousand'd get you a yacht any day."

"Why don't you check that out," she says, "and report back to the group?" Which really pains my ass. If you gonna mess up a perfectly good swim day least you could do is have some answer. "Let's go in," she say like she got something up her sleeve. Only she don't lead the way. So me and Sugar turn the corner to where the entrance is, but when we get there I kinda hang back. Not that I'm scared, what's there to be afraid of, just a toy store. But I feel funny, shame. But what I got to be shamed about? Got as much right to go in as anybody. But somehow I can't seem to get hold of the door, so I step away for Sugar to lead. But she hangs back too. And I look at her and she looks at me and this is ridiculous. I mean, damn, I have never ever been shy about doing nothing or going nowhere. But then Mercedes steps up and then Rosie Giraffe and Big Butt crowd in behind and shove, and next thing we all stuffed into the doorway with only Mercedes squeezing past us, smoothing out her jumper and walking right down the aisle. Then the rest of us tumble in like a glued-together jigsaw done all wrong. And people lookin at us. And it's like the time me and Sugar crashed into the Catholic church on a dare. But once we got in there and everything so hushed and holy and the candles and the bowin and the handkerchiefs on all the drooping heads, I just couldn't go through with the plan. Which was for me to run up to the altar and do a tap dance while Sugar played the nose flute and messed around in the holy water. And Sugar kept givin me the elbow. Then later teased me so bad I tied her up in the shower and turned it on and locked her in. And she'd be there till this day if Aunt Gretchen hadn't finally figured I was lyin about the boarder takin a shower.

Same thing in the store. We all walkin on tiptoe and hardly touchin the games and puzzles and things. And I watched Miss Moore who is steady watchin us like she waitin for a sign. Like Mama Drewery watches the sky and sniffs the air and takes note of just how much slant is in the bird formation. Then me and Sugar bump smack into each other, so busy gazing at the toys, 'specially the sailboat. But we don't laugh

and go into our fat-lady bump-stomach routine. We just stare at that price tag. Then Sugar run a finger over the whole boat. And I'm jealous and want to hit her. Maybe not her, but I sure want to punch somebody in the mouth.

"Watcha bring us here for, Miss Moore?"

"You sound angry, Sylvia. Are you mad about something?" Givin me one of them grins like she tellin a grown-up joke that never turns out to be funny. And she's lookin very closely at me like maybe she plannin to do my portrait from memory. I'm mad, but I won't give her that satisfaction. So I slouch around the store bein very bored and say, "Let's go."

Me and Sugar at the back of the train watchin the tracks whizzin by large then small then gettin gobbled up in the dark. I'm thinkin about this tricky toy I saw in the store. A clown that somersaults on a bar then does chin-ups just cause you yank lightly at his leg. Cost $35. I could see me askin my mother for a $35 birthday clown. "You wanna who that costs what?" she'd say, cocking her head to the side to get a better view of the hole in my head. Thirty-five dollars could buy new bunk beds for Junior and Gretchen's boy. Thirty-five dollars and the whole household could go visit Granddaddy Nelson in the country. Thirty-five dollars would pay for the rent and the piano bill too. Who are these people that spend that much for performing clowns and $1,000 for toy sailboats? What kinda work they do and how they live and how come we ain't in on it? Where we are is who we are, Miss Moore always pointin out. But it don't necessarily have to be that way, she always adds then waits for somebody to say that poor people have to wake up and demand their share of the pie and don't none of us know what kind of pie she talkin about in the first damn place. But she ain't so smart cause I still got her four dollars from the taxi and and she sure ain't gettin it. Messin up my day with this shit. Sugar nudges me in my pocket and winks.

152

Miss Moore lines us up in front of the mailbox where we started from, seem like years ago, and I got a headache for thinkin so hard. And we lean all over each other so we can hold up under the draggy-ass lecture she always finishes us off with at the end before we thank her for borin us to tears. But she just looks at us like she readin tea leaves. Finally she say, "Well, what did you think of F.A.O. Schwartz?"

Rosie Giraffe mumbles, "White folks crazy."

"I'd like to go there again when I get my birthday money," says Mercedes, and we shove her out the pack so she has to lean on the mailbox by herself.

"I'd like a shower. Tiring day," say Flyboy.

Then Sugar surprises me by sayin, "You know, Miss Moore, I don't think all of us here put together eat in a year what that sailboat costs." And Miss Moore lights up like somebody goosed her. "And?" she say, urging Sugar on. Only I'm standin on her foot so she don't continue.

"Imagine for a minute what kind of society it is in which some people can spend on a toy what it would cost to feed a family of six or seven. What do you think?"

"I think," say Sugar pushing me off her feet like she never done before, cause I whip her ass in a minute, "that this is not much of a democracy if you ask me. Equal chance to pursue happiness means an equal crack at the dough, don't it?" Miss Moore is besides herself and I am disgusted with Sugar's treachery. So I stand on her foot one more time to see if she'll shove me. She shuts up, and Miss Moore looks at me, sorrowfully I'm thinkin. And somethin weird is goin on, I can feel it in my chest.

"Anybody else learn anything today?" lookin dead at me. I walk away and Sugar has to run to catch up and don't even seem to notice when I shrug her arm off my shoulder.

"Well, we got four dollars anyway," she says.

"Uh hunh."

"We could go to Hascombs and get half a chocolate layer and then go to the Sunset and still have plenty money for potato chips and ice-cream sodas."

"Uh hunh."

"Race you to Hascombs," she say.

We start down the block and she gets ahead which is O.K. by me cause I'm goin to the West End and then over to the Drive to think this day through. She can run if she want to and even run faster. But ain't nobody gonna beat me at nuthin.

Good kid's pt. of view

They do learn in spite of their outward hatred for Miss Moore. What is she to them.

POETRY

Poetry is an instrument to transform the world.

GABRIEL CELAYA (BASQUE)

Politics is about grievances that something can be done about. And poetry is about grief that nothing can be done about.

ROBERT FROST

Poetry is an act of mischief.

THEODORE ROETHKE

Poetry is a response to the daily necessity of getting the world right.

WALLACE STEVENS

The poet is not to be limited by the literal truth . . . he is not trying to tell the truth: he is trying to make it.

JAMES DICKEY

Five Poems

None of these five short poems rhymes. They do not even deal with what you might think of as "poetic" subjects (a lost love or death, for example). A poem may simply try to make you see something you have never really seen before—a red wheelbarrow, "glazed" with rainwater, beside white chickens—and realize that it is worth seeing. In the following pages we will introduce terms that should help you understand how poems work. Any poem, whether simple or complex, can be discussed in terms of its basic elements: diction (the words it uses), patterns of sound, the tone the poet establishes, and the metaphors or images that the poet creates. Finally, we will discuss some of the more important verse forms that poets have used in the past and continue to use.

WILLIAM CARLOS WILLIAMS (1883–1963)

THE RED WHEELBARROW

so much depends
upon

a red wheel
barrow

5   glazed with rain
water

beside the white
chickens

WALT WHITMAN (1819–1892)

A FARM PICTURE

Through the ample open door of the peaceful country barn,
A sun-lit pasture field, with cattle and horses feeding;
And haze, and vista, and the far horizon, fading away.

GARY SNYDER (1930–)

NORTH BEACH ALBA

waking half-drunk in a strange pad
making it out to the cool gray
    san francisco dawn—
white gulls over white houses,
5   fog down the bay,
tamalpais a fresh green hill in the new sun,
driving across the bridge in a beat old car
    to work.

BASHO (1644–1694)

HAIKU

The sea darkening . . .
   Oh voices of the wild ducks
Crying, whirling, white

ANONYMOUS CHIPPEWA INDIAN

LOVE SONG

A loon I thought it was
But it was
My love's
Splashing oar.

1. By using plain, concrete language, Williams comes as close as a poet can to presenting a scene as a photographer might; yet he makes a point about how we see, or can see. *What* depends upon the red wheelbarrow?

2. Poets usually *interpret* the scenes they compose by their choice of words. What words indicate Whitman's attitude toward his farm "picture"?

3. How important are the first and last lines in establishing the mood that Snyder creates? Why are these particular details included (fog, white gulls, etc.)?

4. Do you "see" the scene in the fourth poem? What does it suggest that a photograph could not? To what extent does the meaning of the poem depend upon the imagination of the reader?

5. Like the Japanese haiku by Basho, this Indian poem leaves much unsaid. What kind of mood does it suggest?

Diction

Many people still expect poetry to use a language removed from common speech, made up of especially "poetic" words such as those used by Edgar Allan Poe (1809–1849) in his poem, "To Helen":

> Helen, thy beauty is to me
>   Like those Nicèan barks of yore,
> That gently, o'er a perfumed sea,
>   The weary, way-worn wanderer bore
> 5   To his own native shore.
>
> On desperate seas long wont to roam,
>   Thy hyacinth hair, thy classic face,
> Thy Naiad airs have brought me home
>   To the glory that was Greece,
> 10   And the grandeur that was Rome.
>
> Lo! in yon brilliant window-niche
>   How statue-like I see thee stand,
>   The agate lamp within thy hand!
> Ah! Psyche, from the regions which
> 15   Are Holy-Land!

Even in the middle of the nineteenth century, when Poe wrote, such words as "thy," "o'er," and "yore" were old-fashioned and literary. Poe stiffly addresses the Helen of his imagination as "thee" and pictures her only in the most general terms ("Thy hyacinth hair, thy classic face"). The language and movement of the poem remove it from the concerns of the world we know, taking the reader away "o'er a perfumed sea" into a reverie over the legendary beauty of Helen of Troy. The poems that follow suggest how dramatically some contemporary poets have broken with old assumptions about the proper language and form of poetry. Instead of lulling the reader, they startle him by combining ordinary words in original and often explosive ways.

IN THE POCKET: NFL

Going backward
All of me and some
Of my friends are forming a shell   my arm is looking
Everywhere and some are breaking
5   In   breaking down
And out   breaking
Across, and one is going deep   deeper
Than my arm.   Where is Number One hooking
Into the violent green alive
10   With linebackers?   I cannot find him he cannot beat
His man   I fall back more
Into the pocket   it is raging and breaking
Number Two has disappeared into the chalk
Of the sideline   Number Three is cutting with half
15   A step of grace   my friends are crumbling
Around me the wrong color
Is looming   hands are coming
Up and over between
My arm and Number Three: throw it hit him in the middle
20   Of his enemies   hit move scramble
Before death and the ground
Come up   LEAP STAND KILL DIE STRIKE

Dickey offers a poetic "instant replay" of a few seconds of action from a quarterback's point of view. What was he trying to capture? Imagine the poem rewritten so that all the lines begin at an even left margin. Would it affect you differently?

BUFFALO BILL'S

Buffalo Bill's
defunct
        who used to
        ride a watersmooth-silver
5   stallion
and break onetwothreefourfive pigeonsjustlikethat
                                                    Jesus
        he was a handsome man
                                and what i want to know is
10   how do you like your blueeyed boy
Mister Death

Cummings runs some words together, for example "onetwothreefourfive." How does this affect the way you read the poem?

FUNNY FANTASIES

    funny fantasies are never so real as oldstyle romances
           where the hero has a heroine who has
              long black braids and lets
                                  nobody
5   kiss her ever
                        and everybody's trying all the time to
         run away with her
                        and the hero is always drawing his
          (sic) sword and
10   tilting at ginmills and
                                      forever telling her he
           loves her and has only honorable intentions and
       honorable mentions
                        and no one ever beats him at
15   anything
              but then finally one day
                             she who has always been so timid
         offs with her glove and says
                             (though not in so many big words)
20   Let's lie down somewheres
                                  baby

Why does Ferlinghetti like "oldstyle romances"? What does the heroine's comment at the end do to the rest of the poem?

Tone

A poem may be joyful or melancholy, questioning or cynical. Sometimes the tone of a poem is difficult to label. An attitude may emerge only in the course of the poem as the poet develops a mood or explores the implications of his subject. Sometimes the tone is obvious, as in Ferlinghetti's playful description of "oldstyle romances" or Thomas Gray's (1716–1771) meditation on the poor in his "Elegy Written in a Country Churchyard":

> Let not Ambition mock their useful toil,
>   Their homely joys, and destiny obscure;
>   Nor Grandeur hear with a disdainful smile
>   The short and simple annals of the poor.

Gray's moralizing lines must be read in a solemn tone of voice. A poet may use an ironic tone to convey a critical attitude toward his subject. To make sense of such poems the reader must grasp the irony, which may be blatant or extremely subtle. For example, in reading Robert Frost's "Provide, Provide" it is necessary to decide how to take the urgings of the speaker. This speaker should not be identified with Frost. Poets often create a character whom they imagine as the speaker of a particular poem.

ROBERT FROST (1874–1963)

PROVIDE, PROVIDE

> The witch that came (the withered hag)
> To wash the steps with pail and rag
> Was once the beauty Abishag,
>
> The picture pride of Hollywood.
> 5   Too many fall from great and good
> For you to doubt the likelihood.
>
> Die early and avoid the fate.
> Or if predestined to die late,
> Make up your mind to die in state.
>
> 10   Make the whole stock exchange your own!
> If need be occupy a throne,
> Where nobody can call *you* crone.

Some have relied on what they knew,
Others on being simply true.
15 What worked for them might work for you.

No memory of having starred
Atones for later disregard
Or keeps the end from being hard.

Better to go down dignified
20 With boughten friendship at your side
Than none at all. Provide, provide!

What assumptions lie behind the speaker's pragmatic advice? How does Frost use his exaggerations to criticize the values of a materialistic society?

Robert Browning wrote a number of dramatic monologues in which a speaker unconsciously displays his own faults. In the most famous of these, "My Last Duchess," Browning's irony works in subtle ways to expose the coldness of the Duke, who appears fonder of his late wife's portrait than he was of her. How does the poem progressively reveal the Duke's character?

ROBERT BROWNING (1812–1889)

MY LAST DUCHESS

Ferrara

That's my last Duchess painted on the wall,
Looking as if she were alive. I call
That piece a wonder, now: Frà Pandolf's hands
Worked busily a day, and there she stands.
5 Will't please you sit and look at her? I said
"Frà Pandolf" by design, for never read
Strangers like you that pictured countenance,
The depth and passion of its earnest glance,
But to myself they turned (since none puts by
10 The curtain I have drawn for you, but I)
And seemed as they would ask me, if they durst,
How such a glance came there; so, not the first
Are you to turn and ask thus. Sir, 'twas not
Her husband's presence only, called that spot
15 Of joy into the Duchess' cheek: perhaps
Frà Pandolf chanced to say "Her mantle laps
Over my Lady's wrist too much," or "Paint
Must never hope to reproduce the faint
Half-flush that dies along her throat": such stuff
20 Was courtesy, she thought, and cause enough
For calling up that spot of joy. She had
A heart—how shall I say?—too soon made glad,
Too easily impressed; she liked whate'er
She looked on, and her looks went everywhere.

25 Sir, 'twas all one! My favour at her breast,
The dropping of the daylight in the West,
The bough of cherries some officious fool
Broke in the orchard for her, the white mule
She rode with round the terrace—all and each
30 Would draw from her alike the approving speech,
Or blush, at least. She thanked men,—good! but thanked
Somehow—I know not how—as if she ranked
My gift of a nine-hundred-years-old name
With anybody's gift. Who'd stoop to blame
35 This sort of trifling? Even had you skill
In speech—(which I have not)—to make your will
Quite clear to such an one, and say "Just this
Or that in you disgusts me; here you miss,
Or there exceed the mark"—and if she let
40 Herself be lessoned so, nor plainly set
Her wits to yours, forsooth, and made excuse,
—E'en then would be some stooping, and I choose
Never to stoop. Oh, Sir, she smiled, no doubt,
Whene'er I passed her; but who passed without
45 Much the same smile? This grew; I gave commands;
Then all smiles stopped together. There she stands
As if alive. Will't please you rise? We'll meet
The company below, then. I repeat,
The Count your master's known munificence
50 Is ample warrant that no just pretence
Of mine for dowry will be disallowed;
Though his fair daughter's self, as I avowed
At starting, is my object. Nay, we'll go
Together down, Sir! Notice Neptune, tho',
55 Taming a sea-horse, thought a rarity,
Which Claus of Innsbruck cast in bronze for me!

164

Metaphor

Poets rely on figurative language, especially metaphor and simile, to express insights for which literal language is inadequate. Metaphor is a way of associating seemingly unlike things to generate new meanings. For example, by speaking of an "old man's eagle mind" Yeats suggests that an old man's mind can be strong and far-seeing. The metaphor challenges our normal habits of thought.

Poets continually remake our world by finding fresh and illuminating relationships. In an essay entitled "Metaphor as Pure Adventure," James Dickey has described the process of discovering metaphors as "not so much a way of understanding the world but a perpetually exciting way of recreating it from its own parts." By using metaphors to show us new ways of perceiving human experience, poets give life, in Dickey's words, "the fullest and most electric sense of being."

The following poem by the Mexican poet Octavio Paz (1914–   ) consists of a series of metaphors. Which do you think are the most "electric"? Why?

YOUR EYES

Your eyes are the land of lightning and the tear,
silence that speaks,
hurricanes without wind, sea without waves,
trapped birds, sleepy golden beasts,
5   dazzle of topaz shocking as the truth,
autumn in a clearing of the woods where light sings on
   the shoulder of a tree whose leaves are birds,
beach that morning discovers starred with springs,
basket of fruits of fire,
10   a lie that nourishes,
mirrors of this world, doors to the beyond,
the easy heartbeat of the sea at noon,
the absolute, quivering,
cold uplands.

Translated by Muriel Rukeyser

What do the comparisons in the following poems by Ezra Pound (1885–1972) suggest? What associations do you have with the words Pound uses? How do these associations affect the way you read the poems? One poem relies on a metaphor, the other on a simile (a metaphor introduced by "like" or "as").

IN A STATION OF THE METRO

The apparition of these faces in the crowd;
Petals on a wet, black bough.

ALBA*

As cool as the pale wet leaves
       of lily-of-the-valley
She lay beside me in the dawn.

*Provençal word for "dawn." Also a kind of poem composed by troubadour poets in medieval France that usually dealt with the parting of lovers at sunrise.

The metaphor and simile in these poems can also be described as *images*. Pound's line, "Petals on a wet, black bough," presents an image, a word-picture that appeals to the senses. This image functions as a metaphor, because it offers a figurative description of faces in the subway. But not all images are metaphoric. Williams's red wheelbarrow "glazed with rain water" and Snyder's "white gulls over white houses" are images that exist simply for their own sake and not to suggest relationships.

Some images are clearly symbolic, pointing to meanings beyond the literal sense of the verse. The images in the following poem by William Blake (1757–1827) make only a limited appeal to the senses; their primary function is to express Blake's sense of the way organized religion (suggested by "Priests in black gowns") represses and kills the desires freely expressed in childhood. What kind of existence does the Garden of Love suggest? What has happened to it in the last stanza?

THE GARDEN OF LOVE

I went to the Garden of Love,
And saw what I never had seen:
A Chapel was built in the midst,
Where I used to play on the green.

5   And the gates of this Chapel were shut,
And "Thou shalt not" writ over the door;
So I turn'd to the Garden of Love
That so many sweet flowers bore;

And I saw it was filled with graves,
10   And tomb-stones where flowers should be;
And Priests in black gowns were walking their rounds,
And binding with briars my joys & desires.

The Sound of Poetry

I wanted to write poetry in the beginning because I had fallen in love with words. The first poems I knew were nursery rhymes, and before I could read them for myself I had come to love just the words of them, the words alone. What the words stood for, symbolized, or meant, was of very secondary importance. What mattered was the sound of them as I heard them for the first time on the lips of the remote and incomprehensible grown-ups who seemed, for some reason, to be living in my world. And these words were, to me, as the notes of bells, the sounds of musical instruments, the noises of wind, sea, and rain, the rattle of milkcarts, the clopping of hooves on cobbles, the fingering of branches on a window pane, might be to someone, deaf from birth, who has miraculously found his hearing.

DYLAN THOMAS (1914–1953)

A child is more likely than an adult to be alive to the magic of spoken words. Confronted everywhere by the printed word, we rapidly lose our fascination with the sound of language. We hardly ever take the time to read a poem aloud, even though its power may depend upon the patterns of sounds it creates. In nursery rhymes, and in many popular songs, the sound of the words counts for more than their sense:

> Ride a cock-horse to Banbury Cross
> To see a fine lady upon a white horse.
> With rings on her fingers and bells on her toes,
> She shall have music wherever she goes.

Here the rhymes hold our attention, and the bouncing rhythm of the verse moves us along from line to line. Sometimes rhyme underscores the sense of verse. In the following example it heightens the humorous effect the poet tries to achieve.

OGDEN NASH (1902–1971)

THE TURTLE

> The turtle lives 'twixt plated decks
> Which practically conceal its sex.
> I think it clever of the turtle
> In such a fix to be so fertile.

When verse has a regular rhythm, it is called metrical. The simplest way to determine the meter of a poem is to listen for stressed (accented) syllables:

That tíme of yéar thou máyst in mé behóld
When yéllow léaves, or nóne, or féw, do háng
Upón those bóughs which sháke agaínst the cóld . . .

Lines of metrical verse can be divided into "feet," each consisting of a stressed syllable and one or more unstressed syllables. These particular lines are iambic pentameter. The basic metrical unit is the iamb, which consists of an unstressed followed by a stressed syllable (˘´), and the line has five iambic feet:

Thăt tíme | ŏf yéar | thŏu máyst | ĭn mé | bĕhóld

Not all verse observes a meter so strictly. In fact, good poets usually keep their verse from becoming monotonously regular. Shakespeare, in the fourth line of the poem from which the above lines are taken, included an unusual number of stressed syllables to slow the line down and give it added emphasis:

Báre ruíned choírs whĕre láte thĕ swéet bírds sáng.

Most of the mistakes made by beginners in marking stressed and unstressed syllables result from wrenching the natural accents of words to make them fit a regular pattern (reading "yĕllów" instead of "yéllŏw," for example). The other basic meters besides iambic (˘ ´) are trochaic (´ ˘), anapestic (˘ ˘ ´), and dactylic (´ ˘ ˘). Less common kinds of feet are the pyrrhic (˘ ˘) and spondaic (´ ´).

People sometimes disagree over how a line should be divided into feet, and over whether a particular word is stressed or not (some distinguish between lightly and heavily stressed syllables). For example, one could read John Donne's phrase "Teach me how to repent" with the first stress on either "Teach" or "me." Here there is room for argument over what Donne intended to emphasize. Such areas of disagreement are usually small, however.

You may not need to mark accents in order to get a feeling for the rhythm of a poem. But the better you understand the way the meter of a poem works, the likelier you are to understand and respond to the effects that the sounds of the words produce. The best way to develop an ear for this rhythm—so that you can put the emphases in the right places—is to read poems aloud.

Alexander Pope (1688–1744) argued that in poetry "the sound must seem an echo to the sense," and then went on to illustrate his own rule:

Soft is the strain when Zephyr gently blows,
And the smooth stream in smoother numbers flows;
But when loud surges lash the sounding shore,
The hoarse, rough verse should like the torrent roar;
When Ajax strives some rock's vast weight to throw,
The line too labors, and the words move slow;
Not so, when swift Camilla scours the plain,
Flies o'er the unbending corn, and skims along the main.

Alexander Pope, *An Essay on Criticism*

The effect of these lines depends upon rhyme, skillful metrical variations, and patterns of sounds within lines. One of the commonest sound patterns used by poets is alliteration, which is usually the repetition of initial consonants (notice Pope's use of *s* in the first three lines). Another common sound pattern is assonance, the repetition of similar vowel sounds ("hoarse," "rough," "torrent," "roar"). Some of the most complicated effects depend upon subtle combinations of consonant and vowel sounds:

> The moan of doves in immemorial elms,
> And murmuring of innumerable bees.

> Alfred, Lord Tennyson, *The Princess*

Harsh, discordant sound patterns can be effective in their own way, as in this description of fierce winds (called by their classical names):

> Bursting their brazen Dungeon, arm'd with ice
> And snow and hail and stormy gust and flaw,
> *Boreas* and *Caecias* and *Argestes* loud
> And *Thrascias* rend the Woods and Seas upturn.

> John Milton, *Paradise Lost*

Consider the ways in which sound echoes sense in the following poems.

> There is sweet music here that softer falls
> Than petals from blown roses on the grass,
> Or night-dews on still waters between walls
> Of shadowy granite, in a gleaming pass;
> Music that gentlier on the spirit lies,
> Than tired eyelids upon tired eyes;
> Music that brings sweet sleep down from the blissful skies.
> Here are cool mosses deep,
> And through the moss the ivies creep,
> And in the stream the long-leaved flowers weep,
> And from the craggy ledge the poppy hangs in sleep.

> Alfred, Lord Tennyson, *The Lotos Eaters*

How many examples of *s* alliteration can you find? How do you respond to Tennyson's use of assonance in such phrases as "blown roses" and "tired eyes"? Are you reacting to the associations of the words as well as to their sounds?

GOD'S GRANDEUR

The world is charged with the grandeur of God.
　　It will flame out, like shining from shook foil;
　　It gathers to a greatness, like the ooze of oil
Crushed. Why do men then now not reck his rod?
5　Generations have trod, have trod, have trod;
　　And all is seared with trade; bleared, smeared with toil;
　　And wears man's smudge and shares man's smell: the soil
Is bare now, nor can foot feel, being shod.

　　And for all this, nature is never spent;
10　　There lives the dearest freshness deep down things;
And though the last lights off the black West went
　　Oh, morning, at the brown brink eastward, springs—
Because the Holy Ghost over the bent
　　World broods with warm breast and with ah! bright wings.

Often Hopkins appears to have chosen a word ("ooze" and "bleared") more for its sound than for its exact meaning. What effect does he achieve by rhyming "seared," "bleared," and "smeared"? By repeating "have trod"? By breaking the flow of the last line with an exclamation ("ah")?

THE DANCE

In Breughel's great picture, The Kermess,
the dancers go round, they go round and
around, the squeal and the blare and the
tweedle of bagpipes, a bugle and fiddles
5　tipping their bellies (round as the thick-
sided glasses whose wash they impound)
their hips and their bellies off balance
to turn them. Kicking and rolling about
the Fair Grounds, swinging their butts, those
10　shanks must be sound to bear up under such
rollicking measures, prance as they dance
in Breughel's great picture, The Kermess.

How does Williams capture the energetic movement of Breughel's picture of peasants dancing?

Poetic Forms

Robert Frost said that writing free verse—that is, poetry without rhyme or meter—is like playing tennis with the net down. Although few contemporary poets would insist, like Frost, on the discipline that rhyme and meter provide, most would agree that a poem defines itself by observing limits of some kind. C. Day Lewis (1904–   ) described the process by which a poem evolves this way:

> A poem, settling to its form,
> Finds there no jailer, but a norm
> Of conduct, and a fitting sphere
> Which stops it wandering everywhere.

Even free verse finds internal limits to keep it from wandering everywhere. Poems written in traditional forms simply observe much stricter, external limits, which to some degree shape their meaning.

When a poet works with rhyme, he must satisfy the demands of the form he chooses. These are relatively simple in the case of couplets (rhymed pairs of lines) or quatrains (four-line stanzas), but more taxing in the case of a complex form such as the sonnet. Jonathan Swift (1667–1745) used couplets to string together a series of brief impressions of eighteenth-century London life in a fast-moving, humorous poem.

A DESCRIPTION OF THE MORNING

Now hardly here and there an hackney-coach
Appearing, show'd the ruddy morn's approach.
Now Betty from her master's bed had flown,
And softly stole to discompose her own.
5   The slipshod prentice from his master's door,
Had par'd the dirt, and sprinkled round the floor.
Now Moll had whirl'd her mop with dext'rous airs,
Prepar'd to scrub the entry and the stairs.

The youth with broomy stumps began to trace
10   The kennel-edge, where wheels had worn the place.
The small-coal man was heard with cadence deep,
'Till drown'd in shriller notes of chimney-sweep,
Duns at his lordship's gate began to meet,
And brickdust Moll had scream'd through half the street.
15   The turnkey now his flock returning sees,
Duly let out a-nights to steal for fees:
The watchful bailiffs take their silent stands;
And school-boys lag with satchels in their hands.

Quatrains allow a poem to develop in a more leisurely way, through separate units of thought. In the following poem William Wordsworth (1770–1850) introduces his subject in the first quatrain, characterizes her with two suggestive images in the second, and expresses his grief in the third.

SHE DWELT AMONG THE UNTRODDEN WAYS

She dwelt among the untrodden ways
   Beside the springs of Dove,
A maid whom there were none to praise
   And very few to love:

5 A violet by a mossy stone
   Half hidden from the eye!
—Fair as a star, when only one
   Is shining in the sky.

She lived unknown, and few could know
10   When Lucy ceased to be;
But she is in her grave, and, oh,
   The difference to me!

Some poets have chosen blank verse, unrhymed iambic pentameter, for their most serious efforts. By using blank verse a poet can employ the rhythmic patterns of a regular rhyme scheme while avoiding the restraints imposed by rhyme. John Milton (1608–1674), who rejected what he called the "bondage" of rhyme, chose this form for his epic, *Paradise Lost*, which ends with the departure of Adam and Eve from paradise.

Some natural tears they dropp'd, but wip'd them soon;
The World was all before them, where to choose
Their place of rest, and Providence their guide:
They hand in hand with wand'ring steps and slow,
Through *Eden* took their solitary way.

The lyric, the epigram, the ballad, and the sonnet are four traditional poetic forms that are still very much alive. The term "lyric" originally referred to a kind of Greek poetry meant to be sung to musical accompaniment; it has since come to refer to short poems that express a feeling, or mood, whether or not they have the "singing line" of lyric poetry written for music. C. Day Lewis described the way this feeling can become more than a purely individual expression:

A lyric is impersonal, not because the poet has deliberately screened personal feelings or memories out of it, but because he has broken through them to the ground of their being, a ground which is the fruitful compost made by numberless human experiences of a like nature.

How do the following lyrics break through to universal human feelings? What moods are developed in them?

WESTERN WIND, WHEN WILT THOU BLOW

Western wind, when wilt thou blow,
The small rain down can rain?
Christ, if my love were in my arms,
And I in my bed again!

WILLIAM SHAKESPEARE (1564–1616)

OH MISTRESS MINE

Oh mistress mine! where are you roaming?
Oh! stay and hear; your true love's coming,
    That can sing both high and low.
Trip no further, pretty sweeting;
5 Journeys end in lovers meeting,
    Every wise man's son doth know.

What is love? 'tis not hereafter;
Present mirth hath present laughter;
    What's to come is still unsure:
10 In delay there lies no plenty;
Then come kiss me, sweet and twenty,
    Youth's a stuff will not endure.

ALFRED, LORD TENNYSON (1809–1892)

BREAK, BREAK, BREAK

Break, break, break,
  On thy cold gray stones, O Sea!
And I would that my tongue could utter
  The thoughts that arise in me.

5 O, well for the fisherman's boy,
  That he shouts with his sister at play!
O, well for the sailor lad,
  That he sings in his boat on the bay!

And the stately ships go on
10   To their haven under the hill;
But O for the touch of a vanished hand,
  And the sound of a voice that is still!

Break, break, break,
  At the foot of thy crags, O sea!
15 But the tender grace of a day that is dead
  Will never come back to me.

COUNTING THE BEATS

You, love, and I,
(He whispers) you and I,
And if no more than only you and I
What care you or I?

5 Counting the beats,
Counting the slow heart beats,
The bleeding to death of time in slow heart beats,
Wakeful they lie.

Cloudless day,
10 Night, and a cloudless day,
Yet the huge storm will burst upon their heads one day
From a bitter sky.

Where shall we be,
(She whispers) where shall we be,
15 When death strikes home, O where then shall we be
Who were you and I?

Not there but here,
(He whispers) only here,
As we are, here, together, now and here,
20 Always you and I.

Counting the beats,
Counting the slow heart beats,
The bleeding to death of time in slow heart beats,
Wakeful they lie.

The epigram, one of the oldest poetic forms, evolved from inscriptions on tombstones. The term came to refer to any terse, pointed statement in verse. Here are an eighteenth-century epigram by Alexander Pope and a contemporary example by J. V. Cunningham (1911–):

ENGRAVED ON THE COLLAR OF A DOG
WHICH I GAVE TO HIS ROYAL HIGHNESS

I am his Highness' dog at Kew;
Pray tell me, sir, whose dog are you?

EPIGRAM

I married in my youth a wife.
She was my own, my very first.
She gave the best years of her life.
I hope nobody gets the worst.

The ballad is a form that is well known to admirers of folk songs, old and new. A ballad tells a story, usually tragic and often involving supernatural happenings, by means of dialogue or a series of dramatic scenes. The older ballads, transmitted orally from singer to singer, are anonymous and impersonal, without the sort of explanatory or sentimental commentary on the action that an individual poet might supply. Below are three ballads, one that has come down through folk tradition, one a literary ballad that captures something of the spirit of older ballads, and the last a stark narrative of a contemporary tragedy.

ANONYMOUS

EDWARD

"Why dois your brand[1] sae[2] drap wi bluid,
                Edward, Edward?
Why dois your brand sae drap wi bluid,
    And why sae sad gang[3] yee, O?"
5 "O I hae killed my hauke sae guid,
                Mither, mither,

O I hae killed my hauke sae guid,
And I had nae mair bot hee, O."

"Your haukis bluid, was nevir sae reid,[4]
10   Edward, Edward,
Your haukis bluid was nevir sae reid,
    My deir son, I tell thee, O."
"O I hae killed my reid-roan steid,
                Mither, mither.

15 O I hae killed my reid-roan steid.
That erst was sae fair and frie, O."

"Your steid was auld, and ye hae gat mair,
                Edward, Edward,
Your steid was auld, and ye hae gat mair;
20   Sum other dule[5] ye drie,[6] O."
"O I hae killed my fadir deir,
                Mither, mither.

O I hae killed my fadir deir,
Alas, and wae[7] is mee, O!"

    [1]Sword. [2]So. [3]Go. [4]Red. [5]Grief. [6]Suffer. [7]Woe.

25   "And whatten[8] penance wul ye drie for that,

                                  Edward, Edward?

   And whatten penance wul ye drie for that,

      My deir son, now tell me, O?"

"Ile set my feit in yonder boat,

30   Mither, mither,

   Ile set my feit in yonder boat,

   And Ile fare ovir the sea, O."

   "And what wul ye doe wi your towirs and your ha,[9]

                                    Edward, Edward?

35   And what wul ye doe wi your towirs and your ha,

      That were sae fair to see, O?"

"Ile let thame stand tul they doun fa,[10]

                                   Mither, mither,

   Ile let thame stand tul they doun fa,

40   For here nevir mair[11] maun[12] I bee, O."

   "And what wul ye leive to your bairns[13] and your wife,

                                    Edward, Edward?

   And what wul ye leive to your bairns and your wife,

      Whan ye gang ovir the sea, O?"

45   "The warldis[14] room, late them beg thrae[15] life,

                                   Mither, mither,

   The warldis room, late them beg thrae life,

   For thame nevir mair wul I see, O."

   "And what wul ye leive to your ain mither deir,

50   Edward, Edward?

   And what wul ye leive to your ain mither deir,

      My deir son, now tell me, O?"

"The curse of hell frae[16] me sall[17] ye beir,

                                   Mither, mither,

55   The curse of hell frae me sall ye beir.

   Sic[18] counseils ye gave to me, O."

[8]What. [9]Hall. [10]Fall. [11]More. [12]Must. [13]Children. [14]World's. [15]Through. [16]From. [17]Shall. [18]Such.

Ballads characteristically work through understatement, forcing the reader to piece together for himself the tragic story and the motives behind it. What is the effect of delaying the explanation of the blood on Edward's sword? How does Edward feel about going into exile? Why does he turn on his mother in the end?

LA BELLE DAME SANS MERCI[1]

O what can ail thee, Knight at arms,
    Alone and palely loitering?
The sedge has withered from the Lake
    And no birds sing!

5 O what can ail thee, Knight at arms,
    So haggard, and so woebegone?
The squirrel's granary is full
    And the harvest's done.

I see a lily on thy brow
10   With anguish moist and fever dew,
And on thy cheeks a fading rose
    Fast withereth too.

I met a Lady in the Meads,
    Full beautiful, a faery's child,
15 Her hair was long, her foot was light
    And her eyes were wild.

I made a Garland for her head,
    And bracelets too, and fragrant Zone;[2]
She looked at me as she did love
20   And made sweet moan.

I set her on my pacing steed
    And nothing else saw all day long,
For sidelong would she bend and sing
    A faery's song.

25 She found me roots of relish sweet,
    And honey wild, and manna dew,
And sure in language strange she said
    "I love thee true."

She took me to her elfin grot[3]
30   And there she wept and sighed full sore,
And there I shut her wild wild eyes
    With kisses four.

[1] The lovely lady without pity. [2] Belt. [3] Grotto.

And there she lulléd me asleep,
And there I dreamed, Ah Woe betide!
35 The latest[4] dream I ever dreamt
On the cold hill side.

I saw pale Kings, and Princes too,
Pale warriors, death-pale were they all;
They cried, "La belle dame sans merci
40 Thee hath in thrall!"

I saw their starved lips in the gloam
With horrid warning gapéd wide,
And I awoke, and found me here
On the cold hill's side.

45 And this is why I sojourn here,
Alone and palely loitering;
Though the sedge is withered from the Lake
And no birds sing.

[4]Last.

Keats' ballad retells the old story of a man ruined by his love for a supernatural enchantress. Why does Keats invent a bleak setting for this encounter ("The sedge has withered from the Lake/And no birds sing!")? What about the lady suggests that she is more than mortal? How does she destroy her victims?

GWENDOLYN BROOKS (1917–)

THE BALLAD OF RUDOLPH REED

Rudolph Reed was oaken.
His wife was oaken too.
And his two good girls and his good little man
Oakened as they grew.

5 "I am not hungry for berries.
I am not hungry for bread.
But hungry hungry for a house
Where at night a man in bed

"May never hear the plaster
10 Stir as if in pain.
May never hear the roaches
Falling like fat rain.

"Where never wife and children need
Go blinking through the gloom.
15 Where every room of many rooms
Will be full of room.

"Oh my home may have its east or west
Or north or south behind it.
All I know is I shall know it,
20 And fight for it when I find it."

It was in a street of bitter white
That he made his application.
For Rudolph Reed was oakener
Than others in the nation.

25 The agent's steep and steady stare
Corroded to a grin.
Why, you black old, tough old hell of a man,
Move your family in!

Nary a grin grinned Rudolph Reed,
30 Nary a curse cursed he,
But moved in his House. With his dark little wife,
And his dark little children three.

A neighbor would *look*, with a yawning eye
That squeezed into a slit.
35 But the Rudolph Reeds and the children three
Were too joyous to notice it.

For were they not firm in a home of their own
With windows everywhere
And a beautiful banistered stair
40 And a front yard for flowers and a back yard for grass?

The first night, a rock, big as two fists.
The second, a rock big as three.
But nary a curse cursed Rudolph Reed.
(Though oaken as man could be.)

45 The third night, a silvery ring of glass.
Patience ached to endure.
But he looked, and lo! small Mabel's blood
Was staining her gaze so pure.

Then up did rise our Rudolph Reed
50 And pressed the hand of his wife,
And went to the door with a thirty-four
And a beastly butcher knife.

He ran like a mad thing into the night.
And the words in his mouth were stinking.
55 By the time he had hurt his first white man
He was no longer thinking.

By the time he had hurt his fourth white man
Rudolph Reed was dead.
His neighbors gathered and kicked his corpse.
60 "Nigger——" his neighbors said.

Small Mabel whimpered all night long,
For calling herself the cause.
Her oak-eyed mother did no thing
But change the bloody gauze.

How does the ballad form allow Miss Brooks to bring out the force of this story? What does the adjective "oak-eyed" in the last stanza mean?

One of the more demanding forms is the sonnet, which enjoyed its greatest vogue in England at the end of the sixteenth century but has been attempted at some time or another by most poets since then. Sonnets consist of fourteen lines of iambic pentameter verse and generally conform to one of two basic rhyme schemes, the Shakespearean (English) or the Petrarchan (Italian). The Shakespearean sonnet breaks down into three quatrains and a couplet, rhyming *abab cdcd efef gg* (each new letter stands for a new rhyme). The Petrarchan sonnet contains an octave (an eight-line unit) and a sestet (six lines), usually rhyming *abba abba cdecde* (or *cdcdcd*, though the last two lines occasionally form a couplet). In each case the rhyme units frequently correspond to units of thought; for example, the octave of a Petrarchan sonnet will present one movement, the sestet an answering or contrasting movement. Consider how the writers of the following sonnets—the first two Shakespearean, the next three Petrarchan—make use of the sonnet form. Shakespeare's sonnet is the most regular of the group, using each quatrain to present a separate image and concluding with a summarizing couplet. MacLeish runs his first two quatrains together, without pausing at the end of many lines, and introduces a sharp break between the eighth and ninth lines. Donne's sonnet observes the natural break between octave and sestet that is encouraged by the Petrarchan form, but Milton's slides over this break, creating a momentum that carries the reader through the poem without stopping. The last poem, by Cummings, is a very free sonnet that does not conform to either of the traditional patterns.

WILLIAM SHAKESPEARE (1564–1616)

THAT TIME OF YEAR THOU MAYST IN ME BEHOLD

That time of year thou mayst in me behold
When yellow leaves, or none, or few, do hang
Upon those boughs which shake against the cold,
Bare ruined choirs where late the sweet birds sang.
5   In me thou see'st the twilight of such day
As after sunset fadeth in the west,
Which by and by black night doth take away,
Death's second self, that seals up all in rest.
In me thou see'st the glowing of such fire,
10   That on the ashes of his youth doth lie
As the deathbed whereon it must expire,
Consumed with that which it was nourished by.
This thou perceivest, which makes thy love more strong,
To love that well which thou must leave ere long.

ARCHIBALD MACLEISH (1892–)

THE END OF THE WORLD

Quite unexpectedly as Vasserot
The armless ambidextrian was lighting
A match between his great and second toe
And Ralph the lion was engaged in biting
5   The neck of Madame Sossman while the drum
Pointed, and Teeny was about to cough
In waltz-time swinging Jocko by the thumb—
Quite unexpectedly the top blew off:
And there, there overhead, there, there, hung over
10   Those thousands of white faces, those dazed eyes,
There in the starless dark the poise, the hover,
There with vast wings across the canceled skies,
There in the sudden blackness the black pall
Of nothing, nothing, nothing—nothing at all.

JOHN DONNE (1572–1631)

AT THE ROUND EARTH'S IMAGINED CORNERS

At the round earth's imagin'd corners, blow
Your trumpets, angels, and arise, arise
From death, you numberless infinities
Of souls, and to your scatter'd bodies go,
5   All whom the flood did, and fire shall o'erthrow,
All whom war, dearth, age, agues, tyrannies,
Despair, law, chance hath slain, and you whose eyes
Shall behold God and never taste death's woe.
But let them sleep, Lord, and me mourn a space,
10   For if above all these my sins abound,
'Tis late to ask abundance of thy grace
When we are there. Here on this lowly ground
Teach me how to repent, for that's as good
As if thou'dst seal'd my pardon with thy blood.

JOHN MILTON (1608–1674)

WHEN I CONSIDER

When I consider how my light is spent,
  Ere half my days, in this dark world and wide,
  And that one Talent[1] which is death to hide,
  Lodg'd with me useless, though my Soul more bent
5 To serve therewith my Maker, and present
    My true account, lest he returning chide,
    Doth God exact day-labour, light deni'd,
    I fondly[2] ask; But patience to prevent
That murmur, soon replies, God doth not need
10   Either man's work or his own gifts, who best
    Bear his mild yoke, they serve him best, his State
Is Kingly. Thousands[3] at his bidding speed
    And post o'er Land and Ocean without rest:
    They also serve who only stand and wait.

[1]An allusion to the parable of the talents, Matt. 25, in which a talent is a piece of money.
[2]Foolishly. [3]Angelic messengers.

JOHN KEATS (1795–1821)

ON FIRST LOOKING INTO CHAPMAN'S HOMER[1]

Much have I travell'd in the realms of gold,
And many goodly states and kingdoms seen;
Round many western islands have I been
Which bards in fealty to Apollo[2] hold.
5   Oft of one wide expanse had I been told
That deep-brow'd Homer ruled as his demesne;
Yet did I never breathe its pure serene
Till I heard Chapman speak out loud and bold:
Then felt I like some watcher of the skies
10   When a new planet swims into his ken;
Or like stout Cortez,[3] when with eagle eyes
He star'd at the Pacific—and all his men
Look'd at each other with a wild surmise—
Silent, upon a peak in Darien.[4]

[1]George Chapman was an Elizabethan poet whose translations of Homer enjoyed considerable popularity. [2]The god of the sun. [3]It makes little difference to the sense of the poem, but it was Balboa who first looked at the Pacific. [4]A region in Panama.

E. E. CUMMINGS (1894–1962)

I LIKE MY BODY WHEN IT IS WITH YOUR BODY

i like my body when it is with your
body. It is so quite new a thing
Muscles better and nerves more.
i like your body. i like what it does,
5   i like its hows. i like to feel the spine
of your body and its bones, and the trembling
-firm-smooth ness and which i will
again and again and again
kiss, i like kissing this and that of you,
10   i like, slowly stroking the, shocking fuzz
of your electric fur, and what-is-it comes
over parting flesh . . . . And eyes big love-crumbs,

and possibly i like the thrill

of under me you so quite new

What Are Poems For?

We usually read poems without wondering why they were written. It is enough to try to understand them. But occasionally it makes sense to ask questions about the purpose a poem seems to serve. At different times, and in different cultures, poems may satisfy very different needs. The following examples suggest that poems can function in various ways: the Eskimo poem and the two Indian poems that use words as part of a religious ritual, and the two poems by contemporary black poets that reflect new conceptions of the ends of poetry.

The poems by Archibald MacLeish and Jorge Luis Borges make statements about the kinds of truth and permanence that any poetry can offer. In their different ways they attempt to define the nature of poetry and to justify its existence. The final poem, Wallace Stevens's "Thirteen Ways of Looking at a Blackbird," affords a glimpse of the poetic imagination at work finding various ways of dealing with the reality of a simple subject.

ANONYMOUS ESKIMO

INTO MY HEAD ROSE

> Into my head rose
> the nothings
> my life day after day
> but I am leaving the shore
> 5 in my skin boat
> It came to me that I was in danger
> and now the small troubles
> look big
> and the ache
> 10 that comes from the things
> I have to do every day
> big
>
> But only one thing
> is great
> 15 only one
> This
> In the hut by the path
> to see the day
> coming out of its mother
> 20 and the light filling the world

> *Translated by W. S. Merwin*

1. What are the "nothings" the poet is talking about?

2. Why is the dawn the only "great" thing?

For the American Indian the word possessed magical powers. Chants and songs had a well-defined ritualistic function: to heal, to protect one against the arrows of enemies, to appease the powers responsible for rain or good harvests. By repeating the proper words the Indian sought to experience the creative processes of nature and thus share in its renewal. How are the forces of nature presented in the Navajo chant? In the Tewa song? How does the Indian singer relate to these forces in each poem? What is the effect of the repetitions?

ANONYMOUS NAVAJO

A PRAYER OF THE NIGHT CHANT

Tségíhi*
House made of dawn.
House made of evening light.
House made of the dark cloud.
5   House made of male rain.
House made of dark mist.
House made of female rain.
House made of pollen.
House made of grasshoppers.
10   Dark cloud is at the door.
The trail out of it is dark cloud.
The zigzag lightning stands high upon it.
Male deity!
Your offering I make.
15   I have prepared a smoke for you.
Restore my feet for me.
Restore my legs for me.
Restore my body for me.
Restore my mind for me.
20   This very day take out your spell for me.
Your spell remove for me.
You have taken it away for me.
Far off it has gone.
Happily I recover.
25   Happily my interior becomes cool.
Happily I go forth.
My interior feeling cool, may I walk.
No longer sore, may I walk.
Impervious to pain, may I walk.
30   With lively feelings may I walk.
As it used to be long ago, may I walk.
Happily may I walk.
Happily, with abundant dark clouds, may I walk.

185

Happily, with abundant showers, may I walk.
35 Happily, with abundant plants, may I walk.
Happily, on a trail of pollen, may I walk.
Happily may I walk.
Being as it used to be long ago, may I walk.
May it be beautiful before me.
40 May it be beautiful behind me.
May it be beautiful below me.
May it be beautiful above me.
May it be beautiful all around me.
In beauty it is finished.

Translated by Washington Matthews

*A canyon often mentioned in Navajo myths as the home of gods who lived in cliff-houses.

ANONYMOUS TEWA

SONG OF THE SKY LOOM

O our Mother the Earth, O our Father the Sky,
Your children are we, and with tired backs
We bring you the gifts you love.
Then weave for us a garment of brightness;
5 May the warp be the white light of morning,
May the weft be the red light of evening,
May the fringes be the falling rain,
May the border be the standing rainbow.
Thus weave for us a garment of brightness,
10 That we may walk fittingly where birds sing,
That we may walk fittingly where grass is green,
O our Mother the Earth, O our Father the Sky.

CALVIN C. HERNTON (1933–)

THE DISTANT DRUM

I am not a metaphor or symbol.
This you hear is not the wind in the trees,
Nor a cat being maimed in the street.
It is I being maimed in the street.
5 It is I who weep, laugh, feel pain or joy.
I speak this because I exist.
This is my voice.

186

These words are my words, my mouth
Speaks them, my hand writes—
10 I am a poet.
It is my fist you hear beating
Against your ear.

What is Hernton's conception of the role of the poet?

ETHERIDGE KNIGHT (1933–)

FOR BLACK POETS
WHO THINK OF SUICIDE

Black Poets should live—not leap
From steel bridges (like the white boys do.
Black Poets should *live*—not lay
Their necks on railroad tracks (like the white boys do.
5 Black Poets should seek—but not search too much
In sweet dark caves, nor hunt for snipes
Down psychic trails (like the white boys do.

For Black Poets belong to Black People. Are
The Flutes of Black Lovers. Are
10 The Organs of Black Sorrows. Are
The Trumpets of Black Warriors.
Let all Black Poets die as trumpets,
And be buried in the dust of marching feet.

DENISE LEVERTOV (1923–)

THE SECRET

Two girls discover
the secret of life
in a sudden line of
poetry.

5 I who don't know the
secret wrote
the line. They
told me

(through a third person)
10 they had found it
but not what it was
not even

what line it was. No doubt
by now, more than a week
15 later, they have forgotten
the secret,

the line, the name of
the poem. I love them
for finding what
20 I can't find,

and for loving me
for the line I wrote,
and for forgetting it
so that

25 a thousand times, till death
finds them, they may
discover it again, in other
lines

in other
30 happenings. And for
wanting to know it,
for

assuming there is
such a secret, yes,
35 for that
most of all.

How does Miss Levertov feel about the girls who find a special meaning in her poem?
Is it all right to find meanings in a poem that the poet was not aware of?

ARS POETICA*

A poem should be palpable and mute
As a globed fruit,

Dumb
As old medallions to the thumb,

5   Silent as the sleeve-worn stone
Of casement ledges where the moss has grown—

A poem should be wordless
As the flight of birds.

*   *   *

A poem should be motionless in time
10   As the moon climbs.

Leaving, as the moon releases
Twig by twig the night-entangled trees,

Leaving, as the moon behind the winter leaves,
Memory by memory the mind—

15   A poem should be motionless in time
As the moon climbs

*   *   *

A poem should be equal to:
Not true

For all the history of grief
20   An empty doorway and a maple leaf

For love
The leaning grasses and the two lights above the sea—

A poem should not mean
But be

*The art of poetry; also the title of a work on poetry by the Roman poet Horace (65–18 B.C.)

According to MacLeish, what kind of meaning should a poem avoid (by being "silent," "motionless," etc.)? What should a poem offer?

ARS POETICA

To gaze at the river made of time and water
And recall that time itself is another river,
To know we cease to be, just like the river,
And that our faces pass away, just like the water.

5   To feel that waking is another sleep
That dreams it does not sleep and that death,
Which our flesh dreads, is that very death
Of every night, which we call sleep.

To see in the day or in the year a symbol
10 Of mankind's days and of his years,
To transform the outrage of the years
Into a music, a rumor and a symbol,

To see in death a sleep, and in the sunset
A sad gold, of such is Poetry
15 Immortal and a pauper. For Poetry
Returns like the dawn and the sunset.

At times in the afternoons a face
Looks at us from the depths of a mirror;
Art must be like that mirror
20 That reveals to us this face of ours.

They tell how Ulysses, glutted with wonders,
Wept with love to descry his Ithaca
Humble and green. Art is that Ithaca
Of green eternity, not of wonders.

25 It is also like an endless river
That passes and remains, a mirror for one same
Inconstant Heraclitus,* who is the same
And another, like an endless river.

Translated by Harold Morland

---

*Heraclitus was an early Greek philosopher who believed that the basic principle of life was change.

1. What does Borges see art as offering man?

2. How is the artist an "inconstant Heraclitus"?

3. Why, in the fifth stanza, does Borges describe looking into a mirror in the *afternoon*?

4. How does Borges justify the activity of creating works of art?

WALLACE STEVENS (1879–1955)

THIRTEEN WAYS OF
LOOKING AT A BLACKBIRD

I

Among twenty snowy mountains,
The only moving thing
Was the eye of the blackbird.

II

I was of three minds,
5 Like a tree
In which there are three blackbirds.

III

The blackbird whirled in the autumn winds.
It was a small part of the pantomime.

IV

A man and a woman
10 Are one.
A man and a woman and a blackbird
Are one.

V

I do not know which to prefer,
The beauty of inflections
15 Or the beauty of innuendoes,
The blackbird whistling
Or just after.

VI

Icicles filled the long window
With barbaric glass.
20 The shadow of the blackbird
Crossed it, to and fro.
The mood
Traced in the shadow
An indecipherable cause.

VII

25 O thin men of Haddam,[1]
Why do you imagine golden birds?
Do you not see how the blackbird
Walks around the feet
Of the women about you?

[1] Town in Connecticut.

VIII

30 I know noble accents
And lucid, inescapable rhythms;
But I know, too,
That the blackbird is involved
In what I know.

IX

35 When the blackbird flew out of sight,
It marked the edge
Of one of many circles.

X

At the sight of blackbirds
Flying in a green light,
40 Even the bawds of euphony
Would cry out sharply.

XI

He rode over Connecticut
In a glass coach.
Once, a fear pierced him,
45 In that he mistook
The shadow of his equipage
For blackbirds.

XII

The river is moving.
The blackbird must be flying.

XIII

50 It was evening all afternoon.
It was snowing
And it was going to snow.
The blackbird sat
In the cedar-limbs.

Places

ROBERT LOWELL (1917–   )

WATER

It was a Maine lobster town—
each morning boatloads of hands
pushed off for granite
quarries on the islands,

5   and left dozens of bleak
white frame houses stuck
like oyster shells
on a hill of rock,

and below us, the sea lapped
10 the raw little match-stick
mazes of a weir,
where the fish for bait were trapped.

Remember? We sat on a slab of rock.
From this distance in time,
15 it seems the color
of iris, rotting and turning purpler,

but it was only
the usual gray rock
turning the usual green
20 when drenched by the sea.

The sea drenched the rock
at our feet all day,
and kept tearing away
flake after flake.

25 One night you dreamed
you were a mermaid clinging to a wharf-pile,
and trying to pull
off the barnacles with your hands.

We wished our two souls
30 might return like gulls
    to the rock. In the end,
    the water was too cold for us.

1. How does Lowell differentiate between the actual place and the place as existing in memory and in dream?

2. What is the significance of the last sentence?

LOUIS SIMPSON (1923–)

A FARM IN MINNESOTA

The corn rows walk the earth,
crowding like mankind between the fences,
feeding on sun and rain;
are broken down by hail,
5 or perish of incalculable drought.

And we who tend them
from the ground up—lieutenants
of this foot cavalry, leaning on fences
to watch our green men never move an inch—
10 who cares for us?

Our beds are sold at auction.
The Bible, and a sword—these are bequeathed
to children who prefer a modern house.
Our flesh has been consumed
15 only to make more lives.

But when our heads are planted.
under the church, from those empty pods
we rise in the fields of death,
and are gathered by angels,
20 and shine in the hands of God.

1. How does the speaker characterize the farm? What relationships between the farmers and the crops are suggested?

2. How is the last stanza related to the first three stanzas?

WILLIAM STAFFORD (1914–)

LETTER FROM OREGON

Mother, here there are shadowy salmon;
ever their sides argue up the falls.
Watching them plunge with fluttering gills,
I thought back through Wyoming where I came from.

5   The gleaming sides of my train glimmered
up over passes and arrowed through shoals
of aspen fluttering in a wind of yellow,
Only the sky stayed true; I turned,

Justifying space through those miles of Wyoming
10 till the wave of the land was quelled by the stars;
then tunnels of shadow led me far
through doubt, and I was home.

Mother, even home was doubtful;
many slip into the sea and are gone for years.
15 just as I boarded the six-fifteen there.
Over the bar I have leaped outward.

Somewhere in the ocean beyond Laramie
when that grass folded low in the dark
a lost fin waved, and I felt the beat
20 of the old neighborhood stop, on our street.

1. According to the poem, how are the poet's life and the salmon's similar?

2. In what ways does the poet's description of the landscape relate to his description of salmon? How do the specific details of landscape relate to the poet's life?

ANNE STEVENSON (1933–)

SIERRA NEVADA

For Margaret Elvin

Landscape without regrets whose weakest junipers
strangle and split granite, whose hard, clean light
is utterly without restraint, whose mountains can purify
and dazzle, and every minute excite us but
5 never can offer us commiseration, never can tell us
anything about ourselves except that we are dispensable . . .

The rocks and water.
The glimmering rocks and the hundreds
and hundreds of blue lakes ought to be mythical,
10 while the great trees, as soon as they die,
immediately become ghosts,
stalk upright among the living with awful composure.
But even these bones that the light has taken and twisted,
with their weird gesticulations and shadows that look
15 as if they had been carved out of dust, even these
have nothing to do with what we have done or not done.

Now, as we climb on the high bare slopes, we find
the most difficult earth supports and the most delicate flowers:
Gilia and harebells, kalmia and larkspur, everywhere
20 the lupin's tight blue spires
and fine-fingered handshaped leaves.
Daintiest of all, the low mariposa, lily of the mountain,
with its honey stained cup and no imperfect dimension.
Strangest and highest, purple and yellow mosses
25 drink from their own furry stems.

If we stand in the fierce but perfectly transparent wind
we can look down over the boulders, over the drifted scree
with its tattered collar of manzanita,
over the groves of hemlock,
30 the tip of each tree resembling an arm
extended to a drooping forefinger,
down, down, over the whole, dry, difficult
train of the ascent, down to the lake
with its narrow, swarming edges where the little white boats
35 are moving their oars like waterbugs.

Nothing but the wind makes noise.
The lake, transparent to its greeny brown floor,
is everywhere else bluer than the sky.
The boats hardly seem to touch its surface. Just as
40 this granite is something that does not really touch us,
although we stand on it and see the color of its flowers.
The wind is strong without knowing that it is wind.
The twisted tree that is not warning or supplicating
never considers that it is not wind.
45 We think that if we were to stay here for a long time,
lie here like wood on these waterless beaches,
we would forget our names, would remember that
what we first wanted had something to do with stones,
the sun, the thousand colors of water,
50 brilliances,   blues.

ROBINSON JEFFERS (1887–1962)

NOVEMBER SURF

Some lucky day each November great waves awake and are
    drawn
Like smoking mountains bright from the west
And come and cover the cliff with white violent cleanness: then
    suddenly
The old granite forgets half a year's filth:
5 The orange-peel, eggshells, papers, pieces of clothing, the clots
Of dung in corners of the rock, and used
Sheaths that make light love safe in the evenings: all the droppings
    of the summer
Idlers washed off in a winter ecstasy:
I think this cumbered continent envies its cliff then. . . . But all
    seasons
10 The earth, in her childlike prophetic sleep,
Keeps dreaming of the bath of a storm that prepares up the long
    coast
Of the future to scour more than her sea-lines:
The cities gone down, the people fewer and the hawks more
    numerous,
The rivers mouth to source pure; when the two-footed
15 Mammal, being someways one of the nobler animals, regains
The dignity of room, the value of rareness.

1. What attitudes toward modern America underlie this poem?

2. What sort of storm does Jeffers imagine preparing "up the long coast/of the future"?

ROBERT HAYDEN (1913–   )

"SUMMERTIME AND THE LIVING . . ."*

Nobody planted roses, he recalls,
but sunflowers gangled there sometimes,
tough-stalked and bold
and like the vivid children there unplanned.
5 There circus-poster horses curveted
in trees of heaven
above the quarrels and shattered glass,
and he was bareback rider of them all.

No roses there in summer—
10 oh, never roses except when people died—
and no vacations for his elders,
so harshened after each unrelenting day
that they were shouting-angry.
But summer was, they said, the poor folks' time
15 of year. And he remembers
how they would sit on broken steps amid

The fevered tossings of the dusk, the dark,
wafting hearsay with funeral-parlor fans
or making evening solemn by
20 their quietness. Feels their Mosaic eyes
upon him, though the florist roses
that only sorrow could afford
long since have bidden them Godspeed.

Oh, summer summer summertime—

25 Then grim street preachers shook
their tambourines and Bibles in the face
of tolerant wickedness;
then Elks parades and big splendiferous
Jack Johnson in his diamond limousine
30 set the ghetto burgeoning
with fantasies
of Ethiopia spreading her gorgeous wings.

*An interview with Robert Hayden appears on page 305.

LUCILLE CLIFTON (1937–   )

RUNNING ACROSS TO THE LOT

running across to the lot
in the middle of the cement days
to watch the big boys trembling
as the dice made poets of them
5 if we remembered to despair
i forget

i forget
while the streetlights were blooming

and the sharp birdcall
10   of the iceman and his son
and the ointment of the ragman's horse
sang spring
our fathers were dead and
our brothers were dying

What is the poet's attitude toward her experiences in the city? Is there a difference between the child's attitude and the adult's?

LUCILLE CLIFTON (1937–)

IN THE INNER CITY

in the inner city
or
like we call it
home
5   we think a lot about uptown
and the silent nights
and the houses straight as
dead men
and the pastel lights
10   and we hang on to our no place
happy to be alive
and in the inner city
or
like we call it
15   home

What is the poet's attitude toward "uptown"? How does "uptown" differ from the "inner city"?

VICTOR HERNANDEZ CRUZ (1949–)

RITMO I

everybody passed the drummer/drummers in the park
drummers in the sky/
      we went up six flights
      looking down at garages
5   & stores & listening to
      drums/all the way from
      the park/all the way from
      the sky

everybody
10   staring out/riding the roofs/look at the lights
of palisades/the round circles in the black sky
float all the way to the edge of the park/standing
by the river   the blue lights & red lights of
commerce/the windows of brooklyn/

15   monk dropped his glass
on someone's head/cause
that's what he wanted to
do/all over a shirt/& what
about it

20   everybody
hanging on like clothes on the line/drummers
writing poems in the sky/drummers   pulling off
their shirts/the trees echo the passages/& we on
the roof quietly resting/looking at summer/at
25   the lights that the city creates/the airplanes
shoot by   over highways   & rivers/

everybody
passed by the drummers/roofs & windows over
head & eyes on fire

1. What kind of impression of city life is conveyed by the details that Cruz chooses?

2. How do the short line breaks (/) between phrases affect the way you read the poem aloud?

AL YOUNG (1939–   )

LONESOME IN THE COUNTRY

How much of me is sandwiches radio beer?
How much pizza traffic & neon messages?
I take thoughtful journeys to supermarkets,
philosophize about the newest good movie,
5   camp out at magazine racks & on floors,
catch humanity leering back in laundromats,
invent shortcuts by the quarter hour

There's meaning to all this itemization
& I'd do well to look for it in woodpiles
10   or in hills & springs or trees in the woods
instead of staying in the shack all the time
imagining too much
                  falling asleep in old chairs

All that childhood I spent in farmhouses
& still can't tell one bush from another—
15 Straight wilderness would wipe me out
faster than cancer from cigarette smoke

Meantime my friends are out all day long
stomping thru the woods all big-eyed
& that's me walking the road afternoons
head in a book
20   all that hilly sweetness wasting

Creatures

TED HUGHES (1930–   )

THE JAGUAR

The apes yawn and adore their fleas in the sun.
The parrots shriek as if they were on fire, or strut
Like cheap tarts to attract the stroller with the nut.
Fatigued with indolence, tiger and lion

5   Lie still as the sun. The boa-constrictor's coil
Is a fossil. Cage after cage seems empty, or
Stinks of sleepers from the breathing straw.
It might be painted on a nursery wall.

But who runs like the rest past these arrives
10   At a cage where the crowd stands, stares, mesmerized,
As a child at a dream, at a jaguar hurrying enraged
Through prison darkness after the drills of his eyes

On a short fierce fuse. Not in boredom—
The eye satisfied to be blind in fire,
15   By the bang of blood in the brain deaf the ear—
He spins from the bars, but there's no cage to him

More than to the visionary his cell:
His stride is wildernesses of freedom:
The world rolls under the long thrust of his heel.
20   Over the cage floor the horizons come.

1. Why does Hughes first introduce all of the other animals?

2. Why does the jaguar seem to escape or transcend his prison?

WILLIAM BLAKE (1757–1827)

THE TIGER

[handwritten: Vehicle]

[handwritten left margin: Symbol: The power might, and cunning of creation.]

Tiger, tiger, burning bright
In the forests of the night,
What immortal hand or eye
Could frame thy fearful symmetry?

5 In what distant deeps or skies
Burnt the fire of thine eyes?
On what wings dare he aspire?
What the hand dare seize the fire?

And what shoulder, and what art,
10 Could twist the sinews of thy heart?
And when thy heart began to beat,
What dread hand and what dread feet?

What the hammer? What the chain?
In what furnace was thy brain?
15 What the anvil? What dread grasp
Dare its deadly terrors clasp?

When the stars threw down their spears,
And watered heaven with their tears,
Did He smile His work to see?
20 Did He who made the lamb make thee?

Tiger, tiger, burning bright
In the forests of the night,
What immortal hand or eye
Dare frame thy fearful symmetry?

1. Why does Blake describe the tiger as "burning"?

2. What conception of God emerges from this poem? Why does Blake replace "could" with "dare" in the last line?

RICHARD EBERHART (1904–   )

SEA-HAWK

The six-foot nest of the sea-hawk,
Almost inaccessible,
Surveys from the headland the lonely, the violent waters.

I have driven him off,
5   Somewhat foolhardily,
And look into the fierce eye of the offspring.

It is an eye of fire,
An eye of icy crystal,
A threat of ancient purity,

10   Power of an immense reserve,
An agate-well of purpose,
Life before man, and maybe after.

How many centuries of sight
In this piercing, inhuman perfection
15   Stretch the gaze off the rocky promontory,

To make the mind exult
At the eye of a sea-hawk,
A blaze of grandeur, permanence of the impersonal.

1. Hughes describes the jaguar's eyes as "drills"; Blake talks about the "fire" of the tiger's eyes. What does Eberhart find in the "fierce eye" of the young sea-hawk's offspring?

2. Why does the poet admire the "permanence" of the sea-hawk's gaze?

ROBINSON JEFFERS (1887–1962)

HURT HAWKS

I

The broken pillar of the wing jags from the clotted shoulder,
The wing trails like a banner in defeat,
No more to use the sky forever but live with famine
And pain a few days: cat nor coyote
5 Will shorten the week of waiting for death, there is game without talons.
He stands under the oak-bush and waits
The lame feet of salvation; at night he remembers freedom
And flies in a dream, the dawns ruin it.
He is strong and pain is worse to the strong, incapacity is worse.
10 The curs of the day come and torment him
At distance, no one but death the redeemer will humble that head,
The intrepid readiness, the terrible eyes.
The wild God of the world is sometimes merciful to those
That ask mercy, not often to the arrogant.
15 You do not know him, you communal people, or you have forgotten him;
Intemperate and savage, the hawk remembers him;
Beautiful and wild, the hawks, and men that are dying, remember him.

II

I'd sooner, except the penalties, kill a man than a hawk; but the great redtail
Had nothing left but unable misery
20 From the bone too shattered for mending, the wing that trailed under his talons when he moved.
We had fed him six weeks, I gave him freedom,
He wandered over the foreland hill and returned in the evening, asking for death,
Not like a beggar, still eyed with the old
Implacable arrogance. I gave him the lead gift in the twilight. What fell was relaxed,
25 Owl-downy, soft feminine feathers; but what
Soared: the fierce rush: the night-herons by the flooded river cried fear at its rising
Before it was quite unsheathed from reality.

What does Jeffers think of the "implacable arrogance" of the redtail hawk?

TED HUGHES (1930–)

HAWK ROOSTING

I sit in the top of the wood, my eyes closed.
Inaction, no falsifying dream
Between my hooked head and hooked feet:
Or in sleep rehearse perfect kills and eat

5 The convenience of the high trees!
The air's buoyancy and the sun's ray
Are of advantage to me;
And the earth's face upward for my inspection.

My feet are locked upon the rough bark.
10 It took the whole of Creation
To produce my foot, my each feather:
Now I hold Creation in my foot

Or fly up, and revolve it all slowly—
I kill where I please because it is all mine.
15 There is no sophistry in my body:
My manners are tearing off heads—

The allotment of death.
For the one path of my flight is direct
Through the bones of the living.
20 No arguments assert my right:

The sun is behind me.
Nothing has changed since I began.
My eye has permitted no change.
I am going to keep things like this.

1. Why does Hughes make the hawk the speaker in this poem?

2. What is the morality of the hawk?

THEODORE ROETHKE (1908–1963)

SNAKE

I saw a young snake glide
Out of the mottle shade
And hang, limp on a stone:
A thin mouth, and a tongue
5 Stayed, in the still air.

It turned; it drew away;
Its shadow bent in half;
It quickened, and was gone.

I felt my slow blood warm.
10   I longed to be that thing,
The pure, sensuous form.

And I may be, some time.

D. H. LAWRENCE (1885–1930)

SNAKE

A snake came to my water-trough
On a hot, hot day, and I in pyjamas for the heat,
To drink there.

In the deep, strange-scented shade of the great dark carob-tree
5   I came down the steps with my pitcher
And must wait, must stand and wait, for there he was at the
    trough before me.

He reached down from a fissure in the earth-wall in the gloom
And trailed his yellow-brown slackness soft-bellied down, over
    the edge of the stone trough
And rested his throat upon the stone bottom,
10   And where the water had dripped from the tap, in a small
    clearness,
He sipped with his straight mouth,
Softly drank through his straight gums, into his slack long body,
Silently.

Someone was before me at my water-trough,
15   And I, like a second comer, waiting.

He lifted his head from his drinking, as cattle do,
And looked at me vaguely, as drinking cattle do,
And flickered his two-forked tongue from his lips, and mused a
    moment,
And stooped and drank a little more,
20   Being earth-brown, earth-golden from the burning
    bowels of the earth
On the day of Sicilian July, with Etna smoking.

The voice of my education said to me
He must be killed,
For in Sicily the black, black snakes are innocent, the gold are
      venomous.

25   And voices in me said, If you were a man
      You would take a stick and break him now, and finish him off.

      But I must confess how I liked him,
      How glad I was he had come like a guest in quiet, to drink at
            my water-trough
      And depart peaceful, pacified, and thankless,
30   Into the burning bowels of this earth.

      Was it cowardice, that I dared not kill him?
      Was it perversity, that I longed to talk to him?
      Was it humility, to feel so honoured?
      I felt so honoured.

35   And yet those voices:
      If you were not afraid, you would kill him!

      And truly I was afraid, I was most afraid,
      But even so, honoured still more
      That he should seek my hospitality
40   From out the dark door of the secret earth.
      He drank enough
      And lifted his head, dreamily, as one who has drunken,
      And flickered his tongue like a forked night on the air, so black,
      Seeming to lick his lips,
45   And looked around like a god, unseeing, into the air,
      And slowly turned his head,
      And slowly, very slowly, as if thrice adream,
      Proceeded to draw his slow length curving round
      And climb again the broken bank of my wall-face.

50   And as he put his head into that dreadful hole,
      And as he slowly drew up, snake-easing his shoulders, and
            entered farther,
      A sort of horror, a sort of protest against his withdrawing into
            that horrid black hole,
      Deliberately going into the blackness, and slowly drawing himself
            after,
      Overcame me now his back was turned.

55   I looked round, I put down my pitcher,
      I picked up a clumsy log
      And threw it at the water-trough with a clatter.

I think it did not hit him,
But suddenly that part of him that was left behind convulsed in
    undignified haste,
60 Writhed like lightning, and was gone
Into the black hole, the earth-lipped fissure in the wallfront,
At which, in the intense still noon, I stared with fascination.

And immediately I regretted it.
I thought how paltry, how vulgar, what a mean act!
65 I despised myself and the voices of my accursed human education.

And I thought of the albatross,
And I wished he would come back, my snake.

For he seemed to me again like a king,
Like a king in exile, uncrowned in the underworld,
70 Now due to be crowned again.

And so, I missed my chance with one of the lords
Of life.
And I have something to expiate;
A pettiness.

1. Why does Lawrence hear voices telling him to kill the snake? What does the snake
come to symbolize for him?

2. Why does he regret throwing the log? What kind of "chance" does he feel he has
missed?

WENDELL BERRY (1934–)

THE PEACE OF WILD THINGS

When despair for the world grows in me
and I wake in the night at the least sound
in fear of what my life and my children's lives may be,
I go and lie down where the wood drake
5 rests in his beauty on the water, and the great heron feeds.
I come into the peace of wild things
who do not tax their lives with forethought
of grief. I come into the presence of still water.
And I feel above me the day-blind stars
10 waiting with their light. For a time
I rest in the grace of the world, and am free.

DIANE WAKOSKI (1937–   )

ANTICIPATION OF SHARKS

stay silent
keep away from sharks. stay
away from blood,
you will not be able to deal with a missing leg,
5   in the water/you will bleed to death,
you will be the pain of a yard strewn with brown leaves,
and the shark will rake you clean,
strip your bones to their earth.

stay silent,
10   when you are in danger. The night is deep water.
The dark is a path of sharks,
their teeth flash
as the constellations,

The lonely night passes over me
15   as a submarine.
I am always lonely, will be
until I find someone to share my life with.
How lucky you are, good friend, to have taken up trout fishing.
I swim with sharks. They mistake me
20   for relatives.
We have nothing cold in common
but we glitter at each other.

And I stay silent,
as I swim in these waters,
25   more alone
than if I were by myself.

Portraits

E. A. ROBINSON (1869–1935)

RICHARD CORY

Whenever Richard Cory went down town,
  We people on the pavement looked at him:
He was a gentleman from sole to crown,
  Clean favored, and imperially slim.

5 And he was always quietly arrayed,
  And he was always human when he talked;
But still he fluttered pulses when he said,
  "Good-morning," and he glittered when he walked.

And he was rich—yes, richer than a king,
10 And admirably schooled in every grace:
In fine, we thought that he was everything
  To make us wish that we were in his place.

So on we worked, and waited for the light,
  And went without the meat, and cursed the bread;
15 And Richard Cory, one calm summer night,
  Went home and put a bullet through his head.

R. S. THOMAS (1913–)

WALTER LLYWARCH

I am, as you know, Walter Llywarch,
Born in Wales of approved parents,
Well goitred, round in the bum,*
Sure prey of the slow virus
5 Bred in quarries of grey rain.

*British slang for buttocks.

Born in autumn at the right time
For hearing stories from the cracked lips
Of old folk dreaming of summer,
I piled them on to the bare hearth
10 Of my own fancy to make a blaze
To warm myself, but achieved only
The smoke's acid that brings the smart
Of false tears into the eyes.

Months of fog, months of drizzle;
15 Thought wrapped in the grey cocoon
Of race, of place, awaiting the sun's
Coming, but when the sun came,
Touching the hills with a hot hand,
Wings were spread only to fly
20 Round and round in a cramped cage
Or beat in vain at the sky's window.

School in the week, on Sunday chapel:
Tales of a land fairer than this
Were not so tall, for others had proved it
25 Without the grave's passport, they sent
The fruit home for ourselves to taste.

Walter Llywarch—the words were a name
On a lost letter that never came
For one who waited in the long queue
30 Of life that wound through a Welsh valley.
I took instead, as others had done
Before, a wife from the back pews
In chapel, rather to share the rain
Of winter evenings, than to intrude
35 On her pale body; and yet we lay
For warmth together and laughed to hear
Each new child's cry of despair.

1. What is Walter Llywarch's attitude toward his life?

2. How does Thomas contrast Walter Llywarch's dreams with the facts of his life in a
Welsh valley?

3. What does Llywarch find in marriage?

DEREK WALCOTT (1930–)

THE GLORY TRUMPETER

Old Eddie's face, wrinkled with river lights,
Looked like a Mississippi man's. The eyes,
Derisive and avuncular at once,
Swivelling, fixed me. They'd seen
5   Too many wakes, too many cathouse nights.
The bony, idle fingers on the valves
Of his knee-cradled horn could tear
Through 'Georgia on My Mind' or 'Jesus Saves'
With the same fury of indifference,
10   If what propelled such frenzy was despair.

Now, as the eyes sealed in the ashen flesh,
And Eddie, like a deacon at his prayer,
Rose, tilting the bright horn, I saw a flash
Of gulls and pigeons from the dunes of coal
15   Near my grandmother's barracks on the wharves,
I saw the sallow faces of those men
Who sighed as if they spoke into their graves
About the Negro in America. That was when
The Sunday comics sprawled out on her floor,
20   Sent from the States, had a particular odour,
A smell of money mingled with man's sweat.

And yet, if Eddie's features held our fate,
Secure in childhood I did not know then
A jesus-ragtime or gut-bucket blues
25   To the bowed heads of lean, compliant men
Back from the States in their funereal serge,
Black, rusty Homburgs and limp waiters' ties
With honey accents and lard-coloured eyes
Was Joshua's ram's horn wailing for the Jews
30   Of patient bitterness or bitter siege.

Now it was that as Eddie turned his back
On our young crowd out fêteing, swilling liquor,
And blew, eyes closed, one foot up, out to sea,
His horn aimed at those cities of the Gulf,
35   Mobile and Galveston and sweetly meted
The horn of plenty through a bitter cup,
In lonely exaltation blaming me
For all whom race and exile have defeated,
For my own uncle in America,
40   That living there I never could look up.

1. What does "Old Eddie" express through his horn-playing? What does the title mean?

2. What does the poem suggest happens to the West Indians who go to the United States? Why does Eddie turn his back on the "young crowd"?

ETHERIDGE KNIGHT (1933–)

HE SEES THROUGH STONE

He sees through stone
he has the secret
eyes this old black one
who under prison skies
5   sits pressed by the sun
against the western wall
his pipe between purple gums

the years fall
like overripe plums
10   bursting red flesh
on the dark earth

his time is not my time
but I have known him
in a time gone

15   he led me trembling cold
into the dark forest
taught me the secret rites
to take a woman
to be true to my brothers
20   to make my spear drink
the blood
of my enemies

now black cats circle him
flash white teeth
25   snarl at the air
mashing green grass beneath
shining muscles
ears peeling his words
he smiles
30   he knows
the hunt the enemy
he has the secret eyes
he sees through stone

1. What does the title of the poem mean?

2. Why are the old man's eyes "secret"? Who is he, and how does he know so much?

3. What continuity does the poet see between African and Afro-American culture?

ROBERT HAYDEN (1913–)

AUNT JEMIMA OF THE OCEAN WAVES

I

Enacting someone's notion of themselves
(and me), The One And Only Aunt Jemima
and Kokimo The Dixie Dancing Fool
do a bally for the freak show.

5   I watch a moment, then move on,
pondering the logic that makes of them
(and me) confederates
of The Spider Girl, The Snake-skinned Man . . .

Poor devils have to live somehow.

10   I cross the boardwalk to the beach,
lie in the sand and gaze beyond
the clutter at the sea.

II

Trouble you for a light?
I turn as Aunt Jemima settles down
15   beside me, her blue-rinsed hair
without the red bandanna now.

I hold the lighter to her cigarette.
Much obliged. Unmindful (perhaps)
of my embarrassment, she looks
20   at me and smiles: You sure

do favor a friend I used to have.
Guess that's why I bothered you
for a light. So much like him that I—
She pauses, watching white horses rush

25   to the shore. Way them big old waves
come slamming whopping in,
sometimes it's like they mean to smash
this no-good world to hell.

Well, it could happen. A book I read—
30   Crossed that very ocean years ago.
London, Paris, Rome,
Constantinople too—I've seen them all.

Back when they billed me everywhere
as the Sepia High Stepper.
35   Crowned heads applauded me.
Years before your time. Years and years.

I wore me plenty diamonds then,
and counts or dukes or whatever they were
would fill my dressing room
40   with the costliest flowers. But of course

there was this one you resemble so.
Get me? The sweetest gentleman.
Dead before his time. Killed in the war
to save the world for another war.

45   High-stepping days for me
were over after that. Still I'm not one
to let grief idle me for long.
I went out with a mental act—

mind-reading—Mysteria From
50   The Mystic East—veils and beads
and telling suckers how to get
stolen rings and sweethearts back.

One night he was standing by my bed,
seen him plain as I see you,
55   and warned me without a single word:
Baby, quit playing with spiritual stuff.

So here I am, so here I am,
fake mammy to God's mistakes.
And that's the beauty part,
60 I mean, ain't that the beauty part.

She laughs, but I do not, knowing what
her laughter shields. And mocks.
I light another cigarette for her.
She smokes, not saying any more.

65 Scream of children in the surf,
adagios of sun and flashing foam,
the sexual glitter, oppressive fun. . . .
An antique etching comes to mind:

"The Sable Venus" naked on
70 a baroque Cellini shell—voluptuous
imago floating in the wake
of slave-ships on fantastic seas.

Jemima sighs, Reckon I'd best
be getting back. I help her up.
75 Don't you take no wooden nickels, hear?
Tin dimes neither. So long, pal.

T. S. ELIOT (1888–1965)

AUNT HELEN

Miss Helen Slingsby was my maiden aunt,
And lived in a small house near a fashionable square
Cared for by servants to the number of four.
Now when she died there was silence in heaven
5 And silence at her end of the street.
The shutters were drawn and the undertaker wiped his feet—
He was aware that this sort of thing had occurred before.
The dogs were handsomely provided for,
But shortly afterwards the parrot died too.
10 The Dresden clock continued ticking on the mantelpiece,
And the footman sat upon the dining-table
Holding the second housemaid on his knees—
Who had always been so careful while her mistress lived.

THE LOVE SONG OF J. ALFRED PRUFROCK

S'io credesse che mia risposta fosse
a persona che mai tornasse al mondo,
questa fiamma staria senza più scosse.
Ma perciòcche giammai di questo fondo
non tornò vivo alcun, s'i'odo il vero,
senza tema d'infamia ti rispondo.*

Let us go then, you and I,
When the evening is spread out against the sky
Like a patient etherized upon a table;
Let us go, through certain half-deserted streets,
5 The muttering retreats
Of restless nights in one-night cheap hotels
And sawdust restaurants with oyster-shells:
Streets that follow like a tedious argument
Of insidious intent
10 To lead you to an overwhelming question. . .
Oh, do not ask, 'What is it?'
Let us go and make our visit.

In the room the women come and go
Talking of Michelangelo.

15 The yellow fog that rubs its back upon the window-panes,
The yellow smoke that rubs its muzzle on the window-panes,
Licked its tongue into the corners of the evening,
Lingered upon the pools that stand in drains,
Let fall upon its back the soot that falls from chimneys,
20 Slipped by the terrace, made a sudden leap,
And seeing that it was a soft October night,
Curled once about the house, and fell asleep.

---

*"If I thought my answer were to one who would ever return to the world, this flame should stay without another movement; but since none ever returned from this depth, if what I hear is true, I answer you without fear of infamy." From Dante's *Inferno*, XXVII, 61–66. The speaker, Count Guido of Montefeltro, tells Dante why he is being punished.

And indeed there will be time
For the yellow smoke that slides along the street
25 Rubbing its back upon the window-panes;
There will be time, there will be time
To prepare a face to meet the faces that you meet;
There will be time to murder and create,
And time for all the works and days of hands
30 That lift and drop a question on your plate;
Time for you and time for me,
And time yet for a hundred indecisions,
And for a hundred visions and revisions,
Before the taking of a toast and tea.

35 In the room the women come and go
Talking of Michelangelo.

And indeed there will be time
To wonder, 'Do I dare?' and, 'Do I dare?'
Time to turn back and descend the stair,
40 With a bald spot in the middle of my hair—
(They will say: 'How his hair is growing thin!')
My morning coat, my collar mounting firmly to the chin,
My necktie rich and modest, but asserted by a simple pin—
(They will say: 'But how his arms and legs are thin!')
45 Do I dare
Disturb the universe?
In a minute there is time
For decisions and revisions which a minute will reverse.

For I have known them all already, known them all—
50 Have known the evenings, mornings, afternoons,
I have measured out my life with coffee spoons;
I know the voices dying with a dying fall
Beneath the music from a farther room.
    So how should I presume?

55 And I have known the eyes already, known them all—
The eyes that fix you in a formulated phrase,
And when I am formulated, sprawling on a pin,
When I am pinned and wriggling on the wall,
Then how should I begin
60 To spit out all the butt-ends of my days and ways?
    And how should I presume?

And I have known the arms already, known them all—
Arms that are braceleted and white and bare
(But in the lamplight, downed with light brown hair!)
65 Is it perfume from a dress
That makes me so digress?
Arms that lie along a table, or wrap about a shawl.
        And should I then presume?
        And how should I begin?

        .   .   .   .   .

70 Shall I say, I have gone at dusk through narrow streets
And watched the smoke that rises from the pipes
Of lonely men in shirt-sleeves, leaning out of windows? . . .

I should have been a pair of ragged claws
Scuttling across the floors of silent seas.

        .   .   .   .   .

75 And the afternoon, the evening, sleeps so peacefully!
Smoothed by long fingers,
Asleep . . . tired . . . or it malingers,
Stretched on the floor, here beside you and me.
Should I, after tea and cakes and ices,
80 Have the strength to force the moment to its crisis?
But though I have wept and fasted, wept and prayed,
Though I have seen my head (grown slightly bald) brought in upon a platter,
I am no prophet—and here's no great matter;
I have seen the moment of my greatness flicker,
85 And I have seen the eternal Footman hold my coat, and snicker,
And in short, I was afraid.

And would it have been worth it, after all,
After the cups, the marmalade, the tea,
Among the porcelain, among some talk of you and me,
90 Would it have been worth while,
To have bitten off the matter with a smile,
To have squeezed the universe into a ball
To roll it towards some overwhelming question,
To say: 'I am Lazarus, come from the dead,
95 Come back to tell you all, I shall tell you all'—
If one, settling a pillow by her head,
        Should say: 'That is not what I meant at all.
        That is not it, at all.'

And would it have been worth it, after all,
100 Would it have been worth while,

After the sunsets and the dooryards and the sprinkled streets,
After the novels, after the teacups, after the skirts that trail along the floor—
And this, and so much more?—
It is impossible to say just what I mean!
105 But as if a magic lantern threw the nerves in patterns on a screen:
Would it have been worth while
If one, settling a pillow or throwing off a shawl,
And turning toward the window, should say:
   'That is not it at all,
110   That is not what I meant, at all.'

     . . . .

No! I am not Prince Hamlet, nor was meant to be;
Am an attendant lord, one that will do
To swell a progress, start a scene or two,
Advise the prince; no doubt, an easy tool,
115 Deferential, glad to be of use,
Politic, cautious, and meticulous;
Full of high sentence, but a bit obtuse;
At times, indeed, almost ridiculous—
Almost, at times, the Fool.

120 I grow old . . . I grow old . . .
I shall wear the bottoms of my trousers rolled.

Shall I part my hair behind? Do I dare to eat a peach?
I shall wear white flannel trousers, and walk upon the beach.
I have heard the mermaids singing, each to each.

125 I do not think that they will sing to me.

I have seen them riding seaward on the waves
Combing the white hair of the waves blown back
When the wind blows the water white and black.

We have lingered in the chambers of the sea
130 By sea-girls wreathed with seaweed red and brown
Till human voices wake us, and we drown.

1. What kind of social world does J. Alfred Prufrock belong to?

2. What in the poem suggests Prufrock's dissatisfaction with his life? His insecurity? Why can't he "force the moment to its crisis"?

3. How does Prufrock feel about being an "attendant lord" rather than a "Prince Hamlet"? Does Prufrock ever appear ridiculous?

4. What kind of lover is Prufrock? Why does he dream of mermaids?

Youth and Age

DYLAN THOMAS (1914–1953)

FERN HILL

Now as I was young and easy under the apple boughs
About the lilting house and happy as the grass was green,
 The night above the dingle starry,
  Time let me hail and climb
5 Golden in the heydays of his eyes,
And honoured among wagons I was prince of the apple towns
And once below a time I lordly had the trees and leaves
  Trail with daisies and barley
 Down the rivers of the windfall light.

10 And as I was green and carefree, famous among the barns
About the happy yard and singing as the farm was home,
  In the sun that is young once only,
   Time let me play and be   .
  Golden in the mercy of his means,
15 And green and golden I was huntsman and herdsman, the calves
Sang to my horn, the foxes on the hills barked clear and cold,
  And the sabbath rang slowly
  In the pebbles of the holy streams.

All the sun long it was running, it was lovely, the hay
20 Fields high as the house, the tunes from the chimneys, it was air
  And playing, lovely and watery
   And fire green as grass.
  And nightly under the simple stars
As I rode to sleep the owls were bearing the farm away,
25 All the moon long I heard, blessed among stables, the nightjars
  Flying with the ricks, and the horses
   Flashing into the dark.

And then to awake, and the farm, like a wanderer white
With the dew, come back, the cock on his shoulder: it was all
30 Shining, it was Adam and maiden,
   The sky gathered again
  And the sun grew round that very day.
So it must have been after the birth of the simple light
In the first, spinning place, the spellbound horses walking warm
35 Out of the whinnying green stable
   On to the fields of praise.

And honoured among foxes and pheasants by the gay house
Under the new made clouds and happy as the heart was long,
   In the sun born over and over,
40   I ran my heedless ways,
   My wishes raced through the house high hay
And nothing I cared, at my sky blue trades, that time allows
In all his tuneful turning so few and such morning songs
   Before the children green and golden
45   Follow him out of grace,

Nothing I cared, in the lamb white days, that time would take me
Up to the swallow thronged loft by the shadow of my hand,
   In the moon that is always rising,
      Nor that riding to sleep
50   I should hear him fly with the high fields
And wake to the farm forever fled from the childless land.
Oh as I was young and easy in the mercy of his means,
   Time held me green and dying
   Though I sang in my chains like the sea.

1. Why does Thomas describe himself as "happy as the grass was green"?

2. How does he convey to the reader his childhood perception of his surroundings?

3. How does the view of "Time" change in the course of the poem?

JAMES DICKEY (1923–)

IN THE TREE HOUSE AT NIGHT

   And now the green household is dark.
   The half-moon completely is shining
   On the earth-lighted tops of the trees.
   To be dead, a house must be still.
5 The floor and the walls wave me slowly;
   I am deep in them over my head.
   The needles and pine cones about me

   Are full of small birds at their roundest,
   Their fists without mercy gripping
10 Hard down through the tree to the roots
   To sing back at light when they feel it.
   We lie here like angels in bodies,
   My brothers and I, one dead,
   The other asleep from much living,

15 In mid-air huddled beside me.
   Dark climbed to us here as we climbed

Up the nails I have hammered all day
Through the sprained, comic rungs of the ladder
Of broom handles, crate slats, and laths
20   Foot by foot up the trunk to the branches
Where we came out at last over lakes

Of leaves, of fields disencumbered of earth
That move with the moves of the spirit.
Each nail that sustains us I set here;
25   Each nail in the house is now steadied
By my dead brother's huge, freckled hand.
Through the years, he has pointed his hammer
Up into these limbs, and told us

That we must ascend, and all lie here.
30   Step after step he has brought me,
Embracing the trunk as his body,
Shaking its limbs with my heartbeat,
Till the pine cones danced without wind
And fell from the branches like apples.
35   In the arm-slender forks of our dwelling

I breathe my live brother's light hair.
The blanket around us becomes
As solid as stone, and it sways.
With all my heart, I close
40   The blue, timeless eye of my mind.
Wind springs, as my dead brother smiles
And touches the tree at the root;

A shudder of joy runs up
The trunk; the needles tingle;
45   One bird uncontrollably cries.
The wind changes round, and I stir
Within another's life. Whose life?
Who is dead? Whose presence is living?
When may I fall strangely to earth,

50   Who am nailed to this branch by a spirit?
Can two bodies make up a third?
To sing, must I feel the world's light?
My green, graceful bones fill the air
With sleeping birds. Alone, alone
55   And with them I move gently.
I move at the heart of the world.

1. What does the speaker feel in the tree house that he could not on the ground? Why must he climb to the tree house?

2. Why does he feel that he moves, with the sleeping birds, "at the heart of the world"?

D. H. LAWRENCE (1885–1930)

PIANO

Softly, in the dusk, a woman is singing to me;
Taking me back down the vista of years, till I see
A child sitting under the piano, in the boom of the tingling strings
And pressing the small, poised feet of a mother who smiles as she sings.

5 In spite of myself, the insidious mastery of song
Betrays me back, till the heart of me weeps to belong
To the old Sunday evenings at home, with winter outside
And hymns in the cozy parlor, the tinkling piano our guide.

So now it is vain for the singer to burst into clamor
10 With the great black piano appassionato. The glamour
Of childish days is upon me, my manhood is cast
Down in the flood of remembrance, I weep like a child for the past.

Why does the speaker "weep like a child for the past"?

THEODORE ROETHKE (1908–1963)

MY PAPA'S WALTZ

The whiskey on your breath
Could make a small boy dizzy;
But I hung on like death:
Such waltzing was not easy.

5 We romped until the pans
Slid from the kitchen shelf;
My mother's countenance
Could not unfrown itself.

The hand that held my wrist
10 Was battered on one knuckle;
At every step you missed
My right ear scraped a buckle.

You beat time on my head
With a palm caked hard by dirt,
15 Then waltzed me off to bed
Still clinging to your shirt.

How does the speaker feel about his father?

ROBERT HAYDEN (1913–   )

THOSE WINTER SUNDAYS

Sundays too my father got up early
and put his clothes on in the blueblack cold,
then with cracked hands that ached
from labor in the weekday weather made
5   banked fires blaze. No one ever thanked him.

I'd wake and hear the cold splintering, breaking.
When the rooms were warm, he'd call,
and slowly I would rise and dress,
fearing the chronic angers of that house,

10   Speaking indifferently to him,
who had driven out the cold
and polished my good shoes as well.
What did I know, what did I know
of love's austere and lonely offices?

What is the effect of the question at the end? Of the repetition of "What did I know, what did I know"?

W. D. SNODGRASS (1926–   )

HOME TOWN

I go out like a ghost,
nights, to walk the streets
I walked fifteen years younger—
seeking my old defeats,
5   devoured by the old hunger;
I had supposed

this longing and upheaval
had left me with my youth.
Fifteen years gone: once more,
10   the old lies are the truth:
I must prove I dare,
and the world, and love, is evil.

I have had loves, had such
honors as freely came;
15   it does not seem to matter.

225

Boys swagger just the same
along the curbs, or mutter
among themselves and watch.

They're out for the same prize.
20 And, as the evening grows,
the young girls take the street,
hard, in harlequin clothes,
with black shells on their feet
and challenge in their eyes.

25 Like a young bitch in her season
she walked the carnival
tonight, trailed by boys;
then, stopped at a penny stall
for me; by glittering toys
30 the pitchman called the reason

to come and take a chance,
try my hand, my skill.
I could not look; bereft
of breath, against my will,
35 I walked ahead and left
her there without one glance.

Pale soul, consumed by fear
of the living world you haunt
have you learned what habits lead you
40 to hunt what you don't want;
learned who does not need you;
learned you are no one here?

1. Why does the speaker walk the streets again? Why doesn't he "take a chance"?

2. What, by the end, does the speaker recognize about himself?

THOMAS KINSELLA (1928–   )

MIRROR IN FEBRUARY

The day dawns with scent of must and rain,
Of opened soil, dark trees, dry bedroom air.
Under the fading lamp, half dressed—my brain
Idling on some compulsive fantasy—
5 I towel my shaven lip and stop, and stare
Riveted by a dark exhausted eye,
A dry downturning mouth.

It seems again that it is time to learn,
In this untiring, crumbling place of growth
10 To which, for the time being, I return.
Now plainly in the mirror of my soul
I read that I have looked my last on youth
And little more; for they are not made whole
That reach the age of Christ.

15 Below my window the awakening trees
Hacked clean for better bearing stand defaced
Suffering their brute necessities,
And how should the flesh not quail that span for span
Is mutilated more? In slow distaste
20 I fold my towel with what grace I can,
Not young and not renewable, but man.

1. What is the significance of the fact that the speaker is looking in the mirror at dawn?
In February?

2. To what extent does the speaker see himself as resembling the trees below his window?

WILLIAM BUTLER YEATS (1865–1939)

AN ACRE OF GRASS

Picture and book remain,
An acre of green grass
For air and exercise,
Now strength of body goes;
5 Midnight, an old house
Where nothing stirs but a mouse.

My temptation is quiet.
Here at life's end
Neither loose imagination,
10 Nor the mill of the mind
Consuming its rag and bone,
Can make the truth known.

Grant me an old man's frenzy,
Myself must I remake
15 Till I am Timon and Lear*
Or that William Blake
Who beat upon the wall
Till Truth obeyed his call;

A mind Michael Angelo knew
20 That can pierce the clouds,
Or inspired by frenzy
Shake the dead in their shrouds;
Forgotten else by mankind,
An old man's eagle mind.

*The title characters, both old men, of Shakespeare's plays, *Timon of Athens* and *King Lear*.

1. How does Yeats imagine life failing in old age?

2. What is "an old man's frenzy"?

JUST AS I USED TO SAY

Just as I used to say
               love comes harder to the aged
because they've been running
               on the same old rails too long
5   and then when the sly switch comes along
               they miss the turn
    and burn up the wrong rail while
               the gay caboose goes flying
    and the steamengine driver don't recognize
10   them new electric horns
and the aged run out on the rusty spur
               which ends up in
        the dead grass where
    the rusty tincans and bedsprings and old razor
15   blades and moldy mattresses
               lie
     and the rail breaks off dead
           right there
    though the ties go on awhile
20   and the aged
say to themselves
       Well
         this must be the place
      we were supposed to lie down
25   And they do
         while the bright saloon careens along away
    on a high
       hilltop
         its windows full of bluesky and lovers
30   with flowers
        their long hair streaming
           and all of them laughing
     and waving and
           whispering to each other
35   and looking out and
          wondering what that graveyard
    where the rails end
       is

W. S. MERWIN (1927–   )

GRANDFATHER IN THE
OLD MEN'S HOME

Gentle, at last, and as clean as ever,
He did not even need drink any more,
And his good sons unbent and brought him
Tobacco to chew, both times when they came
5   To be satisfied he was well cared for.
And he smiled all the time to remember
Grandmother, his wife, wearing the true faith
Like an iron nightgown, yet brought to birth
Seven times and raising the family
10   Through her needle's eye while he got away
Down the green river, finding directions

For boats. And himself coming home sometimes
Well-heeled but blind drunk, to hide all the bread
And shoot holes in the bucket while he made
15   His daughters pump. Still smiled as kindly in
His sleep beside the other clean old men
To see Grandmother, every night the same,
Huge in her age, with her thumbed-down mouth, come
Hating the river, filling with her stare
20   His gliding dream, while he turned to water,
While the children they both had begotten,
With old faces now, but themselves shrunken
To child-size again, stood ranged at her side,
Beating their little Bibles till he died.

1. In what sense has Grandfather become one of the "clean old men"?

2. Why does Grandmother haunt his dreams? What do his children think of him?

Love

from THE SONG OF SONGS

Maiden:

2:3 As the apple tree among the trees of the wood,
So is my beloved among the sons.
I sat down under his shadow with great delight,
And his fruit was sweet to my taste.

4 He brought me to the banqueting house,
And his banner over me was love.

5 Stay me with flagons, comfort me with apples:
For I am sick of love.

6 His left hand is under my head,
And his right hand doth embrace me.

7 I charge you, O ye daughters of Jerusalem,
By the roes, and by the hinds of the field,
That ye stir not up, nor awake my love,
Till he please.

8 The voice of my beloved! behold, he cometh
Leaping upon the mountains, skipping upon the hills.

9 My beloved is like a roe or a young hart:
Behold, he standeth behind our wall,
He looketh forth at the windows,
Showing himself through the lattice.

10 My beloved spake, and said unto me,
Rise up, my love, my fair one, and come away.

11 For, lo, the winter is past,
The rain is over and gone;

12 The flowers appear on the earth;
The time of the singing of birds is come,
And the voice of the turtle is heard in our land; ⁱ

13 The fig tree putteth forth her green figs,
And the vines with the tender grape give a good smell.
Arise, my love, my fair one, and come away.

14 O my dove, that art in the clefts of the rocks, in the secret places of the stairs,
Let me see thy countenance, let me hear thy voice;
For sweet is thy voice, and thy countenance is comely.

15 Take us the foxes,
   The little foxes, that spoil the vines:
   For our vines have tender grapes.
16 My beloved is mine, and I am his:
   He feedeth among the lilies.
17 Until the day break, and the shadows flee away,
   Turn, my beloved,
   And be thou like a roe or a young hart
   Upon the mountains of Bether. . . .

Youth:

4:7 Thou art all fair, my love; there is no spot in thee.
  8 Come with me from Lebanon, my spouse, with me from Lebanon:
    Look from the top of Amana, from the top of Shenir and Hermon,
    From the lions' dens, from the mountains of the leopards.
  9 Thou hast ravished my heart, my sister, my spouse;
    Thou hast ravished my heart with one of thine eyes,
    With one chain of thy neck.
 10 How fair is thy love, my sister, my spouse!
    How much better is thy love than wine!
    And the smell of thine ointments than all spices!
 11 Thy lips, O my spouse, drop as the honeycomb:
    Honey and milk are under thy tongue;
    And the smell of thy garments is like the smell of Lebanon.
 12 A garden inclosed is my sister, my spouse;
    A spring shut up, a fountain sealed.
 13 Thy plants are an orchard of pomegranates, with pleasant fruits;
    Camphire, with spikenard,
 14 Spikenard and saffron;
    Calamus and cinnamon, with all trees of frankincense;
    Myrrh and aloes, with all the chief spices:
 15 A fountain of gardens, a well of living waters,
    And streams from Lebanon.

Maiden:

 16 Awake, O north wind; and come, thou south;
    Blow upon my garden, that the spices thereof may flow out.
    Let my beloved come into his garden,
    And eat his pleasant fruits.

Youth:

5:1 I am come into my garden, my sister, my spouse:
    I have gathered my myrrh with my spice;
    I have eaten my honeycomb with my honey;
    I have drunk my wine with my milk.

The Song of Songs is actually a collection of love lyrics first written down in the third century B.C. This erotic poetry, accepted as part of the Bible because it was thought to have been written by Solomon, came to be interpreted as an allegory illustrating Christ's love for his church.

1. What does the comparison of the lover to a "roe or a young hart" (2:9) tell the reader about him? About the young woman?

2. What do the references to spring contribute to the mood of the poetry?

3. What do the various images of fruits and spices suggest about the nature of passion?

FRANCESCO PETRARCH (1304–1374)

IN WHAT DIVINE IDEAL

In what divine ideal, what lofty sphere
    Is found the pattern from which Nature made
    That face so fair wherein she might parade
    Proof of her heavenly power to mortals here?
5 Were ringlets ever loosed of gold more sheer
    To wayward breeze by nymph in pool or glade?
    Was every virtue in one soul displayed
    Ere now—and how the noblest costs me dear!
Who knows her not can never realize
10   How beauty may the heart of man beguile,
    And who looks not upon my Laura's eyes
Knows not how love can kill and otherwhile
    May heal us; let him hear how soft she sighs
    And gently speaks, oh, let him see her smile!

Translated by T. G. Bergin

FRANCESCO PETRARCH

NOW WHILE THE WIND

Now while the wind and earth and heavens rest,
    While sleep holds beast and feathered bird in fee
    And high above a calm and waveless sea
    The silent stars obey the night's behest,
5 I lie awake and yearning, sore distressed
    And racked by thoughts of my sweet enemy,
    Yet though her face recalled brings death to me
    'Tis only with such dreams I soothe my breast.

So from one living fountain, gushing clear,
10   Pour forth alike the bitter and the sweet,
And one same hand can deal me good or ill.
Whence every day I die anew of fear
And live again to find that hope's a cheat,
And peace of heart or mind escapes me still.

Translated by T. G. Bergin

The sonnets written in the fourteenth century by the Italian poet Petrarch established a view of woman and of courtship that remained popular in Renaissance love poetry. Petrarch built upon and extended a chivalric code of courtly love established in southern France during the twelfth century, according to which a knight must go through elaborate rituals of serious courtship to please an aloof and superior lady. Petrarch presents his Laura as an unattainable ideal, a paragon of beauty and virtue. His unsatisfied love for her is ennobling, but "bitter" as well as "sweet"; many of his sonnets deal with the anguish caused him by his "sweet enemy." The following poems by Shakespeare and Donne challenge the idealization of woman perpetuated by imitators of Petrarch.

WILLIAM SHAKESPEARE (1564–1616)

MY MISTRESS' EYES ARE NOTHING LIKE THE SUN

My mistress' eyes are nothing like the sun;
Coral is far more red than her lips' red;
If snow be white, why then her breasts are dun;
If hairs be wires, black wires grow on her head.
5   I have seen roses damasked, red and white,
But no such roses see I in her cheeks;
And in some perfumes is there more delight
Than in the breath that from my mistress reeks.
I love to hear her speak; yet well I know
10   That music hath a far more pleasing sound:
I grant I never saw a goddess go;
My mistress, when she walks, treads on the ground.
  And yet, by heaven, I think my love as rare
  As any she belied with false compare.

In this sonnet Shakespeare mocks the conventional ways in which Elizabethan sonneteers, imitating Petrarch, praised their ladies (all of whom, consequently, were indistinguishable). How does Shakespeare establish the validity of his own praise?

JOHN DONNE (1572–1631)

THE APPARITION

When by thy scorn, O murd'ress, I am dead,
  And that thou thinkst thee free
From all solicitation from me,
Then shall my ghost come to thy bed,
5 And thee, fained vestal, in worse arms shall see;
Then thy sick taper will begin to wink,
And he, whose thou art then, being tired before,
Will, if thou stir, or pinch to wake him, think
  Thou call'st for more,
10 And in false sleep will from thee shrink,
And then, poor aspen wretch, neglected thou
Bathed in a cold quicksilver* sweat wilt lie,
  A verier ghost than I;
What I will say, I will not tell thee now,
15 Lest that preserve thee; and since my love is spent,
I had rather thou shouldst painfully repent,
Than by my threat'nings rest still innocent.

*Quicksilver (mercury) was used in Donne's time to treat venereal disease.

How does Donne's technique of imagining an actual scene in which the speaker appears as a ghost rather than as an admiring suitor enable him to undermine the Petrarchan view of love?

SIR THOMAS WYATT (1503–1542)

THEY FLEE FROM ME

They flee from me that sometime did me seek
With naked foot stalking in my chamber.
I have seen them gentle, tame, and meek
That now are wild and do not remember
5 That sometime they put themselves in danger
To take bread at my hand; and now they range
Busily seeking with a continual change.

Thankéd be Fortune, it hath been otherwise
Twenty times better; but once in special,
10 In thin array after a pleasant guise,
When her loose gown from her shoulders did fall,
And she me caught in her arms long and small;
And therewithall sweetly did me kiss,
And softly said, "Dear heart, how like you this?"

15 It was no dream; I lay broad waking.
    But all is turned through my gentleness
    Into a strange fashion of forsaking;
    And I have leave to go of her goodness,
    And she also to use newfangleness.
20 But since that I so kindely am served,
    I fain would know what she hath deserved.

Sir Thomas Wyatt wrote poems based upon his experiences in the worldly court of Henry VIII. What are the implications of Wyatt's comparison of his former lovers with deer? Why is his description of an actual encounter in the second stanza effective? How does he get back at his lover in the final stanza?

WILLIAM SHAKESPEARE (1564–1616)

WHEN MY LOVE SWEARS
THAT SHE IS MADE OF TRUTH

When my love swears that she is made of truth
I do believe her, though I know she lies,
That she might think me some untutored youth,
Unlearnèd in the world's false subtleties.
5   Thus vainly thinking that she thinks me young,
Although she knows my days are past the best,
Simply I credit her false-speaking tongue;
On both sides thus is simple truth suppressed.
But wherefore says she not she is unjust?*
10 And wherefore say not I that I am old?
O, love's best habit is in seeming trust,
And age in love loves not to have years told.
    Therefore I lie with her and she with me,
    And in our faults by lies we flattered be.

*Unfaithful.

Shakespeare often explored in his sonnets the psychological and moral nuances of a difficult relationship. How does he establish the pattern of deceit by which he and his unfaithful lover preserve their relationship? How does he feel about their "love"?

The following three poems exemplify the motif of *carpe diem*, in which the speaker urges his lady to "seize the day" and make love. Campion's poem is an imitation, or loose translation, of a much older poem by the Roman poet Catullus (84?–54? B.C.). What is the effect of Campion's repeated reference to the "ever-during night" that awaits everyone?

MY SWEETEST LESBIA

My sweetest Lesbia, let us live and love,
And though the sager sort our deeds reprove,
Let us not weigh them. Heaven's great lamps do dive
Into their west, and straight again revive,
5   But soon as once set is our little light,
Then must we sleep one ever-during night.

If all would lead their lives in love like me,
Then bloody swords and armor should not be;
No drum nor trumpet peaceful sleeps should move,
10   Unless alarm came from the camp of love.
But fools do live, and waste their little light,
And seek with pain their ever-during night.

When timely death my life and fortune ends,
Let not my hearse be vexed with mourning friends,
15   But let all lovers, rich in triumph, come
And with sweet pastimes grace my happy tomb;
And Lesbia, close up thou my little light,
And crown with love my ever-during night.

ROBERT HERRICK (1591–1674)

CORINNA'S GOING A-MAYING

Get up! get up for shame! the blooming morn
Upon her wings presents the god unshorn.[1]
 See how Aurora[2] throws her fair
 Fresh-quilted colors through the air:
5   Get up, sweet slug-a-bed, and see
 The dew bespangling herb and tree.
Each flower has wept and bowéd toward the east
Above an hour since, yet you not dressed;
 Nay, not so much as out of bed?
10   When all the birds have matins said,
 And sung their thankful hymns, 'tis sin,
 Nay, profanation to keep in,
Whenas a thousand virgins on this day
Spring, sooner than the lark, to fetch in May.[3]

[1] Apollo, the sun god, whose locks are rays. [2] Goddess of the dawn. [3] By gathering boughs of white hawthorn to decorate the town on May Day.

15 Rise, and put on your foliage, and be seen
To come forth, like the springtime, fresh and green,
And sweet as Flora.[4] Take no care
For jewels for your gown or hair;
Fear not; the leaves will strew
20 Gems in abundance upon you;
Besides, the childhood of the day has kept,
Against[5] you come, some orient pearls unwept;
Come and receive them while the light
Hangs on the dew-locks of the night,
25 And Titan[6] on the eastern hill
Retires himself, or else stands still
Till you come forth. Wash, dress, be brief in praying:
Few beads are best when once we go a-Maying.

Come, my Corinna, come; and, coming mark
30 How each field turns a street, each street a park
Made green and trimmed with trees; see how
Devotion gives each house a bough
Or branch: each porch, each door ere this,
An ark, a tabernacle is,
35 Made up of whitethorn neatly interwove,
As if here were those cooler shades of love.
Can such delights be in the street
And open fields, and we not see 't?
Come, we'll abroad; and let's obey
40 The proclamation made for May,
And sin no more, as we have done, by staying;
But, my Corinna, come, let's go a-Maying.

There's not a budding boy or girl this day
But is got up and gone to bring in May;
45 A deal of youth, ere this, is come
Back, and with whitethorn laden home.
Some have dispatched their cakes and cream
Before that we have left to dream;
And some have wept, and wooed, and plighted troth,
50 And chose their priest, ere we can cast off sloth.
Many a green-gown[7] has been given,
Many a kiss, both odd and even,
Many a glance, too, has been sent
From out the eye, love's firmament;
55 Many a jest told of the keys betraying
This night, and locks picked; yet we're not a-Maying.

Come, let us go while we are in our prime,
And take the harmless folly of the time.

---

[4]Goddess of the flowers. [5]Until. [6]The sun. [7]Grass-stained dress.

We shall grow old apace, and die
60 Before we know our liberty.
Our life is short, and our days run
As fast away as does the sun;
And, as a vapor or a drop of rain
Once lost, can ne'er be found again;
65 So when or you or I are made
A fable, song, or fleeting shade,
All love, all liking, all delight
Lies drowned with us in endless night.
Then while time serves, and we are but decaying,
70 Come, my Corinna, come, let's go a-Maying.

1. How does the picture of spring presented by the speaker reinforce his argument?

2. How does the speaker convey a sense of urgency? In what ways does he make his point in the last stanza that life is short?

ANDREW MARVELL (1621–1678)

TO HIS COY MISTRESS

Had we but world enough, and time,
This coyness, lady, were no crime.
We would sit down and think which way
To walk, and pass our long love's day;
5 Thou by the Indian Ganges[1] side
Shouldst rubies find; I by the tide
Of Humber[2] would complain. I would
Love you ten years before the Flood;
And you should, if you please, refuse
10 Till the conversion of the Jews.
My vegetable love should grow
Vaster than empires, and more slow.
An hundred years should go to praise
Thine eyes, and on thy forehead gaze;
15 Two hundred to adore each breast,
But thirty thousand to the rest;
An age at least to every part,
And the last age should show your heart.
For, lady, you deserve this state,
20 Nor would I love at lower rate.

[1] A river sacred to the Hindus, flowing from the Himalayas in northern India into the bay of Bengal. [2] An estuary of the Ouse and Trent rivers in England.

But at my back I always hear
Time's wingèd chariot hurrying near;
And yonder all before us lie
Deserts of vast eternity.
25 Thy beauty shall no more be found,
Nor in thy marble vault shall sound
My echoing song; then worms shall try
That long preserved virginity,
And your quaint honor turn to dust,
30 And into ashes all my lust.
The grave's a fine and private place,
But none, I think, do there embrace.
    Now therefore, while the youthful hue
Sits on thy skin like morning dew,
35 And while thy willing soul transpires
At every pore with instant fires,
Now let us sport us while we may;
And now, like am'rous birds of prey,
Rather at once our time devour,
40 Than languish in his slow-chapped[3] power.
Let us roll all our strength, and all
Our sweetness, up into one ball;
And tear our pleasures with rough strife
Through the iron gates of life.
45 Thus, though we cannot make our sun
Stand still, yet we will make him run.

[3]Slow-jawed.

1. Why does the speaker begin with such extravagant claims?

2. How do the initial impressions of time and space established by the poem change in the second stanza?

3. What view of love do the images of the last stanza present?

MATTHEW ARNOLD (1822–1888)

DOVER BEACH

The sea is calm to-night.
The tide is full, the moon lies fair
Upon the straits;—on the French coast, the light
Gleams and is gone; the cliffs of England stand,
5 Glimmering and vast, out in the tranquil bay.

Come to the window, sweet is the night air!
Only, from the long line of spray
Where the sea meets the moon-blanch'd land,
Listen, you hear the grating roar
10 Of pebbles which the waves draw back, and fling,
At their return, up the high strand,
Begin, and cease, and then again begin,
With tremulous cadence slow, and bring
The eternal note of sadness in.

15 Sophocles[1] long ago
Heard it on the Aegean,[2] and it brought
Into his mind the turbid ebb and flow
Of human misery; we
Find also in the sound a thought,
20 Hearing it by this distant northern sea.

The Sea of Faith
Was once, too, at the full, and round earth's shore
Lay like the folds of a bright girdle furl'd.
But now I only hear
25 Its melancholy, long, withdrawing roar,
Retreating, to the breath
Of the night-wind, down the vast edges drear
And naked shingles[3] of the world.

Ah, love, let us be true
30 To one another! for the world, which seems
To lie before us like a land of dreams,
So various, so beautiful, so new,
Hath really neither joy, nor love, nor light,
Nor certitude, nor peace, nor help for pain;
35 And we are here as on a darkling plain
Swept with confused alarms of struggle and flight,
Where ignorant armies clash by night.

[1]A Greek dramatist, 495?–406? B.C. [2]Sea between Greece and Asia Minor. [3]Beaches.

1. What is the "eternal note of sadness" created by the grating roar of the pebbles?

2. How do the images at the end of the second and third stanzas convey the speaker's uncertainties and fears? How does his sense of being on "a darkling plain" intensify his love?

THOMAS HARDY (1840–1928)

NEUTRAL TONES

We stood by a pond that winter day,
And the sun was white, as though chidden[1] of God,
And a few leaves lay on the starving sod;
   They had fallen from an ash, and were gray.

5 Your eyes on me were as eyes that rove
Over tedious riddles solved years ago;
And some words played between us to and fro
   On which lost the more by our love.

The smile on your mouth was the deadest thing
10 Alive enough to have strength to die;
And a grin of bitterness swept thereby
   Like an ominous bird a-wing. . . .

Since then, keen lessons that love deceives,
And wrings with wrong, have shaped to me
15 Your face, and the God-curst sun, and a tree,
   And a pond edged with grayish leaves.

[1] Scolded.

1. What has the speaker learned about love? What is his attitude toward the person he is addressing?

2. How does the setting of the poem reflect the speaker's feelings?

THEODORE ROETHKE (1908–1963)

I KNEW A WOMAN

I knew a woman, lovely in her bones,
When small birds sighed, she would sigh back at them;
Ah, when she moved, she moved more ways than one:
The shapes a bright container can contain!
5 Of her choice virtues only gods should speak,
Or English poets who grew up on Greek
(I'd have them sing in chorus, cheek to cheek).

How well her wishes went! She stroked my chin,
She taught me Turn, and Counter-turn, and Stand;
10 She taught me Touch, that undulant white skin;
I nibbled meekly from her proffered hand;
She was the sickle; I, poor I, the rake,
Coming behind her for her pretty sake
(But what prodigious mowing we did make).

15 Love likes a gander, and adores a goose:
Her full lips pursed, the errant note to seize;
She played it quick, she played it light and loose;
My eyes, they dazzled at her flowing knees;
Her several parts could keep a pure repose,
20 Or one hip quiver with a mobile nose
(She moved in circles, and those circles moved).

Let seed be grass, and grass turn into hay:
I'm martyr to a motion not my own;
What's freedom for? To know eternity.
25 I swear she cast a shadow white as stone.
But who would count eternity in days?
These old bones live to learn her wanton ways:
(I measure time by how a body sways).

1. How does Roethke convey the woman's sensuousness?

2. What do *double entendres* (double meanings with sexual overtones) contribute to the
poem? What kind of commitment does Roethke express in the last two lines?

DONALD HALL (1928–)

THE COAL FIRE

A coal fire burned in a basket grate.
We lay in front of it
while ash collected on the firebrick
like snow.
5 I looked at you, in the small light
of the coal fire: back
delicate, yet with the form of the skeleton,
cheekbones and chin
carved, mouth full,
10 and breasts like hills of flowers.

The fire was tight and small and endured
when we added a chunk every hour.
The new piece blazed at first
from the bulky shadow of fire,
15 turning us bright and dark.
Old coals red at the center
warmed us all night.
If we watched all night
we could not tell the new coal
20 When it flaked into ash.

1. What mood does the first stanza convey?

2. What does the description of the coal fire in the second stanza suggest about their lovemaking?

3. Why does the speaker say they could not tell when the new coal "flaked into ash"?

OCTAVIO PAZ (1914–)

FORGOTTEN

Close your eyes and lose yourself in shadows
under the shadows of your eyelids' red-leaf forest.

Go down among those spirals
of sound humming and falling
5 and sounding faraway, remote,

all the way to the eardrum,
a deafened waterfall.

Send your self down to the shadows,
drown yourself in your skin,
10 further, in your entrails:
let the bone, with its livid spark,
dazzle and blind you,
and among chasms and the gulfs of shadow
open its blue panache,[1] will-o'-the-wisp.

15 And in this liquid shadow of the dream
now bathe your nakedness;
relinquish your form, your foam
(nobody knows who flung it on the shore);

[1] Dashing self-confidence.

243

lose yourself in your self, infinity
20 in your infinite being,
sea losing itself in another sea:
forget yourself and forget me.

In that forgetfulness ageless and endless
lips, kisses, love, all, born again:
25 the stars are daughters of the night.

Translated by Muriel Rukeyser

1. Why does the speaker urge his lover to "forget" herself? What kind of inner journey does this process involve? How is it like a dream?

2. What is the meaning of the last line?

W. D. SNODGRASS (1926–)

LEAVING THE MOTEL

Outside, the last kids holler
Near the pool: they'll stay the night.
Pick up the towels; fold your collar
Out of sight.

5 Check: is the second bed
Unrumpled, as agreed?
Landlords have to think ahead
In case of need,

Too. Keep things straight: don't take
10 The matches, the wrong keyrings—
We've nowhere we could keep a keepsake—
Ashtrays, combs, things

That sooner or later others
Would accidentally find.
15 Check: take nothing of one another's
And leave behind

Your license number only,
Which they won't care to trace;
We've paid. Still, should such things get lonely,
20 Leave in their vase

244

An aspirin to preserve
Our lilacs, the wayside flowers
We've gathered and must leave to serve
A few more hours;

25 That's all. We can't tell when
We'll come back, can't press claims;
We would no doubt have other rooms then,
Or other names.

What does the poem suggest about the psychology of motel sex?

GREGORY CORSO (1930–   )

MARRIAGE

Should I get married? Should I be good?
Astound the girl next door
with my velvet suit and faustus hood?
Don't take her to movies but to cemeteries
5   tell all about werewolf bathtubs and forked clarinets
then desire her and kiss her and all the preliminaries
and she going just so far and I understand why
not getting angry saying You must feel! It's beautiful to feel!
Instead take her in my arms lean against an old crooked tombstone
10   and woo her the entire night the constellations in the sky—

When she introduces me to her parents
back straightened, hair finally combed, strangled by a tie,
should I sit knees together on their 3rd-degree sofa
and not ask.Where's the bathroom?
15   How else to feel other than I am,
often thinking Flash Gordon soap—
Oh how terrible it must be for a young man
seated before a family and the family thinking
We never saw him before! He wants our Mary Lou!
20   After tea and homemade cookies they ask What do you do for a
living?
Should I tell them? Would they like me then?
Say All right get married, we're losing a daughter
but we're gaining a son—
And should I then ask Where's the bathroom?

25   O God, and the wedding! All her family and her friends
     and only a handful of mine all scroungy and bearded
     just waiting to get at the drinks and food—
     And the priest! he looking at me as if I masturbated
     asking me do you take this woman for your lawful wedded wife?
30   And I, trembling what to say say Pie Glue!

     I kiss the bride all those corny men slapping me on the back:
     She's all yours, boy! Ha-ha-ha!
     And in their eyes you could see some obscene honeymoon going on—
     Then all that absurd rice and clanky cans and shoes
35   Niagara Falls! Hordes of us! Husbands! Wives! Flowers! Chocolates!
     All streaming into cozy hotels
     All going to do the same thing tonight
     The indifferent clerk he knowing what was going to happen
     The lobby zombies they knowing what
40   The whistling elevator man he knowing
     The winking bellboy knowing
     Everybody knows! I'd be almost inclined not to do anything!
     Stay up all night! Stare that hotel clerk in the eye!
     Screaming: I deny honeymoon! I deny honeymoon!
45   running rampant into those almost climactic suites
     yelling Radio belly! Cat shovel!
     O I'd live in Niagara forever! in a dark cave beneath the Falls
     I'd sit there the Mad Honeymooner
     devising ways to break marriages, a scourge of bigamy
50   a saint of divorce—

     But I should get married I should be good
     How nice it'd be to come home to her
     and sit by the fireplace and she in the kitchen
     aproned young and lovely wanting my baby
55   and so happy about me she burns the roast beef
     and comes crying to me and I get up from my big papa chair
     saying Christmas teeth! Radiant brains! Apple deaf!
     God what a husband I'd make! Yes, I should get married!
     So much to do! like sneaking into Mr. Jones' house late at night
60   and cover his golf clubs with 1920 Norwegian books
     Like hanging a picture of Rimbaud[1] on the lawnmower
     Like pasting Tannu Tuva postage stamps all over the picket fence
     Like when Mrs. Kindhead comes to collect for the Community Chest
     grab her and tell her There are unfavorable omens in the sky!
65   And when the mayor comes to get my vote tell him
     When are you going to stop people killing whales!
     And when the milkman comes leave him a note in the bottle
     Penguin dust, bring me penguin dust, I want penguin dust—

Yet if I should get married and it's Connecticut and snow
70 and she gives birth to a child and I am sleepless, worn,
up for nights, head bowed against a quiet window, the past behind me
finding myself in the most common of situations a trembling man
knowledged with responsibility not twig-smear nor Roman coin soup
O what would that be like!
75 Surely I'd give it for a nipple a rubber Tacitus[2]
For a rattle a bag of broken Bach records
Tack Della Francesca[3] all over its crib
Sew the Greek alphabet on its bib
And build for its playpen a roofless Parthenon

80 No, I doubt I'd be that kind of father
not rural not snow no quiet window
but hot smelly tight New York City
seven flights up, roaches and rats in the walls
a fat Reichian[4] wife screeching over potatoes Get a job!
85 And five nose-running brats in love with Batman
And the neighbors all toothless and dry haired
like those hag masses of the 18th century
all wanting to come in and watch TV
The landlord wants his rent

90 Grocery store Blue Cross Gas & Electric Knights of Columbus
Impossible to lie back and dream Telephone snow, ghost parking—
No! I should not get married I should never get married!
But—imagine if I were married to a beautiful sophisticated woman
tall and pale wearing an elegant black dress and long black gloves
95 holding a cigarette holder in one hand and a highball in the other
and we live high up in a penthouse with a huge window
from which we could see all of New York and even further on clearer
days
No, can't imagine myself married to that pleasant prison dream—

O but what about love! I forget love
100 not that I am incapable of love
it's just that I see love as odd as wearing shoes—
I never wanted to marry a girl who was like my mother
And Ingrid Bergman was always impossible
And there's maybe a girl now but she's already married
105 And I don't like men and—
but there's got to be somebody!
Because what if I'm 60 years old and not married,
all alone in a furnished room with pee stains on my underwear
and everybody else is married! All the universe married but me!

110   Ah, yet well I know that were a woman possible as I am possible
        then marriage would be possible—
        Like SHE in her lonely alien gaud waiting her Egyptian lover
        so I wait—bereft of 2,000 years and the bath of life.

[1]French poet, 1854–1891. [2]Roman historian who lived about 55–120. [3]Piero della Francesca (1415?–1492), Italian painter and geometrician. [4]Wilhelm Reich was an Austrian psychiatrist who died in 1957.

ROBERT CREELEY (1926–   )

A MARRIAGE

The first retainer
he gave to her
was a golden
wedding ring.

5   The second—late at night
he woke up,
leaned over on an elbow,
and kissed her.

The third and the last—
10   he died with
and gave up loving
and lived with her.

ANDREI VOZNESENSKY (1935–   )

FIRST ICE

In the phone booth, a girl
cold in her shivery coat,
all tears, her face a
chaos of smudgy make-up.
5 She tries to blow warmth
into her paper-thin palms.
Her fingers—small lumps of ice.
Yes, earrings. But now
She has to go back, alone,
10   down the frozen street.

First ice. First ice.
First ice of cold
   clichés on the telephone.
The frozen tracks
15   shimmering on her cheeks.
First ice humiliation.

Translated by Anselm Hollo

MIROSLAV HOLUB (1923–   )

LOVE

Two thousand cigarettes.
A hundred miles
from wall to wall.
An eternity and a half of vigils
5 blanker than snow.

Tons of words
old as the tracks
of a platypus in the sand.

A hundred books we didn't write.
10 A hundred pyramids we didn't build.

Sweepings.
Dust.

Bitter
as the beginning of the world.

15 Believe me when I say
it was beautiful.

Translated by Ian Milner

ERICA JONG

THE MAN UNDER THE BED

The man under the bed
The man who has been there for years waiting
The man who waits for my floating bare foot
The man who is silent as dustballs riding the darkness
5   The man whose breath is the breathing of small white
                                     butterflies
The man whose breathing I hear when I pick up the phone
The man in the mirror whose breath blackens silver
The boneman in closets who rattles the mothballs
The man at the end of the end of the line

10   I met him tonight   I always meet him
He stands in the amber air of a bar
When the shrimp curl like beckoning fingers
& ride through the air on their toothpick skewers
When the ice cracks & I am about to fall through
15   he arranges his face around its hollows
he opens his pupilless eyes at me
For years he has waited to drag me down
& now he tells me
he has only waited to take me home
20   We waltz through the street like death & the maiden
We float through the wall of the wall of my room

If he's my dream he will fold back into my body
His breath writes letters of mist on the glass of my cheeks
I wrap myself around him like the darkness
25   I breathe into his mouth
& make him real

War

WALT WHITMAN (1819–1892)

BEAT! BEAT! DRUMS!

Beat! beat! drums—blow! bugles! blow!
Through the windows—through doors—burst like a ruthless force,
Into the solemn church, and scatter the congregation,
Into the school where the scholar is studying;
5 Leave not the bridegroom quiet—no happiness must he have now
    with his bride,
Nor the peaceful farmer any peace, ploughing his field or gathering
    his grain,
So fierce you whirr and pound you drums—so shrill you bugles
    blow.

Beat! beat! drums!—blow! bugles! blow!
Over the traffic of cities—over the rumble of wheels in the streets;
10 Are beds prepared for sleepers at night in the houses? no sleepers
    must sleep in those beds,
No bargainers' bargains by day—no brokers or speculators—would
    they continue?
Would the talkers be talking? would the singer attempt to sing?
Would the lawyer rise in the court to state his case before the
    judge?
Then rattle quicker, heavier drums—you bugles wilder blow.

15 Beat! beat! drums!—blow! bugles! blow!
Make no parley—stop for no expostulation,
Mind not the timid—mind not the weeper or prayer,
Mind not the old man beseeching the young man,

Let not the child's voice be heard, nor the mother's entreaties,
20 Make even the trestles to shake the dead where they lie awaiting
    the hearses,
So strong you thump O terrible drums—so loud you bugles blow.

1. Why does the poet urge that the drums and bugles be loud and strong?

2. What do they suggest about the nature of war? What is Whitman's attitude toward war?

STEPHEN CRANE (1871–1900)

WAR IS KIND

Do not weep, maiden, for war is kind.
Because your lover threw wild hands toward the sky
And the affrighted steed ran on alone,
Do not weep.
5 War is kind.

      Hoarse, booming drums of the regiment,
      Little souls who thirst for fight,
      These men were born to drill and die.
      The unexplained glory flies above them,
10   Great is the battle-god, great, and his kingdom—
      A field where a thousand corpses lie.

Do not weep, babe, for war is kind.
Because your father tumbled in the yellow trenches,
Raged at his breast, gulped and died,
15 Do not weep.
War is kind.

      Swift blazing flag of the regiment,
      Eagle with crest of red and gold,
      These men were born to drill and die.
20   Point for them the virtue of slaughter,
      Make plain to them the excellence of killing
      And a field where a thousand corpses lie.

Mother whose heart hung humble as a button
On the bright splendid shroud of your son,
25 Do not weep.
War is kind.

1. What is the effect of the ironic refrain, "war is kind"?

2. What does Crane say about the glory of war?

WILFRED OWEN (1893–1918)

DULCE ET DECORUM EST

Bent double, like old beggars under sacks,
Knock-kneed, coughing like hags, we cursed through sludge,
Till on the haunting flares we turned our backs

And towards our distant rest began to trudge.
5   Men marched asleep. Many had lost their boots
But limped on, blood-shod. All went lame; all blind;
Drunk with fatigue; deaf even to the hoots
Of tired, outstripped Five-Nines that dropped behind.

Gas! Gas! Quick, boys!—An ecstasy of fumbling,
10 Fitting the clumsy helmets just in time;
But someone still was yelling out and stumbling
And flound'ring like a man in fire or lime . . .
Dim, through the misty panes and thick green light,
As under a green sea, I saw him drowning.

15 In all my dreams, before my helpless sight,
He plunges at me, guttering, choking, drowning.

If in some smothering dreams you too could pace
Behind the wagon that we flung him in,
And watch the white eyes writhing in his face,
20 His hanging face, like a devil's sick of sin;
If you could hear, at every jolt, the blood
Come gargling from the froth-corrupted lungs,
Obscene as cancer, bitter as the cud
Of vile, incurable sores on innocent tongues,—

25 My friend, you would not tell with such high zest
To children ardent for some desperate glory,
The old Lie: Dulce et decorum est
Pro patria mori.[1]

---

[1] "It is sweet and fitting to die for your country." From Horace, a Roman poet who wrote during the reign of Augustus Caesar.

What is the relationship between the title of the poem and the grotesque details?

LOSSES

It was not dying: everybody died.
It was not dying: we had died before
In the routine crashes—and our fields
Called up the papers, wrote home to our folks,
5   And the rates rose, all because of us.
We died on the wrong page of the almanac,
Scattered on mountains fifty miles away;
Diving on haystacks, fighting with a friend,
We blazed up on the lines we never saw.
10 We died like aunts or pets or foreigners.
(When we left high school nothing else had died
For us to figure we had died like.)

In our new planes, with our new crews, we bombed
The ranges by the desert or the shore,
15 Fired at towed targets, waited for our scores—
And turned into replacements and woke up
One morning, over England, operational.
It wasn't different: but if we died
It was not an accident but a mistake
20 (But an easy one for anyone to make).
We read our mail and counted up our missions—
In bombers named for girls, we burned
The cities we had learned about in school—
Till our lives wore out; our bodies lay among
25 The people we had killed and never seen.
When we lasted long enough they gave us medals;
When we died they said, "Our casualties were low."
They said, "Here are the maps"; we burned the cities.

It was not dying—no, not ever dying;
30 But the night I died I dreamed that I was dead,
And the cities said to me: "Why are you dying?
We are satisfied, if you are; but why did I die?"

1. What is the effect of repeating the line, "It was not dying"?

2. How does the poem convey the impersonality of war?

3. Why does the speaker refer to what he learned in high school?

DENISE LEVERTOV (1923–)

WHAT WERE THEY LIKE?

Did the people of Viet Nam
use lanterns of stone?
Did they hold ceremonies
to reverence the opening of buds?
5   Were they inclined to quiet laughter?
Did they use bone and ivory,
jade and silver, for ornament?
Had they an epic poem?
Did they distinguish between speech and singing?

10   Sir, their light hearts turned to stone.
It is not remembered whether in gardens
stone lanterns illumined pleasant ways.
Perhaps they gathered once to delight in blossom,
but after the children were killed
15   there were no more buds.
Sir, laughter is bitter to the burned mouth.
A dream ago, perhaps. Ornament is for joy.
All the bones were charred.
It is not remembered. Remember,
20   most were peasants; their life
was in rice and bamboo.
When peaceful clouds were reflected in the paddies
and the water buffalo stepped surely along terraces,
maybe fathers told their sons old tales.
25   When bombs smashed those mirrors
there was time only to scream.
There is an echo yet
of their speech which was like a song.
It was reported their singing resembled
30   the flight of moths in moonlight.
Who can say? It is silent now.

1. Why do you suppose the poet chose this question and answer format?

2. Who answers the questions? In what tone?

3. How do the answers collectively make a statement about the war in Vietnam?

Protest

WILLIAM BLAKE (1757–1827)

LONDON

I wander thro' each charter'd[1] street,
Near where the charter'd Thames does flow,
And mark in every face I meet
Marks of weakness, marks of woe.

5   In every cry of every Man,
In every Infant's cry of fear,
In every voice, in every ban,[2]
The mind-forg'd manacles I hear.

How the Chimney-sweeper's cry
10   Every blackning Church appalls;
And the hapless Soldier's sigh
Runs in blood down Palace walls.

But most thro' midnight streets I hear
How the youthful Harlot's curse
15   Blasts the new-born Infant's tear,
And blights with plagues the Marriage hearse.

[1]Leased under a patent granted by the king. [2]Prohibition.

1. What connections do you see between chartered streets, bans, and "mind-forg'd manacles"?

2. What is the reason for the cries and fears?

3. What is the relationship between chimney-sweeper and church, soldier and palace, harlot and marriage?

PERCY BYSSHE SHELLEY (1792–1822)

SONG TO THE MEN OF ENGLAND

I

Men of England, wherefore plough
For the lords who lay ye low?
Wherefore weave with toil and care
The rich robes your tyrants wear?

II

5 Wherefore feed, and clothe, and save,
From the cradle to the grave,
Those ungrateful drones who would
Drain your sweat—nay, drink your blood?

Wherefore, Bees of England, forge
10 Many a weapon, chain, and scourge,
That these stingless drones may spoil
The forced produce of your toil?

IV

Have ye leisure, comfort, calm,
Shelter, food, love's gentle balm?
15 Or what is it ye buy so dear
With your pain and with your fear?

V

The seed ye sow, another reaps;
The wealth ye find, another keeps;
The robes ye weave, another wears;
20 The arms ye forge, another bears.

VI

Sow seed,—but let no tyrant reap;
Find wealth,—let no impost   heap;
Weave robes,—let not the idle wear;
Forge arms,—in your defence to bear.

VII

25 Shrink to your cellars, holes, and cells;
In halls ye deck another dwells.
Why shake the chains ye wrought? Ye see
The steel ye tempered glance on ye.

VIII

With plough and spade, and hoe and loom,
30 Trace your grave, and build your tomb,
And weave your winding sheet, till fair
England be your sepulchre.

1. Who are Shelley's "Men of England"?

2. Is the spirit of the poem democratic? Revolutionary?

DOLOR

I have known the inexorable sadness of pencils,
Neat in their boxes, dolor of pad and paper-weight,
All the misery of manila folders and mucilage,
Desolation in immaculate public places,
5 Lonely reception room, lavatory, switchboard,
The unalterable pathos of basin and pitcher,
Ritual of multigraph, paper-clip, comma,
Endless duplication of lives and objects.
And I have seen dust from the walls of institutions,
10 Finer than flour, alive, more dangerous than silica,
Sift, almost invisible, through long afternoons of tedium,
Dropping a fine film on nails and delicate eyebrows,
Glazing the pale hair, the duplicate gray standard faces.

1. What is Roethke protesting?

2. What is the relationship between the "duplicate gray standard faces" and the details in the rest of the poem?

AWARD

*A Gold Watch to the FBI Man who has followed me
for 25 years*

Well, old spy
looks like I
led you down some pretty blind alleys,
took you on several trips to Mexico,
5 fishing in the high Sierras,
jazz at the Philharmonic.
You've watched me all your life,
I've clothed your wife,
put your two sons through college.
10 what good has it done?
the sun keeps rising every morning.
ever see me buy an Assistant President?
or close a school?
or lend money to Trujillo?
15 ever catch me rigging airplane prices?
I bought some after-hours whiskey in L.A.
but the Chief got his pay.
I ain't killed no Koreans

or fourteen-year-old boys in Mississippi.
20 neither did I bomb Guatemala,
    or lend guns to shoot Algerians.
    I admit I took a Negro child
    to a white rest room in Texas,
    but she was my daughter, only three,
25 who had to pee.

What attitudes is Durem criticizing?

W. H. AUDEN (1907-1973)

THE UNKNOWN CITIZEN

*(To JS/07/M/378
This Marble Monument
Is Erected by the State)*

He was found by the Bureau of Statistics to be
One against whom there was no official complaint,
And all the reports on his conduct agree
That, in the modern sense of an old-fashioned word, he was a saint,
5   For in everything he did he served the Greater Community.
Except for the War till the day he retired
He worked in a factory and never got fired,
But satisfied his employers, Fudge Motors Inc.
Yet he wasn't a scab or odd in his views,
10 For his Union reports that he paid his dues,
(Our report on his Union shows it was sound)
And our Social Psychology workers found
That he was popular with his mates and liked a drink.
The Press are convinced that he bought a paper every day
15 And that his reactions to advertisements were normal in every way.
Policies taken out in his name prove that he was fully insured,
And his Health-card shows he was once in hospital but left it cured.
Both Producers Research and High-Grade Living declare
He was fully sensible to the advantages of the Instalment Plan
20 And had everything necessary to the Modern Man,
A phonograph, a radio, a car and a frigidaire.
Our researchers into Public Opinion are content
That he held the proper opinions for the time of year;
When there was peace, he was for peace; when there was war, he went.
25 He was married and added five children to the population,
Which our Eugenist says was the right number for a parent of his generation,
And our teachers report that he never interfered with their education.
Was he free? Was he happy? The question is absurd:
Had anything been wrong, we should certainly have heard.

259

THE UNITED FRUIT CO.

When the trumpet sounded, it was
all prepared on the earth,
the Jehovah parcelled out the earth
to Coca Cola, Inc., Anaconda,
5   Ford Motors, and other entities:
The Fruit Company, Inc.
reserved for itself the most succulent,
the central coast of my own land,
the delicate waist of America.
10   It rechristened its territories
as the "Banana Republics"
and over the sleeping dead,
over the restless heroes
who brought about the greatness,
15   the liberty and the flags,
it established the comic opera:
abolished the independencies,
presented crowns of Caesar,
unsheathed envy, attracted
20   the dictatorship of the flies,
Trujillo flies, Tacho flies,
Carias flies, Martinez flies,
Ubico flies, damp flies
of modest blood and marmelade,
25   drunken flies who zoom
over the ordinary graves,
circus flies, wise flies
well trained in tyranny.

Among the blood-thirsty flies
30   the Fruit Company lands its ships,
taking off the coffee and the fruit;
the treasure of our submerged
territories flow as though
on plates into the ships.

35   Meanwhile Indians are falling
into the sugared chasms
of the harbors, wrapped
for burial in the mist of the dawn:
a body rolls, a thing
40   that has no name, a fallen cipher,
a cluster of dead fruit
thrown down on the dump.

Translated by Robert Bly

TED JOANS (1928–   )

THE UBIQUITOUS LIONS

There are four lions   at Trafalgar Square   stolen symbols
    that do not
bare   any-kinda   resemblance   to European   royalty
These four lions   at Trafalgar Square   with whom European
    queens and
· kings   try to identify   are African   and very very BLACK
5 The four lions at Trafalgar Square   sit regally/lazy/
    and cooly gaze
whilst mini-skirted tourists slide between their wide spread paws
although they have a hip sneer   across their majestic black jaws
These four lions at Trafalgar Square   bigger than young elephants
heavier than fourteen Rolls Royces   have nothing a-tall to do with
10 chalk-white kings or Europeans horses   an auto roar imitates their
    black voices
These four black lions   of Africa   now sitting in London
    dreary town
lookout in four directions   at international tourists
    pose near   or
around   for the photo shot   these lions DO NOT FROWN!
The four black lions   at Trafalgar Square   have heard and seen
15 white demonstrations/meeting & rally lost and won
they've witnessed white man's pro & con   white guilt & fears
Nearby stands the South African Building and closer still is
    a Hippy church
For U.S.A. Civil Rites   and Biafra white nigger crocodile shed tears
There are four lions   at Trafalgar Square   they are black   and
    like lions everywhere
20 on European buildings   pedestals and government seals
These black lions must be free   to attack imperialism and destroy
    that evil deal
Sic'em sic'em lions   git them   white devils who dared to identify
    with thy!

MORNING HALF-LIFE BLUES

Girls buck the wind in the grooves toward work
in fuzzy coats promised to be warm as fur.
The shop windows snicker
flashing them hurrying over dresses they cannot afford:
5   you are not pretty enough, not pretty enough.

Blown with yesterday's papers through the boiled coffee
   morning
they dream of the stop on the subway without a name,
the door in the heart of the grove of skyscrapers,
that garden where we nestle to the teats of a furry world,
10 lie in mounds of peony eating grapes,
and need barter ourselves for nothing,
not by the hour, not by the pound, not by the skinful,
that party to which no one will give or sell them the key
though we have all thought briefly we had found it
15 drunk or in bed.

Black girls with thin legs and high necks stalking like herons,
plump girls with blue legs and green eyelids and strawberry
   breasts,
swept off to be frozen in fluorescent cubes,
the vacuum of your jobs sucks your brains dry
20 and fills you with the ooze of melted comics.
Living is later. This is your rented death.
You grasp at specific commodities and vague lusts
to make up, to pay for each day
which opens like a can and is empty, and then another,
25 afternoons like dinosaur eggs stuffed with glue.

Girls of the dirty morning, ticketed and spent,
you will be less at forty than at twenty.
Your living is a waste product of somebody's mill.
I would fix you like buds to a city where people work
30 to make and do things necessary and good,
where work is real as bread and babies and trees in parks
and you would blossom slowly and ripen to sound fruit.

Death

EMILY DICKINSON (1830–1886)

BECAUSE I COULD NOT STOP FOR DEATH

Because I could not stop for Death—
He kindly stopped for me—
The Carriage held but just Ourselves—
And Immortality.

5   We slowly drove—He knew no haste
And I had put away
My labor and my leisure too,
For His Civility—

We passed the School, where Children strove
10   At Recess—in the Ring—
We passed the Fields of Gazing Grain—
We passed the Setting Sun—

Or rather—He passed Us—
The Dews drew quivering and chill—
15   For only Gossamer, my Gown—
My Tippet[1]—only Tulle—

We paused before a House that seemed
A Swelling of the Ground—
The Roof was scarcely visible—
20   The Cornice—in the Ground—

Since then—'tis Centuries—and yet
Feels shorter than the Day
I first surmised the Horses Heads
Were toward Eternity—

[1] Scarf.

1. What do the first two lines mean? Why "kindly"?

2. What is the nature of the carriage ride taken by the speaker and Death?

3. What attitude toward death does the poem convey?

'OUT, OUT—'

The buzz saw snarled and rattled in the yard
And made dust and dropped stove-length sticks of wood,
Sweet-scented stuff when the breeze drew across it.
And from there those that lifted eyes could count
5   Five mountain ranges one behind the other
Under the sunset far into Vermont.
And the saw snarled and rattled, snarled and rattled,
As it ran light, or had to bear a load.
And nothing happened: day was all but done.
10 Call it a day, I wish they might have said
To please the boy by giving him the half hour
That a boy counts so much when saved from work.
His sister stood beside them in her apron
To tell them 'Supper.' At the word, the saw,
15 As if to prove saws knew what supper meant,
Leaped out at the boy's hand, or seemed to leap—
He must have given the hand. However it was,
Neither refused the meeting. But the hand!
The boy's first outcry was a rueful laugh,
20 As he swung toward them holding up the hand
Half in appeal, but half as if to keep
The life from spilling. Then the boy saw all—
Since he was old enough to know, big boy
Doing a man's work, though a child at heart—
25 He saw all spoiled. 'Don't let him cut my hand off—
The doctor, when he comes. Don't let him, sister!'
So. But the hand was gone already.
The doctor put him in the dark of ether.
He lay and puffed his lips out with his breath.
30 And then—the watcher at his pulse took fright.
No one believed. They listened at his heart.
Little—less—nothing!—and that ended it.
No more to build on there. And they, since they
Were not the one dead, turned to their affairs.

1. Why does Frost narrate the incident in such a matter-of-fact way?

2. How does Frost contrast the buzz saw with the Vermont setting? Does the buzz saw seem sinister to you?

HERE LIES A LADY

Here lies a lady of beauty and high degree.
Of chills and fever she died, of fever and chills,
The delight of her husband, her aunt, an infant of three,
And of medicos marveling sweetly on her ills.

5   For either she burned, and her confident eyes would blaze,
And her fingers fly in a manner to puzzle their heads—
What was she making? Why, nothing; she sat in a maze
Of old scraps of laces, snipped into curious shreds—

Or this would pass, and the light of her fire decline
10   Till she lay discouraged and cold, like a thin stalk white and
    blown,
And would not open her eyes, to kisses, to wine;
The sixth of these states was her last; the cold settled down.

Sweet ladies, long may ye bloom, and toughly I hope ye may thole,[1]
But was she not lucky? In flowers and lace and mourning,
15   In love and great honor we bade God rest her soul
After six little spaces of chill, and six of burning.

[1] A Scottish word meaning to suffer, bear, endure.

1. What was the lady like? *Was* she lucky?

2. What is the speaker's attitude toward her illness? Toward the "sweet ladies" he addresses in the last stanza?

DO NOT GO GENTLE INTO THAT GOOD NIGHT

Do not go gentle into that good night,
Old age should burn and rave at close of day;
Rage, rage against the dying of the light.
Though wise men at their end know dark is right,
5   Because their words had forked no lightning they
Do not go gentle into that good night.

Good men, the last wave by, crying how bright
Their frail deeds might have danced in a green bay,
Rage, rage against the dying of the light.

10 Wild men who caught and sang the sun in flight,
And learn, too late, they grieved it on its way,
Do not go gentle into that good night.

Grave men, near death, who see with blinding sight
Blind eyes could blaze like meteors and be gay,
15 Rage, rage against the dying of the light.

And you, my father, there on the sad height,
Curse, bless, me now with your fierce tears, I pray.
Do not go gentle into that good night.
Rage, rage against the dying of the light.

1. What does Thomas suggest that men recognize at the point of death? Why does he
urge them to "rage against the dying of the light"?

2. How does the opposition of light and dark work in the poem?

BEN JONSON (1573–1637)

ON MY FIRST SON

Farewell, thou child of my right hand, and joy;
My sin was too much hope of thee, loved boy,
Seven years thou wert lent to me, and I thee pay,
Exacted by thy fate, on the just day.
5 O, could I lose all father now. For why
Will man lament the state he should envy?
To have so soon 'scaped world's and flesh's rage,
And, if no other misery, yet age?
Rest in soft peace, and, asked, say, "Here doth lie
10 Ben Jonson his best piece of poetry."
For whose sake henceforth all his vows be such,
As what he loves may never like too much.

W. H. AUDEN (1907–1973)

IN MEMORY OF W. B. YEATS

(d. Jan. 1939)

I

He disappeared in the dead of winter:
The brooks were frozen, the air-ports almost deserted,
And snow disfigured the public statues;
The mercury sank in the mouth of the dying day.
5   O all the instruments agree
The day of his death was a dark cold day.

Far from his illness
The wolves ran on through the evergreen forests,
The peasant river was untempted by the fashionable quays;[1]
10   By mourning tongues
The death of the poet was kept from his poems.

But for him it was his last afternoon as himself,
An afternoon of nurses and rumours;
The provinces of his body revolted,
15   The squares of his mind were empty,
Silence invaded the suburbs,
The current of his feeling failed: he became his admirers.

Now he is scattered among a hundred cities
And wholly given over to unfamiliar affections;
20   To find his happiness in another kind of wood
And be punished under a foreign code of conscience.
The words of a dead man
Are modified in the guts of the living.

But in the importance and noise of to-morrow
25   When the brokers are roaring like beasts on the floor of the
        Bourse,[2]
And the poor have the sufferings to which they are fairly
        accustomed,
And each in the cell of himself is almost convinced of his
        freedom;
A few thousand will think of this day
As one thinks of a day when one did something slightly unusual.
30   O all the instruments agree
The day of his death was a dark cold day.

[1] Docks. [2] Paris Stock Exchange.

II

You were silly like us; your gift survived it all;
The parish of rich women, physical decay,
Yourself; mad Ireland hurt you into poetry.
35 Now Ireland has her madness and her weather still,
For poetry makes nothing happen: it survives
In the valley of its saying where executives
Would never want to tamper; it flows south
From ranches of isolation and the busy griefs,
40 Raw towns that we believe and die in; it survives,
A way of happening, a mouth.

III

Earth, receive an honoured guest;
William Yeats is laid to rest:
Let the Irish vessel lie
45 Emptied of its poetry.

Time that is intolerant
Of the brave and innocent,
And indifferent in a week
To a beautiful physique,

50 Worships language and forgives
Everyone by whom it lives;
Pardons cowardice, conceit,
Lays its honours at their feet.

Time that with this strange excuse
55 Pardoned Kipling[3] and his views,
And will pardon Paul Claudel,[4]
Pardons him for writing well.

In the nightmare of the dark
All the dogs of Europe bark,
60 And the living nations wait,
Each sequestered in its hate;

Intellectual disgrace
Stares from every human face,
And the seas of pity lie
65 Locked and frozen in each eye.

Follow, poet, follow right
To the bottom of the night,
With your unconstraining voice
Still persuade us to rejoice;

70   With the farming of a verse
　　　　　Make a vineyard of the curse,
　　　　　Sing of human unsuccess
　　　　　In a rapture of distress;

　　　　　In the deserts of the heart
75   Let the healing fountain start,
　　　　　In the prison of his days
　　　　　Teach the free man how to praise.

[3]Kipling championed British imperialism. [4]Claudel, a French dramatist, was an extreme conservative.

1. What does Part I suggest about the significance of Yeats's death?

2. How does Auden attempt to demonstrate, in Part II, that poetry makes nothing happen?

3. How does Auden honor Yeats in Part III? What does he see poetry as accomplishing?

GWENDOLYN BROOKS (1915–　)

MALCOLM X

For Dudley Randall

Original.
Ragged-round.
Rich-robust.

He had the hawk-man's eyes.
5 We gasped. We saw the maleness.
The maleness raking out and making guttural the air
and pushing us to walls.

And in a soft and fundamental hour
a sorcery devout and vertical
10 beguiled the world.

He opened us—
who was a key,

who was a man.

269

ANNE SEXTON (1928–1974)

THE ABORTION

Somebody who should have been born
is gone.

Just as the earth puckered its mouth,
each bud puffing out from its knot,
5   I changed my shoes, and then drove south.

Up past the Blue Mountains, where
Pennsylvania humps on endlessly,
wearing, like a crayoned cat, its green hair,

its roads sunken in like a gray washboard;
10   where, in truth, the ground cracks evilly,
a dark socket from which the coal has poured,

Somebody who should have been born
is gone.

the grass as bristly and stout as chives,
15   and me wondering when the ground would break,
and me wondering how anything fragile survives;

up in Pennsylvania, I met a little man,
not Rumpelstiltskin, at all, at all . . .
he took the fullness that love began.

20   Returning north, even the sky grew thin
like a high window looking nowhere.
The road was as flat as a sheet of tin.

Somebody who should have been born
is gone.

25   Yes, woman, such logic will lead
to loss without death. Or say what you meant,
you coward . . . this baby that I bleed.

Cycles

JOHN KEATS (1795–1821)

TO AUTUMN

Season of mists and mellow fruitfulness,
    Close bosom-friend of the maturing sun;
Conspiring with him how to load and bless
    With fruit the vines that round the thatch-eves run;
5 To bend with apples the mossed cottage-trees,
    And fill all fruit with ripeness to the core;
      To swell the gourd, and plump the hazel shells
With a sweet kernel; to set budding more,
    And still more, later flowers for the bees,
10   Until they think warm days will never cease,

      For Summer has o'er-brimmed their clammy cells.
Who hath not seen thee oft amid thy store?
    Sometimes whoever seeks abroad may find
Thee sitting careless on a granary floor,
15   Thy hair soft-lifted by the winnowing wind;
Or on a half-reaped furrow sound asleep,
    Drowsed with the fume of poppies, while the hook
      Spares the next swath and all its twinéd flowers:
And sometimes like a gleaner thou dost keep
20 Steady thy laden head across a brook;
    Or by a cider-press, with patient look,
      Thou watchest the last oozings hours by hours.

Where are the songs of Spring? Aye, where are they?
    Think not of them, thou hast thy music too—
25 While barréd clouds bloom the soft-dying day,
    And touch the stubble-plains with rosy hue;
Then in a wailful choir the small gnats mourn
    Among the river sallows, borne aloft
      Or sinking as the light wind lives or dies;
30 And full-grown lambs loud bleat from hilly bourn;
    Hedge crickets sing; and now with treble soft
    The redbreast whistles from a garden croft;
    And gathering swallows twitter in the skies.

1. How does Keats characterize Autumn's fertility in the first stanza?

2. What does Keats's personification of Autumn in the second stanza suggest about the season?

3. What attitude toward Autumn does the poem express? How would you describe the "music" of Autumn?

IN HARDWOOD GROVES

The same leaves over and over again!
They fall from giving shade above,
To make one texture of faded brown
And fit the earth like a leather glove.

5   Before the leaves can mount again
To fill the trees with another shade,
They must go down past things coming up.
They must go down into the dark decayed.

They *must* be pierced by flowers and put
10 Beneath the feet of dancing flowers.
However it is in some other world
I know that this is the way in ours.

1. Why "must" the leaves go down and "be pierced"?

2. What does the poem assert about life and death?

ROBERT FROST (1874–1963)

AFTER APPLE-PICKING

My long two-pointed ladder's sticking through a tree
Toward heaven still,
And there's a barrel that I didn't fill
Beside it, and there may be two or three
5   Apples I didn't pick upon some bough.
But I am done with apple-picking now.
Essence of winter sleep is on the night,
The scent of apples: I am drowsing off.
I cannot rub the strangeness from my sight
10 I got from looking through a pane of glass
I skimmed this morning from the drinking trough
And held against the world of hoary grass.
It melted, and I let it fall and break.
But I was well
15 Upon my way to sleep before it fell,
And I could tell
What form my dreaming was about to take.
Magnified apples appear and disappear,
Stem end and blossom end,

20 And every fleck of russet showing clear.
My instep arch not only keeps the ache,
It keeps the pressure of a ladder-round.
I feel the ladder sway as the boughs bend.
And I keep hearing from the cellar bin
25 The rumbling sound
Of load on load of apples coming in.
For I have had too much
Of apple-picking: I am overtired
Of the great harvest I myself desired.
30 There were ten thousand thousand fruit to touch,
Cherish in hand, lift down, and not let fall.
For all
That struck the earth,
No matter if not bruised or spiked with stubble,
35 Went surely to the cider-apple heap
As of no worth.
One can see what will trouble
This sleep of mine, whatever sleep it is.
Were he not gone,
40 The woodchuck could say whether it's like his
Long sleep, as I describe its coming on,
Or just some human sleep.

1. What does the title mean? In what sense is the poem (and its title) an extended metaphor? Why does the speaker say that he is "done with apple-picking now"?

2. What kind of sleep is the poet talking about?

WILLIAM BUTLER YEATS (1865–1939)

THE WILD SWANS AT COOLE

The trees are in their autumn beauty,
The woodland paths are dry,
Under the October twilight the water
Mirrors a still sky;
5 Upon the brimming water among the stones
Are nine-and-fifty swans.

The nineteenth autumn has come upon me
Since I first made my count;
I saw, before I had well finished,
10 All suddenly mount
And scatter wheeling in great broken rings
Upon their clamorous wings.

I have looked upon these brilliant creatures,
And now my heart is sore.
15 All's changed since I, hearing at twilight,
The first time on this shore,
The bell-beat of their wings above my head,
Trod with a lighter tread.

Unwearied still, lover by lover,
20 They paddle in the cold,
Companionable streams or climb the air;
Their hearts have not grown old;
Passion or conquest, wander where they will,
Attend upon them still.

25 But now they drift on the still water
Mysterious, beautiful;
Among what rushes will they build,
By what lake's edge or pool
Delight men's eyes when I awake some day
30 To find they have flown away?

1. Why is the poem set in autumn?

2. How does the speaker contrast his life with that of the swans? Why does he say that "All's changed" since the first time he was in the presence of the swans?

THOMAS HARDY (1840–1928)

DURING WIND AND RAIN

They sing their dearest songs—
He, she, all of them—yea,
Treble and tenor and bass,
  And one to play;
5   With the candles mooning each face. . . .
  Ah, no; the years O!
How the sick leaves reel down in throngs!

They clear the creeping moss—
Elders and juniors—aye,
10   Making the pathways neat
  And the garden gay;
And they build a shady seat. . . .
  Ah, no; the years, the years;
See, the white stormbirds wing across!

15　They are blithely breakfasting all—
　　Men and maidens—yea,
　　Under the summer tree,
　　　With a glimpse of the bay,
　　While pet fowl come to the knee. . . .
20　　　Ah, no; the years O!
　　And the rotten rose is ripped from the wall.

　　They change to a high new house,
　　He, she, all of them—aye,
　　Clocks and carpets and chairs
25　　　On the lawn all day,
　　And brightest things that are theirs. . . .
　　　Ah, no; the years, the years;
　　Down their carved names the raindrop plows.

1. What kind of life does Hardy picture in the various scenes he sketches?

2. What does the refrain suggest in each stanza?

PABLO NERUDA (1904–1973)

from "THE HEIGHTS OF MACCHU PICCHU[1]"

Then up the ladder of the earth I climbed
through the barbed jungle's thickets
until I reached you Macchu Picchu.

Tall city of stepped stone,
5　home at long last of whatever earth
had never hidden in her sleeping clothes.
In you two lineages[2] that had run parallel
met where the cradle both of man and light
rocked in a wind of thorns.

10　Mother of stone and sperm of condors.

High reef of the human dawn.

Spade buried in primordial sand.

This was the habitation, this is the site:
here the fat grains of maize grew high
15　to fall again like red hail.

The fleece of the vicuña was carded here
to clothe men's loves in gold, their tombs and mothers,
the king, the prayers, the warriors.

275

Up here men's feet found rest at night
20 near eagles' talons in the high
meat-stuffed eyries. And in the dawn
with thunder steps they trod the thinning mists,
touching the earth and stones that they might recognize
that touch come night, come death.

25 I gaze at clothes and hands,
traces of water in the booming cistern,
a wall burnished by the touch of a face
that witnessed with my eyes the earth's carpet of tapers,
oiled with my hands the vanished wood:
30 for everything, apparel, skin, pots, words,
wine, loaves, has disappeared,
fallen to earth.

And the air came in with lemon blossom fingers
to touch those sleeping faces:
35 a thousand years of air, months, weeks of air,
blue wind and iron cordilleras[3]—
these came with gentle footstep hurricanes
cleansing the lonely precinct of the stone.

Translated by Nathaniel Tarn

---

[1] The lost Incan city high in the Peruvian Andes, the existence of which was unknown until 1911. [2] The lineage of men, represented by centuries of births and deaths, and the lineage of nature, represented by the enduring stone and the generations of condors. [3] Mountain ranges.

1. How does Neruda suggest the great age of Macchu Picchu?

2. What is his attitude toward the former inhabitants of the place? Why does he identify with them?

*NGO CHI LAN**

WINTER

Lighted brazier
small silver pot
cup of Lofu wine to break the cold of the morning.
The snow
5 makes it feel colder inside the flimsy screens.
Wind lays morsels of frost on the icy pond.
Inside the curtains
inside her thoughts
a beautiful woman.
10 The cracks of doors and windows
all pasted over.
One shadowy wish to restore the spring world:
a plum blossom already open on the hill.

Translated by W. S. Merwin with Nguyen Ngoc Bich

*A fifteenth-century Vietnamese poet.

GERARD MANLEY HOPKINS (1844–1889)

SPRING AND FALL

To a Young Child

Márgarét, are you gríeving
Over Goldengrove unleaving?
Leáves, líke the things of man, you
With your fresh thoughts care for, can you?
5 Áh! ás the heart grows older
It will come to such sights colder
By and by, nor spare a sigh
Though worlds of wanwood leafmeal[1] lie;
And yet you wíll weep and know why.
10 Now no matter, child, the name:
Sórrow's spríngs áre the same.
Nor mouth had, no nor mind, expressed
What heart heard of, ghost guessed:
It ís the blight man was born for,
15 It is Margaret you mourn for.

[1] A compost made of rotting leaves; wanwood suggests "bloodless."

WALLACE STEVENS (1879–1955)

SUNDAY MORNING

I

Complacencies of the peignoir, and late
Coffee and oranges in a sunny chair,
And the green freedom of a cockatoo
Upon a rug mingle to dissipate
5   The holy hush of ancient sacrifice.
She dreams a little, and she feels the dark
Encroachment of that old catastrophe,
As a calm darkens among water-lights.
The pungent oranges and bright, green wings
10   Seem things in some procession of the dead,
Winding across wide water, without sound.
The day is like wide water, without sound,
Stilled for the passing of her dreaming feet
Over the seas, to silent Palestine,
15   Dominion of the blood and sepulchre.

II

Why should she give her bounty to the dead?
What is divinity if it can come
Only in silent shadows and in dreams?
Shall she not find in comforts of the sun,
20   In pungent fruit and bright, green wings, or else
In any balm or beauty of the earth,
Things to be cherished like the thought of heaven?
Divinity must live within herself:
Passions of rain, or moods in falling snow;
25   Grievings in loneliness, or unsubdued
Elations when the forest blooms; gusty
Emotions on wet roads on autumn nights;
All pleasures and all pains, remembering
The bough of summer and the winter branch.
30   These are the measures destined for her soul.

III

Jove[1] in the clouds had his inhuman birth.
No mother suckled him, no sweet land gave
Large-mannered motions to his mythy mind.
He moved among us, as a muttering king,
35   Magnificent, would move among his hinds,
Until our blood, commingling, virginal,

[1]The supreme deity in classical mythology.

With heaven, brought such requital to desire
The very hinds discerned it, in a star.
Shall our blood fail? Or shall it come to be
40 The blood of paradise? And shall the earth
Seem all of paradise that we shall know?
The sky will be much friendlier then than now,
A part of labor and a part of pain,
And next in glory to enduring love,
45 Not this dividing and indifferent blue.

IV

She says, "I am content when wakened birds,
Before they fly, test the reality
Of misty fields, by their sweet questionings;
But when the birds are gone, and their warm fields
50 Return no more, where, then, is paradise?"
There is not any haunt of prophecy,
Nor any old chimera of the grave,
Neither the golden underground, nor isle
Melodious, where spirits gat them home,
55 Nor visionary south, nor cloudy palm
Remote on heaven's hill, that has endured
As April's green endures; or will endure
Like her remembrance of awakened birds,
Or her desire for June and evening, tipped
60 By the consummation of the swallow's wings.

V

She says, "But in contentment I still feel
The need of some imperishable bliss."
Death is the mother of beauty; hence from her,
Alone, shall come fulfilment to our dreams
65 And our desires. Although she strews the leaves
Of sure obliteration on our paths,
The path sick sorrow took, the many paths
Where triumph rang its brassy phrase, or love
Whispered a little out of tenderness,
70 She makes the willow shiver in the sun
For maidens who were wont to sit and gaze
Upon the grass, relinquished to their feet.
She causes boys to pile new plums and pears
On disregarded plate. The maidens taste
75 And stray impassioned in the littering leaves.

VI

Is there no change of death in paradise?
Does ripe fruit never fall? Or do the boughs
Hang always heavy in that perfect sky,

Unchanging, yet so like our perishing earth,
80 With rivers like our own that seek for seas
They never find, the same receding shores
That never touch with inarticulate pang?
Why set the pear upon those river-banks
Or spice the shores with odors of the plum?
85 Alas, that they should wear our colors there,
The silken weavings of our afternoons,
And pick the strings of our insipid lutes!
Death is the mother of beauty, mystical,
Within whose burning bosom we devise
90 Our earthly mothers waiting, sleeplessly.

VII

Supple and turbulent, a ring of men
Shall chant in orgy on a summer morn
Their boisterous devotion to the sun,
Not as a god, but as a god might be,
95 Naked among them, like a savage source.
Their chant shall be a chant of paradise,
Out of their blood, returning to the sky;
And in their chant shall enter, voice by voice,
The windy lake wherein their lord delights,
100 The trees, like serafin,[2] and echoing hills,
That choir among themselves long afterward.
They shall know well the heavenly fellowship
Of men that perish and of summer morn.
And whence they came and whither they shall go
105 The dew upon their feet shall manifest.

VIII

She hears, upon that water without sound,
A voice that cries, "The tomb in Palestine
Is not the porch of spirits lingering.
It is the grave of Jesus, where he lay."
110 We live in an old chaos of the sun,
Or old dependency of day and night,
Or island solitude, unsponsored, free,
Of that wide water, inescapable.
Deer walk upon our mountains, and the quail
115 Whistle about us their spontaneous cries;
Sweet berries ripen in the wilderness;
And, in the isolation of the sky,
At evening, casual flocks of pigeons make
Ambiguous undulations as they sink,
120 Downward to darkness, on extended wings.

[2] Seraphim, the highest order of angels.

Further Poems

JOHN KEATS (1795–1821)

ODE TO A NIGHTINGALE

My heart aches, and a drowsy numbness pains
  My sense, as though of hemlock I had drunk,
Or emptied some dull opiate to the drains
  One minute past, and Lethe-wards[1] had sunk:
5 'Tis not through envy of thy happy lot,
  But being too happy in thy happiness,—
    That thou, light-wingéd Dryad of the trees,
      In some melodious plot
Of beechen green, and shadows numberless,
10 Singest of summer in full-throated ease.

O for a draught of vintage, that hath been
  Cooled a long age in the deep-delvéd earth,
Tasting of Flora[2] and the country green,
  Dance, and Provençal song,[3] and sun-burnt mirth!
15 O for a beaker full of the warm South,
  Full of the true, the blushful Hippocrene,[4]
    With beaded bubbles winking at the brim,
      And purple-stainéd mouth;
That I might drink, and leave the world unseen,
20 And with thee fade away into the forest dim:

Fade far away, dissolve, and quite forget
  What thou among the leaves hast never known,
The weariness, the fever, and the fret
  Here, where men sit and hear each other groan;
25 Where palsy shakes a few, sad, last gray hairs,
  Where youth grows pale, and spectre-thin, and dies;
    Where but to think is to be full of sorrow
      And leaden-eyed despairs;
Where beauty cannot keep her lustrous eyes,
30 Or new love pine at them beyond tomorrow.

Away! away! for I will fly to thee,
  Not charioted by Bacchus[5] and his pards,
But on the viewless wings of Poesy,
  Though the dull brain perplexes and retards:
35 Already with thee! tender is the night,
    And haply the Queen-Moon is on her throne,
      Clustered around by all her starry fays;
          But here there is no light,
    Save what from heaven is with the breezes blown
40   Through verdurous glooms and winding mossy ways.

I cannot see what flowers are at my feet,
  Nor what soft incense hangs upon the boughs,
But, in embalmed darkness, guess each sweet
  Wherewith the seasonable month endows
45 The grass, the thicket, and the fruit-tree wild;
    White hawthorn, and the pastoral eglantine;
      Fast-fading violets covered up in leaves;
          And mid-May's eldest child,
    The coming musk-rose, full of dewy wine,
50   The murmurous haunt of flies on summer eves.

Darkling I listen; and for many a time
  I have been half in love with easeful Death,
Called him soft names in many a mused rhyme,
  To take into the air my quiet breath;
55 Now more than ever seems it rich to die,
    To cease upon the midnight with no pain,
      While thou art pouring forth thy soul abroad
          In such an ecstasy!
    Still wouldst thou sing, and I have ears in vain—
60   To thy high requiem become a sod.

Thou wast not born for death, immortal bird!
  No hungry generations tread thee down;
The voice I hear this passing night was heard
  In ancient days by emperor and clown:
65 Perhaps the self-same song that found a path
    Through the sad heart of Ruth,[6] when, sick for home,
      She stood in tears amid the alien corn;
          The same that oft-times hath
    Charmed magic casements, opening on the foam
70   Of perilous seas, in faery lands forlorn.

Forlorn! the very word is like a bell
 To toll me back from thee to my sole self!
Adieu! the fancy cannot cheat so well
 As she is famed to do, deceiving elf.
75 Adieu! adieu! thy plaintive anthem fades
 Past the near meadows, over the still stream,
  Up the hill-side; and now 'tis buried deep
   In the next valley-glades:
 Was it a vision, or a waking dream?
80 Fled is that music:—do I wake or sleep?

---

[1] The water of the river Lethe, in Hades, causes forgetfulness. [2] The goddess of flowers. [3] Provence, in southern France, was associated with troubador singers in the Middle Ages. [4] The fountain of the Muses, associated with poetic inspiration. [5] The god of wine. [6] A young widow whose story is given in the Book of Ruth in the Bible.

EMILY DICKINSON (1830–1886)

THE SOUL SELECTS HER OWN SOCIETY

The Soul selects her own Society—
Then—shuts the Door—
To her divine Majority—
Present no more—

5 Unmoved—she notes the Chariots—pausing—
At her low Gate—
Unmoved—an Emperor be kneeling
Upon her Mat—

I've known her—from an ample nation—
10 Choose One—
Then—close the Valves of her attention—
Like Stone—

WILLIAM WORDSWORTH (1770–1850)

THE WORLD IS TOO MUCH WITH US

The world is too much with us; late and soon,
Getting and spending, we lay waste our powers:
Little we see in Nature that is ours;

We have given our hearts away, a sordid boon!
5   The Sea that bares her bosom to the moon;
The winds that will be howling at all hours,
And are up-gathered now like sleeping flowers;
For this, for everything, we are out of tune;
It moves us not.—Great God! I'd rather be
10 A Pagan suckled in a creed outworn;
So might I, standing on this pleasant lea,
Have glimpses that would make me less forlorn;
Have sight of Proteus* rising from the sea;
Or hear old Triton* blow his wreathèd horn.

*Proteus and Triton are sea gods.

GERARD MANLEY HOPKINS (1844–1889)

THE WINDHOVER

To Christ Our Lord

I caught this morning morning's minion,[1] king-
   dom of daylight's dauphin,[2] dapple-dawn-drawn Falcon, in his riding
  Of the rolling level underneath him steady air, and striding
High there, how he rung upon the rein of a wimpling[3] wing
In his ecstasy! then off, off forth on swing,
5   As a skate's heel sweeps smooth on a bow-bend; the hurl and gliding
  Rebuffed the big wind. My heart in hiding
Stirred for a bird,—the achieve of, the mastery of the thing!

Brute beauty and valor and act, oh, air, pride, plume, here
  Buckle! AND the fire that breaks from thee then, a billion
10 Times told lovelier, more dangerous, O my chevalier![4]

No wonder of it; shéer plód makes plough down sillion[5]
Shine, and blue-bleak embers, ah my dear,
  Fall, gall themselves; and gash gold-vermilion.

[1] Darling. [2] The eldest son of a king of France. [3] Rippling. [4] Knight. [5] An archaic word, meaning the ridge between two furrows of a plowed field.

WALLACE STEVENS (1879–1955)

THE SNOW MAN

One must have a mind of winter
To regard the frost and the boughs
Of the pinetrees crusted with snow;

And have been cold a long time
5 To behold the junipers shagged with ice,
The spruces rough in the distant glitter

Of the January sun; and not to think
Of any misery in the sound of the wind,
In the sound of a few leaves,

10 Which is the sound of the land
Full of the same wind
That is blowing in the same bare place

For the listener, who listens in the snow,
And, nothing himself, beholds
15 Nothing that is not there and the nothing that is.

WILLIAM BUTLER YEATS (1865–1939)

SAILING TO BYZANTIUM

I

That is no country for old men. The young
In one another's arms, birds in the trees
—Those dying generations—at their song,
The salmon-falls, the mackerel-crowded seas,
5 Fish, flesh, or fowl, commend all summer long
Whatever is begotten, born, and dies.
Caught in that sensual music all neglect
Monuments of unaging intellect.

*Yeats regarded Byzantium, famous for its mosaics and work in gold, as a symbol of a world of art and artifice, opposed to the real world dominated by time.

An aged man is but a paltry thing,
10 A tattered coat upon a stick, unless
Soul clap its hands and sing, and louder sing
For every tatter in its mortal dress,
Nor is there singing school but studying
Monuments of its own magnificence;
15 And therefore I have sailed the seas and come
To the holy city of Byzantium.

3

O sages standing in God's holy fire
As in the gold mosaic of a wall,
Come from the holy fire, perne in a gyre,
20 And be the singing-masters of my soul.
Consume my heart away; sick with desire
And fastened to a dying animal
It knows not what it is; and gather me
Into the artifice of eternity.

4

25 Once out of nature I shall never take
My bodily form from any natural thing,
But such a form as Grecian goldsmiths make
Of hammered gold and gold enameling
To keep a drowsy Emperor awake;
30 Or set upon a golden bough to sing
To lords and ladies of Byzantium
Of what is past, or passing, or to come.

WILLIAM BUTLER YEATS (1865–1939)

LEDA AND THE SWAN*

A sudden blow: the great wings beating still
Above the staggering girl, her thighs caressed
By the dark webs, her nape caught in his bill,
He holds her helpless breast upon his breast.

---

*In classical mythology Zeus, in the form of a swan, made love to Leda, who in turn gave birth to Pollux and Helen. By her husband, Tyndareus, Leda also gave birth to Castor and Clytemnestra. It was Helen's abduction by Paris which started the Trojan War. Agamemnon, the King of Mycenae who led the Greeks in the Trojan War, was murdered by his wife, Clytemnestra. Thus, one of Leda's offspring precipitated the Trojan War and the other murdered her husband, Agamemnon.

5 How can those terrified vague fingers push
  The feathered glory from her loosening thighs?
  And how can body, laid in that white rush,
  But feel the strange heart beating where it lies?

  A shudder in the loins engenders there
10 The broken wall, the burning roof and tower
  And Agamemnon dead.
                      Being so caught up,
  So mastered by the brute blood of the air,
  Did she put on his knowledge with his power
  Before the indifferent beak could let her drop?

RUBÉN DARÍO (1867–1916)

LEDA

The swan in shadow seems to be of snow;
his beak is translucent amber in the daybreak;
gently that first and fleeting glow of crimson
tinges his gleaming wings with rosy light.

5 And then, on the azure waters of the lake,
  when dawn has lost its colors, then the swan,
  his wings outspread, his neck a noble arc,
  is turned to burnished silver by the sun.

  The bird from Olympus,[1] wounded by love, swells out
10 his silken plumage, and clasping her in his wings
  he ravages Leda there in the singing water,
  his beak seeking the flower of her lips.

  She struggles, naked and lovely, and is vanquished,
  and while her cries turn sighs and die away,
15 the screen of teeming foliage parts and the wild
  green eyes of Pan[2] stare out, wide with surprise.

Translated by Lysander Kemp

[1] A mountain in Greece thought to be the home of the gods. [2] The Greek god Pan, half-goat and half-man, was at home in forests and mountains, where he played his reed pipes and pursued nymphs. He was associated with revelry and was sometimes thought of as "universal Pan," the god of all nature and giver of fertility.

THE NEGRO SPEAKS OF RIVERS

I've known rivers:
I've known rivers ancient as the world and older than the
flow of human blood in human veins.

My soul has grown deep like the rivers.

I bathed in the Euphrates when dawns were young.
5 I built my hut near the Congo and it lulled me to sleep.
I looked upon the Nile and raised the pyramids above it.
I heard the singing of the Mississippi when Abe Lincoln
went down to New Orleans, and I've seen its muddy
bosom turn all golden in the sunset.

I've known rivers:
Ancient, dusky rivers.

10 My soul has grown deep like the rivers.

MUSEE DES BEAUX ARTS[1]

About suffering they were never wrong,
The Old Masters: how well they understood
Its human position; how it takes place
While someone else is eating or opening a window or just walking
dully along;
5 How, when the aged are reverently, passionately waiting
For the miraculous birth, there always must be
Children who did not specially want it to happen, skating
On a pond at the edge of the wood:
They never forgot
10 That even the dreadful martyrdom must run its course
Anyhow in a corner, some untidy spot
Where the dogs go on with their doggy life and the torturer's horse
Scratches its innocent behind on a tree.
In Brueghel's *Icarus*,[2] for instance: how everything turns away

[1] Museum of Fine Arts. [2] The painting by Brueghel (1525?–1569) depicting the death of Icarus. When Icarus flew too close to the sun, wax holding on the wings made by his father Daedalus melted, and he fell into the sea.

15 Quite leisurely from the disaster; the ploughman may
Have heard the splash, the forsaken cry,
But for him it was not an important failure; the sun shone
As it had to on the white legs disappearing into the green
Water; and the expensive delicate ship that must have seen
20 Something amazing, a boy falling out of the sky,
Had somewhere to get to and sailed calmly on.

ROBERT LOWELL (1917–)

FOR THE UNION DEAD

"Relinquunt Omnia Servare Rem Publicam."[1]

The old South Boston Aquarium stands
in a Sahara of snow now. Its broken windows are boarded.
The bronze weathervane cod has lost half its scales.
The airy tanks are dry.

5 Once my nose crawled like a snail on the glass;
my hand tingled
to burst the bubbles
drifting from the nose of the cowed, compliant fish.

My hand draws back. I often sigh still
10 for the dark downward and vegetating kingdom
of the fish and reptile. One morning last March,
I pressed against the new barbed and galvanized

fence on the Boston Common. Behind their cage,
yellow dinosaur steamshovels were grunting
15 as they cropped up tons of mush and grass
to gouge their underworld garage.

Parking spaces luxuriate like civic
sandpiles in the heart of Boston.
A girdle of orange, Puritan-pumpkin colored girders
20 braces the tingling Statehouse,

shaking over the excavations, as it faces Colonel Shaw
and his bell-cheeked Negro infantry
on St. Gaudens'[2] shaking Civil War relief,
propped by a plank splint against the garage's earthquake.

25   Two months after marching through Boston,
     half the regiment was dead;
     at the dedication,
     William James[3] could almost hear the bronze Negroes breathe.

     Their monument sticks like a fishbone
30   in the city's throat.
     Its Colonel is as lean
     as a compass-needle.

     He has an angry wrenlike vigilance,
     a greyhound's gentle tautness;
35   he seems to wince at pleasure,
     and suffocate for privacy.

     He is out of bounds now. He rejoices in man's lovely,
     peculiar power to choose life and die—
     when he leads his black soldiers to death,
40   he cannot bend his back.

     On a thousand small town New England greens,
     the old white churches hold their air
     of sparse, sincere rebellion; frayed flags
     quilt the graveyards of the Grand Army of the Republic.

45   The stone statues of the abstract Union Soldier
     grow slimmer and younger each year—
     wasp-wasted, they doze over muskets
     and muse through their sideburns . . .

     Shaw's father wanted no monument
50   except the ditch,
     where his son's body was thrown
     and lost with his "niggers."

     The ditch is nearer.
     There are no statues for the last war here;
55   on Boylston Street, a commercial photograph
     shows Hiroshima boiling

     over a Mosler Safe, the "Rock of Ages"
     that survived the blast. Space is nearer.
     When I crouch to my television set,
60   the drained faces of Negro school-children rise like balloons.

     Colonel Shaw
     is riding on his bubble,
     he waits
     for the blesséd break.

65   The Aquarium is gone. Everywhere,
      giant finned cars nose forward like fish;
      a savage servility
      slides by on grease.

[1]They left everything to serve the state. [2]Nineteenth-century American sculptor. [3]American psychologist (1842–1910).

RICHARD WILBUR (1921–)

YEAR'S-END

    Now winter downs the dying of the year,
    And night is all a settlement of snow;
    From the soft street the rooms of houses show
    A gathered light, a shapen atmosphere,
5   Like frozen-over lakes whose ice is thin
    And still allows some stirring down within.

    I've known the wind by water banks to shake
    The late leaves down, which frozen where they fell
    And held in ice as dancers in a spell
10 Fluttered all winter long into a lake;
    Graved on the dark in gestures of descent,
    They seemed their own most perfect monument.

    There was perfection in the death of ferns
    Which laid their fragile cheeks against the stone
15 A million years. Great mammoths overthrown
    Composedly have made their long sojourns,
    Like palaces of patience, in the grey
    And changeless lands of ice. And at Pompeii

    The little dog lay curled and did not rise
20 But slept the deeper as the ashes rose
    And found the people incomplete, and froze
    The random hands, the loose unready eyes
    Of men expecting yet another sun
    To do the shapely thing they had not done.

25 These sudden ends of time must give us pause,
    We fray into the future, rarely wrought
    Save in the tapestries of afterthought.
    More time, more time. Barrages of applause
    Come muffled from a buried radio.
30 The New-year bells are wrangling with the snow.

EDWARD FIELD (1924–)

AFTER THE MOON WALK

I

When they landed on the moon
what we really wanted
was for strange creatures to seize them.

We wanted them to take off their helmets
5 and discover they could breathe,
that science was wrong
and there was air there.

We wanted people to be there,
tiny people who got that way
10 because they failed to develop usefully
and finally were banished
into a universe of rejected experiments.
And insects, perhaps the giant ancestors
of our own ants and bees.

15 When they took the first step on the moon
we wanted green insect men with mandibles and pincers
to rush out and right on television
drag them off to glass-enclosed cities,
or to underground factories and mines
20 where a humanoid race toils
that once ruled the moon
but invented nuclear weapons and destroyed it
and are now the slaves of giant ants who took over—
all this revealed before our eyes—
25 and an appeal for funds
to build a fleet of airships to attack the moon
and rescue our astronauts in captivity.

II

Instead what happened
was more like the way we once came to this continent
30 seeing nothing of value in the lives of the people here
and ruined them and their world,
like a renegade cell invading another
(though I want to believe the cancer cell obeys laws
even if they are still beyond our understanding).

35 Our earth-probe succeeded
in breaking through the moon's defenses
destroying forever what it was,
but opening a path for settlers,
colonies of infection, the beginning of life.

40 And if it is not yet a living world in our sense,
(though what in the universe is dead: It is all alive),
we have sent the germ cells of our biosystem
to start multiplying there.
Even now air seeds are growing
45 an atmosphere like ours.

If the moon was an egg
and the astronauts sperm-germs burrowing in
and if we chose them right for the task
(which I doubt, all white and macho as they are,
50 with those degenerate vibrations),
even so, it may be the beginning of a new planet.

And when it is ready to be on its own,
to search for its own orbit,
what great wrenching away is ahead for it, and us,
55 and dislocations of the stars
tidal waves and firestorms on earth,
repeating the destruction of continents
when the moon was born like a baby from our oceans.

What was begun—and it began long ago,
60 the necessity for a moon—
must continue to the end, everything always does.
And we'll go on sitting as long as we can,
glued to our TV sets,
watching it all.

ROBERT BLY (1926–   )

THINKING OF "THE AUTUMN FIELDS"

I.

Already autumn begins here in the mossy rocks.
The sheep bells moving from the wind are sad.
I have left my wife foolishly in a flat country,
I have set up my table looking over a valley.
5 There are fish in the lake but I will not fish;
I will sit silently at my table by the window.
From whatever appears on my plate,
I will give a little away to the birds and the grass.

2.

How easy to see the road the liferiver takes!
10 Hard to move one living thing from its own path.
The fish adores being in the deep water;
The bird easily finds a tree to live in.
In the second half of life a man accepts poverty and illness;
praise and blame belong to the glory of the first half.
15 Although cold wind blows against my walking stick,
I will never get tired of the ferns on this mountain.

3.

Music and chanting help me overcome my faults;
the mountains and woods keep my body fiery.
I have two or three books only in my room.
20 The sun shining off the empty bookcase warms my back.
Going out I pick up the pine cones the wind has thrown away.
When night comes, I will open a honeycomb.
On the floor-throw covered with tiny red and blue flowers,
I bring my stocking feet close to the faint incense.

FRANK O'HARA (1926–1966)

THE DAY LADY DIED[1]

It is 12:20 in New York a Friday
three days after Bastille day,[2] yes
it is 1959 and I go get a shoeshine
because I will get off the 4:19 in Easthampton
5 at 7:15 and go straight to dinner
and I don't know the people who will feed me

I walk up the muggy street beginning to sun
and have a hamburger and a malted and buy
an ugly NEW WORLD WRITING to see what the poets
10 in Ghana are doing these days
                    I go on to the bank
and Miss Stillwagon (first name Linda I once heard)
doesn't even look up my balance for once in her life
and in the GOLDEN GRIFFIN I get a little Verlaine[3]
for Patsy with drawings by Bonnard although I do
15 think of Hesiod,[4] trans. Richmond Lattimore or
Brendan Behan's new play or *Le Balcon* or *Les Nègres*
of Genet, but I don't, I stick with Verlaine
after practically going to sleep with quandariness

and for Mike I just stroll into the PARK LANE
20   Liquor Store and ask for a bottle of Strega and
then I go back where I came from to 6th Avenue
and the tobacconist in the Ziegfeld Theatre and
casually ask for a carton of Gauloises and a carton
of Picayunes, and a NEW YORK POST with her face on it

25   and I am sweating a lot by now and thinking of
leaning on the john door in the 5 SPOT
while she whispered a song along the keyboard
to Mal Waldron and everyone and I stopped breathing

---

[1]The blues singer Billie Holiday, known as "Lady Day." [2]The anniversary of the beginning of the French revolution, July 14, [3]Paul Verlaine, late nineteeth-century French poet. [4]Greek poet of the eight century B.C.

DAVID DIOP (1927–1960)

TO A BLACK DANCER

Negress my warm rumour of Africa
My land of mystery and my fruit of reason
You are the dance by the naked joy of your smile
By the offering of your breasts and secret powers
5   You are the dance by the golden tales of marriage nights
By new tempos and more secular rhythms
Negress repeated triumph of dreams and stars
Passive mistress to the koras' assault
You are the dance of giddyness
10   By the magic of loins restarting the world
You are the dance
And the myths burn around me
Around me the wigs of learning
In great fires of joy in the heaven of your steps
15   You are the dance
And burn false gods in your vertical flame
You are the face of the initiate
Sacrificing his childhood before the tree-god
You are the idea of All and the voice of the Ancient
20   Gravely rocketed against our fears
You are the Word which explodes
In showers of light upon the shores of oblivion.

295

THE BEAR

1

In late winter
I sometimes glimpse bits of steam
coming up from
some fault in the old snow
5   and bend close and see it is lung-colored
and put down my nose
and know
the chilly, enduring odor of bear.

2

I take a wolf's rib and whittle
10 it sharp at both ends
and coil it up
and freeze it in blubber and place it out
on the fairway of the bears.

And when it has vanished
15 I move out on the bear tracks,
roaming in circles
until I come to the first, tentative, dark
splash on the earth.

And I set out
20 running, following the splashes
of blood wandering over the world.
At the cut, gashed resting places
I stop and rest,
at the crawl-marks

25 where he lay out on his belly
to overpass some stretch of bauchy ice
I lie out
dragging myself forward with bear-knives in my fists.

3

On the third day I begin to starve,
30 at nightfall I bend down as I knew I would
at a turd sopped in blood,
and hesitate, and pick it up,
and thrust it in my mouth, and gnash it down,
and rise
35 and go on running.

4

On the seventh day,
living by now on bear blood alone,
I can see his upturned carcass far out ahead, a scraggled,
steamy hulk,
40 the heavy fur riffling in the wind.

I come up to him
and stare at the narrow-spaced, petty eyes,
the dismayed
face laid back on the shoulder, the nostrils
45 flared, catching
perhaps the first taint of me as he
died.

I hack
a ravine in his thigh, and eat and drink,
50 and tear him down his whole length
and open him and climb in
and close him up after me, against the wind,
and sleep.

5

And dream
55 of lumbering flatfooted
over the tundra,
stabbed twice from within,
splattering a trail behind me,
splattering it out no matter which way I lurch,
60 no matter which parabola of bear-transcendence,
which dance of solitude, I attempt,
which gravity-clutched leap,
which trudge, which groan.

6

Until one day I totter and fall—
65 fall on this
stomach that has tried so hard to keep up,
to digest the blood as it leaked in,
to break up
and digest the bone itself: and now the breeze
70 blows over me, blows off
the hideous belches of ill-digested bear blood
and rotted stomach
and the ordinary, wretched odor of bear,

blows across
75 my sore, lolled tongue a song
or screech, until I think I must rise up
and dance. And I lie still.

7

I awaken I think. Marshlights
reappear, geese
80 come trailing again up the flyway.
In her ravine under old snow the dam-bear
lies, licking
lumps of smeared fur
and drizzly eyes into shapes
85 with her tongue. And one
hairy-soled trudge stuck out before me,
the next groaned out,
the next,
the next,
90 the rest of my days I spend
wandering: wondering
what, anyway,
was that sticky infusion, that rank flavor of blood, that
poetry, by which I lived?

THOM GUNN (1929–   )

BLACK JACKETS

In the silence that prolongs the span
Rawly of music when the record ends,
The red-haired boy who drove a van
In weekday overalls but, like his friends,

5   Wore cycle boots and jacket here
To suit the Sunday hangout he was in,
Heard, as he stretched back from his beer,
Leather creak softly round his neck and chin.

Before him, on a coal-black sleeve
10   Remote exertion had lined, scratched, and burned
Insignia that could not revive
The heroic fall or climb where they were earned.

On the other drinkers bent together,
15   Concocting selves for their impervious kit,
He saw it as no more than leather
Which, taut across the shoulders grown to it,

Sent through the dimness of a bar
As sudden and anonymous hints of light
As those that shipping give, that are
20 Now flickers in the Bay, now lost in night.

He stretched out like a cat, and rolled
The bitterish taste of beer upon his tongue,
And listened to a joke being told:
The present was the things he stayed among.

25 If it was only loss he wore,
He wore it to assert, with fierce devotion,
Complicity and nothing more.
He recollected his initiation,

And one especially of the rites.
30 For on his shoulders they had put tattoos:
The group's name on the left, The Knights,
And on the right the slogan Born To Lose.

MILLER WILLIAMS (1930–   )

THE CATERPILLAR

Today on the lip of a bowl in the backyard
we watched a caterpillar caught in the circle
of his larval assumptions

my daughter counted
5 27 times he went around
before rolling back and laughing
I'm a caterpillar, look
she left him
measuring out his slow green way to some place
10 there must have been a picture of inside him

After supper
coming from putting the car up
we stopped to look
figured he crossed the yard
15 once every hour
and left him
when we went to bed
wrinkling no closer to my landlord's leaves
than when he somehow fell to his private circle

20 Later I followed
barefeet and doorclicks of my daughter
to the yard   the bowl
a milkwhite moonlight eye
in the black grass

25 *it died*

I said honey they don't live very long

In bed again
re-covered and re-kissed
she locked her arms and mumbling love to mine
30 until turning she slipped
into the deep bone-bottomed dish
of sleep

Stumbling drunk around the rim
I hold
35 the words she said to me across the dark

*I think he thought he was
going in a straight line*

.

SYLVIA PLATH (1932–1963)

TULIPS

The tulips are too excitable, it is winter here.
Look how white everything is, how quiet, how snowed-in.
I am learning peacefulness, lying by myself quietly
As the light lies on these white walls, this bed, these hands.
5 I am nobody; I have nothing to do with explosions.
I have given my name and my day-clothes up to the nurses
And my history to the anaesthetist and my body to surgeons.

They have propped my head between the pillow and the sheet-cuff
Like an eye between two white lids that will not shut.
10 Stupid pupil, it has to take everything in.
The nurses pass and pass, they are no trouble,
They pass the way gulls pass inland in their white caps,
Doing things with their hands, one just the same as another,
So it is impossible to tell how many there are.

15 My body is a pebble to them, they tend it as water
Tends to the pebbles it must run over, smoothing them gently.
They bring me numbness in their bright needles, they bring me
sleep.
Now I have lost myself I am sick of baggage—
My patent leather overnight case like a black pillbox,
20 My husband and child smiling out of the family photo;
Their smiles catch onto my skin, little smiling hooks.

I have let things slip, a thirty-year-old cargo boat
Stubbornly hanging on to my name and address.
They have swabbed me clear of my loving associations.
25 Scared and bare on the green plastic-pillowed trolley
I watched my tea-set, my bureaus of linen, my books
Sink out of sight, and the water went over my head.
I am a nun now, I have never been so pure.

I didn't want any flowers, I only wanted
30 To lie with my hands turned up and be utterly empty.
How free it is, you have no idea how free—
The peacefulness is so big it dazes you,
And it asks nothing, a name tag, a few trinkets.
It is what the dead close on, finally; I imagine them
35 Shutting their mouths on it, like a Communion tablet.

The tulips are too red in the first place, they hurt me.
Even through the gift paper I could hear them breathe
Lightly, through their white swaddlings, like an awful baby.
Their redness talks to my wound, it corresponds.
40 They are subtle: they seem to float, though they weigh me down,
Upsetting me with their sudden tongues and their colour,
A dozen red lead sinkers round my neck.

Nobody watched me before, now I am watched.
The tulips turn to me, and the window behind me
45 Where once a day the light slowly widens and slowly thins,
And I see myself, flat, ridiculous, a cut-paper shadow
Between the eye of the sun and the eyes of the tulips,
And I have no face, I have wanted to efface myself.
The vivid tulips eat my oxygen.

50 Before they came the air was calm enough,
Coming and going, breath by breath, without any fuss.
Then the tulips filled it up like a loud noise.
Now the air snags and eddies round them the way a river
Snags and eddies round a sunken rust-red engine.
55 They concentrate my attention, that was happy
Playing and resting without committing itself.

The walls, also, seem to be warming themselves.
The tulips should be behind bars like dangerous animals;
They are opening like the mouth of some great African cat,
60 And I am aware of my heart: it opens and closes
Its bowl of red blooms out of sheer love of me.
The water I taste is warm and salt, like the sea,
And comes from a country far away as health.

LEROI JONES (1934–)

YOUNG SOUL

First, feel, then feel, then
read, or read, then feel, then
fall, or stand, where you
already are. Think
5 of your self, and the other
selves . . . think
of your parents, your mothers
and sisters, your bentslick
father, then feel, or
10 fall, on your knees
if nothing else will move you,

                    then read
                    and look deeply
                    into all matters
15   come close to you
                    city boys—
                    country men

                    Make some muscle
                    in your head, but
20   use the muscle
                    in yr heart

WOLE SOYINKA (1935–)

TELEPHONE CONVERSATION

The price seemed reasonable, location
Indifferent. The landlady swore she lived
Off premises. Nothing remained
But self-confession. 'Madam,' I warned,
5 'I hate a wasted journey—I am African.'
Silence. Silenced transmission of
Pressurized good-breeding. Voice, when it came,
Lipstick coated, long gold-rolled
Cigarette-holder pipped. Caught I was, foully.
10 'HOW DARK?' . . . I had not misheard. . . . 'ARE YOU
     LIGHT
OR VERY DARK?' Button B. Button A. Stench
Of rancid breath of public hide-and-speak.
Red booth. Red pillar-box. Red double-tiered
Omnibus squelching tar. It *was* real! Shamed
15 By ill-mannered silence, surrender
Pushed dumbfoundment to beg simplification.
Considerate she was, varying the emphasis—
'ARE YOU DARK? OR VERY LIGHT?' Revelation came.
'You mean—like plain or milk chocolate?'
20 Her assent was clinical, crushing in its light
Impersonality. Rapidly, wave-length adjusted,
I chose. 'West African sepia'—and as afterthought,
'Down in my passport.' Silence for spectroscopic
Flight of fancy, till truthfulness clanged her accent
25 Hard on the mouthpiece. 'WHAT'S THAT?' conceding
'DON'T KNOW WHAT THAT IS.' 'Like brunette.'
'THAT'S DARK, ISN'T IT?' 'Not altogether.
Facially, I am brunette, but madam, you should see
The rest of me. Palm of my hand, soles of my feet
30 Are a peroxide blonde. Friction, caused—
Foolishly madam—by sitting down, has turned
My bottom raven black—One moment madam!'—sensing
Her receiver rearing on the thunderclap
About my ears—'Madam,' I pleaded, 'wouldn't you
    rather
35 See for yourself?'

SEDUCTION

one day
you gonna walk in this house
and i'm gonna have on a long African
gown
5   you'll sit down and say "The Black . . . "
and i'm gonna take one arm out
then you—not noticing me at all—will say "What about
this brother . . . "
and i'm going to be slipping it over my head
10 and you'll rapp on about "The revolution . . . "
while i rest your hand against my stomach
you'll go on—as you always do—saying
"I just can't dig . . . "
while i'm moving your hand up and down
15 and i'll be taking your dashiki off
then you'll say "What we really need . . . "
and i'll be licking your arm
and "The way I see it we ought to . . . "
and unbuckling your pants
20 "And what about the situation . . . "
and taking your shorts off
then you'll notice
your state of undress
and knowing you you'll just say
25 "Nikki,
isn't this counterrevolutionary . . . ?"

Commentary by Robert Hayden*

MC CLUSKEY : A poet chooses an image, as a matter of fact each word, to convey a specific meaning or impression. When you read your poems to others, or discuss them with others, do you usually find that you have been successful in conveying the exact impression you had in mind?

HAYDEN : For the most part, yes. But a poem is often a complex of meanings, of primary and secondary and even tertiary meanings. If you write with enough care and precision, the reader will no doubt get out of the poem what you originally intended. He may also find other things, and if the context justifies these discoveries, all well and good. Too often, I'm afraid, people read their own meanings into a poem, ignoring connotations, the way certain key images function, the tone. But I would say, to answer your question more specifically, that on the whole my poems seem to be interpreted correctly, with some exceptions. I have occasionally been surprised by the interpretations readers and critics have come up with.

· · · · ·

MC CLUSKEY : When you begin to write a poem, do you think about form, or does a form suggest itself as you set your thoughts down?

HAYDEN : I would answer yes to both parts of the question. I always hope, as I've said before, that there's going to be a close relationship between form and content. Occasionally, I will have a definite pattern in mind before I begin writing. This was true of the Douglass sonnet. If I'm in luck, if the Muse is not too recalcitrant, I can manage. (Note the "if's"; writing poetry, let's face it, is an "iffy," sometime thing!) Usually, though, I have to try a variety of forms and methods before I arrive at something that seems right. That's why each poem is for me an experiment. At the beginning, I'm not always sure of what the "shape of the content"—to borrow from Ben Shahn—is going to be. And I don't know how a poem is going to end much of the time. A pattern begins to emerge, very often, as I write, and it affects the meaning. Once I see the pattern clearly, I let it guide me. "Sub Specie Aeternitatis," I recall, was hard to organize. It didn't succeed when it was freer, more "open" than it subsequently became. It just didn't work at all. It was loose, needed considerable tightening. In the early drafts the lines were arranged differently. Some were short, and some were longer than they are now. Eventually, the varying lengths of the lines suggested a stanza pattern I was able to work with, and then the poem began to, well, began to be a real poem.

MC CLUSKEY : You told me earlier that you hear your poems. Does hearing them help you to determine their form?

*From an interview with Robert Hayden by Paul McCluskey.

305

HAYDEN: I suppose it does, in a general sort of way. I've not thought much about it, actually. What I can say definitely is that I'm concerned with phrasing, with cadences, pauses, with tone. And these certainly contribute to the structure as well as to the meaning of my poems. Maybe this is as good a place as any to say something I feel is rather important, and that is: a poem should have silences. For me the silences of a poem are as meaningful as its sounds. All my best poems have silences in them. There are things in them that are not expressed, that are all the more strongly suggested because they are not stated.

· · · · ·

MC CLUSKEY: What advice do you give the student poets you work with?

HAYDEN: I too encourage them to use their own experiences, to write about what they know. But although I encourage them to look in their own hearts and write, as Sir Philip Sidney's Muse urged him to do, I am at pains to get them to see that self-expression—writing from the heart—is not all that's required. Knowledge is important. Craftsmanship is essential. And so are dedication and the willingness to work hard. For the most part, I try not to interfere too much with a young poet, once I'm convinced he's really a poet. I don't expect him to write or think as I do. And I want to let him discover some things for himself. I do demand quality, however, demand that he write better than he thinks he can. (I demand this of myself as well, I might say.) I encourage him to read as widely as possible, advise him to spend as much time writing as he can. And of course I read his poems and discuss them with him in detail. I don't theorize much, except in the most general sort of way, because I have very little patience with poetic theories. What I tell my students comes largely from my own experience as a poet. I'll say, for example, that a poem, like any other form of art, establishes its own laws and fails or succeeds in direct proportion to the poet's ability to carry them out. And I'll emphasize the point that there's always material for poetry, no lack of it, because there's poetry everywhere and in everything, waiting like the angel in the block of marble to be released.

· · · · ·

"SUMMERTIME AND THE LIVING . . . "*

MC CLUSKEY: Would you comment on the images in the poem? Did they come readily to mind?

HAYDEN: Most of them were down in my subconscious—that's where most of what I need for a poem is—and when I came to write "Summertime," why, they rose to the surface. Jack Johnson's "diamond limousine," for example. The sunflowers, the circus posters, and, yes, the quarrels and broken glass, even those fans, certainly came readily to mind, and writing was a part of the process of remembering them. As for the contrasts, they developed out of the material without my deliberately working toward them at first. For ghetto life as I knew it was full of contrasts. Violence and ugliness and cruelty. We kids were exposed to the grim realities, to coin a phrase, in spite of all our elders could do to protect us. But there was beauty, there was gentleness,

*The poem appears on page 197.

too. There was a vividness of life, an intensity of being—something I tried to suggest in the poem. And there were people who retained a—"sheltering" is the word to describe it—a sheltering spiritual beauty and dignity—my mother and my foster father among them—despite sordid and disheartening circumstances. I love the memory of those people, and "Summertime" is partly an elegy for them. The contrast between fantasy and reality, apart from the particular significance it has in this poem, is a favorite theme of mine. What is fantasy? What is reality? And can we always distinguish one from the other?

MC CLUSKEY: The sunflower appears rather often in your poetry, and is even used to illustrate your *Selected Poems*. Is the sunflower a symbol?

HAYDEN: Very much so, and one I'm in imminent danger of using too often. To me, the sunflower symbolizes life, vitality, hope in the midst of deprivation. I associate it with the kind of life I knew as a young person. It was the one flower I was likely to see in my neighborhood. It grew without too much attention, I guess. I had a sunflower poem in my very first book, and maybe some day I'll revise it for my collected poems, because it has some images I still like.

MC CLUSKEY: Much of the effectiveness of this poem depends upon folklore.

HAYDEN: It actually doesn't contain any folklore—not folklore as such. But we could say it reflects folk ways, aspects of folk life, attitudes. The last line, for instance, adapts a quotation from the Bible I used to heat often when people got to discussing the racial situation. "And Ethiopia shall stretch forth her hands to God" is the passage, if I remember correctly. And whatever the original meaning might have been, it had a specific meaning for us—our future glory as a God-fearing race, our freedom from oppression. "But summer was . . . the poor folks' time of year" suggests something I also heard the old folks in my neighborhood say from time to time. The street preachers I mention were in the folk tradition, with their fire-and-brimstone sermons full of horrendous imagery, their spirituals and gospel songs accompanied by tambourines. Jack Johnson was something of a folk-hero, and ghetto people admired him as a symbol of the strength and power of the black race, just as they admired Joe Louis years later. His victories were their own vicarious triumphs over the oppressor. And they saw his eventual fall as the result of a plot to destroy him because he had dared to defy the conventions of the white world.

MC CLUSKEY: This poem is a reminiscence. Was the act of remembering a slow process? Were there many revisions to this poem?

HAYDEN: "Summertime," as I recall, grew out of strong emotions. I can't tell you what triggered them. A conversation with my wife about our childhood days in Detroit? An old photograph? A letter from my mother? I've forgotten what it was that quickened old memories and started me writing. At first, I was emotionally involved with my subject, but as I continued working I began to feel detached. I might very well have produced nothing but sentimental twaddle otherwise. I know we can't safely generalize about the poetic process, but I believe, from my own experience, that it's one whereby the expression of a strong emotion becomes the means of release from that emotion. Didn't T.S. Eliot say something similar? And I would say, further, that the emotion out of which a poem grows is objectified in the process of writing the poem. I wrote several versions of "Summertime" before I was satisfied with it. I'm sure that much of its effect depends on tone, pitch, and one of my problems was to keep the tone consistent. As with every poem I've written, I rewrote and revised for several years. "Summertime" was first published in *A Ballad of Remembrance*, then revised for *Selected Poems*. Everything I originally wished to get into the poem now seems to be there, and so I think I'm through with it—at least for awhile.

DRAMA

What the drama can do, and what it actually does, is to take this un-meaning haphazard show of life, that means nothing to you, and arrange it in an intelligible order, and arrange it in such a way as to make you think very much more deeply about it than you ever dreamed of thinking about actual incidents that come to your knowledge.

GEORGE BERNARD SHAW

Introductory

The dramatist's task is to bring events to life by presenting them on a stage. Instead of describing the characters, as a writer of fiction might, he sets them in motion through dialogue, gesture, and action. "The first thing I try to do," writes the Irish playwright Sean O'Casey, "is to make a play live: live as a part of life, and live in its own right as a work of drama."

In order to bring his characters to life, the dramatist has them speak in particular ways, make certain gestures, and exhibit certain habits, idiosyncrasies, and mannerisms; their personalities are steadily revealed through their responses to events and to each other. Characters are brought to life, in other words, not only through their main actions, but through the little things they say and do.

A dramatist shapes his play, gives it a structure, in such a way as to hold the audience's interest. The writers of Greek tragedies such as *Oedipus Rex* used a five-part structure: introduction, rising action, climax, falling action, catastrophe. The introduction to the tragedy brings the audience into the presence of a particular world: we meet most of the characters, see the setting which is provided for them, and sense (through hints which the dramatist provides) that some kind of conflict is either present or can be expected. As the play develops further through a series of events (rising action), we arrive at a turning point in the story (climax). Then further events (falling action) lead to a disastrous conclusion (catastrophe)—Oedipus blinds himself and goes into exile; Hedda Gabler shoots herself in the head with a pistol. Not all plays present a neat five-part structure, however, and thus you should always try to decide for yourself the ways in which, and the sequence in which, the events of a play unfold.

LeRoi Jones's one-act play, *Dutchman*, an example of what Jones calls "Revolutionary Theatre," is meant to shock and challenge its audience. In reading it, you can forget any conventional assumptions about the structure and subject matter of a play. A screenplay, too, should be read with regard for its special nature. In the screenplay of *The Seventh Seal*, Ingmar Bergman (who wrote and directed the film) provides detailed descriptions of scenes that should help you to think in visual terms. But, of course, it's best to see the film if possible.

311

Greek Tragedy

Sophocles's *Oedipus Rex* is not only a representative Greek tragedy but also the best known and most widely read. The terms we use to describe Greek tragedy were presented by Aristotle, and we have not really improved them. The central character is known as the "tragic hero." He has some kind of "flaw," the root cause of which is usually pride ("hubris"), which results, finally, in his downfall. At the moment of his final punishment, or death, he becomes more honestly aware of his limitations and of the nature of his world. Through his suffering, he has achieved a better sense of self. In Greek tragedy the dramatist intentionally attempts to make the members of the audience share in the tragic hero's suffering. By experiencing both pity and fear, the person watching the play purges himself—undergoes a "catharsis"—of those emotions.

In most Greek tragedies, and especially those written by Sophocles, there is a great deal of dramatic irony—that is, irony which involves a difference between what the audience knows about the characters and what the characters know about themselves. When Sophocles wrote *Oedipus Rex*, for example, he relied upon the audience's familiarity with the Oedipal legend.* The audience, but not Oedipus, knows from the beginning of the play that Oedipus has unknowingly murdered his father and married his mother. The dramatic irony is always present; when Oedipus curses the murderer of his father, for example, the audience knows that he is cursing himself.

One of the conventional elements of Greek tragedy is the chorus—which speaks onstage along with the other characters. The members of the chorus

*Oedipus did not know that he had not been raised by his own father, for at his birth he had been left on a hillside to die; however, a shepherd found him and took him to an old couple to raise. Apollo had warned Laios, the king of Thebes, and his wife, Iocaste, that their son would kill Laïos and marry Iocaste—that is, he would commit fratricide and incest. Oedipus himself was warned by the oracle of Apollo at Delphi of the same thing. On his way home from Delphi, Oedipus got into a fight and killed Laios, not knowing he was his father; later on, Oedipus was able to solve a riddle and thereby accept the reward of marriage to Iocaste, not knowing that she was his mother. Oedipus ruled Thebes well and had four children by his mother. Then a plague broke out, at which point *Oedipus Rex* begins.

312

are not involved in the action of the play; nothing *happens* because of their presence. Much of the chorus's commentary on the characters and events in the play has to do with the role of the gods in human affairs; the gods, in Greek tragedy, always know the destiny of the characters, but they do not cause the events or their results. The chorus, in contrast to the gods, does *not* know everything at the beginning; they learn gradually and, by voicing their increasing apprehension over what they see going on, they prepare the audience for the catastrophe. For example, when the chorus reveals shock at Oedipus's blasphemous defiance of the gods, they are voicing what might be the typical reaction of the Greek audience. The chorus, in short, reminds the audience that human beings simply cannot know their own fates as the gods know them.

Greek tragedies such as *Oedipus Rex* were performed at the ancient amphitheatre in Athens, a huge semi-circle of tiered stone rows which held eighteen thousand people (imagine one half of a typical college football stadium). At the center of this enormous semi-circle was a circular area, the "orchestra"; beyond it was a raised platform for the actors to stand on, and beyond the platform was a third structure in which the actors could get into costume. Actors usually wore long robes and leggings called "buskins," and also usually wore high-soled shoes and large masks so that people in the most distant seats could see them. Where we go to rock festivals, the youth of Sophocles's day (and their elders) went to Athens for a five-day festival of tragedy—and they brought along plenty of food and wine. When you read the speeches in *Oedipus Rex*, imagine them being shouted to the enormous open-air crowd; imagine the stylized gestures and the masks necessary to clarify words and actions to eighteen thousand people. Try to transport yourself to the amphitheatre on the southeastern slope of the Acropolis in ancient Athens.

OEDIPUS REX

An English Version
by Dudley Fitts and Robert Fitzgerald

PERSONS REPRESENTED

OEDIPUS	TEIRESIAS	SHEPHERD OF LAÏOS
A PRIEST	IOCASTE	SECOND MESSENGER
CREON	MESSENGER	CHORUS OF THEBAN ELDERS

The Scene: Before the palace of Oedipus, King of Thebes. A central door and two lateral doors open onto a platform which runs the length of the facade. On the platform, right and left, are altars; and three steps lead down into the "orchestra," or chorus-ground. At the beginning of the action these steps are crowded by SUPPLIANTS *who have brought branches and chaplets of olive leaves and who lie in various attitudes of despair.* OEDIPUS *enters.*

PROLOGUE

OEDIPUS. My children, generations of the living
In the line of Kadmos, nursed at his ancient hearth:
Why have you strewn yourselves before these altars
In supplication, with your boughs and garlands?
5 The breath of incense rises from the city
With a sound of prayer and lamentation.
                                        Children,
I would not have you speak through messengers,
And therefore I have come myself to hear you—
I, Oedipus, who bear the famous name.
(*To a* PRIEST.) You, there, since you are eldest in the company,
10 Speak for them all, tell me what preys upon you,
Whether you come in dread, or crave some blessing:
Tell me, and never doubt that I will help you
In every way I can; I should be heartless
Were I not moved to find you suppliant here.
15 PRIEST: Great Oedipus, O powerful King of Thebes!
You see how all the ages of our people

Cling to your altar steps: here are boys
Who can barely stand alone, and here are priests
By weight of age, as I am a priest of God,
20 And young men chosen from those yet unmarried;
As for the others, all that multitude,
They wait with olive chaplets in the squares,
At the two shrines of Pallas, and where Apollo
Speaks in the glowing embers.
                       Your own eyes
25 Must tell you: Thebes is in her extremity
And can not lift her head from the surge of death.
A rust consumes the buds and fruits of the earth;
The herds are sick; children die unborn,
And labor is vain. The god of plague and pyre
30 Raids like detestable lightning through the city,
And all the house of Kadmos is laid waste,
All emptied, and all darkened: Death alone
Battens upon the misery of Thebes.

You are not one of the immortal gods, we know;
35 Yet we have come to you to make our prayer
As to the man of all men best in adversity
And wisest in the ways of God. You saved us
From the Sphinx, that flinty singer, and the tribute
We paid to her so long; yet you were never
40 Better informed than we, nor could we teach you:
It was some god breathed in you to set us free.

Therefore, O mighty King, we turn to you:
Find us our safety, find us a remedy,
Whether by counsel of the gods or men.
45 A king of wisdom tested in the past
Can act in a time of troubles, and act well.
Noblest of men, restore
Life to your city! Think how all men call you
Liberator for your triumph long ago;
50 Ah, when your years of kingship are remembered,
Let them not say *We rose, but later fell*—
Keep the State from going down in the storm!
Once, years ago, with happy augury,
You brought us fortune; be the same again!
55 No man questions your power to rule the land:
But rule over men, not over a dead city!
Ships are only hulls, citadels are nothing,
When no life moves in the empty passageways.
OEDIPUS: Poor children! You may be sure I know
60 All that you longed for in your coming here.
I know that you are deathly sick; and yet,

[handwritten margin notes: "Pitiful, dark city ills"; "Gods as forces in Nature (Multiple meanings)"; "Appeal of history, awareness of future generations."; "Irony"]

315

Sick as you are, not one is as sick as I.
Each of you suffers in himself alone
His anguish, not another's; but my spirit

Irony

65 Groans for the city, for myself, for you.

I was not sleeping, you are not waking me.
No, I have been in tears for a long while
And in my restless thought walked many ways.
In all my search, I found one helpful course,

70 And that I have taken: I have sent Creon,
Son of Menoikeus, brother of the Queen,
To Delphi, Apollo's place of revelation,
To learn there, if he can,
What act or pledge of mine may save the city.

75 I have counted the days, and now, this very day,
I am troubled, for he has overstayed his time.
What is he doing? He has been gone too long.

Suspense

Yet whenever he comes back, I should do ill
To scant whatever hint the god may give.

80 PRIEST: It is a timely promise. At this instant
They tell me Creon is here.
OEDIPUS: O Lord Apollo!
May his news be fair as his face is radiant!
PRIEST: It could not be otherwise: he is crowned with bay,
The chaplet is thick with berries.
OEDIPUS: We shall soon know;
He is near enough to hear us now.

(*Enter* CREON.)

85   O Prince:
Brother: son of Menoikeus:
What answer do you bring us from the god?
CREON: It is favorable. I can tell you, great afflictions
Will turn out well, if they are taken well.

90 OEPIDUS: What was the oracle? These vague words

Irony

Leave me still hanging between hope and fear.
CREON: Is it your pleasure to hear me with all these
Gathered around us? I am prepared to speak,
But should we not go in?
OEDIPUS: Let them all hear it.

Kingly care + Irony

95 It is for them I suffer, more than for myself.
CREON: Then I will tell you what I heard at Delphi.

In plain words
The god commands us to expel from the land of Thebes
An old defilement that it seems we shelter.

100 It is a deathly thing, beyond expiation.

316

We must not let it feed upon us longer.

OEDIPUS: What defilement? How shall we rid ourselves of it?

CREON: By exile or death, blood for blood. It was
Murder that brought the plague-wind on the city.

105 OEDIPUS: Murder of whom? Surely the god has named him?

CREON: My Lord: long ago Laïos was our king,
Before you came to govern us.

OEDIPUS: I know;
I learned of him from others; I never saw him.

CREON: He was murdered; and Apollo commands us now

110 To take revenge upon whoever killed him.

OEDIPUS: Upon whom? Where are they? Where shall we find a clue
To solve that crime, after so many years?

CREON: Here in this land, he said.

                              If we make enquiry,
We may touch things that otherwise escape us.

115 OEDIPUS: Tell me: Was Laïos murdered in his house,
Or in the fields, or in some foreign country?

CREON: He said he planned to make a pilgrimage.
He did not come home again.

OEDIPUS: And was there no one,
No witness, no companion, to tell what happened?

120 CREON: They were all killed but one, and he got away
So frightened that he could remember one thing only.

OEDIPUS: What was that one thing? One may be the key
To everything, if we resolve to use it.

CREON: He said that a band of highwaymen attacked them,

125 Outnumbered them, and overwhelmed the King.

OEDIPUS: Strange, that a highwayman should be so daring—
Unless some faction here bribed him to do it.

CREON: We thought of that. But after Laïos' death
New troubles arose and we had no avenger.

130 OEDIPUS: What troubles could prevent your hunting down the killers?

CREON: The riddling Sphinx's song
Made us deaf to all mysteries but her own.

OEDIPUS: Then once more I must bring what is dark to light.
It is most fitting that Apollo shows,

135 As you do, this compunction for the dead.
You shall see how I stand by you, as I should,
To avenge the city and the city's god,
And not as though it were for some distant friend,
But for my own sake, to be rid of evil.

140 Whoever killed King Laïos might—who knows?—
Decide at any moment to kill me as well.
By avenging the murdered king I protect myself.   *Socially, religiously*
Come, then, my children: leave the altar steps,
Lift up your olive boughs!

One of you go

145 And summon the people of Kadmos to gather here.
I will do all that I can; you may tell them that.

(Exit a PAGE.*)*

So, with the help of God,
We shall be saved—or else indeed we are lost.
PRIEST: Let us rise, children. It was for this we came,
150 And now the King has promised it himself.
Phoibos has sent us an oracle; may he descend
Himself to save us and drive out the plague.

Handwritten margin note: Sun-god.

(Exeunt OEDIPUS *and* CREON *into the palace by the central door. The* PRIEST *and the* SUPPLIANTS *disperse R and L. After a short pause the* CHORUS *enters the orchestra.)*

PARODOS

[STROPHE 1

CHORUS: What is God singing in his profound
Delphi of gold and shadow?
What oracle for Thebes, the sunwhipped city?
Fear unjoints me, the roots of my heart tremble.
5 Now I remember, O Healer, your power, and wonder;
Will you send doom like a sudden cloud, or weave it
Like nightfall of the past?
Speak, speak to us, issue of holy sound:
Dearest to our expectancy: be tender!

[ANTISTROPHE 1

10 Let me pray to Athenê, the immortal daughter of Zeus,
And to Artemis her sister
Who keeps her famous throne in the market ring,
And to Apollo, bowman at the far butts of heaven—

Handwritten margin note: Water/fire

O gods, descend! Like three streams leap against
15 The fires of our grief, the fires of darkness;
Be swift to bring us rest!

As in the old time from the brilliant house
Of air you stepped to save us, come again!

[STROPHE 2

Now our afflictions have no end,
20 Now all our stricken host lies down
And no man fights off death with his mind;

318

The noble plowland bears no grain,
And groaning mothers can not bear—

See, how our lives like birds take wing,
25 Like sparks that fly when a fire soars,
To the shore of the god of evening.

[ANTISTROPHE 2

The plague burns on, it is pitiless,
Though pallid children laden with death   *New generations attacked*
Lie unwept in the stony ways,

30 And old gray women by every path
Flock to the strand about the altars

There to strike their breasts and cry
Worship of Phoibos in wailing prayers:
Be kind, God's golden child!

[STROPHE 3

35 There are no swords in this attack by fire,
No shields, but we are ringed with cries.
Send the besieger plunging from our homes
Into the vast sea-room of the Atlantic
Or into the waves that foam eastward of Thrace—
40 For the day ravages what the night spares—

Destroy our enemy, lord of the thunder!
Let him be riven by lightning from heaven!

[ANTISTROPHE 3

Phoibos Apollo, stretch the sun's bowstring,
That golden cord, until it sing for us,
45 Flashing arrows in heaven!
                    Artemis, Huntress,
Race with flaring lights upon our mountains!

O scarlet god, O golden-banded brow,
O Theban Bacchos in a storm of Maenads,

(*Enter* OEDIPUS, *C.*)

(Prayer for deliverance from the plague)

Whirl upon Death, that all the Undying hate!
50 Come with blinding cressets, come in joy!

SCENE I

OEDIPUS: Is this your prayer? It may be answered. Come,
Listen to me, act as the crisis demands,
And you shall have relief from all these evils.

319

Until now I was a stranger to this tale,
5 As I had been a stranger to the crime.
Could I track down the murderer without a clue?
But now, friends,
As one who became a citizen after the murder,
I make this proclamation to all Thebans:
10 If any man knows by whose hand Laïos, son of Labdakos,
Met his death, I direct that man to tell me everything,
No matter what he fears for having so long withheld it.
Let it stand as promised that no further trouble
Will come to him, but he may leave the land in safety.

15 Moreover: If anyone knows the murderer to be foreign,
Let him not keep silent: he shall have his reward from me.
However, if he does conceal it; if any man
Fearing for his friend or for himself disobeys this edict,
Hear what I propose to do:

20 I solemnly forbid the people of this country,
Where power and throne are mine, ever to receive that man
Or speak to him, no matter who he is, or let him
Join in sacrifice, lustration, or in prayer.
I decree that he be driven from every house,
25 Being, as he is, corruption itself to us: the Delphic
Voice of Zeus has pronounced this revelation.
Thus I associate myself with the oracle
And take the side of the murdered king.

As for the criminal, I pray to God—
30 Whether it be a lurking thief, or one of a number—
I pray that that man's life be consumed in evil and wretchedness.
And as for me, this curse applies no less
If it should turn out that the culprit is my guest here,
Sharing my hearth.
                    You have heard the penalty.
35 I lay it on you now to attend to this
For my sake, for Apollo's, for the sick
Sterile city that heaven has abandoned.
Suppose the oracle had given you no command:
Should this defilement go uncleansed for ever?
40 You should have found the murderer: your king,
A noble king, had been destroyed!
                              Now I,
Having the power that he held before me,
Having his bed, begetting children there
Upon his wife, as he would have, had he lived—
45 Their son would have been my children's brother,
If Laïos had had luck in fatherhood!

320

(But surely ill luck rushed upon his reign)—
I say I take the son's part, just as though
I were his son, to press the fight for him

50 And see it won! I'll find the hand that brought
Death to Labdakos' and Polydoros' child,
Heir of Kadmos' and Agenor's line.
And as for those who fail me,
May the gods deny them the fruit of the earth,

55 Fruit of the womb, and may they rot utterly!
Let them be wretched as we are wretched, and worse!

For you, for loyal Thebans, and for all   *Justice-seeking theme*
Who find my actions right, I pray the favor
Of justice, and of all the immortal gods.

60 CHORAGOS: Since I am under oath, my lord, I swear
I did not do the murder, I can not name
The murderer. Might not the oracle
That has ordained the search tell where to find him?
OEDIPUS: An honest question. But no man in the world

65 Can make the gods do more than the gods will.
CHORAGOS: There is one last expedient—
OEDIPUS: Tell me what it is.
Though it seem slight, you must not hold it back.
CHORAGOS: A lord clairvoyant to the lord Apollo,
As we all know, is the skilled Teiresias.

70 One might learn much about this from him, Oedipus.
OEDIPUS: I am not wasting time:
Creon spoke of this, and I have sent for him—
Twice, in fact; it is strange that he is not here.
CHORAGOS: The other matter—that old report—seems useless.

75 OEDIPUS: Tell me. I am interested in all reports.
CHORAGOS: The King was said to have been killed by highwaymen.
OEDIPUS: I know. But we have no witnesses to that.
CHORAGOS: If the killer can feel a particle of dread,
Your curse will bring him out of hiding!
OEDIPUS: No.   *He tried to defy the oracle before!*

80 The man who dared that act will fear no curse.

(*Enter the blind seer* TEIRESIAS, *led by a* PAGE.)

CHORAGOS: But there is one man who may detect the criminal.
This is Teiresias, this is the holy prophet
In whom, alone of all men, truth was born.
OEDIPUS: Teiresias: seer: student of mysteries,

85 Of all that's taught and all that no man tells,
Secrets of Heaven and secrets of the earth:
Blind though you are, you know the city lies

321

Sick with plague; and from this plague, my lord,
We find that you alone can guard or save us.

90 Possibly you did not hear the messengers?
Apollo, when we sent to him,
Sent us back word that this great pestilence
Would lift, but only if we established clearly
The identity of those who murdered Laïos.
95 They must be killed or exiled.

                                        Can you use
Birdflight or any art of divination
To purify yourself, and Thebes, and me
From this contagion? We are in your hands.
There is no fairer duty
100 Than that of helping others in distress.
TEIRESIAS: How dreadful knowledge of the truth can be
When there's no help in truth! I knew this well,
But did not act on it: else I should not have come.
OEDIPUS: What is troubling you? Why are your eyes so cold?
105 TEIRESIAS: Let me go home. Bear your own fate, and I'll
Bear mine. It is better so: trust what I say.
OEDIPUS: What you say is ungracious and unhelpful
To your native country. Do not refuse to speak.
TEIRESIAS: When it comes to speech, your own is neither temperate
110 Nor opportune. I wish to be more prudent.
OEDIPUS: In God's name, we all beg you—
TEIRESIAS: You are all ignorant.
No; I will never tell you what I know.
Now it is my misery; then, it would be yours.
OEDIPUS: What! You do know something, and will not tell us?
115 You would betray us all and wreck the State?
TEIRESIAS: I do not intend to torture myself, or you.
Why persist in asking? You will not persuade me.
OEDIPUS: What a wicked old man you are! You'd try a stone's
Patience! Out with it! Have you no feeling at all?
120 TEIRESIAS: You call me unfeeling. If you could only see
The nature of your own feelings . . .
OEDIPUS: Why,
Who would not feel as I do? Who could endure
Your arrogance toward the city?
TEIRESIAS: What does it matter!
Whether I speak or not, it is bound to come.
125 OEDIPUS: Then, if "it" is bound to come, you are bound to tell me.
TEIRESIAS: No, I will not go on. Rage as you please.
OEDIPUS: Rage? Why not!
                              And I'll tell you what I think:
You planned it, you had it done, you all but
Killed him with your own hands: if you had eyes,

322

130   I'd say the crime was yours, and yours alone.

TEIRESIAS: So? I charge you, then,
Abide by the proclamation you have made:
From this day forth
Never speak again to these men or to me;

135   You yourself are the pollution of this country.

OEDIPUS: You dare say that! Can you possibly think you have
Some way of going free, after such insolence?

TEIRESIAS: I have gone free. It is the truth sustains me.

OEDIPUS: Who taught you shamelessness? It was not your craft.

140   TEIRESIAS: You did. You made me speak. I did not want to.

OEDIPUS: Speak what? Let me hear it again more clearly.

TEIRESIAS: Was it not clear before? Are you tempting me?

OEDIPUS: I did not understand it. Say it again.

TEIRESIAS: I say that you are the murderer whom you seek.

145   OEDIPUS: Now twice you have spat out infamy. You'll pay for it!

TEIRESIAS: Would you care for more? Do you wish to be really angry?

OEDIPUS: Say what you will. Whatever you say is worthless.

TEIRESIAS: I say you live in hideous shame with those
Most dear to you. You can not see the evil.

150   OEDIPUS: It seems you can go on mouthing like this for ever.

TEIRESIAS: I can, if there is power in truth.

OEDIPUS: There is:
But not for you, not for you,
You sightless, witless, senseless, mad old man!

TEIRESIAS: You are the madman. There is no one here

155   Who will not curse you soon, as you curse me.

OEDIPUS: You child of endless night! You can not hurt me
Or any other man who sees the sun.

TEIRESIAS: True: it is not from me your fate will come.
That lies within Apollo's competence,

160   As it is his concern.

OEDIPUS: Tell me:
Are you speaking for Creon, or for yourself?

TEIRESIAS: Creon is no threat. You weave your own doom.

OEDIPUS: Wealth, power, craft of statesmanship!
Kingly position, everywhere admired!

165   What savage envy is stored up against these,
If Creon, whom I trusted, Creon my friend,
For this great office which the city once
Put in my hands unsought—if for this power
Creon desires in secret to destroy me!

170   He has bought this decrepit fortune-teller, this
Collector of dirty pennies, this prophet fraud—
Why, he is no more clairvoyant than I am!

                                                  Tell us:
Has your mystic mummery ever approached the truth?

When that hellcat the Sphinx was performing here,
175 What help were you to these people?
Her magic was not for the first man who came along:
It demanded a real exorcist. Your birds—
What good were they? or the gods, for the matter of that?
But I came by,
180 Oedipus, the simple man, who knows nothing—
I thought it out for myself, no birds helped me!
And this is the man you think you can destroy,
That you may be close to Creon when he's king!
Well you and your friend Creon, it seems to me,
185 Will suffer most. If you were not an old man,
You would have paid already for your plot.
CHORAGOS: We can not see that his words or yours
Have been spoken except in anger, Oedipus,
And of anger we have no need. How can God's will
190 Be accomplished best? That is what most concerns us.
TEIRESIAS: You are a king. But where argument's concerned
I am your man, as much a king as you.
I am not your servant, but Apollo's.
I have no need of Creon to speak for me.

195 Listen to me. You mock my blindness, do you?
But I say that you, with both your eyes, are blind:
You can not see the wretchedness of your life,
Nor in whose house you live, no, nor with whom.
Who are your father and mother? Can you tell me?
200 You do not even know the blind wrongs
That you have done them, on earth and in the world below.
But the double lash of your parents' curse will whip you
Out of this land some day, with only night
Upon your precious eyes.
205 Your cries then—where will they not be heard?
What fastness of Kithairon will not echo them?
And that bridal-descant of yours—you'll know it then,
The song they sang when you came here to Thebes
And found your misguided berthing.
210 All this, and more, that you can not guess at now,
Will bring you to yourself among your children.

Be angry, then. Curse Creon. Curse my words.
I tell you, no man that walks upon the earth
Shall be rooted our more horribly than you.
215 OEDIPUS: Am I to bear this from him?—Damnation
Take you! Out of this place! Out of my sight!
TEIRESIAS: I would not have come at all if you had not asked me.
OEDIPUS: Could I have told that you'd talk nonsense, that
You'd come here to make a fool of yourself, and of me?

220 TEIRESIAS: A fool? Your parents thought me sane enough.
OEDIPUS: My parents again!—Wait: who were my parents?
TEIRESIAS: This day will give you a father, and break your heart.
OEDIPUS: Your infantile riddles! Your damned abracadabra!
TEIRESIAS: You were a great man once at solving riddles.
225 OEDIPUS: Mock me with that if you like; you will find it true.
TEIRESIAS: It was true enough. It brought about your ruin.   *He begins to believe, it seems.*
OEDIPUS: But if it saved this town?
TEIRESIAS (*to the* PAGE):

                Boy, give me your hand.
OEDIPUS: Yes, boy; lead him away.

                —While you are here
We can do nothing. Go; leave us in peace.
230 TEIRESIAS: I will go when I have said what I have to say.
How can you hurt me? And I tell you again:
The man you have been looking for all this time,
The damned man, the murderer of Laïos,
That man is in Thebes. To your mind he is foreignborn,
235 But it will soon be shown that he is a Theban,
A revelation that will fail to please.

                A blind man,
Who has his eyes now; a penniless man, who is rich now;
And he will go tapping the strange earth with his staff;
To the children with whom he lives now he will be
240 Brother and father—the very same; to her
Who bore him, son and husband—the very same
Who came to his father's bed, wet with his father's blood.

Enough. Go think that over.
If later you find error in what I have said,
245 You may say that I have no skill in prophecy.

(*Exit* TEIRESIAS, *led by his* PAGE. OEDIPUS *goes into the palace.*)

ODE I

[STROPHE 1

CHORUS: The Delphic stone of prophecies
Remembers ancient regicide
And a still bloody hand.
That killer's hour of flight has come.
5 He must be stronger than riderless
Coursers of untiring wind,
For the son of Zeus armed with his father's thunder   *Light/dark*
Leaps in lightning after him;
And the Furies follow him, the sad Furies. — *Avengers*

10 Holy Parnassos' peak of snow
Flashes and blinds that secret man,
That all shall hunt him down:
Though he may roam the forest shade
Like a bull gone wild from pasture
15 To rage through glooms of stone.
Doom comes down on him; flight will not avail him;
For the world's heart calls him desolate,
And the immortal Furies follow, for ever follow.

But now a wilder thing is heard
20 From the old man skilled at hearing Fate in the wingbeat of a bird.
Bewildered as a blown bird, my soul hovers and can not find
Foothold in this debate, or any reason or rest of mind.
But no man ever brought—none can bring
Proof of strife between Thebes' royal house,
25 Labdakos' line, and the son of Polybos;
And never until now has any man brought word
Of Laïos' dark death staining Oedipus the King.

Divine Zeus and Apollo hold
Perfect intelligence alone of all tales ever told;
30 And well though this diviner works, he works in his own night;
No man can judge that rough unknown or trust in second sight,
For wisdom changes hands among the wise.
Shall I believe my great lord criminal
At a raging word that a blind old man let fall?
35 I saw him, when the carrion woman faced him of old,
Prove his heroic mind! These evil words are lies.

Chorus: How they depend on their king as guide in the moral sense.

Lack of trust in Teiresias rather than doubting Gods or King.

(sphinx curse)

SCENE II

CREON: Men of Thebes:
I am told that heavy accusations
Have been brought against me by King Oedipus.

I am not the kind of man to bear this tamely.

5 If in these present difficulties
He holds me accountable for any harm to him
Through anything I have said or done—why, then,
I do not value life in this dishonor.

It is not as though this rumor touched upon

10 Some private indiscretion. The matter is grave.
The fact is that I am being called disloyal
To the State, to my fellow citizens, to my friends.
CHORAGOS: He may have spoken in anger, not from his mind.
CREON: But did you not hear him say I was the one

15 Who seduced the old prophet into lying?
CHORAGOS: The thing was said; I do not know how seriously.
CREON: But you were watching him! Were his eyes steady?
Did he look like a man in his right mind?
CHORAGOS: I do not know. *Decline to intervene*
I can not judge the behavior of great men.

20 But here is the King himself.

(*Enter* OEDIPUS.)

OEDIPUS: So you dared come back.
Why? How brazen of you to come to my house,
You murderer!
                    Do you think I do not know
That you plotted to kill me, plotted to steal my throne?
Tell me, in God's name: am I coward, a fool,

25 That you should dream you could accomplish this?
A fool who could not see your slippery game?
A coward, not to fight back when I saw it?
You are the fool, Creon, are you not? hoping
Without support or friends to get a throne?

30 Thrones may be won or bought: you could do neither.
CREON: Now listen to me. You have talked; let me talk, too.
You can not judge unless you know the facts.
OEDIPUS: You speak well: there is one fact; but I find it hard
To learn from the deadliest enemy I have.

35 CREON: That above all I must dispute with you.
OEDIPUS: That above all I will not hear you deny.
CREON: If you think there is anything good in being stubborn
Against all reason, then I say you are wrong.
OEDIPUS: If you think a man can sin against his own kind] *Condemns himself through his condemnation of Creon.*

40 And not be punished for it, I say you are mad.
CREON: I agree. But tell me: what have I done to you?
OEDIPUS: You advised me to send for that wizard, did you not?
CREON: I did. I should do it again.
OEDIPUS: Very well. Now tell me;
How long has it been since Laïos—
CREON: What of Laïos?

45 OEDIPUS: Since he vanished in that onset by the road?
CREON: It was long ago, a long time.
OEDIPUS: And this prophet,
Was he practicing here then?

327

CREON: He was; and with honor, as now.

OEDIPUS: Did he speak of me at that time?

CREON: He never did;
At least, not when I was present.

OEDIPUS: But . . . the enquiry?
50   I suppose you held one?

CREON: We did, but we learned nothing.

OEDIPUS: Why did the prophet not speak against me then?

CREON: I do not know; and I am the kind of man
Who holds his tongue when he has no facts to go on.

OEDIPUS: There's one fact that you know, and you could tell it.
55   CREON: What fact is that? If I know it, you shall have it.

OEDIPUS: If he were not involved with you, he could not say
That it was I who murdered Laïos.

CREON: If he says that, you are the one that knows it!—
But now it is my turn to question you.

60   OEDIPUS: Put your questions. I am no murderer.

CREON: First, then: You married my sister?

OEDIPUS: I married your sister

CREON: And you rule the kingdom equally with her?

OEDIPUS: Everything that she wants she has from me.

CREON: And I am the third, equal to both of you?

65   OEDIPUS: That is why I call you a bad friend.

CREON: No. Reason it out, as I have done.
Think of this first. Would any sane man prefer
Power, with all a king's anxieties,
To that same power and the grace of sleep?
70   Certainly not I.
I have never longed for the king's power—only his rights.
Would any wise man differ from me in this?
As matters stand, I have my way in everything
With your consent, and no responsibilities.
75   If I were king, I should be a slave to policy.

How could I desire a scepter more
Than what is now mine—untroubled influence?
No, I have not gone mad; I need no honors,
Except those with the perquisites I have now.
80   I am welcome everywhere; every man salutes me,
And those who want your favor seek my ear,
Since I know how to manage what they ask.
Should I exchange this ease for that anxiety?
Besides, no sober mind is treasonable.
85   I hate anarchy
And never would deal with any man who likes it.

Test what I have said. Go to the priestess
At Delphi, ask if I quoted her correctly.

328

And as for this other thing: if I am found
90 Guilty of treason with Teiresias,
Then sentence me to death! You have my word
It is a sentence I should cast my vote for—
But not without evidence!
                    You do wrong
When you take good men for bad, bad men for good.
95 A true friend thrown aside—why, life itself
Is not more precious!
                    In time you will know this well:
For time, and time alone, will show the just man,
Though scoundrels are discovered in a day.

Repetition of the "before this day is over" foreshadowing.

CHORAGOS: This is well said, and a prudent man would ponder it.
100 Judgments too quickly formed are dangerous.
OEDIPUS: But is he not quick in his duplicity?
And shall I not be quick to parry him?
Would you have me stand still, hold my peace, and let
This man win everything, through my inaction?
105 CREON: And you want—what is it, then? To banish me?
OEDIPUS: No, not exile. It is your death I want,
So that all the world may see what treason means.
CREON: You will persist, then? You will not believe me?
OEDIPUS: How can I believe you?
CREON: Then you are a fool.
110 OEDIPUS: To save myself?
CREON: In justice, think of me.
OEDIPUS: You are evil incarnate.
CREON: But suppose that you are wrong?
OEDIPUS: Still I must rule.
CREON: But not if you rule badly.
OEDIPUS: O city, city!
CREON: It is my city, too!
CHORAGOS: Now, my lords, be still. I see the Queen,
115 Iocaste, coming from her palace chambers;
And it is time she came, for the sake of you both.
This dreadful quarrel can be resolved through her.

(*Enter* IOCASTE.)

IOCASTE: Poor foolish men, what wicked din is this?
With Thebes sick to death, is it not shameful
120 That you should rake some private quarrel up?
(*To* OEDIPUS.) Come into the house.
                              —And you, Creon, go now:
Let us have no more of this tumult over nothing.
CREON: Nothing? No, sister: what your husband plans for me
Is one of two great evils: exile or death.
125 OEDIPUS: He is right.

Why, woman I have caught him squarely

Plotting against my life.

CREON: No! Let me die

Accurst if ever I have wished you harm!

IOCASTE: Ah, believe it, Oedipus!

In the name of the gods, respect this oath of his

130 For my sake, for the sake of these people here!

[STROPHE 1

CHORAGOS: Open your mind to her, my lord. Be ruled by her, I beg
you!

OEDIPUS: What would you have me do?

CHORAGOS: Respect Creon's word. He has never spoken like a fool,
And now he has sworn an oath.

OEDIPUS: You know what you ask?

CHORAGOS: I do.

OEDIPUS: Speak on, then.

135 CHORAGOS: A friend so sworn should not be baited so,
In blind malice, and without final proof.

OEDIPUS: You are aware, I hope, that what you say
Means death for me, or exile at the least.

[STROPHE 2

CHORAGOS: No, I swear by Helios, first in Heaven!

140   May I die friendless and accurst,
The worst of deaths, if ever I meant that!
        It is the withering fields
            That hurt my sick heart:
        Must we bear all these ills,

145   And now your bad blood as well?

OEDIPUS: Then let him go. And let me die, if I must,
Or be driven by him in shame from the land of Thebes.
It is your unhappiness, and not his talk,
That touches me.
                    As for him—

150 Wherever he is, I will hate him as long as I live.

CREON: Ugly in yielding, as you were ugly in rage!
Natures like yours chiefly torment themselves.

OEDIPUS: Can you not go? Can you not leave me?

CREON: I can.

You do not know me; but the city knows me,

155 And in its eyes I am just, if not in yours.

(*Exit* CREON.)

[ANTISTROPHE 1

CHORAGOS: Lady Iocaste, did you not ask the King to go to his chambers?

IOCASTE: First tell me what has happened.

CHORAGOS: There was suspicion without evidence; yet it rankled
As even false charges will.

IOCASTE: On both sides?

CHORAGOS: On both.

IOCASTE: But what was said?

160 CHORAGOS: Oh let it rest, let it be done with!
Have we not suffered enough?

OEDIPUS: You see to what your decency has brought you:
You have made difficulties where my heart saw none.

[ANTISTROPHE 2

CHORAGOS: Oedipus, it is not once only I have told you—
165   You must know I should count myself unwise
To the point of madness, should I now forsake you—
            You, under whose hand,
                In the storm of another time,
            Our dear land sailed out free.
170   But now stand fast at the helm!

IOCASTE: In God's name, Oedipus, inform your wife as well:
Why are you so set in this hard anger?

OEDIPUS: I will tell you, for none of these men deserves
My confidence as you do. It is Creon's work,
175 His treachery, his plotting against me.

IOCASTE: Go on, if you can make this clear to me.

OEDIPUS: He charges me with the murder of Laïos.

IOCASTE: Has he some knowledge? Or does he speak from hearsay?

OEDIPUS: He would not commit himself to such a charge,
180 But he has brought in that damnable soothsayer
To tell his story.

IOCASTE: Set your mind at rest.
If it is a question of soothsayers, I tell you
That you will find no man whose craft gives knowledge
Of the unknowable.

                Here is my proof:

185 An oracle was reported to Laïos once
(I will not say from Phoibos himself, but from
His appointed ministers, at any rate)
That his doom would be death at the hands of his own son—
His son, born of his flesh and of mine!

190 Now, you remember the story: Laïos was killed
By marauding strangers where three highways meet;
But his child had not been three days in this world
Before the King had pierced the baby's ankles
And left him to die on a lonely mountainside.

195 Thus, Apollo never caused that child
To kill his father, and it was not Laïos' fate
To die at the hands of his son, as he had feared.
This is what prophets and prophecies are worth!
Have no dread of them.
                                        It is God himself
200 Who can show us what he wills, in his own way.

OEDIPUS: How strange a shadowy memory crossed my mind,
Just now while you were speaking; it chilled my heart.

IOCASTE: What do you mean? What memory do you speak of?

OEDIPUS: If I understand you, Laïos was killed
At a place where three roads meet.

205 IOCASTE: So it was said;
We have no later story.

OEDIPUS: Where did it happen?

IOCASTE: Phokis, it is called: at a place where the Theban Way
Divides into the roads towards Delphi and Daulia.

OEDIPUS: When?

IOCASTE: ' We had the news not long before you came
210 And proved the right to your succession here.

OEDIPUS: Ah, what net has God been weaving for me?

IOCASTE: Oedipus! Why does this trouble you?

OEDIPUS: Do not ask me yet.
First, tell me how Laïos looked, and tell me
How old he was.

IOCASTE: He was tall, his hair just touched
215 With white; his form was not unlike your own.

OEDIPUS: I think that I myself may be accurst
By my own ignorant edict.

IOCASTE: You speak strangely.
It makes me tremble to look at you, my King.

OEDIPUS: I am not sure that the blind man can not see.
220 But I should know better if you were to tell me—

IOCASTE: Anything—though I dread to hear you ask it.

OEDIPUS: Was the King lightly escorted, or did he ride
With a large company, as a ruler should?

IOCASTE: There were five men with him in all: one was a herald;
225 And a single chariot, which he was driving.

OEDIPUS: Alas, that makes it plain enough!
                                        But who—
Who told you how it happened?

IOCASTE: A household servant,
The only one to escape.

OEDIPUS: And is he still
A servant of ours?

IOCASTE: No; for when he came back at last
230 And found you enthroned in the place of the dead king,
He came to me, touched my hand with his, and begged

332

That I would send him away to the frontier district
Where only the shepherds go—
As far away from the city as I could send him.

235 I granted his prayer; for although the man was a slave,
He had earned more than this favor at my hands.
OEDIPUS: Can he be called back quickly?
IOCASTE: Easily.
But why?
OEDIPUS: I have taken too much upon myself
Without enquiry; therefore I wish to consult him.
240 IOCASTE: Then he shall come.
                                          But am I not one also
To whom you might confide these fears of yours?
OEDIPUS: That is your right; it will not be denied you,
Now least of all; for I have reached a pitch
Of wild foreboding. Is there anyone
245 To whom I should sooner speak?
Polybos of Corinth is my father.
My mother is a Dorian: Meropê.
I grew up chief among the men of Corinth
Until a strange thing happened—
250 Not worth my passion, it may be, but strange.

At a feast, a drunken man maundering in his cups
Cries out that I am not my father's son!

I contained myself that night, though I felt anger
And a sinking heart. The next day I visited
255 My father and mother, and questioned them. They stormed,
Calling it all the slanderous rant of a fool;
And this relieved me. Yet the suspicion
Remained always aching in my mind;
I knew there was talk; I could not rest;
260 And finally, saying nothing to my parents,
I went to the shrine at Delphi.
The god dismissed my question without reply;
He spoke of other things.
                                          Some were clear,
Full of wretchedness, dreadful, unbearable:
265 As, that I should lie with my own mother, breed
Children from whom all men would turn their eyes;
And that I should be my father's murderer.

I heard all this, and fled. And from that day
Corinth to me was only in the stars
270 Descending in that quarter of the sky,
As I wandered farther and farther on my way
To a land where I should never see the evil

Sung by the oracle. And I came to this country
Where, so you say, King Laïos was killed.

275   I will tell you all that happened there, my lady.

There were three highways
Coming together at a place I passed;
And there a herald came towards me, and a chariot
Drawn by horses, with a man such as you describe
280   Seated in it. The groom leading the horses
Forced me off the road at his lord's command;
But as this charioteer lurched over towards me
I struck him in my rage. The old man saw me
And brought his double goad down upon my head
As I came abreast.
285   He was paid back, and more!
Swinging my club in this right hand I knocked him
Out of his car, and he rolled on the ground.
                                                    I killed him.

I killed them all.
Now if that stranger and Laïos were—kin,
290   Where is a man more miserable than I?
More hated by the gods? Citizen and alien alike
Must never shelter me or speak to me—
I must be shunned by all.
                                    And I myself
Pronounced this malediction upon myself!

295   Think of it: I have touched you with these hands,
These hands that killed your husband. What defilement!

Am I all evil, then? It must be so,
Since I must flee from Thebes, yet never again
See my own countrymen, my own country,
300   For fear of joining my mother in marriage
And killing Polybos, my father.
                                                    Ah,
If I was created so, born to this fate,
Who could deny the savagery of God?

O holy majesty of heavenly powers!
305   May I never see that day! Never!
Rather let me vanish from the race of men
Than know the abomination destined me!
CHORAGOS: We too, my lord, have felt dismay at this.
But there is hope: you have yet to hear the shepherd.
310   OEDIPUS: Indeed, I fear no other hope is left me.

334

IOCASTE: What do you hope from him when he comes?

OEDIPUS: This much:
If his account of the murder tallies with yours,
Then I am cleared.

IOCASTE: What was it that I said
Of such importance?

OEDIPUS: Why, "marauders," you said,
315 Killed the King, according to this man's story.
If he maintains that still, if there were several,
Clearly the guilt is not mine: I was alone.
But if he says one man, singlehanded, did it,
Then the evidence all points to me.

320 IOCASTE: You may be sure that he said there were several;
And can he call back that story now? He can not.
The whole city heard it as plainly as I.
But suppose he alters some detail of it:
He can not ever show that Laïos' death
325 Fulfilled the oracle: for Apollo said
My child was doomed to kill him; and my child—
Poor baby!—it was my child that died first.
No. From now on, where oracles are concerned,   *Questioning the truth in oracles.*
I would not waste a second thought on any.

330 OEDIPUS: You may be right.
                                But come: let someone go
For the shepherd at once. This matter must be settled.

IOCASTE: I will send for him.
I would not wish to cross you in anything,
And surely not in this.—Let us go in.

(*Exeunt into the palace.*)

ODE II

CHORUS: Let me be reverent in the ways of right,
Lowly the paths I journey on;
Let all my words and actions keep
The laws of the pure universe
5 From highest Heaven handed down.
For Heaven is their bright nurse,
Those generations of the realms of light;
Ah, never of mortal kind were they begot,
Nor are they slaves of memory, lost in sleep:
10 Their Father is greater than Time, and ages not.

The tyrant is a child of Pride
Who drinks from his great sickening cup

335

Recklessness and vanity,
Until from his high crest headlong
15 He plummets to the dust of hope.
That strong man is not strong.
But let no fair ambition be denied;
May God protect the wrestler for the State
In government, in comely policy,
20 Who will fear God, and on His ordinance wait.

Haughtiness and the high hand of disdain
Tempt and outrage God's holy law;
And any mortal who dares hold
No immortal Power in awe
25 Will be caught up in a net of pain:
The price for which his levity is sold.
Let each man take due earnings, then,
And keep his hands from holy things,
And from blasphemy stand apart—
30 Else the crackling blast of heaven
Blows on his head, and on his desperate heart;
Though fools will honor impious men,
In their cities no tragic poet sings.

Shall we lose faith in Delphi's obscurities,
35 We who have heard the world's core
Discredited, and the sacred wood
Of Zeus at Elis praised no more?
The deeds and the strange prophecies
Must make a pattern yet to be understood.
40 Zeus, if indeed you are lord of all,
Throned in light over night and day,
Mirror this in your endless mind:
Our masters call the oracle
Words on the wind, and the Delphic vision blind!
45 Their hearts no longer know Apollo,
And reverence for the gods has died away.

SCENE III

Enter IOCASTE.

IOCASTE: Prince of Thebes, it has occurred to me
To visit the altars of the gods, bearing
These branches as a suppliant, and this incense.

Our King is not himself: his noble soul
5 Is overwrought with fantasies of dread,
Else he would consider
The new prophecies in the light of the old.
He will listen to any voice that speaks disaster,
And my advice goes for nothing.

(*She approaches the altar, R.*)

          To you, then, Apollo,
10 Lycean lord, since you are nearest, I turn in prayer.
Receive these offerings, and grant us deliverance
From defilement. Our hearts are heavy with fear
When we see our leader distracted, as helpless sailors
Are terrified by the confusion of their helmsman.

(ship-state-helmsman imagery)

(*Enter* MESSENGER.)

15 MESSENGER: Friends, no doubt you can direct me:
Where shall I find the house of Oedipus,
Or, better still, where is the King himself?
CHORAGOS: It is this very place, stranger; he is inside.
This is his wife and mother of his children.
20 MESSENGER: I wish her happiness in a happy house,
Blest in all the fulfillment of her marriage.
IOCASTE: I wish as much for you: your courtesy
Deserves a like good fortune. But now, tell me:
Why have you come? What have you to say to us?
25 MESSENGER: Good news, my lady, for your house and your husband.
IOCASTE: What news? Who sent you here?
MESSENGER: I am from Corinth.
The news I bring ought to mean joy for you,
Though it may be you will find some grief in it.
IOCASTE: What is it? How can it touch us in both ways?
30 MESSENGER: The people of Corinth, they say,
Intend to call Oedipus to be their king.

Father who raised him

IOCASTE: But old Polybos—is he not reigning still?
MESSENGER: No. Death holds him in his sepulchre.
IOCASTE: What are you saying? Polybos is dead?
35 MESSENGER: If I am not telling the truth, may I die myself.
IOCASTE (*to a* MAIDSERVANT): Go in, go quickly; tell this to your master.

O riddlers of God's will, where are you now!
This was the man whom Oedipus, long ago,
Feared so, fled so, in dread of destroying him—
40 But it was another fate by which he died.

(Enter OEDIPUS, *C.)*

OEDIPUS: Dearest Iocaste, why have you sent for me?

IOCASTE: Listen to what this man says, and then tell me
What has become of the solemn prophecies.

OEDIPUS: Who is this man? What is his news for me?

45 IOCASTE: He has come from Corinth to announce your father's death!

OEDIPUS: Is it true, stranger? Tell me in your own words.

MESSENGER: I can not say it more clearly: the King is dead.

OEDIPUS: Was it by treason? Or by an attack of illness?

MESSENGER: A little thing brings old men to their rest.

50 OEDIPUS: It was sickness, then?

MESSENGER: Yes, and his many years.

OEDIPUS: Ah!
Why should a man respect the Pythian hearth, or
Give heed to the birds that jangle above his head?
They prophesied that I should kill Polybos,

55 Kill my own father; but he is dead and buried,
And I am here—I never touched him, never,
Unless he died of grief for my departure,
And thus, in a sense, through me. No. Polybos
Has packed the oracles off with him underground.

60 They are empty words.

IOCASTE: Had I not told you so?

OEDIPUS: You had; it was my faint heart that betrayed me.

IOCASTE: From now on never think of those things again.

OEDIPUS: And yet—must I not fear my mother's bed?

IOCASTE: Why should anyone in this world be afraid,

65 Since Fate rules us and nothing can be foreseen?
A man should live only for the present day.

Have no more fear of sleeping with your mother:
How many men, in dreams, have lain with their mothers!
No reasonable man is troubled by such things.

70 OEDIPUS: That is true; only—
If only my mother were not still alive!
But she is alive. I can not help my dread.

IOCASTE: Yet this news of your father's death is wonderful.

OEDIPUS: Wonderful. But I fear the living woman.

75 MESSENGER: Tell me, who is this woman that you fear?

OEDIPUS: It is Meropê, man; the wife of King Polybos.

MESSENGER: Meropê? Why should you be afraid of her?

OEDIPUS: An oracle of the gods, a dreadful saying.

MESSENGER: Can you tell me about it or are you sworn to silence?

80 OEDIPUS: I can tell you, and I will.
Apollo said through his prophet that I was the man
Who should marry his own mother, shed his father's blood
With his own hands. And so, for all these years

338

I have kept clear of Corinth, and no harm has come—
85 Though it would have been sweet to see my parents again.
MESSENGER: And is this the fear that drove you out of Corinth?
OEDIPUS: Would you have me kill my father?
MESSENGER: As for that
You must be reassured by the news I gave you.
OEDIPUS: If you could reassure me, I would reward you.
90 MESSENGER: I had that in mind, I will confess: I thought
I could count on you when you returned to Corinth.
OEDIPUS: No: I will never go near my parents again.
MESSENGER: Ah, son, you still do not know what you are doing—
OEDIPUS: What do you mean? In the name of God tell me!
95 MESSENGER: If these are your reasons for not going home.
OEDIPUS: I tell you, I fear the oracle may come true.
MESSENGER: And guilt may come upon you through your parents?
OEDIPUS: That is the dread that is always in my heart.
MESSENGER: Can you not see that all your fears are groundless?
100 OEDIPUS: How can you say that? They are my parents, surely?
MESSENGER: Polybos was not your father.
OEDIPUS: Not my father?
MESSENGER: No more your father than the man speaking to you.
OEDIPUS: But you are nothing to me!
MESSENGER: Neither was he.
OEDIPUS: Then why did he call me son?
MESSENGER: I will tell you:
105 Long ago he had you from my hands, as a gift.
OEDIPUS: Then how could he love me so, if I was not his?
MESSENGER: He had no children, and his heart turned to you.
OEDIPUS: What of you? Did you buy me? Did you find me by chance?
MESSENGER: I came upon you in the crooked pass of Kithairon.
110 OEDIPUS: And what were you doing there?
MESSENGER: Tending my flocks.
OEDIPUS: A wandering shepherd?
MESSENGER: But your savior, son, that day.
OEDIPUS: From what did you save me?
MESSENGER: Your ankles should tell you that.
OEDIPUS: Ah, stranger, why do you speak of that childhood pain?
MESSENGER: I cut the bonds that tied your ankles together.
115 OEDIPUS: I have had the mark as long as I can remember.
MESSENGER: That was why you were given the name you bear.
OEDIPUS: God! Was it my father or my mother who did it?
Tell me!
MESSENGER: I do not know. The man who gave you to me
120 Can tell you better than I.
OEDIPUS: It was not you that found me, but another?
MESSENGER: It was another shepherd gave you to me.
OEDIPUS: Who was he? Can you tell me who he was?
MESSENGER: I think he was said to be one of Laïos' people.

OEDIPUS: You mean the Laïos who was king here years ago?

MESSENGER: Yes; King Laïos; and the man was one of his herdsmen.

OEDIPUS: Is he still alive? Can I see him?

MESSENGER: These men here
Know best about such things.

OEDIPUS: Does anyone here
Know this shepherd that he is talking about?

130 Have you seen him in the fields, or in the town?
If you have, tell me. It is time things were made plain.

CHORAGOS: I think the man he means is that same shepherd
You have already asked to see. Iocaste perhaps
Could tell you something.

OEDIPUS: Do you know anything

135 About him, Lady? Is he the man we have summoned?
Is that the man this shepherd means?

IOCASTE: Why think of him?
Forget this herdsman. Forget it all.
This talk is a waste of time.

OEDIPUS: How can you say that,
When the clues to my true birth are in my hands?

140 IOCASTE: For God's love, let us have no more questioning!
Is your life nothing to you?
My own is pain enough for me to bear.

OEDIPUS: You need not worry. Suppose my mother a slave,
And born of slaves: no baseness can touch you.

145 IOCASTE: Listen to me, I beg you: do not do this thing!

OEDIPUS: I will not listen; the truth must be made known.

IOCASTE: Everything that I say is for your own good!

OEDIPUS: My own good
Snaps my patience, then; I want none of it.

IOCASTE: You are fatally wrong! May you never learn who you are!

150 OEDIPUS: Go, one of you, and bring the shepherd here.
Let us leave this woman to brag of her royal name.

IOCASTE: Ah, miserable!
That is the only word I have for you now.
That is the only word I can ever have.

(Exit into the palace.)

155 CHORAGOS: Why has she left us, Oedipus? Why has she gone
In such a passion of sorrow? I fear this silence:
Something dreadful may come of it.

OEDIPUS: Let it come!
However base my birth, I must know about it.
The Queen, like a woman, is perhaps ashamed

160 To think of my low origin. But I
Am a child of Luck; I can not be dishonored.
Luck is my mother; the passing months, my brothers,

Have seen me rich and poor.

If this is so,

How could I wish that I were someone else?
165 How could I not be glad to know my birth?

ODE III

CHORUS: If ever the coming time were known
To my heart's pondering,
Kithairon, now by Heaven I see the torches
At the festival of the next full moon,
5 And see the dance, and hear the choir sing
A grace to your gentle shade:
Mountain where Oedipus was found,
O mountain guard of a noble race!
May the god who heals us lend his aid,
10 And let that glory come to pass
For our king's cradling-ground.

Of the nymphs that flower beyond the years,
Who bore you, royal child,
To Pan of the hills or the timberline Apollo,
15 Cold in delight where the upland clears,
Or Hermês for whom Kyllenê's heights are piled?
Or flushed as evening cloud,
Great Dionysos, roamer of mountains,
He—was it he who found you there,
20 And caught you up in his own proud
Arms from the sweet god-ravisher
Who laughed by the Muses' fountains?

SCENE IV

OEDIPUS: Sirs: though I do not know the man,
I think I see him coming, this shepherd we want:
He is old, like our friend here, and the men
Bringing him seem to be servants of my house.
5 But you can tell, if you have ever seen him.

(*Enter* SHEPHERD *escorted by servants.*)

CHORAGOS: I know him, he was Laïos' man. You can trust him.
OEDIPUS: Tell me first, you from Corinth: is this the shepherd
We were discussing?

MESSENGER: This is the very man.

OEDIPUS (*to* SHEPHERD): Come here. No, look at me. You must answer
10 Everything I ask.—You belonged to Laïos?

SHEPHERD: Yes, born his slave, brought up in his house.

OEDIPUS: Tell me: what kind of work did you do for him?

SHEPHERD: I was a shepherd of his, most of my life.

OEDIPUS: Where mainly did you go for pasturage?

15 SHEPHERD: Sometimes Kithairon, sometimes the hills near-by.

OEDIPUS: Do you remember ever seeing this man out there?

SHEPHERD: What would he be doing there? This man?

OEDIPUS: This man standing here. Have you ever seen him before?

SHEPHERD: No. At least, not to my recollection.

20 MESSENGER: And that is not strange, my lord. But I'll refresh
His memory: he must remember when we two
Spent three whole seasons together, March to September,
On Kithairon or thereabouts. He had two flocks;
I had one. Each autumn I'd drive mine home
25 And he would go back with his to Laïos' sheepfold.—
Is this not true, just as I have described it?

SHEPHERD: True, yes; but it was all so long ago.

MESSENGER: Well, then: do you remember, back in those days
That you gave me a baby boy to bring up as my own?

30 SHEPHERD: What if I did? What are you trying to say?

MESSENGER: King Oedipus was once that little child.

SHEPHERD: Damn you, hold your tongue!

OEDIPUS: No more of that!
It is your tongue needs watching, not this man's.

SHEPHERD: My King, my Master, what is it I have done wrong?

35 OEDIPUS: You have not answered his question about the boy.

SHEPHERD: He does not know . . . He is only making trouble . . .

OEDIPUS: Come, speak plainly, or it will go hard with you.

SHEPHERD: In God's name, do not torture an old man!

OEDIPUS: Come here, one of you; bind his arms behind him.

40 SHEPHERD: Unhappy king! What more do you wish to learn?

OEDIPUS: Did you give this man the child he speaks of?

SHEPHERD: I did.
And I would to God I had died that very day.

OEDIPUS: You will die now unless you speak the truth.

SHEPHERD: Yet if I speak the truth, I am worse than dead.

45 OEDIPUS: Very well; since you insist upon delaying—

SHEPHERD: No! I have told you already that I gave him the boy.

OEDIPUS: Where did you get him? From your house? From somewhere
       else?

SHEPHERD: Not from mine, no. A man gave him to me.

OEDIPUS: Is that man here? Do you know whose slave he was?

50 SHEPHERD: For God's love, my King, do not ask me any more!

OEDIPUS: You are a dead man if I have to ask you again.

SHEPHERD: Then . . . Then the child was from the palace of Laïos.

342

OEDIPUS: A slave child? or a child of his own line?

SHEPHERD: Ah, I am on the brink of dreadful speech!

55 OEDIPUS: And I of dreadful hearing. Yet I must hear.

SHEPHERD: If you must be told, then . . .

                       They said it was Laïos' child,

But it is your wife who can tell you about that.

OEDIPUS: My wife!—Did she give it to you?

SHEPHERD: My lord, she did.

OEDIPUS: Do you know why?

SHEPHERD: I was told to get rid of it.

60 OEDIPUS: An unspeakable mother!

SHEPHERD: There had been prophecies . . .

OEDIPUS: Tell me.

SHEPHERD: It was said that the boy would kill his own father.

OEDIPUS: Then why did you give him over to this old man?

SHEPHERD: I pitied the baby, my King,

And I thought that this man would take him far away

65 To his own country.

             He saved him—but for what a fate!

For if you are what this man says you are,

No man living is more wretched than Oedipus.

OEDIPUS: Ah God!

It was true!

         All the prophecies!

                    —Now,

70 O Light, may I look on you for the last time!

I, Oedipus,

Oedipus, damned in his birth, in his marriage damned,

Damned in the blood he shed with his own hand!

(*He rushes into the palace.*)

ODE IV

[STROPHE 1

CHORUS: Alas for the seed of men.

What measure shall I give these generations
That breathe on the void and are void
And exist and do not exist?

5 Who bears more weight of joy
Than mass of sunlight shifting in images,
Or who shall make his thought stay on
That down time drifts away?

Your splendor is all fallen.

343

10 O naked brow of wrath and tears,
   O change of Oedipus!
   I who saw your days call no man blest—
   Your great days like ghósts góne.

   That mind was a strong bow.
15 Deep, how deep you drew it then, hard archer,
   At a dim fearful range,
   And brought dear glory down!

   You overcame the stranger—
   The virgin with her hooking lion claws—
20 And though death sang, stood like a tower
   To make pale Thebes take heart.

   Fortress against our sorrow!

   Divine king, giver of laws,
   Majestic Oedipus!
25 No prince in Thebes had ever such renown,
   No prince won such grace of power.

   And now of all men ever known
   Most pitiful is this man's story:
   His fortunes are most changed, his state
30 Fallen to a low slave's
   Ground under bitter fate.

   O Oedipus, most royal one!
   The great door that expelled you to the light
   Gave at night—ah, gave night to your glory:
35 As to the father, to the fathering son.

   All understood too late.

   How could that queen whom Laïos won,
   The garden that he harrowed at his height,
   Be silent when that act was done?

40 But all eyes fail before time's eye,
   All actions come to justice there.
   Though never willed, though far down the deep past,
   Your bed, your dread sirings,
   Are brought to book at last.
45 Child by Laïos doomed to die,

Then doomed to lose that fortunate little death,
Would God you never took breath in this air
That with my wailing lips I take to cry:

For I weep the world's outcast.

50 I was blind, and now I can tell why:
Asleep, for you had given ease of breath
To Thebes, while the false years went by.

Some good was done, though it may have been lucky & brief.

EXODOS

Enter, from the palace, SECOND MESSENGER.

SECOND MESSENGER: Elders of Thebes, most honored in this land,
What horrors are yours to see and hear, what weight
Of sorrow to be endured, if, true to your birth,
You venerate the line of Labdakos!
5   I think neither Istros nor Phasis, those great rivers,
Could purify this place of the corruption
It shelters now, or soon must bring to light—
Evil not done unconsciously, but willed.

The greatest griefs are those we cause ourselves.
10 CHORAGOS: Surely, friend, we have grief enough already;
What new sorrow do you mean?
SECOND MESSENGER: The Queen is dead.
CHORAGOS: Iocaste? Dead? But at whose hand?
SECOND MESSENGER: Her own.
The full horror of what happened you can not know,
For you did not see it; but I, who did, will tell you
15 As clearly as I can how she met her death.

When she had left us,
In passionate silence, passing through the court,
She ran to her apartment in the house,
Her hair clutched by the fingers of both hands.
20 She closed the doors behind her; then, by that bed
Where long ago the fatal son was conceived—
That son who should bring about his father's death—
We heard her call upon Laïos, dead so many years,
And heard her wail for the double fruit of her marriage,
25 A husband by her husband, children by her child.

Exactly how she died I do not know:
For Oedipus burst in moaning and would not let us

345

Keep vigil to the end: it was by him
As he stormed about the room that our eyes were caught.
30 From one to another of us he went, begging a sword,
Cursing the wife who was not his wife, the mother
Whose womb had carried his own children and himself.
I do not know: it was none of us aided him,
But surely one of the gods was in control!
35 For with a dreadful cry
He hurled his weight, as though wrenched out of himself,
At the twin doors: the bolts gave, and he rushed in.
And there we saw her hanging, her body swaying
From the cruel cord she had noosed about her neck.
40 A great sob broke from him, heartbreaking to hear,
As he loosed the rope and lowered her to the ground.

I would blot out from my mind what happened next!
For the King ripped from her gown the golden brooches
That were her ornament, and raised them, and plunged them down
45 Straight into his own eyeballs, crying, "No more,
No more shall you look on the misery about me,
The horrors of my own doing! Too long you have known
The faces of those whom I should never have seen,
Too long been blind to those for whom I was searching!
50 From this hour, go in darkness!" And as he spoke,
He struck at his eyes—not once, but many times;
And the blood spattered his beard,
Bursting from his ruined sockets like red hail.

So from the unhappiness of two this evil has sprung,
55 A curse on the man and woman alike. The old
Happiness of the house of Labdakos
Was happiness enough: where is it today?
It is all wailing and ruin, disgrace, death—all
The misery of mankind that has a name—
60 And it is wholly and for ever theirs.
CHORAGOS: Is he in agony still? Is there no rest for him?
SECOND MESSENGER: He is calling for someone to lead him to the gates
So that all the children of Kadmos may look upon
His father's murderer, his mother's—no,
65 I can not say it!
        And then he will leave Thebes,
Self-exiled, in order that the curse
Which he himself pronounced may depart from the house.
He is weak, and there is none to lead him,
So terrible is his suffering.
        But you will see:
70 Look, the doors are opening; in a moment
You will see a thing that would crush a heart of stone.

346

(The central door is opened; OEDIPUS, *blinded, is led in.)*

CHORAGOS: Dreadful indeed for men to see.
Never have my own eyes
Looked on a sight so full of fear.

75 Oedipus!
What madness came upon you, what daemon
Leaped on your life with heavier
Punishment than a mortal man can bear?
No: I can not even
80 Look at you, poor ruined one.
And I would speak, question, ponder,
If I were able. No.
You make me shudder.
OEDIPUS: God.   God.
85 Is there a sorrow greater?
Where shall I find harbor in this world?
My voice is hurled far on a dark wind.
What has God done to me?
CHORAGOS: Too terrible to think of, or to see.

[STROPHE I

90 OEDIPUS: O cloud of night,
Never to be turned away: night coming on,
I can not tell how: night like a shroud!

My fair winds brought me here.
                              Oh God. Again
The pain of the spikes where I had sight,
95 The flooding pain
Of memory, never to be gouged out.
CHORAGOS: This is not strange.
You suffer it all twice over, remorse in pain,
Pain in remorse.

Physical and Psychological

[ANTISTROPHE I

100 OEDIPUS: Ah dear friend
Are you faithful even yet, you alone?
Are you still standing near me, will you stay here,
Patient, to care for the blind?
                              The blind man!
Yet even blind I know who it is attends me,
105 By the voice's tone—
Though my darkness hide the comforter.
CHORAGOS: Oh fearful act!
What god was it drove you to rake black
Night across your eyes?

347

110 OEDIPUS: Apollo. Apollo. Dear
Children, the god was Apollo.
He brought my sick, sick fate upon me.
But the blinding hand was my own!
How could I bear to see
115 When all my sight was horror everywhere?
CHORAGOS: Everywhere; that is true.
OEDIPUS: And now what is left?
Images? Love? A greeting even,
Sweet to the senses? Is there anything?
120 Ah, no, friends: lead me away.
Lead me away from Thebes.

                                    Lead the great wreck
And hell of Oedipus, whom the gods hate.
CHORAGOS: Your fate is clear, you are not blind to that.
Would God you had never found it out!

Knowledge
and Fate

125 OEDIPUS: Death take the man who unbound
My feet on that hillside
And delivered me from death to life! What life?
If only I had died,
This weight of monstrous doom
130 Could not have dragged me and my darlings down.
CHORAGOS: I would have wished the same.
OEDIPUS: Oh never to have come here
With my father's blood upon me! Never
To have been the man they call his mother's husband!
135 Oh accurst! Oh child of evil,
To have entered that wretched bed—

                                  the selfsame one!
More primal than sin itself, this fell to me.
CHORAGOS: I do not know how I can answer you.
You were better dead than alive and blind.
140 OEDIPUS: Do not counsel me any more. This punishment
That I have laid upon myself is just.
If I had eyes,
I do not know how I could bear the sight
Of my father, when I came to the house of Death,
145 Or my mother: for I have sinned against them both
So vilely that I could not make my peace
By strangling my own life.

                              Or do you think my children,
Born as they were born, would be sweet to my eyes?
Ah never, never! Nor this town with its high walls,
150 Nor the holy images of the gods.

348

For I,

Thrice miserable—Oedipus, noblest of all the line
Of Kadmos, have condemned myself to enjoy
These things no more, by my own malediction
Expelling that man whom the gods declared
155 To be a defilement in the house of Laïos.
After exposing the rankness of my own guilt,
How could I look men frankly in the eyes?
No, I swear it,
If I could have stifled my hearing at its source,
160 I would have done it and made all this body
A tight cell of misery, blank to light and sound:
So I should have been safe in a dark agony
Beyond all recollection.
Ah Kithairon!

Why did you shelter me? When I was cast upon you,
165 Why did I not die? Then I should never
Have shown the world my execrable birth.

Ah Polybos! Corinth, city that I believed
The ancient seat of my ancestors: how fair
I seemed, your child! And all the while this evil
170 Was cancerous within me!
For I am sick

In my daily life, sick in my origin.

O three roads, dark ravine, woodland and way
Where three roads met: you, drinking my father's blood,
My own blood, spilled by my own hand: can you remember
175 The unspeakable things I did there, and the things
I went on from there to do?
O marriage, marriage!

The act that engendered me, and again the act
Performed by the son in the same bed—
Ah, the net

Of incest, mingling fathers, brothers, sons,
180 With brides, wives, mothers: the last evil
That can be known by men: no tongue can say
How evil!
No. For the love of God, conceal me

Somewhere far from Thebes; or kill me; or hurl me
Into the sea, away from men's eyes for ever.

185 Come, lead me. You need not fear to touch me.
Of all men, I alone can bear this guilt.

(*Enter* CREON.)

CHORAGOS: We are not the ones to decide; but Creon here

[handwritten margin note: Questions—why, why. Can fate be questioned? Is it better not to know? But he couldn't resist questioning his parentage.]

May fitly judge of what you ask. He only
Is left to protect the city in your place.

190 OEDIPUS: Alas, how can I speak to him? What right have I
To beg his courtesy whom I have deeply wronged?

CREON: I have not come to mock you, Oedipus,
Or to reproach you, either.
(*To* ATTENDANTS.)   —You, standing there:
If you have lost all respect for man's dignity,

195 At least respect the flame of Lord Helios:
Do not allow this pollution to show itself
Openly here, an affront to the earth
And Heaven's rain and the light of day. No, take him
Into the house as quickly as you can.

200 For it is proper
That only the close kindred see his grief.

OEDIPUS: I pray you in God's name, since your courtesy
Ignores my dark expectation, visiting
With mercy this man of all men most execrable:

205 Give me what I ask—for your good, not for mine.

CREON: And what is it that you would have me do?

OEDIPUS: Drive me out of this country as quickly as may be
To a place where no human voice can ever greet me.

CREON: I should have done that before now—only,

210 God's will had not been wholly revealed to me.

OEDIPUS: But his command is plain: the parricide
Must be destroyed. I am that evil man.

CREON: That is the sense of it, yes; but things are,
We had best discover clearly what is to be done.

215 OEDIPUS: You would learn more about a man like me?

CREON: You are ready now to listen to the god.

OEDIPUS: I will listen. But it is to you
That I must turn for help. I beg you, hear me.

The woman in there—

220 Give her whatever funeral you think proper:
She is your sister.
            —But let me go, Creon!
Let me purge my father's Thebes of the pollution
Of my living here, and go out to the wild hills,
To Kithairon, that has won such fame with me,

225 The tomb my mother and father appointed for me,
And let me die there, as they willed I should.
And yet I know
Death will not ever come to me through sickness
Or in any natural way: I have been preserved

230 For some unthinkable fate. But let that be.
As for my sons, you need not care for them.
They are men, they will find some way to live.

But my poor daughters, who have shared my table,
Who never before have been parted from their father—
235 Take care of them, Creon; do this for me.
And will you let me touch them with my hands
A last time, and let us weep together?
Be kind, my lord,
Great prince, be kind!

Could I but touch them,
240 They would be mine again, as when I had my eyes.

(*Enter* ANTIGONE *and* ISMENE, *attended.*)

Ah, God!
Is it my dearest children I hear weeping?
Has Creon pitied me and sent my daughters?
CREON: Yes, Oedipus: I knew that they were dear to you
245 In the old days, and know you must love them still
OEDIPUS: May God bless you for this—and be a friendlier
Guardian to you than he has been to me!

Children, where are you?
Come quickly to my hands; they are your brother's—
250 Hands that have brought your father's once clear eyes
To this way of seeing—

Ah dearest ones,
I had neither sight nor knowledge then, your father
By the woman who was the source of his own life!
And I weep for you—having no strength to see you—,
255 I weep for you when I think of the bitterness
That men will visit upon you all your lives.
What homes, what festivals can you attend
Without being forced to depart again in tears?
And when you come to marriageable age,
260 Where is the man, my daughters, who would dare
Risk the bane that lies on all my children?
Is there any evil wanting? Your father killed
His father; sowed the womb of her who bore him;
Engendered you at the fount of his own existence!
That is what they will say of you.
265 Then, whom
Can you ever marry? There are no bridegrooms for you,
And your lives must wither away in sterile dreaming.
O Creon, son of Menoikeus!
You are the only father my daughters have,
270 Since we, their parents, are both of us gone for ever.
They are your own blood: you will not let them
Fall into beggary and loneliness;
You will keep them from the miseries that are mine!

Take pity on them; see, they are only children,
275 Friendless except for you. Promise me this,
Great Prince, and give me your hand in token of it.

(CREON *clasps his right hand.*)

Children:
I could say much, if you could understand me,
But as it is, I have only this prayer for you:
280 Live where you can, be as happy as you can—
Happier, please God, than God has made your father!
CREON: Enough. You have wept enough. Now go within.
OEDIPUS: I must, but it is hard.
CREON: Time eases all things.
OEDIPUS: But you must promise—
CREON: Say what you desire.
OEDIPUS: Send me from Thebes!
285 CREON: God grant that I may!
OEDIPUS: But since God hates me . . .
CREON: No, he will grant your wish.
OEDIPUS: You promise?
CREON: I can not speak beyond my knowledge.
OEDIPUS: Then lead me in.
CREON: Come now, and leave your children.
OEDIPUS: No! Do not take them from me!
CREON: Think no longer
290 That you are in command here, but rather think
How, when you were, you served your own destruction.

(*Exeunt into the house all but the* CHORUS; *the* CHORAGOS *chants directly to the audience.*)

CHORAGOS: Men of Thebes: look upon Oedipus.

This is the king who solved the famous riddle
And towered up, most powerful of men.
205 No mortal eyes but looked on him with envy,
Yet in the end ruin swept over him.
Let every man in mankind's frailty
Consider his last day; and let none
Presume on his good fortune until he find
300 Life, at his death, a memory without pain.

1. In writing *Oedipus Rex* Sophocles relied upon his audience's familiarity with the Oedipus legend. What are some of the effects of the story's being known?

2. How would you summarize what happens to Oedipus? What sort of knowledge does he have by the end of the play? Why does he blind himself?

3. Why is Oedipus blasphemous toward the gods? How does the chorus react to his blasphemy?

4. What revelations are presented by the messenger? How do they contribute to the play's development?

5. What is the blind seer Teiresias' function in the play? How does he contrast with the chorus?

6. How does the final speech summarize and amplify the events of the play?

Introduction to King Lear

Shakespeare greatly enlarged the scope of tragedy, especially in *King Lear*, the richest and most powerful of his plays. While Sophocles' plot moves in a straight line to its resolution, Shakespeare's becomes increasingly complex as it unfolds, interweaving the story of Gloucester with that of Lear himself. The action requires numerous scenes, moving from the palace to the heath to the fields of Dover, as compared to Sophocles' use of a single setting and a severely limited time span. Shakespeare's play demands that the audience accept coincidences, the use of disguise, and such wildly improbable scenes as the one in which Lear, his fool, and someone posing as a mad beggar conduct a mock trial in a hut where they have taken shelter. This scene and others almost as grotesque (the blinding of Gloucester, for example) enable Shakespeare to ask fundamental questions about the nature of justice and of the human capacity for cruelty. By showing families and a whole society disintegrating under the pressure of elemental drives for power and sexual satisfaction—released by Lear's initial act of giving up the throne—Shakespeare suggests how people are unable to predict the course of events and how vulnerable they are.

The tragic experience of Lear holds the play together. Like Oedipus, he errs through pride and is forced to recognize his folly, but the stripping away of pretensions is more complete and more violent in Shakespeare's play. Lear finds himself thrust out into the storm by his "wolvish" daughters and is forced for the first time to come to terms with his human condition. His discovery that he is no better than "poor Tom" the beggar gives him a new sympathy for his fellow creatures and a lucidity which, in the midst of the madness his ordeal brings on, enables him to see through the "robes and furred gowns" that conceal vice in the rich and powerful. Yet the most remarkable thing about Lear and the play is that he has to endure so much before he can die. Edgar says all that can be said in the face of such suffering: "we that are young / Shall never see so much, nor live so long." With its vision of a world reduced to chaos, and individuals resisting the evil and disorder around them by acts of love and loyalty, *King Lear* speaks as directly to our time as it did to Shakespeare's.

The language of the play demands close attention. It ranges from the regal formality of Lear at the beginning to the riddling speeches of the Fool, and relies heavily upon metaphor. Yet if this language is compressed and difficult at times, it can also be simple; often it is most powerful when it is simplest, as in Edgar's "Ripeness is all" or Cordelia's quiet words of forgiveness, "No cause, no cause." Shakespeare did not write for an intellectual elite, but for people of all kinds, who came in vast numbers to watch plays performed without the aid of lighting or scenery. He had to conjure up worlds by the power of his language, as spoken by a troupe of actors using young boys to play the parts of women. The great success of his plays, and the robustness of the Elizabethan theater in general, speaks well for the imaginative capacity of his audience and for their human sympathies. Shakespeare flourished at a time when the drama was bursting with new life and when the people were ready to respond to it.

KING LEAR

CAST OF CHARACTERS

LEAR, *king of Britain.*
KING OF FRANCE.
DUKE OF BURGUNDY.
DUKE OF CORNWALL.
DUKE OF ALBANY.
EARL OF KENT.
EARL OF GLOUCESTER.
EDGAR, *son to Gloucester.*
EDMUND, *bastard son to Gloucester.*
CURAN, *a courtier.*
OLD MAN, *tenant to Gloucester.*
DOCTOR.
FOOL.

OSWALD, *steward to Goneril.*
A CAPTAIN *employed by Edmund.*
GENTLEMAN *attendant on Cordelia.*
A HERALD.
SERVANTS *to Cornwall.*
GONERIL,
REGAN, } *daughters to Lear.*
CORDELIA,
KNIGHTS *of Lear's train,* CAPTAINS, MESSENGERS, SOLDIERS, *and* ATTENDANTS.

SCENE: *Britain.*

ACT ONE

SCENE I. KING LEAR's *palace.*

[*Enter* KENT, GLOUCESTER, *and* EDMUND.]

KENT. I thought the king had more affected the Duke of Albany than Cornwall.

GLOU. It did always seem so to us: but now, in the division of the kingdom, it appears not which of the dukes he values most; for equalities are so weighed, that curiosity in neither can make choice of either's moiety.   7

KENT. Is not this your son, my lord?

GLOU. His breeding, sir, hath been at my charge: I have so often blushed to acknowledge him, that now I am brazed to it.   11

KENT. I cannot conceive you.

GLOU. Sir, this young fellow's mother could: whereupon she grew round-wombed, and had, indeed, sir, a son for her cradle ere she had a husband for her bed. Do you smell a fault?

KENT. I cannot wish the fault undone, the issue of it being so proper.   18

GLOU. But I have, sir, a son by order of law, some year elder than this, who yet is no dearer in my account: though this knave came something saucily into the world before he was sent for, yet was his mother fair; there was good sport at his making, and the whoreson must be acknowledged. Do you know this noble gentleman, Edmund?   25

EDM. No, my lord.

GLOU. My lord of Kent: remember him hereafter as my honourable friend.

EDM. My services to your lordship.

KENT. I must love you, and sue to know you better.   31

EDM. Sir, I shall study deserving.

GLOU. He hath been out nine years, and away he shall again. The king is coming.

[*Sennet. Enter* KING LEAR, CORNWALL, ALBANY, GONERIL, REGAN, CORDELIA, *and* ATTENDANTS.]

LEAR. Attend the lords of France and Burgundy, Gloucester.   35

---

12. **conceive,** understand. 18. **proper,** handsome. 19-20. **by . . . law,** legally. 20. **some year,** about a year. 22. **something,** somewhat. 24. **whoreson,** lit., son of a whore, hence bastard. 32. **deserving,** i.e., to deserve your favor. 33. **out,** i.e., of England, abroad. **s.d. sennet,** a series of notes sounded on a trumpet.

Act 1, Scene i: 1. **affected,** favored. 2. **Albany,** an old name for Scotland. 6. **equalities . . . weighed,** shares are so (evenly) balanced. 7. **curiosity . . . moiety,** careful examination, cannot decide which portion (moiety) is to be preferred. 10. **charge,** expense. 11. **brazed,** hardened.

GLOU. I shall, my liege.

[*Exeunt* GLOUCESTER *and* EDMUND.

LEAR. Meantime we shall express our darker purpose.
Give me the map there. Know that we have divided
In three our kingdom: and 'tis our fast intent
To shake all cares and business from our age;						40
Conferring them on younger strengths, while we
Unburthen'd crawl toward death. Our son of Cornwall,
And you, our no less loving son of Albany,
We have this hour a constant will to publish
Our daughters' several dowers, that future strife						45
May be prevented now. The princes, France and Burgundy,
Great rivals in our youngest daughter's love,
Long in our court have made their amorous sojourn,
And here are to be answer'd. Tell me, my daughters,—
Since now we will divest us, both of rule,	50
Interest of territory, cares of state,—
Which of you shall we say doth love us most?
That we our largest bounty may extend
Where nature doth with merit challenge. Goneril,
Our eldest-born, speak first.						55
GON. Sir, I love you more than words can wield the matter;
Dearer than eye-sight, space, and liberty;
Beyond what can be valued, rich or rare;
No less than life, with grace, health, beauty, honour;
As much as child e'er loved, or father found;
A love that makes breath poor, and speech unable;						61
Beyond all manner of so much I love you.
COR. [*Aside*] What shall Cordelia do? Love, and be silent.

LEAR. Of all these bounds, even from this line to this,
With shadowy forests and with champains rich'd,						65
With plenteous rivers and wide-skirted meads,
We make thee lady: to thine and Albany's issue
Be this perpetual. What says our second daughter,
Our dearest Regan, wife to Cornwall? Speak.
REG. Sir, I am made						70
Of the self-same metal that my sister is,
And prize me at her worth. In my true heart
I find she names my very deed of love;
Only she comes too short: that I profess
Myself an enemy to all other joys,						75
Which the most precious square of sense possesses;
And find I am alone felicitate
In your dear highness' love.
COR.					[*Aside*] Then poor Cordelia!
And yet not so; since, I am sure, my love's
More richer than my tongue.						80
LEAR. To thee and thine hereditary ever
Remain this ample third of our fair kingdom;
No less in space, validity, and pleasure,
Than that conferr'd on Goneril. Now, our joy,
Although the last, not least; to whose young love						85
The vines of France and milk of Burgundy
Strive to be interess'd; what can you say to draw
A third more opulent than your sisters? Speak.
COR. Nothing, my lord.
LEAR. Nothing!						90
COR. Nothing.
LEAR. Nothing will come of nothing: speak again.
COR. Unhappy that I am, I cannot heave
My heart into my mouth. I love your majesty
According to my bond; nor more nor less. 95
LEAR. How, how, Cordelia! mend your speech a little,

37. darker, more secret. 39. fast intent, firm purpose. 44. constant, firm; publish, make known. 46. prevented, forestalled; France, King of France; Burgundy, Duke of Burgundy. 51. interest of, claim to. 54. Where . . . challenge, where your merit and my natural affection lay equal claim (to my generosity). 56. wield the matter, serve to express the fact. 57. space, freedom from imprisonment; liberty, i.e., of action. 59. grace, favor. 60. found, i.e., in a child's love. 62. all . . . much, every sort of similar comparison. 65. champains . . . rich'd,
enriched with fertile fields. 72. And . . . worth, and estimate my value to be the same as hers. 73. very . . . love, my love as it actually is. 74. that, in that. 76. which . . . possesses, which the most delicate test of feeling takes for joys. 77. felicitate, made happy. 78. dear . . . love, love of your dear highness. 80. More . . . tongue, i.e., greater than I can express in words. 83. validity, value. 86. milk, i.e., pastures. 87. to be interess'd, to have a right in. 95. bond, obligation (as a daughter).

Lest it may mar your fortunes.

COR.   Good my lord,
You have begot me, bred me, loved me: I
Return those duties back as are right fit,
Obey you, love you, and most honour
    you.   100
Why have my sisters husbands, if they say
They love you all? Haply, when I shall wed,
That lord whose hand must take my plight
    shall carry
Half my love with him, half my care and
    duty:
Sure, I shall never marry like my sisters, 105
To love my father all.

LEAR. But goes thy heart with this?

COR.   Ay, good my lord.

LEAR. So young, and so untender?

COR. So young, my lord, and true.

LEAR. Let it be so; thy truth, then, be thy
    dower.   110
For, by the sacred radiance of the sun,
The mysteries of Hecate, and the night;
By all the operation of the orbs
From whom we do exist, and cease to be;
Here I disclaim all my paternal care,   115
Propinquity and property of blood,
And as a stranger to my heart and me
Hold thee, from this, for ever. The barbar-
    ous Scythian,
Or he that makes his generation messes
To gorge his appetite, shall to my bosom 120
Be as well neighbour'd, pitied, and relieved,
As thou my sometime daughter.

KENT.   Good my liege,—

LEAR. Peace, Kent!
Come not between the dragon and his wrath.
I loved her most, and thought to set my rest
On her kind nursery. Hence, and avoid my
    sight!   126
So be my grave my peace, as here I give
Her father's heart from her! Call France; who
    stirs?
Call Burgundy. Cornwall and Albany,
With my two daughters' dowers digest this
    third: 130

Let pride, which she calls plainness, marry
    her.
I do invest you jointly with my power,
Pre-eminence, and all the large effects
That troop with majesty. Ourself, by monthly
    course,
With reservation of an hundred knights, 135
By you to be sustain'd, shall our abode
Make with you by due turns. Only we still
    retain
The name, and all the additions to a king;
The sway, revenue, execution of the rest,
Belovèd sons, be yours: which to confirm, 140
This coronet part betwixt you.

                                 [*Giving the crown.*

KENT.   Royal Lear,
Whom I have ever honour'd as my king,
Loved as my father, as my master follow'd,
As my great patron thought on in my
    prayers,—

LEAR. The bow is bent and drawn, make
    from the shaft.   145

KENT. Let it fall rather, though the fork
    invade
The region of my heart: be Kent unman-
    nerly,
When Lear is mad. What wilt thou do, old
    man?
Think'st thou that duty shall have dread to
    speak,
When power to flattery bows? To plainness
    honour's bound,   150
When majesty stoops to folly. Reverse thy
    doom;
And, in thy best consideration, check
This hideous rashness: answer my life my
    judgement,
Thy youngest daughter does not love thee
    least;
Nor are those empty-hearted whose low
    sound   155
Reverbs no hollowness.

LEAR.   Kent, on thy life, no more.

KENT. My life I never held but as a pawn
To wage against thy enemies; nor fear to
    lose it,

99. **as are right fit,** which are most fitting (for a daughter).
102. **love you all,** i.e., give you all their love. 103. **plight,**
pledge. 112. **mysteries,** secret religious rites; **Hecate,** goddess of the lower world, of witchcraft and of magic. 113.
operation, influence; **orbs,** stars. 116. **property,** identity.
118. **Scythian,** inhabitant of Southern Russia, since classical times regarded as complete barbarians. 119. **generation
messes,** food of his children. 124. **dragon,** i.e., his crest;
his wrath, object of his wrath. 125. **set my rest,** rely
entirely. 126. **nursery,** nursing; **avoid,** leave. 130. **digest,**
assimilate, combine. 131. **plainness,** frankness. 133. **large
effects,** lavish manifestations. 134. **troop with,** march in
company with. 138. **additions,** titles. 139. **rest,** i.e., of my
royal prerogatives. 145. **make . . . shaft,** avoid the arrow
(of my anger). 146. **fall,** fly; **fork,** i.e., arrowhead. 151.
answer . . . judgement, i.e., I'll stake my life on the
correctness of my opinion. 156. **Reverbs,** reverberates
with. 158. **wage,** stake.

Thy safety being the motive.

LEAR.   Out of my sight!

KENT. See better, Lear; and let me still remain   160

The true blank of thine eye.

LEAR. Now, by Apollo,—

KENT.   Now, by Apollo, king,
Thou swear'st thy gods in vain.

LEAR.   O, vassal! miscreant!

[*Laying his hand on his sword.*

ALB.
CORN. } Dear sir, forbear.

KENT. Do;   165
Kill thy physician, and the fee bestow
Upon thy foul disease. Revoke thy doom;
Or, whilst I can vent clamour from my
throat,
I'll tell thee thou dost evil.

LEAR.   Hear me, recreant!
On thine allegiance, hear me!   170
Since thou hast sought to make us break our
vow,
Which we durst never yet, and with strain'd
pride
To come between our sentence and our
power,
Which nor our nature nor our place can bear,
Our potency made good, take thy reward. 175
Five days we do allot thee, for provision
To shield thee from diseases of the world;
And on the sixth to turn thy hated back
Upon our kingdom: if, on the tenth day fol-
lowing,
Thy banish'd trunk be found in our
dominions,   180
The moment is thy death. Away! by Jupiter,
This shall not be revoked.

KENT. Fare thee well, king: sith thus thou
wilt appear,
Freedom lives hence, and banishment is here.
[*To* CORDELIA] The gods to their dear shelter
take thee, maid,   185
That justly think'st, and hast most rightly
said!
[*To* REGAN *and* GONERIL] And your large
speeches may your deeds approve,
That good effects may spring from words of
love.

Thus Kent, O princes, bids you all adieu;
He'll shape his old course in a country new.
[*Exit.*

[*Flourish. Re-enter* GLOUCESTER, *with*
FRANCE, BURGUNDY, *and* ATTENDANTS.]

GLOU. Here's France and Burgundy, my
noble lord.   191
LEAR. My lord of Burgundy,
We first address towards you, who with this
king
Hath rivall'd for our daughter: what, in the
least,
Will you require in present dower with
her,   195
Or cease your quest of love?

BUR.   Most royal majesty,
I crave no more than what your highness
offer'd,
Nor will you tender less.

LEAR.   Right noble Burgundy,
When she was dear to us, we did hold her so;
But now her price is fall'n. Sir, there she
stands: 200
If aught within that little seeming substance,
Or all of it, with our displeasure pieced,
And nothing more, may fitly like your grace,
She's there, and she is yours.

BUR.   I know no answer.
LEAR. Will you, with those infirmities she
owes,   205
Unfriended, new-adopted to our hate,
Dower'd with our curse, and stranger'd with
our oath,
Take her, or leave her?

BUR.   Pardon me, royal sir;
Election makes not up on such conditions.
LEAR. Then leave her, sir; for, by the power
that made me,   120
I tell you all her wealth. [*To* FRANCE] For
you, great king,
I would not from your love make such a
stray,
To match you where I hate; therefore be-
seech you
To avert your liking a more worthier way 214

161. blank, white center of a target. 163. miscreant, vile
wretch. 169. recreant, breaker of your oath (of allegiance
to me). 172. strain'd, excessive. 175. potency, authority;
good, effective. 176. for provision, to provide means.

177. diseases, distresses, pains. 183. sith, since. 187.
approve, justify. 190. course, conduct. 201. that . . .
substance, that little person who only seems to be genuine.
203. like, please. 205. infirmities, defects; owes, owns.
209. Election . . . conditions, i.e., choice of wife is not
made under such conditions. 211. For, as for. 214. avert
. . . liking, turn your affection.

Than on a wretch whom nature is ashamed
Almost to acknowledge hers.

    FRANCE.   This is most strange,
That she, that even but now was your best
    object,
The argument of your praise, balm of your
    age,
Most best, most dearest, should in this trice
    of time   219
Commit a thing so monstrous, to dismantle
So many folds of favour. Sure, her offence
Must be of such unnatural degree,
That monsters it, or your fore-vouch'd af-
    fection
Fall'n into taint: which to believe of her, 224
Must be a faith that reason without miracle
Could never plant in me.

    COR.   I yet beseech your majesty,—
If for I want that glib and oily art,
To speak and purpose not; since what I well
    intend,
I'll do 't before I speak,—that you make
    known
It is no vicious blot, murder, or foulness, 230
No unchaste action, or dishonour'd step,
That hath deprived me of your grace and
    favour;
But even for want of that for which I am
    richer,
A still-soliciting eye, and such a tongue
As I am glad I have not, though not to have
    it   235
Hath lost me in your liking.

    LEAR.   Better thou
Hadst not been born than not to have pleased
    me better.

    FRANCE. Is it but this,—a tardiness in nature
Which often leaves the history unspoke
That it intends to do? My lord of Bur-
    gundy,   240
What say you to the lady? Love's not love
When it is mingled with regards that stand
Aloof from the entire point. Will you have
    her?
She is herself a dowry.

    BUR.   Royal Lear,

Give but that portion which yourself pro-
    posed,   245
And here I take Cordelia by the hand,
Duchess of Burgundy.

    LEAR. Nothing: I have sworn; I am firm.

    BUR. I am sorry, then, you have so lost a
    father
That you must lose a husband.

    COR.   Peace be with Burgundy!
Since that respects of fortune are his love, 251
I shall not be his wife.

    FRANCE. Fairest Cordelia, that art most rich,
    being poor;
Most choice, forsaken; and most loved, de-
    spised!
Thee and thy virtues here I seize upon: 255
Be it lawful I take up what's cast away.
Gods, gods! 'tis strange that from their
    cold'st neglect
My love should kindle to inflamed respect.
Thy dowerless daughter, king, thrown to my
    chance,
Is queen of us, of ours, and our fair France:
Not all the dukes of waterish Burgundy 261
Can buy this unprized precious maid of me.
Bid them farewell, Cordelia, though unkind:
Thou losest here, a better where to find.

    LEAR. Thou hast her, France: let her be
    thine; for we   265
Have no such daughter, nor shall ever see
That face of hers again. Therefore be gone
Without our grace, our love, our benison.
Come, noble Burgundy.

    [*Flourish. Exeunt all but* FRANCE,
    GONERIL, REGAN, *and* CORDELIA.]

    FRANCE. Bid farewell to your sisters. 270

    COR. The jewels of our father, with wash'd
    eyes
Cordelia leaves you: I know you what you
    are;
And like a sister am most loath to call
Your faults as they are named. Use well our
    father:
To your professèd bosoms I commit him: 275
But yet, alas, stood I within his grace,
I would prefer him to a better place.

---

liking, i.e., made me lose your affection. **238. tardiness
in nature**, natural reticence. **242-3. regards . . . point**,
considerations that have nothing to do with the essence
of the matter. **251. respects**, considerations. **258. inflamed**,
heightened. **261. waterish**, marshy. **262. unprized**, unap-
preciated. **268. grace**, favor; **benison**, blessing. **274. as
. . . named**, by their proper names. **275. professed**, full of
professions (of love). **277. prefer**, recommend.

---

217. your best object, the main object of your love.
218. argument, topic. **219. Trice**, instant. **220. To**, as to.
223. monsters, makes monstrous. **224. taint**, decay. **227.
for**, because. **228. purpose not**, i.e., not to mean
what one says. **230. vicious blot**, stain· made by a vice;
foulness, lack of chastity. **233. for which**, for lack of
which. **234. still-soliciting**, ever-begging. **236. lost . . .**

So, farewell to you both.

REG. Prescribe not us our duties.

GON.   Let your study
Be to content your lord, who hath received
    you   280
At fortune's alms. You have obedience
    scanted,
And well are worth the want that you have
    wanted.

COR. Time shall unfold what plaited cun-
    ning hides:
Who cover faults, at last shame them derides.
Well may you prosper!

FRANCE.   Come, my fair Cordelia. 285
        [*Exeunt* FRANCE *and* CORDELIA.

GON. Sister, it is not a little I have to say
of what most nearly appertains to us both.
I think our father will hence to-night.

REG. That's most certain, and with you;
next month with us.   290

GON. You see how full of changes his age
is; the observation we have made of it hath
not been little: he always loved our sister
most; and with what poor judgement he hath
now cast her off appears too grossly.

REG. 'Tis the infirmity of his age: yet he
hath ever but slenderly known himself.   297

GON. The best and soundest of his time
hath been but rash; then must we look to
receive from his age, not alone the imper-
fections of long-engraffed condition, but
therewithal the unruly waywardness that
infirm and choleric years bring with them. 303

REG. Such unconstant starts are we like to
have from him as this of Kent's banishment.

GON. There is further compliment of leave-
taking between France and him. Pray you,
let's hit together: if our father carry authority with such dispositions as he bears, this last
surrender of his will but offend us.   310

REG. We shall further think on't.

GON. We must do something, and i' the
    heat.   [*Exeunt.*

281. At . . . alms, i.e., when Fortune was giving alms,
i.e., petty gifts; scanted, grudged. 282. And . . . wanted,
and well deserved that lack of affection (from your husband) in which you have been lacking. 283. plaited, folded.
295. grossly, obviously. 298. the . . . time, the best and
soundest time of his life. 299. rash, headlong, hasty. 301.
long-engraffed condition, temperament that has long been
deeply imbedded in his nature. 302. therewithal, with it.
304. unconstant starts, freakish sudden impulses; like,
likely. 306. compliment, ceremony. 308. hit, agree. 310.
offend, injure. 312. i' the heat, i.e., while the iron is hot.
Scene ii: 3. Stand . . . custom, occupy a position in
which I suffer from disabilities dictated by mere custom.

SCENE II. *The* EARL OF GLOUCESTER'S
                    castle

[*Enter* EDMUND, *with a letter.*]

EDM. Thou, nature, art my goddess; to thy
    law
My services are bound. Wherefore should I
Stand in the plague of custom, and permit
The curiosity of nations to deprive me,
For that I am some twelve or fourteen moon-
    shines   5
Lag of a brother? Why bastard? wherefore
    base?
When my dimensions are as well compact,
My mind as generous, and my shape as true,
As honest madam's issue? Why brand they
    us
With base? with baseness? bastardy? base,
    base?   10
Who, in the lusty stealth of nature, take
More composition and fierce quality
Than doth, within a dull, stale, tired bed,
Go to the creating a whole tribe of fops,
Got 'tween asleep and wake? Well, then,   15
Legitimate Edgar, I must have your land:
Our father's love is to the bastard Edmund
As to the legitimate: fine word,—legitimate!
Well, my legitimate, if this letter speed,   19
And my invention thrive, Edmund the base
Shall top the legitimate. I grow; I prosper:
Now, gods, stand up for bastards!

[*Enter* GLOUCESTER.]

GLOU. Kent banish'd thus! and France in
    choler parted!
And the king gone to-night! subscribed his
    power!
Confined to exhibition! All this done   25
Upon the gad! Edmund, how now! what
    news?

EDM. So please your lordship, none.
                [*Putting up the letter.*

GLOU. Why so earnestly seek you to put up
    that letter?

4. curiosity of nations, nice distinction of universal law;
deprive me, i.e., of my just inheritance. 6. lag of, behind.
7. dimensions . . . compact, structure of my body is as
well built. 8. generous, noble; true, regular. 9. honest,
chaste. 12. more composition, a stronger constitution.
19. speed, succeed. 20. invention, scheme. 23. parted, departed. 24. subscribed his power, his power signed away.
25. exhibition, an allowance. 26. gad, spur (of the moment).

EDM. I know no news, my lord.

GLOU. What paper were you reading? 30

EDM. Nothing, my lord.

GLOU. No? What needed, then, that terrible dispatch of it into your pocket? the quality of nothing hath not such need to hide. itself. Let's see: come, if it be nothing, I shall not need spectacles. 36

EDM. I beseech you, sir, pardon me: it is a letter from my brother, that I have not all o'er-read; and for so much as I have perused, I find it not fit for your o'er-looking. 40

GLOU. Give me the letter, sir.

EDM. I shall offend, either to detain or give it. The contents, as in part I understand them, are to blame.

GLOU. Let's see, let's see. 45

EDM. I hope, for my brother's justification, he wrote this but as an essay or taste of my virtue.

GLOU. [Reads] "This policy and reverence of age makes the world bitter to the best of our times; keeps our fortunes from us till our oldness cannot relish them. I begin to find an idle and fond bondage in the oppression of aged tyranny; who sways, not as it hath power, but as it is suffered. Come to me, that of this I may speak more. If our father would sleep till I waked him, you should enjoy half his revenue for ever, and live the beloved of your brother, 57
"EDGAR."

Hum—conspiracy!—"Sleep till I waked him, —you should enjoy half his revenue,"—My son Edgar! Had he a hand to write this? a heart and brain to breed it in?—When came this to you? who brought it? 62

EDM. It was not brought me, my lord; there's the cunning of it; I found it thrown in at the casement of my closet.

GLOU. You know the character to be your brother's?

EDM. If the matter were good, my lord, I durst swear it were his; but, in respect of that, I would fain think it were not. 70

GLOU. It is his.

EDM. It is his hand, my lord; but I hope his heart is not in the contents.

GLOU. Hath he never heretofore sounded you in this business?

EDM. Never, my lord: but I have heard him oft maintain it to be fit, that, sons at perfect age, and fathers declining, the father should be as ward to the son, and the son manage his revenue. 79

GLOU. O villain, villain! His very opinion in the letter! Abhorred villain! Unnatural, detested, brutish villain! worse than brutish! Go, sirrah, seek him; I'll apprehend him: abominable villain! Where is he? 84

EDM. I do not well know, my lord. If it shall please you to suspend your indignation against my brother till you can derive from him better testimony of his intent, you shall run a certain course; where, if you violently proceed against him, mistaking his purpose, it would make a great gap in your own honour, and shake in pieces the heart of his obedience. I dare pawn down my life for him, that he hath wrote this to feel my affection to your honour, and to no further pretence of danger. 95

GLOU. Think you so?

EDM. If your honour judge it meet, I will place you where you shall hear us confer of this, and by an auricular assurance have your satisfaction; and that without any further delay than this very evening. 101

GLOU. He cannot be such a monster—

EDM. Nor is not, sure.

GLOU. To his father, that so tenderly and entirely loves him. Heaven and earth! Edmund, seek him out; wind me into him, I pray you: frame the business after your own wisdom. I would unstate myself, to be in a due resolution.

EDM. I will seek him, sir, presently; convey the business as I shall find means, and acquaint you withal. 111

GLOU. These late eclipses in the sun and moon portend no good to us: though the

33. terrible dispatch of it, frantic haste to put it. 34. quality, nature. 37. pardon me, excuse my not sharing it with you. 42. detain, withhold. 44. to blame, blameworthy. 47. essay, trial. 48. policy and reverence, established convention of revering the old. 48. best . . . times, best part of our life. 52. idle . . . bondage, a useless and foolish servitude. 53-4. who . . . suffered, which prevails not by virtue of its power, but as a result of our submission. 65. closet, private room. 66. character, handwriting. 68. matter, subject matter. 69. respect of, regard to. 78. perfect age, full maturity; declining, growing old. 89. where, whereas. 94-5. feel my affection, test my feeling. 95. pretence of danger, dangerous intention. 106. wind . . . him, worm your way into his confidence for my sake. 108. unstate myself, surrender the privileges of my rank. 109. due resolution, proper certainty. 109. presently, at once. 109-10. convey, manage secretly.

wisdom of nature can reason it thus and thus, yet nature finds itself scourged by the sequent effects: love cools, friendship falls off, brothers divide: in cities, mutinies; in 116 countries, discord; in palaces, treason; and the bond cracked 'twixt son and father. This villain of mine comes under the prediction; there's son against father: the king falls from bias of nature; there's father against child. We have seen the best of our time: machinations, hollowness, treachery, and all ruinous disorders, follow us disquietly to our graves. Find out this villain, Edmund; it shall lose thee nothing; do it carefully. And the noble and true-hearted Kent banished! his offence, honesty! 'Tis strange.   127
[*Exit.*

EDM. This is the excellent foppery of the world, that, when we are sick in fortune,—often the surfeit of our own behaviour,— we make guilty of our disasters the sun, the moon, and the stars: as if we were villains by necessity; fools by heavenly compulsion; knaves, thieves, and treachers, by spherical predominance; drunkards, liars, and adulterers, by an enforced obedience of plane- 135 tary influence; and all that we are evil in, by a divine thrusting on: an admirable evasion of whoremaster man, to lay his goatish disposition to the charge of a star! My father compounded with my mother under the dragon's tail; and my nativity was under Ursa major; so that it follows, I am rough and lecherous. Tut, I should have been that I am, had the maidenliest star in the firmament winkled on my bastardizing. Edgar–145

[*Enter* EDGAR.]

and pat he comes like the catastrophe of the old comedy: my cue is villanous melancholy, with a sigh like Tom o' Bedlam. O, these eclipses do portend these divisions! fa, sol, la, mi.

EDG. How now, brother Edmund! what serious contemplation are you in?   151

EDM. I am thinking, brother, of a predic-

tion I read this other day, what should follow these eclipses.   154

EDG. Do you busy yourself about that?

EDM. I promise you, the effects he writes of succeed unhappily; as of unnaturalness between the child and the parent; death, dearth, dissolutions of ancient amities; divisions in state, menaces and maledictions against king and nobles; needless diffidences, banishment of friends, dissipation of cohorts, nuptial breaches, and I know not what. 163

EDG. How long have you been a sectary astronomical?

EDM. Come, come; when saw you my father last?

EDG. Why, the night gone by.

EDM. Spake you with him?

EDG. Ay, two hours together.   170

EDM. Parted you in good terms? Found you no displeasure in him by word or countenance?

EDG. None at all.

EDM. Bethink yourself wherein you may have offended him: and at my entreaty forbear his presence till some little time hath qualified the heat of his displeasure; which at this instant so rageth in him, that with the mischief of your person it would scarcely allay.   179

EDG. Some villain hath done me wrong.

EDM. That's my fear. I pray you, have a continent forbearance till the speed of his rage goes slower; and, as I say, retire with me to my lodging, from whence I will fitly bring you to hear my lord speak: pray ye, go; there's my key: if you do stir abroad, go armed.   186

EDG. Armed, brother!

EDM. Brother, I advise you to the best; go armed: I am no honest man if there be any good meaning towards you: I have told you what I have seen and heard; but faintly, nothing like the image and horror of it: pray you, away.   192

EDG. Shall I hear from you anon?

with. 142-3. that I am, what I am. 146. pat, opportunely. 148. Tom o' Bedlam, common name of lunatics of Bethlehem Hospital (Bedlam), an insane asylum, who were sent out to beg. 157. succeed, follow. 159. dearth, famine. 161. diffidences, suspicions. 162. dissipation of cohorts, breaking up of military organizations. 164-5. sectary astronomical, believer in astrology. 175. forbear, avoid. 177. qualified, lessened. 179. mischief . . . person, harm to your body. 182. continent, restrained. 184. fitly, opportunely. 192. image and horror, the horrible truth. 193. anon, shortly.

114. wisdom of nature, scientific theory. 115-6. sequent effects, results which follow. 116. mutinies, tumults. 121. bias, the curve of a bowling ball, hence "tendency." 128. foppery, foolishness. 130. surfeit, overeating, indigestion. 133. treachers, traitors. 133-4. spherical predominance, because of the controlling influence of some planet. 138. goatish, licentious. 140. compounded with, came to terms

EDM. I do serve you in this business.

[*Exit* EDGAR.]

A credulous father! and a brother noble, 195
Whose nature is so far from doing harms,
That he suspects none; on whose foolish honesty
My practices ride easy! I see the business.
Let me, if not by birth, have lands by wit:
All with me's meet that I can fashion fit. 200

[*Exit.*

SCENE III. *The* DUKE OF ALBANY's *palace.*

[*Enter* GONERIL, *and* OSWALD, *her steward.*]

GON. Did my father strike my gentleman for chiding of his fool?

OSW. Yes, madam.

GON. By day and night he wrongs me; every hour
He flashes into one gross crime or other,
That sets us all at odds: I'll not endure it: 5
His knights grow riotous, and himself upbraids us
On every trifle. When he returns from hunting,
I will not speak with him; say I am sick:
If you come slack of former services,
You shall do well; the fault of it I'll answer. 10

OSW. He's coming, madam; I hear him.

[*Horns within.*

GON. Put on what weary negligence you please,
You and your fellows; I'ld have it come to question:
If he dislike it, let him to our sister,
Whose mind and mine, I know, in that are one, 15
Not to be over-ruled. Idle old man,
That still would manage those authorities
That he hath given away! Now, by my life,
Old fools are babes again; and must be used
With checks as flatteries,—when they are seen abused. 20
Remember what I tell you.

OSW.   Well, madam.

GON. And let his knights have colder looks among you;
What grows of it, no matter; advise your fellows so:
I would breed from hence occasions, and I shall
That I may speak: I'll write straight to my sister, 25
To hold my very course. Prepare for dinner.

[*Exeunt.*

SCENE IV. *A hall in the same.*

[*Enter* KENT, *disguised.*]

KENT. If but as well I other accents borrow,
That can my speech defuse, my good intent
May carry through itself to that full issue
For which I razed my likeness. Now, banish'd Kent,
If thou canst serve where thou dost stand condemn'd, 5
So may it come, thy master, whom thou lovest,
Shall find thee full of labours.

[*Horns within. Enter* LEAR, KNIGHTS, *and* ATTENDANTS.]

LEAR. Let me not stay a jot for dinner; go get it ready. [*Exit an* ATTENDANT.] How now! what art thou? 10

KENT. A man, sir.

LEAR. What dost thou profess? what wouldst thou with us?

KENT. I do profess to be no less than I seem; to serve him truly that will put me in trust; to love him that is honest; to converse with him that is wise, and says little; to fear judgement; to fight when I cannot choose: and to eat no fish. 18

LEAR. What art thou?

KENT. A very honest-hearted fellow, and as poor as the king.

LEAR. If thou be as poor for a subject as he is for a king, thou art poor enough. What wouldst thou? 24

KENT. Service.

LEAR. Who wouldst thou serve?

KENT. You.

---

198. practices, plots. 200. fashion fit, make fitting by fraudulent management. Scene iii: 13. to question, i.e., to a showdown. 16. Idle, foolish. 19. used, managed. 20. checks as, rebukes as well as; abused, deceived. 23. advise . . . so, tell your servants to act the same way. 24. occasions, opportunities. Scene iv: 2. defuse, disguise. 4. razed my likeness, erased any likeness to myself.

5. serve, act as a servant. 12. What . . . profess? What is your profession? 16. converse, associate. 18. choose, i.e., help it; eat no fish, i.e., a Protestant and not disloyal like the fish-eating Catholics.

LEAR. Dost thou know me, fellow?

KENT. No, sir; but you have that in your countenance which I would fain call master.

LEAR. What's that? 31

KENT. Authority.

LEAR. What services canst thou do?

KENT. I can keep honest counsel, ride, run, mar a curious tale in telling it, and deliver a plain message bluntly: that which ordinary men are fit for, I am qualified in; and the best of me is diligence.

LEAR. How old art thou? 39

KENT. Not so young, sir, to love a woman for singing, nor so old to dote on her for any thing: I have years on my back forty eight.

LEAR. Follow me; thou shalt serve me: if I like thee no worse after dinner, I will not part from thee yet. Dinner, ho, dinner! Where's my knave? my fool? Go you, and call my fool hither. [*Exit an* ATTENDANT.] 47

[*Enter* OSWALD.]

You, you, sirrah, where's my daughter?

OSW. So please you,— [*Exit.*

LEAR. What says the fellow there? Call the clotpoll back. [*Exit a* KNIGHT.] Where's my fool, ho? I think the world's asleep. 52

[*Re-enter* KNIGHT.]

How now! where's that mongrel?

KNIGHT. He says, my lord, your daughter is not well. 55

LEAR. Why came not the slave back to me when I called him?

KNIGHT. Sir, he answered me in the roundest manner, he would not.

LEAR. He would not! 60

KNIGHT. My lord, I know not what the matter is; but, to my judgement, your highness is not entertained with that ceremonious affection as you were wont; there's a great abatement of kindness appears as well in the general dependants as in the duke himself also and your daughter. 67

LEAR. Ha! sayest thou so?

KNIGHT. I beseech you, pardon me, my lord, if I be mistaken; for my duty cannot be silent when I think your highness wronged. 71

LEAR. Thou but rememberest me of mine own conception: I have perceived a most faint neglect of late; which I have rather blamed as mine own jealous curiosity than as a very pretence and purpose of unkindness: I will look further into 't. But where's my fool? I have not seen him this two days.

KNIGHT. Since my young lady's going into France, sir, the fool hath much pined 80 away.

LEAR. No more of that; I have noted it well. Go you, and tell my daughter I would speak with her. [*Exit an* ATTENDANT.] Go you, call hither my fool. [*Exit an* ATTENDANT.]

[*Re-enter* OSWALD.]

O, you sir, you, come you hither, sir: who am I, sir?

OSW. My lady's father.

LEAR. "My lady's father!" my lord's knave: you whoreson dog! you slave! you cur!

OSW. I am none of these, my lord; I beseech your pardon. 91

LEAR. Do you bandy looks with me, you rascal? [*Striking him.*

OSW. I'll not be struck, my lord.

KENT. Nor tripped neither, you base football player.

[*Tripping up his heels.*

LEAR. I thank thee, fellow; thou servest me, and I'll love thee. 98

KENT. Come, sir, arise, away! I'll teach you differences: away, away! If you will measure your lubber's length again, tarry: but away! go to; have you wisdom? so. 102

[*Pushes* OSWALD *out.*

LEAR. Now, my friendly knave, I thank thee: there's earnest of thy service. 104

[*Giving* KENT *money.*

[*Enter* FOOL.]

FOOL. Let me hire him too: here's my coxcomb. [*Offering* KENT *his cap.*

LEAR. How now, my pretty knave! how dost thou?

30. countenance, bearing. 34. keep honest counsel, keep an honorable secret. 35. curious, elaborate. 46. knave, boy. 51. clotpoll, blockhead. 59. roundest, plainest. 63. entertained, treated. 63-4. ceremonious affection, the affection which shows itself in formal respect. 66. general dependants, the house-servants. 72. rememberest, remind.

73. conception, idea. 74. faint, half-hearted. 75. jealous curiosity, overscrupulous watchfulness (for slights). 76. very pretence, deliberate intention. 92. bandy, strike a ball back and forth (as in tennis). 100. differences, proper distinctions in rank. 101. lubber's, awkward lout's. 104. earnest of, advance payment for.

FOOL. Sirrah, you were best take my cox-comb.

KENT. Why, fool?   110

FOOL. Why, for taking one's part that's out of favour: nay, an thou canst not smile as the wind sits, thou'lt catch cold shortly: there, take my coxcomb: why, this fellow has banished two on 's daughters, and did the third a blessing against his will; if thou follow him, thou must needs wear my coxcomb. How now, nuncle! Would I had two coxcombs and two daughters!

LEAR. Why, my boy?   119

FOOL. If I gave them all my living, I'ld keep my coxcombs myself. There's mine; beg another of thy daughters.

LEAR. Take heed, sirrah; the whip.   123

FOOL. Truth's a dog must to kennel; he must be whipped out, when Lady the brach may stand by the fire and stink.

LEAR. A pestilent gall to me!

FOOL. Sirrah, I'll teach thee a speech.

LEAR. Do.

FOOL. Mark it, nuncle: 130
    Have more than thou showest,
    Speak less than thou knowest,
    Lend less than thou owest,
    Ride more than thou goest,
    Learn more than thou trowest,   135
    Set less than thou throwest;
    Leave thy drink and thy whore,
    And keep in-a-door,
    And thou shalt have more
    Than two tens to a score.   140

KENT. This is nothing, fool.

FOOL. Then 'tis like the breath of an un-fee'd lawyer; you gave me nothing for 't. Can you make no use of nothing, nuncle?

LEAR. Why, no, boy; nothing can be made out of nothing.

FOOL. [To KENT] Prithee, tell him, so much the rent of his land comes to: he will not believe a fool.

LEAR. A bitter fool!   150

FOOL. Dost thou know the difference, my boy, between a bitter fool and a sweet fool?

LEAR. No lad, teach me.

FOOL. That lord that counsell'd thee
    To give away thy land,   155
    Come place him here by me,
    Do thou for him stand:
    The sweet and bitter fool
    Will presently appear;
    The one in motley here,   160
    The other found out there.

LEAR. Dost thou call me fool, boy?

FOOL. All thy other titles thou hast given away; that thou wast born with.   164

KENT. This is not altogether fool, my lord.

FOOL. No, faith, lords and great men will not let me; if I had a monopoly out, they would have part on't: and ladies too, they will not let me have all fool to myself; they'll be snatching. Give me an egg, nuncle, and I'll give thee two crowns.   171

LEAR. What two crowns shall they be?

FOOL. Why, after I have cut the egg i' the middle, and eat up the meat, the two crowns of the egg. When thou clovest thy crown i' the middle, and gavest away both parts, thou borest thy ass on thy back o'er the dirt: thou hadst little wit in thy bald crown, when thou gavest thy golden one away. If I speak like myself in this, let him be whipped that first finds it so.   180
[Singing] Fools had ne'er less wit in a year;
    For wise men are grown foppish,
    They know not how their wits to wear,
    Their manners are so apish.

LEAR. When were you wont to be so full of songs, sirrah?   186

FOOL. I have used it, nuncle, ever since thou madest thy daughters thy mother: for when thou gavest them the rod, and put'st down thine own breeches,   190
[Singing] Then they for sudden joy did weep,
    And I for sorrow sung,
    That such a king should play bo-peep,
    And go the fools among.   194

---

108. **were best,** had better; **coxcomb,** the hood crested with red like a cock's comb, worn by the professional fool. 112. **an,** if. 115. **on's,** of his. 118. **nuncle,** contraction for "mine uncle." 125. **brach,** bitch, personifying flattery. 127. **pestilent gall,** annoying irritation. 133. **owest,** ownest. 134. **goest,** walkest. 135. **trowest,** knowest. 136. **set,** stake; **throwest,** have a chance to throw, i.e., don't bet your all. 138. **in-a-door,** indoors, i.e., at home. 154. **That lord,** perhaps a reference to the Lord Skalligi in the old **King Lear** who suggests the love test. Nobody in this play gives Lear this stupid advice. 157. **for him stand,** impersonate him. 159. **presently,** immediately. 167. **monopoly,** a royal patent granting a monopoly on something; **out,** granted me. 167-8. **they . . . on't,** the lords who helped him get the monopoly would demand a share in it. 179-80. **like myself,** i.e., outspokenly. 182. **foppish,** foolish. 181-2. **Fools . . . foppish,** there is nothing left for fools to do, now that wise men have become fools. 187. **I . . . it,** it has been my custom. 193. **play bo-peep,** be so childish as play "Hide and Go Seek."

Prithee, nuncle, keep a schoolmaster that can teach thy fool to lie: I would fain learn to lie.

LEAR. An you lie, sirrah, we'll have you whipped. 198

FOOL. I marvel what kin thou and thy daughters are: they'll have me whipped for speaking true, thou'lt have me whipped for lying; and sometimes I am whipped for holding my peace. I had rather be any kind o' thing than a fool: and yet I would not be thee, nuncle; thou hast pared thy wit o' both sides, and left nothing i' the middle: here comes one o' the parings. 206

[*Enter* GONERIL.]

LEAR. How now, daughter! what makes that frontlet on? Methinks you are too much of late i' the frown. 209

FOOL. Thou wast a pretty fellow when thou hadst no need to care for her frowning; now thou art an O without a figure; I am better than thou art now; I am a fool, thou art nothing. [*To* GON.] Yes, forsooth, I will hold my tongue; so your face bids me, though you say nothing. Mum, mum, 216

  He that keeps nor crust nor crum,
  Weary of all, shall want some.

[*Pointing to* LEAR] That's a shealed peas-cod.

GON. Not only, sir, this your all-licensed fool,
But other of your insolent retinue 221
Do hourly carp and quarrel; breaking forth
In rank and not-to-be-endurèd riots. Sir,
I had thought, by making this well known unto you,
To have found a safe redress; but now grow fearful, 225
By what yourself too late have spoke and done,
That you protect this course, and put it on
By your allowance; which if you should, the fault
Would not 'scape censure, nor the redresses sleep, 229
Which, in the tender of a wholesome weal,
Might in their working do you that offence,

Which else were shame, that then necessity
Will call discreet proceeding.

FOOL. For, you know, nuncle,
  The hedge-sparrow fed the cuckoo so long, 235
  That it had it head bit off by it young.
So, out went the candle, and we were left darkling.

LEAR. Are you our daughter?

GON. Come, sir,
I would you would make use of that good wisdom, 240
Whereof I know you are fraught; and put away
These dispositions, that of late transform you
From what you rightly are.

FOOL. May not an ass know when the cart draws the horse? Whoop, Jug! I love thee.

LEAR. Doth any here know me? This is not Lear: 246
Doth Lear walk thus? speak thus? Where are his eyes?
Either his notion weakens, his discernings
Are lethargied—Ha! waking? 'tis not so.
Who is it that can tell me whom I am? 250

FOOL. Lear's shadow.

LEAR. I would learn that; for, by the marks of sovereignty, knowledge, and reason, I should be false persuaded I had daughters.

FOOL. Which they will make an obedient father. 256

LEAR. Your name, fair gentlewoman?

GON. This admiration, sir, is much o' the savour
Of other your new pranks. I do beseech you
To understand my purposes aright: 260
As you are old and reverend, you should be wise.
Here do you keep a hundred knights and squires;
Men so disorder'd, so debosh'd and bold,
That this our court, infected with their manners,
Shows like a riotous inn: epicurism and lust 265

208. frontlet, band worn on the forehead, here = frown. 211. an O, cipher. 219. shealed peas-cod, shelled pea pod. 222. carp, find fault. 227. put it on, encourage it. 228. by your allowance, with your approval. 229. redresses, acts of redress. 230. in the tender . . . weal, in our care to make the commonwealth sound. 232-3. which . . . proceedings, which would be shameful but which the demands (of the situation) would force

one to call prudent action (discreet procedure). 235. cuckoo, the cuckoo lays its eggs in other birds' nests. 236. it . . . it, it . . . its. 237. darkling, in the dark. 241. fraught, stored. 245. Whoop, Jug! . . . thee, the tag of some song. The fool takes refuge in nonsense whenever he suspects that one of his sallies has been too impertinent. 248. notion, understanding. 249. lethargied, paralyzed; waking? Am I awake? 256. which, whom. 258. admiration, pretended astonishment. 263. debosh'd, debauched. 265. epicurism, unrestrained indulgence.

Make it more like a tavern or a brothel
Than a graced palace. The shame itself doth
    speak
For instant remedy: be then desired
By her, that else will take the thing she begs,
A little to disquantity your train;   270
And the remainder, that shall still depend,
To be such men as may besort your age,
And know themselves and you.
        LEAR.   Darkness and devils!
Saddle my horses; call my train together.
Degenerate bastard! I'll not trouble thee:
Yet have I left a daughter.   276
    GON. You strike my people; and your dis-
        order'd rabble
Make servants of their betters.

            [Enter ALBANY.]

    LEAR. Woe, that too late repents,—
[To ALB.]
        O, sir, are you come?
Is it your will? Speak, sir. Prepare my horses.
Ingratitude, thou marble-hearted fiend,   281
More hideous when thou show'st thee in a
    child
Than the sea-monster!
        ALB.   Pray, sir, be patient.
    LEAR. [To GON.] Detested kite! thou liest:
My train are men of choice and rarest parts,
That all particulars of duty know,   286
And in the most exact regard support
The worships of their name. O most small
    fault,
How ugly didst thou in Cordelia show!
That, like an engine, wrench'd my frame of
    nature   290
From the fix'd place; drew from my heart all
    love,
And added to the gall. O Lear, Lear, Lear!
Beat at this gate, that let thy folly in,
                        [Striking his head.]
And thy dear judgement out! Go, go, my
    people.
    ALB. My lord, I am guiltless, as I am ignor-
        ant   295
Of what hath moved you.

    LEAR.   It may be so, my lord.
Hear, nature, hear; dear goddess, hear!
Suspend thy purpose, if thou didst intend
To make this creature fruitful!
Into her womb convey sterility!   300
Dry up in her the organs of increase;
And from her derogate body never spring
A babe to honour her! If she must teem,
Create her child of spleen; that it may live,
And be a thwart disnatured torment to
    her!   305
Let it stamp wrinkles in her brow of youth;
With cadent tears fret channels in her cheeks;
Turn all her mother's pains and benefits
To laughter and contempt; that she may feel
How sharper than a serpent's tooth it is   310
To have a thankless child! Away, away!
                                              [Exit.
    ALB. Now, gods that we adore, whereof
        comes this?
    GON. Never afflict yourself to know the
        cause;
But let his disposition have that scope
That dotage gives it.   315

            [Re-enter LEAR.]

    LEAR. What, fifty of my followers at a clap!
Within a fortnight!
    ALB.   What's the matter, sir?
    LEAR. I'll tell thee: [To GON.] Life and
        death! I am ashamed
That thou hast power to shame my manhood
    thus;
That these hot tears, which break from me
    perforce,   320
Should make thee worth them. Blasts and fogs
    upon thee!
The untented woundings of a father's curse
Pierce every sense about thee! Old fond eyes,
Beweep this cause again, I'll pluck ye out,
And cast you, with the waters that you lose,
To temper clay. Yea, is it come to this?   326
Let it be so: yet have I left a daughter,
Who, I am sure, is kind and comfortable:
When she shall hear this of thee, with her
    nails

267. graced, honored. 270. disquantity, reduce the numbers
of. 271. still depend, remain as your dependents. 272.
besort, befit. 283. the sea-monster, (1) perhaps the hippo-
potamus, which had a reputation for ingratitude, or (2)
any sea monster of classical mythology; be patient, exercise self-control. 285. parts, accomplishments. 287-8. And
. . . name, And in the smallest details uphold the honorable
names they bear. 290. like . . . nature, like a powerful piece
of mechanism, dislodged the whole structure of my nature.

301. increase, child-bearing. 302. derogate, deteriorated,
blighted. 303. teem, be fruitful. 304. her, for her; spleen,
malice. 305. thwart, perverse; disnatured, unnatural. 307.
cadent, falling; fret, wear. 314. disposition, mood. 321.
fogs, fogs and mists were supposed to be laden with the
seeds of pestilence. 322. untented, too deep to be cleansed
with a tent (a piece of lint). 323. fond, foolish. 326.
temper, soften. 328. comfortable, bringing comfort.

She'll flay thy wolvish visage. Thou shalt
find   330
That I'll resume the shape which thou dost
think
I have cast off for ever: thou shalt, I warrant
thee.
      [Exeunt LEAR, KENT, *and* ATTENDANTS.
GON. Do you mark that, my lord?
ALB. I cannot be so partial, Goneril,
To the great love I bear you,—   335
  GON. Pray you, content. What, Oswald, ho!
[*To the* FOOL] You, sir, more knave than fool,
  after your master.
  FOOL. Nuncle Lear, nuncle Lear, tarry and
take the fool with thee.
     A fox, when one has cought her,   340
     And such a daughter,
     Should sure to the slaughter,
     If my cap would buy a halter:
     So the fool follows after.   [*Exit.*
  GON. This man hath had good counsel:—a
hundred knights!   345
'Tis politic and safe to let him keep
At point a hundred knights: yes, that, on
  every dream,
Each buzz, each fancy, each complaint, dis-
  like,
He may enguard his dotage with their
  powers,   349
And hold our lives in mercy. Oswald, I say!
  ALB. Well, you may fear too far.
  GON.   Safer than trust too far:
Let me still take away the harms I fear,
Not fear still to be taken: I know his heart.
What he hath utter'd I have writ my sister:
If she sustain him and his hundred knights,
When I have show'd the unfitness,—   356

       [Re-enter OSWALD.]

               How now, Oswald!
What, have you writ that letter to my sister?
  OSW. Yes, madam.
  GON. Take you some company, and away
  to horse:
Inform her full of my particular fear;   360
And thereto add such reasons of your own
As may compact it more. Get you gone;
And hasten your return. [*Exit* OSWALD.] No,
  no, my lord,

This milky gentleness and course of yours
Though I condemn not, yet, under pardon,
You are much more attask'd for want of
  wisdom   366
Than praised for harmful mildness.
  ALB. How far your eyes may pierce I can-
  not tell:
Striving to better, oft we mar what's well.
  GON. Nay, then—   370
  ALB. Well, well; the event.   [*Exeunt.*

SCENE V. *Court before the same.*

    [*Enter* LEAR, KENT, *and* FOOL.]

  LEAR. Go you before to Gloucester with
these letters. Acquaint my daughter no further with any thing you know than comes
from her demand out of the letter. If your
diligence be not speedy, I shall be there afore
you.   5
  KENT. I will not sleep, my lord, till I have
delivered your letter.   [*Exit.*
  FOOL. If a man's brains were in 's heels,
were't not in danger of kibes?
  LEAR. Ay, boy.   10
  FOOL. Then, I prithee, be merry; thy wit
shall ne'er go slip-shod.
  LEAR. Ha, ha, ha!
  FOOL. Shalt see thy other daughter will use
thee kindly; for though she's as like this as a
crab's like an apple, yet I can tell what I can
tell.   16
  LEAR. Why, what canst thou tell, my boy?
  FOOL. She will taste as like this as a crab
does to a crab. Thou canst tell why one's
nose stands i' the middle on 's face?   20
  LEAR. No.
  FOOL. Why, to keep one's eyes of either
side's nose; that what a man cannot smell out,
he may spy into.
  LEAR. I did her wrong—   25
  FOOL. Canst tell how an oyster makes his
shell?
  LEAR. No.
  FOOL. Nor I neither; but I can tell why a
snail has a house.   30

---

336. content, be satisfied. **346.** politic, prudent. **347.** At point, completely equipped. **348.** buzz, rumor. **350.** in mercy, at his mercy. **352-3.** Let . . . taken, let me always remove what I fear will harm me, rather than always live in fear of being attacked by some harm. **353.** still, al-

ways. **362.** compact it more, give it more substance, i.e., make the argument more convincing. **364.** milky . . . course, mild gentleness of this course. **366.** attask'd, to be blamed. **371.** the event, i.e., let's see what will be the outcome. Scene v: **9.** kibes, chilblains. **11.** slip-shod, in slippers (and so in danger of chilblains). **15.** kindly, (1) according to her nature, (2) with kindness. **15.** crab's, crab-apple's.

LEAR. Why?

FOOL. Why, to put his head in; not to give it away to his daughters, and leave his horns without a case. 34

LEAR. I will forget my nature. So kind a father! Be my horses ready?

FOOL. Thy asses are gone about 'em. The reason why the seven stars are no more than seven is a pretty reason.

LEAR. Because they are not eight? 40

FOOL. Yes, indeed: thou wouldst make a good fool.

LEAR. To take 't again perforce! Monster ingratitude!

FOOL. If thou wert my fool, nuncle, I'ld have thee beaten for being old before thy time. 46

LEAR. How's that?

FOOL. Thou shouldst not have been old till thou hadst been wise.

LEAR. O, let me not be mad, not mad, sweet heaven! 50
Keep me in temper: I would not be mad!

[*Enter* GENTLEMAN.]

How now! are the horses ready?

GENT. Ready, my lord.

LEAR. Come, boy.

FOOL. She that's a maid now, and laughs at my departure,
Shall not be a maid long, unless things be cut shorter. [*Exeunt.*

ACT TWO

SCENE I. *The* EARL OF GLOUCESTER'S
castle

[*Enter* EDMUND, *and* CURAN *meets him.*]

EDM. Save thee, Curan.

CUR. And you, sir. I have been with your father, and given him notice that the Duke of Cornwall and Regan his duchess will be here with him this night. 5

EDM. How comes that?

CUR. Nay, I know not. You have heard of the news abroad; I mean the whispered ones, for they are yet but ear-kissing arguments?

EDM. Not I: pray you, what are they? 10

CUR. Have you heard of no likely wars toward, 'twixt the Dukes of Cornwall and Albany?

EDM. Not a word.

CUR. You may do, then, in time. Fare you well, sir. [*Exit.* 15

EDM. The duke be here to-night? The better! best!
This weaves itself perforce into my business.
My father hath set guard to take my brother;
And I have one thing, of a queasy question,
Which I must act: briefness and fortune, work! 20
Brother, a word; descend: brother I say!

[*Enter* EDGAR.]

My father watches: O sir, fly this place;
Intelligence is given where you are hid;
You have now the good advantage of the night:
Have you not spoken 'gainst the Duke of Cornwall? 25
He's coming hither; now, i' the night, i' the haste,
And Regan with him: have you nothing said
Upon his party 'gainst the Duke of Albany?
Advise yourself.

EDG. I am sure on 't, not a word. 29

EDM. I hear my father coming: pardon me;
In cunning I must draw my sword upon you:
Draw; seem to defend yourself; now quit you well.
Yield: come before my father. Light, ho, here!
Fly, brother. Torches, torches! So, farewell.
[*Exit* EDGAR.]
Some blood drawn on me would beget opinion [*Wounds his arm.*]
Of my more fierce endeavour: I have seen drunkards 36
Do more than this in sport. Father, father!
Stop, stop! No help?

38. seven stars, Pleiades. 43. To . . . perforce, I will recover my kingdom by force. 51. temper, natural emotional equilibrium, i.e., sane. Act II, Scene i: 9. ear-kissing arguments. whispered remarks. 16. the better, so much the better. 19. of . . . question, of a ticklish nature. 21. descend, Edgar is in the balcony which represents Edmund's room. 31. In cunning, as a pretense. 32. quit you, acquit yourself. 35. beget opinion, give the impression. 36. drunkards, an Elizabethan gallant, when a little drunk, sometimes cut his arm to mix his blood with wine, to be drunk to his mistress's health.

[*Enter* GLOUCESTER, *and* SERVANTS *with torches.*]

GLOU. Now, Edmund, where's the villain?

EDM. Here stood he in the dark, his sharp
      sword out,   40
Mumbling of wicked charms, conjuring the
      moon
To stand auspicious mistress,—

GLOU.   But where is he?

EDM. Look, sir, I bleed.

GLOU.   Where is the villain, Edmund?

EDM. Fled this way, sir. When by no means
      he could—

GLOU. Pursue him, ho! Go after. [*Exeunt
some* SERVANTS.] By no means what?   45

EDM. Persuade me to the murder of your
      lordship;
But that I told him, the revenging gods
'Gainst parricides did all their thunders bend;
Spoke, with how manifold and strong a bond
The child was bound to the father; sir, in
      fine,   50
Seeing how loathly opposite I stood
To his unnatural purpose, in fell motion,
With his preparèd sword, he charges home
My unprovided body, lanced mine arm:
But when he saw my best alarum'd spirits, 55
Bold in the quarrel's right, roused to the en-
      counter,
Or whether gasted by the noise I made,
Full suddenly he fled.

GLOU.   Let him fly far:
Not in this land shall he remain uncaught;
And found—dispatch. The noble duke my
      master,   60
My worthy arch and patron, comes to-night:
By his authority I will proclaim it,
That he which finds him shall deserve our
      thanks,
Bringing the murderous coward to the stake;
He that conceals him, death.   65

EDM. When I dissuaded him from his intent,
And found him pight to do it, with curst
      speech
I threaten'd to discover him: he replied,
"Thou unpossessing bastard! dost thou think,

47. that, when. 48. bend, aim. 51. loathly opposite,
loathingly opposed. 52. fell motion, fierce thrust. 53. prepared, drawn. 54. unprovided, undefended. 55. my . . .
spirits, my best energies aroused (as by a call to arms).
57. gasted, terrified. 60. dispatch, finish him off. 61.
arch and patron, chief patron. 67. pight, determined;
curst, angry. 68. discover him, reveal his plan. 72. faith'd,
believed. 74. character, handwriting. 75. practice, plotting.

If I would stand against thee, would the re-
      posal   70
Of any trust, virtue, or worth in thee
Make thy words faith'd? No: what I should
      deny,—
As this I would; ay, though thou didst pro-
      duce
My very character,—I'ld turn it all   74
To thy suggestion, plot, and damnèd practice:
And thou must make a dullard of the world,
If they not thought the profits of my death
Were very pregnant and potential spurs
To make thee seek it."

GLOU.   Strong and fasten'd villain!
Would he deny his letter? I never got him. 80
                              [*Tucket within.*]
Hark, the duke's trumpets! I know not why
      he comes.
All ports I'll bar; the villain shall not 'scape;
The duke must grant me that: besides, his
      picture
I will send far and near, that all the kingdom
May have due note of him; and of my land,
Loyal and natural boy, I'll work the means 86
To make thee capable.

[*Enter* CORNWALL, REGAN, *and* ATTENDANTS.]

CORN. How now, my noble friend! since I
      came hither,
Which I can call but now, I have heard
      strange news.

REG. If it be true, all vengeance comes too
      short   90
Which can pursue the offender. How dost,
      my lord?

GLOU. O, madam! my old heart is crack'd,
      is crack'd!

REG. What, did my father's godson seek
      your life?
He whom my father named? your Edgar?

GLOU. O, lady, lady, shame would have it
      hid!   95

REG. Was he not companion with the riot-
      ous knights
That tend upon my father?

GLOU. I know not, madam: 'tis too bad, too
      bad.

EDM. Yes, madam, he was of that consort.

78. pregnant and potential, cogent and powerful. 79.
fasten'd, confirmed. 80. got, begot. s.d. tucket, a flourish
on the trumpet, a fanfare. 82. ports, sea-ports; bar,
guard. 87. capable, i.e., of inheriting, i.e., he promises to
legitimize him. 99. consort, company.

REG. No marvel, then, though he were ill
    affected: 100
'Tis they have put him on the old man's
    death,
To have the expense and waste of his reve-
    nues.
I have this present evening from my sister
Been well inform'd of them; and with such
    cautions,
That if they come to sojourn at my house,
I'll not be there.   106
    CORN.   Nor I, assure thee, Regan.
Edmund, I hear that you have shown your
    father
A child-like office.
    EDM.   'Twas my duty, sir.
    GLOU. He did bewray his practice; and re-
    ceived
This hurt you see, striving to apprehend
    him.   110
    CORN. Is he pursued?
    GLOU.   Ay, my good lord.
    CORN. If he be taken, he shall never more
Be fear'd of doing harm: make your own
    purpose,
How in my strength you please. For you,
    Edmund,   114
Whose virtue and obedience doth this instant
So much commend itself, you shall be ours:
Natures of such deep trust we shall much
    need;
You we first seize on.
    EDM.   I shall serve you, sir,
Truly, however else.
    GLOU.   For him I thank your grace.
    CORN. You know not why we came to visit
    you,—   120
    REG. Thus out of season, threading dark-
    eyed night:
Occasions, noble Gloucester, of some poise,
Wherein we must have use of your advice:
Our father he hath writ, so hath our sister,
Of difference, which I least thought it fit 125
To answer from our home; the several mes-
    sengers
From hence attend dispatch. Our good old
    friend,

100. though, if; ill affected, evilly disposed. 101. put him
on, incited him to. 102. expense, expenditure. 106. assure
thee, be assured. 108. child-like office, filial service. 109.
bewray, disclose; practice, plot. 113. purpose, plans. 114.
How . . . please, using my authority however you please.
121. threading, passing through. 122. poise, weight. 125.
differences, quarrels; which, i.e., letters. 126. from,
away from. 127. attend dispatch, wait to be sent.

Lay comforts to your bosom; and bestow
Your needful counsel to our business,
Which craves the instant use.
    GLOU.   I serve you, madam: 130
Your graces are right welcome.   [Exeunt.

SCENE II. *Before* GLOUCESTER'S *castle*.

[*Enter* KENT *and* OSWALD, *severally*.]

OSW. Good dawning to thee, friend: art of
this house?
    KENT. Ay.
    OSW. Where may we set our horses?
    KENT. I' the mire.   5
    OSW. Prithee, if thou lovest me, tell me.
    KENT. I love thee not.
    OSW. Why, then, I care not for thee.
    KENT. If I had thee in Lipsbury pinfold, I
would make thee care for me.   10
    OSW. Why dost thou use me thus? I know
thee not.
    KENT. Fellow, I know thee.
    OSW. What dost thou know me for?
    KENT. A knave; a rascal; an eater of broken
meats; a base, proud, shallow, beggarly, three-
suited, hundred-pound, filthy, worsted-stock-
ing knave; a lily-livered, action-taking knave,
a whoreson, glass-gazing, super-serviceable,
finical rogue; one-trunk-inheriting slave; 20
one that wouldst be a bawd, in way of good
service, and art nothing but the composition
of a knave, beggar, coward, pandar, and the
son and heir of a mongrel bitch: one whom I
will beat into clamorous whining, if thou de-
niest the least syllable of thy addition.   26
    OSW. Why, what a monstrous fellow art
thou, thus to rail on one that is neither known
of thee nor knows thee!   29
    KENT. What a brazen-faced varlet art thou,
to deny thou knowest me! Is it two days ago
since I tripped up thy heels, and beat thee
before the king? Draw, you rogue: for,
though it be night, yet the moon shines; I'll

130. the instant use, to be carried out instantly. Scene ii:
9. Lipsbury pinfold, pinfold is a pound for stray animals.
Regarding Lipsbury pinfold, says Nares: "The enclosure
adjacent to my teeth, in my jaws," so, in my clutches.
17. three-suited, alludes to the three suits a year regularly
allowed to a man-servant. 18. lily-livered, a white liver
was devoid of blood, i.e., of courage; action-taking, a
man who settles his quarrels by going to the law. 19.
glass-gazing, vain. 19-20. super-serviceable, one who serves
in ways other than honorable, e.g., as a bawd. 20. finical,
fussy; one . . . inheriting, whose possessions would fill
only one trunk. 23. composition, mixture. 26. addition,
descriptive titles.

make a sop o' the moonshine of you: draw, you whoreson cullionly barber-monger, draw.   [*Drawing his sword.*

osw. Away! I have nothing to do with thee.   37

KENT. Draw, you rascal: you come with letters against the king; and take Vanity the puppet's part against the royalty of her father: draw, you rogue, or I'll so carbonado your shanks: draw, you rascal; come your ways.

osw. Help, ho! murder! help!   43

KENT. Strike you slave; stand, rogue, stand; you neat slave, strike.   [*Beating him.*

osw. Help, ho! murder! murder!   46

[*Enter* EDMUND, *with his rapier drawn*, CORN-WALL, REGAN, GLOUCESTER, *and* SERVANTS.]

EDM. How now! What's the matter?

KENT. With you, goodman boy, an you please: come, I'll flesh ye: come on, young master.

GLOU. Weapons! arms! What's the matter here?   51

CORN. Keep peace, upon your lives; He dies that strikes again. What is the matter?

REG. The messengers from our sister and the king.   55

CORN. What is your difference? speak.

osw. I am scarce in breath, my lord.

KENT. No marvel, you have so bestirred your valour. You cowardly rascal, nature disclaims in thee: a tailor made thee.   60

CORN. Thou art a strange fellow: a tailor make a man?

KENT. Ay, a tailor, sir: a stone-cutter or a painter could not have made him so ill, though he had been but two hours at the trade.

CORN. Speak yet, how grew your quarrel?

osw. This ancient ruffian, sir, whose life I have spared at suit of his gray beard,— 68

KENT. Thou whoreson zed! thou unnecessary letter! My lord, if you will give me leave, I will tread this unbolted villain into mortar, and daub the walls of a jakes with him. Spare my gray beard, you wagtail?

CORN. Peace, sirrah!   74
You beastly knave, know you no reverence?

KENT. Yes, sir; but anger hath a privilege.

CORN. Why art thou angry?

KENT. That such a slave as this should wear a sword,
Who wears no honesty. Such smiling rogues as these,
Like rats, oft bite the holy cords a-twain 80
Which are too intrinse t' unloose; smooth every passion
That in the natures of their lords rebel;
Bring oil to fire, snow to their colder moods;
Renege, affirm, and turn their halcyon beaks
With every gale and vary of their masters, 85
Knowing nought, like dogs, but following.
A plague upon your epileptic visage!
Smile you my speeches, as I were a fool?
Goose, if I had you upon Sarum plain,
I'ld drive ye cackling home to Camelot.   90

CORN. What, art thou mad, old fellow?

GLOU. How fell you out? say that.

KENT. No contraries hold more antipathy Than I and such a knave.

CORN. Why dost thou call him knave?
What's his offence?   95

KENT. His countenance likes me not.

CORN. No more, perchance, does mine, nor his, nor hers.

KENT. Sir, 'tis my occupation to be plain: I have seen better faces in my time Than stands on any shoulder that I see 100
Before me at this instant.

CORN.   This is some fellow, Who, having been praised for bluntness, doth affect
A saucy roughness, and constrains the garb Quite from his nature: he cannot flatter, he,

---

35. **make . . . of you**, steep you in moonshine, i.e., steep you in your own blood even if we fight by the uncertain light of the moon. 36. **cullionly . . . monger**, rascally haunter of barber shops (where he was beautified). 39-40. **Vanity . . . part**, Lady Vanity was a character in the morality-like puppet plays. 41. **carbonado**, slash. 42. **come your ways**, come on then. 45. **neat**, foppish. 49. **flesh**, feed with flesh for the first time, i.e., initiate you. 53. **the matter**, cause of the quarrel. 56. **difference**, dispute. 60. **disclaims**, disowns; **a . . . thee**, i.e., you are nothing but clothes. 69. **zed**, i.e., the letter "z"; unnecessary, because "s" can express its sound. 71. **unbolted**, unsifted, coarse.

72. **jakes**, privy. 73. **wagtail**, a ridiculously active bird. 79. **honesty**, sense of honor. 80. **holy cords**, sacred family bonds. 81. **intrinse**, intricately tied; **smooth**, flatter (into uncontrolled expression). 84. **Renege**, deny; **halcyon beaks**, it was believed that if a halcyon (Kingfisher) were hung by the neck, he would turn his beak into the wind. 85. **gale and vary**, varying gale. 87. **epileptic**, distorted by a (frightened) smile. 88. **fool**, professional jester. 89. **Sarum plain**, Salisbury plain where geese were bred. 90. **Camelot**, the site of King Arthur's Court. 96. **His . . . not**, I do not like his face. 98. **plain**, plain-spoken. 103. **constrains the garb**, forces himself to assume a bearing. 104. **Quite from**, completely foreign to.

An honest mind and plain, he must speak
    truth!   105
An they will take it, so; If not, he's plain.
These kind of knaves I know, which in this
    plainness
Harbour more craft and more corrupter ends
Than twenty silly ducking observants
That stretch their duties nicely.   110
    KENT. Sir, in good sooth, in sincere verity,
Under the allowance of your great aspect,
Whose influence, like the wreath of radiant
    fire
On flickering Phœbus' front,—
    CORN.   What mean'st by this? 114
    KENT. To go out of my dialect, which you
discommend so much. I know, sir, I am no
flatterer: he that beguiled you in a plain ac-
cent was a plain knave; which for my part I
will not be, though I should win your dis-
pleasure to entreat me to 't.   120
    CORN. What was the offence you gave him?
    OSW. I never gave him any:
It pleased the king his master very late
To strike at me, upon his misconstruction;
When he, conjunct, and flattering his dis-
    pleasure,   125
Tripp'd me behind; being down, insulted,
    rail'd,
And put upon him such a deal of man,
That worthied him, got praises of the king
For him attempting who was self-subdued;
And, in the fleshment of this dread exploit,
Drew on me here again.   131
    KENT.   None of these rogues and
    cowards
But Ajax is their fool.
    CORN.   Fetch forth the stocks!
You stubborn ancient knave, you reverend
    braggart,
We'll teach you—
    KENT.   Sir, I am too old to learn:
Call not your stocks for me: I serve the king;
On whose employment I was sent to you: 136
You shall do small respect, show too bold
    malice
Against the grace and person of my master,
Stocking his messenger.

    CORN. Fetch forth the stocks! As I have life
    and honour,   140
There shall he sit till noon.
    REG. Till noon! till night, my lord; and all
    night too.
    KENT. Why, madam, if I were your father's
    dog,
You should not use me so.
    REG.   Sir, being his knave, I will.
    CORN. This is a fellow of the self-same
    colour   145
Our sister speaks of. Come, bring away the
    stocks!   [*Stocks brought out.*
    GLOU. Let me beseech your grace not to
    do so:
His fault is much, and the good king his
    master
Will check him for 't: your purposed low cor-
    rection   149
Is such as basest and contemned'st wretches
For pilferings and most common trespasses
Are punish'd with: the king must take it ill,
That he's so slightly valued in his messenger,
Should have him thus restrain'd.
    CORN.   I'll answer that.
    REG. My sister may receive it much more
    worse,   155
To have her gentleman abused, assaulted,
For following her affairs. Put in his legs.
    [KENT *is put in the stocks.*]
Come, my good lord, away.
    [*Exeunt all but* GLOUCESTER *and* KENT.
    GLOU. I am sorry for thee, friend; 'tis the
    duke's pleasure,
Whose disposition, all the world well knows,
Will not be rubb'd nor stopp'd: I'll entreat
    for thee.   161
    KENT. Pray, do not, sir: I have watched
    and travell'd hard;
Some time I shall sleep out, the rest I'll
    whistle.
A good man's fortune may grow out at heels:
Give you good morrow!   165
    GLOU. The duke's to blame in this; 'twill
    be ill taken.   [*Exit.*

gered. **128. worthied him**, as made him appear worthy.
129. For . . . self-subdued, for assailing one who makes
no self-defence. **130. fleshment**, ferocious excitement. **132.
Ajax . . . fool**, the cowardly swashbuckler Ajax is vastly
inferior to them (in braggart talk). **144. should not**,
surely would not. **145. colour**, sort. **146. away**, along.
149. check, reprove. **154. answer**, be responsible for. **161.
rubb'd**, obstructed; a "rub" in bowling was anything that
deflected the course of the ball. **162. watched**, stayed
awake. **164. A good man's**, Even a good man's. **165. Give
you**, God give you.

106. so, well and good; **plain**, frank. **109. ducking observants**, obsequious (continually bowing) courtiers. **110.
nicely**, punctiliously. **111. Sir, etc.**, Kent parodies the
speech of "ducking observants." **112. aspect**, an astro-
logical term. **114. front**, forehead. **124. misconstruction**,
misapprehending [me]. **125. conjunct**, joined with him
(Lear). **127. deal of man**, lot of manhood, i.e., he swag-

KENT. Good king, that must approve the common saw,
Thou out of heaven's benediction comest
To the warm sun!
Approach, thou beacon to this under globe,
That by thy comfortable beams I may 171
Peruse this letter! Nothing almost sees miracles
But misery: I know 'tis from Cordelia,
Who hath most fortunately been inform'd
Of my obscurèd course; [*Reads*] "And shall find time 175
From this enormous state, seeking to give
Losses their remedies." All weary and o'erwatch'd,
Take vantage, heavy eyes, not to behold
This shameful lodging.
Fortune, good night: smile once more; turn thy wheel! [*Sleeps.* 180

SCENE III. *A wood.*

[*Enter* EDGAR.]

EDG. I heard myself proclaim'd;
And by the happy hollow of a tree
Escaped the hunt. No port is free; no place,
That guard, and most unusual vigilance,
Does not attend my taking. Whiles I may 'scape, 5
I will preserve myself: and am bethought
To take the basest and most poorest shape
That ever penury, in contempt of man,
Brought near to beast: my face I 'll grime with filth;
Blanket my loins; elf all my hair in knots; 10
And with presented nakedness out-face
The winds and persecutions of the sky.
The country gives me proof and precedent
Of Bedlam beggars, who, with roaring voices,
Strike in their numb'd and mortified bare arms 15
Pins, wooden pricks, nails, sprigs of rosemary;
And with this horrible object, from low farms,
Poor pelting villages, sheep-cotes, and mills,

Sometime with lunatic bans, sometime with prayers,
Enforce their charity. Poor Turlygod! poor Tom! 20
That's something yet: Edgar I nothing am.
[*Exit.*

SCENE IV. *Before* GLOUCESTER'S *castle.*
KENT *in the stocks.*

[*Enter* LEAR, FOOL, *and* GENTLEMAN.]

LEAR, 'Tis strange that they should so depart from home,
And not send back my messenger.
GENT.   As I learn'd.
The night before there was no purpose in them
Of this remove.
KENT.   Hail to thee, noble master!
LEAR, Ha!   5
Makest thou this shame thy pastime?
KENT.   No, my lord.
FOOL. Ha, ha! he wears cruel garters. Horses are tied by the heads, dogs and bears by the neck, monkeys by the loins, and men by the legs: when a man's over-lusty at legs, then he wears wooden nether-stocks. 11
LEAR. What's he that hath so much thy place mistook
To set thee here?
KENT.   It is both he and she;
Your son and daughter.
LEAR. No.   15
KENT. Yes.
LEAR. No, I say.
KENT. I say, yea.
LEAR. No, no, they would not.
KENT. Yes, they have.   20
LEAR. By Jupiter, I swear, no.
KENT. By Juno, I swear, ay.
LEAR.   They durst not do 't;
They could not, would not do 't; 'tis worse than murder,

375

To do upon respect such violent outrage:
Resolve me, with all modest haste, which way
Thou mightst deserve, or they impose, this
usage,   26
Coming from us.
    KENT.   My lord, when at their home
I did commend your highness' letters to them,
Ere I was risen from the place that show'd
My duty kneeling, came there a reeking
post,   30
Stew'd in his haste, half breathless, panting
forth
From Goneril his mistress salutations;
Deliver'd letters, spite of intermission,
Which presently they read: on whose con-
tents,
They summon'd up their meiny, straight took
horse;   35
Commanded me to follow, and attend
The leisure of their answer; gave me cold
looks:
And meeting here the other messenger,
Whose welcome, I perceived, had poison'd
mine,—
Being the very fellow that of late   40
Display'd so saucily against your highness,—
Having more man than wit about me, drew:
He raised the house with loud and coward
cries.
Your son and daughter found this trespass
worth
The shame which here it suffers.   45
    FOOL. Winter's not gone yet, if the wild-
geese fly that way.
        Fathers that wear rags
           Do make their children blind;
        But fathers that bear bags   50
           Shall see their children kind.
        Fortune, that arrant whore,
        Ne'er turns the key to the poor.
But, for all this, thou shalt have as many
dolours for thy daughters as thou canst tell in
a year.   55
    LEAR. O, how this mother swells up toward
my heart!

Hysterica passio, down, thou climbing sorrow,
Thy element's below! Where is this daughter?
    KENT. With the earl, sir, here within.
    LEAR.   Follow me not;
Stay here.   [*Exit.* 60
    GENT. Made you no more offence but what
you speak of?
    KENT. None.
How chance the king comes with so small a
train?
    FOOL. An thou hadst been set i' the stocks
for that question, thou hadst well deserved it.
    KENT. Why, fool?   67
    FOOL. We'll set thee to school to an ant, to
teach thee there's no labouring i' the winter.
All that follow their noses are led by their
eyes but blind men; and there's not a nose
among twenty but can smell him that's stinking. Let go thy hold when a great wheel runs
down a hill, lest it break thy neck with following it; but the great one that goes up the
hill, let him draw thee after. When a wise
man gives thee better counsel give me mine
again: I would have none but knaves follow it,
since a fool gives it.

        That sir which serves and seeks for gain,
           And follows but for form,   80
        Will pack when it begins to rain,
           And leave thee in the storm.
        But I will tarry; the fool will stay,
           And let the wise man fly:
        The knave turns fool that runs away;   85
           The fool no knave, perdy.

    KENT. Where learned you this fool?
    FOOL. Not i' the stocks, fool.

      [*Re-enter* LEAR, *with* GLOUCESTER.]

    LEAR. Deny to speak with me? They are
sick? they are weary?
They have travell'd all the night? Mere
fetches;   90
The images of revolt and flying off.

Fetch me a better answer.

GLOU.   My dear lord,
You know the fiery quality of the duke;
How unremoveable and fix'd he is
in his own course.   95

LEAR. Vengeance! plague! death! confusion!
Fiery? what quality? Why, Gloucester, Glou-
     cester,
I'ld speak with the Duke of Cornwall and his
     wife.

GLOU. Well, my good lord, I have inform'd
     them so.

LEAR. Inform'd them! Dost thou understand
     me, man?   100

GLOU. Ay, my good lord.

LEAR. The king would speak with Cornwall;
     the dear father
Would with his daughter speak, commands
     her service:
Are they inform'd of this? My breath and
     blood!
Fiery? the fiery duke? Tell the hot duke
     that—   105
No, but not yet: may be he is not well:
Infirmity doth still neglect all office
Whereto our health is bound; we are not our-
     selves
When nature, being oppress'd, commands the
     mind
To suffer with the body: I'll forbear;   110
And am fall'n out with my more headier will,
To take the indisposed and sickly fit
For the sound man. Death on my state!
     wherefore   [Looking on KENT.]
Should he sit here? This act persuades me
That this remotion of the duke and her   115
Is practice only. Give me my servant forth.
Go tell the duke and 's wife I'ld speak with
     them,
Now, presently: bid them come forth and
     hear me,
Or at their chamber-door I'll beat the drum
Till it cry sleep to death.   120

GLOU. I would have all well betwixt you.
                                     [Exit.

LEAR. O me, my heart, my rising heart! but,
     down!

FOOL. Cry to it, nuncle, as the cockney did

to the eels when she put 'em i' the paste alive;
she knapped 'em o' the coxcombs with a stick,
and cried "Down, wantons, down." 'Twas her
brother that, in pure kindness to his horse,
buttered his hay.   128

[Enter CORNWALL, REGAN, GLOUCESTER, and
                SERVANTS.]

LEAR. Good morrow to you both.

CORN.   Hail to your grace!
                    [KENT is set at liberty.

REG. I am glad to see your highness.   130

LEAR. Regan, I think you are; I know what
     reason
I have to think so: if thou shouldst not be
     glad,
I would divorce me from thy mother's tomb,
Sepulchring an adultress. [To KENT] O, are
     you free?
Some other time for that. Belovèd Regan,
Thy sister's naught: O Regan, she hath
     tied   136
Sharp-tooth'd unkindness, like a vulture,
     here: [Points to his heart.]
I can scarce speak to thee; thou'lt not believe
With how depraved a quality—O Regan!

REG. I pray you, sir, take patience: I have
     hope   140
You less know how to value her desert
Than she to scant her duty.

LEAR.   Say, how is that?

REG. I cannot think my sister in the least
Would fail her obligation: if, sir, perchance
She have restrain'd the riots of your follow-
     ers,   145
'Tis on such ground, and to such wholesome
     end,
As clears her from all blame.

LEAR. My curses on her!

REG.   O, sir, you are old;
Nature in you stands on the very verge
Of her confine: you should be ruled and
     led   150
By some discretion, that discerns your state
Better than you yourself. Therefore, I pray
     you,
That to our sister you do make return;
Say you have wrong'd her, sir.

---

107. office, duty. 11. headier, impulsive. 112. to take, for taking. 113. state, royal power. 115. remotion, removal. 116. practice, trickery. 118. presently, at once. 120. cry . . . death, murder sleep. 123. cockney, cook, perhaps a London cook who knows nothing about eels. 125. knapped, rapped; coxcombs, jocular for heads.

129. grace, i.e., Majesty. 134. sepulchring, i.e., as containing. 136. naught, wicked. 139. quality, character. 140. take patience, be calm. 150. confine, assigned boundary. 151. state, i.e., mental state.

LEAR.   Ask her forgiveness?
Do you but mark how this becomes the
    house: 155
"Dear daughter, I confess that I am old;
                        [*Kneeling.*]
Age is unnecessary: on my knees I beg
That you'll vouchsafe me raiment, bed, and
    food."
    REG. Good sir, no more; these are unsightly
    tricks:
Return you to my sister.
    LEAR.   [*Rising*] Never, Regan: 160
She hath abated me of half my train;
Look'd black upon me; struck me with her
    tongue,
Most serpent-like, upon the very heart:
All the stored vengeances of heaven fall
On her ingrateful top! Strike her young
    bones,   165
You taking airs, with lameness!
    CORN.   Fie, sir, fie!
    LEAR. You nimble lightnings, dart your
    blinding flames
Into her scornful eyes! Infect her beauty,
You fen-suck'd fogs, drawn by the powerful
    sun,
To fall and blast her pride!   170
    REG. O the blest gods! so will you wish on
    me,
When the rash mood is on.
    LEAR. No, Regan, thou shalt never have
    my curse:
Thy tender-hefted nature shall not give
Thee o'er to harshness: her eyes are fierce;
    but thine   175
Do comfort and not burn. 'Tis not in thee
To grudge my pleasures, to cut off my train,
To bandy hasty words, to scant my sizes,
And in conclusion to oppose the bolt
Against my coming in: thou better know'st
The offices of nature, bond of childhood, 181
Effects of courtesy, dues of gratitude;
Thy half o' the kingdom hast thou not for-
    got,
Wherein I thee endow'd.
    REG.   Good sir, to the purpose.
    LEAR. Who put my man i' the stocks?
                        [*Tucket within.*]

CORN.   What trumpet's that?
    REG. I know 't, my sister's: this approves
    her letter,   186
That she would soon be here.

                [*Enter* OSWALD.]

                        Is your lady come?
    LEAR. This is a slave, whose easy-borrow'd
    pride
Dwells in the fickle grace of her he follows.
Out, varlet, from my sight!
    CORN.   What means your grace?
    LEAR. Who stock'd my servant? Regan, I
    have good hope   191
Thou didst not know on 't. Who comes here?
    O heavens,

                [*Enter* GONERIL.]

If you do love old men, if your sweet sway
Allow obedience, if yourselves are old,
Make it your cause; send down, and take my
    part!   195
[*To* GON.] Art not ashamed to look upon this
    beard?
O Regan, wilt thou take her by the hand?
    GON. Why not by the hand, sir? How have
    I offended?
All's not offence that indiscretion finds
And dotage terms so.
    LEAR.   O sides, you are too tough;
Will you yet hold? How came my man i'
    the stocks?   201
    CORN. I set him there, sir: but his own dis-
    orders
Deserved much less advancement.
    LEAR.   You! did you?
    REG. I pray you, father, being weak, seem
    so.
If, till the expiration of your month,   205
You will return and sojourn with my sister,
Dismissing half your train, come then to me:
I am now from home, and out of that pro-
    vision
Which shall be needful for your entertain-
    ment.
    LEAR. Return to her, and fifty men dis-
    miss'd?   210
No, rather I abjure all roofs, and choose

---

155. becomes the house, is a fitting family relationship.
157. Age is unnecessary, old people are of no use.
161. abated . . . train, reduced my retinue by half. 165.
young, bones, i.e., Goneril's youthful figure. 166. taking,
infecting. 170. fall, fall upon. 174. tender-hefted, swayed
by tender feelings. 178. sizes, allowances. 181. offices,
duties; bond of childhood, the duties of a child to its
parents. 182. Effects of courtesy, courteous action. 184.
to the purpose, talk sense. 188. easy-borrow'd, easily
assumed. 190. varlet, scoundrel. 194. allow, approve.
203. advancement, honor. 209. entertainment, maintenance.

To wage against the enmity o' the air;
To be a comrade with the wolf and owl,—
Necessity's sharp pinch! Return with her?
Why, the hot-blooded France, that dowerless took   215
Our youngest born, I could as well be brought
To knee his throne, and, squire-like, pension beg
To keep base life afoot. Return with her?
Persuade me rather to be slave and sumpter
To this detested groom. [*Pointing at* OSWALD.
    GON.   At your choice, sir.
    LEAR. I prithee, daughter, do not make me mad: 221
I will not trouble thee, my child; farewell:
We'll no more meet, no more see one another:
But yet thou art my flesh, my blood, my daughter;
Or rather a disease that's in my flesh,   225
Which I must needs call mine: thou art a boil,
A plague-sore, an embossèd carbuncle,
In my corrupted blood. But I'll not chide thee;
Let shame come when it will, I do not call it:
I do not bid the thunder-bearer shoot,   230
Nor tell tales of thee to high-judging Jove:
Mend when thou canst; be better at thy leisure:
I can be patient; I can stay with Regan,
I and my hundred knights.
    REG.   Not altogether so:
I look'd not for you yet, nor am provided   235
For your fit welcome. Give ear, sir, to my sister;
For those that mingle reason with your passion
Must be content to think you old, and so—
But she knows what she does.
    LEAR.   Is this well spoken?
    REG. I dare avouch it, sir: what, fifty followers?   240
Is it not well? What should you need of more?
Yea, or so many, sith that both charge and danger
Speak 'gainst so great a number? How, in one house,

Should many people, under two commands,
Hold amity? 'Tis hard; almost impossible.
    GON. Why might not you, my lord, receive attendance   246
From those that she calls servants or from mine?
    REG. Why not, my lord? If then they chanced to slack you,
We could control them. If you will come to me,—
For now I spy a danger,—I entreat you   250
To bring but five and twenty: to no more
Will I give place or notice.
    LEAR. I gave you all—
    REG.   And in good time you gave it.
    LEAR. Made you my guardians, my depositaries;
But kept a reservation to be follow'd   255
With such a number. What, must I come to you
With five and twenty, Regan? said you so?
    REG. And speak 't again, my lord; no more with me.
    LEAR. Those wicked creatures yet do look well-favour'd,
When others are more wicked; not being the worst   260
Stands in some rank of praise. [*To* GON.]
    I'll go with thee:
Thy fifty yet doth double five-and-twenty,
And thou art twice her love.
    GON.   Hear me, my lord:
What need you five and twenty, ten, or five,
To follow in a house where twice so many
Have a command to tend you?   266
    REG.   What need one?
    LEAR. O, reason not the need: our basest beggars
Are in the poorest thing superfluous:
Allow not nature more than nature needs,
Man's life as cheap as beast's: thou art a lady;
If only to go warm were gorgeous,   271
Why, nature needs not what thou gorgeous wear'st,
Which scarcely keeps thee warm. But, for true need,—
You heavens, give me that patience, patience I need!

light of reason. **240. avouch,** affirm. **242. charge,** expense. **248. slack,** neglect. **252. notice,** recognition. **254. depositaries,** trustees. **259. well-favour'd,** handsome. **267. reason,** discuss. **268. Are . . . superfluous,** have in their most meagre possessions more than the barest necessities. **274. patience,** endurance.

212. wage, wage war with. **217. knee,** kneel before; **squire-like,** as if I were a servant. **219. sumpter,** packhorse, drudge. **220. groom,** menial. **227. embossed,** swollen. **237. mingle . . . passion,** consider your violence in the

379

You see me here, you gods, a poor old man,
As full of grief as age; wretched in both! 276
If it be you that stir these daughters' hearts
Against their father, fool me not so much
To bear it tamely; touch me with noble anger,
And let not women's weapons, water-drops,
Stain my man's cheeks! No, you unnatural
      hags, 281
I will have such revenges on you both,
That all the world shall—I will do such
      things,—
What they are, yet I know not; but they
      shall be
The terrors of the earth. You think I'll weep;
No, I'll not weep: 286
I have full cause of weeping; but this heart
Shall break into a hundred thousand flaws,
Or ere I'll weep. O fool, I shall go mad!
      [*Exeunt* LEAR, GLOUCESTER, KENT *and* FOOL.
                              Storm and tempest.
  CORN. Let us withdraw; 'twill be a storm
  REG. This house is little: the old man and
      his people 291
Cannot be well bestow'd
  GON. 'Tis his own blame; hath put himself
      from rest,
And must needs taste his folly.
  REG. For his particular, I'll receive him
      gladly, 295
But not one follower.
  GON.   So am I purposed.
Where is my lord of Gloucester?
  CORN. Follow'd the old man forth: he is
      return'd.
              [*Re-enter* GLOUCESTER.]
  GLOU. The king is in high rage.
  CORN.   Whither is he going?
  GLOU. He calls to horse; but will I know
      not whither. 300
  CORN. 'Tis best to give him way; he leads
      himself.
  GON. My lord, entreat him by no means to
      stay.
  GLOU. Alack, the night comes on, and the
      bleak winds
Do sorely ruffle; for many miles about
There's scarce a bush.

  REG.   O, sir, to wilful men, 305
The injuries that they themselves procure
Must be their schoolmasters. Shut up your
      doors:
He is attended with a desperate train;
And what they may incense him to, being
      apt 309
To have his ear abused, wisdom bids fear.
  CORN. Shut up your doors, my lord; 'tis a
      wild night:
My Regan counsels well: come out o' the
      storm.   [*Exeunt.*

ACT THREE

SCENE I. *A heath.*

[*Storm still. Enter* KENT *and a* GENTLEMAN,
      meeting.]

  KENT. Who's there, besides foul weather?
  GENT. One minded like the weather, most
      unquietly.
  KENT. I know you. Where's the king?
  GENT. Contending with the fretful element;
Bids the wind blow the earth into the sea, 5
Or swell the curlèd waters 'bove the main,
That things might change or cease; tears his
      white hair,
Which the impetuous blasts, with eyeless rage,
Catch in their fury, and make nothing of;
Strives in his little world of man to out-
      scorn 10
The to-and-fro-conflicting wind and rain.
This night, wherein the cub-drawn bear
      would couch,
The lion and the belly-pinched wolf
Keep their fur dry, unbonneted he runs,
And bids what will take all.
  KENT.   But who is with him?
  GENT. None but the fool; who labours to
      out-jest 16

278-9. fool . . . tamely, do not make me so much of a
weakling as to endure it tamely. 285. The . . . earth,
deeds to terrify the whole world. 288. flaws, fragments.
292. bestow'd, lodged. 293. blame, fault. 294. taste,
i.e., digest. 295. For his particular, as for him alone.
304. ruffle, bluster. 309. incense, incite; apt, ready.

310. abused, deceived. Act III, Scene i: 6. main, main-
land. 7. things, world. 8. eyeless, hence undirected, in-
discriminate. 9. make nothing of, show no respect for.
10. little . . . man, man was regarded as a universe
(macrocosm) in miniature (microcosm). 12. cub-drawn,
sucked dry by her cubs; couch, lie protected from the
storm. 14. unbonneted, without a hat. 15. take all, the
cry of a gambler when he stakes his last penny; so a
gesture of desperation.

His heart-struck injuries.

KENT.   Sir, I do know you;
And dare, upon the warrant of my note,
Commend a dear thing to you. There is division,
Although as yet the face of it be cover'd   20
With mutual cunning, 'twixt Albany and
    Cornwall;
Who have—as who have not, that their great
    stars
Throned and set high?—servants, who seem
    no less,
Which are to France the spies and specula-
    tions
Intelligent of our state; what hath been
    seen,   25
Either in snuffs and packings of the dukes,
Or the hard rein which both of them have
    borne
Against the old kind king; or something
    deeper,
Whereof perchance these are but furnishings;
But, true it is, from France there comes a
    power   30
Into this scatter'd kingdom; who already,
Wise in our negligence, have secret feet
In some of our best ports, and are at point
To show their open banner. Now to you:
If on my credit you dare build so far   35
To make your speed to Dover, you shall find
Some that will thank you, making just report
Of how unnatural and bemadding sorrow
The king hath cause to plain.
I am a gentleman of blood and breeding; 40
And, from some knowledge and assurance,
    offer
This office to you.

GENT. I will talk further with you.

KENT.   No, do not.
For confirmation that I am much more
Than my out-wall, open this purse, and
    take   45
What it contains. If you shall see Cordelia,—
As fear not but you shall,—show her this
    ring;
And she will tell you who your fellow is

That yet you do not know. Fie on this storm!
I will go seek the king.   50

GENT. Give me your hand: have you no
    more to say?

KENT. Few words, but, to effect, more than
    all yet;
That, when we have found the king,—in
    which your pain
That way, I'll this,—he that first lights on
    him
Holla the other.   [*Exeunt severally.* 55

SCENE II. *Another part of the heath.*
Storm still.

[*Enter* LEAR *and* FOOL.]

LEAR. Blow, winds, and crack your cheeks!
    rage! blow!
You cataracts and hurricanoes, spout
Till you have drench'd our steeples, drown'd
    the cocks!
You sulphurous and thought-executing fires,
Vaunt-couriers to oak-cleaving thunderbolts,
Singe my white head! And thou, all-shaking
    thunder,   6
Smite flat the thick rotundity o' the world!
Crack nature's moulds, all germens spill at
    once,
That make ingrateful man!   9

FOOL. O nuncle, court holy-water in a dry
house is better than this rain-water out o'
door. Good nuncle, in, and ask thy daughters' blessing: here's a night pities neither wise
man nor fool.

LEAR. Rumble thy bellyful! Spit, fire! spout,
    rain!
Nor rain, wind, thunder, fire, are my daugh-
    ters: 15
I tax not you, you elements, with unkindness;
I never gave you kingdom, call'd you chil-
    dren,
You owe me no subscription: then let fall
Your horrible pleasure; here I stand, your
    slave,

18. note, knowledge (of the situation). 19. Commend . . .
thing, entrust a momentous matter. 23. no less, not more
nor less than servants. 24. speculations, observers. 25.
Intelligent . . . state, giving information about our political situation. 26. snuffs, resentments; packings, plots. 29.
furnishings, deceptive shows. 30. power, armed force.
31. scatter'd, divided. 32. feet, infantry. 33. at point, all
ready. 35. my credit, your trust in me. 36. To, as to.

37. making just, if you make accurate. 39. plain, complain. 42. office, duty. 45. out-wall, exterior, i.e., the
garb of a serving man. 48. fellow, companion. 52. to
effect, in their importance. 53-4. your . . . way,
i.e., your efforts to find him lie in that direction. Scene
ii: 2. hurricanoes, water-spouts. 3. cocks, weathercocks.
4. thought-executing, having the speed of thought. 8.
Vaunt-couriers, forerunners. 8. nature's moulds, i.e.,
molds in which nature fashions men; germens, seeds; spill,
destroy. 10. court holy-water, i.e., flattery. 16. tax, reproach. 18. subscription, obedience.

A poor, infirm, weak, and despised old man:
But yet I call you servile ministers,   21
That have with two pernicious daughters
   join'd
Your high engender'd battles 'gainst a head
So old and white as this. O! O! 'tis foul!

FOOL. He that has a house to put 's head
in has a good head-piece.

   The cod-piece that will house
     Before the head has any,
   The head and he shall louse;
     So beggars marry many.   30
   The man that makes his toe
     What he his heart should make
   Shall of a corn cry woe,
     And turn his sleep to wake.
For there was never yet fair woman but she
made mouths in a glass.   36

LEAR. No, I will be the pattern of all
   patience;
I will say nothing.

          [*Enter* KENT.]

KENT. Who's there?

FOOL. Marry, here's grace and a cod-piece;
that's a wise man and a fool.   41

KENT. Alas, sir, are you here? things that
   love night
Love not such nights as these; the wrathful
   skies
Gallow the very wanderers of the dark,
And make them keep their caves: since I was
   man,   45
Such sheets of fire, such bursts of horrid
   thunder,
Such groans of roaring wind and rain, I never
Remember to have heard: man's nature can-
   not carry
The affliction nor the fear.

LEAR.   Let the great gods,
That keep this dreadful pother o'er our
   heads,   50
Find out their enemies now. Tremble, thou
   wretch,
That hast within thee undivulgèd crimes,

Unwhipp'd of justice: hide thee, thou bloody
   hand;
Thou perjured, and thou simular man of
   virtue
That art incestuous: caitiff, to pieces shake, 55
That under covert and convenient seeming
Hast practised on man's life: close pent-up
   guilts,
Rive your concealing continents, and cry
These dreadful summoners grace. I am a man
More sinn'd against than sinning.

KENT.   Alack, bare-headed!   60
Gracious my lord, hard by here is a hovel;
Some friendship will it lend you 'gainst the
   tempest:
Repose you there; while I to this hard
   house—
More harder than the stones whereof 'tis
   raised;
Which even but now, demanding after
   you,   65
Denied me to come in—return, and force
Their scanted courtesy.

LEAR.   My wits begin to turn.
Come on, my boy: how dost, my boy? art
   cold?
I am cold myself. Where is this straw, my
   fellow?
The art of our necessities is strange,   70
That can make vile things precious. Come,
   your hovel.
Poor fool and knave, I have one part in my
   heart
That's sorry yet for thee.

FOOL. [*Singing*] He that has and a little tiny
   wit,—   74
     With hey, ho, the wind and the rain,—
     Must make content with his fortunes fit,
     For the rain it raineth every day.

LEAR. True, my good boy. Come, bring us
   to this hovel.   [*Exeunt* LEAR *and* KENT.

FOOL. This is a brave night to cool a
   courtezan.
I'll speak a prophecy ere I go: 80
   When priests are more in word than mat-
     ter;

21. ministers, agents. 23. high-engender'd, engendered on high; battles, battalions. 27-9. The cod-piece . . . louse, the man who begets children before he has a house will live a lousy existence; cod-piece, an appendage worn on the front of men's trousers. 31. The . . . makes, the man who puts his heart where his toe should be. 36. made . . . glass, grimaced before a looking-glass. 40. grace, an honorable gentleman. 44. gallow, terrify. 48. carry, bear. 49. affliction, the bodily pain. 50. pother, uproar. 54. simular

man of, pretender to. 55. caitiff, despicable creature. 56. seeming, hypocrisy. 57. practised on, plotted against. 58. Rive . . . continents, rip open your coverings. 58-9. cry . . . grace, beg for mercy. 59. summoners, police of an ecclesiastical court. 62. lend, afford. 63. hard, cruel. 65. demanding after, asking for. 66. Denied, forbade. 70. art, a reference to alchemy. 79. brave, fine. 81. more . . . matter, better in their talk than in deeds.

When brewers mar their malt with water;
When nobles are their tailors' tutors;
No heretics burn'd, but wenches' suitors;
When every case in law is right;   85
No squire in debt, nor no poor knight;
When slanders do not live in tongues;
Nor cutpurses come not to throngs;
When usurers tell their gold i' the field;
And bawds and whores do churches
     build;   90
Then shall the realm of Albion
Come to great confusion:
Then comes the time, who lives to see 't,
That going shall be used with feet.
This prophecy Merlin shall make; for I live
     before his time.   [*Exit.* 95

SCENE III. GLOUCESTER'S *castle.*

[*Enter* GLOUCESTER *and* EDMUND.]

GLOU. Alack, alack, Edmund, I like not
this unnatural dealing. When I desired their
leave that I might pity him, they took from
me the use of mine own house; charged me,
on pain of their perpetual displeasure, neither
to speak of him, entreat for him, nor any
way sustain him.   6
  EDM. Most savage and unnatural!
  GLOU. Go to; say you nothing. There's a
division betwixt the dukes; and a worse
matter than that: I have received a letter
this night; 'tis dangerous to be spoken; I
have locked the letter in my closet: these
injuries the king now bears will be revenged
home, there's part of a power already footed:
we must incline to the king. I will seek him,
and privily relieve him: go you and main- 15
tain talk with the duke, that my charity be
not of him perceived: if he ask for me, I am
ill, and gone to bed. Though I die for it, as
no less is threatened me, the king my old
master must be relieved. There is some
strange thing toward, Edmund; pray you, be
careful.   [*Exit.* 21
  EDM. This courtesy, forbid thee, shall the
     duke
Instantly know; and of that letter too:

This seems a fair deserving, and must draw
     me
That which my father loses; no less than
     all: 25
The younger rises when the old doth fall.
                               [*Exit.*

SCENE IV. *The heath. Before a hovel.*

[*Enter* LEAR, KENT, *and* FOOL.]

  KENT. Here is the place, my lord; good my
     lord, enter:
The tyranny of the open night's too rough
For nature to endure.   [*Storm still.*
  LEAR.   Let me alone.
  KENT. Good my lord, enter here.
  LEAR.   Wilt break my heart?
  KENT. I had rather break mine own. Good
     my lord, enter.
  LEAR. Thou think'st 'tis much that this con-
     tentious storm
Invades us to the skin: so 'tis to thee;
But where the greater malady is fix'd,
The lesser is scarce felt. Thou 'ldst shun a
     bear;
But if thy flight lay toward the raging sea, 10
Thou 'ldst meet the bear i' the mouth. When
     the mind's free,
The body's delicate: the tempest in my mind
Doth from my senses take all feeling else
Save what beats there. Filial ingratitude!
Is it not as this mouth should tear this hand 15
For lifting food to 't? But I will punish
     home:
No, I will weep no more. In such a night
To shut me out! Pour on; I will endure.
In such a night as this! O Regan, Goneril!
Your old kind father, whose frank heart gave
     all,—   20
O, that way madness lies; let me shun that;
No more of that.
  KENT.   Good my lord, enter here.
  LEAR. Prithee, go in thyself; seek thine own
     ease:
This tempest will not give me leave to ponder
On things would hurt me more. But I'll go
     in.   25

89. tell, count. 91. Albion, Britain. 92. confusion, ruin.
94. going, walking. 95. Merlin, magician and prophet of
King Arthur's Court. Scene iii: 6. sustain, relieve. 13.
home, fully. 13. power, army; footed, landed. 14. incline
to the King, take the King's part. 15. privily, secretly.

20. toward, in preparation. 22. forbid thee, forbidden to
thee. 24. This . . . deserving, this will seem a meritorious
action. Scene iv: 2. open night, night in the open. 11. i'
the mouth, face to face; free, i.e., from trouble. 12. delicate, sensitive. 15. as, as if. 20. frank, generous.

[*To the* FOOL] In, boy; go first. You house-
　　less poverty,—
Nay, get thee in. I'll pray, and then I'll sleep.
　　　　　　　　　　　　[FOOL *goes in.*]
Poor naked wretches, wheresoe'er you are,
That bide the pelting of this pitiless storm,
How shall your houseless heads and unfed
　　sides,　　　　　　　　　　　　　　30
Your loop'd and window'd raggedness, de-
　　fend you
From seasons such as these? O, I have ta'en
Too little care of this! Take physic, pomp;
Expose thyself to feel what wretches feel,
That thou mayst shake the superflux to
　　them,　　　　　　　　　　　　　　35
And show the heavens more just.

EDG. [*Within*] Fathom and half, fathom
and half! Poor Tom!
　　　　　　[*The* FOOL *runs out from the hovel.*
FOOL. Come not in here, nuncle, here's a
spirit. Help me, help me!　　　　　　40
　　KENT. Give me thy hand. Who's there?
FOOL. A spirit, a spirit: he says his name's
poor Tom.
　　KENT. What art thou that dost grumble
there i' the straw? Come forth.

　　[*Enter* EDGAR *disguised as a madman.*]

EDG. Away! the foul fiend follows me!
Through the sharp hawthorn blows the cold
　　wind.
Hum! go to thy cold bed, and warm thee.
　　LEAR. Hast thou given all to thy two
　　daughters?
And art thou come to this?　　　　　　50
EDG. Who gives any thing to poor Tom?
whom the foul fiend hath led through fire and
through flame, through ford and whirlpool,
o'er bog and quagmire; that hath laid knives
under his pillow, and halters in his pew; set
ratsbane by his porridge; made him proud of
heart, to ride on a bay trotting-horse over
four-inched bridges, to course his own
shadow for a traitor. Bless thy five wits!　59
Tom's a-cold,—O, do de, do de, do de. Bless
thee from whirlwinds, star-blasting, and

taking! Do poor Tom some charity, whom
the foul fiend vexes: there could I have him
now,—and there,—and there again, and there.
　　　　　　　　　　　　[*Storm still.*
　　LEAR. What, have his daughters brought
　　him to this pass?　　　　　　　　65
Couldst thou save nothing? Didst thou give
　　them all?
FOOL. Nay, he reserved a blanket, else we
had been all shamed.
LEAR. Now, all the plagues that in the pen-
　　dulous air
Hang faded o'er men's faults light on thy
　　daughters!　　　　　　　　　　70
　　KENT. He hath no daughters, sir.
LEAR. Death, traitor! nothing could have
　　subdued nature
To such a lowness but his unkind daughters.
Is it the fashion, that discarded fathers　74
Should have thus little mercy on their flesh?
Judicious punishment! 'twas this flesh begot
Those pelican daughters.

EDG. Pillicock sat on Pillicock-hill:
Halloo, halloo, loo, loo!
FOOL. This cold night will turn us all to
fools and madmen.　　　　　　　　81
EDG. Take heed o' the foul fiend: obey thy
parents; keep thy word justly; swear not;
commit not with man's sworn spouse; set
not thy sweet heart on proud array. Tom's
a-cold.
　　LEAR. What hast thou been?　　　86
EDG. A serving-man, proud in heart and
mind; that curled my hair; wore gloves in my
cap; served the lust of my mistress' heart
and did the act of darkness with her; swore
as many oaths as I spake words, and broke
them in the sweet face of heaven: one that
slept in the contriving of lust, and waked to
do it: wine loved I deeply, dice dearly; and in
woman out-paramoured the Turk: false of
heart, light of ear, bloody of hand; hog in
sloth, fox in stealth, wolf in greediness, dog in
madness, lion in prey. Let not the creaking
of shoes nor the rustling of silks betray thy
poor heart to woman: keep thy foot out of

29. bide, endure. 31. loop'd and window'd, the two words
are synonymous, meaning "full of holes." 35. superflux,
superfluity (i.e., what pomp does not need). 37. Fathom,
etc., Tom pretends to be a sailor, taking soundings
in a storm at sea. 54-5. knives . . . pillow, i.e., tempted
him to commit suicide. 55. pew, a gallery of a house,
not a church pew. 58. course, chase. 62. taking, infection. 63. there . . . him, i.e., he snatches at vermin.

69. pendulous, overhanging. 72. subdued, reduced; nature,
i.e., man's nature. 75. mercy . . . flesh, Edgar has stuck
thorns or skewers into his flesh. 77. pelican daughters, it
was believed that young pelicans fed on their mother's
blood. 78. Pillicock, suggested by pelican, meant darling.
84. commit, i.e., commit adultery. 88-9. gloves . . . cap,
a gallant often wore his lady's glove in his hat. 94. out-
paramoured, had more mistresses than; the Turk, the
Sultan. 95. light of ear, foolishly credulous of evil gossip.

brothels, thy hand out of plackets, thy pen from lenders' books, and defy the foul fiend. 101

Still through the hawthorn blows the cold wind:

Says suum, mun, ha, no, nonny.

Dolphin my boy, my boy, sessa! let him trot by. [*Storm still.*

LEAR. Why, thou wert better in thy grave than to answer with thy uncovered body this extremity of the skies. Is man no more than this? Consider him well. Thou owest the worm no silk, the beast no hide, the sheep no wool, the cat no perfume. Ha! here's three 110 on's are sophisticated! Thou art the thing itself: unaccommodated man is no more but such a poor, bare, forked animal as thou art. Off, off, you lendings! come, unbutton 114 here. [*Tearing off his clothes.*

FOOL. Prithee, nuncle, be contented; 'tis a naughty night to swim in. Now a little fire in a wild field were like an old lecher's heart; a small spark, all the rest on 's body cold. Look, here comes a walking fire. 119

[*Enter* GLOUCESTER, *with a torch.*]

EDG. This is the foul fiend Flibbertigibbet: he begins at curfew, and walks till the first cock; he gives the web and the pin, squints the eye, and makes the hare-lip; mildews the white wheat, and hurts the poor creature of earth.

Saint Withold footed thrice the 'old; 125
He met the night-mare, and her nine-fold;
   Bid her alight,
   And her troth plight,
And, aroint thee, witch, aroint thee!

KENT. How fares your grace? 130

LEAR. What's he?

KENT. Who's there? What is 't you seek?

GLOU. What are you there? Your names?

EDG. Poor Tom; that eats the swimming frog, the toad, the tadpole, the wall-newt 135 and the water; that in the fury of his heart,

when the foul fiend rages, eats cow-dung for sallets; swallows the old rat and the ditch-dog; drinks the green mantle of the standing pool; who is whipped from tithing to tithing, and stock-punished, and imprisoned; who hath had three suits to his back, six shirts to his body, horse to ride, and weapon to wear; 143

   But mice and rats, and such small deer,
   Have been Tom's food for seven long year.

Beware my follower. Peace, Smulkin; peace, thou fiend!

GLOU. What, hath your grace no better company?

EDG. The prince of darkness is a gentleman:

Modo he's call'd, and Mahu.

GLOU. Our flesh and blood is grown so vile, my lord, 150
That it doth hate what gets it.

EDG. Poor Tom's a-cold.

GLOU. Go in with me: my duty cannot suffer
To obey in all your daughters' hard commands:
Though their injunction be to bar my doors,
And let this tyrannous night take hold upon you, 156
Yet have I ventured to come seek you out,
And bring you where both fire and food is ready.

LEAR. First let me talk with this philosopher.
What is the cause of thunder? 160

KENT. Good my lord, take his offer; go into the house.

LEAR. I'll talk a word with this same learned Theban.
What is your study?

EDG. How to prevent the fiend, and to kill vermin. 164

LEAR. Let me ask you one word in private.

KENT. Importune him once more to go, my lord;
His wits begin to unsettle.

GLOU. Canst thou blame him? [*Storm still.*]

99. plackets, slits in petticoats. 103. Dolphin, my boy, reference to a ballad ridiculing the French Dauphin; sessa, hurry, go it. 106. answer, oppose. 107. extremity . . . skies, violence of the storm. 110. cat, civet cat. 112. unaccommodated man, man unprovided with clothes and other furnishings of civilization. 114. lendings, lent by art to the natural man. 116. naughty, very wicked. 122. web and the pin, old term for "cataract." 124. white, i.e., ripening. 125. Withold, i.e., St. Vitalis; footed, walked across; old, wold, an upland plain. 126. night-mare, a demon; nine-fold, nine offspring. 128. her troth plight, pledge her faith (to do no harm). 129. aroint, begone. 130. grace, majesty. 135-6. wall . . . water, the wall lizard and the water lizard. 137. sallets, salads. 139. mantle, scum; standing, stagnant. 140. tithing to tithing, parish to parish. 139-40. stock-punished, put in the stocks. 144. deer, animal. 146. follower, attendant friend. 151. gets, begets. 153. suffer, permit me. 159. philosopher, scientist. 162. Theban, i.e., Greek philosopher. 163. study, specialty. 164. prevent, forestall.

His daughters seek his death; ah, that good
    Kent!
He said it would be thus, poor banish'd man!
Thou say'st the king grows mad; I'll tell thee,
    friend,   170
I am almost mad myself: I had a son,
Now outlaw'd from my blood; he sought my
    life,
But lately, very late: I loved him, friend:
No father his son dearer: truth to tell thee,
The grief hath crazed my wits. What a night's
    this!   175
I do beseech your grace,—

LEAR.   O, cry you mercy, sir.
Noble philosopher, your company.

EDG. Tom's a-cold.

GLOU. In, fellow, there, into the hovel: keep
    thee warm.

LEAR. Come, let's in all.

KENT.   This way, my lord.

LEAR.   With him;
I will keep still with my philosopher.   181

KENT. Good my lord, soothe him; let him
    take the fellow.

GLOU. Take him you on.

KENT. Sirrah, come on; go along with us.

LEAR. Come, good Athenian.   185

GLOU. No words, no words: hush.

EDG. Child Rowland to the dark tower came,
    His word was still,—Fie, foh, and fum,
      I smell the blood of a British man.
                     [*Exeunt.*

SCENE V. GLOUCESTER'S *castle.*

[*Enter* CORNWALL *and* EDMUND.]

CORN. I will have my revenge ere I depart
his house.

EDM. How, my lord, I may be censured,
that nature thus gives way to loyalty, something fears me to think of.   5

CORN. I now perceive, it was not altogether your brother's evil disposition made
him seek his death; but a provoking merit,
set a-work by a reproveable badness in himself.   9

EDM. How malicious is my fortune, that I
must repent to be just! This is the letter he
spoke of, which approves him an intelligent
party to the advantages of France. O heavens!
that this treason were not, or not I the de-
tector!   14

CORN. Go with me to the duchess.

EDM. If the matter of this paper be certain, you have mighty business in hand.

CORN. True or false, it hath made thee
earl of Gloucester. Seek out where thy father
is, that he may be ready for our apprehension.   20

EDM. [*Aside*] If I find him comforting the
king, it will stuff his suspicion more fully.—I
will persevere in my course of loyalty, though
the conflict be sore between that and my
blood.   24

CORN. I will lay trust upon thee; and thou
shalt find a dearer father in my love. [*Exeunt.*

SCENE VI. *A chamber in a farmhouse
adjoining the castle.*

[*Enter* GLOUCESTER, LEAR, KENT, FOOL, *and*
EDGAR.]

GLOU. Here is better than the open air;
take it thankfully. I will piece out the comfort with what addition I can: I will not be
long from you.

KENT. All the power of his wits have given
way to his impatience: the gods reward your
kindness!   [*Exit* GLOUCESTER. 6

EDG. Frateretto calls me; and tells me Nero
is an angler in the lake of darkness. Pray,
innocent, and beware the foul fiend.

FOOL. Prithee, nuncle, tell me whether a
madman be a gentleman or a yeoman? 11

LEAR. A king, a king!

FOOL. No, he's a yeoman that has a gentleman to his son; for he's a mad yeoman that
sees his son a gentleman before him. 15

LEAR. To have a thousand with red burn-
    ing spits
Come hissing in upon 'em,—

176. cry you mercy, beg your pardon (for not paying attention). 181. still, always. 182. soothe, humor. 187.
Child, a candidate for knighthood; Rowland, Charle-
magne's nephew and legendary hero. The line is probably
a snatch from a lost ballad. Scene v: 3. censured,
judged. 4-5. something fears me, I am somewhat frightened. 8. provoking merit, i.e., the fact that your father

deserved to die also incited him. 9. himself, i.e., Gloucester. 11. just, righteous. 12. approves, proves. 12-3.
intelligent party, a spy. 13. France, King of France.
20. apprehension, arrest. 21. comforting, giving aid and
comfort. 24. blood, natural instincts. Scene vi: 7.
Frateretto, the name of a fiend. 9. innocent, simpleton.
11. yeoman, a small landed proprietor, in rank lower than
a gentleman. 15. before him, before he is one.

EDG. The foul fiend bites my back.

FOOL. He's mad that trusts in the tameness of a wolf, a horse's health, a boy's love, or a whore's oath.   21

LEAR. It shall be done; I will arraign them straight.

[*To* EDGAR] Come, sit thou here, most learned justicer;

[*To the* FOOL] Thou, sapient sir, sit here. Now, you she foxes!

EDG. Look, where he stands and glares!   25
Wantest thou eyes at trial, madam?

Come o'er the bourn, Bessy, to me,—

FOOL. Her boat hath a leak,
        And she must not speak
    Why she dares not come over to thee.   30

EDG. The foul fiend haunts poor Tom in the voice of a nightingale. Hopdance cries in Tom's belly for two white herring. Croak not, black angel; I have no food for thee.

KENT. How do you, sir? Stand you not so amazed: 35
Will you lie down and rest upon the cushions?

LEAR. I'll see their trial first. Bring in the evidence.

[*To* EDGAR] Thou robed man of justice, take thy place;

[*To the* FOOL] And thou, his yoke-fellow of equity,

Bench by his side: [*To* KENT] you are o' the commission,   40
Sit you too.

EDG. Let us deal justly.

    Sleepest or wakest thou, jolly shepherd?
        Thy sheep be in the corn;
    And for one blast of thy minikin mouth,
        Thy sheep shall take no harm.   46
Pur! the cat is gray.

LEAR. Arraign her first; 'tis Goneril. I here take my oath before this honourable assembly, she kicked the poor king her father.   50

FOOL. Come hither, mistress. Is your name Goneril?

LEAR. She cannot deny it.

FOOL. Cry you mercy, I took you for a joint-stool.   55

LEAR. And here's another, whose warp'd looks proclaim
What store her heart is made on. Stop her there!
Arms, arms, sword, fire! Corruption in the place!
False justicer, why hast thou let her 'scape?

EDG. Bless thy five wits!   60

KENT. O pity! Sir, where is the patience now,
That you so oft have boasted to retain?

EDG. [*Aside*] My tears begin to take his part so much,
They'll mar my counterfeiting.

LEAR. The little dogs and all,   65
Tray, Blanch, and Sweet-heart, see, they bark at me.

EDG. Tom will throw his head at them. Avaunt, you curs!

    Be thy mouth or black or white,
    Tooth that poisons if it bite;   70
    Mastiff, greyhound, mongrel grim,
    Hound or spaniel, brach or lym,
    Or bobtail tike or trundle-tail,
    Tom will make them weep and wail:
    For, with throwing thus my head,   75
    Dogs leap the hatch, and all are fled.
Do de, de, de. Sessa! Come, march to wakes and fairs and market-towns. Poor Tom, thy horn is dry.   79

LEAR. Then let them anatomize Regan; see what breeds about her heart. Is there any cause in nature that makes these hard hearts? [*To* EDGAR] You, sir, I entertain for one of my hundred; only I do not like the fashion of your garments: you will say they are Persian attire; but let them be changed.

KENT. Now, good my lord, lie here and rest awhile.   88

LEAR. Make no noise, make no noise; draw the curtains: so, so, so. We'll go to supper i' the morning. So, so, so.   91

FOOL. And I'll go to bed at noon.

[*Re-enter* GLOUCESTER.]

GLOU. Come hither, friend: where is the king my master?

KENT. Here, sir; but trouble him not, his wits are gone.

GLOU. Good friend, O prithee, take him in thy arms;   95
I have o'erheard a plot of death upon him:
There is a litter ready; lay him in 't,
And drive towards Dover, friend, where thou shalt meet
Both welcome and protection. Take up thy master: 99
If thou shouldst dally half an hour, his life,
With thine, and all that offer to defend him,
Stand in assurèd loss: take up, take up;
And follow me, that will to some provision
Give thee quick conduct.

KENT.   Oppressèd nature sleeps;
This rest might yet have balm'd thy broken sinews,   105
Which, if convenience will not allow,
Stand in hard cure. [*To the* FOOL] Come, help to bear thy master;
Thou must not stay behind.

GLOU.   Come, come, away.
[*Exeunt all but* EDGAR.

EDG. When we our betters see bearing our woes,
We scarcely think our miseries our foes.   110
Who alone suffers suffers most i' the mind,
Leaving free things and happy shows behind:
But then the mind much sufferance doth o'erskip,
When grief hath mates, and bearing fellow-ship.
How light and portable my pain seems now,   115
When that which makes me bend makes the king bow,
He childed as I father'd! Tom, away!
Mark the high noises; and thyself bewray,
When false opinion, whose wrong thought defiles thee,

In thy just proof, repeals and reconciles thee.
What will hap more to-night, safe 'scape the king!   121
Lurk, lurk.   [*Exit.*

SCENE VII. GLOUCESTER'S *castle.*

[*Enter* CORNWALL, REGAN, GONERIL, EDMUND, *and* SERVANTS.]

CORN. Post speedily to my lord your husband; show him this letter: the army of France is landed. Seek out the villain Gloucester.   [*Exeunt some of the* SERVANTS.

REG. Hang him instantly.

GON. Pluck out his eyes.

CORN. Leave him to my displeasure. Edmund, keep you our sister company: the revenges we are bound to take upon your traitorous father are not fit for your beholding. Advise the duke, where you are going, to a most festinate preparation: we are   10
bound to the like. Our posts shall be swift and intelligent betwixt us. Farewell, dear sister: farewell, my lord of Gloucester.

[*Enter* OSWALD.]

How now! where's the king?   14

OSW. My lord of Gloucester hath convey'd him hence:
Some five or six and thirty of his knights,
Hot questrists after him, met him at gate;
Who, with some other of the lords dependants,
Are gone with him towards Dover; where they boast   19
To have well-armèd friends.

CORN.   Get horses for your mistress.

GON. Farewell, sweet lord, and sister.

CORN. Edmund, farewell.
[*Exeunt* GONERIL, EDMUND, *and* OSWALD.]
                                   Go seek the traitor Gloucester,
Pinion him like a thief, bring him before us.
[*Exeunt other* SERVANTS.]
Though well we may not pass upon his life
Without the form of justice, yet our power

---

96. upon, against. 100. dally, delay. 102. Stand ... loss, are sure to be lost. 103. provision, i.e., for safety. 105. balm'd ... sinews, healed your racked nerves. 107. Stand ... cure, are hard to cure. 112. free, carefree; happy shows, appearances of happiness. 113. sufferance, suffering; o'er-skip, escape. 114. bearing, i.e., of sorrow. 115. portable, endurable. 117. childed ... father'd, having children like my father (in cruelty). 118. high noises, sounds of discord among the high and mighty; bewray, you reveal yourself, i.e., put off your disguise. 120. In ... proof,

on proof that you are guiltless; repeals, restores (i.e., to favor). 121. what, whatever. 122. Lurk, hide. Scene vii: 10. to ... preparation, to make a most hasty preparation (for war). 11. bound to the like, getting ready for the like preparation; posts, messengers. 12. intelligent, carry information. 13. Lord of Gloucester, i.e., Edmund, who has been given the title as a reward for his treachery. 15. Lord of Gloucester, the old Earl. 17. questrists, searchers. 23. pinion, i.e., bind his elbows together. 24. pass, pass judgment.

Shall do a courtesy to our wrath, which men
May blame, but not control. Who's there?
   the traitor?

[Enter GLOUCESTER, *brought in by two or
three.]*

REG. Ingrateful fox! 'tis he.
CORN. Bind fast his corky arms.
GLOU. What mean your graces? Good my
   friends, consider   30
You are my guests: do me no foul play,
   friends.
CORN. Bind him, I say.
                  *[*SERVANTS *bind him.*
REG.   Hard, hard. O filthy traitor!
GLOU. Unmerciful lady as you are, I'm none.
CORN. To this chair bind him. Villain,
   thou shalt find—   *[*REGAN *Plucks his
                          beard.*
GLOU. By the kind gods, 'tis most ignobly
   done   35
To pluck me by the beard.
REG. So white, and such a traitor!
GLOU.   Naughty lady,
These hairs, which thou dost ravish from my
   chin,
Will quicken, and accuse thee: I am your
   host:
With robbers' hands my hospitable fa-
   vours   40
You should not ruffle thus. What will you do?
CORN. Come, sir, what letters had you late
   from France?
REG. Be simple answerer, for we know the
   truth.
CORN. And what confederacy have you with
   the traitors
Late footed in the kingdom?   45
REG. To whose hands have you sent the
   lunatic king?
Speak.
GLOU.   I have a letter guessingly set
   down,
Which came from one that's of a neutral
   heart,
And not from one opposed.
CORN.   Cunning.

REG.   And false.
CORN. Where hast thou sent the king?   50
GLOU. To Dover.
REG. Wherefore to Dover? Wast thou not
   charged at peril—
CORN. Wherefore to Dover? Let him first
   answer that.
GLOU. I am tied to the stake, and I must
   stand the course.
REG. Wherefore to Dover, sir?   55
GLOU. Because I would not see thy cruel
   nails
Pluck out his poor old eyes; nor thy fierce
   sister
In his anointed flesh stick boarish fangs.
The sea, with such a storm as his bare head
In hell-black night endured, would have
   buoy'd up,   60
And quench'd the stelled fires:
Yet, poor old heart, he help the heavens to
   rain.
If wolves had at thy gate howl'd that stern
   time,
Thou shouldst have said "Good porter, turn
   the key,"
All cruels else subscribed: but I shall see   65
The wingèd vengeance overtake such chil-
   dren.
CORN. See 't shalt thou never. Fellows,
   hold the chair.
Upon these eyes of thine I'll set my foot.
GLOU. He that will think to live till he be
   old,
Give me some help! O cruel! O you gods! 70
REG. One side will mock another; the other
   too.
CORN. If you see vengeance,—
FIRST SERV.   Hold your hand,
   my lord:
I have served you ever since I was a child;
But better service have I never done you
Than now to bid you hold.
REG.   How now, you dog!
FIRST SERV. If you did wear a beard upon
   your chin,   76
I'd shake it on this quarrel. What do you
   mean?

---

26. **do a courtesy,** act in accordance with. 29. **corky,** withered. 37. **Naughty,** wicked. 39. **quicken,** come to life. 40. **hospitable favours,** the features of your host. 41. **ruffle,** treat with violence. 43. **simple,** straightforward. 45. **footed,** landed. 52. **at peril,** under peril (of death). 54. **course,** attack (of the dogs in bear-baiting). 58. **anointed,** i.e., with the consecrated oil at his coronation. 60. **buoy'd up,** heaved aloft. 61. **stelled fires,** the fires of the stars. 62. **holp,** helped. 63. **howl'd,** i.e., for shelter. 65. **All . . . subscribed,** all other cruel creatures except you gave way (to their need for shelter). 71. **one . . . another,** i.e., one good eye will mock the other blind one. 77. **quarrel,** this cause (over which I quarrel with you).

CORN. My villain!   [*They draw and fight.*
FIRST SERV. Nay, then, come on, and take
    the chance of anger.
REG. Give me thy sword. A peasant stand
    up thus!   80
        [*Takes a sword, and runs at him behind.*
FIRST SERV. O, I am slain! My lord, you
    have one eye left
To see some mischief on him. O!
                                        [*Dies.*
CORN. Lest it see more, prevent it. Out,
    vile jelly!
Where is thy lustre now?
    GLOU. All dark and comfortless. Where's
    my son Edmund?   85
Edmund, enkindle all the sparks of nature,
To quit this horrid act.
    REG.   Out, treacherous villain!
Thou call'st on him that hates thee: it was he
That made the overture of thy treasons to
    us;
Who is too good to pity thee.   90
    GLOU. O my follies! then Edgar was abused.
Kind gods, forgive me that, and prosper him!
    REG. Go thrust him out at gates, and let
    him smell
His way to Dover. [*Exit one with* GLOUCES-
    TER.] How is 't, my lord? how look you?
    CORN. I have received a hurt: follow me,
    lady.   95
Turn out that eyeless villain; throw this
    slave
Upon the dunghill. Regan, I bleed apace:
Untimely comes this hurt: give me your arm.
        [*Exit* CORNWALL, *led by* REGAN.
SEC. SERV. I'll never care what wickedness
    I do,
If this man come to good.
    THIRD SERV.   If she live long,   100
And in the end meet the old course of
    death,
Women will all turn monsters.
    SEC. SERV. Let's follow the old earl, and get
    the Bedlam
To lead him where he would: his roguish
    madness
Allows itself to any thing.   105

THIRD SERV. Go thou: I'll fetch some flax
    and whites of eggs
To apply to his bleeding face. Now, heaven
    help him!   [*Exeunt severally.*

ACT FOUR

SCENE I. *The heath.*

[*Enter* EDGAR.]

EDG. Yet better thus, and known to be
    contemn'd,
Than still contemn'd and flatter'd. To be
    worst,
The lowest and most dejected thing of for-
    tune,
Stands still in esperance, lives not in fear:
The lamentable change is from the best;   5
The worst returns to laughter. Welcome,
    then,
Thou unsubstantial air that I embrace!
The wretch that thou hast blown unto the
    worst
Owes nothing to thy blasts. But who comes
    here?

[*Enter* GLOUCESTER, *led by an* OLD MAN.]

My father, poorly led? World, world, O
    world!   10
But that thy strange mutations make us hate
    thee,
Life would not yield to age.
    OLD MAN. O, my good lord, I have been
your tenant, and your father's tenant, these
fourscore years.   15
    GLOU. Away, get thee away; good friend,
    be gone:
Thy comforts can do me no good at all;
Thee they may hurt.
    OLD MAN. Alack, sir, you cannot see your
way.
    GLOU. I have no way, and therefore want
    no eyes;   20

---

78. villain, bondman, serf. 82. mischief, harm. 83. prevent,
forestall. 87. quit, repay, revenge. 89. overture, dis-
closure. 91. abused, deceived (by Edmund). 92. that, i.e.,
my treatment of Edgar. 97. apace, fast. 98. Untimely,
inopportunely. 102. Women . . . monsters, because they
will know there is no divine justice. 103. Bedlam, lunatic,
i.e., Edgar. 105. Allows . . . thing, permits him to do

anything with impunity. Act IV, Scene i: 1. contemn'd,
despised. 4. esperance, hope. 6. returns to laughter,
changes to happiness. 10. poorly led, led by one poor old
man, instead of his former attendants. 11. mutations,
changes (of fortune). 20. I . . . way, i.e., no course in
life is left me.

I stumbled when I saw: full oft 'tis seen,
Our means secure us, and our mere defects
Prove our commodities. O dear son Edgar,
The food of thy abusèd father's wrath!
Might I but live to see thee in my touch, 25
I'ld say I had eyes again!

OLD MAN. How now! Who's there?

EDG. [*Aside*] O gods! Who is 't can say "I
am at the worst"?
I am worse than e'er I was.

OLD MAN. 'Tis poor mad Tom.

EDG. [*Aside*] And worse I may be yet: the
worst is not
So long as we can say "This is the worst." 30

OLD MAN. Fellow, where goest?

GLOU. Is it a beggar-man?

OLD MAN. Madman and beggar too.

GLOU. He has some reason, else he could
not beg.
I' the last night's storm I such a fellow saw;
Which made me think a man a worm: my
son 35
Came then into my mind; and yet my mind
Was then scarce friends with him: I have
heard more since.
As flies to wanton boys, are we to the gods,
They kill us for their sport.

EDG. [*Aside*] How should this be?
Bad is the trade that must play fool to sorrow, 40
Angering itself and others.—Bless thee, master!

GLOU. Is that the naked fellow?

OLD MAN. Ay, my lord.

GLOU. Then, prithee, get thee gone: if, for
my sake,
Thou wilt o'ertake us, hence a mile or twain,
I' the way toward Dover, do it for ancient
love; 45
And bring some covering for this naked soul,
Who I'll entreat to lead me.

OLD MAN. Alack, sir, he is mad.

GLOU. 'Tis the times' plague, when mad-
men lead the blind.
Do as I bid thee, or rather do thy pleasure;
Above the rest, be gone. 50

OLD MAN. I'll bring him the best 'parel that
I have,
Come on 't what will. [*Exit.*

GLOU. Sirrah, naked fellow,—

EDG. Poor Tom's a-cold. [*Aside*] I cannot
daub it further.

GLOU. Come hither, fellow. 55

EDG. [*Aside*] And yet I must.—Bless thy
sweet eyes, they bleed.

GLOU. Knowst thou the way to Dover?

EDG. Both stile and gate, horse-way and
foot-path. Poor Tom hath been scared out of
his good wits: bless thee, good man's son,
from the foul fiend! five fiends have been in
poor Tom at once; of lust, as Obidicut;
Hobbididance, prince of dumbness; Mahu, of
stealing; Modo, of murder; Flibbertigibbet,
of mopping and mowing, who since possesses
chambermaids and waiting-women. So, bless
thee, master! 66

GLOU. Here, take this purse, thou whom
the heavens' plagues
Have humbled to all strokes: that I am
wretched
Makes thee the happier: heavens, deal so
still!
Let the superfluous and lust-dieted man, 70
That slaves your ordinance, that will not see
Because he doth not feel, feel your power
quickly;
So distribution should undo excess,
And each man have enough. Dost thou know
Dover?

EDG. Ay, master. 75

GLOU. There is a cliff, whose high and bend-
ing head
Looks fearfully in the confinèd deep
Bring me but to the very brim of it,
And I'll repair the misery thou dost bear
With something rich about me: from that
place 80
I shall no leading need.

EDG. Give me thy arm:
Poor Tom shall lead thee. [*Exeunt.*

22. **Our . . . secure us**, prosperity makes us careless and overconfident. 22-3. **our mere . . . commodities**, our very depriva-
tions prove to be benefits. 24. **food**, i.e., object; **abused**, deceived. 38. **wanton**, playful. 41. **Angering**, distressing. 48.
times' plague, world's calamity. 49. **thy pleasure**, what you
wish. 50. **above the rest**, above all. 54. **daub it**, dissem-
ble. 65. **mopping and mowing**, grimacing and making
faces; **since**, i.e., since a long time ago. 68. **Have . . .
strokes**, have humbled you so that you accept every sort
of adversity. 69. **deal so still**, i.e., continue to treat men
overconfident in their prosperity as you have me. 70.
superfluous, the man who has all that he needs, all that he
lusts after. 71. **slaves your ordinance**, that makes heaven's
will subservient to his own. 73. **distribution**, distributive
justice; **undo**, correct. 77. **fearfully**, in a way to arouse
terror in anyone who looks over it down to the sea;
confined deep, i.e., the Straits of Dover; **confined**, shut in.

SCENE II. *Before the* DUKE OF ALBANY'S *palace.*

[*Enter* GONERIL *and* EDMUND.]

GON. Welcome, my lord: I marvel our mild husband
Not met us on the way.

[*Enter* OSWALD.]

                Now, where's your master?
OSW. Madam, within; but never man so changed.
I told him of the army that was landed;
He smiled at it: I told him you were coming;
His answer was "The worse:" of Gloucester's
    treachery,   6
And of the loyal service of his son,
When I inform'd him, then he call'd me sot,
And told me I had turn'd the wrong side out:
What most he should dislike seems pleasant
    to him;   10
What like, offensive.
    GON. [*To* EDM.] Then shall you go no further.
It is the cowish terror of his spirit,
That dares not undertake: he'll not feel
    wrongs
Which tie him to an answer. Our wishes on
    the way
May prove effects. Back, Edmund, to my
    brother;   15
Hasten his musters and conduct his powers:
I must change arms at home, and give the
    distaff
Into my husband's hands. This trusty servant
Shall pass between us: ere long you are like
    to hear,
If you dare venture in your own behalf, 20
A mistress's command. Wear this; spare
    speech;   [*Giving a favor.*]
Decline your head: this kiss, if it durst speak,
Would stretch thy spirits up into the air:
Conceive, and fare thee well.
    EDM. Yours in the ranks of death.
    GON.   My most dear Gloucester!
                      [*Exit* EDMUND.]

O, the difference of man and man!   26
To thee a woman's services are due:
My fool usurps my body.
    OSW.   Madam, here comes my lord.
                      [*Exit.*]

[*Enter* ALBANY.]

    GON. I have been worth the whistle.
    ALB.   O Goneril!
You are not worth the dust which the rude
    wind   30
Blows in your face. I fear your disposition:
That nature, which contemns it origin,
Cannot be border'd certain in itself;
She that herself will sliver and disbranch
From her material sap, perforce must wither
And come to deadly use.   36
    GON. No more; the text is foolish.
    ALB. Wisdom and goodness to the vile seem
    vile:
Filths savour but themselves. What have you
    done?
Tigers, not daughters, what have you per-
    form'd?   40
A father, and a gracious agèd man,
Whose reverence even the head-lugg'd bear
    would lick,
Most barbarous, most degenerate! have you
    madded.
Could my good brother suffer you to do it?
A man, a prince, by him so benefited!   45
If that the heavens do not their visible spirits
Send quickly down to tame these vile of-
    fences,
It will come,
Humanity must perforce prey on itself,
Like monsters of the deep.
    GON.   Milk-liver'd man! 50
That bear'st a cheek for blows, a head for
    wrongs:
Who hast not in thy brows an eye discerning
Thine honour from thy suffering; that not
    know'st
Fools do those villains pity who are punish'd

Scene ii: 8. sot, fool. 9. turn'd . . . out, completely misin-
terpreted the situation. 12. cowish, cowardly. 13. undertake, take the initiative. 14. on the way, expressed on our
way here. 15. prove effects, come to pass. 16. powers,
forces. 17. change, exchange; arms, emblems of our professions. 24. Conceive, understand. 28. fool, i.e., fool of a
husband; usurps, possesses without right. 29. the whistle,
whistling for. 31. disposition, temperament. 33. Cannot
. . . itself, can have no sure restraints in its own nature.
34. sliver and disbranch, both mean "break off." 35. material sap, its nourishing substance (i.e., the sap of the
tree). 36. deadly use, i.e., to destruction. 39. Filths . . .
themselves, everything tastes filthy to the filthy. 41.
gracious, kindly. 42. head-lugg'd, pulled along by the
head, showing he is surly. 43. madded, driven insane.
46. visible, in visible form. 48. It will come, this will be
the result. 50. milk-liver'd, white-livered, cowardly. 52.
discerning, able to distinguish. 53. Thine honour, things
you can endure with honor. 54. Fools, i.e., only fools.

Ere they have done their mischief. Where's
  thy drum?   55
France spreads his banners in our noiseless
  land,
With plumèd helm thy state begins to threat;
Whiles thou, a moral fool, sit'st still, and
  criest
"Alack, why does he so?"
ALB.   See thyself, devil!
Proper deformity seems not in the fiend   60
So horrid as in woman.
  GON.   O vain fool!
ALB. Thou changèd and self-cover'd thing,
  for shame,
Be-monster not thy feature. Were 't my fit-
  ness
To let these hands obey my blood,
They art apt enough to dislocate and tear 65
Thy flesh and bones: howe'er thou art a fiend,
A woman's shape doth shield thee.
  GON. Marry, your manhood now—

[*Enter a* MESSENGER.]

ALB. What news?
MESS. O, my good lord, the Duke of Corn-
  wall's dead;   70
Slain by his servant, going to put out
The other eye of Gloucester.
  ALB.   Gloucester's eyes!
MESS. A servant that he bred, thrill'd with
  remorse,
Opposed against the act, bending his sword
To his great master; who, thereat enraged, 75
Flew on him, and amongst them fell'd him
  dead;
But not without that harmful stroke, which
  since
Hath pluck'd him after.
  ALB.   This shows you are above,
You justicers, that these our nether crimes
So speedily can venge! But, O poor Glouces-
  ter!   80
Lost he his other eye?
  MESS.   Both, both, my lord.
This letter, madam, craves a speedy answer;
'Tis from your sister.

GON. [*Aside*] One way I like this well;
But being widow, and my Gloucester with
  her,   85
May all the building in my fancy pluck
Upon my hateful life: another way,
The news is not so tart.—I'll read, and answer.
                                      [*Exit.*
ALB. Where was his son when they did
  take his eyes?
MESS. Come with my lady hither.
ALB.   He is not here.   90
MESS. No, my good lord; I met him back
  again.
ALB. Knows he the wickedness?
MESS. Ay, my good lord; 'twas he inform'd
  against him;
And quit the house on purpose, that their
  punishment
Might have the freer course.
  ALB.   Gloucester, I live 95
To thank thee for the love thou show'dst the
  king,
And to revenge thine eyes. Come hither,
  friend:
Tell me what more thou know'st. [*Exeunt.*

SCENE III. *The French camp near
            Dover.*

[*Enter* KENT *and a* GENTLEMAN.]

KENT. Why the King of France is so suddenly gone back, know you the reason?
GENT. Something he left imperfect in the
state, which since his coming forth is thought
of; which imports to the kingdom so much
fear and danger that his personal return was
most required and necessary.   7
KENT. Who hath he left behind him general?
GENT. The Marshal of France, Monsieur
La Far.   10
KENT. Did your letters pierce the queen to
any demonstration of grief?
GENT. Ay, sir; she took them, read them in
my presence;

And now and then an ample tear trill'd down
Her delicate cheek; it seem'd she was a queen
Over her passion; who, most rebel-like,   16
Sought to be king o'er her.
    KENT.   O, then it moved her.
    GENT. Not to a rage: patience and sorrow strove
Who should express her goodliest. You have seen
Sunshine and rain at once: her smiles and tears   20
Were like a better way: those happy smilets,
That play'd on her ripe lip, seem'd not to know
What guests were in her eyes; which parted thence,
As pearls from diamonds dropp'd. In brief,
Sorrow would be a rarity most beloved,   25
If all could so become it.
    KENT.   Made she no verbal question?
    GENT. 'Faith, once or twice she heaved the name of "father"
Pantingly forth, as if it press'd her heart;
Cried "Sisters! sisters! Shame of ladies! sisters!
Kent! father! sisters! What, i' the storm? i' the night?   30
Let pity not be believed!" There she shook
The holy water from her heavenly eyes,
And clamour moisten'd: then away she started
To deal with grief alone.
    KENT.   It is the stars,
The stars above us, govern our conditions;   35
Else one self mate and mate could not beget
Such different issues. You spoke not with her since?
    GENT. No.
    KENT. Was this before the king return'd?
    GENT.   No, since.
    KENT. Well, sir, the poor distressèd Lear's i' the town;   40
Who sometime, in his better tune, remembers
What we are come about, and by no means
Will yield to see his daughter.

---

14. trill'd, trickled. 16. passion, emotion, i.e., grief. 18. rage, outburst (of grief). 19. express her goodliest, give her the most beautiful expression. 21. like . . . way, like mingled sunshine and rain, only more beautiful; smilets, little smiles. 23. which, i.e., the tears. 26. all . . . become it, it were so becoming to all (as to her); Made . . . question? Did she say nothing? question, speech. 31. believed, believed in. 33. clamour moisten'd, moistened her cries of grief (by weeping). 35. conditions, temperaments. 36. one self, one and the same. 41. sometime, sometimes; better tune, more lucid intervals. 43. yield, assent. 44. sovereign, overmastering; elbows, stands at his elbow. 45. benediction, parting blessing. 46. foreign casualties,

GENT.   Why, good sir?
    KENT. A sovereign shame so elbows him: his own unkindness,
That stripp'd her from his benediction, turn'd her   45
To foreign casualties, gave her dear rights
To his dog-hearted daughters, these things sting
His mind so venomously, that burning shame
Detains him from Cordelia.
    GENT.   Alack, poor gentleman!
    KENT. Of Albany's and Cornwall's powers you heard not?   50
    GENT. 'Tis so, they are afoot.
    KENT. Well, sir, I'll bring you to our master Lear,
And leave you to attend him: some dear cause
Will in concealment wrap me up awhile;
When I am known aright, you shall not grieve
Lending me this acquaintance. I pray you, go   56
Along with me.   [Exeunt.

SCENE IV. *The same. A tent.*

[*Enter, with drum and colours,* CORDELIA,
DOCTOR, *and* SOLDIERS.]

    COR. Alack, 'tis he: why, he was met even now
As mad as the vex'd sea; singing aloud;
Crown'd with rank fumiter and furrow-weeds,
With bur-docks, hemlock, nettles, cuckoo-flowers,
Darnel, and all the idle weeds that grow   5
In our sustaining corn. A century send forth;
Search every acre in the high-grown field,
And bring him to our eye. [*Exit an* OFFICER.]
          What can man's wisdom
In the restoring his bereavèd sense?
He that helps him take all my outward worth.
    DOCT. There is means, madam: 11
Our foster-nurse of nature is repose,
The which he lacks; that to provoke in him,

---

hazards in a foreign land. 50. powers, troops. 53. dear, important. 56. Lending me, for having granted me. Scene iv: 3. rank . . . furrow-weeds, luxuriant fumitory (earth-smoke) and weeds growing in furrows of a plowed field. 4. cuckoo-flowers, flowers blooming when the cuckoo is abroad, i.e., in April and May—perhaps cowslips. 5. idle, useless. 6. sustaining corn, wheat that gives sustenance; century, detail of a hundred men. 8. What . . . wisdom, what can science do. 10. worth, property. 12. Our foster . . . of, the nurse that fosters our nature. 13. provoke, induce.

Are many simples operative, whose power
Will close the eye of anguish.

COR.   All blest secrets, 15
All you unpublish'd virtues of the earth,
Spring with my tears! be aidant and remediate
In the good man's distress! Seek, seek for
    him;
Lest his ungovern'd rage dissolve the life
That wants the means to lead it.

[Enter a MESSENGER.]

MESS.   News, madam; 20
The British powers are marching hitherward.
    COR. 'Tis known before; our preparation
        stands
In expectation of them. O dear father,
It is thy business that I go about;
Therefore great France 25
My mourning and important tears hath pitied.
No blown ambition doth our arms incite,
But love, dear love, and our aged father's
    right:
Soon may I hear and see him!   *[Exeunt.*

SCENE V. GLOUCESTER'S *castle.*

[Enter REGAN *and* OSWALD.]

REG. But are my brother's powers set forth?
OSW.   Ay, madam.
REG. Himself in person there?
OSW.   Madam, with much ado:
Your sister is the better soldier.
    REG. Lord Edmund spake not with your
        lord at home?
OSW. No, madam.   5
REG. What might import my sister's letter
    to him?
OSW. I know not, lady.
    REG. 'Faith, he is posted hence on serious
        matter.
It was great ignorance, Gloucester's eyes
    being out,
To let him live: where he arrives he moves 10
All hearts against us: Edmund, I think, is
    gone,
In pity of his misery, to dispatch
His nighted life; moreover, to descry

The strength o' the enemy.
    OSW. I must needs after him, madam, with
        my letter.   15
    REG. Our troops set forth to-morrow: stay
        with us;
The ways are dangerous.
    OSW.   I may not, madam:
My lady charged my duty in this business.
    REG. Why should she write to Edmund?
        Might not you
Transport her purposes by word? Belike, 20
Something—I know not what: I'll love thee
    much,
Let me unseal the letter.
    OSW.   Madam, I had rather—
    REG. I know your lady does not love her
        husband;
I am sure of that: and at her late being here
She gave strange œillades and most speaking
    looks   25
To noble Edmund. I know you are of her
    bosom.
    OSW. I, madam?
    REG. I speak in understanding; you are, I
        know 't:
Therefore I do advise you, take this note:
My lord is dead; Edmund and I have talk'd;
And more convenient is he for my hand 31
Than for your lady's: you may gather more.
If you do find him, pray you, give him this;
And when your mistress hears thus much
    from you,
I pray, desire her call her wisdom to her. 35
So, fare you well.
If you do chance to hear of that blind traitor,
Preferment falls on him that cuts him off.
    OSW. Would I could meet him, madam! I
        should show
What party I do follow.
    REG.   Fare thee well. *[Exeunt.* 40

SCENE VI. *Fields near Dover.*

[Enter GLOUCESTER, *and* EDGAR *dressed like a
peasant.*]

GLOU. When shall we come to the top of
    that same hill?

---

14. simples operative, effective medicinal herbs. 15. secrets,
private remedies. 16. unpublish'd virtues, secret efficacious
medicinal plants. 17. be . . . remediate, be helpful and
remedial. 19. rage, delirium. 20. the means, i.e., his
reason. 23. In . . . of, ready to meet. 26. important,
importunate. 27. blown, swollen. Scene v: 2. with much
ado, as a result of much effort. 6. import, mean. 8. is
posted, has ridden fast; matter, business. 9. ignorance,
stupidity. 20. Belike, probably. 25. œillades, amorous
glances. 26. of her bosom, in her confidence. 30. have
talk'd, have come to an understanding (about marrying).
31. convenient, suitable. 32. gather more, i.e., make
further references. 34. thus much, as much as I have told
you. 38. Preferment, advancement.

EDG. You do climb up it now: look, how we labour.

GLOU. Methinks the ground is even.

EDG.   Horrible steep.
Hark, do you hear the sea?

GLOU.   No, truly.

EDG. Why, then your other senses grow imperfect   5
By your eyes' anguish.

GLOU.   So may it be, indeed:
Methinks thy voice is alter'd; and thou speak'st
In better phrase and matter than thou didst.

EDG. You're much deceived: in nothing am I changed
But in my garments.

GLOU. Methinks you're better spoken.   10

EDG. Come on, sir; here's the place: stand still. How fearful
And dizzy 'tis, to cast one's eyes so low!
The crows and choughs that wing the midway air
Show scarce so gross as beetles: half way down
Hangs one that gathers samphire, dreadful trade!   15
Methinks he seems no bigger than his head:
The fishermen, that walk upon the beach,
Appear like mice; and yond tall anchoring bark,
Diminish'd to her cock; her cock, a buoy
Almost too small for sight: the murmuring surge,   20
That on the unnumber'd idle pebbles chafes,
Cannot be heard so high. I'll look no more;
Lest my brain turn, and the deficient sight
Topple down headlong.

GLOU.   Set me where you stand.

EDG. Give me your hand: you are now within a foot   25
Of the extreme verge: for all beneath the moon
Would I not leap upright.

GLOU.   Let go my hand.
Here, friend, 's another purse; in it a jewel

Well worth a poor man's taking: fairies and gods
Prosper it with thee! Go thou farther off;   30
Bid me farewell, and let me hear thee going.

EDG. Now fare you well, good sir.

GLOU.   With all my heart.

EDG. Why I do trifle thus with his despair
Is done to cure it.

GLOU. [Kneeling] O you mighty gods!
This world I do renounce, and in your sights,
Shake patiently my great affliction off: 36
If I could bear it longer, and not fall
To quarrel with your great opposeless wills,
My snuff and loathèd part of nature should
Burn itself out. If Edgar live, O, bless him!   40
Now, fellow, fare thee well. [He falls forward.

EDG.   Gone, sir: farewell.
And yet I know not how conceit may rob
The treasury of life, when life itself
Yields to the theft: had he been where he thought,
By this, had thought been past. Alive or dead?
Ho, you sir! friend! Hear you, sir! speak!   46
Thus might he pass indeed: yet he revives.
What are you, sir?

GLOU.   Away, and let me die.

EDG. Hadst thou been aught but gossamer, feathers, air,
So many fathom down precipitating,   50
Thou 'dst shiver'd like an egg: but thou dost breathe;
Hast heavy substance; bleed'st not; speak'st; art sound.
Ten masts at each make not the altitude
Which thou hast perpendicularly fell:
Thy life's a miracle. Speak yet again.   55

GLOU. But have I fall'n, or no?

EDG. From the dread summit of this chalky bourn.
Look up a-height; the shrill-gorged lark so far
Cannot be seen or heard: do but look up.

GLOU. Alack, I have no eyes.   60
Is wretchedness deprived that benefit,
To end itself by death? 'Twas yet some comfort,
When misery could beguile the tyrant's rage,
And frustrate his proud will.

Scene vi: 10. you're better spoken, i.e., you speak with more propriety. 13. choughs, crow-like birds, something like grackles. 14. gross, large. 15. samphire, an aromatic herb, gathered from the face of cliffs by men lowered by a rope. 19. cock, cock-boat, tender. 21. unnumber'd, innumerable. 21. idle, useless, barren. 23. the . . . sight, my sight failing. 24. Topple, cause me to topple. 27. upright, i.e., even straight up. 29. fairies, because they were supposed to make it increase miraculously.

38. quarrel . . . with, rebel against; opposeless, irresistible. 39. snuff, burnt and smoking wick. 42. conceit, imagination. 43. treasury of life, life's treasury. 44. yields . . . theft, i.e., death's theft of the treasury of life. 47. pass, die. 49. gossamer, floating cobweb. 53. at each, end to end. 57. bourn, boundary. 58. a-height, on high; shrill-gorged, shrill-throated. 63. beguile, cheat.

EDG. Give me your arm:
Up: so. How is 't? Feel you your legs? You
   stand. 65
  GLOU. Too well, too well.
    EDG. This is above all strangeness.
Upon the crown o' the cliff, what thing was
   that
Which parted from you?
  GLOU. A poor unfortunate beggar.
  EDG. As I stood here below, methought his
   eyes
Were two full moons; he had a thousand
   noses, 70
Horns whelk'd and waved like the enridgèd
   sea:
It was some fiend; therefore, thou happy
   father,
Think that the clearest gods, who make them
   honours
Of men's impossibilities, have preserved thee.
  GLOU. I do remember now: henceforth I'll
   bear 75
Affliction till it do cry out itself
"Enough, enough," and die. That thing you
   speak of,
I took it for a man; often 'twould say
"The fiend, the fiend:" he led me to that place.
  EDG. Bear free and patient thoughts. But
   who comes here? 80

[*Enter* LEAR, *fantastically dressed with wild
flowers.*]

The safer sense will ne'er accomodate
His master thus.
  LEAR. No, they cannot touch me for coining;
I am the king himself.
    EDG. O thou side-piercing sight! 85
  LEAR. Nature's above art in that respect.
There's your press-money. That fellow handles his bow like a crow-keeper: draw me a
clothier's yard. Look, look, a mouse! Peace,
peace; this piece of toasted cheese will 90
do 't. There's my gauntlet; I'll prove it on a
giant. Bring up the brown bills. O, well
flown, bird! i' the clout, i' the clout: hewgh!
Give the word.

  EDG. Sweet marjoram.
  LEAR. Pass.
  GLOU. I know that voice. 96
  LEAR. Ha! Goneril, with a white beard!
They flattered me like a dog; and told me I
had white hairs in my beard ere the black
ones were there. To say "ay" and "no" 100
to every thing that I said!— "Ay" and "no" too
was no good divinity. When the rain came
to wet me once, and the wind to make me
chatter; when the thunder would not peace
at my bidding; there I found 'em, there I
smelt 'em out. Go to, they are not men o'
their words: they told me I was every thing;
'tis a lie, I am not ague-proof. 107
  GLOU. The trick of that voice I do well re-
   member:
Is 't not the king?
  LEAR. Ay, every inch a king:
When I do stare, see how the subject quakes.
I pardon that man's life. What was thy
   cause? 111
Adultery?
Thou shalt not die: die for adultery! No:
The wren goes to 't, and the small gilded fly
Does lecher in my sight. 115
Let copulation thrive; for Gloucester's bastard
   son
Was kinder to his father than my daughters
Got 'tween the lawful sheets.
To 't, luxury, pell-mell! for I lack soldiers.
Behold yond simpering dame, 120
Whose face between her forks presages snow;
That minces virtue, and does shake the head
To hear of pleasure's name;
The fitchew, nor the soilèd horse, goes to 't
With a more riotous appetite. 125
Down from the waist they are Centaurs,
Though women all above:
But to the girdle do the gods inherit,
Beneath is all the fiends';
There's hell, there's darkness, there's the sul-
   phurous pit, 130
Burning, scalding, stench, consumption; fie,
fie, fie! pah, pah! Give me an ounce of civet,

71. **whelk'd**, twisted. 73. **clearest**, most glorious. 74.
men's impossibilities, things impossible to men. 80. **free**,
i.e., from grief. 81. **safer**, saner; **accommodate**, equip.
83. **touch**, arrest; **coining**, making counterfeit money. 87.
press-money, money to a recruit pressed into military service. 88. **crow-keeper**, a boy stationed to scare away crows.
89. **clothier's yard**, arrow a cloth-yard in length. 91. **prove**,
defend it by combat. 92. **brown bills**, halberds, painted
brown to prevent rust. 93. **bird**, i.e., arrow; **clout**, bulls-
eye; **hewgh**, imitation of the whizzing of the arrow.
94. **word**, password. 104. **peace**, hold its peace. 108. **trick**,
peculiarity. 119. **luxury**, lust. 121. **snow**, i.e., chastity.
122. **minces virtue**, makes a show of virtue by her mincing
(affected) bearing. 124. **fitchew**, skunk, a supposedly over-
sexed animal; **soiled**, fed full with spring grass. 126.
Centaurs, lustful fabulous monsters, half man, half horse.
128. **But**, only; **inherit**, rule. 132. **civet**, perfume.

good apothecary, to sweeten my imagination: there's money for thee.

GLOU. O, let me kiss that hand! 135

LEAR. Let me wipe it first; it smells of mortality.

GLOU. O ruin'd piece of nature! This great world
Shall so wear out to nought. Dost thou know me?

LEAR. I remember thine eyes well enough. Dost thou squiny at me? No, do thy worst, blind Cupid; I'll not love. Read thou this challenge; mark but the penning of it. 142

GLOU. Were all the letters suns, I could not see one.

EDG. I would not take this from report; it is, And my heart breaks at it. 145

LEAR. Read.

GLOU. What, with the case of eyes?

LEAR. O, ho, are you there with me? No eyes in your head, nor no money in your purse? Your eyes are in a heavy case, your purse in a light: yet you see how this world goes.

GLOU. I see it feelingly. 152

LEAR. What, art mad? A man may see how this world goes with no eyes. Look with thine ears: see how yond justice rails upon yond simple thief. Hark, in thine ear: change places; and, handy-dandy, which is the justice, which is the thief? Thou hast seen a farmer's dog bark at a beggar?

GLOU. Ay, sir. 160

LEAR. And the creature run from the cur? There thou mightst behold the great image of authority: a dog's obeyed in office.
Thou rascal beadle, hold thy bloody hand!
Why dost thou lash that whore? Strip thine own back; 165
Thou hotly lust'st to use her in that kind
For which thou whipp'st her. The usurer hangs the cozener.
Through tatter'd clothes small vices do appear;
Robes and furr'd gowns hide all. Plate sin with gold,

And the strong lance of justice hurtless breaks; 170
Arm it in rags, a pigmy's straw does pierce it.
None does offend, none I say, none; I'll able 'em:
Take that of me, my friend, who have the power
To seal the accuser's lips. Get thee glass eyes;
And, like a scurvy politician, seem 175
To see the things thou dost not. Now, now, now, now:
Pull off my boots: harder, harder: so.

EDG. O, matter and impertinency mix'd!
Reason in madness!

LEAR. If thou wilt weep my fortunes, take my eyes. 180
I know thee well enough; thy name is Gloucester:
Thou must be patient; we came crying hither:
Thou know'st, the first time that we smell the air,
We wawl and cry. I will preach to thee: mark.

GLOU. Alack, alack the day! 185

LEAR. When we are born, we cry that we are come
To this great stage of fools: this's a good block;
It were a delicate stratagem, to shoe
A troop of horse with felt: I'll put 't in proof;
And when I have stol'n upon these sons-in-law, 190
Then, kill, kill, kill, kill, kill, kill!

[Enter a GENTLEMAN, with ATTENDANTS.]

GENT. O, here he is: lay hand upon him. Sir,
Your most dear daughter—

LEAR. No rescue? What, a prisoner? I am even
The natural fool of fortune. Use me well; 195
You shall have ransom. Let me have surgeons;
I am cut to the brains.

GENT.   You shall have any thing.

LEAR. No seconds? all myself?
Why, this would make a man a man of salt,

---

137. piece, masterpiece. 138. Shall . . . nought, shall likewise come to nothing. 140. squiny, squint. 141. blind Cupid, the sign usually hung over a brothel. 144. take, accept, believe. 147. case, sockets. 148. are . . . me? i.e., Is that what you are telling me? 150. heavy case, bad condition, with a pun on case-socket. 156. simple, mere. 157. handy-dandy, "Which hand will you have?" (a formula in a well-known child's game). 162. image, figure.

166. kind, way. 167. cozener, cheater, sharper. 169. Plate . . . with gold, clothe sin in golden armor-plates. 172. able, authorize. 173. that, i.e., an imaginary pardon. 174. glass eyes, spectacles. 175. scurvy politician, vile trickster. 178. matter and impertinency, sense and incoherence. 187. block, hat. 189. put 't in proof, make a trial of it. 195. The . . . fortune, man reduced by fortune to the condition of a fool. 199. of salt, of salt tears.

To use his eyes for garden water-pots, 200
Ay, and laying autumn's dust.
    GENT.   Good sir,—
    LEAR. I will die bravely, like a bridegroom.
What!
I will be jovial: come, come; I am a king,
My masters, know you that.
    GENT. You are a royal one, and we obey
you.   205
    LEAR. Then there's life in 't. Nay, if you
get it, you shall get it with running. Sa, sa,
sa, sa.   [*Exit running;* ATTENDANTS *follow.*
    GENT. A sight most pitiful in the meanest
wretch,
Past speaking of in a king! Thou hast one
daughter,
Who redeems nature from the general curse
Which twain have brought her to.   211
    EDG. Hail, gentle sir.
    GENT.   Sir, speed you: what's your will?
    EDG. Do you hear aught, sir, of a battle
toward?
    GENT. Most sure and vulgar: every one hears
that,
Which can distinguish sound.
    EDG.   But, by your favour, 215
How near's the other army?
    GENT. Near and on speedy foot; the main
descry
Stands on the hourly thought.
    EDG.   I thank you, sir: that's all.
    GENT. Though that the queen on special
cause is here,
Her army is moved on.
    EDG.   I thank you, sir.   220
                    [*Exit* GENT.
    GLOU. You ever-gentle gods, take my breath
from me;
Let not my worser spirit tempt me again
To die before you please!
    EDG.   Well pray you, father.
    GLOU. Now, good sir, what are you?
    EDG. A most poor man, made tame to for-
tune's blows;   225
Who, by the art of known and feeling sorrows,

Am pregnant to good pity. Give me your
hand,
I'll lead you to some biding.
    GLOU.   Hearty thanks:
The bounty and the benison of heaven
To boot, and boot!

           [*Enter* OSWALD.]

    OSW. A proclaim'd prize! Most happy! 230
That eyeless head of thine was first framed
flesh
To raise my fortunes. Thou old unhappy
traitor,
Briefly thyself remember: the sword is out
That must destroy thee.
    GLOU.   Now let thy friendly hand
Put strength enough to 't.
                  [EDGAR *interposes.*
    OSW.   Wherefore, bold peasant, 235
Darest thou support a publish'd traitor?
    Hence;
Lest that the infection of his fortune take
Like hold on thee. Let go his arm.
    EDG. Chill not let go, zir, without vurther
'casion.   240
    OSW. Let go, slave, or thou diest!
    EDG. Good gentleman, go your gait, and let
poor volk pass. An chud ha' bin zwaggered
out of my life, 'twould not ha' bin zo long
as 'tis by a vortnight. Nay, come not near th'
old man; keep out, che vor ye, or ise try
whether your costard or my ballow be the
harder: chill be plain with you.   248
    OSW. Out, dunghill!
    EDG. Chill pick your teeth, zir: come; no
matter vor your foins.
    [*They fight, and* EDGAR *knocks him down.*
    OSW. Slave, thou hast slain me: villain, take
my purse:
If ever thou wilt thrive, bury my body;
And give the letters which thou find'st about
me   254
To Edmund earl of Gloucester; seek him out
Upon the British party: O, untimely death!
                       [*Dies.*
    EDG. I know thee well: a serviceable villain;

As duteous to the vices of thy mistress
As badness would desire.

GLOU.   What, is he dead?

EDG. Sit you down, father; rest you.   260
Let's see these pockets: the letters that he
   speaks of
May be my friends. He's dead; I am only
   sorry
He had no other death's-man. Let us see:
Leave, gentle wax; and, manners, blame us
   not:
To know our enemies' minds, we'ld rip their
   hearts;   265
Their papers, is more lawful.
   [*Reads*] "Let our reciprocal vows be remembered. You have many opportunities to
cut him off: if your will want not, time and
place will be fruitfully offered. There is
nothing done, if he return the conqueror:
then am I the prisoner, and his bed my gaol:
from the loathed warmth whereof deliver me,
and supply the place for your labour.
     "Your—wife, so I would say—   275
         "Affectionate servant,
            "GONERIL."

O undistinguish'd space of woman's will!
A plot upon her virtuous husband's life;
And the exchange my brother! Here, in the
   sands,   280
Thee I'll rake up, the post unsanctified
Of murderous lechers: and in the mature
   time
With this ungracious paper strike the sight
Of the death-practised duke: for him 'tis well
That of thy death and business I can tell.

GLOU. The king is mad: how stiff is my
   vile sense,   286
That I stand up, and have ingenious feeling
Of my huge sorrows! Better I were distract:
So should my thoughts be sever'd from my
   griefs,
And woes by wrong imaginations lose   290
The knowledge of themselves.

EDG.   Give me your hand:
         [*Drum afar off.*]

Far off, methinks, I hear the beaten drum:
Come, father, I'll bestow you with a friend.
         [*Exeunt.*

SCENE VII. *A tent in the French camp.*
LEAR *on a bed asleep, soft music play-*
ing; GENTLEMAN, *and others attending.*

   [*Enter* CORDELIA, KENT, *and* DOCTOR.]

COR. O thou good Kent, how shall I live
   and work,
To match thy goodness? My life will be too
   short,
And every measure fail me.

KENT. To be acknowledged, madam, is o'er-
   paid.
All my reports go with the modest truth;   5
Nor more nor clipp'd, but so.

COR.   Be better suited:
These weeds are memories of those worser
   hours:
I prithee, put them off.

KENT.   Pardon me, dear madam;
Yet to be known shortens my made intent: 9
My boon I make it, that you know me not
Till time and I think meet.

COR. Then be 't so, my good lord. [*To the*
   DOCTOR] How does the king?

DOCT. Madam, sleeps still.

COR. O you kind gods,   14
Cure this great breach in his abusèd nature!
The untuned and jarring senses, O, wind up
Of this child-changèd father!

DOCT.   So please your Majesty
That we may wake the king: he hath slept
   long.

COR. Be govern'd by your knowledge, and
   proceed
I' the sway of your own will. Is he array'd?   20

GENT. Ay, madam, in the heaviness of his
   sleep
We put fresh garments on him.

DOCT. Be by, good madam, when we do
   awake him;
I doubt not of his temperance.

COR.   Very well.

258. duteous, compliant. 263. death's-man, executioner.
264. Leave, allow me. 270. fruitfully, amply. 276. servant,
lover. 278. undistinguish'd space, limitless range; will,
lust. 281. rake up, bury hastily; post, messenger. 282.
in . . . time, when the time is ripe. 283. ungracious,
wicked. 284. death . . . duke, duke whose death is
plotted. 286. stiff . . . sense, strong is my sanity. 287.
ingenious feeling, keen consciousness. 288. distract, insane.
Scene vii: 3. measure, i.e., measuring out (of benefits).
5. modest truth, moderate statement of the facts.

6. clipp'd, abridged; suited, clothed. 7. weeds, garments;
memories, reminders. 9. shortens . . . intent, makes me
fall short of my prearranged plan. 10. my . . . it, I ask
it as a favor to me. 16. wind up, i.e., tighten the strings
(as of a musical instrument) of his untuned senses. 17.
child-changed, whose nature has become childish. 24.
temperance, self-control, i.e., sanity.

DOCT. Please you, draw near. Louder the
    music there!   25
COR. O my dear father! Restoration hang
Thy medicine on my lips; and let this kiss
Repair those violent harms that my two sisters
Have in thy reverence made!
    KENT.   Kind and dear princess!
    COR. Had you not been their father, these
    white flakes   30
Had challenged pity of them. Was this a face
To be opposed against the warring winds?
To stand against the deep dread-bolted thun-
    der?
In the most terrible and nimble stroke
Of quick, cross lighting? to watch—poor
    perdu!—   35
With this thin helm? Mine enemy's dog,
Though he had bit me, should have stood
    that night
Against my fire; and wast thou fain, poor
    father,
To hovel thee with swine, and rogues for-
    lorn,
In short and musty straw? Alack, alack! 40
'Tis wonder that thy life and wits at once
Had not concluded all. He wakes; speak to
    him.
    DOCT. Madam, do you; 'tis fittest.
    COR. How does my royal lord? How fares
    your majesty?
    LEAR. You do me wrong to take me out o'
    the grave: 45
Thou art a soul in bliss; but I am bound
Upon a wheel of fire, that mine own tears
Do scald like molten lead.
    COR.   Sir, do you know me?
    LEAR. You are a spirit, I know: when did
    you die?
    COR. Still, still, far wide!   50
    DOCT. He's scarce awake: let him alone
    awhile.
    LEAR. Where have I been? Where am I?
    Fair daylight?
I am mightily abused. I should e'en die with
    pity,
To see another thus. I know not what to say.
I will not swear these are my hands: let's
    see;   55

I feel this pin prick. Would I were assured
Of my condition!
    COR.   O, look upon me, sir,
And hold your hands in benediction o'er me:
No, sir, you must not kneel.
    LEAR.   Pray, do not mock me:
I am a very foolish fond old man,   60
Fourscore and upward, not an hour more nor
    less;
And, to deal plainly,
I fear I am not in my perfect mind.
Methinks I should know you, and know this
    man;   64
Yet I am doubtful: for I am mainly ignorant
What place this is; and all the skill I have
Remembers not these garments; nor I know
    not
Where I did lodge last night. Do not laugh
    at me;
For, as I am a man, I think this lady
To be my child Cordelia.
    COR.   And so I am, I am.   70
    LEAR. Be your tears wet? yes, 'faith. I pray,
    weep not:
If you have poison for me, I will drink it.
I know you do not love me; for your sisters
Have, as I do remember, done me wrong: 74
You have some cause, they have not.
    COR.   No cause, no cause.
    LEAR. Am I in France?
    KENT.   In your own kingdom, sir.
    LEAR. Do not abuse me.
    DOCT. Be comforted, good madam: the great
    rage,
You see, is kill'd in him: and yet it is danger
To make him even o'er the time he has lost. 80
Desire him to go in; trouble him no more
Till further settling.
    COR. Will 't please your highness walk?
    LEAR.   You must bear with me:
Pray you now, forget and forgive: I am old
    and foolish.
        [*Exeunt all but* KENT *and* GENTLEMAN.
    GENT. Holds it true, sir, that the Duke of
Cornwall was so slain?   86
    KENT. Most certain, sir.
    GENT. Who is conductor of his people?

29. in thy reverence made, done to you to whom they
owe reverence. 33. dread-bolted, with its dreadful bolts.
35. cross, zigzag; perdu, a soldier on an isolated post of
great danger. 36. helm, i.e., hair. 38. fain, glad. 39.
rogues, tramps. 42. concluded all, altogether come to an
end. 47. that, so that. 50. wide, i.e., of the mark. 53.
abused, deluded. 57. condition, situation. 60. fond, doting.
65. mainly, completely. 66. skill, intelligence. 77. abuse,
deceive. 78. rage, delirium. 80. even o'er the time, fill the
interval by recalling what happened. 82. Till . . . settling,
until he becomes calmer. 83. walk, i.e., come with me.

KENT. As 'tis said, the bastard son of Glou-
cester.   90
GENT. They say Edgar, his banished son, is
with the Earl of Kent in Germany.
KENT. Report is changeable. 'Tis time to
look about; the powers of the kingdom ap-
proach apace.   95
GENT. The arbitrement is like to be bloody.
Fare you well, sir.   [*Exit.*
KENT. My point and period will be
    throughly wrought,
Or well or ill, as this day's battle's fought. 99
                                        [*Exit.*

ACT FIVE

SCENE I. *The British camp, near
        Dover.*

[*Enter, with drum and colours,* EDMUND,
REGAN, GENTLEMEN, *and* SOLDIERS.]

EDM. Know of the duke if his last purpose
    hold,
Or whether since he is advised by aught
To change the course: he's full of alteration
And self-reproving: bring his constant pleas-
    ure.   [*To a* GENTLEMAN, *who goes out.*
REG. Our sister's man is certainly miscar-
    ried.   5
EDM.'Tis to be doubted, madam.
REG.   Now, sweet lord,
You know the goodness I intend upon you:
Tell me—but truly—but then speak the truth,
Do you not love my sister?
EDM.   In honour'd love.
REG. But have you never found my
    brother's way   10
To the forfended place?

EDM.   That thought abuses you.
REG. I am doubtful that you have been con-
    junct
And bosom'd with her, as far as we call hers.
EDM. No, by mine honour, madam.
REG. I never shall endure her: dear my
    lord,   15
Be not familiar with her.
EDM.   Fear me not:
She and the duke her husband!

[*Enter, with drum and colours,* ALBANY,
        GONERIL, *and* SOLDIERS.]

GON. [*Aside*] I had rather lose the battle
    than that sister
Should loosen him and me.
ALB. Our very loving sister, well be-met. 20
Sir, this I hear; the king is come to his
    daughter,
With others whom the rigour of our state
Forced to cry out. Where I could not be
    honest,
I never yet was valiant: for this business,
It toucheth us, as France invades our land, 25
Not bolds the king, with others, whom, I
    fear,
Most just and heavy causes make oppose.
EDM. Sir, you speak nobly.
REG.   Why is this reason'd?
GON. Combine together 'gainst the enemy;
For these domestic and particular broils   30
Are not the question here.
ALB.   Let's then determine
With the ancient of war on our proceedings.
EDM. I shall attend you presently at your
tent.
REG. Sister, you'll go with us?
GON. No.   35
REG. 'Tis most convenient; pray you, go
    with us.
GON. [*Aside*] O, ho, I know the riddle.—
    I will go.

[*As they are going out, enter* EDGAR
        disguised.]

94. powers, armed forces. 96. arbitrement, forcing of the
decision. 98. My point and period, the final attainment
of my ends; wrought, worked out. Act V, Scene i:
2. advised, induced. 4. constant pleasure, settled decision.
5. miscarried, come to grief. 11. forfended, forbidden;
abuses, dishonors. 12. am doubtful, suspect; conjunct,
joined. 13. bosom'd, intimate; as . . . hers, i.e., in all
that she has. 16. Fear me not, don't worry about me.
20. be-met, met. 22. state, administration. 23. cry out,

protest; honest, honorable. 24. for, as for. 25. France,
the King of France. 26. bolds, emboldens. 27. heavy
causes, weighty reasons; make oppose, force to oppose us.
28. Why . . . reason'd, Why do you search for reasons
[for an action]? 30. domestic and particular, family and
personal. 32. ancient of war, veteran soldiers. 36. convenient, fitting. 37. riddle, hidden reason (i.e., you want
to be alone with Edmund).

EDG. If e'er your grace had speech with man so poor,
Hear me one word.

ALB. I'll overtake you. Speak.
[*Exeunt all but* ALBANY *and* EDGAR.

EDG. Before you fight the battle, ope this
letter.   40
If you have victory, let the trumpet sound
For him that brought it: wretched though I
seem,
I can produce a champion that will prove
What is avouchèd there. If you miscarry,
Your business of the world hath so an end, 45
And machination ceases. Fortune love you!

ALB. Stay till I have read the letter.

EDG.   I was forbid it.
When time shall serve, let but the herald
cry,
And I'll appear again.

ALB. Why, fare thee well: I will o'erlook
thy paper.   [*Exit* EDGAR. 50

[*Re-enter* EDMUND.]

EDM. The enemy's in view; draw up your
powers.
Here is the guess of their true strength and
forces
By diligent discovery; but your haste
Is now urged on you.

ALB.   We will greet the time. [*Exit.*

EDM. To both these sisters have I sworn
my love;   55
Each jealous of the other, as the stung
Are of the adder. Which of them shall I
take?
Both? one? or neither? Neither can be en-
joy'd,
If both remain alive: to take the widow
Exasperates, makes mad her sister Goneril; 60
And hardly shall I carry out my side,
Her husband being alive. Now then we'll use
His countenance for the battle; which being
done,
Let her who would be rid of him devise
His speedy taking off. As for the mercy   65
Which he intends to Lear and to Cordelia,
The battle done, and they within our power,
Shall never see his pardon; for my state
Stands on me to defend, not to debate.   69
                                        [*Exit.*

44. miscarry, i.e., are killed. 46. machination, intrigue (against you). 50. o'erlook, glance at. 53. discovery, scout-

SCENE II. *A field between the two camps.*

[*Alarum within. Enter, with drum and colours,* LEAR, CORDELIA, *and* SOLDIERS, *over the stage; and exeunt.*]

[*Enter* EDGAR *and* GLOUCESTER.]

EDG. Here, father, take the shadow of this
tree
For your good host; pray that the right may
thrive:
If ever I return to you again,
I'll bring you comfort.

GLOU.   Grace go with you, sir!
                              [*Exit* EDGAR.

[*Alarum and retreat within. Re-enter* EDGAR.]

EDG. Away, old man; give me thy hand;
away!   5
King Lear hath lost, he and his daughter
ta'en:
Give me thy hand; come on.

GLOU. No farther, sir; a man may rot even
here.

EDG. What, in ill thoughts again? Men must
endure
Their going hence, even as their coming
hither: 10
Ripeness is all: come on.

GLOU.   And that's true too. [*Exeunt.*

SCENE III. *The British camp near Dover.*

[*Enter, in conquest, with drum and colours,* EDMUND; LEAR *and* CORDELIA, *prisoners;* CAPTAIN, SOLDIERS, &c.]

EDM. Some officers take them away: good
guard,
Until their greater pleasures first be known
That are to censure them.

COR.   We are not the first

ing; your haste, prompt action on your part. 54. greet the
time, meet the situation. 56. jealous, suspiciously afraid.
61. side, plans. 63. countenance, authority. 68-9. my
state . . . debate, my situation requires defense by arms,
not debate (as to the justification of my actions). Scene
ii: s.d. Alarum, a call to arms. 4. Grace, the protection of
the gods. 11. Ripeness, readiness (for death). Scene iii:
2. their greater pleasures, the wishes of those of higher
rank. 3. censure, pass judgment upon.

Who, with best meaning, have incurr'd the
worst.
For thee, oppressèd king, am I cast down; 5
Myself could else out-frown false fortune's
frown.
Shall we not see these daughters and these
sisters?
    LEAR. No, no, no, no! Come, let's away to
prison:
We two alone will sing like birds i' the cage:
When thou dost ask me blessing, I'll kneel
down,   10
And ask of thee forgiveness: so we'll live,
And pray, and sing, and tell old tales, and
laugh
At gilded butterflies, and hear poor rogues
Talk of court news; and we'll talk with them
too,
Who loses and who wins; who's in, who's
out;   15
And take upon 's the mystery of things,
As if we were God's spies: and we'll wear
out,
In a wall'd prison, packs and sects of great
ones,
That ebb and flow by the moon.
    EDM.   Take them away.
    LEAR. Upon such sacrifices, my Cordelia, 20
The gods themselves throw incense. Have I
caught thee?
He that parts us shall bring a brand from
heaven,
And fire us hence like foxes. Wipe thine
eyes;
The good-years shall devour them, flesh and
fell,
Ere they shall make us weep: we'll see 'em
starve first.   25
Come. [*Exeunt* LEAR *and* CORDELIA, *guarded.*
    EDM. Come hither, captain; hark.
Take thou this note [*giving a paper*]; go fol-
low them to prison:
One step I have advanced thee; if thou dost
As this instructs thee, thou dost make thy
way
To noble fortunes: know thou this, that men

Are as the time is: to be tender-minded 31
Does not become a sword: thy great em-
ployment
Will not bear question; either say thou'lt
do 't,
Or thrive by other means.
    CAPT.   I'll do 't, my lord.
    EDM. About it; and write happy when thou
hast done.   35
Mark, I say, instantly; and carry it so
As I have set it down.
    CAPT. I cannot draw a cart, nor eat dried
oats;
If it be man's work, I'll do it.   [*Exit.*

[*Flourish. Enter* ALBANY, GONERIL, REGAN,
    another CAPTAIN, *and* SOLDIERS.]

    ALB. Sir, you have shown to-day your
valiant strain,   40
And fortune led you well: you have the
captives
That were the opposites of this day's strife:
We do require them of you, so to use them
As we shall find their merits and our safety
May equally determine.
    EDM.   Sir, I thought it fit 45
To send the old and miserable king
To some retention and appointed guard;
Whose age has charms in it, whose title more,
To pluck the common bosom on his side,
And turn our impress'd lances in our eyes 50
Which do command them. With him I sent
the queen;
My reason all the same; and they are ready
To-morrow, or at further space, to appear
Where you shall hold your session. At this
time
We sweat and bleed: the friend hath lost his
friend;   55
And the best quarrels, in the heat, are cursed
By those that feel their sharpness:
The question of Cordelia and her father
Requires a fitter place.
    ALB.   Sir, by your patience,

13. **gilded butterflies,** i.e., dandified courtiers; **rogues,**
wretches. **16. take . . . things,** assume that we can explain
the mysteries of human life. **17. wear out,** i.e., forget.
18. packs, parties. **23. fire . . . foxes,** foxes can be driven
from their holes by smoke and fire. **24. good-years,** evils,
perhaps "pestilence"; **fell,** skin. **27. note,** i.e., an order for
the execution of Lear and Cordelia. **31. As . . . is,** is, as the
situation demands. **33. bear question,** permit discussion.

34. **other means,** i.e., than my favor. 35. **write happy,**
write yourself down as fortunate. 36. **carry it,** carry it out.
40. **strain,** stock. 42. **the opposites of,** our opponents in.
47. **some retention . . . guard,** to the custody of some
guards appointed for the purpose. 49. **pluck . . . bosom,**
enlist the sympathies of the common soldiers. 50. **impress'd lances,** drafted troops. 51. **which,** who. 56.
quarrels, causes. 59. **a fitter place,** i.e., than the battle-
field; **by your patience,** i.e., if you will pardon my plain
talk.

I hold you but a subject of this war, 60
Not as a brother.

REG. That's as we list to grace him.
Methinks our pleasure might have been de-
manded,
Ere you had spoke so far. He led our powers;
Bore the commission of my place and person;
The which immediacy may well stand up, 65
And call itself your brother.

GON. Not so hot:
In his own grace he doth exalt himself,
More than in your addition.

REG. In my rights,
By me invested, he compeers the best.

GON. That were the most, if he should husband you. 70

REG. Jesters do oft prove prophets.

GON. Holla, holla!
That eye that told you so look'd but a-squint.

REG. Lady, I am not well; else I should
answer
From a full-flowing stomach. General,
Take thou my soldiers, prisoners, patri-
mony; 75
Dispose of them, of me, the walls are thine:
Witness the world, that I create thee here
My lord and master.

GON. Mean you to enjoy him?

ALB. The let-alone lies not in your good
will.

EDM. Nor in thine, lord.

ALB. Half-blooded fellow, yes. 80

REG. [To EDMUND] Let the drum strike, and
prove my title thine.

ALB. Stay yet; hear reason. Edmund, I ar-
rest thee
On capital treason; and, in thine attaint,
This gilded serpent [pointing to GON.]. For
your claim, fair sister,
I bar it in the interest of my wife; 85
'Tis she is sub-contracted to this lord,
And I, her husband, contradict your bans.
If you will marry, make your loves to me,
My lady is bespoke.

GON. An interlude!

ALB. Thou art arm'd, Gloucester: let the
trumpet sound: 90
If none appear to prove upon thy head
Thy heinous, manifest, and many treasons,
There is my pledge [throwing down a glove];
I'll prove it on thy heart,
Ere I taste bread, thou art in nothing less
Than I have here proclaim'd thee.

REG. Sick, O, sick!

GON. [Aside] If not, I'll ne'er trust medicine. 96

EDM. There's my exchange [throwing down
a glove]: what in the world he is
That names me traitor, villain-like he lies:
Call by thy trumpet: he that dares approach,
On him, on you, who not? I will maintain 100
My truth and honour firmly.

ALB. A herald, ho!

EDM. A herald, ho, a herald!

ALB. Trust to thy single virtue; for thy
soldiers,
All levied in my name, have in my name 104
Took their discharge.

REG. My sickness grows upon me.

ALB. She is not well; convey her to my
tent. [Exit REGAN, led.]

[Enter a HERALD.]

Come hither, herald,—Let the trumpet
sound,—
And read out this. 108

CAPT. Sound, trumpet! [A trumpet sounds.

HER. [Reads] "If any man of quality or
degree within the lists of the army will maintain upon Edmund, supposed Earl of
Gloucester, that he is a manifold traitor, let
him appear by the third sound of the trumpet:
he is bold in his defence."

EDM. Sound! [First trumpet.

HER. Again! [Second trumpet.

HER. Again! [Third trumpet.
[Trumpet answers within.

[Enter EDGAR, at the third sound, armed,
with a trumpet before him.]

61. That's . . . him, that depends on how far I wish
to honor him. 62. pleasure, wishes in the matter. 64.
Bore . . . person, exercised the authority of my rank
and person. 65. The which immediacy, and this fact
of immediate representation [of me]. 67. own grace,
his personal deserts. 68. your addition, the title you gave
him. 69. compeers, equals. 70. the most, most fully
realized. 72. that eye . . . asquint, a reference to the
proverb, "Love being jealous, makes a good eye look
asquint." 74. stomach, anger. 76. the walls are thine, i.e.,
you have taken my outer defences by storm. 79. let-alone
. . . will, the prohibition does not depend on what you wish.
80. half-blooded, bastard. 81. prove, i.e., by combat. 83. in
. . . attaint, i.e., as a sharer in your corruption. 84. claim,
i.e., to Edmund. 86. is sub-contracted, i.e., has made a
contract depending on the abrogation of a previous one.
89. interlude, comedy (a reference to Albany's elaborate
irony). 94. nothing, no respect. 97. what, whoever and
whatever. 103. virtue, valor. 109. trumpet, trumpeter.
109-10. quality or degree, rank or high social position.

ALB. Ask him his purposes, why he appears
Upon this call o' the trumpet.
HER.   What are you?
Your name, your quality? and why you
        answer   120
This present summons?
EDG.   Know, my name is lost;
By treason's tooth bare-gnawn and canker-
        bit:
Yet am I noble as the adversary
I come to cope.
    ALB.   Which is that adversary?
    EDG. What's he that speaks for Edmund
        Earl of Gloucester?   125
    EDM. Himself: what say'st thou to him?
    EDG.   Draw thy sword,
That, if my speech offend a noble heart,
Thy arm may do thee justice: here is mine.
Behold, it is the privilege of mine honours,
My oath, and my profession: I protest,   130
Maugre thy strength, youth, place, and
        eminence,
Despite thy victor sword and fire-new for-
        tune,
Thy valour and thy heart, thou art a traitor;
False to thy gods, thy brother, and thy father;
Conspirant 'gainst this high-illustrious
        prince;   135
And, from the extremest upward of thy head
To the descent and dust below thy foot,
A most toad-spotted traitor. Say thou "No,"
This sword, this arm, and my best spirits, are
        bent
To prove upon thy heart, whereto I
        speak,   140
Thou liest.
    EDM. In wisdom I should ask thy name;
But, since thy outside looks so fair and war-
        like,
And that thy tongue some say of breeding
        breathes,
What safe and nicely I might well delay 144
By rule of knighthood, I disdain and spurn:
Back do I toss these treasons to thy head;

With the hell-hated lie o'erwhelm thy heart;
Which, for they yet glance by and scarcely
        bruise,
This sword of mine shall give them instant
        way,
Where they shall rest for ever. Trumpets,
        speak!   150
        [Alarums. They fight. EDMUND falls.
    ALB. Save him, save him!
    GON.   This is mere practice, Gloucester:
By the law of arms thou wast not bound to
        answer
An unknown opposite; thou art not van-
        quish'd,
But cozen'd and beguiled.
    ALB.   Shut your mouth, dame,
Or with this paper shall I stop it. Hold, sir;
Thou worse than any name, read thine own
        evil: 156
No tearing, lady; I perceive you know it.
        [Gives the letter to EDMUND.
    GON. Say, if I do, the laws are mine, not
        thine:
Who can arraign me for 't?
    ALB.   Most monstrous! oh!
Know'st thou this paper?
    GON.   Ask me not what I know. [Exit.
    ALB. Go after her: she's desperate; govern
        her.   161
    EDM. What you have charged me with,
        that have I done;
And more, much more; the time will bring it
        out:
'Tis past, and so am I. But what art thou
That hast this fortune on me? If thou'rt
        noble,   165
I do forgive thee.
    EDG.   Let's exchange charity.
I am no less in blood than thou art, Edmund;
If more, the more thou hast wrong'd me.
My name is Edgar, and thy father's son.
The gods are just, and of our pleasant vices
Make instruments to plague us: 171
The dark and vicious place where thee he got
Cost him his eyes.

---

122. canker-bit, eaten away by a canker-worm. 124. cope, cope with. 128. arm, weapon. 129. mine honours, my rank, i.e., as knight. 130. oath, i.e., which I swore when dubbed knight, i.e., to protect the honor of knighthood from such evils as treason. 131. Maugre, in spite of. 132. fire-new, brand-new. 133. heart, courage. 135. Conspirant, conspirator. 136. upward, top. 137. descent, lowest part [of you]. 138. toad-spotted, marked with poisonous spots. 141. In wisdom, i.e., a knight was not obliged to accept the challenge of an unknown opponent. 143. say of

breeding, accent of a gentleman. 144. safe and nicely, safely and punctiliously. 146. treasons, accusations of treason. 147. hell-hated, hateful as hell. 148. for, because. 151. mere practice, out-and-out foul play. 152. answer, accept the challenge of. 153. opposite, opponent. 154. cozen'd, cheated. 155. this paper, i.e., her love letter which Edgar has found on Oswald's body. 158. the laws . . . thine, I, as ruler, make the laws, not you. 161. govern, restrain. 165. fortune, success. 172. got, begot.

EDM. Thou hast spoken right, 'tis true;
The wheel is come full circle; I am here.
   ALB. Methought thy very gait did
     prophesy   175
A royal nobleness: I must embrace thee:
Let sorrow split my heart, if ever I
Did hate thee or thy father!
   EDG.   Worthy prince, I know't.
   ALB. Where have you hid yourself?
How have you known the miseries of your
     father?   180
   EDG. By nursing them, my lord. List a brief
     tale,
And when 'tis told, O, that my heart would
     burst!
The bloody proclamation to escape,
That follow'd me so near,—O, our lives'
     sweetness!
That we the pain of death would hourly
     die   185
Rather than die at once!—taught me to shift
Into a madman's rags; to assume a semblance
That very dogs disdain'd: and in this habit
Met I my father with his bleeding rings,
Their precious stones new lost; became his
     guide,   190
Led him, begg'd for him, saved him from
     despair;
Never,—O fault!—reveal'd myself unto him,
Until some half-hour past, when I was arm'd:
Not sure, though hoping, of this good suc-
     cess,
I ask'd his blessing, and from first to last 195
Told him my pilgrimage: but his flaw'd heart,
Alack, too weak the conflict to support!
'Twixt two extremes of passion, joy and grief,
Burst smilingly.
   EDM. This speech of yours hath moved me,
And shall perchance do good: but speak you
     on;   200
You look as you had something more to say.
   ALB. If there be more, more woeful, hold it
     in;
For I am almost ready to dissolve,
Hearing of this.
   EDG.   This would have seem'd a
     period
To such as love not sorrow; but another, 205

To amplify too much, would make much
     more,
And top extremity.
Whilst I was big in clamour came there in a
     man,
Who, having seen me in my worst estate,
Shunn'd my abhorr'd society; but then, find-
     ing   210
Who 'twas that so endured, with his strong
     arms
He fasten'd on my neck, and bellow'd out
As he'ld burst heaven; threw him on my
     father;
Told the most piteous tale of Lear and him
That ever ear received: which in recount-
     ing   215
His grief grew puissant, and the strings of life
Began to crack: twice then the trumpets
     sounded,
And there I left him tranced.
   ALB.   But who was this?
   EDG. Kent, sir, the banish'd Kent; who in
     disguise
Follow'd his enemy king, and did him serv-
     ice   220
Improper for a slave.

[*Enter a* GENTLEMAN, *with a bloody knife.*]

   GENT. Help, help, O, help!
   EDG.   What kind of help?
   ALB.   Speak, man.
   EDG. What means that bloody knife?
   GENT.   'Tis hot, it smokes;
It came even from the heart of—O, she's
     dead!
   ALB. Who dead? speak, man.   225
   GENT. Your lady, sir, your lady: and her
     sister
By her is poisoned; she hath confess'd it.
   EDM. I was contracted to them both: all
     three
Now marry in an instant.
   EDG.   Here comes Kent.
   ALB. Produce their bodies, be they alive or
     dead: 230
This judgement of the heavens, that makes
     us tremble,
Touches us not with pity. [*Exit* GENTLEMAN.]

---

174. wheel, i.e., of Fortune. 175. gait, bearing. 17l
Worthy, honorable. 183. The . . . escape, in order tᴏ
escape from the proclamation for my arrest. 185-6. That
. . . once, that we prefer to suffer the pain of death hour
by hour than to die at once. 192. fault, mistake.

196. flaw'd, cracked. 203. dissolve, i.e., in tears. 204. period,
end (of sorrow). 207. top extremity, exceed the extreme
limit. 208. big in clamour, loud in lament. 209. estate,
condition. 216. puissant, overpowering; strings of life,
heart-strings. 218. tranced, in a swoon. 221. for, even for.

[*Enter* KENT.]

O, is this he?
The time will not allow the compliment
Which very manners urges.

KENT.   I am come
To bid my king and master aye good
    night: 235
Is he not here?

ALB.   Great thing of us forgot!
Speak, Edmund, where's the king? and
    where's Cordelia?
See'st thou this object, Kent?
        [*The bodies of* GONERIL *and* REGAN *are
                                    brought in.*

KENT. Alack, why thus?

EDM.   Yet Edmund was beloved:
The one the other poison'd for my sake, 240
And after slew herself.

ALB. Even so. Cover their faces.

EDM. I pant for life: some good I mean
    to do,
Despite of mine own nature. Quickly send,
Be brief in it, to the castle; for my writ 245
Is on the life of Lear and on Cordelia:
Nay, send in time.

ALB.   Run, run, O, run!

EDG. To who, my lord! Who hath the of-
    fice? send
Thy token of reprieve.

EDM. Well thought on: take my sword, 250
Give it the captain.

ALB. Haste thee, for thy life. [*Exit* EDGAR.

EDM. He hath commission from thy wife
    and me
To hang Cordelia in the prison, and
To lay the blame upon her own despair,
That she forbid herself.   255

ALB. The gods defend her! Bear him hence
    awhile.   [EDMUND *is borne off.*

[*Re-enter* LEAR, *with* CORDELIA *dead in his
arms;* EDGAR, CAPTAIN, *and others following.*]

LEAR. Howl, howl, howl, howl! O, you are
    men of stones:
Had I your tongues and eyes, I'ld use them
    so
That heaven's vault should crack. She's gone
    for ever!

I know when one is dead, and when one
    lives;   260
She's dead as earth. Lend me a looking-glass;
If that her breath will mist or stain the stone,
Why, then she lives.

KENT.   Is this the promised end?

EDG. Or image of that horror?

ALB.   Fall, and cease!

LEAR. This feather stirs; she lives! if it be
    so,   265
It is a chance which does redeem all sorrows
That ever I have felt.

KENT. [*Kneeling*] O my good master!

LEAR. Prithee, away.

EDG.   'Tis noble Kent, your friend.

LEAR. A plague upon you, murderers,
    traitors all!
I might have saved her; now she's gone for
    ever!   270
Cordelia, Cordelia! stay a little. Ha!
What is 't thou say'st? Her voice was ever
    soft,
Gentle, and low, an excellent thing in woman.
I kill'd the slave that was a-hanging thee.

CAPT. 'Tis true, my lords, he did.

LEAR.   Did I not, fellow?
I have seen the day, with my good biting
    falchion   276
I would have made them skip: I am old now,
And these same crosses spoil me. Who are
    you?
Mine eyes are not o' the best: I'll tell you
    straight.

KENT. If fortune brag of two she loved and
    hated,   280
One of them we behold.

LEAR. This is a dull sight. Are you not
    Kent?

KENT.   The same,
Your servant Kent. Where is your servant
    Caius?

LEAR. He's a good fellow, I can tell you
    that;
He'll strike, and quickly too: he's dead and
    rotten.   285

KENT. No, my good lord; I am the very
    man,—

LEAR. I'll see that straight.

233. compliment, ceremony. 235. aye, forever. 236. of,
by. 255. fordid, destroyed. 262. stone, crystal mirror.
263. promised end, i.e., of the world, the Last Judgment.
264. image, exact likeness; Fall, and cease, i.e., let
Doomsday come and all things cease to be. 266. redeem,
repay. 276. falchion, a curved, broad-bladed sword. 278.
crosses, troubles. 279. straight, straightway. 281. one . . .
behold, certainly no more than two men in all human
history have experienced such violent ups and downs of
Fortune as Lear. 287. see that, see to that.

KENT. That, from your first of difference
and decay,
Have follow'd your sad steps.

LEAR.   You are welcome hither.

KENT. Nor no man else: all's cheerless, dark,
and deadly.   290
Your eldest daughters have fordone themselves,
And desperately are dead.

LEAR.   Ay, so I think.

ALB. He knows not what he says: and vain
it is
That we present us to him.

EDG.   Very bootless.

[*Enter a* CAPTAIN.]

CAP. Edmund is dead, my lord.

ALB.   That's but a trifle here.   295
You lords and noble friends, know our in-
tent.
What comfort to this great decay may come
Shall be applied: for us, we will resign
During the life of this old majesty,
To him our absolute power: [*To* EDGAR *and*
KENT] you, to your rights;   300
With boot, and such addition as your honours
Have more than merited. All friends shall
taste
The wages of their virtue, and all foes
The cup of their deservings. O, see, see!

LEAR. And my poor fool is hang'd! No,
no, no life!   305
Why should a dog, a horse, a rat, have life,
And thou no breath at all? Thou'lt come no
more,

Never, never, never, never, never!
Pray you, undo this button: thank you, sir.
Do you see this? Look on her, look, her
lips,   310
Look there, look there!   [*Dies.*

EDG.   He faints! My lord, my lord!

KENT. Break, heart; I prithee, break!

EDG.   Look up, my lord.

KENT. Vex not his ghost: O, let him pass!
he hates him much
That would upon the rack of this tough
world
Stretch him out longer.

EDG.   He is gone, indeed.   315

KENT. The wonder is, he hath endured so
long:
He but usurp'd his life.

ALB. Bear them from hence. Our present
business
Is general woe. [*To* KENT *and* EDGAR] Friends
of my soul, you twain
Rule in this realm, and the gored state sustain.   320

KENT. I have a journey, sir, shortly to go;
My master calls me, I must not say no.

ALB. The weight of this sad time we must
obey;
Speak what we feel, not what we ought to
say.
The oldest hath borne most: we that are
young   325
Shall never see so much, nor live so long.

[*Exeunt, with a dead march.*

288. from . . . decay, from the beginning of the decline
and decay of your fortunes. 290. No . . . else, not I nor
any one else. 291. foredone, killed. 292. desperately, in
despair. 297. great decay, great man fallen into decay.
300. our absolute power, the sovereign power I now exercise. 301. boot, something given in the bargain. 305. poor
fool, i.e., Cordelia; "fool" was used as a term of endear-
ment. 313. ghost, departing spirit. 317. usurp'd his life,
i.e., lived longer than the usual term of life. 322. calls me,
i.e., to follow him through Death. 325. oldest, i.e., Lear
and Gloucester. 326. Shall . . . long, i.e., even if we shall
live as long as Lear has, we should never experience so
much misery.

1. Why does Lear demand what he does in the opening scene? Is Cordelia justified
   in refusing? Why can't Lear subsequently reach some accommodation with Goneril
   and Regan? Why is he a tragic hero, with a stature that commands respect, and
   not just a senile old man? How does he develop in the course of the play?

2. Why is Kent essential to the play? The Fool? How would you describe the Fool's
   relationship with Lear?

3. What does the Gloucester story add to the play? What are the dramatic advantages
   of having Edgar play the role of "poor Tom"? Why does Shakespeare have Lear
   and Gloucester meet in the fields of Dover?

4. Gloucester at one point says that the gods "kill us for their sport." On the heath Lear looks to the "great gods" that make the thunder for justice. What role do you think the gods play in *King Lear*? (Compare the role of the gods in *Oedipus Rex*.)

5. Critics argue about the meaning of the ending of the play. Does the reconciliation of Lear and Cordelia suggest that love can exist and give meaning to life in the face of evil and unspeakable suffering? Or do the deaths of Lear and Cordelia suggest that we can find no meaningful patterns in human experience? Would the play be better if Cordelia lived to marry Edgar? (The play was actually re-written to end this way in the eighteenth century.)

Introduction to *Hedda Gabler*

Although the action of *Hedda Gabler* takes place in the parlor of an ordinary, middle-class home, the fate of the title character is still as tragic, and as universal in its implications, as that of Sophocles' Oedipus. Generally considered an outstanding example of realistic drama, *Hedda Gabler* contrasts sharply with Greek tragedy. Ibsen's plays were not performed before eighteen thousand spectators, but instead in small indoor theatres, with a proscenium arch, very much like those we are accustomed to today, and his main intention was to make his characters as lifelike as possible. This, he felt, could best be done by writing plays *not* about statesmen and princes (generally the subjects of Greek tragedy), but instead about shopkeepers, bankers, professors, and other members of the middle class. Because the main goal of realistic drama is to break down the barriers between art and life, the dramatist as story-teller presents characters who speak and act like ordinary people. The suffering, the boredom, the vanity, the aspirations, and the fears of Ibsen's characters are more or less the same as those of the middle-class audience.

Ibsen's preliminary notes to *Hedda Gabler* reveal that his characters came to life very slowly and only after a great deal of thought. Ibsen explained the process:

Before I write down one word, I have to have the character in mind through and through. I must penetrate into the last wrinkle of his soul. I always proceed from the individual; the stage setting, the dramatic ensemble, all of that comes naturally and does not cause me any worry, as soon as I am certain of the individual in every aspect of his humanity. But I have to have his exterior in mind also, down to the last button, how he stands and walks, how he conducts himself, what his voice sounds like. Then I do not let him go until his fate is fulfilled.

In short, Ibsen slowly created and perfected his characters before putting them on the stage. He felt that by the last draft of a play (and Ibsen usually wrote many drafts), the characters "are my intimate friends, who will not disappoint me in any way; in the manner in which I see them now, I shall always see them."

Tragedies with middle-class characters and settings are often referred to as "bourgeois" or "domestic" tragedy. Where a "tragic hero" such as Oedipus challenges the gods and is punished by them, Hedda Gabler reacts against a boring husband and middle-class respectability, but both suffer intensely. Although Hedda Gabler is a bored housewife and Oedipus is a king, her crisis is no less dramatic than his.

413

HEDDA GABLER

Translated by Otto Reinert

CAST OF CHARACTERS

JØRGEN TESMAN, *University Research Fellow in History of Civilization.*
HEDDA, *his wife.*
MISS JULIANE TESMAN, *his aunt.*
MRS ELVSTED.
JUDGE BRACK.
EILERT LØVBORG.
BERTE, *the Tesmans' maid.*

SCENE: *The Tesmans' villa in a fashionable residential section of the town.*

ACT ONE

(*A spacious, handsome, tastefully furnished room. Dark décor. In the rear, a wide doorway with open portieres. Beyond is a smaller room, furnished in the same style as the front room. A door, right, leads to the front hall. Left, French doors, with portieres drawn aside, through which can be seen a part of a roofed verandah and trees with autumn foliage. Front center, an oval table covered with a cloth. Chairs around it. Front right, a wide, dark, porcelain stove, a high-backed easy chair, a footstool with a pillow, and two ottomans. In the corner far right, a sofa and a small, round table. Front left, a sofa, set out from the wall. Far left, beyond the French doors, an upright piano. On both sides of the doorway, rear center, whatnots with knickknacks. Against the rear wall of the inner room, a sofa, and in front of it a table and two chairs. Above the sofa, a portrait of a handsome, elderly man in general's uniform. Over the table hangs a lamp with milky, white glass. There are several bouquets of flowers, in vases and glasses, in various*)

places in the front room. Others are lying on the tables. Thick carpets on the floors of both rooms. The morning sun is shining through the French doors.

MISS JULIANE TESMAN, *with hat and parasol, enters right, followed by* BERTE, *who carries a bouquet of flowers wrapped in paper.* MISS TESMAN *is a nice-looking woman of 65, of pleasant mien, neatly but not expensively dressed in a gray suit.* BERTE *is a middle-aged servant girl, of rather plain and countrified appearance.*)

MISS TESMAN (*stops inside the door, listens, says in a low voice*): On my word—I don't think they are even up yet!

BERTE (*also softly*): That's what I told you, miss. When you think how late the steamer got in last night. And afterwards—! Goodness!—all the stuff she wanted unpacked before she turned in.

MISS TESMAN: Well—just let them sleep. But fresh morning air—*that* we can give them when they come in here. (*Goes and opens the French doors wide.*)

BERTE (*by the table, lost, still holding the flowers*): Please, miss—I just don't see a bit of space anywhere! I think I'd better put these over here. (*Puts the flowers down on the piano.*)

MISS TESMAN: Well, well, my dear Berte. So you've got yourself a new mistress now. The good Lord knows it was hard for me to let you go.

BERTE (*near tears*): What about me, then, miss! What shall *I* say? I who have served you and Miss Rina all these blessed years.

MISS TESMAN: We shall just have to make the best of it, Berte. There's nothing else to do.

Jørgen can't do without you, you know. He just can't. You've looked after him ever since he was a little boy.

BERTE: Yes, but miss—I'm ever so worried about leaving Miss Rina. The poor dear lying there all helpless. With that new girl and all! She'll never learn how to make things nice and comfortable for an invalid.

MISS TESMAN: Oh yes, you'll see, I'll teach her. And of course, you know, I'll do most of it myself. So don't worry yourself about my poor sister, Berte.

BERTE: Yes, but there's another thing, too, miss. I'm scared I won't be able to suit young Mrs. Tesman.

MISS TESMAN: Oh, well. Good heavens. So there is a thing or two—Right at first—

BERTE: For I believe she's ever so particular.

MISS TESMAN: Can you wonder? General Gabler's daughter? Just think of the kind of life she was used to when the General was alive. Do you remember when she rode by with her father? That long black riding habit she wore? And the feather in her hat?

BERTE: Oh, I remember, all right. But I'll be blessed if I ever thought she and the young master would make a pair of it.

MISS TESMAN: Nor did I. By the way, while I think of it, Berte. Jørgen has a new title now. From now on you must refer to him as "the Doctor."

BERTE: Yes, the young mistress said something about that, too, last night. Soon as they were inside the door. Then it's really so, miss?

MISS TESMAN: It certainly is. Just think, Berte—they have made him a doctor abroad. During the trip, you know. I hadn't heard a thing about it till last night on the pier.

BERTE: Well, I daresay he could be anything he put his mind to, he could—smart as he is. But I must say I'd never thought he'd turn to doctoring people, too.

MISS TESMAN: Oh, that's not the kind of doctor he is. (*Nods significantly.*) And as far as that is concerned, there is no telling but pretty soon you may have to call him something grander yet.

BERTE: You don't say! What might that be miss?

MISS TESMAN (*smiles*): Wouldn't you like to know! (*Moved.*) Ah yes, indeed—! If only dear Jochum could see from his grave what has become of his little boy! (*Looking around.*) But look, Berte—what's this for? Why have you taken off all the slip covers?

BERTE: She told me to. Said she can't stand slip covers on chairs.

MISS TESMAN: Do you think they mean to make this their everyday living room, then?

BERTE: It sure sounded that way. Mrs. Tesman did, I mean. For he—the doctor—he didn't say anything.

(JØRGEN TESMAN *enters from the right side of the inner room. He is humming to himself. He carries an open, empty suitcase. He is of medium height, youthful-looking thirty-three years old, somewhat stoutish. Round, open, cheerful face. Blond hair and beard. He wears glasses and is dressed in a comfortable, rather casual suit.*)

MISS TESMAN: Good morning, good morning, Jørgen!

TESMAN (*in the doorway*): Auntie! Dearest Aunt Julle! (*Comes forward and shakes her hand.*) All the way out here—as early as this! Hm?

MISS TESMAN: Well—I just had to drop in for a moment. To see how you are getting along, you know.

TESMAN: Even though you haven't had a good night's sleep.

MISS TESMAN: Oh, that doesn't matter at all.

TESMAN: But you did get home from the pier all right, I hope. Hm?

MISS TESMAN: Oh yes, certainly I did, thank you. The Judge was kind enough to see me all the way to my door.

TESMAN: We were so sorry we couldn't give you a ride in our carriage. But you saw for yourself—all the boxes Hedda had.

MISS TESMAN: Yes, she certainly brought quite a collection.

BERTE (*to* TESMAN): Should I go and ask Mrs. Tesman if there's anything I can help her with?

TESMAN: No, thank you, Berte—you'd better not. She said she'll ring if she wants you.

BERTE (*going right*): Well, all right.

TESMAN: But, look—you might take this suitcase with you.

BERTE (*takes it*): I'll put it in the attic.

(*Exits right.*)

TESMAN: Just think, Auntie—that whole suitcase was brimful of copies of old documents. You wouldn't believe me if I told you all the things I have collected from libraries and archives all over. Quaint old items nobody has known anything about.

MISS TESMAN: Well, no, Jørgen. I'm sure you haven't wasted your time on your honeymoon.

TESMAN: No, I think I may say I have not. But take your hat off, Auntie—for goodness' sake. Here! Let me untie the ribbon for you. Hm?

MISS TESMAN (*while he does so*): Ah, God forgive me, if this isn't just as if you were still at home with us!

TESMAN (*inspecting the hat*): My, what a fine-looking hat you've got yourself!

MISS TESMAN: I bought it for Hedda's sake.

TESMAN: For Hedda's sake? Hm?

MISS TESMAN: So she won't need to feel ashamed of me if we ever go out together.

TESMAN (*patting her cheek*): If you don't think of everything, Auntie! (*Puts the hat down on a chair by the table.*) And now—over here to the sofa—we'll just sit and chat for a while till Hedda comes.

(*They seat themselves. She places her parasol in the corner by the sofa.*)

MISS TESMAN (*takes both his hands in hers and gazes at him*): What a blessing it is to have you back again, Jørgen, big as life! You—Jochum's little boy!

TESMAN: For me, too, Aunt Julle. To see you again. For you have been both father and mother to me.

MISS TESMAN: Ah, yes—don't you think I know you'll always keep a spot in your heart for these two old aunts of yours!

TESMAN: So Aunt Rina isn't any better, hm?

MISS TESMAN: Oh no. We mustn't look for improvement in her case, poor dear. She is lying there just as she has been all these years. Just the same, may the good Lord keep her for me a long time yet! For else I just wouldn't know what to do with myself, Jørgen. Especially now, when I don't have you to look after any more.

TESMAN (*pats her back*): There, there, now!

MISS TESMAN (*changing tone*): And to think that you are a married man, Jørgen! And that you were the one to walk off with Hedda Gabler. The lovely Hedda Gabler. Just think! As many admirers as she had!

TESMAN (*hums a little, smiles contentedly*): Yes, I daresay I have quite a few good friends here in town who'd gladly be in my shoes, hm?

MISS TESMAN: And such a lovely, long honeymoon you had! More than five—almost six months!

TESMAN: Well, you know—for me it has been a kind of study tour as well. All the collections I had to go through. And the books I had to read!

MISS TESMAN: Yes, I suppose. (*More confidentially, her voice lowered a little.*) But listen, Jørgen—haven't you got something—something special to tell me?

TESMAN: About the trip?

MISS TESMAN: Yes.

TESMAN: No—I don't know of anything besides what I wrote in my letters. They gave me a doctor's degree down there—but I told you that last night; I'm sure I did.

MISS TESMAN: Well, yes, that sort of thing—What I mean is—don't you have certain—certain—expectations?

TESMAN: Expectations?

MISS TESMAN: Ah for goodness' sake, Jørgen! I am your old Auntie, after all!

TESMAN: Certainly I have expectations.

MISS TESMAN: Well!!

TESMAN: I fully expect to be made a professor one of these days.

MISS TESMAN: Professor—oh yes—

TESMAN: I may even say I am quite certain of it. But dear Aunt Julle—you know this just as well as I do!

MISS TESMAN (*laughing a little*): Of course I do. You're quite right. (*Changing topic.*) But we were talking about the trip. It must have cost a great deal of money—hm, Jørgen?

TESMAN: Well, now; you know that large stipend went quite a long way.

MISS TESMAN: I just don't see how you made it do for both of you, though.

TESMAN: No, I suppose that's not so easy to understand, hm?

MISS TESMAN: Particularly with a lady along. For I have always heard that is ever so much more expensive.

TESMAN: Well, yes, naturally. That *is* rather more expensive. But Hedda had to have this trip, Auntie! She really had to. Nothing less would do.

MISS TESMAN: No, I daresay. For a wedding journey is quite the thing these days. But now tell me—have you had a chance to look around here yet?

TESMAN: I certainly have. I have been up and about ever since dawn.

MISS TESMAN: And what do you think of it all?

TESMAN: Delightful! Perfectly delightful! The only thing is I don't see what we are going to do with the two empty rooms between the second sitting room in there and Hedda's bedroom.

MISS TESMAN (*with a chuckle*): Oh my dear Jørgen—you may find them useful enough—when the time comes!

TESMAN: Of course, you're right, Auntie! As my library expands, hm?

MISS TESMAN: Quite so, my dear boy. It was your library I was thinking of.

TESMAN: But I'm really most happy on Hedda's behalf. For you know, before we were engaged she used to say she wouldn't care to live anywhere but in Secretary Falk's house.

MISS TESMAN: Yes, just think—wasn't that a lucky coincidence, that it was up for sale right after you had left?

TESMAN: Yes, Aunt Julle. We've certainly been lucky. Hm?

MISS TESMAN: But it will be expensive, my dear Jørgen. Terribly expensive—all this.

TESMAN (*looks at her, a bit crestfallen*): Yes, I daresay it will, Auntie.

MISS TESMAN: Heavens, yes!

TESMAN: How much, do you think? Roughly. Hm?

MISS TESMAN: No, I couldn't possibly say till all the bills arrive.

TESMAN: Well, anyway, Judge Brack managed to get very reasonable terms for us. He said so himself in a letter to Hedda.

MISS TESMAN: Yes, and I won't have you uneasy on that account, Jørgen. Besides, I have given security for the furniture and the carpets.

TESMAN: Security? You? But dear Aunt Julle—what kind of security could you give?

MISS TESMAN: The annuity.

TESMAN (*jumps up*): What! Your and Aunt Rina's annuity?

MISS TESMAN: Yes. I didn't know what else to do, you see.

TESMAN (*standing before her*): But are you clear out of your mind, Auntie! That annuity—that's all the two of you have to live on!

MISS TESMAN: Oh well, there's nothing to get so excited about, I'm sure. It's all just a matter of form, you know. That's what the Judge said, too. For he was kind enough to arrange the whole thing for me. Just a matter of form—those were his words.

TESMAN: That's all very well. Still—

MISS TESMAN: For now you'll have your own salary, you know. And, goodness—what if we do have a few expenses—Help out a bit right at first—? That would only be a joy for us—

TESMAN: Oh, Auntie! When will you ever stop making sacrifices for my sake!

MISS TESMAN (*gets up, puts her hands on his shoulders*): But what other happiness do I have in this world than being able to smooth your way a little, my own dear boy? You, who haven't had either father or mother to lean on? And now the goal is in sight,

417

Jørgen. Things may have looked black at times. But heaven be praised: you're on top now!

TESMAN: Yes, it's really quite remarkable the way things have worked out.

MISS TESMAN: Yes—and those who were against you—who tried to block your way—now they are tasting defeat. They are down, Jørgen! He, the most dangerous of them all, his fall was the greatest! He made his bed, and now he is lying in it—poor, lost wretch that he is!

TESMAN: Have you had any news about Eilert? Since I went away, I mean?

MISS TESMAN: Just that he is supposed to have published a new book.

TESMAN: What! Eilert Løvborg? Recently? Hm?

MISS TESMAN: That's what they say. But I wonder if there can be much to it. What do you think? Ah—but when *your* new book comes, that will be something quite different, Jørgen! What is it going to be about?

TESMAN: It will deal with the domestic industries of Brabant during the Middle Ages.

MISS TESMAN: Just think—being able to write about something like that!

TESMAN: But as far as that is concerned, it may be quite some time before it is ready. I have all these collections to put in order first, you see.

MISS TESMAN: Yes, collecting and putting things in order—you certainly know how to do that. In that you are your father's son.

TESMAN: Well, I must say I am looking forward to getting started. Particularly now, that I've got my own delightful home to work in.

MISS TESMAN: And most of all now that you have the one your heart desired, dear Jørgen.

TESMAN (*embracing her*): Oh yes, yes, Aunt Julle! Hedda—she is the most wonderful part of it all! (*Looks toward the doorway.*) There—I think she is coming now, hm?

HEDDA *enters from the left side of the inner room. She is twenty-nine years old. Both features and figure are noble and elegant. Pale, ivory complexion. Steel-gray eyes, expressive of cold, clear calm. Beautiful brown hair, though not particularly ample. She is dressed in a tasteful, rather loose-fitting morning costume.*)

MISS TESMAN (*going toward her*): Good morning, my dear Hedda! A very happy morning to you!

HEDDA (*giving her hand*): Good morning, dear Miss Tesman! So early a call? That is most kind.

MISS TESMAN (*seems slightly embarrassed*): And—has the little lady of the house slept well the first night in her new home?

HEDDA: Passably, thank you.

TESMAN (*laughs*): Passably! You are a good one, Hedda! You were sleeping like a log when I got up.

HEDDA: Fortunately. And then, of course, Miss Tesman, it always takes time to get used to new surroundings. That has to come gradually. (*Looks left.*) Oh dear. The maid has left the verandah doors wide open. There's a veritable flood of sunlight in here.

MISS TESMAN (*toward the doors*): Well, then, we'll just close them.

HEDDA: No, no, not that. Tesman, dear, please pull the curtains. That will give a softer light.

TESMAN (*over by the French doors*): Yes, dear. There, now! Now you have both shade and fresh air, Hedda.

HEDDA: We certainly can use some air in here. Such loads of flowers—But, Miss Tesman, please—won't you be seated?

MISS TESMAN: No thanks. I just wanted to see if everything was all right—and so it is, thank goodness. I had better get back to Rina. I know she is waiting for me, poor thing.

TESMAN: Be sure to give her my love, Auntie. And tell her I'll be around to see her later today.

MISS TESMAN: I'll certainly do that!—Oh my! I almost forgot! (*Searches the pocket of her dress.*) I have something for you, Jørgen. Here.

TESMAN: What's that, Auntie? Hm?

MISS TESMAN (*pulls out a flat parcel wrapped in newspaper and gives it to him*): Here you are, dear.

TESMAN (*opens the parcel*): Well, well, well! So you took care of them for me, Aunt Julle! Hedda! Now, isn't that sweet, hm?

HEDDA (*by the whatnot, right*): If you'd tell me what it is—

TESMAN: My old slippers! *You* know!

HEDDA: Oh really? I remember you often talked about them on the trip.

TESMAN: Yes, for I missed them so. (*Walks over to her.*) Here—now you can see what they're like, Hedda.

HEDDA (*crosses toward stove*): Thanks. I don't know that I really care.

TESMAN (*following*): Just think—Aunt Rina embroidered these slippers for me. Ill as she was. You can't imagine how many memories they hold for me!

HEDDA (*by the table*): Hardly for me.

MISS TESMAN: That's true, you know, Jørgen.

TESMAN: Yes, but—I just thought that now that she's one of the family—

HEDDA (*interrupting*): I don't think we'll get on with that maid, Tesman.

MISS TESMAN: Not get on with Berte?

TESMAN: Whatever makes you say that, dear? Hm?

HEDDA (*points*): Look—she has left her old hat on the chair over there.

TESMAN (*appalled, drops the slippers*): But Hedda—!

HEDDA: What if somebody were to come and see it!

TESMAN: No, no, Hedda—that's Aunt Julle's hat!

HEDDA: Oh?

MISS TESMAN (*picking up the hat*): Yes, indeed it is. And it isn't old either, my dear young lady.

HEDDA: I really didn't look that closely—

MISS TESMAN (*tying the ribbons*): I want you to know that this is the first time I have it on my head. On my word it is!

TESMAN: And very handsome it is, too.

Really a splendid-looking hat!

MISS TESMAN: Oh, I don't know that it is anything so special, Jørgen. (*Looks around.*) My parasol—? Ah, here it is. (*Picks it up.*) For that is mine, too. (*Mutters.*) Not Berte's.

TESMAN: New hat and new parasol! What do you think of that, Hedda!

HEDDA: Very nice indeed.

TESMAN: Yes, don't you think so? Hm? But, Auntie, take a good look at Hedda before you leave. See how pretty and blooming she looks.

MISS TESMAN: Dear me, Jørgen; that's nothing new. Hedda has been lovely all her days.

(*She nods and walks right.*)

TESMAN (*following*): Yes, but have you noticed how full-figured and healthy she looks after the trip? How she has filled out?

HEDDA (*crossing*): Oh—stop it!

MISS TESMAN (*halts, turns around*): Filled out?

TESMAN: Yes, Aunt Julle. You can't see it so well now when she wears that dress. But I, who have the opportunity—

HEDDA (*by the French doors, impatiently*): Oh, you have no opportunity at all!

TESMAN: It must be the mountain air in Tyrol.

HEDDA (*curtly interrupting*): I am just as I was when I left.

TESMAN: Yes, so you say. I just don't think you're right. What do you think, Auntie?

MISS TESMAN (*has folded her hands, gazes at* HEDDA): Lovely—lovely—lovely! that is what Hedda is. (*Goes over to her, inclines her head forward with both her hands, and kisses her hair.*) God bless and keep Hedda Tesman. For Jørgen's sake.

HEDDA (*gently freeing herself*): There, *there*, Now let me go.

MISS TESMAN (*in quiet emotion*): Every single day I'll be over and see you two.

TESMAN: Yes, please do, Auntie. Hm?

MISS TESMAN: Goodbye, goodbye!

(*She leaves through door, right.* TESMAN *sees her out. The door remains ajar.* TESMAN *is heard repeating his greetings for* AUNT RINA *and his thanks for the slippers. In the meantime,* HEDDA *paces up and down, raises her arms, clenching her fists, as in quiet rage. Opens the curtains by the French doors and stands looking out. In a few moments,* TESMAN *re-enters and closes the door behind him.*)

TESMAN (*picking up the slippers*): What are you looking at, Hedda?

HEDDA (*once again calm and controlled*): Just the leaves. They are so yellow. And so withered.

TESMAN (*wrapping the slippers in their paper, putting the parcel down on the table*): Well, you know—we're in September now.

HEDDA (*again restless*): Yes—just think. We are already in—September.

TESMAN: Don't you think Aunt Julle acted strange, Hedda? Almost solemn. I wonder why. Hm?

HEDDA: I hardly know her, you see. Isn't she often like that?

TESMAN: Not the way she was today.

HEDDA (*turning away from the French doors*): Do you think she minded that business with the hat?

TESMAN: Oh, I don't think so. Not much. Perhaps a little bit right at the moment—

HEDDA: Well, I'm sorry, but I must say it strikes me as very odd—putting her hat down here in the living room. One just doesn't do that.

TESMAN: Well, you may be sure Aunt Julle won't ever do it again.

HEDDA: Anyway, I'll make it up to her, somehow.

TESMAN: Oh yes, Hedda; if only you would!

HEDDA: When you go over there today, why don't you ask her over for tonight?

TESMAN: I'll certainly do that. And then there is one other thing you could do that she'd appreciate ever so much.

HEDDA: What?

TESMAN: If you could just bring yourself to call her Auntie. For my sake, Hedda, hm?

HEDDA: No, Tesman, no. You really mustn't ask me to do that. I have already told you I won't. I'll try to call her Aunt Juliane. That will have to do.

TESMAN: All right, if you say so. I just thought that now that you're in the family—

HEDDA: Hmmm—I don't know about that—

(*She walks toward the doorway.*)

TESMAN (*after a brief pause*): Anything the matter, Hedda? Hm?

HEDDA: I'm just looking at my old piano. It doesn't quite go with the other furniture in here.

TESMAN: As soon as I get my first pay check we'll have it traded in.

HEDDA: No—I don't want to do that. I want to keep it. But let's put it in this inner room and get another one for out here. Whenever it's convenient, I mean.

TESMAN (*a little taken back*): Well—yes—we could do that—

HEDDA (*picks up the bouquet from the piano*): These flowers weren't here last night.

TESMAN: I suppose Aunt Julle brought them for you.

HEDDA (*looking at the flowers*): There's a card here. (*Takes it out and reads.*) "Will be back later." Can you guess who it's from?

TESMAN: No. Who? Hm?

HEDDA: Thea Elvsted.

TESMAN: No, really? Mrs. Elvsted! Miss Rysing that was.

HEDDA: That's right. The one with that irritating head of hair she used to show off with. An old flame of yours, I understand.

TESMAN (*laughs*): Well, now—that didn't last long! Anyway, that was before I knew you, Hedda. Just think—her being in town.

HEDDA: Strange, that she'd call on us. I have hardly seen her since we went to school together.

TESMAN: As far as that goes, I haven't seen her either for—God knows how long. I don't see how she can stand living in that out-of-the-way place. Hm?

HEDDA (*suddenly struck by a thought*): Listen, Tesman—isn't it some place near there that he lives—what's his name—Eilert Løvborg?

TESMAN: Yes, that's right. He is up there, too.

(BERTE *enters right.*)

BERTE: Ma'am, she's here again, that

lady who brought those flowers a while back. (*Pointing.*) The flowers you're holding in your hand, ma'am.

HEDDA: Ah, she is? Well, show her in, please.

(BERTE *opens the door for* MRS. ELVSTED *and exits.* MRS. ELVSTED *is of slight build, with a pretty, soft face. Her eyes are light blue, large, round, rather prominent, of a timid and querying expression. Her hair is strikingly light in color, almost whitish, and unusually rich and wavy. She is a couple of years younger than* HEDDA. *She is dressed in a dark visiting dress, tasteful, but not quite in the most recent fashion.*)

HEDDA (*walks toward her. Friendly*): Good morning, my dear Mrs. Elvsted. How very nice to see you again.

MRS. ELVSTED (*nervous, trying not to show it*): Well, yes, it is quite some time since we met.

TESMAN (*shaking hands*): And we, too. Hm?

HEDDA. Thank you for your lovely flowers—

MRS. ELVSTED. Please, don't—I would have come here yesterday afternoon. But I was told you were still traveling—

TESMAN: You've just arrived in town, hm?

MRS. ELVSTED. I got here yesterday, at noon. Oh, I was quite desperate when I learned you weren't home.

HEDDA: Desperate? But why?

TESMAN: But my dear Mrs. Rysing—I mean Mrs. Elvsted—

HEDDA: There is nothing wrong, I hope?

MRS. ELVSTED: Yes there is. And I don't know a single soul other than you that I can turn to here.

HEDDA (*putting the flowers down on the table*): Come—let's sit down here on the sofa.

MRS. ELVSTED: Oh, I'm in no mood to sit!

HEDDA: Of course you are. Come on. (*She pulls* MRS. ELVSTED *over to the sofa and sits down next to her.*)

TESMAN: Well, now, Mrs.—? Exactly what—?

HEDDA: Has something—special happened at home?

MRS. ELVSTED: Well, yes—and no. Oh, but I am so afraid you are going to misunderstand!

HEDDA: In that case, it seems to me you ought to tell us exactly what has happened, Mrs. Elvsted.

TESMAN: After all, that's why you are here. Hm?

MRS. ELVSTED: Yes, yes, of course. Well, then, maybe you already know—Eilert Løvborg is in town.

HEDDA: Is Løvborg—!

TESMAN: No! You don't say! Just think, Hedda—Løvborg's back!

HEDDA: All right. I can hear.

MRS. ELVSTED: He has been here a week already. Imagine—a whole week! In this dangerous place. Alone! With all that bad company around.

HEDDA: But my dear Mrs. Elvsted—why is he a concern of yours?

MRS. ELVSTED (*with an apprehensive look at her, says quickly*): He tutored the children.

HEDDA: Your children?

MRS. ELVSTED: My husband's. I don't have any.

HEDDA: In other words, your stepchildren.

MRS. ELVSTED: Yes.

TESMAN (*with some hesitation*): But was he— I don't quite know how to put this—was he sufficiently—regular—in his way of life to be thus employed? Hm?

MRS. ELVSTED: For the last two years, there hasn't been a thing to object to in his conduct.

TESMAN: No, really? Just think, Hedda!

HEDDA: I hear.

MRS. ELVSTED: Not the least little bit, I assure you! Not in any respect. And yet— knowing he's here—in the big city—And with all that money, too! I'm scared to death!

TESMAN: But in that case, why didn't he remain with you and your husband? Hm?

MRS. ELVSTED: After his book came out, he was too restless to stay.

TESMAN: Ah yes, that's right. Aunt Julle said he has published a new book.

MRS. ELVSTED: Yes, a big new book, about the course of civilization in general. It came out about two weeks ago. And since it has had such big sales and been discussed so much and made such a big splash—

TESMAN: It has, has it? I suppose this is something he has had lying around from better days?

MRS. ELVSTED: You mean from earlier?

TESMAN: Yes.

MRS. ELVSTED: No; it's all been written since he came to stay with us. During this last year.

TESMAN: Well, now! That's very good news, Hedda! Just think!

MRS. ELVSTED: Yes, if it only would last!

HEDDA: Have you seen him since you came to town?

MRS. ELVSTED: No, not yet. I had a great deal of trouble finding his address. But this morning I finally tracked him down.

HEDDA (*looks searchingly at her*): Isn't it rather odd that your husband—hm—

MRS. ELVSTED (*with a nervous start*): My husband! What about him?

HEDDA: That he sends you to town on such an errand? That he doesn't go and look after his friend himself?

MRS. ELVSTED: Oh, no, no—my husband doesn't have time for things like that. Besides, I have some—some shopping to do, anyway.

HEDDA (*with a slight smile*): Well, in that case, of course—

MRS. ELVSTED (*getting up, restlessly*): And now I beg of you, Mr. Tesman—won't you please receive Eilert Løvborg nicely if he calls on you? And I am sure he will. After all—Such good friends as you two used to be. And then you both do the same kind of work—the same studies, as far as I know.

TESMAN: We used to, at any rate.

MRS. ELVSTED: Yes. And that's why I implore you to please, please, try to keep an eye on him—you too. You'll do that, Mr. Tesman, won't you? Promise?

TESMAN: With the greatest pleasure, Mrs. Rysing.

HEDDA: Elvsted.

TESMAN: I'll gladly do as much for Eilert as I possibly can. You may certainly count on that.

MRS. ELVSTED: Oh, how good and kind you are! (*Clasps his hands.*) Thank you, thank you! (*Nervously.*) You see, my husband is so very fond of him.

HEDDA (*getting up*): You ought to write him a note, Tesman. Maybe he won't come without an invitation.

TESMAN: Yes, I suppose that would be the right thing to do, Hedda. Hm?

HEDDA: The sooner the better. Right away I think.

MRS. ELVSTED (*pleadingly*): If only you would!

TESMAN: I'll write this minute. Do you have his address, Mrs.—Mrs. Elvsted?

MRS. ELVSTED: Yes. (*Pulls a slip of paper from her bag and gives it to him.*) Here it is.

TESMAN: Very good. Well, then, if you'll excuse me—(*Looks around.*) By the way—the slippers? Ah, here we are. (*Leaving with the parcel.*)

HEDDA: Be sure you write a nice, warm, friendly letter, Tesman. And a long one, too.

TESMAN: Certainly, certainly.

MRS. ELVSTED: But not a word that it is I who—!

TESMAN: No, that goes without saying, I should think. Hm? (*Goes out right through inner room.*)

HEDDA (*goes over to* MRS. ELVSTED, *smiles, says in a low voice*): There! We've just killed two birds with one stone.

MRS. ELVSTED: What do you mean?

HEDDA: Didn't you see I wanted him out of the room?

MRS. ELVSTED: Yes, to write that letter—

HEDDA: And to speak to you alone.

MRS. ELVSTED (*flustered*): About the same thing?

HEDDA: Exactly.

MRS. ELVSTED (*anxious*): But there *is* nothing more, Mrs. Tesman! Really, there isn't!

HEDDA: Oh yes, there is. There is considerably more. I can see that much. Over here—We are going to have a real, nice, confidential talk, you and I. (*She forces* MRS. ELVSTED *down in the easy chair and seats herself on one of the ottomans.*)

MRS. ELVSTED (*worried, looks at her watch*):

But my dear Mrs. Tesman—I had really thought I would be on my way now.

HEDDA: Oh, I am sure there is no rush. Now, then. Tell me about yourself. How are things at home?

MRS. ELVSTED: That is just what I don't want to talk about.

HEDDA: But to me—! After all, we are old schoolmates.

MRS. ELVSTED: But you were a year ahead of me. And I used to be so scared of you!

HEDDA: Scared of me?

MRS. ELVSTED: Terribly. For when we met on the stairs, you always ruffled my hair.

HEDDA: Did I really?

MRS. ELVSTED: Yes. And once you said you were going to burn it off.

HEDDA: Oh, but you know—I wasn't serious!

MRS. ELVSTED: No, but I was such a silly, then. Anyway. Afterwards we drifted far apart. Our circles are so very different, you know.

HEDDA: All the more reason for getting close again. Listen. In school we called each other by our first names.

MRS. ELVSTED: Oh I'm sure you're wrong—

HEDDA: I'm sure I'm not! I remember it quite clearly. And now we want to be open with one another, just the way we used to. (*Moves the ottoman closer.*) There now! (*Kisses her cheek.*) You call me Hedda.

MRS. ELVSTED (*seizes her hands*): Oh, you are so good and kind! I'm not used to that.

HEDDA: There, there! And I'll call you my dear Thora, just as in the old days.

MRS. ELVSTED: My name is Thea.

HEDDA: So it is. Of course. I meant Thea. (*Looks at her with compassion.*) So you're not much used to goodness and kindness, Thea? Not in your own home?

MRS. ELVSTED: If I even had a home! But I don't. I never have had one.

HEDDA (*looks at her for a moment*): I thought there might be something like this.

MRS. ELVSTED (*helplessly, looking straight ahead*): Yes—yes—yes—

HEDDA: I am not sure if I quite remember—Didn't you first come to your husband as his housekeeper?

MRS. ELVSTED: I was really hired as governess. But his wife—his first wife—was ailing already then and was practically bedridden. So I had to take charge of the household as well.

HEDDA: But in the end you became his wife.

MRS. ELVSTED (*dully*): So I did.

HEDDA: Let's see. How long ago is that?

MRS. ELVSTED: Since my marriage?

HEDDA: Yes.

MRS. ELVSTED: About five years.

HEDDA: Right. It must be that long.

MRS. ELVSTED: Oh, those five years! Or mostly the last two or three! Oh, Mrs. Tesman—if you could just imagine!

HEDDA (*slaps her hand lightly*): Mrs. Tesman? Shame on you!

MRS. ELVSTED: Oh yes, all right; I'll try. Yes—if you could just—conceive—understand—

HEDDA (*casually*): And Eilert Løvborg has been living near you for some three years or so, hasn't he?

MRS. ELVSTED (*looks at her uncertainly*): Eilert Løvborg? Yes—he has.

HEDDA: Did you know him before? Here in town?

MRS. ELVSTED: Hardly at all. That is, of course I did in a way. I mean, I knew *of* him.

HEDDA: But up there—You saw a great deal of him; did you?

MRS. ELVSTED: Yes, he came over to us every day. He was supposed to tutor the children, you see. For I just couldn't do it all by myself.

HEDDA: Of course not. And your husband—? I suppose he travels quite a bit.

MRS. ELVSTED: Well, yes, Mrs. Tes—Hedda —as a public magistrate, you know, he very often has to travel all over his district.

HEDDA (*leaning against the armrest on the easy chair*): Thea—poor, sweet Thea—now you have to tell me everything—just as it is.

MRS. ELVSTED: You'd better ask me, then.

HEDDA: How *is* your husband, Thea? I mean—you know—*really*? To be with. What kind of person is he? Is he good to you?

MRS. ELVSTED (*evasively*): I believe he thinks he does everything for the best.

HEDDA: But isn't he altogether too old for you? He is more than twenty years older, isn't he?

MRS. ELVSTED (*with irritation*): Yes, there is that, too. But there isn't just one thing. Every single little thing about him repels me! We don't have a thought in common, he and I. Not a thing in the world!

HEDDA: But isn't he fond of you all the same? I mean in his own way?

MRS. ELVSTED: I don't know. I think I am just useful to him. And I don't use much money. I am inexpensive.

HEDDA: That is foolish of you.

MRS. ELVSTED (*shakes her head*): Can't be changed. Not with him. I don't think he cares for anybody much except himself. Perhaps the children a little.

HEDDA: And Eilert Løvborg, Thea.

MRS. ELVSTED (*looks at her*): Eilert Løvborg? What makes you think that?

HEDDA: Well, it seems to me that when he sends you all the way to town to look after him—(*with an almost imperceptible smile*). Besides, you said so yourself. To Tesman.

MRS. ELVSTED (*with a nervous twitch*): Did I? I suppose I did. (*With a muted outburst.*) No! I might as well tell you now as later. For it's bound to come out, anyway.

HEDDA: But my dear Thea—?

MRS. ELVSTED: All right. My husband doesn't know I've gone!

HEDDA: What! He doesn't know?

MRS. ELVSTED: He wasn't even home. He's away again. Oh, I just couldn't take it any longer, Hedda! It had become utterly impossible. All alone as I was.

HEDDA: So what did you do?

MRS. ELVSTED: I packed some of my things. Just the most necessary. Without telling anybody. And left.

HEDDA: Just like that?

MRS. ELVSTED: Yes. And took the next train to town.

HEDDA: But dearest Thea—how did you dare to do a thing like that!

MRS. ELVSTED (*rises, walks*): What else could I do?

HEDDA: But what do you think your husband will say when you go back?

MRS. ELVSTED (*by the table; looks at her*): Go back to him?

HEDDA: Yes!

MRS. ELVSTED: I'll never go back.

HEDDA (*rises, approaches her slowly*): So you have really, seriously—left everything?

MRS. ELVSTED: Yes. It seemed to me there was nothing else I could do.

HEDDA: And quite openly, too.

MRS. ELVSTED: You can't keep a thing like that secret, anyway.

HEDDA: But what do you think people will say, Thea?

MRS. ELVSTED: In God's name, let them say whatever they like. (*Sits down on the sofa, dully tired.*) For I have only done what I had to do.

HEDDA (*after a brief silence*): And what do you plan to do with yourself? What sort of work will you do?

MRS. ELVSTED: I don't know yet. I only know I have to live where Eilert Løvborg is. If I am to live at all.

HEDDA (*moves a chair from the table closer to* MRS. ELVSTED, *sits down, strokes her hands*): Thea—tell me. How did this—this friendship between you and Eilert Løvborg—how did it begin?

MRS. ELVSTED: Oh, it grew little by little. I got some sort of power over him.

HEDDA: Oh?

MRS. ELVSTED: He dropped his old ways. Not because I asked him to. I never dared to do that. But I think he must have noticed how I felt about that kind of life. So he changed.

HEDDA (*quickly suppresses a cynical smile*): So you have—rehabilitated him, as they say. Haven't you, Thea?

MRS. ELVSTED: At least, that's what *he* says. On the other hand, he has turned me into a real human being. Taught me to think—and understand—all sorts of things.

HEDDA: Maybe he tutored you, too?

MRS. ELVSTED: No, not tutored exactly. But he talked to me. About so many, many things. And then came that lovely, lovely time when I could share his work with him. He let me help him!

HEDDA: He did?

MRS. ELVSTED: Yes! Whatever he wrote, he wanted us to be together about it.

HEDDA: Just like two good comrades.

MRS. ELVSTED (*with animation*): Comrades! —that's it! Imagine, Hedda—that's just what he called it, too. Oh, I really ought to feel so happy. But I can't. For you see, I don't know if it will last.

HEDDA: You don't trust him any more than that?

MRS. ELVSTED (*heavily*): The shadow of a woman stands between Eilert Løvborg and me.

HEDDA (*tensely, looks at her*): Who?

MRS. ELVSTED: I don't know. Somebody or other from—his past. I don't think he has ever really forgotten her.

HEDDA: What has he told you about it?

MRS. ELVSTED: He has mentioned it only once—just casually.

HEDDA: And what did he say?

MRS. ELVSTED: He said that when they parted she was going to kill him with a gun.

HEDDA (*cold, controlled*): Oh, nonsense. People don't do that sort of thing here.

MRS. ELVSTED: No, I know. And that is why I think it must be that red-headed singer he used to—

HEDDA: Yes, I suppose so.

MRS. ELVSTED: For I remember people said she carried a loaded gun.

HEDDA: Well, then I'm sure it's she.

MRS. ELVSTED (*wringing her hands*): Yes, but just think, Hedda—now I hear that she— that singer—that she's here in town again, too! Oh, I'm just desperate—!

HEDDA (*with a glance toward the inner room*): Shhh; Here's Tesman. (*Rises and whispers.*) Not a word about all this to anybody, Thea!

MRS. ELVSTED (*jumps up*): No, no. For God's sake—!

(TESMAN, *carrying a letter, enters from the right side of the inner room.*)

TESMAN: There, now—here's the missive, all ready to go!

HEDDA: Good. But I believe Mrs. Elvsted wants to be on her way. Wait a moment. I'll see you to the garden gate.

TESMAN: Say, Hedda—do you think Berte could take care of this?

HEDDA (*takes the letter*): I'll tell her. (BERTE *enter right.*)

BERTE: Judge Brack is here and wants to know if you're receiving.

HEDDA: Yes, ask the Judge please to come in. And—here—drop this in a mailbox, will you?

BERTE (*takes the letter*): Yes, ma'am.

(*She opens the door for* JUDGE BRACK *and exits. The* JUDGE *is forty-five years of age. Rather thickset, but well-built and with brisk, athletic movements. Roundish face, aristocratic profile. His hair is short, still almost completely black, very neatly dressed. Lively, sparkling eyes. Thick eyebrows and mustache with cut-off points. He is dressed in an elegant suit, a trifle youthful for his age. He wears pince-nez glasses, attached to a string, and lets them drop from time to time.*)

JUDGE BRACK (*hat in hand, salutes*): May one pay one's respects as early as this?

HEDDA: One certainly may.

TESMAN (*shaking his hand*): You are always welcome. (*Introducing.*) Judge Brack—Miss Rysing—

HEDDA (*groans*).

BRACK (*bowing*): Delighted!

HEDDA (*looks at him, laughs*): How nice it is to see you in daylight, Judge!

BRACK: You find me changed, perhaps?

HEDDA: A bit younger, I think.

BRACK: Much obliged.

TESMAN: But what do you think of Hedda?

Hm? Did you ever see her in such bloom? She positively—

HEDDA: Will you please leave me out of this? You had better thank the Judge for all the trouble he has taken.

BRACK: Oh, nonsense. It's been a pleasure.

HEDDA: Yes, you are indeed a faithful soul. But my friend here is dying to be off. Don't leave, Judge. I'll be back in a minute.

(*Mutual goodbyes.* MRS. ELVSTED *and* HEDDA *exit, right.*)

BRACK: Well, now—your wife—is she tolerably satisfied?

TESMAN: Yes, indeed, and we really can't thank you enough. That is, I understand there will have to be some slight changes made here and there. And there are still a few things—just a few trifles—we'll have to get.

BRACK: Oh? Really?

TESMAN: But we certainly don't want to bother you with that. Hedda said she's going to take care of it herself. But do sit down, hm?

BRACK: Thanks. Maybe just for a moment —(*sits down by the table*). There's one thing I'd like to talk to you about, my dear Tesman.

TESMAN: Oh? Ah, I see. (*Sits down.*) I suppose it's the serious part of the festivities that's beginning now. Hm?

BRACK: Oh—there's no great rush as far as the money is concerned. Though I must say I wish we could have established ourselves a trifle more economically.

TESMAN: Out of the question, my dear fellow! Remember, it's all for Hedda! You, who know her so well—! After all, I couldn't put her up like any little middle-class housewife—

BRACK: No, I suppose—That's just it.

TESMAN: Besides—fortunately—it can't be long now before I receive my appointment.

BRACK: Well, you know—things like that have a way of hanging fire.

TESMAN: Perhaps you have heard something? Something definite? Hm?

BRACK: No, nothing certain—(*interrupting himself*): But that reminds me. I have some news for you.

TESMAN: Oh?

BRACK: Your old friend Eilert Løvborg is back in town.

TESMAN: I know that already.

BRACK: So? Who told you?

TESMAN: The lady who just left.

BRACK: I see. What did you say her name was again? I didn't quite catch—

TESMAN: Mrs. Elvsted.

BRACK: Ah yes—the Commissioner's wife. Yes, it's up in her part of the country that Løvborg has been staying, too.

TESMAN: And just think. I am so glad to hear it. He is quite respectable again.

BRACK: Yes, so they say.

TESMAN: And he has published a new book, hm?

BRACK: Oh yes.

TESMAN: Which is making quite a stir.

BRACK: Quite an unusual stir.

TESMAN: Just think! Isn't that just wonderful! He—with his remarkable gifts. And I was so sure he'd gone under for good.

BRACK: That seems to have been the general opinion.

TESMAN: What I don't understand, though, is what he is going to do with himself. What sort of living can he make? Hm?

(*During the last remark* HEDDA *re-enters, right.*)

HEDDA (*to* BRACK, *with a scornful little laugh*): Tesman is forever worrying about how people are going to make a living.

TESMAN: Well, you see, we are talking about poor Eilert Løvborg, Hedda.

HEDDA (*with a quick look at him*): You are? (*Sits down in the easy chair by the stove and asks casually,*) What is the matter with him?

TESMAN: Well, you see, I believe he's run through his inheritance a long time ago. And I don't suppose he can write a new book every year. Hm? So I really must ask how he is going to make out.

BRACK: Maybe I could help you answer that.

TESMAN: Yes?

BRACK: Remember, he has relatives with considerable influence.

TESMAN: Ah—unfortunately, those relatives have washed their hands of him long ago.

BRACK: Just the same, they used to call him the hope of the family.

TESMAN: Yes, before! But he has ruined all that.

HEDDA: Who knows? (*With a little smile.*) I hear the Elvsteds have rehabilitated him.

BRACK: And then this book—

TESMAN: Well, I certainly hope they will help him to find something or other. I just wrote him a letter. Hedda, dear, I asked him to come out here tonight.

BRACK: Oh dear, I am sorry. Don't you remember—you're supposed to come to my little stag dinner tonight? You accepted last night on the pier, you know.

HEDDA: Had you forgotten, Tesman?

TESMAN: So I had.

BRACK: Oh well. I'm sure he won't come, so it doesn't really make any difference.

TESMAN: Why is that? Hm?

BRACK (*gets up somewhat hesitantly, rests his hands on the back of the chair*): Dear Tesman— and you, too, Mrs. Tesman—I cannot in good conscience let you remain in ignorance of something, which—which—

TESMAN: Something to do with Eilert?

BRACK: With both you and him.

TESMAN: But my dear Judge, do speak!

BRACK: You must be prepared to find that your appointment will not come through as soon as you hope and expect.

TESMAN (*jumps up, nervously*): Something's happened? Hm?

BRACK: It may conceivably be made contingent upon the result of a competition.

TESSMAN: Competition! Just think, Hedda!

HEDDA (*leaning farther back in her chair*): Ah—I see, I see—!

TESMAN: But with whom? Don't tell me with—?

BRACK: Precisely. With Eilert Løvborg.

TESMAN (*claps his hands together*): No, no! This can't be. It is unthinkable! Quite impossible! Hm?

BRACK: All the same, that's the way it may turn out.

TESMAN: No, but Judge, this would amount to the most incredible callousness toward me! (*Waving his arms.*) For just think—I'm a married man! We married on the strength of these prospects, Hedda and I. Got ourselves deep in debt. Borrowed money from Aunt Julle, too. After all, I had practically been promised the post, you know. Hm?

BRACK: Well, well. I daresay you'll get it in the end. If only after a competition.

HEDDA (*motionless in her chair*): Just think, Tesman. It will be like a kind of contest.

TESMAN: But dearest Hedda, how can you be so unconcerned!

HEDDA (*still without moving*): I'm not at all unconcerned. I'm dying to see who wins.

BRACK: In any case, Mrs. Tesman, I'm glad you know the situation for what it is. I mean—before you proceed to make the little additional purchases I understand you threaten us with.

HEDDA: This makes no difference as far as that is concerned.

BRACK: Really? Well, in that case, of course—Goodbye! (*to* TESMAN) I'll pick you up on my afternoon walk.

TESMAN: What? Oh yes, yes, of course. I'm sorry; I'm just all confused.

HEDDA (*without getting up, gives her hand*): Goodbye, Judge. Come back soon.

BRACK: Thanks. Goodbye, goodbye.

TESMAN (*sees him to the door*): Goodbye, my dear Judge. You really must excuse me— (*JUDGE BRACK exits, right.*)

TESMAN (*pacing the floor*): Oh, Hedda, Hedda! One should never venture into fairyland. Hm?

HEDDA (*looks at him, smiles*): Do *you* do that?

TESMAN: Well, yes—it can't be denied—it was most venturesome of me to rush into marriage and set up a home on the strength of mere prospects.

HEDDA: Well, maybe you're right.

TESMAN: Anyway—we do have our own nice, comfortable home, now. Just think,

Hedda—the very home both of us dreamed about. Set our hearts on, I may almost say. Hm?

HEDDA (*rises, slowly, tired*): The agreement was that we were to maintain a certain position—entertain—

TESMAN: Don't I know it! Dearest Hedda— I have been so looking forward to seeing you as hostess in a select circle! Hm? Well, well, well! In the meantime, we'll just have to be content with one another. See Aunt Julle once in a while. Nothing more. And you were meant for such a different kind of life, altogether!

HEDDA: I suppose a footman is completely out of the question.

TESMAN: I'm afraid so. Under the circumstances, you see—we couldn't possibly—

HEDDA: And as for getting my own riding horse—

TESMAN (*aghast*): Riding horse!

HEDDA: I suppose I mustn't even think of that.

TESMAN: Good heavens, no! That goes without saying, I hope!

HEDDA (*walking*): Well—at least I have one thing to amuse myself with in the meantime.

TESMAN (*overjoyed*): Oh thank goodness for that! And what *is* that, Hedda, hm?

HEDDA (*in the doorway, looks at him with suppressed scorn*): My guns—Jørgen!

TESMAN (*in fear*): Your guns!

HEDDA (*with cold eyes*): General Gabler's guns.

(*She exits left, through the inner room.*)

TESMAN (*runs to the doorway, calls after her*): But Hedda! Good gracious! Hedda, dear! Please don't touch those dangerous things! For my sake, Hedda! Hm?

ACT TWO

(*The same room at the TESMANS'. The piano has been moved out and replaced by an elegant little writing desk. A small table has been placed near the sofa, left. Most of the flowers have been removed. MRS. ELVSTED's bouquet is on the big table front center. Afternoon.*

HEDDA, dressed to receive callers, is alone. She is standing near the open French doors loading a revolver. Its mate is lying in an open case on the desk.)

HEDDA (*looking down into the garden, calls*): Hello there, Judge! Welcome back!

JUDGE BRACK (*off-stage*): Thanks, Mrs. Tesman!

HEDDA (*raises the gun, sights*): Now I am going to shoot you, Judge Brack!

BRACK (*calls off-stage*): No—no—no! Don't point the gun at me like that!

HEDDA: That's what you get for sneaking in at the back door! (*Fires.*)

BRACK (*closer*): Are you out of your mind—!

HEDDA: Oh dear—did I hit you?

BRACK (*still off-stage*): Stop that nonsense!

HEDDA: Come on in, then.

(*JUDGE BRACK, dressed for dinner, enters left. He carries a light overcoat over his arm.*)

BRACK: Dammit! Do you still fool around with that thing? What are you shooting at, anyway?

HEDDA: Oh—just firing off into blue air.

BRACK (*gently but firmly taking the gun away from her*): With your permission, Mrs. Tesman. (*Looks at it.*) Ah yes, I remember this gun very well. (*Looks around.*) Where is the case? Ah, here we are. (*Puts the gun in the case and closes it.*) That's enough of that silliness for today.

HEDDA: But in the name of heaven, what do you expect me to do with myself?

BRACK: No callers?

HEDDA (*closing the French doors*): Not a soul. All my close friends are still out of town, it seems.

BRACK: And Tesman is out, too, perhaps?

HEDDA (*by the desk, puts the gun case in a drawer*): Yes. He took off for the aunts' right after lunch. He didn't expect you so early.

BRACK: I should have thought of that. That was stupid of me.

HEDDA (*turns her head, looks at him*): Why stupid?

BRACK: I would have come a little—sooner.

HEDDA (*crossing*): If you had, you wouldn't have found anybody home. For I have been in my room ever since lunch, changing my clothes.

BRACK: And isn't there the tiniest little opening in the door for negotiations?

HEDDA: You forgot to provide one.

BRACK: Another stupidity.

HEDDA: So we'll have to stay in here. And wait. For I don't think Tesman will be back for some time.

BRACK: By all means. I'll be very patient.

(HEDDA *sits on the sofa in the corner.* BRACK *puts his overcoat over the back of the nearest chair and sits down, keeping his hat in his hand. Brief silence. They look at one another.*)

HEDDA: Well?

BRACK (*in the same tone*): Well?

HEDDA: I said it first.

BRACK (*leans forward a little*): All right. Let's have a nice little chat, Mrs. Tesman.

HEDDA (*leans back*): Don't you think it's an eternity since last time we talked? I don't count last night and this morning. That was nothing.

BRACK: You mean—just the two of us?

HEDDA: Something like that.

BRACK: There hasn't been a day I haven't wished you were back again.

HEDDA: My feelings, exactly.

BRACK: Yours? Really, Mrs. Tesman? And I have been assuming you were having such a wonderful time.

HEDDA: I'd say!

BRACK: All Tesman's letters said so.

HEDDA: Oh yes, he! He's happy just poking through old collections of books. And copying old parchments—or whatever they are.

BRACK (*with a touch of malice*): Well, that's his calling, you know. Partly, anyway.

HEDDA: Yes, so it is. And in that case I suppose—But I! Oh, Judge! You've no idea how bored I've been.

BRACK (*with sympathy*): Really? You're serious?

HEDDA: Surely you can understand that? For a whole half year never to see anyone who knows even a little bit about our circle? And talks our language?

BRACK: Yes, I think I would find that trying, too.

HEDDA: And then the most unbearable thing of all—

BRACK: Well?

HEDDA: —everlastingly to be in the company of the same person—

BRACK (*nods in agreement*): Both early and late—yes. I can imagine—at all possible times—

HEDDA: I said everlastingly.

BRACK: All right. Still, it seems to me that with as excellent a person as our Tesman, it ought to be possible—

HEDDA: My dear Judge—Tesman is a specialist.

BRACK: Granted.

HEDDA: And specialists are not at all entertaining travel companions. Not in the long run, at any rate.

BRACK: Not even—the specialist—one happens to love?

HEDDA: Bah! That nauseating word!

BRACK (*puzzled*): Really, now, Mrs. Tesman—?

HEDDA (*half laughing, half annoyed*): You ought to try it some time! Listening to talk about the history of civilization, early and late—

BRACK: Everlastingly—

HEDDA: All right. And then this business about the domestic industry in the Middle Ages—! That's the ghastliest part of it all!

BRACK (*looking searchingly at her*): But in that case—tell me—how I am to explain—?

HEDDA: That Jørgen Tesman and I made a pair of it, you mean?

BRACK: If you want to put it that way—yes.

HEDDA: Come now. Do you really find that so strange?

BRACK: Both yes and no—Mrs. Tesman.

HEDDA: I had danced myself tired, my dear Judge. My season was over—(*gives a slight start*). No, no—I don't really mean that. Won't think it, either!

BRACK: Nor do you have the slightest reason to, I am sure.

HEDDA: Oh—as far as reason is concerned—(*looks at him as if trying to read his mind*). And, after all, Jørgen Tesman must be said to be a most proper young man in all respects.

BRACK: Both proper and substantial. Most certainly.

HEDDA: And one can't say there is anything exactly comical about him. Do you think there is?

BRACK: Comical? No—o. I wouldn't say that—

HEDDA: All right, then. And he is a most assiduous collector. Nobody can deny that. I think it is perfectly possible he may go quite far, after all.

BRACK (*looks at her rather uncertainly*): I assumed that you, like everybody else, were convinced that he will in time become an exceptionally eminent man?

HEDDA (*with a weary expression*): Yes, I was. And then, you see—there he was, wanting so desperately to be allowed to provide for me—I don't know why I shouldn't have accepted?

BRACK: No, certainly. From that point of view—

HEDDA: For you know, Judge, that was considerably more than my other admirers were willing to do.

BRACK (*laughs*): Well! Of course I can't answer for all the others. But as far as I am concerned, I have always had a certain degree of—respect for the bonds of matrimony. You know—as a general proposition, Mrs. Tesman.

HEDDA (*lightly*): Well, I never really counted very heavily on *you*—

BRACK: All I want is a nice, confidential circle, in which I can be of service, both in deed and in counsel. Be allowed to come and go like a true and trusted friend—

HEDDA: You mean, of the master of the house—?

BRACK (*with a slight bow*): To be perfectly frank—rather of the mistress. But by all means—the master, too, of course. Do you know, that kind of—shall I say, triangular?—relationship can really be a great comfort to all parties involved.

HEDDA: Yes, many were the times I missed a second travel companion. To be twosome in the compartment—brrr!

BRACK: Fortunately, the wedding trip is over.

HEDDA (*shakes her head*): There's a long journey ahead. I've just arrived at a station on the way.

BRACK: Well, at the station one gets out and moves around a bit, Mrs. Tesman.

HEDDA: I never get out.

BRACK: Really?

HEDDA: No. For there's always someone around, who—

BRACK (*laughs*): —looks at one's legs; is that it?

HEDDA: Exactly.

BRACK: Oh well, really, now—

HEDDA (*with a silencing gesture*): I won't have it! Rather stay in my seat—once I'm seated. Twosome and all.

BRACK: But what if a third party were to join the couple?

HEDDA: Well, now—*that* would be something altogether different!

BRACK: A proven, understanding friend—

HEDDA: —entertaining in all sorts of lively ways—

BRACK: —and not at all a specialist!

HEDDA (*with audible breath*): Yes, that would indeed be a comfort.

BRACK (*hearing the front door open, looking at her*): The triangle is complete.

HEDDA (*half aloud*): And the train goes on.

(TESMAN, *in gray walking suit and soft hat, enters, right. He carries a pile of paperbound books under his arm. Others are stuffed in his pockets.*)

TESMAN (*walks up to the table in front of the corner sofa*): Puuhh—! Quite some load to carry, all this—and in this heat, too. (*Puts the books down.*) I am positively perspiring, Hedda. Well, well. So you're here already, my dear Judge. Hm? And Berte didn't tell me.

BRACK (*rises*): I came through the garden.

HEDDA: What are all those books?

TESMAN (*leafing through some of them*): Just some new publications in my special field.

HEDDA: Special field, hm?

BRACK: Ah yes—professional publications, Mrs. Tesman. (*He and* HEDDA *exchange knowing smiles.*)

HEDDA: Do you still need more books?

TESMAN: Yes, my dear. There is no such thing as having too many books in one's special field. One has to keep up with what is being written and published, you know.

HEDDA: I suppose.

TESMAN (*searching among the books*): And look. Here is Eilert Løvborg's new book, too. (*Offers it to her.*) Want to take a look at it, Hedda? Hm?

HEDDA: No—thanks just the same. Or perhaps later.

TESMAN: I glanced at it on my way home.

BRACK: And what do you think of it? As a specialist yourself?

TESMAN: It is remarkable for its sobriety. He never wrote like that before. (*Gathers up all the books.*) I just want to take these into my study. I am so much looking forward to cutting them open! And then I'll change. (*to* BRACK) I assume there's no rush to be off, is there?

BRACK: Not at all. We have plenty of time.

TESMAN: In that case, I think I'll indulge myself a little. (*On his way out with the books he halts in the doorway and turns.*) That's right, Hedda—Aunt Julle won't be out to see you tonight, after all.

HEDDA: No? Is it that business with the hat, do you think?

TESMAN: Oh, no—not at all. How can you believe a thing like that about Aunt Julle! Just think! No, it's Aunt Rina. She's feeling very poorly.

HEDDA: Isn't she always?

TESMAN: Yes, but it's especially bad today, poor thing.

HEDDA: Well, in that case I suppose she ought to stay home. I shall have to put up with it; that's all.

TESMAN: And you have no idea how perfectly delighted Aunt Julle was, even so. Because of how splendid you look after the trip, Hedda!

HEDDA (*half aloud, rising*): Oh, these everlasting aunts!

TESMAN: Hm?

HEDDA (*walks over to the French doors*): Nothing.

TESMAN: No? All right. Well, excuse me. (*Exits right, through inner room.*)

BRACK: What is this about a hat?

HEDDA: Oh, something with Miss Tesman this morning. She had put her hat down on the chair over there. (*Looks at him, smiles.*) So I pretended to think it was the maid's.

BRACK (*shakes his head*): But my dear Mrs. Tesman—how could you do a thing like that! And to that excellent old lady, too!

HEDDA (*nervously pacing the floor*): Well, you see—something just takes hold of me at times. And then I can't help myself— (*throws herself down in the easy chair near the stove*). Oh I can't explain it even to myself.

BRACK (*behind her chair*): You aren't really happy—that's the trouble.

HEDDA (*staring into space*): I don't know any reason why I should be. Do you?

BRACK: Well, yes—partly because you've got the home you've always wanted.

HEDDA (*looks up at him and laughs*): So you too believe that story about my great desire?

BRACK: You mean, there is nothing to it?

HEDDA: Well, yes; there is *something* to it.

BRACK: Well?

HEDDA: There is this much to it, that last summer I used Tesman to see me home from evening parties.

BRACK: Unfortunately—my route was in quite a different direction.

HEDDA: True. You walked other roads last summer.

BRACK (*laughs*): Shame on you, Mrs.

Tesman! So, all right—you and Tesman—?

HEDDA: One evening we passed by here. And Tesman, poor thing, was practically turning himself into knots trying to find something to talk about. So I felt sorry for all that erudition—

BRACK (*with a doubting smile*): You did? Hm—

HEDDA: I really did. So, just to help him out of his misery, I happened to say that I'd like to live in this house.

BRACK: Just that?

HEDDA: That was all—*that* evening.

BRACK: But afterwards—?

HEDDA: Yes, my frivolity had consequences, Judge.

BRACK: Unfortunately—that's often the way with frivolities. It happens to all of us, Mrs. Tesman.

HEDDA: Thanks! So in our common enthusiasm for Mr. Secretary Falk's villa Tesman and I found each other, you see! The result was engagement and wedding and honeymoon abroad and all the rest of it. Well, yes, my dear Judge—I've made my bed—I almost said.

BRACK: But this is priceless! And you didn't really care for the house at all?

HEDDA: Certainly not.

BRACK: Not even now? After all, we've set up quite a comfortable home for you here, haven't we?

HEDDA: Oh—it seems to me I smell lavender and rose sachets in all the rooms. But maybe that's a smell Aunt Julle brought with her.

BRACK (*laughs*): My guess is rather the late lamented Secretary's wife.

HEDDA: It smells of mortality, whoever it is. Like corsages—the next day. (*Clasps her hands behind her neck, leans back, looks at him.*) Judge, you have no idea how dreadfully bored I'll be—out here.

BRACK: But don't you think life may hold some task for you, too, Mrs. Tesman?

HEDDA: A task? With any kind of appeal?

BRACK: Preferably that, of course.

HEDDA: Heaven knows what kind of task that might be. There are times when I wonder if—(*interrupts herself*). No; I'm sure that wouldn't work, either.

BRACK: Who knows? Tell me.

HEDDA: It has occurred to me that maybe I could get Tesman to enter politics.

BRACK (*laughs*): Tesman! No, really—I must confess that—politics doesn't strike me as being exactly Tesman's line.

HEDDA: I agree. But suppose I were to prevail on him, all the same?

BRACK: What satisfaction could you possibly find in that? If he can't succeed—why do you want him even to try?

HEDDA: Because I am bored, I tell you! (*After a brief pause.*) So you think it's quite out of the question that Tesman could ever become prime minister?

BRACK: Well, you see, Mrs. Tesman—to do that he'd first of all have to be a fairly wealthy man.

HEDDA (*getting up, impatiently*): Yes! There we are! These shabby circumstances I've married into! (*Crosses the floor.*) That's what makes life so mean. So outright ludicrous! For that's what it is, you know.

BRACK: Personally I believe something else is to blame.

HEDDA: What?

BRACK: You've never been through anything that's really stirred you.

HEDDA: Something serious, you mean?

BRACK: If you like. But maybe it's coming now.

HEDDA (*with a toss of her head*): You are thinking of that silly old professorship! That's Tesman's business. I refuse to give it a thought.

BRACK: As you wish. But now—to put it in the grand style—now when a solemn challenge of responsibility will be posed? Demands made on you? (*Smiles.*) New demands, Mrs. Tesman.

HEDDA (*angry*): Quiet! You'll never see anything of the kind.

BRACK (*cautiously*): We'll talk about this a year from now—on the outside.

HEDDA (*curtly*): I'm not made for that

sort of thing, Judge! No demands for me!

BRACK: But surely you, like most women, are made for a duty, which—

HEDDA (*over by the French doors*): Oh, do be quiet! Often it seems to me there's only one thing in the world that I am made for.

BRACK (*coming close*): And may I ask what that is?

HEDDA (*looking out*): To be bored to death. Now you know. (*Turns, looks toward the inner room, laughs.*) Just as I thought. Here comes the professor.

BRACK (*warningly, in a low voice*): Steady now, Mrs. Tesman!

(TESMAN, *dressed for a party, carrying his hat and gloves, enters from the right side of the inner room.*)

TESMAN: Hedda, any word yet from Eilert Løvborg that he isn't coming, hm?

HEDDA: No.

TESMAN: In that case, I wouldn't be a bit surprised if we have him here in a few minutes.

BRACK: You really think he'll come?

TESMAN: I am almost certain he will. For I'm sure it's only idle gossip what you told me this morning.

BRACK: Oh?

TESMAN: Anyway, that's what Aunt Julle said. She doesn't for a moment believe he'll stand in my way. Just think!

BRACK: I'm very glad to hear that.

TESMAN (*puts his hat and his gloves down on a chair, right*): But you must let me wait for him as long as possible.

BRACK: By all means. We have plenty of time. Nobody will arrive at my place before seven—seven-thirty, or so.

TESMAN: And in the meantime we can keep Hedda company. Take our time. Hm?

HEDDA (*carrying* BRACK's *hat and coat over to the sofa in the corner*): And if worst comes to worst, Mr. Løvborg can stay here with me.

BRACK (*trying to take the things away from her*): Let me, Mrs. Tesman—What do you mean—"if worst comes to worst?"

HEDDA: If he doesn't want to go with you and Tesman.

TESMAN (*looks dubiously at her*): But, dearest Hedda—do you think that will quite do? He staying here with you? Hm? Remember, Aunt Julle won't be here.

HEDDA: No, but Mrs. Elvsted will. The three of us will have a cup of tea together.

TESMAN: Oh yes; *that* will be perfectly all right!

BRACK (*with a smile*): And perhaps the wiser course of action for him.

HEDDA: What do you mean?

BRACK: Begging your pardon, Mrs. Tesman—you've often enough looked askance at my little stag dinners. It's been your opinion that only men of the firmest principles ought to attend.

HEDDA: I should think Mr. Løvborg is firm-principled enough now. A reformed sinner—

(BERTE *appears in door, right.*)

BERTE: Ma'am—there's a gentleman here who asks if—

HEDDA: Show him in, please.

TESMAN (*softly*): I'm sure it's he! Just think!

(EILERT LØVBORG *enters, right. He is slim, gaunt. Of* TESMAN's *age, but he looks older and somewhat dissipated. Brown hair and beard. Pale, longish face, reddish spots on the cheekbones. Dressed for visiting in elegant, black, brand-new suit. He carries a silk hat and dark gloves in his hand. He remains near the door, makes a quick bow. He appears a little embarrassed.*)

TESMAN (*goes over to him, shakes his hand*): My dear Eilert—at last we meet again!

EILERT LØVBORG (*subdued voice*): Thanks for your note, Jørgen! (*Approaching* HEDDA.) Am I allowed to shake your hand, too, Mrs. Tesman?

HEDDA (*accepting his proffered hand*): I am very glad to see you, Mr. Løvborg. (*With a gesture.*) I don't know if you two gentlemen—

LØVBORG (*with a slight bow*): Judge Brack, I believe.

BRACK (*also bowing slightly*): Certainly. Some years ago—

TESMAN (*to* LØVBORG, *both hands on his shoulders*): And now I want you to feel quite at home here, Eilert! Isn't that right, Hedda? For you plan to stay here in town, I understand. Hm?

LØVBORG: Yes, I do.

TESMAN: Perfectly reasonable. Listen—I just got hold of your new book, but I haven't had a chance to read it yet.

LØVBORG: You may save yourself the trouble.

TESMAN: Why do you say that?

LØVBORG: There's not much to it.

TESMAN: Just think—you saying that!

BRACK: Nevertheless, people seem to have very good things to say about it.

LØVBORG: That's exactly why I wrote it—so everybody would like it.

BRACK: Very wise of you.

TESMAN: Yes, but Eilert—!

LØVBORG: For I am trying to rebuild my position. Start all over again.

TESMAN (*with some embarrassment*): Yes, I suppose you are, aren't you? Hm?

LØVBORG (*smiles, puts his hat down, pulls a parcel out of his pocket*): When *this* appears—Jørgen Tesman—this you must read. For this is the real thing. This is me.

TESMAN: Oh really? And what is it?

LØVBORG: The continuation.

TESMAN: Continuation? Of what?

LØVBORG: Of this book.

TESMAN: Of the new book?

LØVBORG: Of course.

TESMAN: But Eilert—you've carried the story all the way up to the present!

LØVBORG: So I have. And this is about the future.

TESMAN: The future! But, heavens—we don't know a thing about the future!

LØVBORG: No, we don't. But there are a a couple of things to be said about it all the same. (*Unwraps the parcel.*) Here, let me show you—

TESMAN: But that's not your handwriting.

LØVBORG: I have dictated it. (*Leafs through portions of the manuscript.*) It's in two parts. The first is about the forces that will shape the civilization of the future. And the second (*riffling through more pages*)—about the course that future civilization will take.

TESMAN: How remarkable! It would never occur to me to write anything like that.

HEDDA (*over by the French doors, her fingers drumming the pane*): Hmm—No—

LØVBORG (*replacing the manuscript in its wrappings and putting it down on the table*): I brought it along, for I thought maybe I'd read parts of it aloud to you this evening.

TESMAN: That's very good of you, Eilert. But this evening—? (*Looks at* BRACK.) I'm not quite sure how to arrange that—

LØVBORG: Some other time, then. There's no hurry.

BRACK: You see, Mr. Løvborg, there's a little get-together over at my house tonight. Mainly for Tesman, you know—

LØVBORG (*looking for his hat*): In that case, I certainly won't—

BRACK: No, listen. Won't you do me the pleasure to join us?

LØVBORG (*firmly*): No, I won't. But thanks all the same.

BRACK: Oh come on! Why don't you do that? We'll be a small, select circle. And I think I can promise you a fairly lively evening, as Hed—as Mrs. Tesman would say.

LØVBORG: I don't doubt that. Nevertheless—

BRACK: And you may bring your manuscript along and read aloud to Tesman over at my house. I have plenty of room.

TESMAN: Just think, Eilert! Wouldn't that be nice, hm?

HEDDA (*intervening*): But can't you see that Mr. Løvborg doesn't want to? I'm sure he would rather stay here and have supper with me.

LØVBORG (*looks at her*): With you, Mrs. Tesman?

HEDDA: And with Mrs. Elvsted.

LØVBORG: Ah—! (*Casually.*) I ran into her at noon today.

HEDDA: Oh? Well, she'll be here tonight. So you see your presence is really required,

Mr. Løvborg. Otherwise she won't have anybody to see her home.

LØVBORG: True. All right, then, Mrs. Tesman—I'll stay, thank you.

HEDDA: Good. I'll just tell the maid. (*She rings for* BERTE *over by the door, right.*)

(BERTE *appears just off-stage.* HEDDA *talks with her in a low voice, points toward the inner room.* BERTE *nods and exits.*)

TESMAN (*while* HEDDA *and* BERTE *are talking, to* LØVBORG): Tell me, Eilert—is it this new subject—about the future—is that what you plan to lecture on?

LØVBORG: Yes.

TESMAN: For the bookseller told me you have announced a lecture series for this fall.

LØVBORG: Yes. I have. I hope you won't mind too much.

TESMAN: Of course not! But—

LØVBORG: For of course I realized it is rather awkward for you.

TESMAN (*unhappily*): Oh well—I certainly can't expect—that just for my sake—

LØVBORG: But I will wait till you receive your appointment.

TESMAN: Wait? But—but—but—you mean you aren't going to compete with me? Hm?

LØVBORG: No. Just triumph over you. In people's opinion.

TESMAN: Oh, for goodness' sake! Then Aunt Julle was right, after all! I knew it all the time. Hedda! Do you hear that! Just think—Eilert Løvborg isn't going to stand in our way after all.

HEDDA (*tersely*): Our? I have nothing to do with this. (*She walks into the inner room, where* BERTE *is bringing in a tray with decanters and glasses.* HEDDA *nods her approval and comes forward again.*)

TESMAN (*during the foregoing business*): How about that, Judge? What do you say to this? Hm?

BRACK: I say that moral victory and all that—hm—may be glorious enough and beautiful enough—

TESMAN: Oh, I agree. All the same—

HEDDA (*looks at* TESMAN *with a cold smile*):

You look as if the lightning had hit you.

TESMAN: Well, I am—pretty much—I really believe—

BRACK: After all, Mrs. Tesman, that was quite a thunderstorm that just passed over.

HEDDA (*points to the inner room*): How about a glass of cold punch, gentlemen?

BRACK (*looks at his watch*): A stirrup cup. Not a bad idea.

TESMAN: Splendid, Hedda. Perfectly splendid. In such a light-hearted mood as I am now—

HEDDA: Please. You, too, Mr. Løvborg.

LØVBORG (*with a gesture of refusal*): No, thanks. Really. Nothing for me.

BRACK: Good heavens, man! Cold punch isn't poison, you know!

LØVBORG: Perhaps not for everybody.

HEDDA: I'll keep Mr. Løvborg company in the meantime.

TESMAN: All right, Hedda. You do that.

(*He and* BRACK *go into the inner room, sit down, drink punch, smoke cigarettes, and engage in lively conversation during the next scene.* EILERT LØVBORG *remains standing near the stove.* HEDDA *walks over to the desk.*)

HEDDA (*her voice a little louder than usual*): I'll show you some pictures, if you like. You see—Tesman and I, we took a trip through Tyrol on our way back.

(*She brings an album over to the table by the sofa. She sits down in the far corner of the sofa.* LØVBORG *approaches, stops, looks at her. He takes a chair and sits down at her left, his back toward the inner room.*)

HEDDA (*opens the album*): Do you see these mountains, Mr. Løvborg? They are the Ortler group. Tesman has written their name below. Here it is: "The Ortler group near Meran."

LØVBORG (*has looked steadily at her all this time. Says slowly*): Hedda—Gabler!

HEDDA (*with a quick glance sideways*): Not that! Shhh!

LØVBORG (*again*): Hedda Gabler!

HEDDA (*looking at the album*): Yes, that used to be my name. When—when we two knew each other.

LØVBORG: And so from now on—for the whole rest of my life—I must get used to never again saying Hedda Gabler.

HEDDA (*still occupied with the album*): Yes, you must. And you might as well start right now. The sooner the better, I think.

LØVBORG (*with indignation*): Hedda Gabler married? And married to—Jørgen Tesman!

HEDDA: Yes—that's the way it goes.

LØVBORG: Oh, Hedda, Hedda—how could you throw yourself away like that!

HEDDA (*with a fierce glance at him*): What's this? I won't have any of that!

LØVBORG: What do you mean?

(TESMAN *enters from the inner room.*)

HEDDA (*hears him coming and remarks casually*): And this here, Mr. Løvborg, this is from somewhere in the Ampezzo valley. Just look at those peaks over there. (*With a kindly look at* TESMAN.) What did you say those peaks were called, dear?

TESMAN: Let me see. Oh, they—they are the Dolomites.

HEDDA: Right, Those are the Dolomites, Mr. Løvborg.

TESMAN: Hedda, I thought I'd just ask you if you don't want me to bring you some punch, after all? For you, anyway? Hm?

HEDDA: Well, yes; thanks. And a couple of cookies, maybe.

TESMAN: No cigarettes?

HEDDA: No.

TESMAN: All right.

(*He returns to the inner room, then turns right.* BRACK *is in there, keeping an eye on* HEDDA *and* LØVBORG *from time to time.*)

LØVBORG (*still in a low voice*): Answer me, Hedda. How could you do a thing like that?

HEDDA (*apparently engrossed in the album*): If you keep on using my first name I won't talk to you.

LØVBORG: Not even when we're alone?

HEDDA: No. You may think it, but you must not say it.

LØVBORG: I see. It offends your love for—Jørgen Tesman.

HEDDA (*glances at him, smiles*): Love? That's a good one!

LØVBORG: Not love, then.

HEDDA: But no infidelities, either! I won't have it.

LØVBORG: Hedda—answer me just this one thing—

HEDDA: Shhh!

(TESMAN *enters with a tray from the inner room.*)

TESMAN: Here! Here are the goodies. (*Puts the tray down.*)

HEDDA: Why don't you get Berte to do it?

TESMAN (*pouring punch*): Because I think it's so much fun waiting on you, Hedda.

HEDDA: But you've filled both glasses. And Mr. Løvborg didn't want any—

TESMAN: I know, but Mrs. Elvsted will soon be here, won't she?

HEDDA: That's right. So she will.

TESMAN: Had you forgotten about her? Hm?

HEDDA: We've been so busy looking at this. (*Shows him a picture.*) Remember this little village?

TESMAN: That's the one just below the Brenner Pass, isn't it? We spent the night there—

HEDDA: —and ran into that lively crowd of summer guests.

TESMAN: Right! Just think—if we only could have had you with us, Eilert! Oh well.

(*Returns to the inner room, sits down, and resumes his conversation with* BRACK.)

LØVBORG: Just tell me this, Hedda—

HEDDA: What?

LØVBORG: Wasn't there love in your feelings for me, either? Not a touch—not a shimmer of love? Wasn't there?

HEDDA: I wonder. To me, we seemed to be simply two good comrades. Two close friends. (*smiles*) You, particularly, were very frank.

LØVBORG: You wanted it that way.

HEDDA: And yet—when I think back upon it now, there was something beautiful, something thrilling, something brave, I think,

436

about the secret frankness—that comradeship that not a single soul so much as suspected.

LØVBORG: Yes, wasn't there, Hedda? Wasn't there? When I called on your father in the afternoons—And the General sat by the window with his newspapers—his back turned—

HEDDA: And we two in the sofa in the corner—

LØVBORG: —always with the same illustrated magazine—

HEDDA: —for want of an album, yes—

LØVBORG: Yes, Hedda—and then when I confessed to you—! Told you all about myself, things the others didn't know. Sat and told you about all my orgies by day and night. Dissipation day in and day out! Oh, Hedda—what sort of power in you was it that forced me to tell you things like that?

HEDDA: You think there was some power in me?

LØVBORG: How else can I explain it? And all those veiled questions you asked—

HEDDA: —which you understood so perfectly well—

LØVBORG: That you could ask such questions as that! With such complete frankness!

HEDDA: *Veiled*, if you please.

LØVBORG: But frankly all the same. All about—that!

HEDDA: And to think that you answered, Mr. Løvborg!

LØVBORG: Yes, that's just what I can't understand—now, afterwards. But tell me, Hedda; wasn't love at the bottom of our whole relationship? Didn't you feel some kind of urge to—purify me—when I came to you in confession? Wasn't that it?

HEDDA: No, not quite.

LØVBORG: Then what made you do it?

HEDDA: Do you find it so very strange that a young girl—when she can do so, without anyone knowing—

LØVBORG: Yes—?

HEDDA: —that she wants to take a peek into a world which—

LØVBORG: —which—?

HEDDA: —she is not supposed to know anything about?

LØVBORG: So that was it!

HEDDA: That, too. That, too—I think—

LØVBORG: Companionship in the lust for life. But why couldn't *that* at least have continued?

HEDDA: That was your own fault.

LØVBORG: You were the one who broke off.

HEDDA: Yes, when reality threatened to enter our relationship. Shame on you, Eilert Løvborg! How could you want to do a thing like that to your frank and trusting comrade!

LØVBORG (*clenching his hands*): Oh, why didn't you do it! Why didn't you shoot me down, as you said you would!

HEDDA: Because I'm scared of scandal.

LØVBORG: Yes, Hedda. You are really a coward.

HEDDA: A terrible coward. (*Changing her tone.*) But that was your good luck, wasn't it? And now the Elvsteds have healed your broken heart very nicely.

LØVBORG: I know what Thea has told you.

HEDDA: Perhaps you have told her about us?

LØVBORG: Not a word. She is too stupid to understand.

HEDDA: Stupid?

LØVBORG: In things like that.

HEDDA: And I'm a coward. (*Leans forward, without looking in his eyes, whispers.*) But now I am going to confess something to you.

LØVBORG (*tense*): What?

HEDDA: That I didn't dare to shoot—

LØVBORG: Yes—?

HEDDA: —that was not the worst of my cowardice that night.

LØVBORG (*looks at her a moment, understands, whispers passionately*): Oh, Hedda! Hedda Gabler! Now I begin to see what was behind the companionship! You and I! So it *was* your lust for life—!

HEDDA (*in a low voice, with an angry glance*): Take care! Don't you believe that!

437

(*Darkness is falling. The door, right, is opened, and* BERTE *enters.*)

HEDDA (*closing the album, calls out, smiling*): At last! So there you are, dearest Thea! Come in!

(MRS. ELVSTED *enters. She is dressed for a party.* BERTE *exits, closing the door behind her.*)

HEDDA (*in the sofa, reaching out for* MRS. ELVSTED): Sweetest Thea, you have no idea how I've waited for you.

(*In passing,* MRS. ELVSTED *exchanges quick greetings with* TESMAN *and* BRACK *in the inner room. She walks up to the table and shakes* HEDDA's *hand.* EILERT LØVBORG *rises. He and* MRS. ELVSTED *greet one another with a silent nod.*)

MRS. ELVSTED: Maybe I ought to go in and say hello to your husband?

HEDDA: No, never mind that. Let them be. They're soon leaving, anyway.

MRS. ELVSTED: Leaving?

HEDDA: They're off to a spree.

MRS. ELVSTED (*quickly, to* LØVBORG): Not you?

LØVBORG: No.

HEDDA: Mr. Løvborg stays here with us.

MRS. ELVSTED (*pulls up a chair, is about to sit down next to* LØVBORG): Oh, how wonderful it is to be here!

HEDDA: Oh no, little Thea. Not that. Not there. Over here by me, please. I want to be in the middle.

MRS. ELVSTED: Just as you like. (*She walks in front of the table and seats herself on the sofa, on* HEDDA's *right.* LØVBORG *sits down again on his chair.*)

LØVBORG (*after a brief pause, to* HEDDA): Isn't she lovely to look at?

HEDDA (*gently stroking her hair*): Just to look at?

LØVBORG: Yes. For you see—she and I— we are real comrades. We have absolute faith in one another. And we can talk together in full freedom.

HEDDA: Unveiled, Mr. Løvborg?

LØVBORG: Well—

MRS. ELVSTED (*in a low voice, clinging to* HEDDA): Oh, I am so happy, Hedda! For just think—he says I have inspired him, too!

HEDDA (*looks at her with a smile*): No, really! He says that?

LØVBORG: And she has such courage, Mrs. Tesman! Such courage of action.

MRS. ELVSTED: Oh, my God—courage—! I!

LØVBORG: Infinite courage—when it concerns the comrade.

HEDDA: Yes, courage—if one only had that.

LØVBORG: What then?

HEDDA: Then maybe life would be tolerable, after all. (*Changing her tone.*) But now, dearest Thea, you want a glass of nice, cold punch.

MRS. ELVSTED: No, thanks. I never drink things like that.

HEDDA: Then what about you, Mr. LØVBORG?

LØVBORG: Thanks. Nothing for me, either.

MRS. ELVSTED: No, nothing for him, either.

HEDDA (*looks firmly at him*): If I say so?

LØVBORG: Makes no difference.

HEDDA (*laughs*): Poor me! So I have no power over you at all. Is that it?

LØVBORG: Not in that respect.

HEDDA: Seriously, though; I really think you should. For your own sake.

MRS. ELVSTED: No, but Hedda—!

LØVBORG: Why so?

HEDDA: Or rather for people's sake.

LØVBORG: Oh?

HEDDA: For else they might think you don't really trust yourself—That you lack self-confidence—

MRS. ELVSTED (*softly*): Don't, Hedda!

LØVBORG: People may think whatever they like for all I care—for the time being.

MRS. ELVSTED (*happy*): Exactly!

HEDDA: I could easily tell from watching Judge Brack just now.

LØVBORG: Tell what?

HEDDA: He smiled so contemptuously when you didn't dare to join them in there.

LØVBORG: Didn't I dare to! It's just that I'd much rather stay here and talk with you!

438

MRS. ELVSTED: But that's only natural, Hedda.

HEDDA: The Judge had no way of knowing that. And I also noticed he smiled and looked at Tesman when you didn't dare to go to his silly old party.

LØVBORG: Didn't dare! Are you saying I didn't dare?

HEDDA: *I* am not. But that's how Judge Brack understood it.

LØVBORG: Let him.

HEDDA: So you're not going?

LØVBORG: I'm staying here with you and Thea.

MRS. ELVSTED: Of course, he is, Hedda!

HEDDA (*smiles, nods approvingly*): That's what I call firm foundations. Principled forever; that's the way a man ought to be! (*Turning to* MRS. ELVSTED, *stroking her cheek.*) What did I tell you this morning—when you came here, quite beside yourself—?

LØVBORG (*puzzled*): Beside herself?

MRS. ELVSTED (*in terror*): Hedda—Hedda—don't!

HEDDA: Now do you see? There was no need at all for that mortal fear of yours—(*interrupting herself*). There, now! Now we can all three relax and enjoy ourselves.

LØVBORG (*startled*): What's all this, Mrs. Tesman?

MRS. ELVSTED: Oh, God, Hedda—what are you saying? What are you doing?

HEDDA: Please be quiet. That horrible Judge is looking at you.

LØVBORG: In mortal fear? So that's it. For my sake.

MRS. ELVSTED (*softly, wailing*): Oh, Hedda—if you only knew how utterly miserable you have made me!

LØVBORG (*stares at her for a moment. His face is distorted*): So that was the comrade's happy confidence in me!

MRS. ELVSTED: Oh, my dearest friend—listen to me first—!

LØVBORG (*picks up one of the glasses of punch, raises it, says hoarsely*): Here's to you, Thea! (*Empties the glass, puts it down, picks up the other one.*)

MRS. ELVSTED (*softly*): Hedda, Hedda—why did you want to do this?

HEDDA: Want to! I! Are you mad?

LØVBORG: And here's to you, too, Mrs. Tesman! Thanks for telling me the truth. Long live the truth! (*He drains the glass and is about to fill it again.*)

HEDDA (*restrains him*): That's enough for now. Remember you are going to a party.

MRS. ELVSTED: No, no, no!

HEDDA: Shhh! They are looking at you.

LØVBORG (*puts his glass down*): Listen, Thea—tell me the truth—

MRS. ELVSTED: I will, I will!

LØVBORG: Did your husband know you were coming after me?

MRS. ELVSTED (*wringing her hands*): Oh, Hedda—do you hear what he's asking?

LØVBORG: Did the two of you agree that you were to come here and look after me? Maybe it was his idea, even? Did he send you? Ah, I know what it was—he missed me in the office, didn't he? Or was it at the card table?

MRS. ELVSTED (*softly, in agony*): Oh, Løvborg, Løvborg!

LØVBORG (*grabs a glass and is about to fill it*): Here's to the old Commissioner, too!

HEDDA (*stops him*): No more now. You're supposed to read aloud for Tesman tonight—remember?

LØVBORG (*calm again, puts the glass down*): This was silly of me, Thea. I'm sorry. To take it this way. Please, don't be angry with me. You'll see—both you and all those others—that even if I have been down—! With your help, Thea—dear comrade.

MRS. ELVSTED (*beaming*): Oh, thank God—! (*In the meantime,* BRACK *has looked at his watch. He and* TESMAN *get up and come forward.*)

BRACK (*picking up his coat and hat*): Well, Mrs. Tesman; our time is up.

HEDDA: I suppose it is.

LØVBORG (*rising*): Mine, too, Judge.

MRS. ELVSTED (*softly, pleadingly*): Oh, Løvborg—don't do it!

HEDDA (*pinches her arm*): They can hear you!

MRS. ELVSTED (*with a soft exclamation*): Ouch!

LØVBORG (*to* BRACK): You were good enough to ask me—

BRACK: So you're coming, after all?

LØVBORG: If I may.

BRACK: I'm delighted.

LØVBORG (*picks up his manuscript and says to* TESMAN): For there are a couple of things here I'd like to show you before I send it off.

TESMAN: Just think! Isn't that nice! But— dearest Hedda—? In that case, how are you going to get Mrs. Elvsted home? Hm?

HEDDA: We'll manage somehow.

LØVBORG (*looking at the two women*): Mrs. Elvsted? I'll be back to pick her up, of course. (*Coming closer.*) About ten o'clock, Mrs. Tesman? Is that convenient?

HEDDA: Certainly. That will be fine.

TESMAN: Then everything is nice and settled. But don't expect me that early, Hedda.

HEDDA: You just stay as long as—as long as you want, dear.

MRS. ELVSTED (*in secret fear*): I'll be waiting for you here, then, Mr. Løvborg.

LØVBORG (*hat in hand*): Of course, Mrs. Elvsted.

BRACK: All aboard the pleasure train, gentlemen! I hope we'll have a lively evening— as a certain fair lady would say.

HEDDA: Ah—if only the fair lady could be present. Invisible.

BRACK: Why invisible?

HEDDA: To listen to some of your unadulterated liveliness, Judge.

BRACK (*laughs*): I shouldn't advise the fair lady to do that!

TESMAN (*also laughing*): You're a good one, Hedda! Just think!

BRACK: Well—good night, ladies!

LØVBORG (*with a bow*): Till about ten, then.

(BRACK, LØVBORG, *and* TESMAN *go out, right. At the same time* BERTE *enters from the inner room with a lighted lamp, which she places on the table, front center. She goes out the same way.*)

MRS. ELVSTED (*has risen and paces restlessly up and down*): Hedda, Hedda—how do you think all this will end?

HEDDA: At ten o'clock he'll be here. I see him already. With vine leaves in his hair. Flushed and confident.

MRS. ELVSTED: I only hope you're right.

HEDDA: For then, you see, he'll have mastered himself. And be a free man for all the days of his life.

MRS. ELVSTED: Dear God—how I hope you are right! That he comes back like that.

HEDDA: That is the way he will come. Not any other way. (*Rises and goes closer to* MRS. ELVSTED.) *You* may doubt as long as you like. I believe in him. And now we'll see—

MRS. ELVSTED: There is something behind all this, Hedda. Some hidden purpose.

HEDDA: Yes, there is! For once in my life I want to have power over a human destiny.

MRS. ELVSTED: But don't you already?

HEDDA: I don't and I never have.

MRS. ELVSTED: But your husband—?

HEDDA: You think that's worth the trouble? Oh, if you knew how poor I am! And you got to be so rich! (*Embraces her passionately.*) I think I'll have to burn your hair off, after all!

MRS. ELVSTED: Let me go! Let me go! You scare me, Hedda!

BERTE (*in the doorway*). Supper is served, ma'am.

HEDDA: Good. We're coming.

MRS. ELVSTED: No, no, no! I'd rather go home by myself! Right now!

HEDDA: Nonsense! You'll have your cup of tea first, you little silly. And then—at ten o'clock—Eilert Løvborg comes—with vine leaves in his hair! (*She almost pulls* MRS. ELVSTED *toward the doorway.*)

ACT THREE

(*The same room at the* TESMANS'. *The doorway and the French windows both have their portieres closed. The lamp, turned half down, is still on the table. The stove is open. Some dying embers can be seen.*

MRS. ELVSTED, *wrapped in a big shawl, is in the easy chair near the stove, her feet on a footstool.* HEDDA, *also dressed, is lying on the sofa, covered by a blanket.*)

MRS. ELVSTED (*after a while suddenly sits up, listens anxiously; then she wearily sinks back in her chair, whimpers softly*): Oh my God, my God— not yet!

(BERTE *enters cautiously, right, carrying a letter.*)

MRS. ELVSTED (*turns and whispers tensely*): Well—has anybody been here?

BERTE (*in a low voice*): Yes. Just now there was a girl with this letter.

MRS. ELVSTED (*quickly, reaches for it*): A letter! Give it to me!

BERTE: No, ma'am. It's for the Doctor.

MRS. ELVSTED: I see.

BERTE: Miss Tesman's maid brought it. I'll leave it here on the table.

MRS. ELVSTED: All right.

BERTE (*puts the letter down*): I'd better put out the lamp. It just reeks.

MRS. ELVSTED: Yes, do that. It must be daylight soon, anyway.

BERTE (*putting out the lamp*): It's light already, ma'am.

MRS. ELVSTED: Light already! And still not back!

BERTE: No, so help us. Not that I didn't expect as much—

MRS. ELVSTED: You did?

BERTE: Yes, when I saw a certain character was back in town. Taking off with them. We sure heard enough about him in the old days!

MRS. ELVSTED: Not so loud. You are waking up Mrs. Tesman.

BERTE (*looks toward the sofa, sighs*): God forbid—! Let her sleep, poor thing. Do you want me to get the fire going again?

MRS. ELVSTED: Not on my account, thank you.

BERTE: All right; I won't then. (*Exits quietly right.*)

HEDDA (*awakened by the closing door*): What's that?

MRS. ELVSTED: Just the maid.

HEDDA (*looks around*): Why in here—? Oh, I remember! (*Sits up, rubs her eyes, stretches.*) What time is it, Thea?

MRS. ELVSTED (*looks at her watch*). Past seven.

HEDDA: When did Tesman get home?

MRS. ELVSTED: He didn't.

HEDDA: Not home yet!

MRS. ELVSTED (*getting up*): Nobody's come.

HEDDA: And we who waited till four!

MRS. ELVSTED (*wringing her hands*): And *how* we waited!

HEDDA (*her hand covering a yawn*): We—ll. We could have saved ourselves that trouble.

MRS. ELVSTED: Did you get any sleep at all?

HEDDA: Yes, I slept pretty well, I think. Didn't you?

MRS. ELVSTED: Not a wink. I just couldn't, Hedda! It was just impossible.

HEDDA (*rises, walks over to her*): Well, now! There's nothing to worry about, for heaven's sake. I know exactly what's happened.

MRS. ELVSTED: Then tell me please. Where do you think they are?

HEDDA: Well, first of all, I'm sure they were terribly late leaving the Judge's—

MRS. ELVSTED: Dear yes. I'm sure you're right. Still—

HEDDA: —and so Tesman didn't want to wake us up in the middle of the night. (*Laughs.*) Maybe he didn't want us to see him, either—after a party like that.

MRS. ELVSTED: But where do you think he has gone?

HEDDA: To the aunts', of course. His old room is still there, all ready for him.

MRS. ELVSTED: No, he can't be there. Just a few minutes ago there came a letter for him from Miss Tesman. It's over there.

HEDDA: Oh? (*Looks at the envelope.*) So it is—Auntie Julle herself. In that case, I suppose he's still at Brack's. And there's Eilert Løvborg, too—reading aloud, with vine leaves in his hair.

MRS. ELVSTED: Oh Hedda—you're only saying things you don't believe yourself.

HEDDA: My, what a little imbecile you really are, Thea!

MRS. ELVSTED: Yes, I suppose I am.

HEDDA: And you look dead tired, too.

MRS. ELVSTED: I *am* dead tired.

HEDDA: Why don't you do as I say. Go into my room and lie down.

MRS. ELVSTED: No, no—I wouldn't be able to go to sleep, anyway.

HEDDA: Of course, you would.

MRS. ELVSTED: And your husband is bound to be home any minute now. And I have to know right away.

HEDDA: I'll let you know as soon as he gets here.

MRS. ELVSTED: You promise me that, Hedda?

HEDDA: I do. You just go to sleep.

MRS. ELVSTED: Thanks. At least I'll try. (*Exits through inner room.*)

(HEDDA *goes to the French doors, opens the portieres. The room is now in full daylight. She picks up a little hand mirror from the desk, looks at herself, smooths her hair. Walks over to door, rings the bell for the maid.* BERTE *presently appears.*)

BERTE: You want something, ma'am?

HEDDA: Yes. You'll have to start the fire again. I'm cold.

BERTE: Yes, ma'am! I'll get it warm in no time. (*Rakes the embers together and puts in another piece of wood. Then she suddenly listens.*) There's the doorbell, ma'am.

HEDDA: All right. See who it is. I'll take care of the stove myself.

BERTE: You'll have a nice blaze going in a minute. (*Exits right.*)

(HEDDA *kneels on the footstool and puts in more pieces of wood. Presently* TESMAN *enters, right. He looks tired and somber. He tiptoes toward the doorway and is about to disappear between the portieres.*)

HEDDA (*by the stove, without looking up*): Good morning.

TESMAN (*turning*): Hedda! (*Comes closer.*) For heaven's sake—you up already! Hm?

HEDDA: Yes, I got up very early this morning.

TESMAN: And I was so sure you'd still be sound asleep! Just think!

HEDDA: Not so loud. Mrs. Elvsted is asleep in my room.

TESMAN: Mrs. Elvsted stayed here all night?

HEDDA: Yes. Nobody came for her, you know.

TESMAN: No, I suppose—

HEDDA (*closes the stove, rises*): Well, did you have a good time at the Judge's?

TESMAN: Were you worried about me? Hm?

HEDDA: I'd never dream of worrying about you. I asked if you had a good time.

TESMAN: Yes, indeed. Nice for a change, anyway. But I think I liked it best early in the evening. For then Eilert read to me. Just think—we were more than an hour early! And Brack, of course, had things to see to. So Eilert read.

HEDDA (*sits down at the right side of the table*): So? Tell me all about it.

TESMAN (*sits down on an ottoman near the stove*): Oh Hedda, you'll never believe what a book that will be! It must be just the most remarkable thing ever written! Just think!

HEDDA: Yes, but I don't really care about that—

TESMAN: I must tell you, Hedda—I have a confession to make. As he was reading—something ugly came over me—

HEDDA: Ugly?

TESMAN: I sat there envying Eilert for being able to write like that! Just think, Hedda!

HEDDA: All right. I'm thinking!

TESMAN: And yet, with all his gifts—he's incorrigible, after all.

HEDDA: I suppose you mean he has more courage for life than the rest of you?

TESMAN: No, no—I don't mean that. I mean he's incapable of exercising moderation in his pleasures.

HEDDA: What happened—in the end?

TESMAN: Well—I would call it a bacchanal, Hedda.

HEDDA: Did he have vine leaves in his hair?

TESMAN: Vine leaves? No, I didn't notice any vine leaves. But he gave a long, muddled speech in honor of the woman who had inspired him in his work. Those were his words.

HEDDA: Did he say her name?

TESMAN: No, he didn't. But I'm sure it must be Mrs. Elvsted. You just wait and see if I'm not right!

HEDDA: And where did you and he part company?

TESMAN: On the way back to town. We left—the last of us did—at the same time. And Brack came along, too, to get some fresh air. Then we decided we'd better see Eilert home. You see, he had had altogether too much to drink!

HEDDA: I can imagine.

TESMAN: But then the strangest thing of all happened, Hedda! Or maybe I should say the saddest. I'm almost ashamed—on Eilert's behalf—even talking about it.

HEDDA: Well—?

TESMAN: You see, on the way back I happened to be behind the others a little. Just for a minute or two—you know—

HEDDA: All right, all right—!

TESMAN: And when I hurried to catch up with them, can you guess what I found by the roadside? Hm?

HEDDA: How can I possibly—?

TESMAN: You mustn't tell this to a living soul, Hedda! Do you hear! Promise me that, for Eilert's sake. (*Pulls a parcel out of his coat pocket.*) Just think—I found this!

HEDDA: Isn't that what he had with him here yesterday?

TESMAN: Yes! It's his whole, precious, irreplaceable manuscript! And he had dropped it—just like that! Without even noticing! Just think, Hedda! Isn't that awfully sad?

HEDDA: But why didn't you give it back to him?

TESMAN: In the condition he was in! Dear— I just didn't dare to.

HEDDA: And you didn't tell any of the others that you had found it, either?

TESMAN: Of course not. I didn't want to, for Eilert's sake—don't you see?

HEDDA: So nobody knows that you have Eilert Løvborg's papers?

TESMAN: Nobody. And nobody must know, either.

HEDDA: And what did you and he talk about afterwards?

TESMAN: I didn't have a chance to talk to him at all after that. For when we came into town, he and a couple of the others simply vanished. Just think!

HEDDA: Oh? I expect they took him home.

TESMAN: I suppose that must be it. And Brack took off on his own, too.

HEDDA: And what have you been doing with yourself since then?

TESMAN: Well, you see, I and some of the others went home with one of the younger fellows and had a cup of early morning coffee. Or night coffee maybe, rather. Hm? And now, after I've rested a bit and poor Eilert's had some sleep, I'll take this back to him.

HEDDA (*reaches for the parcel*): No—don't do that! Not right away, I mean. Let me look at it first.

TESMAN: Dearest Hedda—honestly, I just don't dare to.

HEDDA: Don't you dare to?

TESMAN: No, for I'm sure you realize how utterly desperate he'll be when he wakes up and finds that the manuscript is gone. For he hasn't got a copy, you know. He said so himself.

HEDDA (*looks searchingly at him*): But can't a thing like that be written over again?

TESMAN: Hardly. I really don't think so. For, you see—the inspiration—

HEDDA: Yes, I daresay that's the main thing. (*Casually.*) By the way, here's a letter for you.

TESMAN: Imagine!

HEDDA (*gives it to him*): It came early this morning.

TESMAN: It's from Aunt Julle, Hedda! I wonder what it can be. (*Puts the manuscript down on the other ottoman, opens the letter, skims the content, jumps up.*) Oh Hedda! She says here that poor Aunt Rina is dying!

HEDDA: You know we had to expect that.

TESMAN: And if I want to see her again I had better hurry. I'll rush over right away.

HEDDA (*suppressing a smile*): You'll rush?

TESMAN: Dearest Hedda of mine—if only you could bring yourself to come along! Hm?

HEDDA (*rises, weary, with an air of refusal*): No, no. You mustn't ask me that. I don't want to look at death and disease. I want to be free from all that's ugly.

TESMAN: Well, all right—(*rushing around*).

443

My hat? My coat? Oh—out here in the hall. I just hope I won't be too late, Hedda. Hm?

HEDDA: Oh I'm sure that if you rush—

(BERTE *appears in the door, right.*)

BERTE: Judge Brack is here and wants to know if he may see you.

TESMAN: At this hour! No, no. I can't possibly see him now!

HEDDA: But I can. (*To* BERTE.) Tell the Judge please to come in.

(BERTE *exits.*)

HEDDA (*with a quick whisper*): Tesman! The package! (*She grabs it from the ottoman.*)

TESMAN: Yes! Give it to me!

HEDDA: No, no. I'll hide it for you till later.

(*She walks over to the desk and sticks the parcel among the books on the shelf. In his hurry* TESMAN *is having difficulties getting his gloves on.* JUDGE BRACK *enters right.*)

HEDDA (*nods to him*): If *you* aren't an early bird—

BRACK: Yes, don't you think so? (*To* TESMAN.) You're going out, too?

TESMAN: Yes, I must go and see the aunts. Just think, the invalid—she's dying!

BRACK: Oh, I'm terribly sorry! In that case, don't let me keep you. At such a moment—

TESMAN: Yes, I really must run. Goodbye, goodbye! (*Hurries out, right.*)

HEDDA (*approaching* BRACK): It appears that things were quite lively last night over at your house.

BRACK: Indeed, Mrs. Tesman—I didn't get to bed at all.

HEDDA: You didn't either?

BRACK: As you see. But tell me—what has Tesman told you about the night's adventures?

HEDDA: Just some tiresome story about having coffee with somebody someplace—

BRACK: I believe I know all about that coffee. Eilert Løvborg wasn't one of them, was he?

HEDDA: No, they had taken him home first.

BRACK: Tesman, too?

HEDDA: No. Some of the others, he said.

BRACK (*smiles*): Jørgen Tesman is really an ingenuous soul, you know.

HEDDA: He certainly is. But why do you say that? Is there something more to all this?

BRACK: Yes, there is.

HEDDA: Well! In that case, why don't we make ourselves comfortable, Judge. You'll tell your story better, too.

(*She sits down at the left side of the table,* BRACK *near her at the adjacent side.*)

HEDDA: All right?

BRACK: For reasons of my own I wanted to keep track of my guests' movements last night. Or, rather—some of my guests.

HEDDA: Eilert Løvborg was one of them, perhaps?

BRACK: As a matter of fact—he was.

HEDDA: Now you are really making me curious.

BRACK: Do you know where he and a couple of the others spent the rest of the night, Mrs. Tesman?

HEDDA: No—tell me. If it is at all tellable.

BRACK: Oh, certainly it can be told. They turned up at an exceptionally gay early morning gathering.

HEDDA: Of the lively kind?

BRACK: The very liveliest.

HEDDA: A little more about this, Judge.

BRACK: Løvborg had been invited beforehand. I knew all about that. But he had declined. He is a reformed character, you know.

HEDDA: As of his stay with the Elvsteds—yes. But he went after all?

BRACK: Well, yes, you see, Mrs. Tesman—unfortunately, the spirit moved him over at my house last evening.

HEDDA: Yes, I understand he became inspired.

BRACK: Quite violently inspired. And that, I gather, must have changed his mind. You know, we men don't always have as much integrity as we ought to have.

HEDDA: Oh I'm sure you're an exception, Judge Brack. But about Løvborg—?

BRACK: To make a long story short—he ended up at Miss Diana's establishment.

HEDDA: Miss Diana's?

BRACK: She was the hostess at this gathering

—a select circle of intimate friends, male and female.

HEDDA: Is she a redhead, by any chance?

BRACK: That's correct.

HEDDA: And a singer—of sorts?

BRACK: Yes—that, too. And a mighty huntress—of men, Mrs. Tesman. You seem to have heard of her. Eilert Løvborg used to be one of her most devoted protectors in his more affluent days.

HEDDA: And how did it all end?

BRACK: Not in a very friendly fashion, apparently. It seems that after the tenderest reception Miss Diana resorted to brute force—

HEDDA: Against Løvborg?

BRACK: Yes. He accused her or her woman friends of having stolen something of his. Said his wallet was gone. And other things, too. In brief, he's supposed to have started a pretty wicked row.

HEDDA: With what results?

BRACK: Nothing less than a general free-for-all—men and women both. Fortunately, the police stepped in—

HEDDA: The police—!

BRACK: Yes. I'm afraid this will be an expensive escapade for Eilert Løvborg, crazy fool that he is.

HEDDA: Well!

BRACK: It appears that he made quite violent objection—struck an officer in the ear and tore his coat. So they had to take him along.

HEDDA: How do you know all this?

BRACK: From the police.

HEDDA (*staring straight ahead*): So that's how it was. No vine leaves in his hair.

BRACK: Vine leaves, Mrs. Tesman?

HEDDA (*changing her tone*): But tell me, Judge Brack—why did you keep such a close watch on Eilert Løvborg?

BRACK: Well—for one thing, it is obviously of some concern to me if he testifies that he came straight from my party.

HEDDA: So you think there will be an investigation?

BRACK: Naturally. But I suppose that doesn't really matter too much. However, as a friend of the house I considered it my duty to give you and Tesman a full account of his night-time exploits.

HEDDA: Yes, but why?

BRACK: Because I very strongly suspect that he intends to use you as a kind of screen.

HEDDA: Really! Why do you think that?

BRACK: Oh, come now, Mrs. Tesman! We can use our eyes, can't we? This Mrs. Elvsted—she isn't leaving town right away, you know.

HEDDA: Well, even if there should be something going on between those two, I'd think there would be plenty of other places they could meet.

BRACK: But no home. After last night, every respectable house will once again close its doors to Eilert Løvborg.

HEDDA: And so should mine, you mean?

BRACK: Yes. I admit I would find it more than embarrassing if the gentleman were to become a daily guest here, Mrs. Tesman. If he, as an outsider—a highly dispensable outsider—if he were to intrude himself—

HEDDA: —into the triangle?

BRACK: Precisely. It would amount to homelessness for me.

HEDDA (*smiling*): Sole cock-o'-the-walk—so, that's your goal, is it, Judge?

BRACK (*nods slowly, lowers his voice*): Yes. That is my goal. And for that I will fight with every means at my disposal.

HEDDA (*her smile fading*): You're really a dangerous person, you know—when you come right down to it.

BRACK: You think so?

HEDDA: Yes. I am beginning to think so now. And I must say I am exceedingly glad you don't have any kind of hold on me.

BRACK (*with a noncommital laugh*): Well, well, Mrs. Tesman! Maybe there is something to what you are saying, at that. Who knows what I might do if I did.

HEDDA: Really, now, Judge Brack! Are you threatening me?

BRACK (*rising*):—Nonsense! For the triangle, you see—is best maintained on a voluntary basis.

445

HEDDA: My sentiments, exactly.

BRACK: Well, I have said what I came to say. And now I should get back to town. Goodbye, Mrs. Tesman! (*Walks toward the French doors.*)

HEDDA (*rises*): You're going through the garden?

BRACK: Yes. For me that's a short cut.

HEDDA: Yes, and then it's a back way.

BRACK: Quite true. I have nothing against back ways. There are times when they are most intriguing.

HEDDA: You mean when real ammunition is used?

BRACK (*already in the door, laughs back at her*): Oh good heavens! I don't suppose one shoots one's tame roosters!

HEDDA (*laughs also*): No—not if one has only one—!

(*They nod to each other, both still laughing. He leaves. She closes the door behind him. For a few moments she remains by the door, quite serious now, looking into the garden. Then she walks over to the doorway and opens the portieres wide enough to look into the inner room. Walks to the desk, pulls* LØVBORG's *manuscript from the bookshelf and is about to read in it when* BERTE's *voice, very loud, is heard from the hall, right.* HEDDA *turns around, listens. She hurriedly puts the manuscript into the drawer of the desk and puts the key down on its top.* EILERT LØVBORG, *wearing his coat and with his hat in his hand, flings open the door, right. He looks somewhat confused and excited.*)

LØVBORG (*turned toward the invisible* BERTE *in the hall*): And I say I must! You can't stop me! (*He closes the door, turns, sees* HEDDA, *immediately controls himself, greets her.*)

HEDDA (*by the desk*): Well, well, Mr. Løvborg—aren't you a trifle late coming for Thea?

LØVBORG: Or a trifle early for calling on you. I apologize.

HEDDA: How do you know she is still here?

LØVBORG: The people she is staying with told me she's been gone all night.

HEDDA (*walks over to the table*): Did they seem—strange—when they told you that?

LØVBORG (*puzzled*): Strange?

HEDDA: I mean, did they seem to find it a little—unusual?

LØVBORG (*suddenly understands*): Ah, I see what you mean! Of course! I'm dragging her down with me. But as a matter of fact, I didn't notice anything. I suppose Tesman isn't up yet?

HEDDA: I—I don't think so—

LØVBORG: When did he get home?

HEDDA: Very late.

LØVBORG: Did he tell you anything?

HEDDA: Yes, he said you'd all had quite a time over at Brack's.

LØVBORG: Just that?

HEDDA: I think so. But I was so awfully sleepy—

(MRS. ELVSTED *enters through portieres in the rear.*)

MRS. ELVSTED (*toward him*): Oh, Løvborg! At last!

LØVBORG: Yes, at last. And too late.

MRS. ELVSTED (*in fear*): What is too late?

LØVBORG: Everything is too late now. It's all over with me.

MRS. ELVSTED: Oh no, no! Don't say things like that!

LØVBORG: You'll say the same yourself when you hear—

MRS. ELVSTED: I don't want to hear—!

HEDDA: Maybe you'd rather talk with her alone? I'll leave.

LØVBORG: No, stay—you, too. I beg you to.

MRS. ELVSTED: But I don't want to listen, do you hear?

LØVBORG: It isn't last night I want to talk about.

MRS. ELVSTED: What about then?

LØVBORG: We'll have to part, Thea.

MRS. ELVSTED: Part!

HEDDA (*involuntarily*): I knew it!

LØVBORG: For I don't need you any more.

MRS. ELVSTED: And you can stand there and tell me a thing like that! Don't need me! Why can't I help you the way I did before? Aren't we going to keep on working together?

LØVBORG: I don't intend to work any more.

MRS. ELVSTED (*giving up*): What am I going to do with my life, then?

LØVBORG: You'll have to try to live your life as if you'd never known me.

MRS. ELVSTED: But I can't do that!

LØVBORG: Try, Thea. Go back home.

MRS. ELVSTED (*agitated*): Never again! Where you are I want to be! And you can't chase me away just like that. I want to stay right here! Be with you when the book appears.

HEDDA (*in a tense whisper*): Ah—yes—the book!

LØVBORG (*looks at her*): My book—and Thea's. For that's what it is.

MRS. ELVSTED: That's what I feel, too. And that's why I have the right to be with you when it comes out. I want to see all the honor and all the fame you'll get. And the joy—I want to share the joy, too.

LØVBORG: Thea, our book is never going to come out.

HEDDA: Ah!

MRS. ELVSTED: It won't!

LØVBORG: *Can't* ever appear.

MRS. ELVSTED (*with fearful suspicion*): Løvborg, what have you done with the manuscript?

HEDDA (*watching him tensely*): Yes—what about the manuscript?

MRS. ELVSTED: Where is it?

LØVBORG: Oh Thea—please, don't ask me about that!

MRS. ELVSTED: Yes, yes—I want to be told! I have the right to know—right now!

LØVBORG: All right. I've torn it to pieces.

MRS. ELVSTED (*screams*): Oh, no! No!

HEDDA (*involuntarily*): But that's not—!

LØVBORG (*looks at her*): Not true, you think?

HEDDA (*composing herself*): Well, of course, if you say so. You should know. It just sounds so—so unbelievable.

LØVBORG: All the same, it's true.

MRS. ELVSTED (*hands clenched*): Oh God— oh God, Hedda. He has torn his own work to pieces!

LØVBORG: I have torn my whole life to pieces, so why not my life's work as well?

MRS. ELVSTED: And that's what you did last night?

LØVBORG: Yes, I tell you! In a thousand pieces. And scattered them in the fjord. Far out—where the water is clean and salty. Let them drift there, with wind and current. Then they'll sink. Deep, deep down. Like me, Thea.

MRS. ELVSTED: Do you know, Løvborg— this thing you've done to the book—all the rest of my life I'll think of it as killing a little child.

LØVBORG: You are right. It is like murdering a child.

MRS. ELVSTED: But then, how could you? For the child was mine, too!

HEDDA (*almost soundlessly*): The child—

MRS. ELVSTED (*with a deep sigh*): So it's all over. I'll go now, Hedda.

HEDDA: But you aren't leaving town?

MRS. ELVSTED: Oh, I don't know myself what I'll do. There's only darkness before me. (*Exits, right.*)

HEDDA (*waits for a moment*): Aren't you going to see her home, Mr. Løvborg?

LØVBORG: I? Through the streets? Letting people see her with me?

HEDDA: Of course, I don't know what else may have happened last night. But is it really so absolutely irreparable—?

LØVBORG: Last night is not the end of it. That I know. And yet, I don't really care for that kind of life any more. Not again. She has broken all the courage for life and all the defiance that was in me.

HEDDA (*staring ahead*): So that sweet little goose has had her hand in a human destiny. (*looks at him*) But that you could be so heartless, even so!

LØVBORG: Don't tell me I was heartless!

HEDDA: To ruin everything that's given her soul and mind meaning for such a long, long time! You don't call that heartless!

LØVBORG: Hedda—to you I can tell the truth.

HEDDA: The truth?

447

LØVBORG: But first promise me—give me your word you'll never let Thea know what I'm going to tell you now.

HEDDA: You have it.

LØVBORG: All right. It isn't true what I just told her.

HEDDA: About the manuscript?

LØVBORG: Yes. I have not torn it up. Not thrown it in the sea, either.

HEDDA: But then—where is it?

LØVBORG: I've destroyed it just the same. Really, I have, Hedda!

HEDDA: I don't understand.

LØVBORG: Thea said that what I had done seemed to her like murdering a child.

HEDDA: Yes—she did.

LØVBORG: But killing a child, that's not the worst thing a father can do to it.

HEDDA: No?

LØVBORG: No. And the worst is what I don't want Thea to know.

HEDDA: What *is* the worst?

LØVBORG: Hedda—suppose a man, say, early in the morning, after a stupid, drunken night—suppose he comes home to his child's mother and says: Listen, I've been in such and such a place. I've been here—and I've been there. And I had our child with me. In all those places. And the child is lost. Gone. Vanished! I'll be damned if I know where it is. Who's got hold of it—

HEDDA: Yes—but when all is said and done—it is only a book, you know.

LØVBORG: Thea's pure soul was in that book.

HEDDA: I realize that.

LØVBORG: Then you surely also realize that she and I can have no future together.

HEDDA: Where do you go from here?

LØVBORG: Nowhere. Just finish everything off. The sooner the better.

HEDDA (*a step closer*): Listen—Eilert Løvborg—Couldn't you make sure it's done beautifully?

LØVBORG: Beautifully? (*Smiles.*) With vine leaves in the hair, as you used to say.

HEDDA: Oh no. I don't believe in vine leaves any more. But still beautifully! For once. Goodbye. Go now. And don't come back.

LØVBORG: Goodbye, Mrs. Tesman. Give my regards to Jørgen Tesman. (*He is about to leave.*)

HEDDA: Wait! I want to give you something—a remembrance. (*Goes to the desk, opens the drawer, takes out the gun case. Returns to* LØVBORG *with one of the revolvers.*)

LØVBORG: The gun? That's the remembrance?

HEDDA (*nods slowly*): Do you recognize it? It was pointed at you once.

LØVBORG: You should have used it then.

HEDDA: Take it! *You* use it.

LØVBORG (*pockets the gun*): Thanks!

HEDDA: And beautifully, Eilert Løvborg! That's all I ask!

LØVBORG: Goodbye, Hedda Gabler.

(*Exits, right.*)

(HEDDA *listens by the door for a moment. Then she crosses to the desk, takes out the manuscript, glances inside the cover, pulls some of the pages halfway out and looks at them. Carries the whole manuscript over to the chair by the stove. She sits down with the parcel in her lap. After a moment she opens the stove and then the manuscript.*)

HEDDA (*throws a bundle of sheets into the fire, whispers*): Now I'm burning your child, Thea. You—curlyhead! (*Throws more sheets in.*) Your and Eilert Løvborg's child. (*Throws all the rest of the manuscript into the stove.*) I am burning—I am burning your child.

ACT FOUR

(*The same rooms at the* TESMANS'. *Evening. The front room is dark. The inner room is lighted by the ceiling lamp over the table. Portieres cover the French doors.*)

HEDDA, *in black, is walking up and down in the dark of the front room. She goes into the inner room, turning left in the doorway. She is heard playing a few bars on the piano. She reappears and comes forward again.* BERTE *enters from the right side of the inner room. She carries a lighted lamp, which she puts down on the table in front of the corner sofa. Her eyes show signs of weeping; she wears black ribbons on her uniform. She exits quietly, right.* HEDDA *goes over to the French windows, looks between the portieres into the dark. Presently* MISS TESMAN, *in mourning, with hat and veil, enters, right.* HEDDA *walks over to meet her, gives her her hand.*)

MISS TESMAN: Yes, my dearest Hedda— here you see me in my garb of grief. For now at last my poor sister has fought her fight to the end.

HEDDA: I already know—as you see. Tesman sent word.

MISS TESMAN: Yes, he promised he'd do that. But I thought that to you, Hedda— here in the house of life—I really ought to bring the tidings of death myself.

HEDDA: That is very kind of you.

MISS TESMAN: Ah, but Rina shouldn't have died just now. There should be no mourning in Hedda's house at this time.

HEDDA (*changing the topic*): I understand she had a very quiet end.

MISS TESMAN: Oh so beautiful, so peaceful! She left us so quietly! And then the unspeakable happiness of seeing Jørgen one more time! To say goodbye to him to her heart's content! Isn't he back yet?

HEDDA: No. He wrote I musn't expect him back very soon. But do sit down.

MISS TESMAN: No—no, thanks, my dear, blessed Hedda. Not that I wouldn't like to. But I don't have much time. I must go back and prepare her as best I can. I want her to look right pretty when she goes into her grave.

HEDDA: Is there anything I can help you with?

MISS TESMAN: I won't have you as much as think of it! That's not for Hedda Tesman to lend a hand to. Or lend thoughts to, either. Not now, of all times!

HEDDA: Oh—thoughts! We can't always control our thoughts—

MISS TESMAN (*still preoccupied*): Ah yes— such is life. At home we're making a shroud for Rina. And here, too, there'll be sewing to

do soon, I expect. But of quite different kind, thank God!

(TESMAN *enters, right.*)

HEDDA: So finally you're back!

TESMAN: You here, Aunt Julle? With Hedda? Just think!

MISS TESMAN: I am just about to leave, Jørgen dear. Well—did you do all the things you promised me you'd do?

TESMAN: No, I'm afraid I forgot half of them, Auntie. I'd better run in again tomorrow. I'm all confused today. I can't seem to keep my thoughts together.

MISS TESMAN: But dearest Jørgen—you mustn't take it this way!

TESMAN: Oh, I musn't? How do you mean?

MISS TESMAN: You ought to be joyful in the midst of your sorrow. Glad for what's happened. The way I am.

TESMAN: Oh yes, of course. You're thinking of Aunt Rina.

HEDDA: You're going to feel lonely now, Miss Tesman.

MISS TESMAN: The first few days, yes. But I hope that won't last long. Dear Rina's little parlor won't be empty for long, if I can help it!

TESMAN: Oh? And who do you want to move in there, hm?

MISS TESMAN: Ah—it's not very hard to find some poor soul who needs nursing and comfort.

HEDDA: And you really want to take on such a burden all over again?

MISS TESMAN: Heavens! God forgive you, child—burden? It has not been a burden to me.

HEDDA: Still—a stranger, who—

MISS TESMAN: Oh, it's easy to make friends with sick people. And I sorely need something to live for, I, too. Well, the Lord be praised, maybe soon there'll be a thing or two an old aunt can turn her hand to here.

HEDDA: Please, don't let our affairs worry you—

TESMAN: Yes, just think—how lovely it would be for the three of us, if only—

449

HEDDA: If only—?

TESMAN (*uneasy*): Oh, nothing. I daresay it will all work out. Let's hope it will, hm?

MISS TESMAN: Well, well. I can see that you two have something to talk about. (*With a smile.*) And perhaps Hedda has something to tell *you*, Jørgen! Goodbye! I'm going home to Rina, now. (*Turns around in the door.*) Dear, dear—how strange to think—! Now Rina is both with me and with Jochum!

TESMAN: Yes, just think, Aunt Julle! Hm?

(MISS TESMAN *exits, right.*)

HEDDA (*coldly scrutinizing* TESMAN): I wouldn't be at all surprised if you are not more affected by this death than she is.

TESMAN: Oh, it isn't just Aunt Rina's death, Hedda. It's Eilert I worry about.

HEDDA (*quickly*): Any news about him?

TESMAN: I went over to his room this afternoon to tell him the manuscript is safe.

HEDDA: Well? And didn't you see him?

TESMAN: No. He wasn't home. But I ran into Mrs. Elvsted and she told me he'd been here early this morning.

HEDDA: Yes, right after you'd left.

TESMAN: And he said he'd torn up the manuscript? Did he really say that?

HEDDA: Yes. So he claimed.

TESMAN: But dear God—in that case he really must have been out of his mind! So I assume you didn't give it to him either, hm, Hedda?

HEDDA: No. He didn't get it.

TESMAN: But you told him we had it, of course?

HEDDA: No. (*Quickly.*) Did you tell Mrs. Elvsted?

TESMAN: No, I didn't want to. But you ought to have told him, Hedda. Just think—what if he does something rash—something to hurt himself! Give me the manuscript, Hedda! I want to rush down to him with it right this minute. Where is it?

HEDDA (*cold, motionless, one arm resting on the chair*): I haven't got it any more.

TESMAN: You haven't got it! What do you mean by that?

HEDDA: I burned it—the whole thing.

TESMAN (*jumps up*): Burned it! Burned Eilert's book!

HEDDA: Don't shout. The maid might hear you.

TESMAN: Burned it? But good God—no, no, no!—This can't be—!

HEDDA: It is, all the same.

TESMAN: But do you realize what you've done, Hedda? It's illegal! Willful destruction of lost property! You just ask Judge Brack! He'll tell you!

HEDDA: You'd better not talk about this to anyone—the Judge or anybody else.

TESMAN: But how could you do a thing like that! I never heard anything like it! What came over you? What can possibly have been going on in your head? Answer me! Hm?

HEDDA (*suppresses an almost imperceptible smile*): I did it for your sake, Jørgen.

TESMAN: For my sake!

HEDDA: When you came back this morning and told me he had read aloud to you—

TESMAN: Yes, yes! What then?

HEDDA: You confessed you were jealous of him for having written such a book.

TESMAN: But good gracious—! I didn't mean it as seriously as all that!

HEDDA: All the same. I couldn't stand the thought that somebody else was to overshadow you.

TESMAN (*in an outburst of mingled doubt and joy*): Hedda—oh Hedda! Is it true what you're saying! But—but—but—I never knew you loved me like that! Just think!

HEDDA: In that case, I might as well tell you—that—just at this time—(*breaks off, vehemently*). No, no! You can ask Aunt Julle. She'll tell you.

TESMAN: I almost think I know what you mean, Hedda! (*Claps his hands.*) For goodness' sake! Can that really be so! Hm?

HEDDA: Don't shout so! The maid can hear you.

TESMAN (*laughing with exuberant joy*): The maid! Well, if you don't take the prize, Hedda! The maid—but that's Berte! I'm going to tell Berte myself this very minute!

HEDDA (*her hands clenched in despair*): Oh I'll die—I'll die, in all this!

TESMAN: In what, Hedda? Hm?

HEDDA (*cold and composed*): In all this—ludicrousness, Jørgen.

TESMAN: Ludicrous? That I'm so happy? Still—maybe I oughtn't to tell Berte, after all.

HEDDA: Oh, go ahead. What difference does it make.

TESMAN: No, not yet. But on my word—Aunt Julle must be told. And that you've started to call me "Jørgen," too! Just think! She'll be ever so happy—Aunt Julle will!

HEDDA: Even when you tell her that I have burned Eilert Løvborg's papers?

TESMAN: No, oh no! That's true! That about the manuscript—nobody must know about that. But to think that you'd burn for me, Hedda—I certainly want to tell *that* to Aunt Julle! I wonder now—is that sort of thing usual with young wives, hm?

HEDDA: Why don't you ask Aunt Julle about that, too.

TESMAN: I shall—I certainly shall, when I get the chance. (*Looks uneasy and disturbed again.*) But the manuscript! Good God—I don't dare to think what this is going to do to poor Eilert!

(MRS. ELVSTED, *dressed as on her first visit, wearing hat and coat, enters, right.*)

MRS. ELVSTED (*gives a hurried greeting, is obviously upset*): Oh Hedda, you must forgive me for coming here again!

HEDDA: What has happened, Thea?

TESMAN: Something to do with Eilert Løvborg again? Hm?

MRS. ELVSTED: Yes, yes—I'm so terribly afraid something's happened to him.

HEDDA (*seizing her arm*): Ah—you think so?

TESMAN: Oh dear—why do you think that, Mrs. Elvsted?

MRS. ELVSTED: I heard them talking about him in the boarding house, just as I came in. And people are saying the most incredible things about him today.

TESMAN: Yes, imagine! I heard that, too! And I can testify that he went straight home to bed! Just think!

HEDDA: And what did they say in the boarding house?

MRS. ELVSTED: Oh, I didn't find out anything. Either they didn't know any details or—They all became silent when they saw me. And I didn't dare to ask.

TESMAN (*pacing the floor uneasily*): We'll just have to hope—to hope that you heard wrong, Mrs. Elvsted!

MRS. ELVSTED: No, no. I'm sure it was he they were talking about. And somebody said something about the hospital or—

TESMAN: The hospital—!

HEDDA: Surely, that can't be so!

MRS. ELVSTED: I got so terribly frightened! So I went up to his room and asked for him there.

HEDDA: Could you bring yourself to do that, Thea?

MRS. ELVSTED: What else could I do? For I felt I just couldn't stand the uncertainty any longer.

TESMAN: But I suppose you didn't find him in, either, did you? Hm?

MRS. ELVSTED: No. And the people there didn't know anything about him. He hadn't been home since yesterday afternoon, they said.

TESMAN: Yesterday! Just think! How could they say that!

MRS. ELVSTED: I don't know what else *to* think—something bad must have happened to him!

TESMAN: Hedda, dear—? What if I were to walk down town and ask for him at several places—?

HEDDA: No, no—don't you go and get mixed up in all this.

(JUDGE BRACK, *hat in hand, enters through the door, right, which* BERTE *opens and closes for him. He looks serious and greets the others in silence.*)

TESMAN: So here you are, Judge, hm?

BRACK: Yes. I had to see you this evening.

TESMAN: I can see you have got Aunt Julle's message.

BRACK: That, too—yes.

TESMAN: Isn't it sad, though?

BRACK: Well, my dear Tesman—that depends on how you look at it.

TESMAN (*looks at him uncertainly*): Has something else happened?

BRACK: Yes.

HEDDA (*tense*): Something sad, Judge Brack?

BRACK: That, too, depends on how you look at it, Mrs. Tesman.

MRS. ELVSTED (*bursting out*): Oh, I'm sure it has something to do with Eilert Løvborg!

BRACK (*looks at her for a moment*): Why do you think that, Mrs. Elvsted? Maybe you already know something—?

MRS. ELVSTED (*confused*): No, no; not at all. It's just—

TESMAN: For heaven's sake, Brack, out with it!

BRACK (*shrugging his shoulders*): Well—unfortunately, Eilert Løvborg's in the hospital. Dying.

MRS. ELVSTED (*screams*): Oh God, oh God!

TESMAN: In the hospital! And dying!

HEDDA (*without thinking*): So soon—!

MRS. ELVSTED (*wailing*): And we didn't even part as friends, Hedda!

HEDDA (*whispers*): Thea, Thea—for heaven's sake—!

MRS. ELVSTED (*paying no attention to her*): I want to see him! I want to see him alive!

BRACK: Won't do you any good, Mrs. Elvsted. Nobody can see him.

MRS. ELVSTED: Then tell me what's happened to him! What?

TESMAN: For, surely, he hasn't himself—!

HEDDA: I'm sure he has.

TESMAN: Hedda! How can you—!

BRACK (*observing her all this time*): I am sorry to say that your guess is absolutely correct, Mrs. Tesman.

MRS. ELVSTED: Oh, how awful!

TESMAN: Did it himself! Just think!

HEDDA: Shot himself!

BRACK: Right again, Mrs. Tesman.

MRS. ELVSTED (*trying to pull herself together*): When did this happen, Judge?

BRACK: This afternoon. Between three and four.

TESMAN: But dear me—where can he have done a thing like that? Hm?

BRACK (*a little uncertain*): Where? Well—I suppose in his room. I don't really know—

MRS. ELVSTED: No, it can't have been there. For I was up there sometime between six and seven.

BRACK: Well, then, some other place. I really can't say. All I know is that he was found. He had shot himself—in the chest.

MRS. ELVSTED: Oh, how horrible to think! That he was to end like that!

HEDDA (*to* BRACK): In the chest?

BRACK: Yes—as I just told you.

HEDDA: Not the temple?

BRACK: In the chest, Mrs. Tesman.

HEDDA: Well, well—the chest is a good place, too.

BRACK: How is that, Mrs. Tesman?

HEDDA (*turning aside*): Oh—nothing.

TESMAN: And you say the wound is fatal? Hm?

BRACK: No doubt about it—absolutely fatal. He's probably dead already.

MRS. ELVSTED: Yes, yes! I feel you're right! It's over! It's all over! Oh, Hedda!

TESMAN: But tell me—how do *you* know all this?

BRACK (*tersely*): A man on the force told me. One I had some business with.

HEDDA (*loudly*): At last a deed!

TESMAN (*appalled*): Oh dear—what are you saying, Hedda!

HEDDA: I am saying there is beauty in this.

BRACK: Well, now—Mrs. Tesman—

TESMAN: Beauty—! Just think!

MRS. ELVSTED: Oh, Hedda—how can you talk about beauty in a thing like this!

HEDDA: Eilert Løvborg has settled this

account with himself. He has had the courage to do—what had to be done.

MRS. ELVSTED: But you musn't believe it happened that way! He did it when he was not himself!

TESMAN: In despair! That's how!

HEDDA: He did not. I am certain of that.

MRS. ELVSTED: Yes he did! He was not himself! That's the way he tore up the book, too!

BRACK (*puzzled*): The book? You mean the manuscript? Has he torn it up?

MRS. ELVSTED: Yes, last night.

TESMAN (*whispers*): Oh, Hedda—we'll never get clear of all this!

BRACK: That is strange.

TESMAN (*walking the floor*): To think that this was to be the end of Eilert! Not to leave behind him anything that would have preserved his name—

MRS. ELVSTED: Oh, if only it could be put together again!

TESMAN: Yes, if only it could. I don't know what I wouldn't give—

MRS. ELVSTED: Maybe it can, Mr. Tesman.

TESMAN: What do you mean?

MRS. ELVSTED (*searching her dress pocket*): Look. I have kept these little slips he dictated from.

HEDDA (*a step closer*): Ah—!

TESMAN: You've kept them, Mrs. Elvsted? Hm?

MRS. ELVSTED: Yes. Here they are. I took them with me when I left. And I've had them in my pocket ever since—

TESMAN: Please, let me see—

MRS. ELVSTED (*gives him a pile of small paper slips*): But it's in such a mess. Without any kind of system or order—!

TESMAN: But just think if we could make sense out of them, all the same! Perhaps if we helped each other—

MRS. ELVSTED: Oh yes! Let's try, anyway!

TESMAN: It will work! It *has* to work! I'll stake my whole life on this!

HEDDA: You, Jørgen? Your life?

TESMAN: Yes, or at any rate all the time I can set aside. My own collections can wait.

Hedda, you understand—don't you? Hm? This is something I owe Eilert's memory.

HEDDA: Maybe so.

TESMAN: And now, my dear Mrs. Elvsted, we want to get to work. Good heavens, there's no point brooding over what's happened. Hm? We'll just have to acquire sufficient peace of mind to—

MRS. ELVSTED: All right, Mr. Tesman. I'll try to do my best.

TESMAN: Very well, then. Come over here. Let's look at these slips right away. Where can we sit? Here? No, it's better in the other room. If you'll excuse us, Judge! Come along, Mrs. Elvsted.

MRS. ELVSTED: Oh dear God—if only it were possible—!

(TESMAN *and* MRS. ELVSTED *go into the inner room. She takes off her hat and coat. Both sit down at the table under the hanging lamp and absorb themselves in eager study of the slips.* HEDDA *walks over toward the stove and sits down in the easy chair. After a while,* BRACK *walks over to her.*)

HEDDA (*in a low voice*): Ah, Judge—what a liberation there is in this thing with Eilert Løvborg!

BRACK: Liberation, Mrs. Tesman? Well, yes, for him perhaps one may say there was liberation of a kind—

HEDDA: I mean for me. There is liberation in knowing that there is such a thing in the world as an act of free courage. Something which becomes beautiful by its very nature.

BRACK (*smiles*): Well—dear Mrs. Tesman—

HEDDA: Oh I know what you're going to say! For you see—you really are a kind of specialist, too!

BRACK (*looks at her fixedly*): Eilert Løvborg has meant more to you than perhaps you're willing to admit, even to yourself. Or am I wrong?

HEDDA: I won't answer such questions. All I know is that Eilert Løvborg had the courage to live his own life. And then now—this—magnificence! The beauty of it! Having the strength and the will to get up and leave life's feast—so early—

BRACK: Believe me, Mrs. Tesman, this pains me, but I see it is necessary that I destroy a pretty illusion—

HEDDA: An illusion?

BRACK: Which could not have been maintained very long, anyway.

HEDDA: And what is that?

BRACK: He didn't shoot himself—of his own free will.

HEDDA: Not of his own—!

BRACK: No. To tell the truth, the circumstances of Eilert Løvborg's death aren't exactly what I said they were.

HEDDA (tense): You've held something back? What?

BRACK: For the sake of poor Mrs. Elvsted I used a few euphemisms.

HEDDA: What?

BRACK: First—he is already dead.

HEDDA: In the hospital.

BRACK: Yes. And without regaining consciousness.

HEDDA: What else haven't you told?

BRACK: The fact that it did not happen in his room.

HEDDA: Well, does that really make much difference?

BRACK: Some. You see—Eilert Løvborg was found shot in Miss Diana's bedroom.

HEDDA (is about to jump up, but sinks back): That's impossible, Judge Brack! He can't have been there again today!

BRACK: He was there this afternoon. He came to claim something he said they had taken from him. Spoke some gibberish about a lost child—

HEDDA: So that's why—!

BRACK: I thought maybe he meant his manuscript. But now I hear he has destroyed that himself. So I suppose it must have been something else.

HEDDA: I suppose. So it was there—so they found him there?

BRACK: Yes. With a fired gun in his pocket. Mortally wounded.

HEDDA: Yes—in the chest.

BRACK: No—in the guts.

HEDDA (looks at him with an expression of disgust): That, too! What is this curse that turns everything I touch into something ludicrous and low!

BRACK: There is something else, Mrs. Tesman. Something I'd call—nasty.

HEDDA: And what is that?

BRACK: The gun they found—

HEDDA (breathless): What about it?

BRACK: He must have stolen it.

HEDDA (jumps up): Stolen! That's not true! He didn't!

BRACK: Anything else is impossible. He must have stolen it.—Shhh!

(TESMAN and MRS. ELVSTED have risen from the table and come forward into the front room.)

TESMAN (with papers in both hands): D'you know, Hedda—you can hardly see in there with that lamp! Just think!

HEDDA: I am thinking.

TESMAN: I wonder if you'd let us use your desk, hm?

HEDDA: Certainly, if you like. (Adds quickly.) Wait a minute, though! Let me clear it off a bit first.

TESMAN: Ah, there's no need for that, Hedda. There's plenty of room.

HEDDA: No, no. I want to straighten it up. Carry all this in here. I'll put it on top of the piano for the time being.

(She has pulled an object, covered by note paper, out of the bookcase. She puts several other sheets of paper on top of it and carries the whole pile into the left part of the inner room. TESMAN puts the papers down on the desk and moves the lamp from the corner table over to the desk. He and MRS. ELVSTED sit down and resume their work. HEDDA returns.)

HEDDA (behind MRS. ELVSTED's chair, softly ruffling her hair): Well, little Thea—how is Eilert Løvborg's memorial coming along?

MRS. ELVSTED (looks up at her, discouraged): Oh God—I'm sure it's going to be terribly hard to make anything out of all this.

TESMAN: But we have to. We just don't have a choice. And putting other people's papers in order—that's just the thing for me.

(HEDDA walks over to the stove and sits down

on one of the ottomans. BRACK *stands over her, leaning on the easy chair.*)

HEDDA (*whispers*): What were you saying about the gun?

BRACK (*also softly*): That he must have stolen it.

HEDDA: Why, necessarily?

BRACK: Because any other explanation ought to be out of the question, Mrs. Tesman.

HEDDA: Oh?

BRACK (*looks at her for a moment*): Eilert Løvborg was here this morning, of course. Isn't that so?

HEDDA: Yes.

BRACK: Were you alone with him?

HEDDA: Yes, for a while.

BRACK: You didn't leave the room while he was here?

HEDDA: No.

BRACK: Think. Not at all? Not even for a a moment?

HEDDA: Well—maybe just for a moment—out in the hall.

BRACK: And where was the gun case?

HEDDA: Down in the—

BRACK: Mrs. Tesman?

HEDDA: On the desk.

BRACK: Have you looked to see if both guns are still there?

HEDDA: No.

BRACK: You needn't bother. I saw the gun they found on Løvborg, and I knew it immediately. From yesterday—and from earlier occasions, too.

HEDDA: Perhaps you have it?

BRACK: No, the police do.

HEDDA: What are the police going to do with it?

BRACK: Try to find the owner.

HEDDA: Do you think they will?

BRACK (*leans over her, whispers*): No, Hedda Gabler—not as long as I keep quiet.

HEDDA (*with a hunted look*): And if you don't?

BRACK (*shrugs his shoulders*): Of course, there's always the chance that the gun was stolen.

HEDDA (*firmly*): I'd rather die!

BRACK (*smiles*): People *say* things like that. They don't *do* them.

HEDDA (*without answering*): And if the gun was not stolen—and if they find the owner—then what happens?

BRACK: Well, Hedda—then comes the scandal!

HEDDA: The scandal!

BRACK: Yes—the scandal. That you are so afraid of. You will of course be required to testify. Both you and Miss Diana. Obviously, she'll have to explain how the whole thing happened. Whether it was accident or homicide. Did he try to pull the gun out of his pocket to threaten her? And did it fire accidentally? Or did she grab the gun away from him, shoot him, and put it back in his pocket? She might just possibly have done that. She's a pretty tough girl—Miss Diana.

HEDDA: But this whole disgusting affair has nothing to do with me.

BRACK: Quite so. But you'll have to answer the question: Why did you give Eilert Løvborg the gun? And what inferences will be drawn from the fact that you did?

HEDDA (*lowers her head*): That's true. I hadn't thought of that.

BRACK: Well—luckily, there's nothing to worry about as long as I don't say anything.

HEDDA (*looks up at him*): So then I'm in your power, Judge. From now on you can do anything you like with me.

BRACK (*in an even softer whisper*): Dearest Hedda—believe me, I'll not misuse my position.

HEDDA: In your power, all the same. Dependent on your will. Servant to your demands. Not free. Not free! (*Rises suddenly.*) No—I can't stand that thought! Never!

BRACK (*looks at her, half mockingly*): Most people submit to the inevitable.

HEDDA (*returning his glance*): Perhaps. (*Walks over to the desk. Suppresses a smile and mimics* TESMAN's *way of speaking.*) Well? Do you think you can do it, Jørgen? Hm?

TESMAN: Lord knows, Hedda. Anyway, I can already see it will take months.

HEDDA (*still mimicking*): Just think! (*Runs her hands lightly through* MRS. ELVSTED'S *hair.*) Doesn't this seem strange to you, Thea? Sitting here with Tesman—just the way you used to with Eilert Løvborg?

MRS. ELVSTED: Oh dear—if only I could inspire your husband, too!

HEDDA: Oh, I'm sure that will come—in time.

TESMAN: Well, yes—do you know, Hedda? I really think I begin to feel something of the kind. But why don't you go and talk to the Judge again.

HEDDA: Isn't there anything you two can use me for?

TESMAN: No, not a thing, dear. (*Turns around.*) From now on, you must be good enough to keep Hedda company, my dear Judge!

BRACK (*glancing at* HEDDA): I'll be only too delighted.

HEDDA: Thank you. I'm tired tonight. I think I'll go and lie down for a while on the sofa in there.

TESMAN: Yes, you do that, dear; why don't you? Hm?

(HEDDA *goes into the inner room, closes the portieres behind her. Brief pause. Suddenly, she is heard playing a frenzied dance tune on the piano.*)

MRS. ELVSTED (*jumps up*): Oh God! What's that!

TESMAN (*running to the doorway*): But dearest Hedda—you musn't play dance music tonight, for goodness' sake! Think of Aunt Rina! And Eilert, too!

HEDDA (*peeks in from between the portieres*): And Aunt Julle. And everybody. I'll be quiet.

(*She pulls the portieres shut again.*)

TESMAN (*back at the desk*): I don't think it's good for her to see us at such a melancholy task. I'll tell you what, Mrs. Elvsted. You move in with Aunt Julle, and then I'll come over in the evenings. Then we can sit and work over there. Hm?

MRS. ELVSTED: Maybe that would be better—

HEDDA (*from the inner room*): I hear every word you're saying, Tesman. And how am I going to spend my evenings?

TESMAN (*busy with the papers*): Oh, I'm sure Judge Brack will be good enough to come out and see you, anyway.

BRACK (*in the easy chair, calls out gaily*): Every single night, as far as I'm concerned, Mrs. Tesman! I'm sure we're going to have a lovely time, you and I!

HEDDA (*loud and clear*): Yes, don't you think that would be nice, Judge Brack? You—sole cock-o'-the-walk—

(*A shot is heard from the inner room.* TESMAN, MRS. ELVSTED, *and* JUDGE BRACK *all jump up.*)

TESMAN: There she is, fooling with those guns again.

(*He pulls the portieres apart and runs inside.* MRS. ELVSTED *also.* HEDDA, *lifeless, is lying on the sofa. Cries and confusion.* BERTE, *flustered, enters, right.*)

TESMAN (*shouts to* BRACK): She's shot herself! In the temple! Just think!

BRACK (*half stunned in the easy chair*): But, merciful God—! People don't *do* things like that!

IBSEN'S NOTES FOR *HEDDA GABLER*: COMMENTARY AND QUESTIONS

More of Ibsen's preliminary notes have been preserved for *Hedda Gabler* than for any of his other plays. These notes, which reveal Ibsen's thoughts as he was planning the play, provide the student with a framework for asking further questions:

One evening as Hedda and Tesman, together with some others, were on their way home from a party, Hedda remarked as they walked by a charming house that was where she would like to live. *She meant it, but she said it only to keep the conversation with Tesman going. "He simply cannot carry on a conversation."*

The house was actually for rent or sale. Tesman had been pointed out as the coming young man. And later when he proposed, and let slip that he too had dreamed of living there, she accepted.

He too had liked the house very much.

They get married. And they rent the house. [At this point Ibsen makes the following note to his own notes: *Both of them, each in his and her own way, have seen in their common love for this house a sign of their mutual understanding. As if they sought and were drawn to a common home. Then he rents the house. They get married and go abroad. He orders the house bought and his aunt furnishes it at his expense. Now it is their home. It is theirs and yet it is not, because it is not paid for. Everything depends on his getting the professorship.*]

But when Hedda returns as a young wife with a vague sense of responsibility, the whole thing seems distasteful to her. She conceives a kind of hatred for the house because it has become her home. She confides this to Brack. She evades the question with Tesman.

The play shall deal with "the impossible," that is, to aspire to and strive for something which is against all the conventions, against that which is acceptable to conscious minds—Hedda's included.

1. Ibsen's comments make it clear that the house which Hedda and Tesman move into has a kind of symbolic meaning: it has, initially, brought them together. When they move in, they have already been abroad. Hedda has had a taste of marriage and its restraints, and thus upon settling into the house she perceives it as symbolizing her imprisonment in a dull marriage. Why does Ibsen restrict the setting of *Hedda Gabler* to a single room? What kind of "life style" does the room reflect?

2. Ibsen notes that everything depends on Tesman's getting the professorship. How important to the plot is the potential rivalry between Tesman and Løvborg for the academic position? Why does Hedda tell Brack that she is not concerned with "that silly old professorship"? Does Tesman's attitude toward Løvborg change as the play progresses? How does he respond to Hedda's burning of Løvborg's manuscript?

3. Ibsen explains that before Hedda and Tesman move into the house, it is furnished by Tesman's aunt, Miss Juliana Tesman. How does Hedda feel about Tesman's aunt?

4. Hedda is willing to confide in Judge Brack. What kind of person is he? Why does he want to form a "triangle" with Hedda and Tesman?

5. When Ibsen explains that *Hedda Gabler* is to be about striving for "the impossible," he seems to be thinking about unconventional behavior. Hedda suggests that Løvborg may have "more courage for life than the rest of you." Is she thinking of an unconventional kind of courage? Does Løvborg die courageously? Does Hedda? Would it have taken more courage, given their situations, to continue living? Would that have been the conventional course of action?

6. The final words of the play are those of Judge Brack; "But, merciful God!—people don't *do* things like that!" What kind of "people" is Judge Brack thinking of? Why can't he understand Hedda's suicide? Why do you think the play ends with this statement?

A few more of Ibsen's notes follow:

The feminine imagination is not active and independently creative like the masculine. It needs a bit of reality as a help. A woman needs a man's work to be creative.

457

Løvborg has had inclinations toward "the bohemian life." Hedda is attracted in the same direction, but she does not dare to take the leap.

Buried deep within Hedda there is a level of poetry. But the environment frightens her. Suppose she were to make herself ridiculous!

Hedda realizes that she, much more than Thea, has abandoned her husband . . . she marries Tesman but she devotes her imagination to Eilert Løvborg. She leans back in her chair, and dreams of his adventures . . . . This is the enormous difference: Mrs. Elvsted "works for his moral improvement." But for Hedda he is the object of cowardly, tempting daydreams. In reality she does not have the courage to be a part of anything like that. Then she realizes her condition. Caught! Can't comprehend it. Ridiculous! Ridiculous!

7. In the beginning Hedda thinks that Løvborg's flight from reality and its responsibilities is cowardly. How early in the play does she change her mind? Would you say that when Hedda gives Løvborg the gun she has decided that it is ridiculous for a feeling person to remain imprisoned? Do you agree with Ibsen that the feminine imagination needs more stimulation to action, the example of a Løvborg, before it is able to act?

8. Løvborg's book is about the ways in which truly spiritual human beings can be created, in the future, through new kinds of comradeship between men and women. At one point in his notes, Ibsen writes:

   1. *They (women) are not all made to be mothers.*
   2. *They are passionate but they are afraid of scandal.*
   3. *They perceive that the times are full of missions worth devoting one's life to, but they cannot discover them.*

Ibsen was obviously distressed by the situation of women, much as many women are today. What kind of woman, finally, is Hedda Gabler? How much of the boredom and conflict in her life is due to her environment? To society's conventional attitudes toward women?

Further Plays

DUTCHMAN – why?

[handwritten margin notes: More of a social drama than psychodrama compared to Oedipus Rex & Hedda Gabler?]

[handwritten margin notes: Are these characters "types?!" Reminds me of Zoo Story]

CHARACTERS	RIDERS OF COACH, *white and black*
CLAY, *twenty-year-old Negro*	YOUNG NEGRO
LULA, *thirty-year-old white woman*	CONDUCTOR

In the flying underbelly of the city. Steaming hot, and summer on top, outside. Underground. The subway heaped in modern myth.

Opening scene is a man sitting in a subway seat, holding a magazine but looking vacantly just above its wilting pages. Occasionally he looks blankly toward the window on his right. Dim lights and darkness whistling by against the glass. (Or paste the lights, as admitted props, right on the subway windows. Have them move, even dim and flicker. But give the sense of speed. Also stations, whether the train is stopped or the glitter and activity of these stations merely flashes by the windows.)

The man is sitting alone. That is, only his seat is visible, though the rest of the car is outfitted as a complete subway car. But only his seat is shown. There might be, for a time, as the play begins, a loud scream of the actual train. And it can recur throughout the play, or continue on a lower key once the dialogue starts.

The train slows after a time, pulling to a brief stop at one of the stations. The man looks idly up, until he sees a woman's face staring at him through the window; when it realizes that the man has noticed the face, it begins very premeditatedly to smile. The man smiles too, for a moment, without a trace of self-consciousness. Almost an instinctive though undesirable response. Then a kind of awkwardness or embarrassment sets in, and the man makes to look away, is further embarrassed, so he brings back his eyes to where the face was, but by now the train is moving again, and the face would seem to be left behind by the way the man turns his head to look back through the other windows at the slowly fading platform. He smiles then; more comfortably confident, hoping perhaps that his memory of this brief encounter will be pleasant. And then he is idle again.

SCENE I

Train roars. Lights flash outside the windows.

LULA *enters from the rear of the car in bright, skimpy summer clothes and sandals. She carries a net bag full of paper books, fruit, and other anonymous articles. She is wearing sunglasses, which she pushes up on her forehead from time to time.* LULA *is a tall, slender, beautiful woman with long red hair hanging straight down her back, wearing only loud lipstick in somebody's good taste. She is eating an apple, very daintily. Coming down the car toward* CLAY.

She stops beside CLAY's *seat and hangs languidly from the strap, still managing to eat the apple. It is apparent that she is going to sit in the seat next to* CLAY, *and that she is only waiting for him to notice her before she sits.*

CLAY *sits as before, looking just beyond his magazine, now and again pulling the magazine slowly back and forth in front of his face in a hopeless effort to fan himself. Then he sees the woman hanging there beside him and he looks up into her face, smiling quizzically.*

LULA: Hello.

CLAY: Uh, hi're you?

LULA: I'm going to sit down. . . . O.K.?

CLAY: Sure.

LULA [*Swings down onto the seat, pushing her legs straight out as if she is very weary*]: Oooof! Too much weight.

CLAY: Ha, doesn't look like much to me. [*Leaning back against the window, a little surprised and maybe stiff*]

LULA: It's so anyway. [*And she moves her toes in the sandals, then pulls her right leg up on the left knee, better to inspect the bottoms of the sandals and the back of her heel. She appears for a second not to notice that* CLAY *is sitting next to her or that she has spoken to him just a second before.* CLAY *looks at the magazine, then out the black window. As he does this, she turns very quickly toward him*] Weren't you staring at me through the window?

CLAY: [*Wheeling around and very much stiffened*] What?

LULA: Weren't you staring at me through the window? At the last stop?

CLAY: Staring at you? What do you mean?

LULA: Don't you know what staring means?

CLAY: I saw you through the window . . . if that's what it means. I don't know if I was staring. Seems to me you were staring through the window at me.

LULA: I was. But only after I'd turned around and saw you staring through that window down in the vicinity of my ass and legs.

CLAY: Really?

LULA: Really. I guess you were just taking those idle potshots. Nothing else to do. Run your mind over people's flesh.

CLAY: Oh boy. Wow, now I admit I was looking in your direction. But the rest of that weight is yours.

LULA: I suppose.

CLAY: Staring through train windows is weird business. Much weirder than staring very sedately at abstract asses.

LULA: That's why I came looking through the window . . . so you'd have more than that to go on. I even smiled at you.

461

CLAY: That's right.

LULA: I even got into this train, going some other way than mine. Walked down the aisle . . . searching you out.

CLAY: Really? That's pretty funny.

LULA: That's pretty funny. . . . God, you're dull.

CLAY: Well, I'm sorry, lady, but I really wasn't prepared for party talk.

LULA: No, you're not. What are you prepared for? [*Wrapping the apple core in a Kleenex and dropping it on the floor*]

CLAY: [*Takes her conversation as pure sex talk. He turns to confront her squarely with this idea*] I'm prepared for anything. How about you?

LULA: [*Laughing loudly and cutting it off abruptly*] What do you think you're doing?

CLAY: What?

LULA: You think I want to pick you up, get you to take me somewhere and screw me, huh?

CLAY: Is that the way I look?

LULA: You look like you been trying to grow a beard. That's exactly what you look like. You look like you live in New Jersey with your parents and are trying to grow a beard. That's what. You look like you've been reading Chinese poetry and drinking lukewarm sugarless tea. [*Laughs, uncrossing and recrossing her legs*] You look like death eating a soda cracker.

CLAY: [*Cocking his head from one side to the other, embarrassed and trying to make some comeback, but also intrigued by what the woman is saying . . . even the sharp city coarseness of her voice, which is still a kind of gentle sidewalk throb*] Really? I look like all that?

LULA: Not all of it. [*She feints a seriousness to cover an actual somber tone*] I lie a lot. [*Smiling*] It helps me to control the world.

CLAY: [*Relieved and laughing louder than the humor*] Yeah, I bet.

LULA: But it's true, most of it, right? Jersey? Your bumpy neck?

CLAY: How'd you know all that? Huh? Really, I mean about Jersey . . . and even the beard. I met you before? You know Warren Enright?

LULA: You tried to make it with your sister when you were ten. [CLAY *leans back hard against the back of the seat, his eyes opening now, still trying to look amused*] But I succeeded a few weeks ago. [*She starts to laugh again*]

CLAY: What're you talking about? Warren tell you that? You're a friend of Georgia's?

LULA: I told you I lie. I don't know your sister. I don't know Warren Enright.

CLAY: You mean you're just picking these things out of the air?

LULA: Is Warren Enright a tall skinny black black boy with a phony English accent?

CLAY: I figured you knew him.

LULA: But I don't. I just figured you would know somebody like that. [*Laughs*]

CLAY: Yeah, yeah.

LULA: You're probably on your way to his house now.

CLAY: That's right.

LULA: [*Putting her hand on Clay's closest knee, drawing it from the knee up to the thigh's hinge, then removing it, watching his face very closely, and continuing to laugh, perhaps more gently than before*] Dull, dull, dull. I bet you think I'm exciting.

CLAY: You're O.K.

LULA: Am I exciting you now?

CLAY: Right. That's not what's supposed to happen?

LULA: How do I know? [*She returns her hand, without moving it, then takes it away and plunges it in her bag to draw out an apple*] You want this?

CLAY: Sure.

LULA: [*She gets one out of the bag for herself*] Eating apples together is always the first step. Or walking up uninhabited Seventh Avenue in the twenties on weekends. [*Bites and giggles, glancing at Clay and speaking in loose singsong*] Can get you involved . . . boy! Get us involved. Um-huh. [*Mock seriousness*] Would you like to get involved with me, Mister Man?

CLAY: [*Trying to be as flippant as Lula, whacking happily at the apple*] Sure. Why not? A beautiful woman like you. Huh, I'd be a fool not too.

LULA: And I bet you're sure you know what you're talking about. [*Taking him a little roughly by the wrist, so he cannot eat the apple, then shaking the wrist*] I bet you're sure of almost everything anybody ever asked you about . . . right? [*Shakes his wrist harder*] Right?

CLAY: Yeah, right. . . . Wow, you're pretty strong, you know? Whatta you, a lady wrestler or something?

LULA: What's wrong with lady wrestlers? And don't answer because you never knew any. Huh. [*Cynically*] That's for sure. They don't have any lady wrestlers in that part of Jersey. That's for sure.

CLAY: Hey, you still haven't told me how you know so much about me.

LULA: I told you I didn't know anything about *you* . . . you're a well-known type.

CLAY: Really?

LULA: Or at least I know the type very well. And your skinny English friend too.

CLAY: Anonymously?

LULA: [*Settles back in seat, single-mindedly finishing her apple and humming snatches of rhythm and blues song*] What?

CLAY: Without knowing us specifically?

LULA: Oh boy. [*Looking quickly at Clay*] What a face. You know, you could be a handsome man.

CLAY: I can't argue with you.

LULA: [*Vague, off-center response*] What?

CLAY: [*Raising his voice, thinking the train noise has drowned part of his sentence*] I can't argue with you.

LULA: My hair is turning gray. A gray hair for each year and type I've come through.

CLAY: Why do you want to sound so old?

LULA: But it's always gentle when it starts. [*Attention drifting*] Hugged against tenements, day or night.

CLAY: What?

LULA: [*Refocusing*] Hey, why don't you take me to that party you're going to?

CLAY: You must be a friend of Warren's to know about the party.

LULA: Wouldn't you like to take me to the party? [*Imitates clinging vine*] Oh, come on, ask me to your party.

CLAY: Of course I'll ask you to come with me to the party. And I'll bet you're a friend of Warren's.

LULA: Why not be a friend of Warren's? Why not? [*Taking his arm*] Have you asked me yet?

CLAY: How can I ask you when I don't know your name?

LULA: Are you talking to my name?

CLAY: What is it, a secret?

LULA: I'm Lena the Hyena.

CLAY: The famous woman poet?

LULA: Poetess! The same!

CLAY: Well, you know so much about me . . . what's my name?

LULA: Morris the Hyena.

CLAY: The famous woman poet?

LULA: The same. [*Laughing and going into her bag*] You want another apple?

CLAY: Can't make it, lady. I only have to keep one doctor away a day.

464

LULA: I bet your name is . . . something like . . . uh, Gerald or Walter. Huh?

CLAY: God, no.

LULA: Lloyd, Norman? One of those hopeless colored names creeping out of New Jersey. Leonard? Gag. . . .

CLAY: Like Warren?

LULA: Definitely. Just exactly like Warren. Or Everett.

CLAY: Gag. . . .

LULA: Well, for sure, it's not Willie.

CLAY: It's Clay.

LULA: Clay? Really? Clay what?

CLAY: Take your pick. Jackson, Johnson, or Williams.

LULA: Oh, really? Good for you. But it's got to be Williams. You're too pretentious to be a Jackson or Johnson.

CLAY: Thass right.

LULA: But Clay's O.K.

CLAY: So's Lena.

LULA: It's Lula.

CLAY: Oh?

LULA: Lula the Hyena.

CLAY: Very good.

LULA: [*Starts laughing again*] Now you say to me, "Lula, Lula, why don't you go to this party with me tonight?" It's your turn, and let those be your lines.

CLAY: Lula, why don't you go to this party with me tonight, Huh?

LULA: Say my name twice before you ask, and no huh's

CLAY: Lula, Lula, why don't you go to this party with me tonight?

LULA: I'd like to go, Clay, but how can you ask me to go when you barely know me?

CLAY: That is strange, isn't it?

LULA: What kind of reaction is that? You're supposed to say, "Aw, come on, we'll get to know each other better at the party."

CLAY: That's pretty corny.

LULA: What are you into anyway? [*Looking at him half sullenly but still amused*] What thing are you playing at, Mister? Mister Clay Williams? [*Grabs his thigh, up near the crotch*] What are *you* thinking about?

CLAY: Watch it now, you're gonna excite me for real.

LULA: [*Taking her hand away and throwing her apple core through the window*] I bet. [*She slumps in the seat and is heavily silent*]

CLAY: I thought you knew everything about me? What happened? [LULA *looks at him, then looks slowly away, then over where the other aisle would be. Noise of the train. She reaches in her bag and pulls out one of the paper books. She puts it on her leg and thumbs the pages listlessly.* CLAY *cocks his head to see the title of the book. Noise of the train.* LULA *flips pages and her eyes drift. Both remain silent*] Are you going to the party with me, Lula?

LULA: [*Bored and not even looking*] I don't even know you.

CLAY: You said you know my type.

LULA: [*Strangely irritated*] Don't get smart with me, Buster. I know you like the palm of my hand.

CLAY: The one you eat the apples with?

LULA: Yeh. And the one I open doors late Saturday evening with. That's my door. Up at the top of the stairs. Five flights. Above a lot of Italians and lying Americans. And scrape carrots with. Also . . . [*Looks at him*] the same hand I unbutton my dress with, or let my skirt fall down. Same hand. Lover.

CLAY: Are you angry about something? Did I say something wrong?

LULA: Everything you say is wrong. [*Mock smile*] That's what makes you so attractive. Ha. In that funnybook jacket with all the buttons. [*More animate, taking hold of his jacket*] What've you got that jacket and tie on in all this heat for? And why're you wearing a jacket and tie like that? Did your people ever burn witches or start revolutions over the price of tea? Boy, those narrow-shoulder clothes come from a tradition you ought to feel oppressed by. A three-button suit. What right do you have to be wearing a three-button suit and striped tie? Your grandfather was a slave, he didn't go to Harvard.

CLAY: My grandfather was a night watchman.

LULA: And you went to a colored college where everybody thought they were Averell Harriman.[1]

CLAY: All except me.

LULA: And who did you think you were? Who do you think you are now?

CLAY: [*Laughs as if to make light of the whole trend of the conversation*] Well, in college I thought I was Baudelaire. But I've slowed down since.

LULA: I bet you never once thought you were a black nigger. [*Mock serious, then she howls with laughter.* CLAY *is stunned but after initial reaction, he quickly tries to appreciate the humor.* LULA *almost shrieks*] A black Baudelaire.

CLAY: That's right.

LULA: Boy, are you corny. I take back what I said before. Everything you say is not wrong. It's perfect. You should be on television.

[1] W. Averell Harriman (1891–), a U.S. government official and diplomat.

CLAY: You act like you're on television already.

LULA: That's because I'm an actress.

CLAY: I thought so.

LULA: Well, you're wrong. I'm no actress. I told you I always lie. I'm nothing, honey, and don't you ever forget it. [*Lighter*] Although my mother was a Communist. The only person of my family ever to amount to anything.

CLAY: My mother was a Republican.

LULA: And your father voted for the man rather than the party.

CLAY: Right!

LULA: Yea for him. Yea, yea for him.

CLAY: Yea!

LULA: And yea for America where he is free to vote for the mediocrity of his choice! Yea!

CLAY: Yea!

LULA: And yea for both your parents who even though they differ about so crucial a matter as the body politic still forged a union of love and sacrifice that was destined to flower at the birth of the noble Clay . . . what's your middle name?

CLAY: Clay.

LULA: A union of love and sacrifice that was destined to flower at the birth of the noble Clay Clay Williams. Yea! And most of all yea yea for you, Clay Clay. The Black Baudelaire! Yes! [*And with knifelike cynicism*] My Christ. My Christ. *Heavy?*

CLAY: Thank you, ma'am.

LULA: May the people accept you as a ghost of the future. And love you, that you might not kill them when you can.

CLAY: What?

LULA: You're a murderer, Clay, and you know it. [*Her voice darkening with significance*] You know goddam well what I mean.

CLAY: I do?

LULA: So we'll pretend the air is light and full of perfume.

CLAY: [*Sniffing at her blouse*] It is.

LULA: And we'll pretend the people cannot see you. That is, the citizens. And that you are free of your own history. And I am free of my history. We'll pretend that we are both anonymous beauties smashing along through the city's entrails. [*She yells as loud as she can*] GROOVE! *Social comment? Irony of the play?*

BLACK OUT

467

Scene is the same as before, though now there are other seats visible in the car. And throughout the scene other people get on the subway. There are maybe one or two seated in the car as the scene opens, though neither CLAY *nor* LULA *notices them.* CLAY'S *tie is open.* LULA *is hugging his arm.*

CLAY: The party!

LULA: I know it'll be something good. You can come in with me, looking casual and significant. I'll be strange, haughty, and silent, and walk with long slow strides.

CLAY: Right.

LULA: When you get drunk, pat me once, very lovingly on the flanks, and I'll look at you cryptically, licking my lips.

CLAY: It sounds like something we can do.

LULA: You'll go around talking to young men about your mind, and to old men about your plans. If you meet a very close friend who is also with someone like me, we can stand together, sipping our drinks and exchanging codes of lust. The atmosphere will be slithering in love and half-love and very open moral decision.

CLAY: Great. Great.

LULA: And everyone will pretend they don't know your name, and then . . . [*She pauses heavily*] later, when they have to, they'll claim a friendship that denies your sterling character.

CLAY: [*Kissing her neck and fingers*] And then what?

LULA: Then? Well, then we'll go down the street, late night, eating apples and winding very deliberately toward my house.

CLAY: Deliberately?

LULA: I mean, we'll look in all the shopwindows, and make fun of the queers. Maybe we'll meet a Jewish Buddhist and flatten his conceits over some very pretentious coffee.

CLAY: In honor of whose God?

LULA: Mine.

CLAY: Who is . . .?

LULA: Me . . . and you?

CLAY: A corporate Godhead.

LULA: Exactly. Exactly. [*Notices one of the other people entering*]

CLAY: Go on with the chronicle. Then what happens to us?

468

LULA: [*A mild depression, but she still makes her description triumphant and increasingly direct*] To my house, of course.

CLAY: Of course.

LULA: And up the narrow steps of the tenement.

CLAY: You live in a tenement?

LULA: Wouldn't live anywhere else. Reminds me specifically of my novel form of insanity.

CLAY: Up the tenement stairs.

LULA: And with my apple-eating hand I push open the door and lead you, my tender big-eyed prey, into my . . . God, what can I call it . . . into my hovel.

CLAY: Then what happens?

LULA: After the dancing and games, after the long drinks and long walks, the real fun begins.

CLAY: Ah, the real fun. [*Embarrassed, in spite of himself*] Which is . . .?

LULA: [*Laughs at him*] Real fun in the dark house. Hah! Real fun in the dark house, high up above the street and the ignorant cowboys. I lead you in, holding your wet hand gently in my hand . . .

CLAY: Which is not wet?

LULA: Which is dry as ashes.

CLAY: And cold?

LULA: Don't think you'll get out of your responsibility that way. It's not cold at all. You Fascist! Into my dark living room. Where we'll sit and talk endlessly, endlessly.

CLAY: About what?

LULA: About what? About your manhood, what do you think? What do you think we've been talking about all this time?

CLAY: Well, I didn't know it was that. That's for sure. Every other thing in the world but that. [*Notices another person entering, looks quickly, almost involuntarily up and down the car, seeing the other people in the car.*] Hey, I didn't even notice when those people got on.

LULA: Yea, I know.

CLAY: Man, this subway is slow.

LULA: Yeah, I know.

CLAY: Well, go on. We were talking about my manhood.

LULA: We still are. All the time.

CLAY: We were in your living room.

LULA: My dark living room. Talking endlessly.

CLAY: About my manhood.

LULA: I'll make you a map of it. Just as soon as we get to my house.

CLAY: Well, that's great.

LULA: One of the things we do while we talk. And screw.

CLAY: [*Trying to make his smile broader and less shaky*] We finally got there.

LULA: And you'll call my rooms black as a grave. You'll say, "This place is like Juliet's tomb."

CLAY: [*Laughs*]: I might.

LULA: I know. You've probably said it before.

CLAY: And is that all? The whole grand tour?

LULA: Not all. You'll say to me very close to my face, many, many times, you'll say, even whisper, that you love me.

CLAY: Maybe I will.

LULA: And you'll be lying.

CLAY: I wouldn't lie about something like that.

LULA: Hah. It's the only thing you will lie about.
Especially if you think it'll keep me alive.

CLAY: Keep you alive? I don't understand.

LULA: [*Bursting out laughing, but too shrilly*] Don't understand? Well, don't look at me. It's the path I take, that's all. Where both feet take me when I set them down. One in front of the other.

CLAY: Morbid. Morbid. You sure you're not an actress? All that self-aggrandizement.

LULA: Well, I told you I wasn't an actress . . . but I also told you I lie all the time. Draw your own conclusions.

CLAY: Morbid. Morbid. You sure you're not an actress? All scribed? There's no more?

LULA: I've told you all I know. Or almost all.

CLAY: There's no funny parts?

LULA: I thought it was all funny.

CLAY: But you mean peculiar, not ha-ha.

LULA: You don't know what I mean.

CLAY: Well, tell me the almost part then. You said almost all. What else? I want the whole story.

470

LULA: [*Searching aimlessly through her bag. She begins to talk breathlessly, with a light and silly tone*] All stories are whole stories. All of 'em. Our whole story . . . nothing but change. How could things go on like that forever? Huh? [*Slaps him on the shoulder, begins finding things in her bag, taking them out and throwing them over her shoulder into the aisle*] Except I do go on as I do. Apples and long walks with deathless intelligent lovers. But you mix it up. Look out the window, all the time. Turning pages. Change change change. Till, shit, I don't know you. Wouldn't, for that matter. You're too serious. I bet you're even too serious to be psychoanalyzed. Like all those Jewish poets from Yonkers, who leave their mothers looking for other mothers, or others' mothers, on whose baggy tits they lay their fumbling heads. Their poems are always funny, and all about sex.

CLAY: They sound great. Like movies.

LULA: But you change. [*Blankly*] And things work on you till you hate them. [*More people come into the train. They come closer to the couple, some of them not sitting, but swinging drearily on the straps, staring at the two with uncertain interest*]

CLAY: Wow. All these people, so suddenly. They must all come from the same place.

LULA: Right. That they do.

CLAY: Oh? You know about them too?

LULA: Oh yeah. About them more than I know about you. Do they frighten you?

CLAY: Frighten me? Why should they frighten me?

LULA: 'Cause you're an escaped nigger.

CLAY: Yeah?

LULA: 'Cause you crawled through the wire and made tracks to my side.

CLAY: Wire?

LULA: Don't they have wire around plantations?

CLAY: You must be Jewish. All you can think about is wire. Plantations didn't have any wire. Plantations were big open whitewashed places like heaven, and everybody on 'em was grooved to be there. Just strummin' and hummin' all day.

LULA: Yes, yes.

CLAY: And that's how the blues was born.

LULA: Yes, yes. And that's how the blues was born. [*Begins to make up a song that becomes quickly hysterical. As she sings she rises from her seat, still throwing things out of her bag into the aisle, beginning a rhythmical shudder and twistlike wiggle, which she continues up and down the aisle, bumping into many of the standing people and tripping over the feet of those sitting. Each time she runs into a person she lets out a very vicious piece of profanity, wiggling and stepping all the time*] And that's how the blues was

471

born. Yes. Yes. Son of a bitch, get out of the way. Yes. Quack. Yes. Yes. And that's how the blues was born. Ten little niggers sitting on a limb, but none of them ever looked like him. [*Points to* CLAY, *returns toward the seat, with her hands extended for him to rise and dance with her*] And that's how blues was born. Yes. Come on, Clay. Let's do the nasty. Rub bellies. Rub bellies.

CLAY: [*Waves his hands to refuse. He is embarrassed, but determined to get a kick out of the proceedings*] Hey, what was in those apples? Mirror, mirror on the wall, who's the fairest one of all? Snow White, baby, and don't you forget it.

LULA: [*Grabbing for his hands, which he draws away*] Come on, Clay. Let's rub bellies on the train. The nasty. The nasty. Do the gritty grind, like your ol' rag-head mammy. Grind till you lose your mind. Shake it, shake it, shake it, shake it! OOOOweeee! Come on, Clay. Let's do the choo-choo train shuffle, the navel scratcher.

CLAY: Hey, you coming on like the lady who smoked up her grass skirt.

LULA: [*Becoming annoyed that he will not dance, and becoming more animated as if to embarrass him still further*] Come on, Clay . . . let's do the thing. Uhh! Uhh! Clay! Clay! You middle-class black bastard. Forget your social-working mother for a few seconds and let's knock stomachs. Clay, you liver-lipped white man. You would-be Christian. You ain't no nigger, you're just a dirty white man. Get up, Clay. Dance with me, Clay.

CLAY: Lula! Sit down, now. Be cool.

LULA: [*Mocking him, in wild dance*] Be cool. Be cool. That's all you know . . . shaking that wildroot cream-oil on your knotty head, jackets buttoning up to your chin, so full of white man's words. Christ. God. Get up and scream at these people. Like scream meaningless shit in these hopeless faces. [*She screams at people in train, still dancing*] Red trains cough Jewish underwear for keeps! Expanding smells of silence. Gravy snot whistling like sea birds. Clay. Clay, you got to break out. Don't sit there dying the way they want you to die. Get up.

CLAY: Oh, sit the fuck down. [*He moves to restrain her*] Sit down, goddamn it.

LULA: [*Twisting out of his reach*] Screw yourself, Uncle Tom. Thomas Woolly-head. [*Begins to dance a kind of jig, mocking Clay with loud forced humor*] There is Uncle Tom . . . I mean, Uncle Thomas Woolly-Head. With old white matted mane. He hobbles on his wooden cane. Old Tom. Old Tom. Let the white man hump his ol' mama, and he jes' shuffle off in the woods and hide his gentle gray head. Ol' Thomas Woolly-Head. [*Some of the other riders are laughing now. A drunk gets up and joins* LULA *in her dance, singing, as best he can, her "song."* CLAY *gets up out of his seat and visibly scans the faces of the other riders*]

CLAY: Lula! Lula! [*She is dancing and turning, still shouting as loud as she can. The drunk too is shouting, and waving his hands wildly*] Lula . . . you dumb bitch. Why don't you stop it? [*He rushes half stumbling from his seat, and grabs one of her flailing arms*]

LULA: Let me go! You black son of a bitch. [*She struggles against him*] Let me go! Help! [CLAY *is dragging her towards her seat, and the drunk seeks to interfere.*

472

He grabs CLAY *around the shoulders and begins wrestling with him.* CLAY *clubs the drunk to the floor without releasing* LULA, *who is still screaming.* CLAY *finally gets her to the seat and throws her into it*]

CLAY: Now you shut the hell up. [*Grabbing her shoulders*] Just shut up. You don't know what you're talking about. You don't know anything. So just keep your stupid mouth closed.

LULA: You're afraid of white people. And your father was. Uncle Tom Big Lip!

CLAY: [*Slaps her as hard as he can, across the mouth.* LULA's *head bangs against the back of the seat. When she raises it again,* CLAY *slaps her again*] Now shut up and let me talk. [*He turns toward the other riders, some of whom are sitting on the edge of their seats. The drunk is on one knee, rubbing his head, and singing softly the same song. He shuts up too when he sees* CLAY *watching him. The others go back to newspapers or stare out the windows*] Shit, you don't have any sense, Lula, nor feelings either. I could murder you now. Such a tiny ugly throat. I could squeeze it flat, and watch you turn blue, on a humble. For dull kicks. And all these weak-faced ofays squatting around here, staring over their papers at me. Murder them too. Even if they expected it. That man there . . . [*Points to well-dressed man*] I could rip that *Times* right out of his hand, as skinny and middle-classed as I am, I could rip that paper out of his hand and just as easily rip out his throat. It takes no great effort. For what? To kill you soft idiots? You don't understand anything but luxury.

LULA: You fool!

CLAY: [*Pushing her against the seat*] I'm not telling you again, Tallulah Bankhead! Luxury. In your face and your fingers. You telling me what I ought to do. [*Sudden scream frightening the whole coach*] Well, don't! Don't you tell me anything! If I'm a middle-class fake white man . . . let me be. And let me be in the way I want. [*Through his teeth*] I'll rip your lousy breasts off! Let me be who I feel like being. Uncle Tom. Thomas. Whoever. It's none of your business. You don't know anything except what's there for you to see. An act. Lies. Device. Not the pure heart, the pumping black heart. You don't ever know that. And I sit here, in this buttoned-up suit, to keep myself from cutting all your throats. I mean wantonly. You great liberated whore! You fuck some black man, and right away you're an expert on black people. What a lotta shit that is. The only thing you know is that you come if he bangs you hard enough. And that's all. The belly rub? You wanted to do the belly-rub? Shit, you don't even know how. You don't know how. That ol'dipty-dip shit you do, rolling your ass like an elephant. That's not my kind of belly rub. Belly rub is not Queens. Belly rub is dark places, with big hats and overcoats held up with one arm. Belly rub hates you. Old bald-headed four-eyed ofays popping their fingers . . . and don't know yet what they're doing. They say, "I love Bessie Smith."[2] And don't even understand that Bessie Smith is saying, "Kiss my ass, kiss my black unruly ass." Before love, suffering, desire, anything you can explain, she's saying, and very plainly, "Kiss my black ass." And if you don't know that, it's you that's doing the kissing.

---

[2] (1896?–1937), one of the greatest American blues singers.

Charlie Parker? Charlie Parker.[3] All the hip white boys scream for Bird. And Bird saying, "Up your ass, feeble-minded ofay! Up your ass." And they sit there talking about the tortured genius of Charlie Parker. Bird would've played not a note of music if he just walked up to East Sixty-seventh Street and killed the first ten white people he saw. Not a note! And I'm the great would-be poet. Yes. That's right! Poet. Some kind of bastard literature . . . all it needs is a simple knife thrust. Just let me bleed you, you loud whore, and one poem vanished. A whole people of neurotics, struggling to keep from being sane. And the only thing that would cure the neurosis would be your murder. Simple as that. I mean if I murdered you, then other white people would begin to understand me. You understand? No. I guess not. If Bessie Smith had killed some white people she wouldn't have needed that music. She could have talked very straight and plain about the world. No metaphors. No grunts. No wiggles in the dark of her soul. Just straight two and two are four. Money. Power. Luxury. Like that. All of them. Crazy niggers turning their backs on sanity. When all it needs is that simple act. Murder. Just murder! Would make us all sane. [*Suddenly weary*] Ahhh. Shit. But who needs it? I'd rather be a fool. Insane. Safe with my words, and no deaths, and clean, hard thoughts, urging me to new conquests. My people's madness. Hah! That's a laugh. My people. They don't need me to claim them. They got legs and arms of their own. Personal insanities. Mirrors. They don't need all those words. They don't need any defense. But listen, though, one more thing. And you tell this to your father, who's probably the kind of man who needs to know at once. So he can plan ahead. Tell him not to preach so much rationalism and cold logic to these niggers. Let them alone. Let them sing curses at you in code and see your filth as simple lack of style. Don't make the mistake, through some irresponsible surge of Christian charity, of talking too much about the advantages of Western rationalism, or the great intellectual legacy of the white man, or maybe they'll begin to listen. And then, maybe one day, you'll find they actually do understand exactly what you are talking about, all these fantasy people. All these blues people. And on that day, as sure as shit, when you really believe you can "accept" them into your fold, as half-white trusties late of the subject peoples. With no more blues, except the very old ones, and not a watermelon in sight, the great missionary heart will have triumphed, and all of those ex-coons will be stand-up Western men, with eyes for clean hard useful lives, sober, pious and sane, and they'll murder you. They'll murder you, and have very rational explanations. Very much like your own. They'll cut your throats, and drag you out to the edge of your cities so the flesh can fall away from your bones, in sanitary isolation.

LULA: [*Her voice takes on a different, more businesslike quality*] I've heard enough.

CLAY: [*Reaching for his books*] I bet you have. I guess I better collect my stuff and get off this train. Looks like we won't be acting out that little pageant you outlined before.

LULA: No. We won't. You're right about that, at least. [*She turns to look quickly around the rest of the car*] All right! [*The others respond*]

[3]Charlie ("Bird") Parker (1920– 1955), a renowned jazz saxophonist.

CLAY: [*Bending across the girl to retrieve his belongings*] Sorry, baby, I don't think we could make it. [*As he is bending over her, the girl brings up a small knife and plunges it into* CLAY'S *chest. Twice. He slumps across her knees, his mouth working stupidly*]

LULA: Sorry is right. [*Turning to the others in the car who have already gotten up from their seats*] Sorry is the rightest thing you've said. Get this man off me! Hurry, now! [*The others come and drag* CLAY'S *body down the aisle*] Open the door and throw his body out. [*They throw him off*] And all of you get off at the next stop.

[LULA *busies herself straightening her things. Getting everything in order. She takes out a notebook and makes a quick scribbling note. Drops it in her bag. The train apparently stops and all the others get off, leaving her alone in the coach.*

Very soon a young Negro of about twenty comes into the coach, with a couple of books under his arm. He sits a few seats in back of LULA. *When he is seated she turns and gives him a long slow look. He looks up from his book and drops the book on his lap. Then an old Negro conductor comes into the car, doing a sort of restrained soft shoe, and half mumbling the words of some song. He looks at the young man, briefly, with a quick greeting*]

CONDUCTOR: Hey, brother!

YOUNG MAN: Hey.

[*The conductor continues down the aisle with his little dance and the mumbled song.* LULA *turns to stare at him and follows his movements down the aisle. The conductor tips his hat when he reaches her seat, and continues out the car*]

CURTAIN

That they must remain separate,
(except in death)?
The fight goes on?
Does he see much hope for the union
of blacks and whites beyond
surface talk & surface love?

She acted out his murder. He didn't
understand her.

Art displaces violence
But people are part of art, involved
with it.

Little change in character — just uncovered layers? Or is
there a real shift, when Lula stands up and starts
making a public scene.

475

THE SEVENTH SEAL

A Screenplay

CAST

JONS, THE SQUIRE	GUNNAR BJÖRNSTRAND
DEATH	BENGT EKEROT
JOF	NILS POPPE
THE KNIGHT, ANTONIUS BLOCK	MAX VON SYDOW
MIA	BIBI ANDERSSON
LISA	INGA GILL
TYAN, THE WITCH	MAUD HANSSON
THE KNIGHT'S WIFE	INGA LANDGRÉ
THE GIRL	GUNNEL LINDBLOM
RAVAL	BERTIL ANDERBERG
THE MONK	ANDERS EK
PLOG, THE SMITH	ÅKE FRIDELL
THE CHURCH PAINTER	GUNNAR OLSSON
SKAT	ERIK STRANDMARK
THE MERCHANT	BENKT-ÅKE BENKTSSON
WOMAN AT THE INN	GUDRUN BROST
LEADER OF THE SOLDIERS	ULF JOHANSSON
THE YOUNG MONK	LARS LIND

The night had brought little relief from the heat, and at dawn a hot gust of wind blows across the colourless sea. The KNIGHT, *Antonius Block, lies prostrate on some spruce branches spread over the fine sand. His eyes are wide-open and bloodshot from lack of sleep.*

Nearby his squire JONS *is snoring loudly. He has fallen asleep where he collapsed, at the edge of the forest among the wind-gnarled fir trees. His open mouth gapes towards the dawn, and unearthly sounds come from his throat.*

At the sudden gust of wind the horses stir, stretching their parched muzzles towards the sea. They are as thin and worn as their masters.

The KNIGHT *has risen and waded into the shallow water, where he rinses his sunburned face and blistered lips.*

JONS *rolls over to face the forest and the darkness. He moans in his sleep and vigorously scratches the stubbled hair on his head. A scar stretches diagonally across his scalp, as white as lighting against the grime.*

The KNIGHT *returns to the beach and falls on his knees. With his eyes closed and brow furrowed, he says his morning prayers. His hands are clenched together and his lips form the words silently. His face is sad and bitter. He opens his eyes and stares directly into the morning sun which wallows up from the misty sea like some bloated, dying fish. The sky is grey and immobile, a dome of lead. A cloud hangs mute and dark over the western horizon. High up, barely visible, a seagull floats on motionless wings. Its cry is weird and restless.*

The KNIGHT'S *large grey horse lifts its head and whinnies. Antonius Block turns around.*

Behind him stands a man in black. His face is very pale and he keeps his hands hidden in the wide folds of his cloak.

KNIGHT: Who are you?

DEATH: I am Death.

KNIGHT: Have you come for me?

DEATH: I have been walking by your side for a long time.

KNIGHT: That I know.

DEATH: Are you prepared?

KNIGHT: My body is frightened, but I am not.

DEATH: Well, there is no shame in that.

The KNIGHT *has risen to his feet. He shivers.* DEATH *opens his cloak to place it around the* KNIGHT'S *shoulders.*

KNIGHT: Wait a moment.

DEATH: That's what they all say. I grant no reprieves.

KNIGHT: You play chess, don't you?

A gleam of interest kindles in DEATH'S *eyes.*

DEATH: How did you know that?

KNIGHT: I have seen it in paintings and heard it sung in ballads.

DEATH: Yes, in fact I'm quite a good chess player.

KNIGHT: But you can't be better than I am.

The KNIGHT *rummages in the big black bag which he keeps beside him and takes out a small chessboard. He places it carefully on the ground and begins setting up the pieces.*

DEATH: Why do you want to play chess with me?

KNIGHT: I have my reasons.

DEATH: That is your privilege.

KNIGHT: The condition is that I may live as long as I hold out against you. If I win, you will release me. Is it agreed?

The KNIGHT *holds out his two fists to* DEATH, *who smiles at him suddenly.* DEATH *points to one of the* KNIGHT's *hands; it contains a black pawn.*

KNIGHT: You drew black!

DEATH: Very appropriate. Don't you think so?

The KNIGHT *and* DEATH *bend over the chessboard. After a moment of hesitation, Antonius Block opens with his king's pawn.* DEATH *moves, also using his king's pawn.*

The morning breeze has died down. The restless movement of the sea has ceased, the water is silent. The sun rises from the haze and its glow whitens. The sea gull floats under the dark cloud, frozen in space. The day is already scorchingly hot.

The squire JONS *is awakened by a kick in the rear. Opening his eyes, he grunts like a pig and yawns broadly. He scrambles to his feet, saddles his horse and picks up the heavy pack.*

The KNIGHT *slowly rides away from the sea, into the forest near the beach and up towards the road. He pretends not to hear the morning prayers of his squire.* JONS *soon overtakes him.*

JONS *sings*: Between a strumpet's legs to lie
　　　　　Is the life for which I sigh.

He stops and looks at his master, but the KNIGHT *hasn't heard* JON's *song, or he pretends that he hasn't. To give further vent to his irritation,* JONS *sings even louder.*

JONS *sings*: Up above is God Almighty
　　　　　So very far away,
　　　　　But your brother the Devil
　　　　　You will meet on every level.

JONS *finally gets the* KNIGHT's *attention. He stops singing. The* KNIGHT, *his horse,* JON's *own horse and* JONS *himself know all the songs by heart. The long, dusty journey from the Holy Land hasn't made them any cleaner.*

They ride across a mossy heath which stretches towards the horizon. Beyond it, the sea lies shimmering in the white glitter of the sun.

JONS: In Färjestad everyone was talking about evil omens and other horrible things. Two horses had eaten each other in the night, and, in the churchyard, graves had been opened and the remains of corpses scattered all over the place. Yesterday afternoon there were as many as four suns in the heavens.

The KNIGHT *doesn't answer. Close by, a scrawny dog is whining, crawling towards its master, who is sleeping in a sitting position in the blazing hot sun. A black cloud of flies clusters around his head and shoulders. The miserable-looking dog whines incessantly as it lies flat on its stomach, wagging its tail.*

JONS *dismounts and approaches the sleeping man.* JONS *addresses him politely. When he doesn't receive an answer, he walks up to the man in order to shake him awake. He bends over the sleeping man's shoulder, but quickly pulls back his hand. The man falls backward on the heath, his face turned towards* JONS. *It is a corpse, staring at* JONS *with empty eye sockets and white teeth.*

478

JONS *remounts and overtakes his master. He takes a drink from his waterskin and hands the bag to the knight.*

KNIGHT: Well, did he show you the way?

JONS: Not exactly.

KNIGHT: What did he say?

JONS: Nothing.

KNIGHT: Was he a mute?

JONS: No, sir, I wouldn't say that. As a matter of fact, he was quite eloquent.

KNIGHT: Oh?

JONS: He was eloquent, all right. The trouble is that what he had to say was most depressing.

JONS *sings*: One moment you're bright and lively,
      The next you're crawling with worms.
      Fate is a terrible villain
      And you, my friend, its poor victim.

KNIGHT: Must you sing?

JONS: No.

The KNIGHT *hands his squire a piece of bread, which keeps him quiet for a while. The sun burns down on them cruelly, and beads of perspiration trickle down their faces. There is a cloud of dust around the horses' hooves.*

They ride past an inlet and along verdant groves. In the shade of some large trees stands a bulging wagon covered with a mottled canvas. A horse whinnies nearby and is answered by the KNIGHT'S *horse. The two travellers do not stop to rest under the shade of the trees but continue riding until they disappear at the bend of the road.*

In his sleep, JOF *the juggler hears the neighing of his horse and the answer from a distance. He tries to go on sleeping, but it is stifling inside the wagon. The rays of the sun filtering through the canvas cast streaks of light across the face of* JOF'S *wife,* MIA, *and their one-year-old son,* MIKAEL, *who are sleeping deeply and peacefully. Near them,* JONAS SKAT, *an older man, snores loudly.*

JOF *crawls out of the wagon. There is still a spot of shade under the big trees. He takes a drink of water, gargles, stretches and talks to his scrawny old horse.*

JOF: Good morning. Have you had breakfast? I can't eat grass, worse luck. Can't you teach me how? We're a little hard up. People aren't very interested in juggling in this part of the country.

He has picked up the juggling balls and slowly begins to toss them. Then he stands on his head and cackles like a hen. Suddenly he stops and sits down with a look of utter astonishment on his face. The wind causes the trees to sway slightly. The leaves stir and there is a soft murmur. The flowers and the grass bend gracefully, and somewhere a bird raises its voice in a long warble.

JOF's *face breaks into a smile and his eyes fill with tears. With a dazed expression he sits flat on his behind while the grass rustles softly, and bees and butterflies hum around his head. The unseen bird continues to sing.*

Suddenly the breeze stops blowing, the bird stops singing, JOF's *smile fades, the flowers and grass wilt in the heat. The old horse is still walking around grazing and swishing its tail to ward off the flies.*

JOF *comes to life. He rushes into the wagon and shakes* MIA *awake.*

JOF: Mia, wake up. Wake up! Mia, I've just seen something. I've got to tell you about it!

MIA *sits up terrified*: What is it? What's happened?

JOF: Listen, I've had a vision. No, it wasn't a vision. It was real, absolutely real.

MIA: Oh, so you've had a vision again!

MIA's *voice is filled with gentle irony.* JOF *shakes his head and grabs her by the shoulders.*

JOF: But I did see her!

MIA: Whom did you see?

JOF: The Virgin Mary.

MIA *can't help being impressed by her husband's fervour. She lowers her voice.*

MIA: Did you really see her?

JOF: She was so close to me that I could have touched her. She had a golden crown on her head and wore a blue gown with flowers of gold. She was barefoot and had small brown hands with which she was holding the Child and teaching Him to walk. And then she saw me watching her and she smiled at me. My eyes filled with tears and when I wiped them away, she had disappeared. And everything became so still in the sky and on the earth. Can you understand . . .

MIA: What an imagination you have.

JOF: You don't believe me! But it was real, I tell you, not the kind of reality you see every day, but a different kind.

MIA: Perhaps it was the kind of reality you told us about when you saw the Devil painting our wagon wheels red, using his tail as a brush.

JOF *embarrassed*: Why must you keep bringing that up?

MIA: And then you discovered that you had red paint under your nails.

JOF: Well, perhaps that time I made it up. *Eagerly.* I did it just so that you would believe in my other visions. The real ones. The ones that I didn't make up.

MIA *severely*: You have to keep your visions under control. Otherwise people will think that you're a half-wit, which you're not. At least not yet—as far as I know. But, come to think of it, I'm not so sure about that.

480

JOF *angry*: I didn't ask to have visions. I can't help it if voices speak to me, if the Holy Virgin appears before me and angels and devils like my company.

SKAT *sits up*: Haven't I told you once and for all that I need my morning's sleep! I have asked you politely, pleaded with you, but nothing works. So now I'm telling you to *shut up!*

His eyes are popping with rage. He turns over and continues snoring where he left off. MIA *and* JOF *decide that it would be wisest to leave the wagon. They sit down on a crate.* MIA *has* MIKAEL *on her knees. He is naked and squirms vigorously.* JOF *sits close to his wife. Slumped over, he still looks dazed and astonished. A dry, hot wind blows from the sea.*

MIA: If we would only get some rain. Everything is burned to cinders. We won't have anything to eat this winter.

Drought

JOF *yawning*: We'll get by.

Faith

He says this smilingly, with a casual air. He stretches and laughs contentedly.

MIA: I want Mikael to have a better life than ours.

JOF: Mikael will grow up to be a great acrobat—or a juggler who can do the one impossible trick.

Faith

MIA: What's that?

JOF: To make one of the balls stand absolutely still in the air.

MIA: But that's impossible.

JOF: Impossible for us—but not for him.

MIA: You're dreaming again.

She yawns. The sun has made her a bit drowsy and she lies down on the grass. JOF *does likewise and puts one arm around his wife's shoulders.*

JOF: I've composed a song. I made it up during the night when I couldn't sleep. Do you want to hear it?

MIA: Sing it. I'm very curious.

JOF: I have to sit up first.

He sits with his legs crossed, makes a dramatic gesture with his arms and sings in a loud voice.

JOF: On a lily branch a dove is perched
    Against the summer sky,
    She sings a wondrous song of Christ
    And there's great joy on high.

He interrupts his singing in order to be complimented by his wife.

JOF: Mia! Are you asleep?

MIA: It's a lovely song.

JOF: I haven't finished yet.

MIA: I heard it, but I think I'll sleep a little longer. You can sing the rest to me afterwards.

JOF: All you do is sleep.

JOF *is a bit offended and glances over at his son,* MIKAEL, *but he is also sleeping soundly in the high grass.* JONAS SKAT *comes out from the wagon. He yawns; he is very tired and in a bad humour. In his hands he holds a crudely made death mask.*

SKAT: Is this supposed to be a mask for an actor? If the priests didn't pay us so well, I'd say no thank you.

JOF: Are you going to play Death?

SKAT: Just think, scaring decent folk out of their wits with this kind of nonsense.

JOF: When are we supposed to do this play?

SKAT: At the saints' feast in Elsinore. We're going to perform right on the church steps, believe it or not.

JOF: Wouldn't it be better to play something bawdy? People like it better, and besides, it's more fun.

SKAT: Idiot. There's a rumour going around that there's a terrible pestilence in the land, and now the priests are prophesying sudden death and all sorts of spiritual agonies.

MIA *is awake now and lies contentedly on her back, sucking on a blade of grass and looking smilingly at her husband.*

JOF: And what part am I to play?

SKAT: You're such a damn fool, so you're going to be the Soul of Man.

JOF: That's a bad part, of course.

SKAT: Who makes the decisions around here? Who is the director of this company anyhow?

SKAT, *grinning, holds the mask in front of his face and recites dramatically.*

SKAT: Bear this in mind, you fool. Your life hangs by a thread. Your time is short. *In his usual voice.* Are the women going to like me in this getup. Will I make a hit? No! I feel as if I were dead already.

He stumbles into the wagon muttering furiously. JOF *sits, leaning forward.* MIA *lies beside him on the grass.*

MIA: Jof!

JOF: What is it!

MIA: Sit still. Don't move.

JOF: What do you mean?

MIA: Don't say anything.

482

JOF: I'm as silent as a grave.

MIA: Shh! I love you.

Waves of heat envelop the grey stone church in a strange white mist. The KNIGHT *dismounts and enters. After tying up the horses,* JONS *slowly follows him in. When he comes onto the church porch he stops in surprise. To the right of the entrance there is a large fresco on the wall, not quite finished. Perched on a crude scaffolding is a* PAINTER *wearing a red cap and paint-stained clothes. He has one brush in his mouth, while with another in his hand he outlines a small, terrified human face amidst a sea of other faces.*

JONS: What is this supposed to represent?

PAINTER: The Dance of Death.

JONS: And that one is Death?

PAINTER: Yes, he dances off with all of them.

JONS: Why do you paint such nonsense?

PAINTER: I thought it would serve to remind people that they must die.

— *Doesn't want to look at destruction*

JONS: Well, it's not going to make them feel any happier.

PAINTER: Why should one always make people happy? It might not be a bad idea to scare them a little once in a while.

JONS: Then they'll close their eyes and refuse to look at your painting.

PAINTER: Oh, they'll look. A skull is almost more interesting than a naked woman.

JONS: If you do scare them . . .

PAINTER: They'll think.

JONS: And if they think . . .

PAINTER: They'll become still more scared.

JONS: And then they'll run right into the arms of the priests.

PAINTER: That's not my business.

JONS: You're only painting your Dance of Death.

PAINTER: I'm only painting things as they are. Everyone else can do as he likes.

JONS: Just think how some people will curse you.

PAINTER: Maybe. But then I'll paint something amusing for them to look at. I have to make a living—at least until the plague takes me.

JONS: The plague. That sounds horrible.

PAINTER: You should see the boils on a diseased man's throat. You should see how his body shrivels up so that his legs look like knotted strings—like the man I've painted over there.

The PAINTER *points with his brush.* JONS *sees a small human form writhing in the grass, its eyes turned upwards in a frenzied look of horror and pain.*

JONS: That looks terrible.

PAINTER: It certainly does. He tries to rip out the boil, he bites his hands, tears his veins open with his fingernails and his screams can be heard everywhere. Does that scare you?

JONS: Scare? Me? You don't know me. What are the horrors you've painted over there?

PAINTER: The remarkable thing is that the poor creatures think the pestilence is the Lord's punishment. Mobs of people who call themselves Slaves of Sin are swarming over the country, flagellating themselves and others, all for the glory of God.

JONS: Do they really whip themselves?

PAINTER: Yes, it's a terrible sight. I crawl into a ditch and hide when they pass by.

JONS: Do you have any brandy? I've been drinking water all day and it's made me as thirsty as a camel in the desert.

PAINTER: I think I frightened you after all.

JONS *sits down with the* PAINTER, *who produces a jug of brandy.*

The KNIGHT *is kneeling before a small altar. It is dark and quiet around him. The air is cool and musty. Pictures of saints look down on him with stony eyes. Christ's face is turned upwards, His mouth open as if in a cry of anguish. On the ceiling beam there is a representation of a hideous devil spying on a miserable human being. The* KNIGHT *hears a sound from the confession booth and approaches it. The face of* DEATH *appears behind the grille for an instant, but the* KNIGHT *doesn't see him.*

KNIGHT: I want to talk to you as openly as I can, but my heart is empty.

DEATH *doesn't answer.*

KNIGHT: The emptiness is a mirror turned towards my own face. I see myself in it, and I am filled with fear and disgust.

DEATH *doesn't answer.*

KNIGHT: Through my indifference to my fellow men, I have isolated myself from their company. Now I live in a world of phantoms. I am imprisoned in my dreams and fantasies.

DEATH: And yet you don't want to die.

KNIGHT: Yes, I do.

DEATH: What are you waiting for?

KNIGHT: I want knowledge.

484

DEATH: You want guarantees?

KNIGHT: Call it whatever you like. Is it so cruelly inconceivable to grasp God with the senses? Why should He hide himself in a mist of half-spoken promises and unseen miracles?

DEATH *doesn't answer.*

KNIGHT: How can we have faith in those who believe when we can't have faith in ourselves? What is going to happen to those of us who want to believe but aren't able to? And what is to become of those who neither want to nor are capable of believing?

The KNIGHT *stops and waits for a reply, but no one speaks or answers him. There is complete silence.*

KNIGHT: Why can't I kill God within me? Why does He live on in this painful and humiliating way even though I curse Him and want to tear Him out of my heart? Why, in spite of everything, is He a baffling reality that I can't shake off? Do you hear me?

DEATH: Yes, I hear you.

KNIGHT: I want knowledge, not faith, not suppositions, but knowledge. I want God to stretch out His hand towards me, reveal Himself and speak to me.

DEATH: But He remains silent.

KNIGHT: I call out to Him in the dark but no one seems to be there.

DEATH: Perhaps no one is there.

KNIGHT: Then life is an outrageous horror. No one can live in the face of death, knowing that all is nothingness.

DEATH: Most people never reflect about either death or the futility of life.

KNIGHT: But one day they will have to stand at that last moment of life and look towards the darkness.

DEATH: When *that* day comes . . .

KNIGHT: In our fear, we make an image, and that image we call God.

DEATH: You are worrying . . .

KNIGHT: Death visited me this morning. We are playing chess together. This reprieve gives me the chance to arrange an urgent matter.

DEATH: What matter is that?

KNIGHT: My life has been a futile pursuit, a wandering, a great deal of talk without meaning. I feel no bitterness or self-reproach because the lives of most people are very much like this. But I will use my reprieve for one meaningful deed.

DEATH: Is that why you are playing chess with Death?

KNIGHT: He is a clever opponent, but up to now I haven't lost a single man.

DEATH: How will you outwit Death in your game?

KNIGHT: I use a combination of the bishop and the knight which he hasn't yet discovered. In the next move I'll shatter one of his flanks.

DEATH: I'll remember that.

DEATH *shows his face at the grille of the confession booth for a moment but disappears instantly.*

KNIGHT: You've tricked and cheated me! But we'll meet again, and I'll find a way.

DEATH *invisible*: We'll meet at the inn, and there we'll continue playing.

The KNIGHT *raises his hand and looks at it in the sunlight which comes through the tiny window.*

KNIGHT: This is my hand. I can move it, feel the blood pulsing through it. The sun is still high in the sky and I, Antonius Block, am playing chess with Death.

He makes a fist of his hand and lifts it to his temple.

Meanwhile, JONS *and the* PAINTER *have got drunk and are talking animatedly together.*

JONS: Me and my master have been abroad and have just come home. Do you understand, you little pictor?

PAINTER: The Crusade.

JONS *drunk*: Precisely. For ten years we sat in the Holy Land and let snakes bite us, flies sting us, wild animals eat us, heathens butcher us, the wine poison us, the women give us lice, the lice devour us, the fevers rot us, all for the Glory of God. Our crusade was such madness that only a real idealist could have thought it up. But what you said about the plague was horrible.

PAINTER: It's worse than that.

JONS: Ah me. No matter which way you turn, you have your rump behind you. That's the truth.

PAINTER: The rump behind you, the rump behind you—there's a profound truth.

JONS *paints a small figure which is supposed to represent himself.*

JONS: This is squire Jons. He grins at Death, mocks the Lord, laughs at himself and leers at the girls. His world is a Jons-world, believable only to himself, ridiculous to all including himself, meaningless to Heaven and of no interest to Hell.

The KNIGHT *walks by, calls to his squire and goes out into the bright sunshine.* JONS *manages to get himself down from the scaffolding.*

486

Outside the church, four soldiers and a monk are in the process of putting a woman in the stocks. Her face is pale and child-like, her head has been shaved, and her knuckles are bloody and broken. Her eyes are wide open, yet she doesn't appear to be fully conscious.

JONS and the KNIGHT stop and watch in silence. The soldiers are working quickly and skilfully, but they seem frightened and dejected. The monk mumbles from a small book. One of the soldiers picks up a wooden bucket and with his hand begins to smear a bloody paste on the wall of the church and around the woman. JONS holds his nose.

JONS: That soup of yours has a hell of a stink. What is it good for?

SOLDIER: She has had carnal intercourse with the Evil One.

He whispers this with a horrified face and continues to splash the sticky mess on the wall.

JONS: And now she's in the stocks.

SOLDIER: She will be burned tomorrow morning at the parish boundary. But we have to keep the Devil away from the rest of us.

JONS *holding his nose*: And you do that with this stinking mess?

SOLDIER: It's the best remedy: blood mixed with the bile of a big black dog. The Devil can't stand the smell.

JONS: Neither can I.

JONS *walks over towards the horses. The KNIGHT stands for a few moments looking at the young girl. She is almost a child. Slowly she turns her eyes towards him.*

KNIGHT: Have you seen the Devil?

The MONK stops reading and raises his head.

MONK: You must not talk to her.

KNIGHT: Can that be so dangerous?

MONK: I don't know, but she is believed to have caused the pestilence with which we are afflicted.

KNIGHT: I understand.

He nods resignedly and walks away. The young woman starts to moan as though she were having a horrible nightmare. The sound of her cries follows the two riders for a considerable distance down the road.
The sun stands high in the sky, like a red ball of fire. *noon*

The waterskin is empty and JONS looks for a well where he can fill it.

They approach a group of peasant cottages at the edge of the forest. JONS ties up the horses, slings the skin over his shoulder and walks along the path towards the nearest cottage. As always, his movements are light and almost soundless. The door to the cottage is open. He stops outside, but when no one appears he enters. It is very dark inside and his foot touches a soft object. He looks down. Beside the whitewashed fireplace, a woman is lying with her face to the ground.

At the sound of approaching steps, JONS *quickly hides behind the door. A man comes down a ladder from the loft. He is broad and thick-set. His eyes are black and his face is pale and puffy. His clothes are well cut but dirty and in rags. He carries a cloth sack. Looking around, he goes into the inner room, bends over the bed, tucks something into the bag, slinks along the walls, looking on the shelves, finds something else which he tucks in his bag.*

Slowly he re-enters the outer room, bends over the dead woman and carefully slips a ring from her finger. At that moment a young woman comes through the door. She stops and stares at the stranger.

RAVAL: Why do you look so surprised? I steal from the dead. These days it's quite a lucrative enterprise.

The GIRL *makes a movement as if to run away.*

RAVAL: You're thinking of running to the village and telling. That wouldn't serve any purpose. Each of us has to save his own skin. It's as simple as that.

GIRL: Don't touch me.

RAVAL: Don't try to scream. There's no one around to hear you, neither God nor man.

Slowly he closes the door behind the GIRL. *The stuffy room is now in almost total darkness. But* JONS *becomes clearly visible.*

JONS: I recognize you, although it's a long time since we met. Your name is Raval, from the theological college at Roskilde. You are Dr. Mirabilis, Coelestis et Diabilis.

RAVAL *smiles uneasily and looks around.*

JONS: Am I not right?

The GIRL *stands immobile.*

JONS: You were the one who, ten years ago, convinced my master of the necessity to join a better-class crusade to the Holy Land.

RAVAL *looks around.*

JONS: You look uncomfortable. Do you have a stomach-ache?

RAVAL *smiles anxiously.*

JONS: When I see you, I suddenly understand the meaning of these ten years, which previously seemed to me such a waste. Our life was too good and we were too satisfied with ourselves. The Lord wanted to punish us for our complacency. That is why He sent you to spew out your holy venom and poison the knight.

RAVAL: I acted in good faith.

JONS: But now you know better, don't you? Because now you have turned into a thief. A more fitting and rewarding occupation for scoundrels. Isn't that so?

With a quick movement he knocks the knife out of RAVAL's *hand, gives him a kick so that he falls on the floor and is about to finish him off. Suddenly the* GIRL *screams.* JONS *stops and makes a gesture of generosity with his hand.*

JONS: By all means. I'm not bloodthirsty.

He bends over RAVAL.

RAVAL: Don't beat me.

JONS: I don't have the heart to touch you, Doctor. But remember this: the next time we meet, I'll brand your face the way one does with thieves. *He rises.* What I really came for is to get my waterskin filled.

GIRL: We have a deep well with cool, fresh water. Come, I'll show you.

They walk out of the house. RAVAL *lies still for a few moments, then he rises slowly and looks around. When no one is in sight, he takes his bag and steals away.*

JONS *quenches his thirst and fills his bag with water. The* GIRL *helps him.*

JONS: Jons is my name. I am a pleasant and talkative young man who has never had anything but kind thoughts and has only done beautiful and noble deeds. I'm kindest of all to young women. With them, there is no limit to my kindness.

He embraces her and tries to kiss her, but she holds herself back. Almost immediately he loses interest, hoists the waterbag on his shoulder and pats the GIRL *on the cheek.*

JONS: Goodbye, my girl. I could very well have raped you, but between you and me, I'm tired of that kind of love. It runs a little dry in the end.

He laughs kindly and walks away from her. When he has walked a short distance he turns; the GIRL *is still there.*

JONS: Now that I think of it, I will need a housekeeper. Can you prepare good food? *The* GIRL *nods.* As far as I know, I'm still a married man, but I have high hopes that my wife is dead by now. That's why I need a housekeeper. *The* GIRL *doesn't answer but gets up.* The devil with it! Come along and don't stand there staring. I've saved your life, so you owe me a great deal.

She begins walking towards him, her head bent. He doesn't wait for her but walks towards the KNIGHT, *who patiently awaits his squire.*

The Embarrassment Inn lies in the eastern section of the province. The plague has not yet reached this area on its way along the coast.

The actors have placed their wagon under a tree in the yard of the inn. Dressed in colorful costumes, they perform a farce.

The spectators watch the performance, commenting on it noisily. There are merchants with fat, beer-sweaty faces, apprentices and journeymen, farmhands and milkmaids. A ~~middle class~~ *whole flock of children perch in the trees around the wagon.*

The KNIGHT *and his squire have sat down in the shadow of a wall. They drink beer and doze in the midday heat. The* GIRL *from the deserted village sleeps at* JONS's *side.*

489

SKAT *beats the drums,* JOF *blows the flute,* MIA *performs a gay and lively dance. They perspire under the hot white sun. When they have finished* SKAT *comes forward and bows.*

SKAT: Noble ladies and gentlemen, I thank you for your interest. Please remain standing a little longer, or sit on the ground, because we are now going to perform a tragedia about an unfaithful wife, her jealous husband, and the handsome lover—that's me.

MIA *and* JOF *have quickly changed costumes and again step out on the stage. They bow to the public.*

SKAT: Here is the husband. Here is the wife. If you'll shut up over there, you'll see something splendid. As I said, I play the lover and I haven't entered yet. That's why I'm going to hide behind the curtain for the time being. *He wipes the sweat from his forehead.* It's damned hot. I think we'll have a thunderstorm.

He places his leg in front of JOF *as if to trip him, raises* MIA's *skirt, makes a face as if he could see all the wonders of the world underneath it, and disappears behind the gaudily patched curtains.*

SKAT *is very handsome, now that he can see himself in the reflection of a tin washbowl. His hair is tightly curled, his eyebrows are beautifully bushy, glittering earrings vie for equal attention with his teeth, and his cheeks are flushed rose red.*

He sits out in back on the tailboard of the wagon, dangling his legs and whistling to himself.

In the meantime JOF *and* MIA *play their tragedy; it is not, however, received with great acclaim.*

SKAT *suddenly discovers that someone is watching him as he gazes contentedly into the tin bowl. A woman stands there, stately in both height and volume.*

SKAT *frowns, toys with his small dagger and occasionally throws a roguish but fiery glance at the beautiful visitor. She suddenly discovers that one of her shoes doesn't quite fit. She leans down to fix it and in doing so allows her generous bosom to burst out of its prison—no more than honour and chastity allow, but still enough so that the actor with his experienced eye immediately sees that there are ample rewards to be had here.*

Now she comes a little closer, kneels down and opens a bundle containing several dainty morsels and a skin filled with red wine. JONAS SKAT *manages not to fall off the wagon in his excitement. Standing on the steps of the wagon, he supports himself against a nearby tree, crosses his legs and bows.*

The woman quietly bites into a chicken leg dripping with fat. At this moment the actor is stricken by a radiant glance full of lustful appetites.

When he sees this look, SKAT *makes an instantaneous decision, jumps down from the wagon and kneels in front of the blushing damsel.*

She becomes weak and faint from his nearness, looks at him with a glassy glance and breathes heavily. SKAT *doesn't neglect to press kisses on her small, chubby hands. The sun shines brightly and small birds make noises in the bushes.*

Now she is forced to sit back; her legs seem unwilling to support her any longer. Bewildered,

490

she singles out another chicken leg from the large sack of food and holds it up in front of SKAT *with an appealing and triumphant expression, as if it were her maidenhood being offered as a prize.*

SKAT *hesitates momentarily, but he is still the strategist. He lets the chicken leg fall to the grass, and murmurs in the woman's rosy ear.*

His words seem to please her. She puts her arms around the actor's neck and pulls him to her with such fierceness that both of them lose their balance and tumble down on the soft grass. The small birds take to their wings with frightened shrieks.

JOF *stands in the hot sun with a flickering lantern in his hand.* MIA *pretends to be asleep on a bench which has been pulled forward on the stage.*

JOF: Night and moonlight now prevail
    Here sleeps my wife so frail . . .

VOICE FROM THE PUBLIC: Does she snore?

JOF: May I point out that this is a tragedy, and in tragedies one doesn't snore.

VOICE FROM THE PUBLIC: I think she should snore anyhow.

This opinion causes mirth in the audience. JOF *becomes slightly confused and goes out of character, but* MIA *keeps her head and begins snoring.*

JOF: Night and moonlight now prevail.
    There snores—I mean sleeps—my wife so frail.
    Jealous I am, as never before,
    I hide myself behind this door.
    Faithful is she
    To her lover—not me.
    He soon comes a-stealing
    To awaken her lusty feeling.
    I shall now kill him dead
    For cuckolding me in my bed.
    There he comes in the moonlight,
    His white legs shining bright.
    Quiet as a mouse, here I'll lie,
    Tell him not that he's about to die.

JOF *hides himself.* MIA *immediately ends her snoring and sits up, looking to the left.*

MIA: Look, there he comes in the night
    My lover, my heart's delight.

She becomes silent and looks wide-eyed in front of her.

The mood in the yard in front of the inn has, up to now, been rather lighthearted despite the heat.

Now a rapid change occurs. People who had been laughing and chattering fall silent. Their faces seem to pale under their sunbrowned skins, the children stop their games and stand with gaping mouths and frightened eyes. JOF *steps out in front of the curtain. His painted face bears an expression of horror.* MIA *has risen with* MIKAEL *in her arms.*

Some of the women in the yard have fallen on their knees, others hide their faces, many begin to mutter half-forgotten prayers.

All have turned their faces towards the white road. Now a shrill song is heard. It is frenzied, almost a scream.

A crucified Christ sways above the hilltop.

The cross-bearers soon come into sight. They are Dominican monks, their hoods pulled down over their faces. More and more of them follow, carrying litters with heavy coffins or clutching holy relics, their hands stretched out spasmodically. The dust wells up around their black hoods; the censers sway and emit a thick, ashen smoke which smells of rancid herbs.

After the line of monks comes another procession. It is a column of men, boys, old men, women, girls, children. All of them have steel-edged scourges in their hands with which they whip themselves and each other, howling ecstatically. They twist in pain; their eyes bulge wildly; their lips are gnawed to shreds and dripping with foam. They have been seized by madness. They bite their own hands and arms, whip each other in violent, almost rhythmic outbursts. Throughout it all the shrill song howls from their bursting throats. Many sway and fall, lift themselves up again, support each other and help each other to intensify the scourging.

Now the procession pauses at the crossroads in front of the inn. The monks fall on their knees, hiding their faces with clenched hands, arms pressed tightly together. Their song never stops. The Christ figure on its timbered cross is raised above the heads of the crowd. It is not Christ triumphant, but the suffering Jesus with the sores, the blood, the hammered nails and the face in convulsive pain. The Son of God, nailed on the wood of the cross, suffering scorn and shame.

The penitents have now sunk down in the dirt of the road. They collapse where they stood like slaughtered cattle. Their screams rise with the song of the monks, through misty clouds of incense, towards the white fire of the sun.

A large square monk rises from his knees and reveals his face, which is red-brown from the sun. His eyes glitter; his voice is thick with impotent scorn.

MONK: God has sentenced us to punishment. We shall all perish in the black death. You, standing there like gaping cattle, you who sit there in your glutted complacency, do you know that this may be your last hour? Death stands right behind you. I can see how his crown gleams in the sun. His scythe flashes as he raises it above your heads. Which one of you shall he strike first? You there, who stand staring like a goat, will your mouth be twisted into the last unfinished gasp before nightfall? And you, woman, who bloom with life and self-satisfaction, will you pale and become extinguished before the morning dawns? You back there, with your swollen nose and stupid grin, do you have another year left to dirty the earth with your refuse? Do you know, you insensible fools, that you shall die today or tomorrow, or the next day, because all of you have been sentenced? Do you hear what I say? Do you hear the word? You have been sentenced, sentenced!

The MONK falls silent, looking around with a bitter face and a cold, scornful glance. Now he clenches his hands, straddles the ground and turns his face upwards.

MONK: Lord have mercy on us in our humiliation! Don't turn your face from us in loathing and contempt, but be merciful to us for the sake of your son, Jesus Christ.

He makes the sign of the cross over the crowd and then begins a new song in a strong voice. The monks rise and join in the song. As if driven by some superhuman force, the penitents begin to whip themselves again, still wailing and moaning.

The procession continues. New members have joined the rear of the column; others who were unable to go on lie weeping in the dust of the road.

JONS *the squire drinks his beer.*

JONS: This damned ranting about doom. Is that food for the minds of modern people? Do they really expect us to take them seriously?

The KNIGHT *grins tiredly.*

JONS: Yes, now you grin at me, my lord. But allow me to point out that I've either read, heard or experienced most of the tales which we people tell each other.

KNIGHT *yawns*: Yes, yes.

JONS: Even the ghost stories about God the Father, the angels, Jesus Christ and the Holy Ghost—all these I've accepted without too much emotion.

He leans down over the GIRL *as she crouches at his feet and pats her on the head. The* KNIGHT *drinks his beer silently.*

JONS *contentedly*: My little stomach is my world, my head is my eternity, and my hands, two wonderful suns. My legs are time's damned pendulums, and my dirty feet are two splendid starting points for my philosophy. Everything is worth precisely as much as a belch, the only difference being that a belch is more satisfying.

The beer mug is empty. Sighing, JONS *gets to his feet.*

The GIRL *follows him like a shadow.*

In the yard he meets a large man with a sooty face and a dark expression. He stops JONS *with a roar.*

JONS: What are you screaming about?

PLOG: I am Plog, the smith, and you are the squire Jons.

JONS: That's possible.

PLOG: Have you seen my wife?

JONS: No, I haven't. But if I had seen her and she looked like you, I'd quickly forget that I'd seen her.

PLOG: Well, in that case you haven't seen her.

JONS: Maybe she's run off.

PLOG: Do you know anything?

JONS: I know quite a lot, but not about your wife. Go to the inn. Maybe they can help you.

The SMITH *sighs sadly and goes inside.*

The inn is very small and full of people eating and drinking to forget their newly aroused fears of eternity. In the open fireplace a roasting pig turns on an iron spit. The sun shines outside the casement window, its sharp rays piercing the darkness of the room, which is thick with fumes and perspiration.

MERCHANT: Yes, it's true! The plague is spreading along the west coast. People are dying like flies. Usually business would be good at this time of year, but, damn it, I've still got my whole stock unsold.

WOMAN: They speak of the judgment day. And all these omens are terrible. Worms, chopped-off hands and other monstrosities began pouring out of an old woman, and down in the village another woman gave birth to a calf's head.

OLD MAN: The day of judgment. Imagine.

FARMER: It hasn't rained here for a month. We'll surely lose our crops.

MERCHANT: And people are acting crazy, I'd say. They flee the country and carry the plague with them wherever they go.

OLD MAN: The day of judgment. Just think, just think!

FARMER: If it's as they say, I suppose a person should look after his house and try to enjoy life as long as he can.

WOMAN: But there have been other things too, such things that can't even be spoken of. *Whispers.* Things that mustn't be named—but the priests say that the woman carries it between her legs and that's why she must cleanse herself.

OLD MAN: Judgment day. And the Riders of the Apocalypse stand at the bend in the village road. I imagine they'll come on judgment night, at sundown.

WOMAN: There are many who have purged themselves with fire and died from it, but the priests say that it's better to die pure than to live for hell.

MERCHANT: This is the end, yes, it is. No one says it out loud, but all of us know that it's the end. And people are going mad from fear.

FARMER: So you're afraid too.

MERCHANT: Of course I'm afraid.

OLD MAN: The judgment day becomes night, and the angels descend and the graves open. It will be terrible to see.

They whisper in low tones and sit close to each other.

PLOG, *the smith, shoves his way into a place next to* JOF, *who is still dressed in his costume. Opposite him sits* RAVAL, *leaning slightly forward, his face perspiring heavily.* RAVAL *rolls an armlet out on the table.*

494

RAVAL: Do you want this armlet? You can have it cheap.

JOF: I can't afford it.

RAVAL: It's real silver.

JOF: It's nice. But it's surely too expensive for me.

PLOG: Excuse me, but has anyone here seen my wife?

JOF: Has she disappeared?

PLOG: They say she's run away.

JOF: Has she deserted you?

PLOG: With an actor.

JOF: An actor! If she's got such bad taste, then I think you should let her go.

PLOG: You're right. My first thought, of course, was to kill her.

JOF: Oh. But to murder her, that's a terrible thing to do.

PLOG: I'm also going to kill the actor.

JOF: The actor?

PLOG: Of course, the one she eloped with.

JOF: What has he done to deserve that?

PLOG: Are you stupid?

JOF: The actor! Now I understand. There are too many of them, so even if he hasn't done anything in particular you ought to kill him merely because he's an actor.

PLOG: You see, my wife has always been interested in the tricks of the theatre.

JOF: And that turned out to be her misfortune.

PLOG: Her misfortune, but not mine, because a person who's born unfortunate can hardly suffer from any further misfortune. Isn't that true?

Now RAVAL *enters the discussion. He is slightly drunk and his voice is shrill and evil.*

RAVAL: Listen, you! You sit there and lie to the smith.

JOF: I! A liar!

RAVAL: You're an actor too and it's probably your partner who's run off with Plog's old lady.

PLOG: Are you an actor too?

JOF: An actor! Me! I wouldn't quite call myself that!

RAVAL: We ought to kill you; it's only logical.

JOF *laughs*: You're really funny.

RAVAL: How strange—you've turned pale. Have you anything on your conscience?

JOF: You're funny. Don't you think he's funny? *To Plog.* Oh, you don't.

RAVAL: Maybe we should mark you up a little with a knife, like they do petty scoundrels of your kind.

PLOG *bangs his hands down on the table so that the dishes jump. He gets up.*

PLOG *shouting*: What have you done with my wife?

The room becomes silent. JOF *looks around, but there is no exit, no way to escape. He puts his hands on the table. Suddenly a knife flashes through the air and sinks into the table top between his fingers.*

JOF *snatches away his hands and raises his head. He looks half surprised, as if the truth had just become apparent to him.*

JOF: Do you want to hurt me? Why? Have I provoked someone, or got in the way? I'll leave right now and never come back.

JOF *looks from one face to another, but no one seems ready to help him or come to his defence.*

RAVAL: Get up so everyone can hear you. Talk louder.

Trembling, JOF *rises. He opens his mouth as if to say something, but not a word comes out.*

RAVAL: Stand on your head so that we can see how good an actor you are.

JOF *gets up on the table and stands on his head. A hand pushes him forward so that he collapses on the floor.* PLOG *rises, pulls him to his feet with one hand.*

PLOG *shouts*: What have you done with my wife?

PLOG *beats him so furiously that* JOF *flies across the table.* RAVAL *leans over him.*

RAVAL: Don't lie there moaning. Get up and dance.

JOF: I don't want to. I can't.

RAVAL: Show us how you imitate a bear.

JOF: I can't play a bear.

RAVAL: Let's see if you can't after all.

RAVAL *prods* JOF *lightly with the knife point.* JOF *gets up with cold sweat on his cheeks and forehead, frightened half to death. He begins to jump and hop on top of the tables, swinging his arms and legs and making grotesque faces. Some laugh, but most of the people sit silently.* JOF *gasps as if his lungs were about to burst. He sinks to his knees, and someone pours beer over him.*

RAVAL: Up again. Be a good bear.

JOF: I haven't done any harm. I haven't got the strength to play a bear any more.

At that moment the door opens and JONS *enters.* JOF *sees his chance and steals out.* RAVAL *intends to follow him, but suddenly stops.* JONS *and* RAVAL *look at each other.*

JONS: Do you remember what I was going to do to you if we met again?

RAVAL *steps back without speaking.*

JONS: I'm a man who keeps his word.

JONS *raises his knife and cuts* RAVAL *from forehead to cheek.* RAVAL *staggers towards the wall.*

The hot day has become night. Singing and howling can be heard from the inn. In a hollow near the forest, the light still lingers. Hidden in the grass and the shrubbery, nightingales sing and their voices echo through the stillness.

The players' wagon stands in a small ravine, and not far away the horse grazes on the dry grass. MIA *has sat down in front of the wagon with her son in her arms. They play together and laugh happily.*

Now a soft gleam of light strokes the hilltops, a last reflection from the red clouds over the sea.

Not far from the wagon, the KNIGHT *sits crouched over his chess game. He lifts his head.*

The evening light moves across the heavy wagon wheels, across the woman and the child.

The KNIGHT *gets up.*

MIA *sees him and smiles. She holds up her struggling son, as if to amuse the* KNIGHT.

KNIGHT: What's his name?

MIA: Mikael.

KNIGHT: How old is he?

MIA: Oh, he'll soon be two.

KNIGHT: He's big for his age.

MIA: Do you think so? Yes, I guess he's rather big.

She puts the child down on the ground and half rises to shake out her red skirt. When she sits down again, the KNIGHT *steps closer.*

KNIGHT: You played some kind of show this afternoon.

MIA: Did you think it was bad?

KNIGHT: You are more beautiful now without your face painted, and this gown is more becoming.

MIA: You see, Jonas Skat has run off and left us, so we're in real trouble now.

KNIGHT: Is that your husband?

MIA *laughs*: Jonas! The other man is my husband. His name is Jof.

KNIGHT: Oh, that one.

MIA: And now there's only him and me. We'll have to start doing tricks again and that's more trouble than it's worth.

KNIGHT: Do you do tricks also?

MIA: We certainly do. And Jof is a very skilful juggler.

KNIGHT: Is Mikael going to be an acrobat?

MIA: Jof wants him to be.

KNIGHT: But you don't.

MIA: I don't know *smiling*. Perhaps he'll become a knight.

KNIGHT: Let me assure you, that's no pleasure either.

MIA: No, you don't look so happy.

KNIGHT: No.

MIA: Are you tired?

KNIGHT: Yes.

MIA: Why?

KNIGHT: I have dull company.

MIA: Do you mean your squire?

KNIGHT: No, not him.

MIA: Who do you mean, then?

KNIGHT: Myself.

MIA: I understand.

KNIGHT: Do you, really?

MIA: Yes, I understand rather well. I have often wondered why people torture themselves as often as they can. Isn't that so?

She nods energetically and the KNIGHT *smiles seriously. Now the shrieks and the noise from the inn become louder. Black figures flicker across the grass mound. Someone collapses, gets up and runs. It is* JOF. MIA *stretches out her arms and receives him. He holds his hands in front of his face, moaning like a child, and his body sways. He kneels.* MIA *holds him close to her and sprinkles him with small, anxious questions:* What have you done? How are you? What is it? Does it hurt? What can I do? Have they been cruel to you? *She runs for a rag, which she dips in water, and carefully bathes her husband's dirty, bloody face.*

Eventually a rather sorrowful visage emerges. Blood runs from a bruise on his forehead and his nose, and a tooth has been loosened, but otherwise JOF *seems unhurt.*

JOF: Ouch, it hurts.

MIA: Why did you have to go there? And of course you drank.

MIA's *anxiety has been replaced by a mild anger. She pats him a little harder than necessary.*

JOF: Ouch! I didn't drink anything.

MIA: Then I suppose you were boasting about the angels and devils you consort with. People don't like someone who has too many ideas and fantasies.

JOF: I swear to you that I didn't say a word about angels.

MIA: You were, of course, busy singing and dancing. You can never stop being an actor. People also become angry at that, and you know it.

JOF *doesn't answer but searches for the armlet. He holds it up in front of* MIA *with an injured expression.*

JOF: Look what I bought for you.

MIA: You couldn't afford it.

JOF *angry*: But I got it anyhow.

The armlet glitters faintly in the twilight. MIA *now pulls it across her wrist. They look at it in silence, and their faces soften. They look at each other, touch each other's hands.* JOF *puts his head against* MIA's *shoulder and sighs.*

JOF: Oh, how they beat me.

MIA: Why didn't you beat them back?

JOF: I only become frightened and angry. I never get a chance to hit back. I can get angry, you know that. I roared like a lion.

MIA: Were they frightened?

JOF: No, they just laughed.

Their son MIKAEL *crawls over to them.* JOE *lies down on the ground and pulls his son on top of him.* MIA *gets down on her hands and knees and playfully sniffs at* MIKAEL.

MIA: Do you notice how good he smells?

JOF: And he is so compact to hold. You're a sturdy one. A real acrobat's body.

He lifts MIKAEL *up and holds him by the legs.* MIA *looks up suddenly, remembering the knight's presence.*

MIA: Yes, this is my husband, Jof.

JOF: Good evening.

KNIGHT: Good evening.

JOF *becomes a little embarrassed and rises. All three of them look at one another silently.*

KNIGHT: I have just told your wife that you have a splendid son. He'll bring great joy to you.

JOF: Yes, he's fine.

They become silent again.

JOF: Have we nothing to offer the knight, Mia?

KNIGHT: Thank you, I don't want anything.

MIA *housewifely*: I picked a basket of wild strawberries this afternoon. And we have a drop of milk fresh from a cow . . .

JOF: . . . that we were *allowed* to milk. So, if you would like to partake of this humble fare, it would be a great honour.

MIA: Please be seated and I'll bring the food.

They sit down. MIA *disappears with* MIKAEL.

KNIGHT: Where are you going next?

JOF: Up to the saints' feast at Elsinore.

KNIGHT: I wouldn't advise you to go there.

JOF: Why not, if I may ask?

KNIGHT: The plague has spread in that direction, following the coast line south. It's said that people are dying by the tens of thousands.

JOF: Really! Well, sometimes life is a little hard.

KNIGHT: May I suggest . . . JOF *looks at him, surprised* . . . that you follow me through the forest tonight and stay at my home if you like. Or go along the east coast. You'll probably be safer there.

MIA *has returned with a bowl of wild strawberries and the milk, places it between them and gives each of them a spoon.*

JOF: I wish you good appetite.

KNIGHT: I humbly thank you.

MIA: These are wild strawberries from the forest. I have never seen such large ones. They grow up there on the hillside. Notice how they smell!

She points with a spoon and smiles. The KNIGHT *nods, as if he were pondering some profound thought.* JOF *eats heartily.*

JOF: Your suggestion is good, but I must think it over.

MIA: It might be wise to have company going through the forest. It's said to be full of trolls and ghosts and bandits. That's what I've heard.

JOF *staunchly*: Yes, I'd say that it's not a bad idea, but I have to think about it. Now that Skat has left, I am responsible for the troupe. After all, I have become director of the whole company.

MIA *mimics*: After all, I have become director of the whole company.

JONS *comes walking slowly down the hill, closely followed by the* GIRL. MIA *points with her spoon.*

MIA: Do you want some strawberries?

JOF: This man saved my life. Sit down, my friend, and let us be together.

MIA *stretches herself*: Oh, how nice this is.

KNIGHT: For a short while.

MIA: Nearly always. One day is like another. There is nothing strange about that. The summer, of course, is better than the winter, because in summer you don't have to be cold. But spring is best of all.

JOF: I have written a poem about the spring. Perhaps you'd like to hear it. I'll run and get my lyre. *He sprints towards the wagon.*

MIA: Not now, Jof. Our guests may not be amused by your songs.

JONS *politely*: By all means. I write little songs myself. For example, I know a very funny song about a wanton fish which I doubt that you've heard yet.

The KNIGHT looks at him.

JONS: You'll not get to hear it either. There are persons here who don't appreciate my art and I don't want to upset anyone. I'm a sensitive soul.

JOF *has come out with his lyre, sits on a small, gaudy box and plucks at the instrument, humming quietly, searching for his melody.* JONS *yawns and lies down.*

KNIGHT: People are troubled by so much.

MIA: It's always better when one is two. Have you no one of your own?

KNIGHT: Yes, I think I had someone.

MIA: And what is she doing now?

KNIGHT: I don't know.

MIA: You look so solemn. Was she your beloved?

KNIGHT: We were newly married and we played together. We laughed a great deal. I wrote songs to her eyes, to her nose, to her beautiful little ears. We went hunting together and at night we danced. The house was full of life . . .

MIA: Do you want some more strawberries?

KNIGHT *shakes his head*: Faith is a torment, did you know that? It is like loving someone who is out there in the darkness but never appears, no matter how loudly you call.

MIA: I don't understand what you mean.

KNIGHT: Everything I've said seems meaningless and unreal while I sit here with you and your husband. How unimportant it all becomes suddenly.

He takes the bowl of milk in his hand and drinks deeply from it several times. Then he carefully puts it down and looks up, smiling.

MIA: Now you don't look so solemn.

KNIGHT: I shall remember this moment. The silence, the twilight, the bowls of strawberries and milk, your faces in the evening light. Mikael sleeping, Jof with his lyre. I'll try to remember what we have talked about. I'll carry this memory between my hands as carefully as if it were a bowl filled to the brim with fresh milk. *He turns his face away and looks out towards the sea and the colourless grey sky.* And it will be an adequate sign—it will be enough for me.

He rises, nods to the others and walks down towards the forest. JOF *continues to play on his lyre.* MIA *stretches out on the grass.*

The KNIGHT *picks up his chess game and carries it towards the beach. It is quiet and deserted; the sea is still.*

DEATH: I have been waiting for you.

KNIGHT: Pardon me. I was detained for a few moments. Because I revealed my tactics to you, I'm in retreat. It's your move.

DEATH: Why do you look so satisfied?

KNIGHT: That's my secret.

DEATH: Of course. Now I take your knight.

KNIGHT: You did the right thing.

DEATH: Have you tricked me?

KNIGHT: Of course. You fell right in the trap. Check!

DEATH: What are you laughing at?

KNIGHT: Don't worry about my laughter; save your king instead.

DEATH: You're rather arrogant.

KNIGHT: Our game amuses me.

DEATH: It's your move. Hurry up. I'm a little pressed for time.

KNIGHT: I understand that you've a lot to do, but you can't get out of our game. It takes time.

Death is about to answer him but stops and leans over the board. The KNIGHT *smiles.*

DEATH: Are you going to escort the juggler and his wife through the forest? Those whose names are Jof and Mia and who have a small son?

KNIGHT: Why do you ask?

DEATH: Oh, no reason at all.

The KNIGHT *suddenly stops smiling.* DEATH *looks at him scornfully.*

Immediately after sundown, the little company gathers in the yard of the inn. There is the KNIGHT, JONS *and the* GIRL, JOF *and* MIA *in their wagon. Their son,* MIKAEL, *is already asleep.* JONAS SKAT *is still missing.*

JONS *goes into the inn to get provisions for the night journey and to have a last mug of beer. The inn is now empty and quiet except for a few farmhands and maidens who are eating their evening meal in a corner.*

502

At one of the small windows sits a lonely, hunched-over fellow, with a jug of brandy in his hands. His expression is very sad. Once in a while he is shaken by a gigantic sob. It is PLOG, *the smith, who sits there and whimpers.*

JONS: God in heaven, isn't this Plog, the smith?

PLOG: Good evening.

JONS: Are you sitting here snivelling in loneliness?

PLOG: Yes, yes, look at the smith. He moans like a rabbit.

JONS: If I were in your boots, I'd be happy to get rid of a wife in such an easy way.

JONS *pats the smith on the back, quenches his thirst with beer, and sits down by his side.*

PLOG: Are *you* married?

JONS: *I!* A hundred times and more. I can't keep count of all my wives any longer. But it's often that way when you're a travelling man.

PLOG: I can assure you that *one* wife is worse than a hundred, or else I've had worse luck than any poor wretch in this miserable world, which isn't impossible.

JONS: Yes, it's hell *with* women and hell *without* them. So, however you look at it, it's still best to kill them off while it's most amusing.

PLOG: Women's nagging, the shrieking of children and wet nappies, sharp nails and sharp words, blows and pokes, and the devil's aunt for a mother-in-law. And then, when one wants to sleep after a long day, there's a new song—tears, whining and moans loud enough to wake the dead.

JONS *nods delightedly. He has drunk deeply and talks with an old woman's voice.*

JONS: Why don't you kiss me good night?

PLOG *in the same way*: Why don't you sing a song for me?

JONS: Why don't you love me the way you did when we first met?

PLOG: Why don't you look at my new shift?

JONS: You only turn your back and snore.

PLOG: Oh hell!

JONS: Oh hell. And now she's gone. Rejoice!

PLOG *furious*: I'll snip their noses with pliers, I'll bash in their chests with a small hammer, I'll tap their heads ever so lightly with a sledge.

PLOG *begins to cry loudly and his whole body sways in an enormous attack of sorrow.* JONS *looks at him with interest.*

JONS: Look how he howls again.

PLOG: Maybe I love her.

JONS: So, maybe you love her! Then, you poor misguided ham shank, I'll tell you that love is another word for lust, plus lust, plus lust and a damn lot of cheating, falseness, lies and all kinds of other fooling around.

PLOG: Yes, but it hurts anyway.

JONS: Of course. Love is the blackest of all plagues, and if one could die of it, there would be some pleasure in love. But you almost always get over it.

PLOG: No, no, not me.

JONS: Yes, you too. There are only a couple of poor wretches who die of love once in a while. Love is as contagious as a cold in the nose. It eats away at your strength, your independence, your morale, if you have any. If everything is imperfect in this imperfect world, love is most perfect in its perfect imperfection.

PLOG: You're happy, you with your oily words, and, besides, you believe your own drivel.

JONS: Believe! Who said that I believed it? But I love to give good advice. If you ask me for advice you'll get two pieces for the price of one, because after all I really am an educated man.

JONS *gets up from the table and strokes his face with his hands.* PLOG *becomes very unhappy and grabs his belt.*

PLOG: Listen, Jons. May I go with you through the forest? I'm so lonely and don't want to go home because everyone will laugh at me.

JONS: Only if you don't whimper all the time, because in that case we'll all have to avoid you.

PLOG *gets up and embraces* JONS. *Slightly drunk, the two new friends walk towards the door.*

When they come out in the yard, JOF *immediately catches sight of them, becomes angry and yells a warning to* JONS.

JOF: Jöns! Watch out. That one wants to fight all the time. He's not quite sane.

JONS: Yes, but now he's just snivelling.

PLOG *steps up to* JOF, *who blanches with fear.* PLOG *offers his hand.*

PLOG: I'm really sorry if I hurt you. But I have such a hell of a temper, you know. Shake hands.

JOF *gingerly proffers a frightened hand and gets it thoroughly shaken and squeezed. While* JOF *tries to straighten out his fingers,* PLOG *is seized by great good will and opens his arms.*

PLOG: Come in my arms, little brother.

JOF: Thank you, thank you, perhaps later. But now we're really in a hurry.

JOF *climbs up on the wagon seat quickly and clucks at the horse.*

The small company is on its way towards the forest and the night.

It is dark in the forest.

First comes the KNIGHT *on his large horse. Then* JOF *and* MIA *follow, sitting close to each other in the juggler's wagon.* MIA *holds her son in her arms.* JONS *follows them with his heavily laden horse. He has the smith in tow. The* GIRL *sits on top of the load on the horse's back, hunched over as if asleep.*

The footsteps, the horses' heavy tramp on the soft path, the human breathing—yet it is quiet.

Then the moon sails out of the clouds. The forest suddenly becomes alive with the night's unreality. The dazzling light pours through the thick foliage of the beech trees, a moving, quivering world of light and shadow.

The wanderers stop. Their eyes are dark with anxiety and foreboding. Their faces are pale and unreal in the floating light. It is very quiet.

PLOG: Now the moon has come out of the clouds.

JONS: That's good. Now we can see the road better.

MIA: I don't like the moon tonight.

JOF: The trees stand so still.

JONS: That's because there's no wind.

PLOG: I guess he means that they stand *very* still.

JOF: It's completely quiet.

JONS: If one could hear a fox at least.

JOF: Or an owl.

JONS: Or a human voice besides one's own.

GIRL: They say it's dangerous to remain standing in moonlight.

Suddenly, out of the silence and the dim light falling across the forest road, a ghostlike cart emerges.

It is the WITCH *being taken to the place where she will be burned. Next to her eight soldiers shuffle along tiredly, carrying their lances on their backs. The girl sits in the cart, bound with iron chains around her throat and arms. She stares fixedly into the moonlight. A black figure sits next to her, a monk with his hood pulled down over his head.*

JONS: Where are you going?

SOLDIER: To the place of execution.

JONS: Yes, now I can see. It's the girl who has done it with the Black One. The witch?

The SOLDIER *nods sourly. Hesitantly, the travellers follow.*

The KNIGHT *guides his horse over to the side of the cart.*

The WITCH *seems to be half-conscious, but her eyes are wide open.*

KNIGHT: I see that they have hurt your hands.

The WITCH'S *pale, childish face turns towards the* KNIGHT *and she shakes her head.*

KNIGHT: I have a potion that will stop your pain.

She shakes her head again.

JONS: Why do you burn her at this time of night? People have so few diversions these days.

SOLDIER: Saints preserve us, be quiet! It's said that she brings the Devil with her wherever she goes.

JONS: You are eight brave men, then.

SOLDIER: Well, we've been paid. And this is a volunteer job.

The SOLDIER *speaks in whispers while glancing anxiously at the* WITCH.

KNIGHT *to the* WITCH: What's your name?

TYAN: My name is Tyan, my lord.

KNIGHT: How old are you?

TYAN: Fourteen, my lord.

KNIGHT: And is it true that you have been in league with the Devil?

TYAN *nods quietly and looks away. Now they arrive at the parish border. At the foot of the nearby hills lies a crossroads. The pyre has already been stacked in the centre of the forest clearing. The travellers remain there, hesitant and curious.*

The soldiers have tied up the cart horse and bring out two long wooden beams. They nail rungs across the beams so that it looks like a ladder. TYAN *will be bound to this like an eelskin stretched out to dry.*

The sound of the hammering echoes through the forest. The KNIGHT *has dismounted and walks closer to the cart. Again he tries to catch* TYAN'S *eyes, touches her very lightly as if to waken her.*

Slowly she turns her face towards him.

KNIGHT: They say that you have been in league with the Devil.
TYAN: Why do you ask?

KNIGHT: Not out of curiosity, but for very personal reasons. I too want to meet him.

TYAN: Why?

KNIGHT: I want to ask him about God. He, if anyone, must know.

TYAN: You can see him anytime.

KNIGHT: How?

TYAN: You must do as I tell you.

The KNIGHT *grips the wooden rail of the cart so tightly that his knuckles whiten.* TYAN *leans forward and joins her gaze with his.*

TYAN: Look into my eyes.

The KNIGHT *meets her gaze. They stare at each other for a long time.*

TYAN: What do you see? Do you see *him*?

KNIGHT: I see fear in your eyes, an empty, numb fear. But nothing else.

He falls silent. The soldiers work at the stakes; their hammering echoes in the forest.

TYAN: No one, nothing, no one?

KNIGHT *shakes his head*: No.

TYAN: Can't you see him behind your back?

KNIGHT *looks around*: No, there is no one there.

TYAN: But he is with me everywhere. I only have to stretch out my hand and I can feel his hand. He is with me now too. The fire won't hurt me. He will protect me from everything evil.

KNIGHT: Has he told you this?

TYAN: I know it.

KNIGHT: Has he said it?

TYAN: I know it, I know it. You must see him somewhere, you must. The priests had no difficulty seeing him, nor did the soldiers. They are so afraid of him that they don't even dare touch me.

The sound of the hammers stops. The soldiers stand like black shadows rooted in the moss. They fumble with the chains and pull at the neck iron. TYAN *moans weakly, as if she were far away.*

KNIGHT: Why have you crushed her hands?

SOLDIER *surely*: We didn't do it.

KNIGHT: Who did?

SOLDIER: Ask the monk.

The soldiers pull the iron and the chains. TYAN's *shaven head sways, gleaming in the moonlight. Her blackened mouth opens as if to scream, but no sound emerges.*

They take her down from the cart and lead her towards the ladder and the stake. The KNIGHT *turns to the* MONK, *who remains seated in the cart.*

KNIGHT: What have you done with the child?

DEATH *turns around and looks at him.*

DEATH: Don't you ever stop asking questions?

KNIGHT: No, I'll never stop.

The soldiers chain TYAN *to the rungs of the ladder. She submits resignedly, moans weakly like an animal and tries to ease her body into position.*

507

When they have fastened her, they walk over to light the pyre. The KNIGHT *steps up and leans over her.*

JONS: For a moment I thought of killing the soldiers, but it would do no good. She's nearly dead already.

One of the soldiers approaches. Thick smoke wells down from the pyre and sweeps over the quiet shadows near the crossroads and the hill.

SOLDIER: I've told you to be careful. Don't go too close to her.

The KNIGHT *doesn't heed this warning. He cups his hand, fills it with water from the skin and gives it to* TYAN. *Then he gives her a potion.*

KNIGHT: Take this and it will stop the pain.

Smoke billows down over them and they begin to cough. The soldiers step forward and raise the ladder against a nearby fir tree. TYAN *hangs there motionlessly, her eyes wide open.*

The KNIGHT *straightens up and stands immobile.* JONS *is behind him, his voice nearly choked with rage.*

JONS: What does she see? Can you tell me?

KNIGHT *shakes his head*: She feels no more pain.

JONS: You don't answer my question. Who watches over that child? Is it the angels, or God, or the Devil, or only the emptiness? Emptiness, my lord!

KNIGHT: This cannot be.

JONS: Look at her eyes, my lord. Her poor brain has just made a discovery. Emptiness under the moon.

KNIGHT: No.

JONS: We stand powerless, our arms hanging at our sides, because we see what she sees, and our terror and hers are the same. *An outburst.* That poor little child. I can't stand it, I can't stand it . . .

His voice sticks in his throat and he suddenly walks away. The KNIGHT *mounts his horse. The travellers depart from the crossroads.* TYAN *finally closes her eyes.*

The forest is now very dark. The road winds between the trees. The wagon squeaks and rattles over stones and roots. A bird suddenly shrieks.

JOF *lifts his head and wakes up. He has been asleep with his arms around* MIA'S *shoulders. The* KNIGHT *is sharply silhouetted against the tree trunks.*

His silence makes him seem almost unreal.

JONS *and* PLOG *are slightly drunk and support each other. Suddenly* PLOG *has to sit down. He puts his hands over his face and howls piteously.*

PLOG: Oh, now it came over me again!

JONS: Don't scream. What came over you?

PLOG: My wife, damn it. She is so beautiful. She is so beautiful that she can't be described without the accompaniment of a lyre.

JONS: Now it starts again.

PLOG: Her smile is like brandy. Her eyes like blackberries . . .

PLOG searches for beautiful words. He gestures gropingly with his large hands.

JONS *sighs*: Get up, you tear-drenched pig. We'll lose the others.

PLOG: Yes, of course, of course. Her nose is like a little pink potato; her behind is like a juicy pear—yes, the whole woman is like a strawberry patch. I can see her in front of me, with arms like wonderful cucumbers.

JONS: Saints almighty, stop! You're a very bad poet, despite the fact that you're drunk. And your vegetable garden bores me.

They walk across an open meadow. Here it is a little brighter and the moon shimmers behind a thin sky. Suddenly PLOG points a large finger towards the edge of the forest.

PLOG: Look there.

JONS: Do you see something?

PLOG: There, over there!

JONS: I don't see anything.

PLOG: Hang on to something, my friends. The hour is near! Who is that at the edge of the forest if not my own dearly beloved, with actor attached?

The two lovers discover PLOG and it's too late. They cannot retreat. SKAT immediately takes to his heels. PLOG chases him, swinging his sledge and bellowing like a wild boar.

For a few confusing moments the two rivals stumble among the stones and bushes in the grey gloom of the forest. The duel begins to look senseless, because both of them are equally frightened.

The travellers silently observe this confused performance. LISA screams once in a while, more out of duty than out of impulse.

SKAT *panting*: You miserable stubbleheaded bastard of seven scurvy bitches, if I were in your lousy rags I would be stricken with such eternal shame about my breath, my voice, my arms and legs—in short, about my whole body—that I would immediately rid nature of my own embarrassing self.

PLOG *angry*: Watch out, you perfumed slob, that I don't fart on you and immediately blow you down to the actor's own red-hot hell, where you can sit and recite monologues to each other until the dust comes out of the Devil's ears.

Then LISA throws herself around her husband's neck.

LISA: Forgive me, dear little husband, I'll never do it again. I am so sorry and you can't imagine how terribly that man over there betrayed me.

PLOG: I'll kill him anyway.

LISA: Yes, do that, just kill him. He isn't even a human being.

JONS: Hell, he's an actor.

LISA: He is only a false beard, false teeth, false smiles, rehearsed lines, and he's as empty as a jug. Just kill him.

LISA *sobs with excitement and sorrow.* PLOG *looks around, a little confused.* SKAT *uses this opportunity. He pulls out a dagger and places the point against his breast.*

SKAT: She's right. Just kill me. If you thought that I was going to apologize for being what I am, you are mistaken.

LISA: Look how sickening he is. How he makes a fool of himself, how he puts on an act. Dear Plog, kill him.

SKAT: My friends, you have only to push, and my unreality will soon be transformed into a new, solid reality. An absolutely tangible corpse.

LISA: Do something then. Kill him.

PLOG *embarrassed*: He has to fight me, otherwise I can't kill him.

SKAT: Your life's thread now hangs by a very ragged shred. Idiot, your day is short.

PLOG: You'll have to irritate me a little more to get me as angry as before.

SKAT *looks at the travellers with a pained expression and then lifts his eyes towards the night sky.*

SKAT: I forgive all of you. Pray for me sometimes.

SKAT *sinks the dagger into his breast and slowly falls to the ground. The travellers stand confused.* PLOG *rushes forward and begins to pull at* SKAT's *hands.*

PLOG: Oh dear, dear, I didn't mean it that way! Look, there's no life left in him. I was beginning to like him, and in my opinion Lisa was much too spiteful.

JOF *leans over his colleague.*

JOF: He's dead, totally, enormously dead. In fact, I've never seen such a dead actor.

LISA: Come on, let's go. This is nothing to mourn over. He has only himself to blame.

PLOG: And I have to be married to *her.*

JONS: We must go on.

SKAT *lies in the grass and keeps the dagger pressed tightly to his breast. The travellers depart and soon they have disappeared into the dark forest on the other side of the meadow. When* SKAT *is sure that no one can see him, he sits up and lifts the dagger from his breast. It is a stage dagger with a blade that pushes into the handle.* SKAT *laughs to himself.*

SKAT: Now that was a good scene. I'm really a good actor. After all, why shouldn't I be a little pleased with myself? But where shall I go? I'll wait until it becomes light and then I'll find the easiest way out of the forest. I'll climb up a tree for the time being so that no bears, wolves or ghosts can get at me.

He soon finds a likely tree and climbs up into its thick foliage. He sits down as comfortably as possible and reaches for his food pouch.

SKAT *yawns*: Tomorrow I'll find Jof and Mia and then we'll go to the saints' feast in Elsinore. We'll make lots of money there. *Yawns.* Now, I'll sing a little song to myself:

> I am a little bird
> Who sings whate'er he will,
> And when I am in danger
> I fling out a pissing trill
> As in the carnal thrill.

SKAT *speaks*: It's boring to be alone in the forest tonight.

SKAT *sings*: The terrible night doesn't frighten me . . .

He interrupts himself and listens. The sound of industrious sawing is heard through the silence.

SKAT: Workmen in the forest. Oh well! *Sings.* The terrible night doesn't frighten me . . . Hey, what the devil . . . it's *my* tree they're cutting down.

He peers through the foliage. Below him stands a dark figure diligently sawing away at the base of the tree. SKAT *becomes frightened and angry.*

SKAT: Hey you! Do you hear me, you tricky bastard? What are you doing with my tree?

The sawing continues without a pause. SKAT *becomes more frightened.*

SKAT: Can't you at least answer me? Politeness costs so little. Who are you?

DEATH *straightens his back and squints up at him.* SKAT *cries out in terror.*

DEATH: I'm sawing down your tree because your time is up.

SKAT: It won't do. I haven't got time.

DEATH: So you haven't got time.

SKAT: No, I have my performance.

DEATH: Then it's cancelled because of death.

SKAT: My contract.

DEATH: Your contract is terminated.

SKAT: My children, my family.

DEATH: Shame on you, Skat!

SKAT: Yes, I'm ashamed.

DEATH *begins to saw again. The tree creaks.*

SKAT: Isn't there any way to get off? Aren't there any special rules for actors?

DEATH: No, not in this case.

SKAT: No loopholes, no exceptions?

DEATH *saws*.

SKAT: Perhaps you'll take a bribe.

DEATH *saws*.

SKAT: Help!

DEATH *saws*.

SKAT: Help! Help!

The tree falls. The forest becomes silent again.

Night and then dawn.

The travellers have come to a sort of clearing and have collapsed on the moss. They lie quietly and listen to their own breathing, their heartbeats, and the wind in the tree tops. Here the forest is wild and impenetrable. Huge boulders stick up out of the ground like the heads of black giants. A fallen tree lies like a mighty barrier between light and shadow.

MIA, JOF *and their child have sat down apart from the others. They look at the light of the moon, which is no longer full and dead but mysterious and unstable.*

The KNIGHT *sits bent over his chess game.* LISA *cries quietly behind* PLOG's *back.* JONS *lies on the ground and looks up at the heavens.*

JONS: Soon dawn will come, but the heat continues to hang over us like a smothering blanket.

LISA: I'm so frightened.

PLOG: We feel that something is going to happen to us, but we don't know what.

JONS: Maybe it's the day of judgment.

PLOG: The day of judgment . . .

Now something moves behind the fallen tree. There is a rustling sound and a moaning cry that seems to come from a wounded animal. Everyone listens intently, all faces turned towards the sound.

A voice comes out of the darkness.

RAVAL: Do you have some water?

RAVAL's *perspiring face soon becomes visible. He disappears in the darkness, but his voice is heard again.*

RAVAL: Can't you give me a little water? *Pause.* I have the plague.

JONS: Don't come here. If you do I'll slit your throat. Keep to the other side of the tree.

RAVAL: I'm afraid of death.

No one answers. There is complete silence. RAVAL *gasps heavily for air. The dry leaves rustle with his movements.*

RAVAL: I don't want to die! I don't want to!

No one answers. RAVAL'S *face appears suddenly at the base of the tree. His eyes bulge wildly and his mouth is ringed with foam.*

RAVAL: Can't you have pity on me? Help me! At least talk to me.

No one answers. The trees sigh. RAVAL *begins to cry.*

RAVAL: I am going to die. I. I. *I!* What will happen to me! Can no one console me? Haven't you any compassion? Can't you see that I . . .

His words are choked off by a gurgling sound. He disappears in the darkness behind the fallen tree. It becomes quiet for a few moments.

RAVAL *whispers*: Can't anyone . . . only a little water.

Suddenly the GIRL *gets up with a quick movement, snatches* JONS's *water bag and runs a few steps.* JONS *grabs her and holds her fast.*

JONS: It's no use. It's no use. I know that it's no use. It's meaningless. It's totally meaningless. I tell you that it's meaningless. Can't you hear that I'm consoling you?

RAVAL: Help me, help me!

No one answers, no one moves. RAVAL'S *sobs are dry and convulsive, like a frightened child's. His sudden scream is cut off in the middle.*

Then it becomes quiet.

The GIRL *sinks down and hides her face in her hands.* JONS *places his hand on her shoulder.*

The KNIGHT *is no longer alone.* DEATH *has come to him and he raises his hand.*

DEATH: Shall we play our game to the end?

KNIGHT: Your move!

DEATH *raises his hand and strikes the* KNIGHT's *queen. Antonius Block looks at* DEATH.

DEATH: Now I take your queen.

KNIGHT: I didn't notice that.

The KNIGHT *leans over the game. The moonlight moves over the chess pieces, which seem to have a life of their own.*

Climax of chess game, more than fate, less than faith. Skill.

JOF *has dozed off for a few moments, but suddenly he wakens. Then he sees the* KNIGHT *and* DEATH *together. He becomes very frightened and awakens* MIA.

JOF: Mia!

MIA: Yes, what is it?

513

JOF: I see something terrible. Something I almost can't talk about.

MIA: What do you see?

JOF: The knight is sitting over there playing chess.

MIA: Yes, I can see that too and I don't think it's so terrible.

JOF: But do you see who he's playing with?

MIA: He is alone. You *mustn't* frighten me this way.

JOF: No, no, he isn't alone.

MIA: Who is it, then?

JOF: Death. He is sitting there playing chess with Death himself.

MIA: You mustn't say that.

JOF: We must try to escape.

MIA: One can't do that.

JOF: We must try. They are so occupied with their game that if we move very quickly, they won't notice us.

JOF *gets up carefully and disappears into the darkness behind the trees.* MIA *remains standing, as if paralyzed by fear. She stares fixedly at the* KNIGHT *and the chess game. She holds her son in her arms.*

Now JOF *returns.*

JOF: I have harnessed the horse. The wagon is standing near the big tree. You go first and I'll follow you with the packs. See that Mikael doesn't wake up.

MIA *does what* JOF *has told her. At the same moment, the* KNIGHT *looks up from his game.*

DEATH: It is your move, Antonius Block.

The KNIGHT *remains silent. He sees* MIA *go through the moonlight towards the wagon.* JOF *bends down to pick up the pack and follows at a distance.*

DEATH: Have you lost interest in our game?

The KNIGHT's *eyes become alarmed.* DEATH *looks at him intently.*

KNIGHT: Lost interest? On the contrary.

DEATH: You seem anxious. Are you hiding anything?

KNIGHT: Nothing escapes you—or does it?

DEATH: Nothing escapes me. No one escapes from me.

KNIGHT: It's true that I'm worried.

He pretends to be clumsy and knocks the chess pieces over with the hem of his coat. He looks up at DEATH.

KNIGHT: I've forgotten how the pieces stood.

514

DEATH *laughs contentedly*: But I have not forgotten. You can't get away that easily.

DEATH *leans over the board and rearranges the pieces. The* KNIGHT *looks past him toward the road.* MIA *has just climbed up on the wagon.* JOF *takes the horse by the bridle and leads it down the road.* DEATH *notices nothing; he is completely occupied with reconstructing the game.*

DEATH: Now I see something interesting.

KNIGHT: What do you see?

DEATH: You are mated on the next move, Antonius Block.

KNIGHT: That's true.

DEATH: Did you enjoy your reprieve?

KNIGHT: Yes, I did.

DEATH: I'm happy to hear that. Now I'll be leaving you. When we meet again, you and your companions' time will be up.

KNIGHT: And you will divulge your secrets.

DEATH: I have no secrets.

KNIGHT: So you know nothing.

DEATH: I have nothing to tell.

The KNIGHT *wants to answer, but* DEATH *is already gone.*

A murmur is heard in the tree tops. Dawn comes, a flickering light without life, making the forest seem threatening and evil. JOF *drives over the twisting road.* MIA *sits beside him.*

MIA: What a strange light.

JOF: I guess it's the thunderstorm which comes with dawn.

MIA: No, it's something else. Something terrible. Do you hear the roar in the forest?

JOF: It's probably rain.

MIA: No, it isn't rain. He has seen us and he's following us. He has overtaken us; he's coming towards us.

JOF: Not yet, Mia. In any case, not yet.

MIA: I'm so afraid. I'm so afraid.

The wagon rattles over roots and stones; it sways and creaks. Now the horse stops with his ears flat against his head. The forest sighs and stirs ponderously.

JOF: Get into the wagon, Mia. Crawl in quickly. We'll lie down, Mia, with Mikael between us.

They crawl into the wagon and crouch around the sleeping child.

JOF: It is the Angel of Death that's passing over us, Mia. It's the Angel of Death. *The Angel of Death, and he's very big.*

MIA: Do you feel how cold it is? I'm freezing. I'm terribly cold.

She shivers as if she had a fever. They pull the blankets over them and lie closely together. The wagon canvas flutters and beats in the wind. The roar outside is like a giant bellowing.

The castle is silhouetted like a black boulder against the heavy dawn. Now the storm moves there, throwing itself powerfully against walls and abutments. The sky darkens; it is almost like night.

Antonius Block has brought his companions with him to the castle. But it seems deserted. They walk from room to room. There is only emptiness and quiet echoes. Outside, the rain is heard roaring noisily.

Suddenly the KNIGHT *stands face to face with his wife. They look at each other quietly.*

KARIN: I heard from people who came from the crusade that you were on your way home. I've been waiting for you here. All the others have fled from the plague.

The KNIGHT *is silent. He looks at her.*

KARIN: Don't you recognize me any more?

The KNIGHT *nods, silent.*

KARIN: You also have changed.

She walks closer and looks searchingly into his face. The smile lingers in her eyes and she touches his hand lightly.

KARIN: Now I can see that it's you. Somewhere in your eyes, somewhere in your face, but hidden and frightened, is that boy who went away so many years ago.

KNIGHT: It's over now and I'm a little tired.

KARIN: I see that you're tired.

KNIGHT: Over there stand my friends.

KARIN: Ask them in. They will break the fast with us.

They all sit down at the table in the room, which is lit by torches on the walls. Silently they eat the hard bread and the salt-darkened meat. KARIN *sits at the head of the table and reads aloud from a thick book.*

KARIN: 'And when the Lamb broke the seventh seal, there was silence in heaven for about the space of half an hour. And I saw the seven angels which stood before God; and to them were given seven trumpets. And another . . .'

Three mighty knocks sound on the large portal. KARIN *interrupts her reading and looks up from the book.* JONS *rises quickly and goes to open the door.*

KARIN: 'The first angel sounded, and there followed hail and fire mingled with blood, and they were cast upon the earth; and the third part of the trees was burnt up and all the green grass was burnt up.'

Now the rain becomes quiet. There is suddenly an immense, frightening silence in the large, murky room where the burning torches throw uneasy shadows over the ceiling and the walls. Everyone listens tensely to the stillness.

KARIN: 'And the second angel sounded, and as it were a great mountain burning with fire was cast into the sea; and a third part of the sea became blood . . .'

Steps are heard on the stairs. JONS *returns and sits down silently at his place but does not continue to eat.*

KNIGHT: Was someone there?

JONS: No, my lord. I saw no one.

KARIN *lifts her head for a moment but once again leans over the large book.*

KARIN: 'And the third angel sounded, and there fell a great star from heaven, burning as it were a torch, and it fell upon the third part of the rivers and upon the fountains of waters; and the name of the star is called Wormwood . . .'

They all lift their heads, and when they see who is coming towards them through the twilight of the large room, they rise from the table and stand close together.

KNIGHT: Good morning, noble lord.

KARIN: I am Karin, the knight's wife, and welcome you courteously to my house.

PLOG: I am a smith by profession and rather good at my trade, if I say so myself. My wife Lisa—curtsy for the great lord, Lisa. She's a little difficult to handle once in a while and we had a little spat, so to say, but no worse than most people.

The KNIGHT *hides his face in his hands.*

KNIGHT: From our darkness, we call out to Thee, Lord. Have mercy on us because we are small and frightened and ignorant.

JONS *bitterly*: In the darkness where You are supposed to be, where all of us probably are. . . . In the darkness You will find no one to listen to Your cries or be touched by Your sufferings. Wash Your tears and mirror Yourself in Your indifference.

KNIGHT: God, You who are somewhere, who *must* be somewhere, have mercy upon us.

JONS: I could have given you an herb to purge you of your worries about eternity. Now it seems to be too late. But in any case, feel the immense triumph of this last minute when you can still roll your eyes and move your toes.

KARIN: Quiet, quiet.

JONS: I shall be silent, but under protest.

GIRL *on her knees*: It is the end.

JOF *and* MIA *lie close together and listen to the rain tapping lightly on the wagon canvas, a sound which diminishes until finally there are only single drops.*

They crawl out of their hiding place. The wagon stands on a height above a slope, protected by an enormous tree. They look across ridges, forests, the wide plains, and the sea, which glistens in the sunlight breaking through the clouds.

JOF *stretches his arms and legs.* MIA *dries the wagon seat and sits down next to her husband.* MIKAEL *crawls between* JOF'S *knees.*

A lone bird tests its voice after the storm. The trees and bushes drip. From the sea comes a strong and fragrant wind.

JOF *points to the dark, retreating sky where summer lightning glitters like silver needles over the horizon.*

JOF: I see them, Mia! I see them! Over there against the dark, stormy sky. They are all there. The smith and Lisa and the knight and Raval and Jöns and Skat. And Death, the severe master, invites them to dance. He tells them to hold each other's hands and then they must tread the dance in a long row. And first goes the master with his scythe and hourglass, but Skat dangles at the end with his lyre. They dance away from the dawn and it's a solemn dance towards the dark lands, while the rain washes their faces and cleans the salt of the tears from their cheeks.

He is silent. He lowers his hand.

His son, MIKAEL, *has listened to his words. Now he crawls up to* MIA *and sits down in her lap.*

MIA *smiling*: You with your visions and dreams.

WRITING

ABOUT

LITERATURE

Written responses to literature take many forms. A note in the margin of a book, a diary entry about something we have just read, a letter to a friend mentioning a recent novel, an essay for school, an article in a scholarly journal—all are versions of writing about literature. The first two examples grow out of our internal monolog as we read; the letter is a form of talking to friends about what interests us. The essays and articles start from these monologs and dialogs and result in finished forms that make specific points about specific works. If we see the thinking, jotting, talking, and writing as a continuum—rather than as four separate acts—then we have probably all done some writing about literature. The paper assigned for class is just another phase of reading and responding to literature.

Writing about a work forces us to look at it critically, to pay attention to it in a way that simply reading it does not; writing allows us to "get into" the work as no other method can. We respond to literature with mind, emotions, senses. Writing about those responses requires that we find words for what we feel or intuit as much as for what we intellectually think through. And as we become more familiar with a piece of writing and put responses into words, it is possible to see and understand more of that work and to see and understand more of ourselves.

GETTING STARTED

No one way of starting a paper will work for everyone but there are two general approaches that are helpful. Neither one is "more correct" or "better" than the other. Try both ways and see which one works better for you. You may find that some combination of the two suits you best. The point is the final essay and not how you got there. Both methods depend on your having read the work carefully—with your mind and feelings open—before you begin the paper.

The first method is "focused free writing." It works well for people who cannot get started, who write one word and think immediately of three others that would do the job better. It is a way of getting past the first scary sentence. The second emphasizes "overall aim." It works well for people who need a clear direction before they start to write, whose ideas form better inside their heads than on paper. But do not decide which kind of person you are until you have tried both methods. You may find that one way works better for some papers and the other way for others.

Focused Free Writing

Write continuously for ten to twenty minutes about the work you have read. If you have not done free writing before, write five to ten minutes the first time, but try to build up to twenty minutes. Do not edit what you say, or worry about grammar, punctuation, or spelling. Just write everything that comes into your mind about the work. If you get stuck, keep your pen moving by writing the title of the work until you get unstuck. This writing is just for you, to get your thinking and writing started. Stay focused on the work and on your responses to it. Do not reread the work or what you have written while you are doing the free writing. Write as long as you can, but set a minimum amount of time for writing and stick to it.

When you have finished, go over what you have written. You will almost certainly find a thesis for your paper, probably several to choose among. You may also find whole paragraphs that you can use in slightly rewritten form in your final essay. Free writing is for you, to help you get your responses on paper. It is not a finished essay. To make a finished essay, free writing must be edited, corrected, cut, rewritten, and probably rethought in part.

Free writing is a good way to begin and may lead you to new ideas and responses, to clearer and deeper appreciation of the literary work. If you get stuck in the final writing and just cannot make a point or a paragraph work, try focusing a free writing on that particular problem. It may give you a solution.

One good way to get used to writing about literature is to keep a journal on your reading. Discipline yourself to write a ten-minute focused free writing at least three times a week. The writing will help you clarify your responses by getting ideas and feelings onto paper while they are fresh. It will probably also give you subjects for more themes than you will ever be assigned for class.

Overall Aim

Before you start writing, decide on a clear aim for the paper. You will probably need to do some prewriting, although some writers are able to do much of this work in their heads. If you know what you want to write about as soon as you finish reading, jot down that idea with as many sentences, phrases, and questions, and as much evidence from the text as you can. If you do not know what to write about, go over the points that most interest you or that you respond to most strongly in the work. (Your thinking may be prodded by scanning the rest of this discussion.) After you have drawn up your rough list of ideas, go over it, seeing which ones group together and discarding ones that do not fit. Write a thesis that will serve as a framework for your grouped ideas, or if no thesis appears, write a question your jottings suggest. If you have chosen a question, gather the evidence from the work relating to the question. Then write an answer to your question in a sentence or two. This will be your thesis statement.

Next, in outline or note form, develop the organization of the essay, shifting the points around until each point grows clearly out of the preceding one and leads into the following one. Gather the evidence that you will use to support each point.

This method begins with the overall aim of the paper (thesis statement), fills in details and evidence in outline form, then moves to the writing. If the preliminary work has been fully and thoughtfully done, the writing will flow smoothly to link all the points, responses, and evidence.

The focused-free-writing and overall-aim approaches are general methods of working. They can be used for assigned topics and for ones you must develop yourself. Most writers use a combination of methods: perhaps jotting down an overall aim, using free writing to develop it, making an outline from the ideas that have appeared in the free writing, and then returning to free writing to fill in the outline. Every method ends with careful rewriting, proofreading, and editing.

TOPICS

If you have been assigned a topic for writing, the preceding section and the section called "Writing the Paper" near the end of this discussion may be helpful for composing the paper. If you have not been assigned a specific topic, you might look at the questions following many selections in this book. Most of them would make good subjects for essays of varying lengths, and the idea behind any question might be applied to another work. For instance, "Like the Japanese haiku of Basho, this Indian poem leaves much unsaid. What kind of mood does it suggest?" (p. 158). The question about mood could be applied to almost every work in *Mirrors*. "How does Hedda feel about Tesman's aunt?" (p. 457) is a question that may lead you to ask how any character feels about any other character in a play or a work of fiction. "The point of view in the story is that of the first-person (I) narrator. Point out places in the story where the reader understands things the narrator doesn't" (p. 44). Each of these questions about a particular work could be developed into a brief essay about another work in the text, and each could be varied slightly to yield additional subjects for writing. For instance, one might compare the mood of the Japanese poem with the mood of the Indian one. Or one might enlarge the point-of-view topic by showing just how the narrator's understanding is limited and how that limitation is important to the work.

If you have not been assigned a topic, and none of the questions in the text suits you, then you must find a topic of your own. The topic you choose will vary with the literary form you are writing about and with your own interests and temperament. Some topics are more appropriate to one type of literature than another. For example, a close analysis of language (diction, metaphor, simile) will often be more appropriate to poetry than to fiction. A discussion of setting will usually work better with fiction and drama than with poetry. But these are not hard and fast rules. Metaphors can reveal an author's (or fictional nattator's) attitude toward his or her characters in fiction, and setting may be important in some poems. With these qualifications in mind, the following classification of appropriate subject for specific literary forms may be helpful.

For fiction:

    plot
    character
    setting
    point of view
    irony
    symbolism
    theme

For poetry:

    diction
    tone
    metaphor
    sound (rhythmic patterns)
    poetic forms
    symbolism
    theme

For drama:

    plot
    character
    setting
    symbolism
    theme
    language (If the play is in poetry, like *King Lear*, all the topics listed under poetry can be fruitfully applied.)

Many of the above terms are defined and discussed in the introductions to the sections of *Mirrors*. (See the contents for page numbers.) Theme, a particularly troublesome term, is discussed in the following section. Rereading the introductions and the next section may suggest ways of developing the terms into manageable topics. Just the term *symbolism* is not a manageable topic. It must be narrowed and molded by your interests and insights, and by the unique character of the work or works you are writing about.

Theme

The term *theme* is often used to refer to the general idea or intent of the author and the significant statement the work makes. Because theme is common to all literary works, discussions of it are equally suitable to fiction, poetry, and drama. But defining the theme in a work can be difficult for several reasons. Unlike essayists, authors of poetry, drama, and fiction rarely make a specific statement of the purpose of the work. You will find few if any "thesis statements" in the selections in *Mirrors*. Rather, the reader must infer the author's intention from careful reading. Another difficulty is that some works may have a single theme, but more often several themes are complexly interwoven. No single theme represents the "real" one, although you will probably be wise to narrow your topic to only one of them. A simplistic hunting for themes can wrench ideas out of context and force "messages" where none exist. Yet it is usually helpful to look for unifying ideas that give a work its shape and purpose. In some modern works, the unifying idea may be that there is no unity, that events, people, places, and words occur without pattern.

A theme is not the same as a moral. Thurber gives us a moral in "The Princess and the Tin Box," but it is certainly not one that can be taken seriously. It might be tempting to make a simplistic and moralistic statement about some works, such as "People suffer when they are the victims of unwarranted racial prejudice," which hardly conveys the power of "Telephone Conversation" or reflects the significant statement of the poem. It might also be tempting to reduce a work to a platitude; one might conclude from "Richard Cory" that "You can't tell what a person is like on the inside," but that does not do justice to the meaning of the poem.

Finding one or more unifying ideas in a work should not be difficult. Look for an area of concern that you can identify by an abstract noun (love, injustice, disillusionment) and then try to show how the story, poem, or play deals with that concern. In other words, you might state in general terms a theme of the work and then show in specific terms how that theme is developed. Böll's story "The Balek Scales" is obviously about injustice—the villagers discover that the scales they have trusted for years are rigged—but what does the story say about the effects of this injustice, about the Balek family and others like it, about the remedies available to the people? The success of your paper will depend on how well you trace the particular form taken by the abstract theme (in this case, injustice) in a work. Various headings under which poems are grouped might serve as topics ("War" or "Death," for example). Using "Youth and Age" as a starting place, one might read the poems in that section and decide on a theme that ties them together. A statement such as "Youth seems richer in memory than it might have been in fact" can form the basis for an essay.

To find a theme that might serve as a topic for an essay, look at what seems to be important in a work. In Ellison's "The King of the Bingo Game," the game itself does not matter as much as what happens after bingo is called; yet the title invites one to think about what Ellison is using the game to suggest about society. Sometimes a title is suggestive enough to serve as a topic (for example, Daniel's story "Hands"). One might choose lines from a play, such as these from *King Lear*: "we that are young / Shall never see so much, nor live so long." Often a phrase or sentence embodies the author's principal idea within the work. Then again, the actions of a character or the author's revelation of that character may embody the theme of a work (as in Kafka's "The Hunger Artist").

TYPES OF ESSAYS

Below are five frequently-used types of essays. Under each type are topics that show how that essay form might be used for an essay on literature.

1. Comparison (showing the similarities and differences between two works, or between parts of works, or among a group of works). A good paper would probably have to go beyond comparison to discuss the significance of the differences and how the differences affect the reader's response.

   a. Compare the handling of point of view in two works of fiction.
   b. Compare the rhythmic patterns in one poem with those in another poem.
   c. Compare the responses of two characters in a play to a particular incident or to another character.

2. Analysis (looking closely at the parts of a work or of several works to see how the parts function; this requires breaking a work or elements of a work into constituent parts).

   a. Analyze how the setting of a particular work affects the characters.
   b. Analyze how the metaphors and similes in a poem affect its meaning.
   c. Analyze how an author's portrayal of some characters—women, for instance—does or does not reflect current stereotypes (or stereotypes of the author's period).
   d. Analyze how the plot of a story or play unfolds—what we learn and when. ("A Rose for Emily" is a particularly good work to use with this topic.)
   e. Analyze how a character reveals himself (or herself) through actions and dialog.

525

3. Cause and Effect (showing how a particular facet of a work leads to a particular result).

    a. Discuss how the actions of a character bring about the climax of a play.
    b. Discuss how a group of images in a poem (or verse drama) produces a specific effect on the reader (or viewer).

4. Definition (showing what a term means by establishing boundaries that indicate what is and is not covered by the term). Defining literary forms or elements is difficult, but the topic and its problems may teach you more about the nature of literature and literary forms than any other topic you can choose.

    a. Define a literary form, such as poetry or prose. (The point here is to look for works that do not fit your preconceived ideas of the form—for example, the group of poems that begin the poetry section—and then establish what they share with the works that do fit your idea.)
    b. Define an element of literature, such as plot, setting, or tone. (The problem with this topic is that all elements in literature are interconnected.)

5. Classification (showing why a work does or does not belong in a particular group of works). Sometimes this topic will grow out of definition, but it is generally easier to handle because you may use someone else's definition as your basis.

    a. Discuss why a particular work should or should not be classified as poetry (or drama, or fiction).
    b. Discuss why a particular poem should not be grouped with works on nature (for example, it is really about politics).

WRITING THE PAPER

Openings

Sometimes your subject dictates the opening paragraph of your paper; sometimes you may have an opening paragraph taken from the free writing you have done; often writing is just a matter of starting with the first thing you have to say. Some possible ways of beginning a paper are:

1. Stating your thesis. This does not necessarily have to be done boldly in the opening sentence (all topic sentences do not come first in a paragraph). But it is often helpful to readers, especially if you plan to develop a complex or unusual idea, to tell them what your essay will be about.
2. Showing something unusual or paradoxical about the material you will present. Even though your main thesis is not something startling, you can use this device to catch your reader's attention.

3. Using a brief quotation from the work or works you are writing about or possibly from a critical comment in *Mirrors* or another source. One or two lines from a poem or play may embody much of what you propose to deal with in your theme. Sometimes you will encounter a critic's comment so perfectly phrased that to alter it would be to lessen its meaning. By all means use the quotation, but give proper credit to the source. (See "Support from the Text" (pp. 528–530) for methods of documenting the sources of your quotations.)

5. Challenging some generally-held assumption about your topic or the work you are writing about. If you have decided to argue a view contrary to what others believe, make a statement to that effect immediately. Then you will have prepared the reader to follow your argument and, perhaps, to agree with your conclusion.

Weak Openings

Some ways of beginning an essay should be avoided.

1. Don't repeat the title. It is not the same as the aim of your essay and is certainly not going to be identical to the thesis. If the reader has not been sufficiently observant, the title will remain on the page and it can be seen at any time.

2. Don't ask a question; you might be surprised by the answer the reader will give. Although questions do invite audience participation, it is usually not helpful to invite a reader to respond to a question before you have had a chance to give your information or viewpoint. Also you cannot expect any informed response from a reader at the beginning of an essay.

3. Don't tell what you propose to do in the essay. Especially avoid saying, "In this essay I am going to. . . ." What you are going to write about should become evident as you do it. Repeating something the reader is about to discover makes reading dull.

4. Don't be cute or folksy, unless that style is especially well suited to your thesis or to the literature you are writing about. Generally it will not be.

5. Don't apologize. Get to work and do your best.

Development

The body of your paper is the place to expand your principal idea. If you are concerned with comparisons (similarities and differences), point out and explain those elements here. If you are explaining an idea, this is where you are obligated to provide sufficient information for the reader to understand the points you are making. If you are analyzing something, this is where you point out the parts that comprise the whole of your subject matter. If you are classifying, the body of the essay is the place to show how the literary work (or what you have to say about it) fits into some larger grouping or unit. The content of the body of the essay may be presented in one of several ways:

1. Order of importance. Begin with the most important point you want to make about your subject and lead the reader gradually away from that to less important elements of support. Or work the other way around by beginning with the least important aspect of your subject and leading the reader successively to the most important thing you have to say.

2. Chronology. Some subjects lend themselves to being written about in terms of development in time. For instance, characters often change over the time period encompassed by the literary work. Or you may deal with works from different eras. You might start with either the most recent element you want to write about or the most remote, so long as your procedure is consistent throughout the paper.

3. General to specific. Make an encompassing statement that covers all the ground you want to include, then develop individually those specific elements that led you to the generalization. This method presents the reader with a paper that develops opposite to the way in which you probably did the preliminary work. Give your conclusions initially so that the reader is immediately "let in on" what you want to say and can follow your thought process with you.

4. Specific to general (the opposite of the organizational method just noted). Begin with specific evidence and build toward a general statement based on the evidence. One word of caution about using this form: Do not try to mislead the reader and do not take too long getting to the main idea.

5. Enumeration. Some topics do not require that you follow any of the preceding methods of development. If all elements are equally important and none is more specific or more general than any other, simply write down the individual points you want to convey. If you include like ideas, group them for easy reading.

Your essay may involve comparing works or elements in works. If so, you may organize by the point-by-point method in which you alternate references to the works. Or you may choose to treat first one work and then the other, discussing the same points about each.

Support from the Text

When you write about a literary work, give some evidence from the work to support each point you make. Evidence from the text is what "proves" your point. It convinces your reader that your thesis is true. You might give examples of metaphor of other stylistic devices an author uses. You could refer to the rhyme scheme of a poem or show a character's viewpoint by quoting a speech he or she gives in a play. Or by a series of statements taken from the work you can show an author's attitude toward a particular topic or the ironic turn of a thought. To make these and other kinds of textual references, you will need to know some traditional forms that readers are accustomed to seeing.

References to any textual material must always be identified; if a direct quotation is used, the passage must also be put in quotation marks. The usual bibliographic or reference information should always be included: author, title of work, publisher and location, and date of publication. Specific material should be identified by page number. Line numbers from poems are often used, and passages from plays are designated according to act and scene. Because the reason for noting specific sources is to enable a reader to find the precise reference with ease, a good way to decide how much information you should offer is to consider how much help you can give an interested reader.

Custom dictates that the titles of long works, such as books, plays, and films, be underlined when you write or type them. The titles of shorter works—poems and stories—are enclosed in quotation marks. Punctuation marks usually separate the elements of information within a given reference.

If all references within your essay will be to the same literary work, it is necessary to cite the source only once and to indicate that all future references will be to that work or that particular edition. If the work appears in *Mirrors* (or in another collection), that fact should also be noted if you are being very formal. For example:

All references are to "Of Cabbages and Kings" by James Alan McPherson in John R. Knott, Jr. and Christopher R. Reaske, *Mirrors*, 2nd ed. (San Francisco: Canfield Press, 1975).

This reference would appear within the essay (either in the text or at the bottom of a page in the form of a footnote). It varies slightly from a bibliographic entry (which is alphabetized according to last name of author or editor and contains other punctuation). Subsequent references will consist of the page number in the cited book where the referenced material appears.

Source citations can be enclosed within parentheses and included within the text of your writing; this method simplifies writing and reading. Or the citation may be identified by numerals that refer the reader to notes somewhere other than within the text, usually either at the bottom of the page on which the reference appears or, in long works, in a separate listing of notes at the conclusion of the essay. The latter method (often reserved for research papers) makes typing easy, especially if there are many references, although the former method is more helpful to the reader of a short paper or one with few notes.

A quotation that runs more than three lines in your paper is customarily typed single (rather than double) space using the same textual margins. For instance, if you quoted from "Young Goodman Brown" by Nathaniel Haw-thorne, and the source for that story had already been established, you could use this form:

As nearly as could be discerned, the second traveller was about fifty years old, apparent-ly in the same rank of life as Goodman Brown, and bearing considerable resemblance to him, though perhaps more in expression than in features.[1]

Note that quotation marks are omitted because the different spacing at *the end* of cited materials or passages. Handwritten essays follow the same form with

[1]Page 77.

a change in margins because a change in spacing may not be possible on lined paper.

Poetry quotations longer than three or four lines are customarily written and identified in the same way as the prose passage just noted. However, shorter passages are usually included directly in the text as part of a sentence. A slash mark shows the end of a typographical line and capitalization is retained. Example: When Matthew Arnold wrote "Ah, love, let us the true/ To one another!" he might have been speaking for all youth.

Conclusions

The writer should end an essay when there is nothing left to say. Circumlocution and repetition detract from an otherwise good essay. Here are some ways to conclude.

1. Make a statement about your thesis. Rather than restating it, conclude the paper by referring to the thesis and making a comment derived from its development.
2. Link what you have written to something known, just as you might have done in opening the essay.
3. Use a quotation, if one is especially apt. The quotation may come from the work or works that have been the subject of the essay or from another source. Be sure to credit the source.
4. Return to some initial statement or generalization and show that you have proved, disproved, or enlarged it. This is a form of summary but it will add sharpness and direction to what you have already written.

Poor Endings

1. Don't repeat what has already been said. You are concluding, not beginning again.
2. Don't introduce a new idea. The time for that is past.
3. Don't use the words "And in conclusion . . ." The substance of your writing should make it evident that your statements are completed and that you are now ready to finish.
4. Don't apologize. If you've done your best, there's no need to be apologetic.

534

Index